All inquiries should be addressed to:
Sports Media Group
An imprint of Ann Arbor Media Group, LLC
2500 S. State Street
Ann Arbor, MI  48104

Printed and bound in the United States of America.

09   08   07   06   05        1   2   3   4   5

Library of Congress Cataloging-in-Publication Data

Stewart, Jerry, 1969-
   Pebble Beach : golf and the forgotten men / Jerry Stewart.
   p. cm.
   ISBN-13: 978-1-58726-261-6 (hardcover : alk. paper)
   ISBN-10: 1-58726-261-4 (hardcover : alk. paper)
   1. Pebble Beach Golf Links (Pebble Beach, Calif.)–History.
I. Title.
GV969.P43S74 2005
796.352'06'879476–dc22

For Pop and the Caddies

# Contents

# Acknowledgments

A project such as *Pebble Beach: Golf and the Forgotten Men* would not have been possible without the assistance and support of many individuals.

Those on the tee include the Pebble Beach Company, Pebble Beach Company director of licensing and historian Neal Hotelling, Ann Arbor Media Group publisher Skip DeWall, Ann Arbor Media Group product development manager Lynne Johnson, my editor Carol Bokas, and the past and present caddies of Pebble Beach Golf Links.

Those in the fairway include the *Monterey County Herald,*

Doug Thompson, Scott Brown, Ed Vyeda, Joe Wolfcale, Dave Kellogg, Paul Miller, Scott Houston, William and Alice Englander, and again the caddies.

Those on the green include my mother Helga (Yes, I'm finished Ma), James and Neila Stewart, the Spector Family (Sarah), the Horning Family (Mason and Ian), Shireen and Sarah Garrison (Again, yes I'm done), Susan Adams, Joe "Mojo" Amireault, the Collins Family (Big Al) and the 'men'— Dosie, Boy, Toko, Irie, Skeeter, DJ and Cisco—and again the caddies.

Finally, I'd like to thank my own life caddie, Samantha, for her patience, ever-present support, and direction. Where would I be without you?

# Introduction

*"If you want to walk Pebble Beach, take a cart.*
*If you want to play Pebble Beach . . .*
*take a caddie."*
—Pebble Beach wisdom

There's nothing like walking Pebble Beach Golf Links, as anyone who's experienced it knows. In fact, walking has been described as the only way Pebble Beach can be truly experienced.

There are the Cliffs of Doom hanging precariously over Carmel Bay, the waves licking the lips of world-famous hole No. 7, and the gratifying stroll down the fairway of majestic hole No. 18. Toss in the sunsets and history of the place and each tick of the clock becomes timeless.

It was during the Caddie Cup Challenge II in the winter

of 1999, on a day that defined the adage "Crosby Weather," that I came to watch the walking guides of this "Beauty and the Beast"—the Pebble Beach Golf Links caddies—make their own way around the loop that they call home in an exhibition match against their rival caddies from St. Andrews Links in Scotland.

As I stood cowered beneath skies as dark as molasses and sheltered myself from winds straight from the Kansas set of the *Wizard of Oz,* I found myself wondering why I saw so many smiles among the caddies. I thought, "Who are these guys and why are they so happy to be on a golf course on a day like this?"

After chatting with some of the caddies, the truth began to roll in as easy as a six inch tap-in putt for birdie.

Since Pebble Beach Golf Links opened its fairways in 1919, the caddies of Pebble Beach have been there. They have become as much a part of the tradition and history of golf as Pebble Beach Golf Links itself. Today, they remain as invisible as the right-to-left break on the first green, hiding within the game.

The caddies at Pebble Beach Golf Links have been there through it all—the opening of the famed golf course, the early days of the Crosby Clambake, the dreaded introduction of golf carts, four U.S. Opens (1972, 1982, 1992, and 2000), Mondays through Sundays, the sunny days, and the rainy days.

"I don't think there's any other way to take in the full Pebble Beach experience than to play with a caddie" one Pebble Beach caddie says. "It's the way golf was meant to be played."

"It all comes down to the fact that two heads are better than one," says another caddie. "That's why you see pros out there with caddies."

If you look up "caddie" in the dictionary, you will find the word defined as one who "is hired to assist a golfer, especially one to carry golf clubs."

However, at Pebble Beach Golf Links, the caddie's role gives the term more meaning than a breed of two-legged pack mule. More than anything, they have course knowledge—knowledge that, in a sense, makes Pebble Beach caddies the Albert Einsteins of the golf course. Instead of E = mc², it's "Don't believe the hump. It's two balls to the left of the cup; firm." It's time-tested science as constant as the left-to-right spin on a slice.

"A caddie's real role can be defined in two words: local knowledge," says a Pebble Beach looper.

Having borne witness to this gift on more than one occasion, and having seen the joy in their sharing of this wisdom, I felt it was time to enter the laboratory. After all, the science of knowing how to play golf at Pebble Beach had to have started somewhere, and it had to be going somewhere.

It was through this journey that I found out who the first Pebble Beach caddies were and what they knew. And it was through this journey that I found those experiments that failed and those that succeeded. After all, for every fist-pump and smile resulting from a birdie, there have been hands in the pockets and looks of gloom.

Like Pebble Beach Golf Links itself, the stories behind the caddies of Pebble Beach are endless; so much that, with all apologies, some may be missing.

Nevertheless, the good news is that the caddies of Pebble Beach Golf Links remain where they've always been—and where they should be—on the brink of a new frontier, and in the footsteps of the past.

# PEBBLE BEACH

## GOLF AND THE FORGOTTEN MEN

# 1 The First Caddie

*"I'd move heaven and earth just to break 100," the player said.*
*"Try Heaven," replied his caddie.*
*"You've already moved most of the earth."*
—Anonymous

It was like trying to putt through quicksand. Back in 1917, times were tough. Globally, the world was at war, and here in the United States doughboys from Maine to Washington were busy packing their bags. On California's Monterey Peninsula, most residents were literally hanging on by a thread— that of their fisherman's net.

The now world-famous Cannery Row—which would later be immortalized by Peninsula native John Steinbeck—was peaking, but those not coming home reeking of fish scrambled to make ends meet. On the street, new Dodge cars sold for

$930, and a forty-by-one hundred square-foot lot in the heart of downtown Monterey sold for $125.

However, a short trolley ride across town from the canneries stood a shining beacon of the good life—Hotel Del Monte.

Charles Crocker—who along with Collis Huntington, Leland Stanford, and Mark Hopkins were known as the Big Four due to the quartet's role in building the Central Pacific

*In 1918, Del Monte Golf Course was the best ticket in town for a number of kids. Here, caddie master Mortie Dutra is surrounded by his crew. The young loopers include:* (back row, left to right) *Cam Puget, Magnus Jenses, Henry Puget, Charlie Castro, Francis Parker, Phil Collum, Olin Dutra, Earl Smith, John Zaches;* (middle row, left to right) *Allan Yeager, Glen Monroe, Sidney Artellan, William Lemestres, Mortie Dutra, Nino Balesteri, John Santos, Lyle Yeager;* (front, left to right) *Walter Vierra, Alfred Santos, Henry Pate, Sonny Pate, Denzel Dana, and Chris Jensen.* (Photograph by Fred X. Fry.)

Railroad and developing California's first railway system—had watched Hotel Del Monte quickly grow into a major West Coast vacation destination. Opened in 1880, the resort offered it all for the wealthy—fine dining, luxury suites, equestrian stables, a racetrack, and a lavish bathhouse on the shores of Monterey Bay.

Another resort amenity was Del Monte Golf Course, which began as a nine-hole layout in 1897, but was expanded to eighteen holes in 1903.

For a number of local boys, like brothers Henry and Cam Puget, the golf course at Del Monte would eventually become the best ticket in town. Lugging golf clubs as a caddie, after all, was a lot better than spending all day skinning and gutting fish.

The Pugets, along with their parents, arrived on the Monterey Peninsula in 1917, after moving down from nearby Santa Clara. As for the decision to begin work as a caddie, it was a no-brainer. After all, his family's new home was only 300 yards away from Del Monte's clubhouse.

"Being so close it was a natural fit," said Henry Puget, who was a mere 12 years old in 1917. "We used to get seventy-five cents for eighteen holes, plus tips, which were usually anything from a dime to a quarter."

Sometimes, however, the tip was even less.

"I remember one kid was handed a nickel tip and, in disgust and in sight of the player, threw all his fee and tip over the clubhouse roof," Puget told the *Monterey County Herald* in a 1977 interview. "Afterward though, he ran like blazes around the building to retrieve the money because the other kids had already started climbing the building to grab it."

While it may just be spare change today, back in 1917 that seventy-five cents indeed meant something. That year, a man's raincoat sold for $6.75, while a bar of soap cost a quarter. Gasoline cost on average fifteen cents per gallon.

As for other occupations, a laundry worker earned nine dollars per week, while a factory worker on average made sixty-six cents per hour.

For the Pugets and other kids, looping wasn't the only way to make some money at Del Monte. A number of odd jobs were also available—and taken—even if it meant helping course greenkeeper Chris Augusta fill out his wardrobe.

"I used to earn an extra thirty-five cents an hour shagging balls for (then Del Monte head pro and future Pebble Beach head pro) Peter Hay while he was giving lessons," Henry Puget said. "Plus, before going to school each day I used to set two dozen gopher traps around the course. When I got back from school, I'd check them. The greenkeeper, Chris Augusta, paid me fifteen cents per gopher and fifty cents per mole. He'd cut their tails off so that I couldn't collect twice. From the moles, he made himself a vest. I

*Working the course as kids would later pay off for a number of Monterey Peninsula caddies such as Olin and Mortie Dutra (here shown looping at Del Monte Golf Course in 1912). Olin went on to capture the 1920 PGA Championship and 1934 U.S. Open, while older brother Mortie became the head pro at Pebble Beach Golf Links in the 1920s and later won the 1955 Senior PGA Championship. (Photograph by R. J. Arnold.)*

cleaned the course completely out of gophers. In return, I was allowed to play early Sunday mornings."

For Puget and the other caddies, being on the clock or off didn't matter. Del Monte was the place to be.

"When I wasn't caddying or playing, I used to sit on the fence by the sixteenth fairway, watching other players and studying their game," Puget said.

That extra time analyzing Del Monte golfers paid off not only for Puget and his brother Cam, but also for a group of fellow loopers. So much, in fact, that young Henry and a number of his compatriots later helped put Monterey on the map as a home of champion players.

Among those included in the mix, besides Henry and Cam Puget, were the Dutra boys, Olin and Mortie. In 1932, Olin Dutra captured the PGA Championship at Minnesota-based Keller Golf Club, and in 1934, the U.S. Open held at Merion Cricket Club in Pennsylvania. Mortie Dutra won the 1955 Senior PGA Championship at PGA National Golf Club in Florida.

There were also the Espinosas: Abe, Al, Henry, Ray, and Romeo (who preferred going by Romie). Among the Espinosas' feats to come was Abe Espinosa winning the 1928 Western Open and the 1931 Texas Open and Al finishing runner-up to the legendary Bobby Jones in the 1929 U.S. Open at New York–based Winged Foot Golf Club. Henry, Ray, and Romie became teaching pros in the San Francisco Bay area. Al was also named to the first three Ryder Cup teams.

Olin Dutra, who was 16 years old in 1917, had originally spent most of his days working at a hardware store in downtown Monterey. After introducing the store's manager Bill Adams to golf, however, Dutra and Adams soon began a routine of getting in nine holes before opening the store. Later in the day, Dutra occasionally returned to Del Monte to pick up a loop or two on the side.

"We'd get thirty-five cents for nine holes, and we'd put ten cents away," recalled Olin Dutra, who, in addition to his two Major wins, played on two Ryder Cup teams. "Our father always taught us to save something, so we'd take the other twenty-five cents and go downtown to see two movie serials for fifteen cents."

The big show at the time? Charlie Chaplin flicks.

"After the movies, we'd spend the left-over dime on an ice cream soda," Olin Dutra said.

Like the Dutra brothers, the Puget boys also took advantage of any free golf that could be had.

"If we got caught sneaking onto the course, we'd be fired—usually for about two weeks—so we had to run for the bushes occasionally," Henry Puget said. "One time, I had collected a bag of old balls and was out at the fifteenth practicing. The greenkeeper, Joe Boronda, rode his bicycle around the course to check everything out. One day I saw him coming, so I dropped the bag of balls in order to jump the fence and hide. Then I saw him pick up the bag. He never mentioned it and neither did I."

Still two years away from the opening of Pebble Beach in 1919, the most celebrated remark by a caddie at the time came from fellow Del Monte looper Jack Zaches.

During a fateful round at Del Monte, the player for whom Zaches was looping happened to hit his first drive into the rough along the first fairway. Following a lengthy search, Zaches explained that he couldn't find his player's ball.

"What do you mean, you can't find it?" demanded the player. "You saw where it went. Didn't you mark the spot by anything?"

"Yes," Jack said. "I marked it by a bird. But the bird flew away."

Young Zaches had discovered the first ingredient of being a great caddie—knowing when to say the right thing at the right time. He later saved up enough change as a young looper to pay for an education at Stanford University.

Meanwhile, for Puget and the others, more stories were waiting across the forest as the anticipated opening of a new golf course—Pebble Beach Golf Links—loomed closer.

# Puget's Touch

Thanks to his days learning the ropes as a kid at Del Monte, Henry Puget and the game of golf would eventually forge a relationship that lasted for over seventy years.

Despite becoming the first-ever caddie at Pebble Beach Golf Links, not long after the course opened in 1919, Puget suddenly decided that looping wasn't filling his pockets, so he went to work as a carpenter's apprentice and later as a bus driver. In 1927, however, Puget returned to golf, becoming an assistant professional at Del Monte under head professional Peter Hay. Just a few years later in 1931, Pebble Beach founder and local real estate baron Samuel F.B. Morse offered Puget the job of head professional at recently opened Cypress Point Club, which is just around the corner from Pebble Beach.

"I told him [Morse] at the time that I would only take it for a few years," Puget said in a 1995 article in the *Monterey County Herald*. Those few years ended up almost literally being a lifetime. Puget, the first-ever caddie at Pebble Beach, stayed at Cypress Point as head professional for forty years.

"The first time I played Cypress Point I was five under after seven," said Puget, who died in 1996. "Jack Morris was the pro, and I hit the club he told me to hit off the tee on eight (an inland par 4). I got all of it, but it ended up in a sand trap. It took me four or five shots to get out. I just picked up the ball and put it in my pocket. I played the last ten holes one under."

During other rounds, Puget's extra time spent walking and playing the fairways of Del Monte also showed major dividends. In 1928, he set what was then the course record (65) at Del Monte, and in one month at Cypress Point he recorded three scores of 66 (6 under par).

Nevertheless, his roots as a caddie were never far behind.

"One time in the late 1940s, I was playing with Cam and Babe Zaharias in a golf match at Del Monte," Puget said. "Well, Babe bugged me all the way around, asking me what club she should hit."

Zaharias, at the time, was the hottest female golfer on the planet. Not only did she boast a remarkable seventeen tournament win streak, but she had also captured the 1946 U.S. Women's Amateur and the 1947 British Women's Amateur crowns. Nevertheless, she still wanted the former caddie's sage advice.

"She was on me through the whole eighteen," Puget said. "It was a long day."

During his forty-year tenure (1931–1971) as head professional at Cypress Point, Puget tutored and played with a number of other luminaries, including kings and presidents. He was also on hand for Bing Crosby's ace on the world-famous par-3 sixteenth. "We knew three balls had reached the green— Crosby's, mine, and [five-some member] Dan Searle's, but as we approached the green only two balls were visible. Obviously, one was in the cup. Another member of the five-some ran all the way to the hole to see whose it was and, in his excitement, plucked the ball out of the cup and announced that it was Bing's. Then he carried the ball to Bing, ignoring the etiquette that says that the man who shoots the ace shall pick it out himself," Puget said. "Bing, typically, merely shrugged and smiled."

If the Pebble Beach caddies ever wanted a great act to follow, they got it in Puget.

"He was a great man," said current Cypress Point head professional Jim Langley, who succeeded Puget after his 1971 retirement, "one of the all-time best."

# 2  A New Home: Pebble Beach

*One day, a player entered the caddie shack to pick out his caddie.*
*"Sir, that kid isn't even eight years old," the caddie master said.*
*"Better that way," replied the player.*
*"He probably can't count past ten."*
—Anonymous

While Del Monte Golf Course was the first home for cad-dies on the Monterey Peninsula, Samuel F.B. Morse would soon expand the horizon.

It didn't take very long for Morse, who arrived as the new manager of the Del Monte holdings in 1915, to realize the value of land in Pebble Beach. Originally asked to liquidate properties along the glorious coastline at Pebble Beach, Morse quickly began having different ideas.

Already familiar with the North Carolina golf resort Pinehurst, Morse immediately began to have visions of build-

*In the Pebble Beach pro shop* (left to right) *Peter Hay, Cam Puget, Ray Parga, and Henry Puget, circa 1960.* (Photograph by Julian P. Graham.)

ing a golf course instead of homes along the breathtaking shore at Pebble Beach.

Among the golf course designers who immediately came to Morse's mind were Charlie MacDonald and Donald Ross. MacDonald, regarded as the father of American golf course design and the original source of the term "golf architect," had previously laid out America's first 18-hole golf course—the Chicago Golf Club in 1895. A Scotsman, Ross meanwhile had already put the final touches on what would become another one of America's greatest courses—Pinehurst No. 2 in North Carolina.

In the end, Morse elected to share his vision with two amateur golf champions—Jack Neville and Douglas Grant.

Neville, as Morse knew, was a proven amateur champion. The winner of both the 1912 and 1913 California Amateur Championships, Neville in Morse's eyes was someone who would easily understand the intricacies of building a course. Grant, meanwhile, was also known among the golfing circle as a great player, having beaten Neville 7 & 5 in the 1916 Mid-Winter Championship at Del Monte Golf Course.

In Neville's case, the idea to build a golf course along the shoreline at Pebble Beach was enticing.

"It was all there in plain sight," Neville once said. "Little change was needed."

*Caddie master Ray Parga* (third from left) *poses with loopers* (from left) *Alvin "DiDi" Gonzales, Bill Shumway, Ernie Fermint, Hank Christman, and Manuel Linares in front of the Pebble Beach Golf Links pro shop circa 1950.* (Photograph by Julian P. Graham.)

The project, however, wasn't as easy as it looked. For instance, 17-Mile Drive, which wove through Del Monte Forest, had to be re-routed.

As one could have guessed, when a christening tournament was held in 1918 at Pebble Beach, players didn't exactly gush. Among their concerns were a lack of turf and rocky fairways.

"The course is in an early state of development and it will be many months before all the fairways and greens are in condition for real tournament play," Neville explained afterward.

Neville was right on target. When Pebble Beach Golf Links did finally officially open its fairways on February 22, 1919, the course was ready, as was an eager public.

Pebble Beach founder Samuel F.B. Morse had realized his vision, and it was time for the golfing world to get its first glimpse of what would become one of the game's most hallowed grounds. One of those on hand for the occasion was Sacramento resident R.R. Flint, who christened the opening via the golfer's oath—"We pledge ourselves by our faith in the cherry tree to turn in honest scorecards."

Also riding the wave of enthusiasm, not surprisingly, were the caddies of Del Monte. Stuck for years with only one place to work, they suddenly had two loops—Del Monte and Pebble Beach Golf Links.

Quickly thickening the plot was the fact that only a year after the Pebble Beach welcoming reception, the California Golf Association agreed to include Pebble Beach in the State Amateur Championship, which had previously been contested only at Del Monte. Word spread fast about the new course and its new role; more than 300 players signed up for the 1920 championship to get their glimpse. The need for caddies was immense.

"[Because] every player had to have a caddie, every stevedore, prizefighter, and hobo who could be rounded up between here and San Francisco was pressed into service,"

Henry Puget told the *Monterey County Herald*. "The caddie fees were raised to $1.50 for the event. What a mob!"

With both courses open, most caddies shuffled from one to the other following the championship. However, bright-eyed youngster Ray Parga and a crew of others followed the footsteps of Henry Puget and tried to make a new home at Pebble Beach.

"Back then most of the caddies were kids from 11 to 13 years old," Parga says. "We were eager beavers, but we had some tough characters to cope with—like the older boys who spent their spare time and money playing six-card pyute, put n' take, and chuckaluck in the caddie yard."

As for games, there was also always the signup book, a daily list which designated players' tee times and caddies' assignments.

"The signup book was supposed to show whose turn it was to carry the bag, but most of the older guys would tear the pages out," Parga told the *Monterey County Herald*. "If their name wasn't on it, it was gone."

According to Parga, however, all the caddies were still on the same page when it came to their mission—making a buck. New loops were to be had, but nonetheless, being selective was part of the equation.

"If a player was in the habit of spending more than three-and-a-half hours on a round or was a notorious low-tipper, the caddies would want nothing to do with them," Parga said. "The caddies would run and hide if they saw one of those guys coming."

Like Puget, getting hooked on the bag had been a no-brainer for Parga as well. However, Parga's proximity to the course wasn't a factor; it was the result of his first two loops. That fateful day, he walked away with $2.25.

"It was like a pot of gold," he recalls.

Another caddie who helped set the tone in the new Pebble Beach caddie shack was Alvin "DiDi" Gonzales. Gonzales, one of the few local veterans and older caddies in

*One of the first to set the tone in the Pebble Beach caddie shack was Al 'DiDi' Gonzales.* (Photographs by Julian P. Graham.)

the shack, had been on the bag so long at Del Monte that he had saved enough money to buy what would become the un-official caddie bus: a Model T Ford. Other than Gonzales' Model T, caddies relied on either the streetcar or, later, the bus. That reliance on Gonzales' Model T did not keep some of the kids from having a little fun.

"One day as a gag, the kids rubbed Limburger on the manifold of the Model T, which, as it heated up, gave off a powerful stench," Parga says. "DiDi made them all get out and walk."

In his days as a caddie at Pebble Beach, Parga carried the bags of a number of Hollywood celebrities, including Jack Benny, Danny Kaye, and W.C. Fields. Years later, Gonzales also looped for Bob Hope and Jack Nicklaus.

"One time, Hope was playing with Del Webb, who had DiDi on the bag, and Webb had to quit after nine," Parga told the *Monterey County Herald*. "Well, that left Hope to cover the five-dollar caddie fee for DiDi. 'Five bucks!' Hope screamed in dismay. 'I'm not buying [Gonzales]. I've seen better lines on a porpoise.'"

For the Dogs—During the early days of Pebble Beach, one caddie apparently figured out a way to still earn a buck if work was slow.

"Tamale Joe," who was fond of both wine and his pet Chihuahua, quickly found out that the "new" rubber golf balls (which sold for about three dollars at the time) such as the Spalding ball, the Davey Dimple ball, and the Silver King ball had somewhat the same scent as dog food.

"If he didn't make a loop and any money for the day, Joe would buy a can of dog food and throw it around the green on No. 8," said caddie Roy Drocovich, who worked with Joe. "Along with eating the food, his Chihuahua would also come back with balls that had been lost in the rough. That way, he'd make his money for more dog food, and more importantly a little wine."

After retrieving the balls, Joe would clean them up and re-sell them.

Not too soon after, however, Tamale Joe found himself competing with fellow caddie George "Ponde" Parker, who quickly caught on to the idea.

"Parker found out that someone else living near the course had a dog that would do the same thing," the caddie said. "Thing was, he didn't know the owner. Instead he would end up dog-napping the dog for a few hours almost every day to get his own fill."

# 3 The Early Years: 1920–1940

*"Stop checking your watch all the time," the player said.*
*"It's distracting." "This isn't a watch," the caddie replied.*
*"It's a compass."*
—Anonymous

B y the late 1920s Pebble Beach Golf Links was swinging in full gear thanks to some course enhancements, such as lengthening the now world-famous eighteenth hole to a par 5. As a result, Samuel Morse soon was again on the move. His goal this time? Bringing a national championship to Pebble Beach.

Morse got his wish in 1929, as Pebble Beach was designated host of the U.S. Amateur. Now, the greatest golfers in the world—men like Francis Ouimet and Bobby Jones—would step foot on Morse's playground.

*"Wild" Bill Kynoch, who served as the head professional at Pebble Beach from 1939 to 1942, wasn't just known for his drives as a golfer. He was also known for his "skills" as the driver of the Pebble Beach caddies' bus.* (Photograph by Julian P. Graham.)

For the caddies, it was a chance to work in the spotlight. As it was, however, the hardest part of a caddie's job had nothing to do with the golf course. Most important, among everything, was simply finding a way to get to work.

"In the years following the U.S. Amateur, Del Monte Properties became so desperate for caddies that it provided a local bus to pick them up, starting at 7 A.M.," recalled Joe Solis, who at the time was caddie master of neighbor Cypress Point Club. "The bus would go on to drop guys off at Pebble, Cypress, and Monterey Peninsula Country Club, and then it would return in that order at 5 P.M. to pick them up. If you were on the eighteenth green and the bus was about to leave, you were out of luck. You couldn't walk out on your player, who probably hadn't paid you yet, and the bus driver, "Wild" Bill Kynoch wasn't about to wait. So you had to walk home, which may have taken anywhere from half an hour to an hour and a half."

Pebble Beach caddies that did make the bus still had to contend with Wild Bill, who earned his nickname due to, of all things, his driving skills. As always, from the first step until the drop-off, Wild Bill, who later served as the head pro at Pebble Beach from 1939 to 1942, let the loopers know who was boss.

"When the riders were unruly, Wild Bill would stop on Carmel Hill and offer to throw them all out," Ray Parga said. "There was scarcely any room on the bus for all the kids, and the big guys thought it was funny to try and keep the little ones off."

For the young caddies, there was also the dreaded portable seat.

"The back seat had space for six people and a portable seat was set in the aisle between the next two seats," said Parga in a 1977 article in the *Monterey County Herald*. "You soon learned not to sit on the portable with your back to the back seat, or you'd be pounded black and blue by the six guys who were sitting behind you and kicking you."

For players who occasionally rode the bus along with caddies, the ride was at times just as treacherous.

"Once in a while, a player would want to ride the bus and would take the seat right behind Wild Bill," Parga said. "Then the caddies sitting behind him would start a conversation between themselves about, 'Well, I'm carrying for Mr. So-and-So today. He's paying me two bucks! It sure is great to get two bucks instead of the old one-fifty.' By the time they reached the course, the player riding the bus would be convinced that the going caddie fee was two dollars, when it was still only a buck or so."

Meanwhile, for those caddies who did miss the morning bus—like Dyer Wilson Jr.—an alternative mode of transpor-

*When Jack Nicklaus (shown here blasting out of a bunker on No. 2) arrived at Pebble Beach for the 1961 U.S. Amateur, there to guide him was caddie Alvin "DiDi" Gonzales (left).*
(Photograph by William C. Brooks.)

tation had to be found, and quick. Otherwise, their pockets would only be filled with lint.

"I remember one time Wilson Jr. had an early morning loop scheduled, but somehow missed the daily bus to Pebble Beach," recalled caddie Roy Drocovich. "It was a good loop too, five dollars or so. So Wilson got this great idea to stop by the nearby Cadillac dealership. He went in and asked if he could test-drive one of the cars. He told the dealer that he wanted to buy two cars—one for himself and one for his wife."

The test drive, of course, ended at Pebble Beach Golf Links.

"When they arrived at the course, Wilson told the driver to drop him off at Samuel Morse's house, which was located along hole No. 1," Drocovich said.

Thinking that Wilson would be right out, the dealer waited. And waited. And waited.

"Finally, the dealer came over to a group of us and asked us what the hell was going on. We told the dealer, 'You better forget about any deal. That guy doesn't have two nickels to rub together.'"

Drocovich, who was known as "Droc" in the caddie barn, also recalled the day when Cypress Point caddie master Joe Solis called the shack at Pebble Beach looking for some help.

"It was a rather slow day at Pebble Beach in the 1940s, and a call came in that loopers were needed at nearby Cypress Point Club," Drocovich said. "Problem for most caddies, however, was that they needed to be at Cypress Point as soon as possible, which meant they needed a car. Back then, of course, hardly anyone had a car."

Those who did have cars quickly leapt into battle stations to make the loop.

"Well, one guy with one car wanted to beat another guy who had a car," Drocovich said. "So he stuck a potato in the other guy's tailpipe. As it ended up, the caddie with the potato in the tailpipe couldn't get his car to start. He sat there and tried and tried but it never turned over. In the end, he tried so hard he blew his muffler."

## The Man

If anyone ruled the Pebble Beach caddie shack during the 1930s, it was Alvin "DiDi" Gonzales.

"We used to row a boat out on Stillwater Cove and look for abalone," caddie Adrian Montiel said. "Well, one day I'm out there with DiDi and the boat flips. I later got us both back into the boat, and as we're heading back I tell him, 'Now remember, I saved your life.' He just got this gruff look and then said, 'To hell you did.'"

Although still relatively young at the time, Gonzales had, like Henry Puget, been one of the first Del Monte Golf Course caddies to make the move to Pebble Beach back in 1919.

"DiDi was really the king of the caddies," fellow looper Adrian Montiel says. "He was a funny guy, but he could be mean as well. I remember everyone would say, 'Oh, oh, that's DiDi. Stay away from him.'"

While Puget climbed his way up the ranks and into the pro shop, Gonzales made his moves in the caddie barn. His biggest break would come during the 1929 U.S. Amateur, when he was on the bag of eventual champion Harrison "Jimmy" Johnston. Years later, after serving as a sergeant in the Pacific theater of World War II, Gonzales resumed his roost at Pebble Beach.

Gonzales' greatest moment came at another U.S. Amateur in 1961. That year, Gonzales looped for another champion—Jack Nicklaus. Nicklaus, 20 years old and sporting a crew cut, was setting foot for the first time on Pebble Beach.

"Pebble Beach has a great reputation—and is a great course," Nicklaus has said. "This is the first course on which I haven't been able to judge the distances."

*Following their win at the 1961 U.S. Amateur, caddie Alvin "DiDi" Gonzales would loop for Jack Nicklaus just about every time the young "Bear" set foot on Pebble Beach.* (Photograph by Julian P. Graham.)

There to guide the young Bear was none other than Gonzales.

"DiDi was this tiny, rotund Portuguese man, who always had this big cigar in his mouth," Nicklaus recalls with a laugh. "I would say, 'Where do I hit it DiDi,' and he'd say, 'Inch and a half left, and hit it firm.' He really taught me about the greens. He was terrific. He really knew those greens."

Using Nicklaus' skills and Gonzales' knowledge, the duo found themselves marching their way to victory. In the final thirty-six-hole round, Nicklaus jumped out to a quick 4-up lead over H. Dudley Wysong through the first eighteen holes of match play. The barrage continued later with Nicklaus winning the first four holes in the afternoon, helping carry the young Bear to an impressive 8 & 6 win.

From then on, Gonzales caddied for Nicklaus almost every time he played at Pebble Beach. The duo also teamed up for a win at the 1967 Crosby Pro-Am.

"I will never forget, there was only one time I went against DiDi and what he said," Nicklaus recalls. "One year when we were playing the Crosby I hooked the tee shot almost out of bounds at No. 2. The shot ended up behind the trees, and DiDi said, 'Hit a five-iron out to the fairway and pitch it on.' I said, 'Nah, I'm gonna knock it on the green.' He came back then with, 'No, hit a five-iron into the fairway. Don't be ridiculous.'"

At the time a huge tree stood in the fairway.

"So I said, 'DiDi, I can knock it on the green.' Then he simply said, 'Your game.' Well, I took a three-wood, hooked it around the tree, put it a foot from the hole, and went on to make eagle. And I said, 'How's that, DiDi?' So he turns to me and says, 'You should have played the five-iron.' He was great. One of a kind."

Semi-retired in 1969, Gonzales continued his relationship with Nicklaus, who in 1970 would pay for Gonzales' funeral expenses.

Whatever It Takes—Pebble Beach caddie Dyer Wilson Jr.
and a number of other Pebble Beach loopers felt the after-
shocks when Wall Street collapsed in the fall of 1929.

As unimaginable as it may seem, Pebble Beach was relatively
silent for nearly a decade. Men normally working the course
found work, but it was in spurts. The only major events held at
Pebble Beach were the California State Amateur Championship
and the California Open. As it was in 1917, times were again
tough, but this time no one was untouchable. Morse, as well as
the caddies, felt the effects. So much, in fact, that at the time
the only profitable division of Del Monte Properties Company
was a sand plant located at what, since 1987, has been the
setting for The Links at Spanish Bay, co-designed by PGA Tour
legend Tom Watson, former United States Golf Association
president Sandy Tatum, and renowned golf architect Robert
Trent Jones Jr.

For men like Wilson Jr., the desperation associated with the
Depression called for desperate measures.

"Like many of the caddies back then, Wilson Jr. was fond of the
drink, and at times he would get a little down and out of it,"
Drocovich said. "One time, we heard that during an off day he
was walking around in Ojai (a city in Southern California just
northeast of Los Angeles that is about four hours away from
Pebble Beach) and noticed a few goats on a farm. So he decided
to take them. Turned out, the goats were owned by the Ojai City
Judge. He ended up having to spend ninety days in jail."

Wilson Jr., unfortunately, wasn't alone.

"Back then, guys lived from day-to-day," Drocovich said. "If they
didn't make a loop, they didn't have dinner. They'd end up borrowing money from the guys who did make a loop."

As for finding a daily dose of hooch, caddies also leaned on one
another.

*Johnny Goodman* (left) *poses with legendary Bobby Jones during the 1929 U.S. Amateur. Goodman, a caddie from Nebraska, would go on to defeat Jones 1-up in the championship, sending shockwaves through-out the golf world.* (Photograph by Julian P. Graham.)

"When you'd get a tap on the shoulder first thing in the morning it meant one thing—someone needed money for wine."

Breakthrough—If the Pebble Beach caddies admired anyone at the 1929 U.S. Amateur, it was Johnny Goodman.

Goodman, a caddie in Omaha, Nebraska, landed in the tournament following a trip to California via a railroad cattle car. In the opening round of match play, Goodman found himself going against the greatest player ever, Robert Tyre Jones Jr.

Bobby Jones, who brought in fans from throughout the West, had weeks earlier captured the U.S. Open at Winged Foot against former Pebble Beach caddie Al Espinosa. Omaha caddie Goodman, however, never backed down. After three holes, Goodman found himself 3-up. And after fourteen holes, Goodman still had a 1-up edge. Goodman went on to halve the final four holes, sending Jones packing.

Former Pebble Beach resident Charlie Seaver, who played in the tournament, witnessed the upset first-hand.

"When Jones lost, it was like Moses parting the Red Sea," said Seaver during an interview in 2003. "Most of the fans left. It was a mass exodus."

Goodman, perhaps having lost some steam himself following the huge win, lost in the afternoon to another of the era's up and coming players—Lawson Little.

No flash in the pan, Goodman won the 1933 U.S. Open at North Shore Golf Club in Illinois, becoming the last amateur to win the event. Little, meanwhile, went on to become the only player to capture back-to-back U.S. Amateur and British Amateur championships, winning both events in both 1934 and 1935.

As for winning at Pebble Beach, who knows? Had either pulled DiDi Gonzales on the bag, it might have happened.

# 4   The War Years:
## 1940–1945

*"Golf is a game whose aim it is to hit a very small ball into
an even smaller hole with weapons singularly
ill-designed for the purpose."*
—Winston Churchill

Like the rest of the Monterey Peninsula, Pebble Beach Golf Links was also affected when the United States entered World War II in 1942.

The majority of Peninsula men, who were still laboring in the canneries, suddenly found themselves on ships bound for the Pacific and European fronts. As a result, the number of rounds played at both Del Monte and Pebble Beach dwindled. For the caddies, tough times had returned once again. So tough, in fact, that most left for the Bay Area to find work at the Naval Shipyards in nearby Oakland.

"There weren't many people around in those days, and the lack of players forced many caddies to head out of the area to find better-paying work," recalled Roy Drocovich, who was 13 years old when the war began. "It was very quiet at the time."

By day, the links were usually quiet. At night, however, it was a different story.

*One of the few whom the Pebble Beach caddies could count on to be on hand during the war years was Pebble Beach founder Samuel F.B. Morse.* (Photograph by Julian P. Graham.)

U.S. Army soldiers, based at nearby Fort Ord, had constructed a machine gun nest at the nearby cliffs overlooking Carmel Bay. Another nest was located even closer to Pebble Beach. In the early years of the war, both posts were manned during the evenings in case of a sudden attack.

"They thought the Japanese might come in there at any time," said fellow looper Jack "Li'l Abner" Holt, who was also at Pebble Beach at the time.

For those caddies who did stick around, there still was some work to be had. At the time, military brass from nearby Fort Ord played the course, as did guests of The Lodge at Pebble Beach and Pebble Beach executives.

One of those still getting out was Morse, who only had to walk out of his still-standing house on No. 18 to get in a few holes.

*While things did slow down at Pebble Beach during the war years, there were always caddie recruits waiting in the wings. In this promotional photo, a group of women is instructed in the role of being a caddie.* (Photograph by Julian P. Graham.)

"He [Morse] used to love coming out in the afternoon to play nine holes, and for some reason or another the caddie master [Ray Parga] would always put me with him," said Holt, then 13 and known as "Li'l Abner" because of his fondness for working in a huge pair of boots. "Mr. Morse had this big looping slice, and one day it was just the two of us out there. When we came to the ocean holes [No. 7 through No. 10], which are death for slicers, he sliced three balls into the rough."

Li'l Abner's boots would come in handy. The search was on.

"We looked all over for those balls and came up with nothing," Holt said. "Finally, at the end of the hunt he came up to me and put his arm around me and said, 'Son, my son had the same problem.' He went on to tell me that his son had bad eyesight!"

In addition to carrying for Morse, Holt also spent time on the bags of the elite like banker Charlie Crocker and San Francisco entrepreneur Chris Buckley.

"Buckley loved his cigars, and would always bring his dog with him," Holt said. "At the end of the loop, he'd give us an extra quarter for brushing the dog down."

For many caddies, however, it was still slow, but that didn't mean the extra time would go to waste. In the case of the younger caddies a new school had opened. The ante? Mostly nickels and dimes.

"We played a lot of card games in the shack during those years," Holt said. "DiDi Gonzales, who was by then one of the older caddies still around, was more than happy to teach us how to play blackjack and poker."

"That was my first exposure to those kinds of things," Holt said. "Turned out it was a great way for me to make money for my school clothes."

Looper Dominic "Dom" Canepa, who arrived at Pebble Beach in 1946 at the age of 11, also remembers the action in the shack.

"I was known as the kid who'd rather stay in the shack

and play poker than work," Canepa said. "We had some damn good poker games in there."

Caddie Bill Shumway, who arrived at Pebble Beach a few years later in 1948, recalled one instance when the stakes were a little higher than just spare change.

"I remember there was a group of kids from Monterey who had this grand idea to come to the shack and try to scam the caddies' money," Shumway said. "They used hand signals and everything. Well, the caddies caught on to them, and knew exactly what was going on. Boy did they get in trouble. The older guys took them outside and gave them a whooping."

"It was like getting paid for having fun, and the older guys who had stuck around were all like big brothers to us younger guys," Canepa recalled. "We [the kids] didn't know much about golf, but we all thought we did. I mean, if a guy had a shot from 118 yards, we'd just tell him he was looking at about 100. It all wasn't as serious as today."

Soon everything would again change. After joining Lakeside Golf Club in Los Angeles in 1937, noted entertainer Bing Crosby came up with the idea of staging a Pro-Am competition to give Lakeside members and other golfing friends a chance to play with the pros.

While the "Crosby Clambake" found its early home at Rancho Santa Fe Golf Club outside of San Diego, it would be a mere ten years after its inception in 1937 that Crosby would move his event to the Monterey Peninsula and Pebble Beach Golf Links.


His Honor's Honor—Among those on the bag during the war years was young Dan Albert, who in the early 1940s happened to live near Pebble Beach head professional Peter Hay.

"I remember that a lot of us were just kids, so we didn't really know what we were doing," Albert said. "I mean, we had no idea which way a putt would break. We'd just say it'll do this or that."

Calling the wrong shot or club could have its consequences, however, as Albert found out. Along with catching heat at times from some of the older caddies, Albert recalled being reprimanded by more than one of his loops.

"They [players] would hate it when you couldn't find their ball," Albert said. "Back then a ball was more expensive than the round of golf. When a ball was lost the player would look at you like, 'Well, what are you here for?'"

For Albert, only a few years on the bag ended up being a lesson in life. So much, in fact, that Albert later went on to become mayor of the City of Monterey.

"Looking back, being a caddie helped me a lot with my future," Albert said. "There's a discipline and etiquette to being a caddie, and those qualities are things needed in everyday life."

The nearly five years as a Pebble Beach caddie never paid off for his own game, however. Albert, who has been the mayor of Monterey since 1986, hasn't picked up a club in years.

"I just never played a lot," he said. "People all the time ask me, 'So, being mayor of Monterey, what golf courses do you play?' When I tell them I don't play they can't believe it."


Turkey Time—At Pebble Beach, Thanksgiving Day traditions usually involve a round of golf. A great example was the lawyer who formerly lived near the first green.

"He called the shop saying he had a foursome and said he needed four caddies," said looper Roy Drocovich. "So the four of us go up, and this guy's cooking Thanksgiving dinner."

In both cooking and golf, it turns out, timing is key.

"So he tells us he has a plan for playing, and goes on to tell us that he wants to play a quick loop: No. 1, No. 2, No. 3, No. 17, and No. 18 (the "Whiskey Route"). Well, we ended up going around the loop four times. Each time we'd pass his house, he'd run in to baste the turkey."

Following the golf, Drocovich and his three compatriots got more than their fare and tip; they also got dinner.


A Caddies' Favorite—Undoubtedly, one of the caddies' favorite players during the 1930s and 1940s was San Francisco attorney Chris Buckley. Buckley, an entrepreneur who never had to practice law thanks to inheriting millions, instead spent most of his time on the links of Pebble Beach.

"If ever there was a character, it was Chris Buckley," Roy Drocovich said. "He loved to play golf and loved to drink the hooch."

Buckley's affection for the bottle, in fact, once landed him in the most bizarre of situations.

"As the story goes, Buckley once got so drunk that he ended up in a morgue," Drocovich said laughing. "I mean, they thought he was dead! Well, to everyone's surprise he woke up, so off he goes to the hospital. While he was there, someone got him to bet on the horses. Sure enough, he does and he loses $5,000, which back then was a lot of money. Oh, what a wild one. There were other stories that he'd get drunk and wake up in Paris or Chicago."

As a result of many of his indiscretions, Buckley eventually quit drinking and instead moved to Pebble Beach to play more golf. Every Monday through Thursday at 1 P.M., Buckley was on the tee.

"After he quit drinking he was more mellow, but he still had some fight in him," Drocovich said. "He used to love to take his dog Eagle with him on the course. Thing was, every time we'd get to No. 7 he'd let the dog poop. Then on No. 8 he'd put him back on the leash."

As for gambling, Buckley also quit, at least sort of.

*One of the caddies' favorite players during the 1930s and 1940s was San Francisco attorney Chris Buckley. In this shot taken in 1946, Buckley* (left) *takes a break to pose with fellow millionaires Francis Brown* (center), *a former champion of both the California and Hawaiian Amateurs, and Douglas Grant* (right), *codesigner of Pebble Beach Golf Links.* (Photograph by Julian P. Graham.)

"I remember one time Buckley set up a game with a navy captain," Drocovich said. "The captain was wearing a cap, and Buckley had served in the Navy during World War II. So, the two began bantering over who was more of a Navy man. Eventually, the captain had enough and made a bet. He'd play Buckley for his pants and the hat. Turned out, Buckley didn't win the hat. Instead, he ended having to drive home in his shorts."

## Peter Hay

If there was one bright spot at Pebble Beach during the war years, it was the move of Scotland native Peter Hay from head professional of Del Monte to Pebble Beach in 1943.

During his tenure as head pro (1943–1961), Hay—a former caddie at Royal Aberdeen Golf Club in Scotland and a former caddie master and pro at Del Monte Golf Course—became a legend within the Monterey Peninsula golfing circles. So much, in fact, that at the time the *Monterey County Herald* sports editor Ted Durein described Hay as being "known intimately by royalty and caddies, by golf wizards and duffers."

Indeed, Hay had a wide influence, but as it turns out he wasn't just known for his personality or position.

At six-foot three-inches and 260 pounds, Hay was also known for his imposing stature.

"He was built like a barrel," said longtime Pebble Beach resident Charlie Seaver, who competed in the 1929 U.S. Amateur.

"He was just strong and big," Seaver said. "There has never been anyone else that I've known built like him. I never saw anyone try to take him on. Not in his day."

Looper Dan Albert, for one, learned not to mess with Hay.

"I lived about three houses down from him and remember that we [the kids] liked to stand out in front of his house and goof off," Albert said. "Once he came out and said 'Go home!' though, everyone was gone and on their way home. He was my neighbor and could have given me a lift to work, but I never asked for a ride to the course. I was too scared!"

Caddie Sal Ursino, a fresh, 9-year-old caddie who arrived just after the war at Pebble Beach, also got to know Hay intimately. Ursino, who later became a starter at Del Monte, was Hay's personal shag man at the time.

"One time he was hitting balls to me in the range, and this lady hitting nearby skulled a shot that hit me in the leg," Ursino said. "Being so young I ended up down on my knees crying. Well, the lady started to come over to see if I was all right, but Peter came over, saying, 'Oh no, Miss, he's fine.' Then he went on to tell me, 'Laddie, get up and fetch the ball.'"

Ursino knew, as did the rest of the caddies, that when Peter Hay spoke it was time to follow directions.

*Peter Hay, Cam Puget, Henry Puget, and Bill Kynoch wait to tee off at Del Monte Golf Course circa 1948.* (Photograph by Julian P. Graham.)

*Peter Hay takes a swing. As caddie Sal Ursino and other loopers found out, when Hay spoke, it was time to follow directions.* (Photograph by Julian P. Graham.)

Young boys, however, weren't the only ones intimidated by Hay's imposing presence. A few years after the Ursino incident, professionals Dr. Cary Middlecoff and E.J. "Dutch" Harrison found out how tough Hay could be.

In the 1952 Crosby, which became known as the "Year of the Big Blow," Middlecoff and Harrison and their amateur partners marked the position of their balls on the sixteenth green at Cypress Point and started walking off the course after the wind started howling. They ran into Hay, who asked them where they were going.

"Peter, it's so windy out there you can't keep the ball on the tee," Middlecoff said.

"Sure, and show me in the rule book where it says you have to tee up the ball," replied Hay. "Now get back out there and play."

Middlecoff, Harrison, and their amateur partners, speechless, did just that.

Hay, however, was also known for his biggest muscle—his heart. His biggest passion was teaching the game, especially to kids. In addition to creating the Peter Hay Junior Golf Tournament in 1938, Hay helped construct the nine-hole Peter Hay Golf Course that lies adjacent to Pebble Beach.

Opened in 1957 and featuring nine par 3s that stretch a mere 725 yards combined, the Peter Hay Course is the epitome of a pitch-and-putt course that has over the years helped not only adults learn the game of golf, but also kids. Also known to get in a few rounds are the caddies of Pebble Beach.

"I try to accommodate everyone," Hay once said. "As long as I'm around I may as well keep busy."

Today, the Peter Hay Golf Course hosts thousands of rounds to old and young alike. And that's just the way he would have wanted it.

# 5 The Crosby Pro-Am Arrives: 1950–1960

*"I'm frequently asked, by journalists and others, what event, achievement or success has been the most gratifying to me in my lifetime. Well, the answer is immediate. This golf tournament."*
—Bing Crosby

If the caddies of Pebble Beach ever needed a shot in the arm following World War II, they got it when Bing Crosby decided to move his Clambake to the Monterey Peninsula in 1947.

With Pebble Beach already slated to host the 1947 U.S. Amateur in August, the caddies got an even bigger boost when Monterey resident Jack Dougherty and the *Monterey County Herald* sports editor Ted Durein began courting Crosby to move his tournament to Pebble Beach. Dougherty, owner of the Casa Munras Hotel and president of the Monterey Hotel and Restaurant Association, realized a ball was rolling when Pebble Beach was rewarded both the 1947 U.S. Amateur and 1948 U.S. Women's Amateur. Seizing the excitement, Dougherty coined for the Monterey Peninsula the designation "Golf Capital of the World."

"This slogan could be carried on every piece of business mail leaving here," said Dougherty in an edict to the local Monterey Peninsula business community. "It should be the byline on all envelopes, printed checks, letterheads, advertising folders, and why not on the masthead of each newspaper on the Peninsula, on the radio, in every store show-window."

One of those watching and listening was Bing Crosby.

"In the spring of 1946 I received a letter from Ted Durein," Crosby said. "It read, 'There is a group of sports-minded people on the Monterey Peninsula who would like to bring a big-time tournament here. We wondered if you would be open to a suggestion to hold [the Clambake] on one of our courses.'"

"I turned the project over to my brother Larry and later met with the Monterey people. The original purse was to be $5,000, but the PGA had legislated a $10,000 minimum in the meantime. So we went ahead with a $10,000 payoff.'"

In January of 1947, the stage for the "Greatest Show in Golf" was set, and the caddies, of course, would be among the members in the cast.

One of those on hand for the 1947 Clambake was looper Jack "Li'l Abner" Holt. Holt, still at the time only a teenager, found himself on the bag of a relatively unknown amateur by the name of Doug Ford.

"I remember thinking, 'Who is this guy?'" said Holt of Ford, who would later go on to capture the Green Jacket at Augusta National in 1957 and a Pro-Am title in 1962. "No one really knew who he was at the time."

For both Holt and the golfing world, however, it didn't take long for Ford to make his introduction.

"I remember on No. 4 he [Ford] hit his drive into the trap on the left-side of the fairway," Holt recalled. "On his second he proceeded to hole out for an eagle. He ended up beating the score of his professional partner. After that weekend, I told myself, 'This guy's a player.'"

Meanwhile, looper Byron "Sundown" Brown, who thought he'd already seen it all, also arrived at Pebble Beach Golf Links for the first Crosby. In his second year at Pebble Beach, Brown found himself not only working at the Crosby, but for Crosby himself.

"I remember Jimmy Demaret and Crosby were in the same foursome, and as we came through hole No. 13 at Pebble, Bing looked at me and said, 'There's a small whiskey jug in my bag. Now, I want you to go to that house over there and fill it up so we can make some drinks.'"

A trip to the house, which was located by what was then known as "Millionaire's Row," sounded like a good idea to Brown as well.

"As I went in, a woman offered me a glass of Scotch, which I of course accepted. Then she went on to fill the jug," Brown said. "Not long after I came out and had made some drinks for Crosby and Demaret, some of the other caddies came over and said, 'Look, we know you have a jug of whiskey in that bag.'"

Suffice to say, the hooch was out of the bag, and by the time Brown and company had reached No. 18, Crosby's jug was not only empty, but also floating in the Pacific Ocean.

"By that time, I was a little woozy myself," Brown said.

Following the round, Brown quickly got a wake-up call when Crosby asked for the location of his jug.

"As we're walking off the eighteenth green, Bing asked me where the jug was," Brown said. "When he found out where it was, he told me two words—'You're fired.'"

Suddenly down-and-out, Brown found solace in the arms of a doctor who was standing nearby and overheard the commotion.

"The doctor came over to me, and said, 'I've got a trick.' So he took me to take a cold shower and gave me a shot."

Hours later when the evening arrived, Brown was feeling better, so he decided to try to patch things up with Crosby.

*For Bing Crosby (seen here teeing off), one of the bigger questions surrounding the 1947 Pebble Beach National Pro-Am ended up being, "Where's my jug?"* (Photograph by Julian P. Graham.)

"I figured it was later in the evening and that maybe everything had blown over a bit," Brown said. "Well, when I called, it was apparent that by then Bing had already had some drinks of his own. He wasn't really sure what I was talking about or why I was calling."

The next day, Brown was back on Crosby's bag.

On the other side of the spectrum, meanwhile, was caddie Bill "Billy" Shumway. Shumway, who used to get rides to Pebble Beach from head pro Peter Hay, worked the first Crosby at age 11.

"Well, I spent most of my time as a kid hanging out at the course, and Ray Parga (then caddie master) knew me well," said Shumway. "I was a real little guy and Parga didn't think I'd be able to handle a bag. On my first loop ever, which occurred earlier in 1947, I was with a guy who hit his tee shot on No. 18 into the ocean. Afterward, he threw his driver in the ocean. So I tried to be a good caddie and went wading into the ocean to retrieve his club. My dad had told me that he had never lost a golf ball, so I definitely didn't want to lose a club. I managed to get it, but it didn't help. He still wasn't very happy."

In his Crosby debut, Shumway ended up looping for Chicago pro Felice Torza.

"It worked out great, because he was a young guy himself," Shumway said.

The best inaugural Crosby loop, however, was the one that fell into the lap of caddie Adrian Montiel.

"I lived next door to Ray Parga, and on Sunday he asked me if I wanted to make some money. Of course, I said yes," Montiel said.

Montiel, only 13 years old in 1947, found himself on the bag of then 28-year-old Ed Furgol, who entered the final round only a stroke behind co-leaders Lloyd Mangrum and Dick Metz.

"I remember the guy had one hand that was crippled, but he still could play like the devil," Montiel said.

Furgol, who had suffered a serious arm injury as a child,

did more than just play. On No. 16, he sank a 5-iron from the fairway to climb into a tie atop the leaderboard. With pars on No. 17 and No. 18, Furgol tied George Fazio for the title. Seven years later, he went on to win the U.S. Open at Baltusrol.

"Looking back, I'm sure glad I took that loop," Montiel said. "I mean, for starters, it was the first time I had ever set foot on Pebble Beach; and then to loop for Furgol. What a beautiful day."

Also on hand working the first Crosby was Vince Tomasello. Then only 13 years old, Tomasello looped for amateur Tom LoPresti, who in 1932 become the first head professional at the Sacramento Municipal Golf Course, now known as Haggin Oaks Golf Complex.

"He was a friend of the family, and had grown up with my dad, Joe," Tomasello said. "I remember I looped each day, and afterward Mr. LoPresti handed me a check for one hundred dollars. I felt like a millionaire."

For the caddies of Pebble Beach, a long journey had begun.

## Sundown

Byron "Sundown" Brown's first Clambake wasn't the first time he had rubbed shoulders with the stars. Brown had started his looping career at the Country Club of Greenfield in Massachusetts in 1923 at the tender age of 11.

"In those days, a loop around the country club meant forty-five cents was in your pocket," Brown recalled. And if it was a good round? "Well, maybe an extra nickel would fall in your hand."

A priceless experience, however, was only looming around the corner. In the fall of 1930, Brown, who had since moved on to newly opened Longmeadow Country Club in Massachusetts, found himself on the bag of a certain Bobby Jones. Jones, only months earlier, had set a standard for all who followed him by winning the Grand Slam—the British Open, the British Amateur, the U.S. Amateur, and the U.S. Open Championship.

"The first thing I learned is that he didn't like it when people called him Bobby," Brown said. "He would say that 'in England, a bobby is a policeman.'"

Soon after, however, Brown learned an even bigger lesson.

"As a caddie, the number one rule was to not distract him," Brown said. "If you asked him something on the course, he'd roll his eyes as if to say, 'Look, I've got a golf shot here.'"

Following duty service in World War II, Brown rubbed the shoulders of more stars when, in 1945, he landed at Los Angeles-based Bel Air Country Club. Among his clients were James Stewart, Clark Gable, Gary Cooper, and the man who had assumed Jones' throne—Ben Hogan.

Brown quickly found out that, like Jones, Hogan also preferred to focus on his work.

"Occasionally, he would ask for a distance, but that's the only time he would talk," Brown said. "He spent a lot of time trying to give some of the actors lessons. With Gary Cooper, he'd just keep saying, 'Get that left hip out of the way!'"

"I remember one day a milk-faced kid walked in the caddie shack. We said, 'you want to loop for a pro, huh?'" Brown said. "So we told him he'd be working for Hogan. He just stood there, with his eyes rolling around like marbles."

All of the experiences, according to Brown, led to what became the round of a lifetime.

"I was always one of those guys who wanted to see what was around the corner," Brown said. "After all, that's the bulk and trade of being a caddie. You never know who your next boss is going to be."

"Looking back, I wish I would've come to Pebble Beach earlier," said Brown, who remained a fixture in the Pebble Beach caddie barn until the 1960s. "When my day does come, I think instead of them throwing dirt over me, I'd rather

have my ashes tossed over my favorite all-time golf hole—
No. 18 at Pebble Beach."

Superstitions—Many golfers have their superstitions.
According to caddie Bill Shumway, who once looped for the
attorney who sent Al Capone to Alcatraz, one player had some
superstitions he'd never seen before.

"I remember caddying for this one guy who was extremely
superstitious," Shumway said. "For one, I always had to hand
him his putter with the blade up. He had figured that if the
blade was down, all the luck would drain out of his putter."

Then, there was my baseball cap. Before putting, he'd rub his
putter on my cap for good luck," Shumway said. "Whatever it
took, [as caddies] we were there to do our job."

# 6  Tales of the Clambake

*"To be allowed to stage a golf tournament in such environs is like the Louvre granting choice gallery space to an aspiring artist so he can display his efforts."*
—Bing Crosby

With the Crosby National Pro-Am having found a new home on the Monterey Peninsula in 1947, everything seemed to be in place for the caddies of Pebble Beach Golf Links.

"When we got the news that the Crosby was here, we loved it," said former Pebble Beach looper Adrian Montiel. "It was a chance for us to make some extra money."

Unfortunately, however, not everyone was thrilled. Only a year after the inaugural Monterey Peninsula Clambake, the PGA Tour came knocking on the door.

Its request to Crosby and other Pro-Am officials? Drop the amateurs from tournament play.

"The golf tournament, I believe, was a success if for no other reason than the opportunity it afforded the amateurs to meet and play with some of the great golfers of the day, and for the professionals to establish a social relationship with some of the people who played and supported the game," Crosby said.

Suffice to say, Crosby never budged.

"This is my week for vacation," said 1948 Pro-Am champion Lloyd Mangrum, summing up the feelings of many professionals at the time. "A fellow can't get serious about his golf when Crosby and his gang are around."

Indeed, the early Crosbys of the 1950s were all about having a good time. It was professional golf meets Hollywood, complete with Crosby occasionally belting out a tune or Bob Hope providing the laughs.

And with every step of the way, the caddies were part of the ride.

One caddie who kicked off the 1950s on the right foot was former looper Eddie Cortes.

Cortes, who had begun looping at the age of 10 in the early 1940s, opened the 1951 Crosby alongside "Lord" Byron Nelson.

At the time, Nelson hadn't played the PGA Tour in four years, instead turning his attention to ranching in Texas. Nevertheless, Nelson, then age 38, wasn't quite done.

Nelson opened the event with a 1-under 71, and followed that with a quick 67. On Sunday, he wrapped up the title with another 71, beating Dr. Cary Middlecoff by three strokes.

"I remember you didn't have to say much to him other than carry his clubs," said Cortes, who still resides on the Peninsula. "Every now and then he'd ask my opinion on a club selection, but it didn't really matter. He had already made up his mind."

For Nelson, who had won eleven straight PGA Tour titles in 1945, the win would end up being his last.

"I've got some cows to tend down in Texas," said Nelson following the win. "I'm not going back on Tour."

He never did, only competing when he felt like it.

For young caddie Sal Ursino, the new Clambakes were a chance to rub shoulders with some of Hollywood's biggest stars. Along with once looping for Western movie star Bob Steele (who was the man behind 1930s blockbusters such as *No Man's Range* and *Man from Hell's Edges*), Ursino also got to once carry Tarzan's bag.

"Looping for Johnny Weissmuller was quite an experience," Ursino said. "People kept asking him to do his yell, but he didn't do it. He'd say, 'I'm not going to do that in the middle of a golf course.'"

Another looper who got an inside glimpse at the stars was Dominic Canepa. During a 1950s Clambake, Canepa carried the bag for singer Andy Williams.

"I remember it was another rainy Crosby, and it was cold as hell," Canepa recalled. "Well, on one of the holes, everyone started sipping out of the bottle, just to stay warm. Being a caddie, I didn't expect the bottle to come my way, but sure enough I got a swig. Looking back, it was quite a thrill. I mean, I was only in my teens at the time."

Canepa also will never forget the day he worked in the same Pro-Am foursome as 1958 U.S. Open Champion Tommy "Terrible" Bolt.

Bolt, who had always had a reputation for his temper, gave his caddie a demonstration during a Clambake round.

"We were on the par-3 tenth at Monterey Peninsula Country Club, and the wind was blowing pretty hard," Canepa said. "Well, Bolt asked his caddie what to hit, and his caddie said, '3-iron.' As soon as Bolt hit his ball, the wind died down, and his ball went way over the green. After his shot, Bolt turned around screaming at his caddie. Needless to say, the caddie didn't take it. Instead, he turned around and took off running."

Bolt, according to Canepa, was right there behind him— every step of the way.

"He [Bolt] was running all over, cursing," Canepa said. "What a sight."

Vince Tomasello, who started working the fairways at Pebble Beach at age nine, also got in on the action.

"I used to get excuses from school to work the Crosbys," said Tomasello, who still resides on the Peninsula. "Sometimes, Ray Parga would even call the school to get me out."

Among Tomasello's loops were amateurs Ed Lowery and Johnny Lujack.

*Byron Nelson* (teeing off) *and caddie Emmitt Castro* (background) *paired up during the 1950 Crosby Pro-Am. A year later, Nelson and caddie Eddie Cortes would team up to capture the 1951 Crosby Pro-Am. For Nelson, who won 11 straight PGA Tour titles in 1945, the win would end up being his last.* (Photograph by Julian P. Graham.)

If anyone knew a thing about caddies, it was Lowery. In 1913, at the age of 10, Lowery had been on the bag when Francis Ouimet won the 1913 U.S. Open at The Country Club of Brookline, in Massachusetts, by knocking off Harry Vardon and Edward Ray in an eighteen-hole play-off.

"He was a real good golfer himself," said Tomasello of Lowery, who would end up being one of the biggest automo-

*For the caddies of Pebble Beach, the arrival of the Crosby Pro-Am in 1947 not only meant working with professionals such as George Bayer* (second from left) *and Ed "Porky" Oliver* (far right), *but also celebrities such as James Garner* (far left) *and Johnny "Tarzan" Weissmuller* (second from right). (Photograph by Julian P. Graham.)

bile barons in California. "He could have been playing with the pros."

As for Lujack, the 1947 Heisman Trophy winner also had game.

"For being about a 12-handicap, he was decent," Tomasello said.

The most memorable loop for Tomasello, however, happened after a Crosby round.

"One day it was getting late, and as I'm standing around the pro shop, here comes Bob Hope and three other guys," Tomasello said. "They said they wanted to play ten holes and needed some caddies. I was one of the guys who got the loop. Well, we ended up staying out on the course 'til dark, and then all of a sudden, here comes some limousines. So Hope has all of us pile in the limo and they take us back to the clubhouse. Only problem was, by that time no one was anywhere, so we couldn't even hitch-hike. Let's just say it was a long walk home."

Caddie Noel Shumway, meanwhile, was exposed to his first Pro-Am at the tender age of 11 when he worked the 1959 Crosby.

His first loop? Bing's younger brother, Bob Crosby. The musical director for the Jack Benny Show, Bob Crosby had become a well-known bandleader.

"I was a pretty small guy back then. I mean, the bag was bigger than me," said Shumway, who is the younger brother of fellow former looper Bill Shumway. "So here I go to start my round with Mr. Crosby, and on the first tee, they announce my name along with his! I guess it was because I was such a little guy. I'll never forget it. At that age, things like that stick with you. It was pretty neat."

As it turned out, the round was also unforgettable—especially the last hole.

"On the eighteenth tee, Mr. Crosby hooked a few balls into the ocean," Shumway recalled. "Next thing I know, his driver is flying into the ocean."

A few years later, in the early 1960s, Noel Shumway, who

now resides in the San Francisco Bay area, found himself shagging balls for Byron Nelson.

As for getting to the range, which at the time was located where the Beach and Tennis Club courts now stand (to the right of the fairway of hole No. 2), Shumway found out that Nelson did everything his way.

"I'm outside the pro shop waiting for Byron and I don't see him," Shumway said. "Next thing you know, a Rolls Royce pulls up and he puts me inside to take me down to the range."

For Shumway, who earned one dollar per hour shagging balls, the best was yet to come.

"He just stood in one spot and kept hitting chip shots," Shumway said. "It didn't matter to me. I just watched and got the balls."

In the end, Shumway also got something that made his eyes bulge even more—a twenty-dollar tip.

"When I saw that twenty-dollar bill in my hands, I said 'Holy smokes!'"

For former caddie Mike Maiorana, nothing ever compared to his experience in the 1958 Pro-Am.

That year, Maiorana looped for Iowan Jack Fleck, who only three years earlier in 1955 had pulled off one of golf's greatest upsets ever by defeating Ben Hogan at the U.S. Open at San Francisco's Olympic Club.

"I remember hanging around the shack, and here comes Jack Fleck. So Ray Parga says, 'Do you want to go with him?'" Maiorana said. "I said, 'Of course. Damn right I'll go with him. I mean, whoever this guy was that beat Hogan, I want to watch him play.'"

When the duo hit the course, Maiorana wasn't disappointed. In Thursday's opening round at Pebble Beach, Fleck proceeded to birdie seven of the first eight holes (No. 2 through No. 8).

"He was amazing that day," Maiorana said. "Other than asking me a lot about the greens, he just went along his business."

Fleck, however, finished the day with a 4-under 68, and

even worse apparently had used up all his magic. The next day, he fired a 4-over 76, followed by a 71 on Saturday. In Sunday's final round, he ballooned to a 78.

### Porky's Predicament—For professional Ed "Porky" Oliver the number sixteen was anything but sweet during the third round of the 1953 Crosby.

Playing in fifty-plus miles-per-hour winds at Cypress Point Club, Oliver carded a sixteen on Cypress Point's world-famous par-3 No. 16. After putting five tee shots into the Pacific, Oliver finally made it over the water but ended up in a patch of ice plant.

"He used to joke about it when we came to the hole," said caddie Adrian Montiel, who was on Oliver's bag a year later. "I always let him bring up the subject, however."

Following his sixteen in 1953, a message was waiting for Oliver in the clubhouse—"Call long-distance operator number sixteen."

Oliver did get his laughs, but he wasn't laughing at the time. Despite the sixteen, Oliver went on to card an amazing 4-over 76.

"That was priceless, Porky old boy," San Francisco Examiner columnist Prescott Sullivan told Oliver. "Best laugh we've had in years."

Replied Oliver, "I guess you'd laugh at a broken leg."

### Crime Pays—During the 1950s, one of the Pebble Beach caddies' favorite loops happened to be a notorious East Coast mobster who ran casinos in Havana. According to caddie Roy Drocovich, the mobster's popularity was a reflection of his lifestyle. His motto, by the way, also didn't hurt. "He used to always tell us, 'I may not be the best player, but I'm the best payer.'"

The X-Factor—If any golf tournament or sporting event has an annual intangible, it's the Pebble Beach National Pro-Am. Each year, the weather has played a part in the show.

"Bing's tournament is a real test of endurance," said Bob Hope, who made his Pro-Am debut in 1951. "You expect wind and rain, and usually get it. But one day there were clams in the rain."

The two most memorable weather-related early years, undoubtedly, were exactly ten years apart.

In 1952, which was known as the "Year of the Big Blow," Crosby participants, caddies, and fans were blown away—not by the golf, but by winds up to 45 mph.

"It was similar to when [Tom] Kite later won the U.S. Open in 1992," said former caddie Sal Ursino, who worked the 1952 Pro-Am. "I mean, real bad stuff."

Thanks to the wind and two inches of rain, Saturday's second round was canceled, leaving pro Jimmy Demaret—who had fired a 2-over-par 74 early Friday—all alone in first place after one round.

"It's a little breezy, but in Texas we'd consider this a wonderful day for a picnic," said Demaret, who went on to capture the title with a 71 on Sunday.

For caddies and players, the real kicker, however, was the "Year of the Snow" in 1962. That year, Sunday's final round of the Crosby was postponed due to snow. The majority of players showed up for Monday's re-scheduled final round. Others, however, elected to take off.

One Pebble Beach caddie who was on hand for the occasion was Al Kirby, who that year was carrying the bag of former amateur great Charlie Seaver. Kirby, who began looping Pebble Beach at the age of 11 in 1951, was not surprised by the turn of events.

"Having grown up on the Peninsula, I knew that it was possible.

I'd seen it happen before. Most players just accepted it like a rain-out," Kirby said.

According to lore, Elliott Henry, who was then the West Coast promotions director for ABC, had premonitions of the things to come. As the story goes, Henry went to dinner with publicity man Cliff Dektar that Saturday night. After dinner, Henry, who hailed from Chicago, began sniffing the air.

"I think it's going to snow tonight," Henry said.

"Are you kidding, it hasn't snowed here in forty years," replied Dektar, a native of Los Angeles.

Sure enough, Sunday morning the late Christmas did arrive, prompting pro Jimmy Demaret to ask, "I know I got loaded last night, but how did I end up at Squaw Valley?"

The Invasion—When golf carts first went into production nationwide in 1953, it was only a matter of time before they made their way to Pebble Beach. Sure enough, six arrived at Pebble Beach that same year.

Whether or not they stayed, however, was a different story. Not surprisingly, the caddies weren't very thrilled with their appearance.

"We quickly found out that with those old models, if you didn't set the brake, away they'd go," said longtime Pebble Beach caddie Roy Drocovich. "Needless to say, they all ended up in the ocean."

Most of the first carts, according to Drocovich, "mysteriously" disappeared off No. 18 and other Pebble Beach ocean holes (No. 17, No. 4, No. 7, No. 9, and No. 10). Oddly enough, carts were spared from what could have been their worst fate—the cliffs at the par-4 eighth.

"There were some tough caddies back then," said former looper

Sal Ursino, who began carrying bags at Pebble Beach at the age of nine in 1946. "I'm sure there were some shenanigans once the sun went down."

"The only problem with the mischief was that I was the one who had to retrieve the carts from the water," Drocovich said. "I wanted to leave them there, but it was my job, so I'd have to strip down and get in."

While it took some manpower to get the carts out, trucks were the primary pulling source. In general, Pebble Beach Golf Links features a relatively flat layout inland but the southern side of the ocean holes at Pebble Beach—most specifically holes No. 4 through No. 10—all feature relatively steep drops into Carmel Bay that can exceed forty feet. By far the most dramatic drop-off occurs at No. 8, where players fire their approach shot over a deep chasm that has been cut out by the pounding Pacific Ocean surf.

"I remember there was one occasion in the early 1990s where a player on No. 14 forgot to set the brake before getting out," former caddie master Neil Allen said. "The cart ended up rolling backwards all the way down across hole No. 6 and over the cliff."

While Pebble Beach began using carts in 1953, it wasn't until 1975 that the course featured paved cart paths. The decision to add paved paths was made by Don Marshall, who became the Golf Manager at Pebble Beach in 1975. The key behind Marshall's decision, which at first was considered "desecration of a National Treasure" by the public, was the fact that Pebble Beach continued to attract more and more players. Another factor was that during the 1970s the course almost annually suffered from severe drought. The unpaved cart paths that were in use at the time had basically started to look like the wagon trails of the Old West.

"The real bottom line is the preservation of Pebble Beach so that golf associations and charities of the future may continue to reap the same vast benefits they have been so successful in using Pebble for in the past," said Marshall in defense of his decision to pave the paths.

Today, the paved paths remain at Pebble Beach. And while the paths obviously take golfers to the famed ocean holes, the paths maintain a route along the inland side of the ocean-side fairways, keeping drivers as far away as possible from the cliffs. Governors also have been installed on the carts to mechanically slow down carts if they are moving too fast.

### The Georgia Peach—Former caddie Eddie Leonard will never forget his first taste of The Georgia Peach. One day during the mid-1950s, Leonard, who was then only 16, got word

*Baseball legend Ty Cobb wasn't just fond of swinging a bat. He also, as Pebble Beach caddie Eddie Leonard found out, was fond of swinging a golf club. In this shot, Cobb (right) instructs comedian Oliver Hardy in the finer points of tuning the swing.*
(Photograph by Julian P. Graham.)

from Pebble Beach caddie master Ray Parga that it was time to work.

"Ray just told me that this guy wanted to play, so I decided to take the loop," Leonard recalled.

Through the front nine, Leonard discovered his mystery loop was not only left-handed, but also a pretty damn good player. The older fellow also apparently was a sports nut.

"It was a pretty quiet stroll, but the guy kept on wanting to talk about sports—especially baseball. He really wanted to know what I enjoyed about baseball," Leonard said.

"So the guy finishes his round, which is right around par, and we head on back to the clubhouse. Well, Parga later comes over to me and asks, 'What'd he do out there?' I told him he was right at par."

"Then, he asked, 'Do you know who that was?' I replied, 'No.'"

"So he goes on to tell me, 'That was one of the greatest base-ball players of all time—Ty Cobb.'"

Having heard the news, shockwaves hit Leonard.

"When Parga told me it was Ty Cobb, I froze," Leonard said. "I just got tingly all over. Immediately I started to look for him, but he was gone."

# 7   Changing of the Guard: 1960–1970

*"Why it was called the Clambake? I'll never know, because there wasn't a clam in evidence."*
—Bing Crosby

By the time the 1960s rolled around, America was changing. So was the Crosby Pro-Am.

Gone were professional icons such as Byron Nelson and Ben Hogan, who stopped competing in the 1950s. Also missing from the action was Crosby himself, who like Hogan last competed in the 1956 Pro-Am.

The tournament and the caddies of Pebble Beach, however, kept rolling along.

After all, a number of young professionals—most notably

Ken Venturi, Jack Nicklaus, and Arnold Palmer—were more than ready to assume the vacant thrones.

As for Venturi, caddie Adrian Montiel carried the new star's bag in 1961, only a year after Venturi had continued his rise thanks to a victory at the Crosby. At the 1961 Pro-Am, Venturi was again in the hunt following an opening round 67 at Pebble Beach.

"I had come down from Washington, where I was based in the service, just to work the Crosby," Montiel said. "So here I get Ken Venturi. The main thing I remember was one hole on the old Dunes Course at MPCC. It was No. 18 (a par 5), and by that time I thought I had done another fairly good job."

"So we're walking up the fairway and he says, 'Club me.' I told him, 'You need a three-wood.' As I'm pulling the bag away, people start telling me, 'That's too much club! People have been clearing the green with a three-wood all day.' Sure enough, his ball went sailing way over the green."

Montiel braced himself, but nothing happened.

"He never got angry about it," Montiel said. "He just said, 'I should have known better.'"

Venturi, three years later, garnered even more national attention with his memorable win at the 1964 U.S. Open at Congressional Country Club. Montiel, meanwhile, stayed on Venturi's bag whenever the star played at Pebble Beach.

"In those days, a lot of the Crosby players would head over to nearby Fort Ord to play in exhibition matches at Bayonet Golf Course and he brought me with him a few times," Montiel said. "Hell, I remember he shot a 67 there one time, and he was just goofing around."

For Montiel, the only complaint he ever heard from Venturi—the former lead golf commentator for CBS—surprisingly had something to do with his shoes.

"I had just bought a brand new pair of Foot-Joys," said Montiel, who still resides on the Peninsula. "And I remember him saying, 'Christ, you have better shoes than I do.'"

Former Pebble Beach looper Noel Shumway wasn't so lucky to have someone as established as Venturi. During an early 1960s Pro-Am, Shumway kept trying to figure out just who he was looping for.

*Rising star Ken Venturi* (left) *poses with amateur partner/comedian George Gobel on the eve of the 1961 Crosby Pro-Am.* (Photograph by Julian P. Graham.)

"The guy was very young. I mean in his mid-20s," Shumway recalled. "I also remember he was wearing some huge glasses."

The man behind the frames was none other than Hale Irwin, who would go on to win the 1974 U.S. Open at New

*Longtime Pebble Beach looper Roy Drocovich (seen here as a starter) saw some strange things during his days as a Pebble Beach caddie. Among them was being on hand the year the Crosby Pro-Am was robbed.* (Photograph by Julian P. Graham.)

York–based Winged Foot Golf Club, the 1979 U.S. Open at Inverness Club in Ohio, and the 1990 U.S. Open at Medinah Country Club in Illinois.

"At the time, he was a real no-nonsense kind of guy," said Shumway of Irwin. "You could tell he was just thinking about golf. He was young, but he was focused."

That focus at Pebble Beach would eventually pay off. In 1984, Irwin went on to win one of the most memorable Pro-Ams thanks to a two-hole play-off win over Jim Nelford. With Nelford the leader in the clubhouse at 10-under 278, Irwin came to the eighteenth tee trailing by a stroke. His drive veered left into the rocks, but incredibly ricocheted off a boulder and soared back into the fairway. Given new life, Irwin went on to birdie the hole to force a play-off. In the play-off, after both Irwin and Nelford made par at the fifteenth, Irwin skied a 3-wood tee shot at the sixteenth, ending up in a fairway bunker. From the bunker, Irwin knocked a 2-iron from 213 yards out to within nine feet of the pin. He sank the putt for the win.

For former looper Roy Drocovich, the 1960s Pro-Ams were also memorable.

"I tried to stay away from the pros. The ams always paid better" said Drocovich, who passed away in 2003. "One lesson I learned early was that you always wanted to get paid before the loop. Or at least negotiate a fee before going out. That way you'd know whether or not it was worth your time to hang around. I mean, there were times when I'd get a dollar tip."

The good news was that he at least never suffered the same fate as Dean Martin's caddie.

"I remember during one Pro-Am, Dean Martin sent his caddie about one-hundred yards out in the range to shag balls," Drocovich said. "Well, sure enough, one guy hooks a low drive that slams the poor caddie right between the eyes, dropping him to the ground. A little later an ambulance came over to pick him up."

Other highlights for Drocovich included looping in the same groups with former President Gerald Ford and actor/singer Robert Goulet.

"Now there's two guys who were lethal out there," Drocovich said. "They should have had an ambulance follow those two, because they hit more people than anything else."

For Drocovich, the Dean Martin incident wasn't the last time he heard sirens at Pebble Beach. As the man in charge of cashing all the caddies' paychecks, Drocovich was on hand the year the Crosby Pro-Am was robbed.

"Back then, all of the tournament's proceeds would go straight into a [Pebble Beach Company] office, which was located just across from The Lodge. As for myself, I would head up there to cash the caddies' checks for them. Well, on this particular day, I get up to the office and there are cops all over the place. So I asked someone what the hell was going on, and they tell me there was a stickup."

In the middle of the stickup, however, was quick-thinking accountant Chester Gillette.

"By the time it was over, the robber didn't get anything," Drocovich said.

Gillette, the thinker, apparently had feigned a heart attack during the heist. And when the burglar reached down to loosen his gag to let him breathe, Gillette kicked him in the groin and then fell on him. With the aid of an assistant, Gillette then held the man until police arrived to haul him to jail.

As for Crosby's reaction to the holdup, Bing took it in stride.

"I remember the next morning a bunch of us were sitting around Cypress Point Club, talking about the tournament," said Crosby later. "Included in our number was an old chap named Stuart Haldorn—a very funny man. Didn't say much, but about once every month he'd come up with some wry, dry remark that would convulse everybody."

"We got to talking and someone said it was a wonderful event. Somebody else said, 'Yes, and the weather was superb,' and then someone added, 'and a popular winner.'

"Someone else said, 'Thrilling shots,' and someone said, 'Yes, I think there's no doubt. It's probably the best tournament we've ever had.'"

"At that point, Stuart chimed in, 'Well, I don't know. Seems to me that fella loused up the holdup.'"

As for getting close to some of the greats, former looper Tom Bruno got his chance in the 1964 Pro-Am.

That year, Bruno was on the bag of amateur Father John Durkin, who was paired with rising professional star Tony Lema. Lema, who only a year earlier had finished as runner-up at The Masters, opened the tournament with a 2-under 70, and then made a move with a 64 in the second round and a 70 in the third round. A final round 76 through wind and rain landed Lema the trophy, and gave Bruno the lasting memory of watching a champion in action.

"I was very impressed by what he did and the way he played," Bruno said. "Tony Lema was by far the best player that was in any of my foursomes."

As a preview of things to come, Bruno again witnessed Lema making a run at the 1965 Pro-Am, where he finished second. Months later, the Northern California native won the British Open.

In 1966, however, tragedy struck. Lema, then one of the most popular pros on Tour, died in a plane crash.

"Back then, a lot of people wrote that Tony Lema was a cocky kid," Bruno said. "As far as I'm concerned, he was a perfect gentleman. He also had one of the prettiest swings in all of golf."

## One of a Kind

If anyone defined the party-like atmosphere of the Crosby during the 1950s and 1960s, it was comedian Phil Harris.

Harris, at the time, was the bandleader of the *Jack Benny Show*. He was also, undoubtedly, the tournament's biggest lush.

In the 1951 Crosby, Harris paired up with pro Dutch Harrison to win the pro-am portion, thanks to a huge Harris putt on the historic two-tiered seventeenth green at Pebble Beach. One of those on hand for the occasion was caddie Vince Tomasello, who was looping in the same foursome.

"The flag was back left, and his ball was way over to the right, about 140 feet away," Tomasello said. "So here I am holding the flag, and Harris putts this bomb. It falls right into the cup."

*Not only a Crosby Pro-Am but also a caddie favorite, Phil Harris* (at the microphone) *revs up a gallery that includes Bing Crosby* (seated left). (Photograph by Julian P. Graham.)

According to lore, Harris then headed straight for the clubhouse, letting Harrison clean up a final par for the victory. Later, asked that night if the putt covered such a vast distance, Harris replied, "Hell, it broke that much."

It was then, however that reporters approached not Tomasello, but Harris' personal caddie, Scorpie Doyle.

"I can't say for sure how far it was, but I'd like to have that much footage along Wilshire Boulevard," Doyle said.

Other Harris highlights included a memorable Crosby round at Spyglass Hill, upon which, after a night on the town, Harris came staggering to the first tee. Not surprisingly, he whiffed his first tee shot.

As for the aforementioned Doyle, it was no shocker that he was just as fond of hooch as his boss. In one Pro-Am, Doyle arrived at first tee at Pebble Beach looking a wee bit hungover. Harris, however, didn't notice a thing and proceeded to tee it up.

After taking his swing, Harris turned to his right-hand man and asked, "Where did it go?"

With squinty eyes and a deep sigh, the caddie replied, "Where did WHAT go?"

Later, Harris offered Doyle a deal. For one, extra money if he never took another drink. Being friends with Ben Hogan, Harris said he would also set up Doyle with a job at Hogan's Tamarisk Country Club in Palm Springs.

Doyle, realizing the situation, took the offer. He later became the starter at Tamarisk, a position he held until his death in 2001.

## A Twist of Lemmon

The year 1969 wasn't just the year that man landed on the moon. It was also the year that actor Jack Lemmon landed at Pebble Beach Golf Links.

*The year 1969 wasn't just the year man landed on the moon. It was
also the year that Jack Lemmon landed at Pebble Beach Golf Links.
There to help him along would be a caddie that Lemmon would never
forget.* (Photograph by William C. Brooks.)

As for his first tourney? Let's just say Lemmon was only warming up.

In a story that appears in Dwayne Netland's book *The Crosby: Greatest Show in Golf,* upon arriving on the Monterey Peninsula to make his debut Lemmon received a message stating that his hired caddie would be unable to make it. New to the event and finding himself suddenly pressed for time, he quickly hurried to the Pebble Beach caddie barn to find a replacement.

"I looked around the caddie pen and this fellow, an older guy with a big, heavy overcoat, comes up and says he'd like the job," reported Lemmon. "I learned later that he was one of the great lushes of all time, but at this minute he was sober."

With an 8:46 tee time at Spyglass Hill, Lemmon arrived at eight o'clock the next day at Pebble Beach to pick up his new caddie.

"So I pick him up at Pebble in a car I had rented and we head for Spyglass. His breath is so strong my eyes start to water. It's 8 A.M., and he's smashed."

"Well, on the first tee I hit a pretty good three-wood, take a bow for the gallery and start walking down the fairway, still carrying that three-wood. I'm on top of the world."

"Next thing, I turn around and my caddie is gone. He's searching for my bag. Lost it on the first tee. Finally, he finds it and comes rumbling down the fairway, lurching and stumbling. About a hundred yards off the tee, on a piece of perfectly flat ground, he slips. My clubs fly out of the bag and he's flat on his ass."

The mayhem, it turns out, had just began.

"On the second hole, I hear this tinkling, like jingle bells. I don't know what the hell it is," Lemmon said. "Then, the sun comes out and off comes that big coat, hitting the ground like a ten-ton rock. He had pint bottles stashed away in the lining, four or five of them clanking together on the bottom."

Later in the week, Lemmon's adventure arrived at Pebble Beach—in front of live television.

For starters, there was the par-5 fourteenth, where—as ABC broadcaster Jim McKay explained—Lemmon was getting ready for "that all important eighth shot."

Then there was the par-3 seventeenth.

"When we got to seventeen, we had a little wind behind us," Lemmon said. "I cranked up and hit a driver. It went forty yards over the green."

Standing on rocks amid the ocean, Lemmon's "save" shot went 130 yards further out to sea.

The capper, however, was No. 18. Following two drives into the water, Lemmon reached the par-5 green in nine. He then began surveying his thirty-five-foot putt, and wanting some advice, asked his caddie which way it broke.

Replied Lemmon's caddie—"Who cares?"

"I would rather play Hamlet with no rehearsal in an opera house than play golf on television," Lemmon would say.

From that year on, the Lemmon show continued through twenty-six, Sunday-less Crosbys. And with each passing year and each missed cut, the former favorite looked more and more like Wile E. Coyote. He just couldn't close out the chase.

At the 1998 AT&T Pro-Am, Lemmon and longtime partner Peter Jacobsen stood at 16-under after the first two days of competition, and it appeared they were locks to make the cut. Rain, however, washed out the amateur portion of the tournament and sent Lemmon home empty-handed once again.

"We got gypped," said Lemmon following the postponement.

For both golf fans and Pro-Am fans, the game won't be the same without a twist of Lemmon.

"It's not going to be the same for me without having Jack out there with me," said Jacobsen following Lemmon's death in 2000. "When I stop coming here, I'll think of all the times I've played with Jack."

The King—If any professional left his mark at Pebble Beach and the Crosby Pro-Am during the 1960s, it was Arnold Palmer.

Palmer, who first arrived at the Crosby in 1958, had opened the new decade with a run in the 1961 Pro-Am, eventually tying for fourth place. Two years later, however, the stories really started flowing.

In the third round of the 1963 Pro-Am, Palmer—who had entered the day only three strokes behind co-leaders Dave Hill and Billy Casper—stood on  the majestic, but tough seventeenth tee at Pebble Beach. After surveying the 218-yard par-3 hole, Palmer decided to go with a 2-iron.

Taking his swing, Palmer lashed out, sending the ball over the green, and apparently into the Pacific Ocean. He went on to re-tee and hit another, but as he approached the green, officials relayed the news to Palmer that his first ball was still in play, lying on the rocks of the beach below.

Looking to save strokes, The King went on to play the beached ball. A day later, following his fourth round, the PGA Tour—who had been discussing the previous day's events—suddenly made a statement.

According to officials, Palmer had hit an unauthorized provisional ball. The result? A disqualification.

Turns out, the incident was only the beginning.

In the 1964 Pro-Am, Palmer again found trouble on No. 17 after again hitting his tee shot over the green. Again, the beach was in play, and once again, Palmer took a swipe. One swing. Two swings. Three swings. Four. Palmer was still in the rocks.

"To take an unplayable lie," remarked television broadcaster Jimmy Demaret, "his nearest drop would have been Honolulu."

Palmer, ever charging, kept on swinging and eventually ended up carding a nine. He missed the cut by one stroke.

*If anyone left his mark at Pebble Beach and the Crosby Pro-Am during the 1960s, it was Arnold Palmer. During both the 1963 and 1964 Crosby Pro-Ams, Palmer would find himself playing from the rocks off the green at No. 17. In the 1967 Pro-Am, meanwhile, Palmer dueled with a tree on No. 14.* (Photograph by William C. Brooks.)

"Looking back, it was really kind of amusing," Palmer said. "I hit the tee shot rather poorly and it took off for the ocean. When I found it I elected to play it, but it ended up being somewhat of a fiasco because the ball would wash up and then go back into the water. As it turned out, when I finished my round I headed over to the Tap Room. By the time I got there, the bartender had invented a new drink—"Palmer on the Rocks."

Turns out, however, that No. 17 wasn't Palmer's only problem. In the 1967 Pro-Am, Palmer came to the dog-leg right par-5 No. 14 (555 yards) only a stroke behind rival Jack Nicklaus.

Again trying to charge, Palmer went for the green in two with a 3-wood, with his ball landing in the branches of a tree and bouncing through the out-of-bounds marker on the right. Still less than one-hundred yards from the green, Palmer went for it, but his next shot hit the tree again, again bouncing out-of-bounds. Again, a nine would end up on his card, leaving him seven strokes behind eventual winner Jack Nicklaus.

"Well, I was leading at the time so I elected to go for the green with a 3-wood," Palmer said. "I hit it high and it looked good, but then it hit that tree."

In the end, Palmer got the last laugh. That night, a storm knocked down the infamous tree.

"The next morning as I'm driving in, I saw what had happened to that tree," Palmer said. "Thing was, everyone was blaming me. They thought that I had gone out at night and chopped it down."

On each of the occasions, Palmer's man on the bag had been veteran caddie Bob Blair, who passed away in the early 1990s.

"Bob was a tough guy, but he later reformed," Palmer recalled. "Did he ever say anything to me prior to or after some of those shots? By the time I'd hit them what could he say?"

While Blair's recollections are lost, one man who still knows what it was like to work with Palmer is Ernest "Creamy" Carolan.

During his caddie career, Carolan, who turned 89 in 2004, spent the majority of his time on Palmer's bag. In 2000, Carolan was named to the Professional Caddies Association Hall of Fame.

"Bob Blair was indeed tough. Not only had he been a policeman in Philadelphia, but he also served in World War II at Tarawa," Carolan said. "He was an ex-Marine."

"As for Arnie though, there were times when he did need help. He could make some bad decisions. I remember he'd get mad at you if you were right," Carolan said. "I remember there were shots he had where I'd say, 'No, don't go for it, don't do it.' After listening enough, he'd lay up and then make birdie. Then he'd say, 'Good call, Creamy. Nice one.' Or he'd just still go for it and still make birdie."

"Arnold always did it his way. He was always bold. Sometimes it would work out, and sometimes it didn't. He always did his own thing."

# 8  The Open Arrives:
## The 1972 U.S. Open

*"I never hit a shot, not even in practice, without having a very sharp, in-focus picture of it in my head. First I see the ball where I want it to finish, nice and white and sitting up high on the bright green grass. Then the scene quickly changes, and I see the ball going there: its path, trajectory, and shape, even its behavior on landing. Then there is a sort of fade-out, and the next scene shows me making the kind of swing that will turn the previous images into reality."*
—Jack Nicklaus

Having further honed their skills by working the Bing Crosby National Pro-Am, there was only one major question left for the caddies of Pebble Beach as the 1970s rolled around.

When would they get the chance to work a U.S. Open Championship?

Pebble Beach still had not hosted a U.S. Open, almost half a century after the legendary course opened, despite already having hosted three U.S. Amateurs and two U.S. Women's Amateurs.

As strange as it may now sound, getting the national championship to come to Pebble Beach wasn't easy.

According to USGA officials, there were just too many obstacles standing in the way of having a national championship at Pebble Beach.

Among them, of all things, was the perception that Pebble Beach was a poor and risky location. After all, in the USGA's mind, San Francisco was over one-hundred miles away, which meant that there just wouldn't be enough of a fan base or sponsors to make the event successful.

Another concern for the USGA, meanwhile, was the fact that Pebble Beach was a public golf course. As officials explained it, with the public regularly "hacking" up the course, getting the course ready for an Open would be impossible.

Morse and Del Monte officials, not surprisingly, had their own ideas. With the Open in mind and in hopes of pleasing the USGA, Morse had years earlier (1963) created the Pebble Beach Golf Club, which all but privatized Pebble Beach. Under club rules, Pebble Beach would be open "only to guests of the Del Monte Lodge, residents of the forest and their guests, and to members of Cypress Point Club, Monterey Peninsula Country Club and the Beach Club."

The move to privatization, however, didn't change the USGA's mind. And to make matters worse, residents of the Monterey Peninsula weren't thrilled.

With the 1972 U.S. Open invitation and application deadline nearing, Morse knew he had to change course, and fast.

His first move, which was undoubtedly celebrated by not only Monterey Peninsula golfers but golfers worldwide, was to abandon the Pebble Beach Golf Club and re-open public play. Later, boosted in part by the presence of new USGA Executive Director P.J. Boatwright, Morse sent in his invitation to the USGA, and this time the USGA agreed. Before Morse and Boatwright could sit at the table, however, the then 89-year-old Pebble Beach founder died of a heart attack.

With the Open question still in the air and the competition to host the championship ever-increasing, the burden fell on new Del Monte Properties Company president Aimee G. "Tim" Michaud.

Knowing how badly his predecessor had wanted an Open at Pebble Beach, Michaud came up with the biggest idea he could—a $250,000 minimum guarantee to the USGA no matter what revenue the event would generate.

Suffice to say, the U.S. Open had finally arrived at Pebble Beach. Waiting at the gates were the caddies.

## The Accidental Caddie

When the U.S. Open landed at Pebble Beach in 1972, it didn't really mean much to Monterey Peninsula resident Paul Latzke. At the time, the 30-year-old Latzke was a teacher at Robert Louis Stevenson High School, which sits only a mile or so from Pebble Beach.

"When I heard the U.S. Open was coming, I was interested but not really revved up about it," Latzke said. "I didn't play much golf, and to be honest with you I really didn't know that much about the game."

Little did Latzke know, however, that things were about to drastically change.

Only a few days prior to the championship, then Robert Louis Stevenson High athletic director Wally Goodwin (who would later become the head golf coach at Stanford University), approached Latzke and other faculty members about some news he'd heard.

"Wally told us that there was a need for caddies for the Open," Latzke said. "The pros couldn't use their own caddies, so there were openings. Anyone could throw their name in a box, so Wally told us to get down there."

The caddie and players pool, which basically featured names in a hat, was at the time the USGA's effort to make the championship as fair as possible. In the USGA's mind, profes-

*Jack Nicklaus and caddie Paul Latzke make their way up toward the green of No. 1 during the 1972 U.S. Open at Pebble Beach. Latzke had won the right to be Nicklaus' caddie via a player-caddie lottery held on the eve of the championship.* (Photograph by William C. Brooks.)

sional players who used their own personal caddies would be at an advantage.

As a result, the caddies gathered at the first tee and drew names out of a hat. The player that the caddie drew was his loop for the week. The catch was that the names in the hat weren't always just names. They were also sometimes legends—Chi Chi Rodriguez, Lee Trevino, Jack Nicklaus, and Arnold Palmer.

"Well, I decided that despite my little knowledge, I would enter the pool," Latzke said. "It was the Saturday before the championship began, and here I am waiting for my name to be called so I could go pick my player. Thing was, everyone wanted Jack Nicklaus. He had already won the Masters, and there was all this talk about the grand slam."

Eventually, Latzke's name was called, so he reached for the piece of paper in the hat.

"I remember I picked up the piece of paper that was on top," Latzke said. "Then I looked and when I saw it, I said, 'I got the man.'"

Sure enough, Latzke had drawn Nicklaus.

"There was a huge commotion. Cheering, jeering, laughing—all of it. You see, a lot of the regular caddies, who would've gone nuts had they drawn Nicklaus, knew that I didn't know much about being a caddie," Latzke said. "I remember they were saying, 'What the hell are you going to tell Nicklaus? You're going to be working for the master!'"

Despite all the hubbub, Latzke never flinched.

"I had played in the NFL for six years, so I was used to being near great athletes. I'd known Joe Namath and John Brodie. Everyone else was in awe, but I wasn't. I just knew that I needed to brush up on my caddie skills, and damn fast," Latzke said.

Meanwhile, word of the accidental caddie's feat began spreading. So much, in fact, that local newspapers picked up on the action.

"By Monday, Jack knew who I was," Latzke said. "I guess he'd read about the big pick in the newspaper."

All of Latzke's confidence quickly waned, however. Through the grapevine, he had received word regarding Chi Chi Rodriguez' caddie.

"Someone had told me that Chi Chi had interviewed his pick, and that one of his questions was, 'Have you ever caddied before?' When Chi Chi found out that his caddie had no experience, he fired him on the spot. The first thing I thought after I heard that was, 'Oh no, I'm gonna be fired.'"

The Monday prior to the championship, Latzke met his new boss face-to-face for the first time. His fate was waiting.

"I remember you could see him coming from miles away, because he was surrounded by press people," Latzke said. "As he came towards me, he said, 'So you got me, huh. Well, here's what we're going to do. We're gonna go hit some balls.'"

Minutes later, Latzke was sitting in the backseat of a car headed to the range with Nicklaus in the front.

"So we're on the way up to the range, and he turns around and asks me, 'Have you ever caddied before?' I thought, 'Oh no, here we go.' My heart was in my throat."

With his mind racing, Latzke opted to go with the truth.

"I was honest. I didn't lie. I told him that I'd caddied only a handful of times before and that when I did play I usually shot in the 80s," Latzke said. "So he turns back and says, 'Don't worry about it. I'll tell you everything you need to know.'"

According to Latzke, Nicklaus then laid down the golden rule.

"The first thing he said was to never toss him the ball. Only hand it to him. The reason for that was that according to Jack, 'If you toss me the ball I might hurt my finger. Then I'm out of the tournament.'"

Another rule, according to Latzke, was how Nicklaus' balls should be marked for identification. "He used MacGregor balls that had a picture of a bear on them," Latzke said. "The rule with the balls was that you had to put a pencil mark next to the bear. When I asked why, he said, 'All of the balls I use during practice rounds have that mark. That way, if I lose a ball during a practice round, with that mark there, I won't be confused should I lose a non-marked ball during regulation."

With the verbal lessons over, it was time to get to work.

"So we headed up to the range, and Jack steps into the line of guys hitting balls," Latzke said. "Well, all of the other guys stopped. They just stood there and watched. You could tell they were all in awe."

After taking Tuesday off, Latzke and Nicklaus went back to work on Wednesday. This time, they'd be hitting the course.

"I remember there were some holes where he wouldn't even take a practice swing. He'd just get up to the tee and let it rip," Latzke said. "As we're getting done, he told me my job for Thursday and the rest of the week. It was to walk the eighteen holes prior to his rounds to see where the pins were. He wanted to know exactly where each pin was on the green, down to paces, ten paces, fourteen paces or whatever. The amazing thing was that he already knew the paces from the tee box to the green. And as for knowing what club to hit, forget it. He'd know right away what club to hit. He never once asked me anything like, six-iron or seven-iron?'"

When the championship began, Nicklaus quickly made a move, jumping into a tie for first-place thanks to a first round 1-under-par 71. On day two, Nicklaus slipped to a 1-over 73, but nonetheless still sat in the lead.

"Those first two days everything went really smooth. Thankfully, there weren't a lot of problems," Latzke said. "By then, I had it down. It was clean the clubs and then give them to him, rake the bunkers and replace the divots. It wasn't rocket science."

In the third round, which featured a stiff breeze, Nicklaus continued to keep it going, shooting an even-par 72 to remain in the lead. Entering the final round, he had a one-stroke lead over Lee Trevino, Kermit Zarley, and Bruce Crampton.

"It's nice to be in a position to win," Nicklaus told the press

*Caddie Paul Latzke and Jack Nicklaus wait to putt during the 1972 U.S. Open.* (Courtesy of Paul Latzke Library.)

afterward. "But wait until tomorrow and we'll see if it's an advantage playing last."

Come Sunday morning, Latzke could sense he was about to witness history.

"After being on his bag for a week, I had seen that there was indeed something special about Nicklaus," Latzke said. "He had this ability to focus and concentrate to a point where you could almost physically feel his power of concentration. It was as if radiation was coming off him. Then he'd just cock his chin, give the ball a whap and away the curtain would go."

As for the final round, it looked like funnyman Lee Trevino and Nicklaus would battle it out again. Only a year earlier at Merion Golf Club in Pennsylvania, Trevino had won the U.S. Open thanks to an eighteen-hole play-off win over Nicklaus. Just prior to teeing off in the play-off, Trevino had pulled out a rubber snake to scare Nicklaus as a joke.

"So here we are on the tee, and Jack looks over at Trevino and says, 'What, no snakes?' Trevino got a good laugh, but said, 'No,'" Latzke said. "Right after that, Trevino looked back at Jack and said, 'You know Jack, if I don't win this I want you to. You're the greatest and you've done so much for golf.' That was really a great thing to witness."

By the time the two superstars had reached the third hole, Nicklaus' one-stroke lead over Trevino had grown to three. While Nicklaus was carding a birdie on No. 2, Trevino was scoring a double-bogey thanks to hitting his third shot over the green.

If there was a shaky moment for Nicklaus, it came on No. 10. After testing the wind, Nicklaus teed it up. As he went into his backswing a gust of wind blew. His drive ended up on the beach below the coastline edge, leading to a double-bogey.

"Although his drive went way right, it was like it didn't even faze him," Latzke recalled. "He'd been in cruise control before that, and he knew it. It was as if he was saying to himself, 'Oh, well. Guess I'll just have to hit my next shot from the beach.' He had that much confidence."

Later, Arnold Palmer entered the fray, but again Nicklaus came through thanks to a critical bogey-saving putt on the par-3 twelfth. After holding off the competition for four more holes, the championship came down to the par-3 seventeenth. At the time, Nicklaus held a three-stroke lead over Bruce Crampton.

"As we're headed over to seventeen, a marshal comes over and says, 'Hey Jack, we don't want to alarm you but there's some (Vietnam War) protesters chained to a tree on No. 18.' Jack said, 'Are they armed?' and the marshal said, 'No, I don't think so.' Then Trevino piped in, 'I know how to find the key to that chain—just give me a book of matches.' Then we get to the tee box and all Jack says is, 'I want my 1-iron,'" Latzke said. "That's it. No other words—just going along his business as usual. There's a ton of people there, and as he hits it, there's a huge cheer."

Despite playing directly into heavy winds, the ball landed just a foot away from the cup, bounced once, hit the flagstick and came to rest a mere six inches from the hole. The resulting tap-in birdie all but clinched Nicklaus' thirteenth Major championship, tying him with the great Bobby Jones.

"So we're walking up No. 18, and Jack says, 'Paul, will you do a favor for me. I want you to walk between me and the protesters.' I nodded and told him that I understood," Latzke said. "Then we get up to the green and it's all over. He reaches out of the cup and gives me the ball, shakes my hand, does his thing with his family, and heads off to the press tent."

Nicklaus had finished the job; and so had Latzke.

"I've never talked to Jack since then. He went on to keep playing golf and I went on teaching. I always remember the last thing he ever said to me, though. He said, "Paul, if I can ever be of any assistance to you, please let me know. I'd be more than happy to help. Looking back, it was quite an experience. I mean, there are people who would've handed over their first-born to do what I did."

## The King and I

Like Paul Latzke, Monterey teenager Kit Huston also had no idea what was headed his way.

A football and basketball star at nearby Carmel High School, Huston first began looping at Pebble Beach in 1967, when he was a mere 13 years old. Five years later, the U.S. Open was in town.

"It was a real big deal," Huston recalled. "I mean, the big guys were coming."

Through the years, Huston had already looped for a number of notable amateurs in the Crosby Pro-Am. The 1972 U.S. Open, however, would be an experience for a lifetime.

Having earned a role as a caddie for the Open thanks to his work at the Crosbys, Huston soon found his name in the Open's caddie and players pool. When it was Huston's turn to draw, he walked up, reached in and handed the piece of paper to the announcer: "Arnold Palmer."

"When the announcer said Arnold Palmer, it got real quiet all of a sudden," said Huston, who is now the head professional at Cobb Meadows Golf Club in Napa Valley. "Just appreciation for Mr. Palmer, I guess."

Later, when it came time to meet and greet Mr. Palmer, it was Huston who was in awe.

"No doubt I was a little nervous, but he quickly made me feel right at home," Huston recalled. "Plus, he always had his entourage with him, so that helped to keep things smooth."

As for the job at hand, Huston quickly found out what it was like to be a member of the King's court.

"When we walked through the crowds, I felt like Moses parting the Red Sea," Huston said. "Everyone wanted to see this legend up close, as if brushing me was an extension of him," Huston said. "People adored him. They respected Nicklaus and they enjoyed Trevino, but there was an outpouring of love for Arnold Palmer."

Palmer, meanwhile, gave his caddie some love in the form

of advice. Palmer had seen that Huston was carrying his bag over his shoulder, so he showed him an easier way to carry it over his back instead.

"The Tour bags back then probably weighed seventy or eighty pounds," Huston said. "He was interested in making sure I didn't hurt myself."

As for the championship, when play began Palmer got down to business. Following a shaky first round, he promptly fired a 4-under-par 68 in the second round, tying the low round of the tournament and putting him only one stroke off the lead.

"It could have been better," said Palmer, who began thinking that his luck at Pebble Beach was finally going to change. "I missed makeable putts at five (fifteen feet), six (twelve feet) and seven (six feet), and also the little two-footer at eight. I was madder than I've ever been on a golf course."

As Huston recalled, there was indeed tension on the par-5 sixth hole.

"I remember he smashed this long drive down the left side of the fairway—really kills it. So he asks me, 'Kit, did that go in the bunker?' Well, I said, "No." Turned out it was in the bunker. I had guessed, which looking back wasn't the right thing to do," Huston said. "I could tell that kind of irritated him a little."

Two days later, in the final fourth round, Palmer again made one of his trademark charges. Despite a bogey on No. 10, he had pars on both No. 11 and No. 12, leaving him only two strokes behind the leader, Jack Nicklaus.

By the time Palmer reached the long, difficult par-5 fourteenth, he was still trailing Nicklaus by a mere two strokes. The championship would soon hang in the balance.

While Palmer hit his third shot at No. 14 to within eight feet of the pin, Nicklaus watched his tee shot at the par-3 No. 12 bounce off the green and into a patch of rough. From where he was, Nicklaus tried to chop out, but could only manage to move the ball a few feet. His third shot then rolled eight feet past the cup.

Suddenly, the two legends were each looking at a critical eight-foot putt. If Palmer made his putt and Nicklaus missed, it would mean a three-shot swing that would put Palmer in the lead. With the television cameras showing both moments at the same time on a split-screen for viewers at home, Palmer watched as his putt just missed. Nicklaus' putt, meanwhile, found the bottom of the cup.

From there, Palmer fell to third place. Pebble Beach had won again.

"He had been real steady and real patient all day, and then he missed that putt," Huston said. "You could feel his pain."

For Huston and Palmer, the ride was over. At least on the golf course, that is.

Turns out, that same weekend, Huston was supposed to be at his high school graduation.

Ever the "King," Palmer offered a quick way to get him there.

"I remember he asked me how bad I wanted to be there," Huston said. "He was going to have me flown in by helicopter."

Instead, Huston walked away with a big check (that would later pay for a month in Hawaii) and the memories.

"That whole week was magical for me. I mean, the experience of being with Arnold Palmer; I was in a daze," Huston said. "Do I regret missing my graduation? No, not at all."

## The Man in the Hat

Monterey Peninsula native Chester Gillette was no stranger to carrying a big bag.

This time, though, he'd be working a U.S. Open.

In Gillette's case, the trip to the 1972 U.S. Open began six years earlier in 1966, when at the age of 16 he decided to become a caddie at Pebble Beach.

While many of his first loops were anonymous players, there was one who stood out—actress Joan Fontaine.

Fontaine, 49 at the time, was then (as she was in 2004) a resident of the Monterey Peninsula.

In 1941, Fontaine had won the Academy Award for best actress for her role in the film *Suspicion*, a thriller directed by Alfred Hitchcock that was partially shot in Monterey County. Other major film credits for Fontaine had been *Rebecca* (1940), another Hitchcock film partially shot in Monterey County (including use of the old stairs from Stillwater Cove to the current fifth hole of Pebble Beach Golf Links), *The Constant Nymph* (1943), *Jane Eyre* (1944), and *Voyage to the Bottom of the Sea* (1961).

"Looking back, I didn't really know who she was at the time. I mean, I was still just a teenager," Gillette said. "Ended up I looped for her quite a few times. I remember she was an extremely nice lady and would tell me about the old days at Pebble Beach. She loved to talk about what Pebble Beach had been like in previous years."

Buoyed by previous loops including Fontaine, Gillette also found his name in the caddie and players pool upon the arrival of the 1972 U.S. Open. On his turn to draw from the hat, Gillette pulled out the name Jim Colbert.

In 1972, Colbert, now a star on the Champions Tour, was 31 years old and had been a professional for seven years. Prior to the U.S. Open, his only win on the PGA Tour had come at the now-defunct Monsanto Open Invitational in 1969. The Kansas State graduate was, however, fairly well known. Entering the national championship, Colbert was ranked as one of the Top 40 players on the PGA Tour. At the 1971 U.S. Open at Pennsylvania-based Merion Golf Club, meanwhile, Colbert had finished tied for third.

"He was the same back then as he is today," Gillette said. "He was a very energetic gentleman wearing that pork-pie hat."

Being so young, Gillette found himself being carefully eyed by Colbert early on during the week. Once Colbert saw Gillette at work, however, the two went on with business.

"I remember at first he was very hesitant to having me

out there," Gillette said. "Once he saw that I knew what I was doing, though, he was OK. By the start of the championship, I was reading the greens, giving yardages, doing what a good caddie should do."

Despite Gillette's help, Colbert played two uneven opening rounds to survive the thirty-six-hole cut by two strokes.

By Sunday's final round, Colbert and Gillette were still on the course, but for all intents and purposes were out of the hunt.

"I remember that we were in the first group to go off on Sunday. We were paired with Tommy Aaron," Gillette said. "Well, both (Aaron and Colbert) already knew that they would be taking home some money. So they both played the course as fast as they could."

In the end, Colbert finished the championship well behind eventual champion Jack Nicklaus in what turned out to be an extremely difficult U.S. Open.

Gillette, meanwhile, had worked a U.S. Open.

"We did what we could that week. It just didn't work out," Gillette said. "To this day, I'm still glad I got my shot, though. I was so young, and to get a chance to caddie in a U.S. Open. It's something I'll always remember."

# 9 Another Major: The 1977 PGA Championship

*"I was jumping off the planet, but so was he."*
—Lanny Wadkins

As soon as Pebble Beach had landed its first U.S. Open in 1972, preparations for the big event began.

The USGA's first move was to hire Frank D. "Sandy" Tatum Jr. as the man responsible for course conditions. Tatum, a veteran of the 1947 U.S. Amateur at Pebble Beach and several California amateurs, was more than comfortable on the course, but nonetheless he looked for second opinions.

Knowing that time was crucial, he quickly enlisted the original Pebble Beach co-designer, Jack Neville, as an assistant. For Neville, 81 years old at the time, it was a chance to return to his masterpiece.

Together, Tatum, Neville, and USGA Executive Director P. J. Boatwright went about the task of making Pebble Beach stronger than it had ever been. For starters, the rough was seeded with thickening fescue grass, and the fairways were narrowed. Then, two new tee boxes were constructed on holes No. 2 and No. 10, adding twenty-five yards to the course.

The final touch was the addition and fortification of bunkers. Tatum, who would later go on to co-design The Links at Spanish Bay with Tom Watson, added a new bunker to the front-left side of the green at No. 1 and expanded the large fairway bunker on No. 4. Other changes included extending the bunker on the left side of No. 10 and the addition of three new fairway bunkers on the tough par-4 No. 9.

By the time all was said and done, Pebble Beach passed the test with flying colors. By February of 1972, more than 14,000 season tickets to the championship had been sold at an average of thirty-six dollars apiece. By the end of the championship, ticket sales had topped the $500,000 mark.

## All the Way

Thanks to the overwhelming success of the 1972 U.S. Open, it wasn't long before Pebble Beach hosted another Major championship.

In 1977, despite one of the worst droughts in the course's history, the PGA Championship arrived at Pebble Beach.

"There was never a doubt in my mind . . . what we have learned to call 'adverse' playing conditions today, years ago would have been called ideal," wrote president of the PGA of America Don Padgett in the championship program. "Pebble Beach is a particularly sturdy course . . . a challenging and adaptable course that is always a thrill to play under any conditions. We knew we had one of the greatest courses in the world, and we had history on our side. So enjoy the championship. It had to happen here."

As for the course, the drought had no doubt left its mark. Unlike the 1972 Open, this time around the Pebble Beach fairways played harder and faster, with less rough.

For young up-and-coming long-hitting pros like Lanny Wadkins, the conditions were tailor-made.

That fateful year, Wadkins, now a golf commentator for CBS Sports, had actually been struggling. So much, in fact, that the then 27-year-old Wadkins had to qualify on Mondays to play in regular PGA Tour events. It was a far cry from his 1973 season, when he finished fifth on the money list.

"I was really hoping to just finish in the top eight so I could make The Masters the following year," Wadkins said.

As it turned out, he and professional caddie Ralph Coffey would go on to etch their names into the Pebble Beach history books.

While Wadkins was becoming a veteran, Coffey was already a veteran. Coffey, who hailed from North Carolina, had started his PGA Tour looping career by carrying the bag of Jim Grant in the 1968 Crosby Pro-Am. Only a few weeks later, however, Grant fired Coffey.

"A few weeks after that Pro-Am, we went down to Riviera CC for the Monday qualifier to get into the tournament in Los Angeles," Coffey said. "On the eighth hole the fog comes in and he (Grant) asks me to club him so I tell him it's a nine-iron. He wanted an eight-iron but I said no way. So he hits his shot and it flies over the green. He looks over at me and says, 'I should have listened to you.' Well, he failed to qualify and after the round fired me. So here I am over near the clubhouse and I've got no job, and here comes Deane Beman. So I asked if I could work for him. He says, 'No, I think I have somebody' and he saw me kick my feet. Then he says, 'Wait a sec, let me call and see.' He came out of the clubhouse and told me to be at the course the next day at 9 A.M."

For the now deceased Coffey, a door had opened. Or had it?

"So it ended up we go on to make the cut. We played with Billy Casper on Sunday. Well, we get done and Deane says to me, 'Ralph, I've got to talk to you.' I thought, 'Oh my god, after one week he's going to fire me! So I waited for him to come out and give me the bad news. He came out a little later and before he could say anything I said, 'Deane, I'll do a good job, I think we can win, we may win next weekend.' He looks at me and says, 'Ralph, I'm not going to fire you. I want you to caddy for me. I never did figure out if he was going to fire me until I told him we'd win the next week!" said Coffey, who passed away in early 2004.

As for the Beman-Coffey relationship, that lasted until 1974, when Beman became commissioner of the PGA Tour. It was three years later, however, that Coffey found himself on the bag of Wadkins at the 1977 PGA Championship at Pebble Beach. The duo had hooked up for the first time earlier in 1976 at the Disney World tournament.

"Ralph was very much an old-school guy. By that, I mean he knew what shot needed to be hit at that particular moment," Wadkins said. "He would visualize the shot, and we'd immediately be on the same page. Then we'd go after it."

For the fast playing Wadkins, it wasn't hard to realize he had the right guy on the bag, even if Coffey had his quirks.

"I remember he was always very excitable. He'd get so into it sometimes that he'd repeat himself over and over as we'd be walking along. 'Hit a little fade here, hit a little fade here, hit a little fade here," Wadkins said. "He also had this habit of writing everything down, and I mean everything. I always could tell how nervous he was, because if he was really nervous he'd just act like he was writing something down. That was just the way he liked to do things."

As for the Wadkins-Coffey duo, during the final round of the 1977 PGA Championship Wadkins entered Sunday's final round six strokes behind leader Gene Littler, who had led the tournament from day one.

By Sunday, the then 47-year-old Littler didn't look like he was going to budge, either. Through the first nine holes, Littler still had a five-shot lead over both Wadkins and ever-present Jack Nicklaus.

"I had played with Gene on Saturday and at the time I didn't see how he could lose," Wadkins said. "I remember telling him after the [Saturday] round when he was 10 under par and I was 4 under, 'I hope you win it, Gene.'"

The championship and Wadkins and Coffey's ride, however, were far from over.

*Lanny Wadkins and caddie Ralph Coffey congratulate runner-up Gene Littler following the 1977 PGA Championship at Pebble Beach.* (Photograph by William C. Brooks.)

As soon as Littler made the turn at No. 10, the wheels suddenly came off. On No. 10, he knocked his approach shot into a bunker, leading to a bogey, and following a scrambling par at No. 11, he three-putted the par-3 No. 12 from forty-five feet away. It was his first three-putt of the week.

Then, on No. 13, Littler hit his approach twenty yards over the green for a bogey, and on No. 14 he missed a six-foot putt for par. When he left his approach at No. 15 in a front bunker and failed to salvage par, his lead had evaporated. Nicklaus had pulled even at 6-under-par.

Meanwhile, also suddenly back in the thick of things were Wadkins and Coffey.

"When Gene went down to eight under at the No. 13, I was only two strokes behind him and I began to give it some serious thought," Wadkins said.

As for Wadkins' day, he made two eagles on the front nine—thanks to a laser-beamed 2-iron to within five feet of the pin on No. 2 and a 4-wood to within eight feet at No. 6. In between, he three-putted No. 3 and missed the fifth green to make bogey. After carding eight straight pars, he slipped with another bogey on No. 14, but he got that stroke back with a clutch birdie at No. 18 after knocking a wedge to within a few feet of the cup.

Later, in the clubhouse, with a final round 2-under-par 70 for a four-day total of 282 (6-under) Wadkins and Coffey were left to think—and watch.

Littler made par at both No. 16 and No. 17, but then hit a poor wedge shot at No. 18, leaving his ball thirty-five feet from the hole. Needing a birdie to wrap up the championship, Littler had to settle for a two-putt par.

"I thought I had a good shot at birdie on that last hole but I didn't hit a very good pitch," Littler lamented.

As for Nicklaus, it was No. 17—the same hole where his famous 1-iron shot hit the flagstick to set up the birdie that clinched the 1972 U.S. Open—that was the difference.

This time around, instead of a birdie Nicklaus carded a

bogey. Now to even tie, Nicklaus would need a birdie of his own at No. 18. Like Littler, however, he had to settle for par.

With Nicklaus out, it came down to Wadkins and Littler in what was the first sudden-death play-off ever for a Major championship.

"I remember on that first play-off hole on No. 1, I hit a perfect drive right down the middle," Wadkins said. "Well, I liked to play fast so when we got to the ball I asked Ralph what the yardage into the green was. He was so excited about what was going on he couldn't even get the words out of his mouth. Ended up he had to write it on a piece of paper and gave it to me."

Wadkins nearly lost the first hole thanks to a shoddy chip, but he recovered via a twelve-foot putt for par of which Littler commented, "He had to hit it perfectly, and did."

After both players carded birdies on No. 2, the play-off moved to No. 3. There, both players missed the green, with Wadkins about eight feet away from the pin and Littler around fifteen feet short of the pin.

"By then Littler was already on, so we're looking at a chip shot that needs to get close," Wadkins said. "The ball was really down in the grass. So I looked at Ralph and said, 'I'm going to go with a sand wedge, what do you think? I remember he looked back and said, 'That's a safe, smart play.'"

After both players reached the green, Littler's putt for par skimmed by the hole. Wadkins, however, then drained an eight-footer.

"When I won the thing, Ralph was so excited," Wadkins said. "I mean, I was jumping off the planet, but so was he."

Wadkins, who still can be seen playing on the Champions Tour at times, went on to capture seventeen other PGA Tour events in the next seventeen years, and also played on eight U.S. Ryder Cup squads. As for Majors, however, the 1977 PGA Championship would be his only one.

As for Coffey, the sudden veteran on the bag went on to work mainly for George Burns during the 1980s, picking up yet another win at Pebble Beach when Burns won the 1980 Pro-Am . Overall, Coffey won three times at Pebble Beach: once with Bert Yancey in 1970, once with Burns in 1980, and once with Wadkins in 1977.

"Looking back, when I think of the 1977 PGA Championship one of the first people I still think about is Ralph," Wadkins said. "He was just so into it, and looking back it's cool knowing he was so excited. He was as proud to be out there—in the first sudden-death play-off of a Major—as anyone out there."

One of the Few—When the PGA Championship arrived at Pebble Beach in 1977, the caddie barn wasn't exactly bustling.

"At that time, there weren't even twenty caddies at Pebble Beach," former looper Michael Chapman said. "Most of the guys who were there ended up getting loops, but it was fairly quiet. Unlike the 1972 U.S. Open, professionals could use whomever they wanted as a caddie."

Then a bright-eyed 18-year-old, Chapman was one Pebble Beach caddie who did find work.

Upon the eve of the championship, Chapman was hired by James Ferriell Jr., a 34-year-old club professional from Ohio.

In the 1977 PGA Championship, Ferriell started off with a shaky 6-over-par 78. In the second round, however, his 71 was good enough to make the cut.

"I remember that Saturday morning after the cut we were on the range," Chapman said. "Well, right next to us hitting balls was Arnold Palmer. I knew that Palmer had yet to win the PGA Championship, so at one point I went more to his side and said, 'Go Arnie.' He looked over at me and Ferriell and said, 'I'm gonna beat that guy.' Then he went back to hitting balls."

Ferriell finished in a tie for 66th, Palmer seventeen stokes better in a tie for nineteenth.

"I remember he [Ferriell] was the only club pro to make the cut. That to me was an accomplishment in itself," Chapman said. "It was impressive to see a club pro make the cut in a Major championship."

A mere five years later, Chapman again worked a Major at Pebble Beach—the 1982 U.S. Open.

# 10   The 1982 U.S. Open

*"The person I fear most in the last two rounds is myself."*
—Tom Watson

By the time the 1970s had ended, there were no doubts regarding the championship status of Pebble Beach Golf Links. Within a five-year span (1972–1977), Morse's gem had hosted not only a U.S. Open championship, but also a PGA Championship.

For the caddies of Pebble Beach, things couldn't have been any better. Or could they?

As the caddies of Pebble Beach would soon find out, the championship run wasn't over. Not surprisingly, only five years after the PGA Championship left, the United States Golf Association was ready to come back for more.

The 1982 U.S. Open would return to Pebble Beach. Suffice to say, more history would be waiting for the caddies.


## Tom Terrific

Winning at Pebble Beach, and on a links course for that matter, was nothing new to Tom Watson.

In both 1977 and 1978, Watson walked away with wins at the Pebble Beach National Pro-Am, while in 1975, 1977, and 1980 the Stanford University alumnus captured the British Open.

As for U.S. Open titles, however, entering 1982 Watson was still empty-handed. By then 31 years old, the Kansas native had made some runs in the national championship, but he'd yet to take home the trophy.

In the 1975 U.S. Open at Medinah Country Club in Illinois, Watson held the lead through the first two rounds, but ended up finishing in a tie for ninth place. In 1980 at Baltusrol Golf Club in New Jersey, Watson made a charge over the weekend, jumping from twenty-fifth place to fourth by Sunday. In the end, however, Jack Nicklaus walked away with the championship.

As players got ready to tee off in the 1982 Open at Pebble Beach, Watson was again one of the favorites to make something happen, but there were other contenders as well. Tom Kite and Craig Stadler, who were quickly making names for themselves on the PGA Tour, were hungry for a win, as were Seve Ballesteros and Fred Couples. And there were the veterans, Arnold Palmer, Lee Trevino, and the ever-present Nicklaus, whom Watson had beat in a classic duel to win the 1977 British Open.

"Tom was ready to go," said legendary looper Bruce

Edwards, Watson's caddie at the time. "It was a Major championship, and it was Tom's business to try to win Majors."

On day one, with Pebble Beach weather raising its head, many players struggled right from the go, including Watson. Thanks to three consecutive opening bogeys, Watson began the championship 3-over through three holes.

"He was struggling, but in typical fashion he gutted it out and kept grinding," Edwards said.

By the end of the first round, Watson had indeed recovered. Three birdies on the final four holes had brought him back to even-par 72 for the day, leaving him only two strokes behind co-leaders Bruce Devlin and Bill Rogers.

In the second round, Watson continued to struggle, but again made a late charge thanks to three more late birdies. Having survived the cut with a two-day score of 144 (72-72), Watson was still five strokes off the pace. Devlin, one of the first round co-leaders, had continued his hot play, following up an opening 2-under 70 with an even better 69.

"Looking back, those first two days set the tone for the weekend," Edwards said. "It was tough at times, but he kept finding ways to get back into it. Instead of sucking his thumb, he just kept plugging along."

As Edwards and Watson would quickly find out, they were more than in the hunt. In Saturday's third round, Devlin finally felt the heat, collapsing to a 75 on a day where Watson described the course as "defenseless."

Watson and Edwards were making their charge. While Devlin was crumbling, Watson came to the world-famous tee on No. 18, 3-under-par for the day.

"Tom had played great up to eighteen, but we both knew that eighteen was the biggest hole of the day," Edwards said. "By then, after everything that was happening, we knew that a birdie on No. 18 would put him in the last group for Sunday, and that's what you want to do. That way, you can be the one dictating what's going on."

By the end of the day, Watson had earned that precious

spot in the final pairing. He finished the third round with a 4-under 68, tying him with Rogers for the outright lead.

Others in the chase included defending champion David Graham, Bruce Devlin, George Burns, and Scott Simpson, who were each two strokes off the pace, and Calvin Peete and Nicklaus, who were three back.

Come Sunday morning, the pressure was on.

"So we get to the tee on No. 1 on Sunday, and Tom tees off with a 4-wood," Edwards said. "As he handed me the club I asked, 'Are you nervous?' because I was. He said, 'No.' When he said no, my feeling was that he was in control and welcoming the challenge that was presented to him."

As the leaders began their rounds, three groups ahead was Nicklaus. After opening with a bogey on No. 1 and a par on No. 2, the Golden Bear also welcomed the challenge, carding birdies on the next five consecutive holes.

After a birdie of his own on No. 2, Watson carded a bogey on the par-3 third hole. At that point, Watson, Nicklaus, Rogers, and a recovering Devlin all were in a tie for the lead at four-under. It continued to be a logjam for most of the rest of the day.

"On No. 7, Tom had a great chance for birdie, but missed a three-footer, and then on No. 8 he saved par by sinking a long putt," Edwards said. "By No. 10, he was down on the cliffs and the beach, but he managed to get up on the green and sank a twenty-footer for par. Looking back, those were all key moments."

Standing on the tee at the difficult par-5 No. 14, Watson still was tied for the lead, but now only with Nicklaus.

"His third shot on No. 14 was thin. I mean, it barely cleared the front guarding bunker on the left," Edwards said. "The ball, which by then had a nice smiley cut mark, ended up on back fringe."

Facing a tough thirty-five foot breaking putt for birdie and the outright lead, Edwards and Watson collaborated to get a read on the green. Despite a severe break and a cut ball, Watson drained the putt.

*Tom Watson and legendary professional caddie Bruce Edwards are all smiles following the conclusion of the 1982 U.S. Open at Pebble Beach.* (Photograph by William C. Brooks.)

"It was a hell of a putt. With the ball cut he still made the putt," Edwards said. "After that hole he said, 'Bruce, once I made that my back eased up.' That meant he had taken the pressure off himself."

"It was the putt that won the tournament for me," Watson later said. "The pressure was gone. I had control of the situation, and the game was on. I led Jack by one, with Bill Rogers three behind. It was a two-man battle with Jack going for a record fifth Open and me for my first. I knew what I was trying to do and I was doing it, and I was enjoying myself for the first time in the round. It's the greatest feeling you can have in golf."

The tournament and the drama were, however, far from over. Watson came to the tee at No. 16 still holding the lead by only one stroke.

"When we got to the tee at sixteen, he asked me whether he should go with driver or three-wood. I said driver because the pin was in the front. I figured get the ball out there so you can go into the green with a pitching wedge or sand wedge," recalled Edwards. "That way you can get the ball high in the air and over the front bunkers. Well, he went with driver and he ended up near the fairway bunker on the right. Then his second shot ended up on the back-right portion of the green. He was looking at about an eighty-foot putt."

Three putts later, Watson and Nicklaus (who had failed to score birdie at No. 18) were tied for the lead again. If Watson was to win, he'd have to make something happen at either the par-3 seventeenth or par-5 eighteenth.

No. 17, which plays directly toward the Pacific Ocean, was already tough enough. This time, it was even tougher. For the Open, the USGA used the back tee to stretch the hole to a heart-thumping 209 yards.

"When we got to the tee at No. 17, the first thing I realized was that it was a shot where we were between clubs," said Edwards of the tee shot, which features a lengthy carry over two gaping bunkers. "The decision was to, at all costs, avoid being in the bunker, so Tom went with a two-iron. So he hits, and pulls the shot to the left. As were walking up to the green, he flips the club at me, and says, 'That's dead.'"

Little did Edwards and Watson know, however, that the ball was indeed alive.

*Jack Nicklaus and professional caddie Angelo Argea did everything during the 1982 U.S. Open except beat Tom Watson* (background). (Photograph by William C. Brooks.)

"As we get up to the green, we can see the ball. I told him, 'We can work with this,'" said Edwards.

Watson's ball had landed on the left collar of the green, and from there bounced into the thick rough, eight feet behind the narrow, hourglass shaped green. The pitch shot out of the difficult lie couldn't just be good. It had to be great.

"As he was getting ready to play the shot, I came over and said, 'Now get this close.' Well, he looked up and replied, 'To hell with getting it close—I'm going to make it.'"

With the touch of an artist, Watson slid a sand wedge under the ball. The ball landed softly on the fringe, took a hop, and began tracking to the hole, eventually falling in for a birdie.

"I remember the ball gets on the green and starts rolling. When it's about a foot away from the cup, he looks up at me and says, 'I told you so.' Then the ball goes in and he turns to me again, and says, 'I told you so.' In my opinion, it was the best clutch shot he's ever played. I mean, the U.S. Open was on the line, and with all that pressure. It was one for the ages."

Up ahead, off to the side of the green on No. 18, Nicklaus watched "the shot heard 'round the world" on a television monitor. Only needing a par for the win, Watson made another birdie on No. 18—this time in front of Nicklaus' eyes.

"Why you SOB," Nicklaus exclaimed as he met Watson on the green to congratulate him. "You're something else. I'm really proud of you."


Forever—Prior to the 1982 U.S. Open at Pebble Beach, Bruce Edwards had already spent nearly a decade looping for Tom Watson. It was during the 1982 U.S. Open, however, that the duo would etch their names into the history books together thanks to Watson's heroics on the 71st hole. The win at Pebble Beach would be Watson and Edward's only Major working together as a team. While Watson's history as a player does involve other caddies, not one would eclipse the shadow left by Edwards.

"I think that hug Bruce and I shared at the eighteenth hole at Pebble Beach was probably the most wonderful memory that we shared together," said Watson, who prior to working with Edwards at Pebble Beach in 1982 had used other caddies to win The Masters at Augusta National Golf Club in 1977 and 1981, and the 1975, 1977, and 1980 British Opens at Carnoustie Golf Club, Turnberry GC, and Muirfield GC, respectively. "That would be the only Major Bruce won on my bag. But, you know, that (the U.S. Open) was the Major I wanted most, and he knew that."

Other than a temporary breakup between the two in the late 1980s when Edwards switched to carrying Greg Norman's bag, Edwards, for the most part, was Watson's right-hand man on nearly every tee box, fairway, and green for nearly thirty years.

At the 1999 Ryder Cup at The Country Club at Brookline in Massachusetts, U.S. team captain Ben Crenshaw recognized and tabbed Edwards as the man in charge of the American team's caddies.

It was in 2003, however, that Edwards garnered more attention than Watson. In January of that year, after realizing his speech was slurred and that at times his limbs were trembling, Edwards was diagnosed with amyotrophic lateral sclerosis (ALS), more commonly known as Lou Gehrig's Disease.

Upon the doctors' discovery, Edwards was told by medical personnel that he would have one to three years to live.

"My plan is to carry on," Edwards told *Golf Digest* five weeks later.

Upon the eve of the 2003 U.S. Open at Illinois-based Olympia Fields Country Club later that June, Edwards was indeed carrying on—and Watson was back on the attack.

During the first round of the 2003 U.S. Open, the duo conjured up memories of the 1982 U.S. Open at Pebble Beach by teaming up to blister Olympia Fields to the tune of a magical 5-under-par 65. After the first round, the then 53-year-old Watson was tied for the lead, becoming the oldest player to ever lead a U.S. Open.

Because of his condition, the USGA offered Edwards the opportunity to caddie via a cart. He declined.

Among the highlights of the pair's first round run were Watson holing out from 170 yards for an eagle on No. 12 and Watson draining a forty-foot plus putt for birdie on No. 7. At No. 7, the putt hung on the edge of the cup for several seconds before falling.

"When that ball fell in, it was something special," Watson later told the press. "It stopped short and people were groaning. I'm walking up to it and said, 'That is so close how couldn't it be in?' And then it went in."

Knowing full well at the time that any loop could be Edwards' last, the two went on to complete their round while fighting back emotions. By the time the pair reached the eighteenth green, both were in tears.

"It evoked memories of the past," Edwards told the media afterward. "Like I said, you never know when it's going to be the last one. Tom is my big brother. That's all I can say."

"The galleries were loud and they were genuine," Watson said. "They were pulling not only for me, but also for Bruce. There were a lot of comments about Bruce. 'We're pulling for you. You can beat this.'"

Less than a year later, only hours before Watson teed off in the 2004 Masters, Edwards succumbed to ALS at the age of 49.

"He certainly did his job with aplomb and respect for the game," Watson told the media. "And that made him. . . . the Arnold Palmer of caddies. When a young guy came out, a guy who was a rookie out here, Bruce would not hesitate to tell him the ropes, show him the ropes and say, 'Hey, this is the way you do it.' He didn't hesitate to kick him in the butt when they weren't doing the right thing, too. He'd say, 'Come on, clean up your act. We have an image to uphold out here.'"

A night before his passing at his home in Florida, Edwards was honored by the Golf Writers Association of America with the Ben Hogan Award, an honor annually bestowed upon an individual who, despite a physical handicap or serious illness, continued to contribute to golf.

"If I go in a year or less, I've had a wonderful life," Edwards told the media prior to the 2003 U.S. Open. "I've been lucky. I had one of the greatest golfers in the world. I've had a wonderful ride, a lot of wins, a lot of great moments. It's been fun."

Indeed, it was. Thank you, Bruce.


## Local Motion

Longtime Monterey Peninsula resident and caddie Mike Chapman will never forget the 1982 U.S. Open Championship. Chapman, a native of the area, caddied for one of the Peninsula's most recent great players—Bobby Clampett.

Both pupils of Carmel Valley golf guru Ben Doyle, Chapman and Clampett first became friends while competing head-to-head in the 1975 and 1976 Monterey City Amateur championships. Chapman, who had just gotten out of the service, beat Clampett—a student at Robert Louis Stevenson School at Pebble Beach—1-up in both meetings.

"Back then I was 23 years old, and Bobby was only 15. "Even then, I was impressed with Bobby as a person, and it turned out I ended up giving him a ride home after one of the matches. Needless to say, we got to be good friends," Chapman said. "Being the older guy, I wanted to help him get to where he wanted to go as much as I could."

At the time, Clampett didn't look like he needed much

help. In fact, only two years after their last match at the Monterey City Amateur, Clampett won the first of his two California Amateur crowns. That same year (1978), he was also the low amateur at the U.S. Open, and he finished as runner-up at the annual Spalding Invitational, which is now known as the Callaway Golf Pebble Beach Invitational.

"The thing with Bobby at that time was that even though he was a great golfer, he had a small ego," said Chapman,

*Bobby Clampett and caddie Mike Chapman, both natives of the Monterey Peninsula, head toward the green of world-famous No. 18 during Sunday's final round of the 1982 U.S. Open. Despite a brilliant run, the two longtime friends would end up finishing in third place.* (Courtesy of Mike Chapman.)

who still lives on the Peninsula. "A lot of guys would've started getting a big head. Bobby never did."

In 1979, Clampett's rapid ascent continued. Despite not returning to Pebble Beach to defend his 1978 California Amateur title, Clampett did return to the area for the Spalding Invitational. Again competing as an amateur in the professional division, this time around Clampett won the event, setting a course record 65 at Spyglass Hill in the process.

The good vibes sustained into 1980. Clampett returned to win his second California State Amateur title in three years. A day after his win, the 20-year-old rising star turned professional.

Two years later, the U.S. Open returned to Pebble Beach and Chapman and Clampett were brimming with confidence.

For Clampett, it was a chance to play the national championship on a golf course he called home. Chapman, then a bellman at The Lodge, was also extremely familiar with the layout of Pebble Beach Golf Links. Not only did he play the course, but he also worked on it. In previous years, Chapman had looped for Bob Hope and Willie Mays at the Crosby Pro-Am, and in 1977 he had looped for Jim Ferriell Jr. at the PGA Championship at Pebble Beach.

"In those days I knew Pebble Beach as well as some of the veteran caddies," Chapman said.

With the championship approaching, it was Doyle who brought the two together again. This time, however, they'd be working as partners.

"When Ben said Bobby needed a caddie, I jumped at the chance. I mean, Bobby knew me and he trusted me, and I had played Pebble enough to know it inside out," Chapman said. "In my mind it was a natural fit. You had a guy who had tons of local knowledge about the course, and you had a guy who could play the course. As it turned out, I ended up hooking up with him."

During practice rounds, the two began getting a feel for one another.

"Bobby was very thorough in his preparation," Chapman

said. "We spent a lot of time charting the course to get yardages down as much as possible. I remember it was funny because there were a lot of times, where, without pacing off, we'd pretty much agree what the yardage was. We'd just use sprinklers or bushes. Bobby would say, 'What do you have?' and I'd say, '141.' He'd look over and say, 'I have 142.'"

Over the first two days of competition, the duos' work would pay off. Paired with veteran Ben Crenshaw and fellow young gun Bernhard Langer, Clampett opened the championship with a 1-under 71, following that up with a 1-over 73. Entering the weekend, he was at even par, only a few strokes off the lead.

"At the time, Langer was also coming up through the ranks, so he and Bobby knew one another. I think that helped Bobby feel more comfortable," Chapman said. "Crenshaw, on the other hand, was the veteran. I remember he was kind of pissed off because Bobby tended to play slowly. As usual, though, he was as kind as ever. I remember near the end of the second round he was really bummed out because he was going to miss the cut. Well, as we're walking along I asked him who his favorite golfer was. He said, 'Bobby Jones,' and proceeded to go on and tell me a bunch of stories about Jones."

In the third round, the stakes got higher. Near the top of the leaderboard, Clampett teed off in the same group as then 42-year-old Jack Nicklaus. From the moment the two stepped on the tee, the game was on, according to Chapman.

"So here we go for the third round, and who are we playing with but the greatest golfer ever," Chapman said. "I remember, at the time, Bobby had just signed a contract with the IMG group, who also represented Palmer. Bobby's bag was covered with sponsorships, and Jackie Jr., who was then looping for his dad, looks over at Bobby's bag and starts reading off the sponsors. Then he says, 'What have you ever done to deserve this?' From that first step on the first tee, there was gamesmanship. Jackie Jr. was trying to intimidate Bobby right from the start."

Later in the round, Clampett, now a golf commentator for

CBS Sports, one-upped the Golden Bear. With a birdie on the tricky par-5 fourteenth hole, Clampett jumped to the top of the leaderboard.

"It was an incredible feeling. I mean, Bobby was beating Nicklaus, and Jack was the man back then," Chapman said. "Nicklaus had this way of willing the ball around the course, and here was this young guy beating him."

Following a bogey on No. 17, however, Clampett fell one stroke off the pace.

On the par-5 eighteenth, Clampett's drive landed in a group of trees that have since been removed. Renowned as a great ball striker from his knees, Clampett immediately had visions of getting down on all fours to take a shot. Only two years earlier, at the 1980 U.S. Open, Clampett had played as a marker, and played multiple shots from his knees. So much, in fact, that he was kicked off the course by the USGA.

"His first inclination when he saw his ball under the trees was to get on his knees. I said, 'No way! You can't do that.' He kept telling me he wanted to play it from his knees, but in the end I talked him out of it. Turns out, that's one of the regrets of my life."

Instead of hitting from his knees, Clampett punched out. Two shots later, he was on the green facing a five-foot putt for par. He missed the putt and walked away with a frustrating bogey.

"I often wonder, 'What if?'" Chapman said. "There's no telling what would've happened. If he gets a birdie on eighteen, he's in the final pairing for Sunday. I'll always regret not keeping my mouth shut."

Nevertheless, early in the final round the local favorite made another charge. Through holes No. 1 through No. 7, he was on fire, giving himself ample birdie chances and opportunities to move back up the leaderboard. In fact, when Clampett reached the tee on No. 3 he was the leader.

"Going to the tee at No. 12, we were at 2-under," Chapman recalled. "We were right there."

At No. 12, however, Clampett's charge bogged down in

the rough. His tee shot on the tough par 3 went left and failed to hit the green. Four strokes later, Clampett had carded a double bogey.

Still not out of the hunt, Clampett regrouped and eventually brought his fortunes to the eighteenth. Standing at 1-under, he cranked a driver and fairway wood that left him just short of the green in two. Although his eagle putt ran just past the cup, Clampett made birdie and headed to the clubhouse as the leader at 2-under. An hour later, though, Tom Watson made the "shot heard 'round the world" on No. 17 by pitching in from the rough for birdie.

Clampett's dream would be shattered.

"For a 22-year-old kid to finish third in the U.S. Open is still quite a feat," Chapman said. "There will always be a lot of memories from that Open. Looking back, there were all those little things that made such a huge difference. But then again, that's golf."

## Inside the Ropes

Tom DiMaggio will always be thankful for the 1982 U.S. Open at Pebble Beach. On the eve of the championship, the Monterey Peninsula native was 21 years old. And like many 21-year-olds, DiMaggio was still trying to figure out exactly where he was going.

"I was unemployed and really didn't have any idea what I wanted to do," DiMaggio said. "Then I started thinking, 'Well, my uncle had been a caddie. Maybe I could try it. I did like golf.'"

DiMaggio's uncle, Turk Archdeacon was, from 1940 to 1960, one of the most famous caddies at nearby Cypress Point Club. During his time at Cypress Point, Archdeacon looped for most of the celebrities who played the course, including Dwight Eisenhower, King Leopold III, Prince Baudoin of Belgium, and Prince Bertil of Sweden.

"He'd had a big influence on me when it came to golf," DiMaggio said.

The week of the 1982 U.S. Open, DiMaggio decided to give looping a shot. Hoping to get in on the action, he began hanging out around the caddie barn.

"There weren't a lot of regular Pebble Beach caddies back then, maybe 12 or so," DiMaggio said. "As it turned out, only a few guys got loops."

Still hoping for something to happen, DiMaggio did not get a chance to loop. He was, however, offered the chance to be a forecaddie. As a forecaddie, DiMaggio's duties included tracking players' balls to ensure they were not lost during play and, if needed, warning the gallery of stray shots.

"It was the Tuesday of championship week and into the barn came this woman from ABC television. So she says, 'Does anyone want to forecaddie for the U.S. Open?' I immediately raised my hand and said, 'Yes, ma'am. I want to be a part of this,'" DiMaggio said.

Signed up, a day later both DiMaggio and his younger brother of six years, Vince, attended an orientation meeting at the Monterey Hyatt. During the meeting, Tom and Vince asked officials if they could work the par-5 fourteenth hole. Their request was approved.

"There were a number of reasons we wanted No. 14," DiMaggio said. "For one, it's such a great hole to watch. It can make a round or break a round. Secondly, we figured that when the last group was through and we were done, we could follow them in."

Through the first three days of the championship, Vince worked one side of the fairway, while Tom watched the other side.

Then, Sunday arrived.

Having already seen Jack Nicklaus play through No. 14, the two began waiting for the final group, which included Tom Watson. Following Watson's birdie at No. 14, the two DiMaggios were off and running.

"We were done but still had our forecaddie badges and

flags, so we decided to go watch Nicklaus come in. I was a huge Nicklaus fan," Tom said. "We caught him at No. 17, and I remember because of our badges we could still go inside the ropes. There was a ton of excitement in the air, and we're inside the ropes, just a few feet from Jack Nicklaus."

After watching Nicklaus play No. 17, Tom and Vince headed for the green at No. 18. Again, the duo knew their credentials would get them close to the action.

"So in comes Nicklaus off the eighteenth green. The crowds are massive, and they're going crazy. It looks like he's going to win it and we want his autograph," Tom DiMaggio said. "As we're behind the green we see Nicklaus enter a tent, where he's waiting for Watson to finish. After a bit, there's suddenly a huge roar. It was like the ground was literally shaking."

Watson had made his chip-in at No. 17.

"So Vince and I are still behind the green at eighteen and out of nowhere here comes Nicklaus out of the tent. There were maybe three or four other people there," DiMaggio said. "After walking out of the tent, he just stood there for a bit with this blank expression. Then, all of a sudden he said, 'That little shit did it to me again.'"

"When it was over and Watson came in, I remember Nicklaus was one of the first there to congratulate him," DiMaggio said. "As for what I heard Nicklaus say, I've never thought that it was mean. It was in the spirit of the game. It was a national championship and these two guys had again gone head-to-head. You could tell that Nicklaus had the utmost respect for Watson from the bottom of his heart. Obviously Nicklaus was upset that he lost, but he knew he lost to another great one. To this day, I've never seen anyone lose with such class and dignity. It was neat to see."

Reeled in by the moment and championship week, Tom DiMaggio returned to the caddie barn at Pebble Beach the next day. He's been there ever since.

"After everything that happened in that U.S. Open, I knew

I wanted to be a caddie," DiMaggio said. "Turned out it was one of the best decisions I've ever made."

## Inside the Ropes II

For James Hudgeon, getting a chance to work the 1982 U.S. Open at Pebble Beach began eight years earlier in 1974. Then only 16 years old, Hudgeon was living in Lemoore, California, which is just south of Fresno. That summer, Hudgeon headed to the Monterey Peninsula to not only play golf, but also to look for work as a caddie.

"On a previous trip to the Peninsula, I was out playing the U.S. Navy Golf Course (now Monterey Pines) one day. Tom Hayes, who was the head professional of the Navy course at the time, and I began talking. He told me that I should try to go out and get loops," said Hudgeon, whose father had served in the Navy. "From then on each summer I'd come to the Peninsula looking for work as a caddie."

While in the area he would stay with his brother, Robert Jordan, who was the manager of a local McDonald's. "There were some years where I'd work at the McDonald's and also caddie," said Hudgeon, who, along with occasionally looping Pebble Beach, found work at Laguna Seca Golf Ranch and Corral de Tierra Golf Club. "It was all about trying to make a buck."

It was in the summer of 1982, however, that Hudgeon again headed to the Peninsula—this time with his eyes set on carrying in a U.S. Open. Two years earlier in 1980, Hudgeon had further expanded his caddie horizon by spending a summer working as a looper at The Mid Ocean Golf Club in Bermuda.

"I had seen that Pebble Beach had a caddie program, so I thought I'd hang around to see if something happened," Hudgeon said. "One day during championship week, I had some downtime, so I went to hit a bucket of balls on the range.

Back in those days, there wasn't so much security. Well, as I'm hitting balls a guy comes over to me and asks, 'Are you playing this week?' I said, 'No.' After hearing my answer, his next question was, 'Well, would you like to carry?'"

The "guy" was amateur golfer Gary Marlowe. Marlowe, who later played briefly on the PGA Tour, was in 1982 one of the top amateurs in the country. Two years earlier in 1980, Marlowe had captured the Maryland State Amateur and in 1978 the Maryland State Open.

"He was pumped up and so was I. I'd be carrying in a U.S. Open," Hudgeon said.

For both Marlowe and Hudgeon, the journey in the 1982 U.S. Open was somewhat brief, thanks in part to the world-famous seventh hole at Pebble Beach.

"The one hole that sticks out to me still is No. 7 on Friday," Hudgeon said. "Back then, the green at No. 7 was smaller and shaped more like a kidney bean. In that second round, the pin on No. 7 was back-right, which was a very difficult pin placement. With that pin, the only goal would be to hit your tee shot somewhere around the middle of the green and then hope that your birdie putt went in."

Marlowe hit near the center of the green, but he still faced a difficult putt. "From where he was, there was a safe play and there was a risky play, where he'd have to try and cut an angle to the cup by flirting with the rough. Instead of going the safe route, he decided to try and cut the angle. Upon his stroke, his ball would not only catch the rough, but would fall into a bunker," Hudgeon said. "He would go on to make a bogey."

Unbeknownst to both Marlowe and Hudgeon at the time, that one stroke would cost the pair dearly. Upon the cut, the low seventy players and ties moved on to the final two rounds. Marlowe came in at tied for 71st place in the standings, missing the cut by one stroke.

"When I look back, that extra shot on No. 7 is always the first thing I think about," Hudgeon said. "If there was one stroke that stood out, that was it."

Despite his brief run, Hudgeon—like Tom DiMaggio—was also hooked. He finally found a permanent home as a caddie.

"There were times before the Open where I didn't really know where I was headed," said Hudgeon, who entered his twenty-third year as a Pebble Beach caddie in 2005. "Looking back, I feel like I've been blessed. God sent me in the right direction."

# 11  The 1992 U.S. Open

*"He [Tom Kite] knew he was fighting, but he never got worried.
He was more or less just having fun."*
—Michael Carrick

By the time the 1990s rolled around, caddies at Pebble Beach had just about seen it all; or so they thought. When the U.S. Open returned yet again to Pebble Beach in 1992, caddies found themselves working more than ever for not only Americans, but also Europeans. There was Spaniard Seve Ballesteros, German Bernhard Langer, and Welshman Ian Woosnam.

As the caddies discovered, the times were indeed a-changin'. New faces were there, and a new breed of players was breaking through the ranks. As it had been at the majority of previous U.S. Opens, a Yank would however walk away with the last laugh.

## Major Tom

The premonitions were there, and Michael Carrick knew it. Even weeks before the 1992 U.S. Open at Pebble Beach, the Texas native and longtime professional Tour caddie sensed the feeling in the pit of his stomach. Still weeks and miles away from Pebble Beach, Carrick was for the moment, however, too busy trying to get his man—Tom Kite—through Jack Nicklaus' annual Memorial Tournament at Muirfield Village Golf Club in Ohio.

It was Sunday's final round, and Kite was in the hunt to capture the title.

"I remember looking to Tom that day and saying, 'We have to stay patient. We have a chance here, but we could also have a bigger chance in a few weeks,'" said Carrick, who had been Kite's right-hand man for years. "We ended up finishing in fifth or sixth place there, but I still had this good feeling. I'd never seen him so focused in the present. Pebble Beach was still weeks away, but he'd not only won the Pro-Am there before (1983), he'd set the course record (a 62 during the third round). We walked away feeling pretty good."

Entering the 1992 season, Kite was still empty handed when it came to Major championships, and at the time everyone was more than happy to remind him of his failures. He was 42 years old, and had already tallied up numerous PGA Tour victories. The problem was that none of those wins were in a Major championship. He was "the best player to have never won a Major."

"When you go as long as I did without winning a Major championship, and you had done all the great things that I had done, like winning the Vardon Trophy (lowest scoring

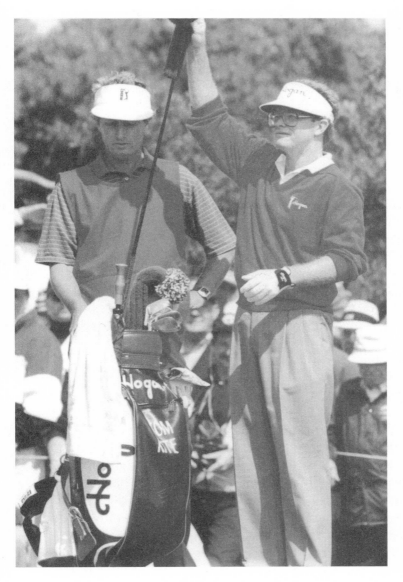

*In 1992, professional caddie Michael Carrick and Tom Kite would team up at Pebble Beach to capture the U.S. Open Championship.* (Photograph by Paul Lester.)

average), playing on Ryder Cup teams and winning multiple events, then I had no problem with that label," Kite said. "It was a fair label that applied to me."

Two weeks after the Memorial, Carrick and Kite would try again at Pebble Beach. It was time to try and tap into those vibes felt in Ohio. Or at least try to.

"We arrived that Monday and went over to the range to hit some balls, and Tom wasn't particularly swinging well so it was a rough start," Carrick said.

During Tuesday's practice round, the mood brightened despite the fact that Kite was still fighting his swing.

"It was just very relaxing," Carrick said. "He knew he was fighting, but he never got worried. He was more or less just having fun."

By Wednesday's practice round, Kite apparently more than won the battle. During the round, the Texas native aced the tough par-3 twelfth at Pebble Beach.

"We didn't really hit a lot of balls that day, but it didn't matter. After that ace we couldn't wait to get started," Carrick said. "The attitude was there and those good vibes were back, big time."

When play in the championship began, Kite, however, found himself quickly looking up the leaderboard at former back-to-back U.S. Open champion Curtis Strange and surprise leader, Dr. Gil Morgan. With an early 5-under-par 67, Strange jumped into the lead, but Morgan responded with an even better 66 after draining a dramatic fifteen-foot birdie on the challenging eighteenth green. Kite, meanwhile, settled for a steady round of 1-under-par 71.

"Nothing spectacular but nothing awful, either," Carrick said. "If there was any good sign it was that he was hitting the ball decently and putting well."

As the second round got underway, Morgan suddenly appeared to be trying to make it a runaway. Buoyed by his opening 66, the Southern College of Optometry grad went out and fired a 69, bringing his two-day total to 9-under, 135.

In second place was Oklahoma pro Andy Dillard at 138 (68-70), while tied for third were 1986 Open champ Raymond Floyd and Wayne Grady with both at 140. Following an even-par 72, Kite was now eight strokes back and appeared out of it. Or was he?

As many of the pros suggested, Morgan was indeed the leader but not yet the winner.

"There's only one player at nine-under. That tells you what

*Kite blasts out of a bunker as caddie Michael Carrick* (left) *looks on. With his win in the 1992 U.S. Open, Kite would shrug off the title as the "best player to have never won a major."* (Courtesy of Pebble Beach Company.)

the golf course is doing to the rest of the field," Floyd said. "All I can say is, you can lose a championship in any one or two rounds. If Gil continues at this level of play all records are going to be broken. It's not likely."

Midway through Saturday's third round, Floyd and the others got more of the same, however. With his third birdie of the day at No. 7, Morgan set a record by becoming the first player to ever reach a score of 12-under-par in a U.S. Open championship. It appeared for the moment that Kite and the others were maybe wasting their time, but suddenly things began changing.

Headed straight for the infamous "Cliffs of Doom" of Pebble Beach—oceanfront holes No. 8, No. 9, and No. 10— Morgan proceeded to card double-bogey, bogey, and another double-bogey. Morgan's once insurmountable lead had been instantly cut to five, and would later be snipped even more following two more bogeys at No. 11 and No. 12 and another double-bogey at the par-5 No. 14.

Only an hour or so earlier, Kite and Carrick had stood on the severely sloped thirteenth green facing a fifteen-foot putt for birdie and a chance to cut even more into the lead.

"By then we had seen what happened with Dr. Gil and knew it was time to try and make something happen," Carrick said. "So we're on the thirteenth green and Tom has this sloping fifteen-footer. He hits a good putt that just misses, but with the slope the ball ends up rolling fifteen feet away from the cup. I remember he looked back at me after that first putt like, 'Can you believe that?' So now he has another fifteen-footer, this time for par. Sure enough he makes it. It was like he was saying, 'Well, if you want to be that way, take that.'"

By the time everyone reached the clubhouse, Morgan was clinging to a slim one-stroke lead with a total score of 3 under. Kite (thanks to a solid 70), Mark Brooks, Ian Woosnam, and Gary Hallberg were now each only a stroke behind.

"When we saw Gil come backwards, it was suddenly like, 'Hey, we're right in the thick of this,'" Carrick said. "It was great for us because it had felt like we weren't pushing all week and now everything was falling into place. There wasn't any pressure."

Come Sunday's final round, Carrick and Kite quickly felt even more at ease. Despite the fact that the skies were clear, the wind had picked up and began taking scorecards with it. In the ABC broadcasting booth, even Jack Nicklaus questioned whether any of the leaders would be able to break par.

"I remember we got down to the course and instantly felt and saw the wind. We were almost excited when we got there," Carrick said. "Tom knew that tougher conditions meant a better chance for him. We were actually joking about how thrilled we were to see the awful conditions."

The duo's excitement soon grew even more. Playing in a group ahead of Morgan, Kite opened the final round with a birdie at No. 1. Moments later though, he dropped two strokes after both he and Morgan double-bogeyed No. 4. This prompted Nicklaus to crown Scotland's Colin Montgomery—who was in with a final score of (70-71-77-70) 288—as the new champion.

"Congratulations, Colin," said Nicklaus to "Monty" in the booth. "How's it feel to win your first Open?"

Following a birdie at No. 6, and at the time unaware of the Nicklaus-Montgomery victory talk, Kite arrived at the par-3 seventh tee. Playing a punch shot into the brutal wind, Kite's tee shot landed just off the green. His following pitch shot landed on the green and rolled directly into the cup for birdie. With Morgan still working behind for a double-bogey at No. 6, Kite suddenly went from being tied to a having a three-stroke cushion.

"When that pitch went in we were more than ecstatic because we knew how much it meant," Carrick said. "Tom wanted to dance but he never did. He knew it still wasn't over."

In fact, the wild ride was only beginning.

Only two holes after his dramatics at No. 7, Kite lost a stroke with a tough but "good" bogey at No. 9. Then, on the par-4 tenth, he couldn't get on the green in two. Kite did save par, however, and carded another par at the par-4 No. 11.

On No. 12, a long, tricky par 3, he knocked his tee shot some thirty feet from the cup and then proceeded to drain the ensuing birdie putt. A par at No. 13 followed.

"At that point I just told myself to stick with the game plan," Kite said later. "Positive shots; one at a time."

No shot would be as big as his tee shot at the long and tough par-5 fourteenth. Still holding precariously to his three-stroke lead, Kite and Carrick stepped onto the tee and instantly began debating exactly which club to hit.

"All week he had been going with a three-wood, so that was the natural call to make," Carrick said. "This time there was a strong wind from left-to-right, though. I remember he asked me, 'What do you think about the driver? It's downwind and if I hit a good one . . .' Well, I was thinking lay up. Eventually he looked at me and said, 'Let's see if we can get up in the (left-side green protecting) bunker.' So he went with the three-wood."

Following a solid drive and testy second shot, Kite ended up right where he wanted to be—just left of the bunker. His ensuing pitch shot landed three feet from the pin leading to an easy birdie and boosting his lead over then clubhouse leader Jeff Sluman to four strokes.

"It was one of the greatest pitch shots he ever made and turned out to be the cushion we needed," Carrick said. "Then again, we knew at the time that it was still far from over."

Now holding a four-stroke lead with only four holes to play, Kite simply had to try and hold on. A great up-and-down from the fringe at No. 15 earned a par, but on No. 16 a bogey resulted after Kite hit his straight-into-the-wind drive into the right-side rough. He reached the green in two, but missed his par putt. The lead was suddenly only three.

"When he missed that putt, he looked over and said, 'That was my worst putt all week,'" Carrick said.

Upon reaching No. 17—a hole already made famous by previous U.S. Open winners at Pebble Beach Tom Watson and

Jack Nicklaus—Kite and Carrick again huddled to think of a game plan. The yardage may have been 209 yards on the card, but both knew the winds were whipping dangerously.

"I had wanted him to go with a driver but he didn't like the idea, so he went with a three-wood," Carrick said.

Kite's tee shot landed in the large bunker protecting the left side of the green. He got on in two after a sensational pitch with his sand wedge, but missed his par putt. The lead had shrunk to two.

"One more hole," Carrick said. "We had to survive eighteen."

As the duo had on the last few holes, it was time for another conference on the tee—ocean on the left; sand and trees on the right—the decision would be critical.

"Our main thought was to just get it somewhere in the fairway," Carrick said. "We'd gone three-wood all week but this time I knew Tom wanted the driver. On fifteen, sixteen, and seventeen we went three-wood and he had pulled it to the left, and on No. 18 at Pebble Beach that's the last thing you want to do. So we went with driver and he pipes it down the middle. Even after that we still weren't breathing easy, though."

Upon reaching his drive, Kite laid-up with a 5-iron. His third shot, a wedge, landed safely on the green. The "best player who had never won a Major" would finally have his day in the sun—or in this case, the wind.

"Once he was on we knew we had it. It was like, 'Finally!'" said Carrick, who still regularly loops on the PGA Tour. "To this day it's the highlight of all my years as a caddie. And to have that special moment at Pebble Beach; what a magical week."

## The Call

For Pebble Beach caddie Michael Moore, getting a chance to loop during the 1992 U.S. Open was just a phone call away.

A native of the Monterey Peninsula, Moore, who began carrying the bag at Pebble Beach in 1989, was originally slated to spend U.S. Open week performing other duties, most specifically coordinating the food and beverage schedule for the Carmel High School District volunteer center.

On the Sunday morning before tournament week, however, Moore suddenly got a phone call from the Pebble Beach pro shop. "They wanted to know if I'd be able to caddie," said Moore, who was born at the former Fort Ord in 1963. "Of course I said yes."

When Moore got to Pebble Beach, he learned his loop would be James Empey. Empey, a club professional who in 1993 became the head golf coach at the University of Southern California, earned a spot in the national championship via open qualifying.

"I remember we headed for a practice round that Sunday afternoon," Moore said. "As we were walking off the first green, he looked over to me and said, 'I want you to caddie for me for the week.'"

Having instantly established a connection, Moore and Empey grew even more entwined a few hours into the round.

"So eventually we're in the fairway at No. 9, and up ahead on the green is Jack Nicklaus. Well, Nicklaus waves us up," Moore said. "We're about 195-yards out, and Empey goes on to hit a perfect two-iron to within six inches of the cup. As we approach the green, Nicklaus looks over and says with a smile, 'Would you like to play the back nine with us?'"

Although just a practice round, a few marshals on hand had captured the moment via photos and a video tape. Today, Moore still has pictures and videotape that capture the moment.

"Ended up I got a copy of the pictures and the video tape," Moore said. "What an experience. I mean, not only did I get a chance to loop the U.S. Open at Pebble Beach, but I got a chance to loop in the same group as someone like Nicklaus. It doesn't matter that it was just a practice round that day. It's something I'll never forget."

## One of the Best

If any professional Tour caddie has found success at Pebble Beach Golf Links, it's looper Andy Martinez. The caddie for now NBC golf analyst Johnny Miller, Martinez was on the bag for seventeen of the Hall of Famer's twenty-four PGA Tour victories, including the 1973 U.S. Open and the 1974, 1987, and 1994 Pebble Beach National Pro-Ams.

It was at Pebble Beach, in fact, that Martinez met Peninsula native Bobby Clampett in 1982 during the Pro-Am. Splitting time on the bag between Miller and Clampett—fifteen tournaments each—Martinez helped lead Clampett to his only

*Caddie Andy Martinez helps eventual champion David Gossett line up a putt during the 1999 U.S. Amateur at Pebble Beach.*
(Courtesy of Pebble Beach Company.)

professional win at the Southern Open in 1982 at Green Island Country Club in Columbus, Georgia.

In 1992, Martinez began looping for Tom Lehman. Four
years later, the Lehman-Martinez tandem won the British
Open. Then, in 1998 the duo came to Pebble Beach and won
the Callaway Golf Pebble Beach Invitational, a prestigious off-
season event. The win was Martinez' second at the Callaway,
since he also helped Bob Gilder win the title in 1988.

In 1999, Martinez was on the bag of 20-year-old David
Gossett, a University of Texas sophomore, when he won the
99th U.S. Amateur at Pebble Beach by easily defeating Sung
Yoon Kim 9 & 8 in the final round.

"I can't explain my success at Pebble Beach," Martinez
said. "It is sort of odd. I guess the course and I sort of speak
to each other."

Whatever their means of communication, the message is
loud and clear.

Under the stress of playing Pebble Beach under championship conditions, Martinez, time and again, has found a way
to make his loop shine brightest. So much, in fact, that many
of his employers have described Martinez as able to see free
and clear of any distractions.

"Andy is by far the most meticulous caddie on the Tour,"
said Lehman prior to the 2000 U.S. Open at Pebble Beach.
"Sometimes he'll tell you to hit, say, a 5-iron. I'll start to argue
with a 'C'mon Andy, let's hit this club'; and then I'll remember
who I'm talking to and just say, 'Sorry, man, a five it is.'"

It was Martinez' attention to detail that brought him to
Gossett. The two met in 1999 at the St. Jude Classic in Memphis.

"In a casual conversation, I asked David if he'd ever been
out to Pebble Beach and if he had a caddie for the week,"
Martinez said. "Then I found out I had the week off."

Later, Martinez confessed he had an ulterior motive.

"I wanted to see Pebble Beach under USGA conditions
on Tom's behalf," Martinez said.

Despite the premise, Martinez committed to the Gossett job with all his heart. The result? Another win.

"At the start of the Amateur, David and Andy were very professional," said Gossett's mother, Pam. "But by Sunday, they were staying up late, playing cards and watching *America's Funniest Home Videos*. Andy was calling David his 'little man.' You just get the sense that he's the best there is when it comes to understanding Pebble Beach and the relaxed mindset it takes to win there."

From Gossett's eventual win, Martinez collected his customary 10 percent of total earnings—which, because it was the U.S. Amateur, accounted to a mere zero dollars. Despite having been over the course hundreds of times, Martinez at least hoped he'd gained a greater sense of Pebble Beach than he had before.

"You always want your guy to be able to play the course, rather than the opponent," Martinez said. "To know Pebble Beach is to have a relationship with it—to feel it. You can't let go and then come back. It always has to be tended to."

Truly Classic—Only a few months before the 1992 U.S. Open, the caddies of Pebble Beach were presented to America via a home-gaming console.

In April of 1992, the Nintendo Gaming Corporation released *True Golf Classics: Pebble Beach Golf Links* for the Super Nintendo Entertainment System.

During game play, console users could tee off at a simulated Pebble Beach Golf Links in stroke play, skins play, match play or practice play. As a bonus, joining the player during the round would be a simulated Pebble Beach caddie who would offer tips and advice.

In a first, the virtual caddies used in *True Golf Classics* were non-fictional. Instead, they were based on real caddies at Pebble Beach.

The Pebble Beach loopers whom players could consult during game play were Robert "Dawg" Robare, Robert "Rocket" Lytle, Dave Quesenberry, Casey Boyns, Michael Moore, and Ray "Foot" Mednis.

Years later, Nintendo gamers voted *True Golf Classics: Pebble Beach Golf Links* as one of the Top 100 Super NES games ever.

# 12 A New Century: The 2000 U.S. Open

*"If Tiger Woods wasn't perfect here this week, in this perfect place, then I don't know that the word should exist."*
—Ernie Els

Somewhere, Pebble Beach Golf Links founder Samuel F.B. Morse had to be laughing. Not only did the arrival of the year 2000 mark a new century of golf in the kingdom, but it also kicked off a new millennium of golf at Pebble Beach.

It was Morse, of course, who had at one time been put on the defensive in regards to whether or not Pebble Beach was indeed a venue worthy of hosting a national championship.

Eighty years after the course first opened its fairways in 1919, Pebble Beach had hosted four U.S. Amateur Championships (1929, 1947, 1961, 1999), one PGA Championship (1977), one Nabisco Championships (1988), and three U.S. Opens (1972, 1982, 1992).

During its first eighty years, the course also hosted the 1940 and 1948 U.S. Women's Amateur Championship and became the home course for the annual AT&T Pebble Beach National Pro-Am, the Callaway Golf Pebble Beach Invitational, and California Golf Association's State Amateur Championship.

Adding to that heritage, Pebble Beach received its greatest compliment in 2000.

Despite a ten-year rotation from 1972 to 1992, Pebble Beach was, in the eyes of the USGA, the perfect place to hold the centennial U.S. Open. One hundred years of U.S. Open history would be celebrated at one of golf's greatest stages, with caddies again being a part of the central cast.

## A Walk in the Park

Professional Tour caddie Steve Williams had been there before, but this would be something entirely different.

For Williams, who's known as the Kiwi Caddie among his peers, the journey first began in 1976 when, despite being only 13 years old at the time, Williams opted to become a caddie in his hometown of Paraparaumu, New Zealand. During that fateful first year on the bag, Williams ended up carrying for 1976 New Zealand Open winner Peter Thompson.

With the win, Williams received $150, a golf bag, and enough golf balls to fill the bag.

"In those days I was getting fifty cents a week pocket money, so I thought there must be something in this caddying lark," Williams told *Golf Today* in a 1998 interview.

As Williams eventually found out, there was much, much more.

Having gained steam as a more than reliable bag man from working with Thompson and others Down Under, Williams, in the early 1980s, moved to Europe, where he first spent a year on the bag of future 1991 British Open champion Ian Baker-Finch. Following the Baker-Finch campaign, it was eight years in the States with the "Great White Shark"—1993 British Open champ and Australian native Greg Norman—

*Waiting for the green to clear at No. 16 are* (left to right) *former Pebble Beach caddie Gavan McCray, Arnold Palmer, Bob Hope, and comedian Phil Harris so they can hit their approach shots. In the background is Hope's caddie.* (Photograph by William C. Brooks.)

before switching to carry for 1986 U.S. Open champion Raymond Floyd.

While Williams had missed out on his previous clients' big wins, he was soon to be arm-in-arm with the biggest jackpot winner in golf history.

In early 1999, while Williams was still looping for Floyd on both the PGA and Champions tours, Tiger Woods suddenly fired his caddie Mike "Fluff" Cowan in a move that many at the time figured revolved around Cowan's sudden celebrity status and his willingness to speak openly with a Tiger Woods hungry media.

Content with his role as the bag man for Floyd, Williams at the time didn't pay much attention to the Woods-Cowan flap.

Then, however, the focus suddenly turned to Williams. Looking for a new caddie, Woods approached Williams through his coach, renowned instructor Butch Harmon.

"I just about fell over," Williams said. "I mean here was Tiger Woods asking me, not me asking Tiger. What made it really satisfying is that almost every American player had an American caddie, and Tiger had gone for me, a Kiwi."

Upon accepting the job with the greatest player in the world, Williams instantly found himself riding shotgun with The Striped-One. Having watched the unfolding of the Cowan affair however, Williams quickly set a tone with the media.

"I'm a caddie. I carry golf clubs," said Williams matter-of-factly.

In other words, there would be no comments. Not then, now, or any other time in the foreseeable future.

Almost exactly a year after taking on Woods' offer, Williams was on the bag when Woods made his 2000 run at a second Masters title at plush Augusta National Golf Club.

From Augusta, it was on to Pebble Beach Golf Links and the centennial 2000 U.S. Open. Despite a fifth place finish at Augusta, Woods was the overwhelming favorite coming into Pebble Beach.

"Everything points to Tiger winning his first Open at

Pebble Beach," said NBC golf analyst Johnny Miller on the eve of the championship. "Everyone else is looking like a pretender."

During day one of the championship, Woods first cracked his way into red numbers after knocking a lob wedge on the par-4 fourth to within a few feet of the cup for birdie.

After tacking on a few more birdies, including one on the always tough par-4 tenth, Woods and Williams headed to the tee at No. 14. Despite a solid drive, Woods hit his second shot into the heavy rough off the left side of the fairway. Facing potential trouble Woods recovered with a brilliant pitch shot out of the thick stuff that would land within two feet of the cup for another birdie.

"That was luck, just blind luck," Woods said afterward. "I was able to knock it within a few feet and get my birdie."

While luck played a role on No. 14, it was skill that pushed Woods onward through round one. By the end of their round, Woods' 6-under-par 65 ranked as the lowest Open round ever recorded at Pebble Beach.

"I saw Steve (Williams) pacing off yardage markers, bunkers, ice cream stands that just shouldn't come into play," said Swede Jesper Parnevik, Woods' playing partner. "He's in a different world."

As for the world of Pebble Beach, not long after Woods posted his score, the course was tucked in a blanket of Monterey Peninsula fog. With some seventy-five players having not completed their first round, many pulled double-time on Friday.

As for Woods, the first round was history, and it was time to get busy again.

Holding a one-stroke lead over Spaniard Miguel Angel Jiminez at the official end of round one on Friday, Woods increased his lead early in the second round after sinking an 18-foot birdie putt for par on the dog-leg left par-4 No. 3 hole at Pebble Beach. Three holes later, Woods again struck pay dirt, this time from the jail of hole No. 6.

Teeing off on the par-5 sixth, Woods lost his drive to the far right into heavy rough.

The decision was either pitch out to the fairway or blast off toward the green. Feeling frisky, Tiger opted for liftoff, remarkably slapping his second shot on to the green. While Woods missed his eagle attempt, another birdie was in hand.

"I had played enough to know what certain lies will do," Woods said. "I squeezed the shot perfectly and it came out hot but high enough on a flat line. Once it got on the green I knew I could two-putt for a birdie."

After another birdie on the par-4 No. 9, Woods was at 9-under for the championship, well ahead of the rest of the field. By the end of round two, Woods (65-69–134) held a six stroke lead over his nearest competitor, Thomas Bjorn of Sweden.

Entering the third round, Woods looked to increase the lead even more, but Pebble Beach would for a moment strike back. On the dog-leg left par-4 third hole, Woods hit his drive too far to the right. His second shot landed in the thick grass edging the greenside bunker protecting the right-front of the green. On his first attempt out, Woods remained incarcerated. He got out on his next shot, but still ended up carding a triple-bogey seven on the hole to suddenly drop his overall score back to a potentially reachable and more reasonable 6 under par.

Moments later, however, Tiger was again on the prowl. A birdie at the par-3 seventh, followed by another birdie on the par-4 ninth, and by the end of round three, Woods tacked on another birdie to finish the first fifty-four holes at a record 10 under par. In being 10 under, Woods not only entered the final round with a more than comfy ten-stroke lead over his nearest competitor, Ernie Els of South Africa, but he was shattering the record books.

For starters, his six-stroke lead over the rest of the field after round two had broken a 97-year-old Open record. The previous thirty-six-hole record was five strokes, set by Willie Anderson in 1903 at Baltusrol Golf Club in New Jersey.

*Despite this awkward shot leading to a rare triple-bogey on the par-4 third hole, the 2000 U.S. Open at Pebble Beach became a walk in the park for Tiger Woods and professional caddie Steve Williams.* (Photograph by Paul Lester.)

As for other feats, his ten-stroke lead after fifty-four holes was the largest ever. The previous record of seven was set by James Barnes in 1921 at Columbia Country Club.

The U.S. Open at Pebble Beach was turning into another Woods' masterpiece, à la his dominating win at the 1997 Masters.

"It surprises me I'm doing this at the U.S. Open," Woods said. "It's just because a U.S. Open is so difficult to go low. Don't get me wrong, at Augusta it's difficult to go low, but there you can see it's possible because there's no rough and you could go bombs away."

As for Woods' final round at Pebble Beach, the week could be summed up by his walk to the courtesy van that Sunday morning. Upon reaching the van, Woods looked over to Williams and asked with a grin, "Having a good time?"

As a sign of the times, Williams simply laughed.

With history in the bag, Williams and Woods went out to complete the most dominant showing in one hundred years of U.S. Open history.

At the end of it all, Woods walked away with his first U.S. Open crown by a record fifteen shots. His seventy-two hole total of 272 was a record low, as was his score (12 under) in relation to par.

"Those who know golf understand that it is a game that consists far more of small failures than of success," Els remarked afterward. "Someone once said, 'Golf is not a game of perfect.' But if Tiger Woods wasn't perfect, in this perfect place, then I don't know that the word should exist."

Indeed, the 2000 U.S. Open at Pebble Beach was an open and shut case.

Following his win at Pebble Beach, Woods went on to capture the 2000 British Open at St. Andrews and the 2000 PGA Championship at Kentucky-based Valhalla Golf Club. Then a win at the 2001 Masters tabbed Woods as the first modern player ever to hold all four Major championships—the modern Grand Slam—at the same time. At the time of his crowning achievement, only four other players had won career Grand Slams—Hall of Famers Gene Sarazen, Ben Hogan, Gary Player, and Jack Nicklaus. The legendary Bobby Jones, the only player to ever win a Grand Slam in the same year, captured the British Open, British Amateur, U.S. Open, and U.S. Amateur championships in 1930.

As for the mum Williams, meanwhile, the Kiwi Caddie became the first caddie to own a Grand Slam. He also earned nearly $900,000 as the bag man for Woods in 2000. The staggering amount—a result of Williams earning eight to ten percent for each Woods win—would have landed Williams at fifty-fourth on the PGA Tour money player's list.

"Steve's been a great caddie," Woods said. "He's very positive and upbeat. If I'm not playing well, he knows exactly what buttons to push to get me going."

Considering what the two have accomplished as a team, no will ever argue that.

## Farewell to a Friend

While there was joy at the 2000 U.S. Open at Pebble Beach Golf Links, there was also sadness. Prior to its arrival, the centennial U.S. Open was to have marked the knighting of Payne Stewart as one of the royalty of Pebble Beach.

It was a year earlier that Stewart had kicked off what would become a run of triumphs by first capturing the title at the 1999 AT&T Pebble Beach National Pro-Am, marking his first victory since winning the 1991 U.S. Open at Hazeltine Golf Club in Minnesota.

Stewart wrapped up day two of a wet and windy Pro-Am tournament with a sizzling 8-under par 64 at Poppy Hills Golf Course to take a three-stroke lead. A day later, Stewart would play always-tough Spyglass Hill, with the conditions getting even worse. Despite the conditions, Stewart again hung tough, this time finishing with a 1-over 73 to cling to a one-stroke lead.

That Saturday night, Pebble Beach was pelted with rain. In the morning, the final round was canceled. Stewart was again a champion.

"I've been on the other side of the 54-hole deal before, and this time on the right side of it," said Stewart, who in 1990 was in second place when the final round of the annual Ohio-based Memorial Tournament was called off due to inclement weather. "I'm not going to lie. It feels pretty good. I did want the opportunity to prove I could win in 72 holes, but I'm going to take this and run. I was low after 54 holes, and that was good enough this week."

With his win at Pebble Beach, Stewart appeared to be back on track, a fact that wasn't lost on his longtime caddie Mike Hicks. Hicks had carried Stewart's bag for 12 years. "By the time the 1999 AT&T Pro-Am rolled around, Payne was ready to go," Hicks said. "He was back. He'd become a great putter."

Following his win at Pebble Beach, Stewart nearly won the MCI Classic at Hilton Head, South Carolina, losing in a play-off. Two months later, however, Stewart got more than back on track by winning the historic 1999 U.S. Open at Pinehurst No. 2.

In the final round, the knickers-clad Stewart dueled with playing partner Phil Mickelson all day long. Finally, Stewart took a one-stroke lead over Mickelson with a birdie on No. 17. On No. 18, the Missouri native would face a difficult putt for par and the win from nearly 15 feet out to win the championship.

With Mickelson, Hicks, and the world looking on, Stewart sank the putt, further etching his name into the history books. "Little did I know I'd be part of one of the greatest moments in sports," Hicks said later. "Payne's stroke was perfect, and I could see the label on his ball just rolling over and over and over until it just disappeared. It was classic Payne."

As for the expected coronation of Stewart at Pebble Beach

in 2000 as returning champion of both the AT&T Pro-Am and the U.S Open, however, the celebration was not to be. On October 25, 1999, Stewart, then 42 years old, would perish along with four others when their Learjet crashed in South Dakota. The plane was en route to Texas, where Stewart was expected to play in the PGA Tour Championship in Houston.

"Payne absolutely loved Pebble Beach. He was a traditionalist, and there's just so much history there," Hicks said.

Stewart loved Pebble Beach, and he had a storied history on the links. Hicks was not on Stewart's bag when Payne made his debut at Pebble Beach, finishing in a tie for fourteenth in the 1983 Pro-Am. Nor was Hicks on the bag in 1986 or 1987 when Stewart finished as runner-up in back-to-back years. But he was on the bag when Stewart came into the 1992 U.S. Open at Pebble Beach as the reigning champion.

"For some reason, Payne could get to a level of focus at the U.S. Open that he could never attain any other week, as much as he tried. Being such a patriotic guy, the U.S. Open was the most important tournament for him" Hicks told *Golf Digest*. "I was really looking forward to going back to Pebble Beach."

Payne was 1-under par and just three strokes back going into the final round of the 1992 U.S. Open. Like so many others, he fell victim to the strong winds. On the final day, when the leaders (other than Tom Kite) averaged over 80, Stewart closed with an 83 and fell out of contention.

"We had started the final round only three back, and as we're walking down the first fairway the wind hit," Hicks said. "By the time we got to No. 3, it was even worse. For Payne, No. 3 was usually a 3-wood and then a wedge. That Sunday, it was a driver and a 3-iron. Later on No. 7 we hit a 6-iron. It was just an extremely difficult day."

The next year, Stewart returned for the 1993 AT&T Pebble Beach National Pro-Am. Although Stewart didn't win the individual championship, he and his playing partner Jim Morris won the Pro-Am team title. Morris, an insurance man from Springfield, Missouri, was not only a close friend of Payne's late father, but was Stewart's godfather.

"That was a very special week for Payne," Hicks said. "Payne and Jim were very close, so he was thrilled."

By all accounts, Stewart would have been one of the favorites entering the 2000 U.S. Open. Yet instead, he was gone. Gone, but not forgotten.

At the 2000 AT&T Pebble Beach National Pro-Am, Stewart was remembered in a number of ways. Along with a moment of silence prior to the 2000 Past Champions Shoot-Out, tournament officials that year wore plaid ribbons in honor of Stewart—the colors being either red-and-green or red-and-black, both of which are historically connected with the Stewart clan in Scotland. In addition, a commemorative bag tag that featured somewhat the same design as the ribbon was given to each of the professional and amateur contestants. Officials also renamed the annual Wednesday youth clinic the Payne Stewart Youth Clinic.

Five months later, at the 2000 U.S. Open, Stewart was immortalized at Pebble Beach Golf Links. On the Wednesday of Open week, a day before the championship teed off, a sunrise service was held followed by a "21-gun salute" along the fairway of No. 18 at Pebble Beach. Upon the call "Ready! Aim! Fire!" 21 golfers, including the likes of Paul Azinger and Tom Lehman and Hicks, hit ceremonious drives into the Pacific Ocean in a tribute to Stewart.

"He (Stewart) did his own thing, and he did it beautifully," Hicks said. "We'll never forget him. I miss him and think about him every day."

## Inside the Bag

Since Tiger Woods' firing of caddie "Fluff" Cowan in early 1999, a large number of caddies on the PGA Tour have adopted the mantra of "Don't ask; don't tell."

It was during Cowan's run with Woods that at one point the grizzled, mustachioed Fluff became somewhat of a celebrity himself. Not only did fans want Tiger to sign autographs, they wanted Cowan to sign.

Cowan became such a familiar face, in fact, that he ended up appearing in more than one television commercial, the most memorable one being for a motel chain that showed him magically popping out of a suitcase.

Although Woods never officially explained why Cowan was canned, and Cowan has also never divulged the inside details, many caddies at the time believed his firing was due to the fact that Fluff had become as much a household word as Tiger.

No matter the real reasons behind it all, since the Woods-Cowan episode Steve Williams and other caddies on the PGA Tour have in recent years clammed up when it comes to media.

"Generally speaking, I think caddies are wary," Andy Martinez said. "Sometimes things don't come out the way you say them. Sometimes they [media] print parts of what you say. Because of that, it can make you look bad or make your player look bad."

"I keep to myself," Greg Norman's longtime caddie Tony Navarro told the *Augusta Chronicle.* "I let Greg do the talking for our team. I think that's the way it should be. Sometimes one little thing taken the wrong way can really ruffle some feathers."

The times have indeed changed.

As for today's gag orders and suspicions, it's of course the caddies' choice whether or not to open up. It's a matter of rolling the dice and missing, rolling and shooting craps or simply walking away.

Said longtime Jim Thorpe caddie and veteran PGA Tour looper Richard "Jelly" Hansberry: "The caddie should keep a low profile. You don't ever want to be in front of the player. You want to be behind him. Players don't mind you talking to the press, but you can't say anything that comes out of your mouth."

## A Homecoming

Pebble Beach caddie Michael Moore wasn't exactly in great spirits on the eve of the 2000 U.S. Open. Despite having already worked the 1992 U.S. Open, Moore was still loopless.

"I remember telling my wife, 'I'm out of here,'" Moore recalled. "I wasn't too happy to say the least."

The Sunday evening of championship week, however, everything changed when Moore received a phone call from Monterey Peninsula golf legend Bobby Clampett.

"It was around 9 P.M. Sunday night, and I suddenly got this phone call," Moore said. "Once the other person spoke, I knew it was Bobby. His first question was, 'Would you like to caddie for me?'"

Clampett, who had finished tied for third in the 1982 U.S. Open at Pebble Beach and had since become a golf commentator for CBS in 1995, hadn't played in an official event in nearly two years. Nonetheless, the one-time prodigy had earned a spot in the centennial U.S. Open via open qualifying.

For Clampett, the trip home had begun with a 73 in local qualifying at North Carolina–based Prestonwood Country Club, good enough to earn a fourth alternate spot for the sectional.

Still, however, Clampett was on the bubble. Or so it seemed.

Three days before the scheduled sectional at Maryland-based Woodmont Country Club, Clampett first saw that PGA Tour professional and good friend Bill Glasson (who had urged Clampett to give qualifying a shot months before) had sent Clampett an e-mail telling him he was going to withdraw from the sectional field, opening up a spot.

Then, upon the day of the sectional, the good news

spread even more when none of the other three alternates showed up.

Clampett ended up getting his shot—playing ironically in Glasson's spot—and promptly went on to fire back-to-back rounds of 68 in the morning and afternoon to stamp his ticket home.

"I had been the fourth alternate and it turned out that Billy [Glasson] was the fourth one to withdraw, so I got his spot," Clampett told the *Monterey County Herald*. "You know, we've been such close friends for so many years. I think he really wanted me to have a chance to come home to Pebble Beach for the U.S. Open."

*Caddie Michael Moore and Bobby Clampett line up a putt during the 2000 U.S. Open.* (Photograph by Michael Moore.)

Upon his return to Pebble Beach, Clampett found Moore more than eager to help with any attempts at another batch of home-cooking.

"He was excited and I was excited," Moore said. "We were ready to go."

Having retired from the PGA Tour in 1995, both Clampett and Moore were indeed ready to roll.

On day one of the national championship, Clampett opened with four birdies through the first ten holes, good enough to at one point share the lead. By the end of the fog-riddled round, Clampett was in at 68, a mere three strokes behind leader Tiger Woods.

"It was like playing golf in heaven," the then 40-year-old Clampett said following his round.

"That first day, he didn't miss a shot through the first twelve holes," Moore said. "We were both in a zone, completely focused. I mean, we were giving each other the yardage, reading the greens together, whatever it took. It was a great team effort."

Despite a fabulous start, Mother Nature stepped on both Clampett and Moore's feet in the second round. Due to continuous weather delays from fog, Clampett didn't tee off in Friday's second round until 4 P.M. The duo ended up getting in fifteen holes at 2 over par for the partial round.

In the wee hours of Saturday morning, Clampett and Moore finished the fog-delayed second round, playing holes No. 16 through No. 18 at 3 over par to finish with a 77. Later that Saturday afternoon, Clampett played round three, again finishing over par at 76.

Sunday's final round offered more of the same. Overall, Clampett finished the championship with a total of 298 (68-77-76-77), three dozen shots behind Woods.

"I remember there was a point over the weekend where everyone on the range was scared of Tiger. It had become more about him than anyone else. The other guys had given up the fight," Moore said. "As for Bobby, we had all intentions of giving it a run. With the delays though, it became a waiting game. This was a guy who hadn't played in years. It's tough to turn it on and off in those conditions. The experience will always stick with me, though. Through those first holes, Bobby could have competed with anyone."

## On the Road

During both the 1992 and 2000 U.S. Opens, the caddies of Pebble Beach Golf Links didn't just work at home.

Due to the ever-growing influence of corporations into the golf circle, more than a dozen Pebble Beach caddies in both 1992 and 2000 found themselves working for U.S. Open guests during championship week at many of the Peninsula's other great golf courses including Spyglass Hill, Spanish Bay, Del Monte, Poppy Hills, Bayonet, Carmel Valley Ranch, and Rancho Canada golf courses.

Included in that group was longtime Pebble Beach looper Al Kirby, whose father Joe Kirby had been a caddie at Plank Hill Country Club in New Jersey during the 1920s.

"Most of the [Pebble Beach] caddies preferred to try and hook up a loop for the whole week of the championship," Kirby said. "What many of the professional players did though was to hire a local caddie only for the practice rounds. They'd want to get a feel and knowledge about the course from someone local. Then, when it came time for the championship to tee off, they'd go back to their regular professional caddie."

With the caddie and players lottery days of the 1972 U.S. Open long gone, most players would indeed turn to their professional caddie. Whether or not some players may have shaved strokes by permanently using a local caddie, one will never know.

"I'm sure there are some players that would have benefited," said Kirby, who in 2004 still carried the bag four days a week at Pebble Beach. "As for myself, I was happy doing what I did. No matter where you are, you're still a caddie."

## Eyes and Ears

While Al Kirby looped at other courses, fellow Pebble Beach caddie Dave Quesenberry spent the 2000 U.S. Open working basically as a caddie for the major networks covering the championship.

During the final three rounds of the championship, the then 32-year-old Quesenberry followed the final group (which included champion Tiger Woods) each day, providing yardages, club selection or whatever other information the associate producers would ask for. Along with working for NBC, Quesenberry also became the on-course eyes and ears for the BBC and Japanese television.

"Basically, I'd be ahead of the players or on the tee, getting the clubs and distances. Then I would relay that info to [NBC analyst] Roger Maltbie, the BBC guy or [Japanese TV's] Isao Aoki," said Quesenberry, who joined the caddie ranks at Pebble Beach in 1987. "I was basically a caddie, but it was obviously different. Instead of being in the middle of everything, I was more on the sidelines. It's not unusual to see professional caddies who are out of regular work ending up working for the networks."

One of the veteran loopers at Pebble Beach, Quesenberry took on the professional ranks in 2003 when he spent a year working with then PGA Tour rookie and fellow Bay Area native Todd Fischer. While the two went winless that season, they did have two top ten finishes—one coming at the FBR Capital Open and the other coming at the Greater Hartford Open.

As of 2004, Quesenberry has returned to work the course he has called home for seventeen years. "I don't know if I'll ever go back on the Tour," Quesenberry said. "Pebble Beach is a tough place to leave."

# 13 Bagging the Beach: Modern Day Caddies

*"Everyone's always nervous at the first hole at Pebble Beach.
I just tell them to relax."*
—Casey Boyns

From the first loop of Henry Puget back in 1919 to today, caddies have been a part of the history at Pebble Beach Golf Links, and they always will be.

"Playing Pebble Beach is an experience in itself," said longtime Pebble Beach looper Scott Houston. "Taking a caddie is part of that experience. You can meet someone from Paris, France or Paris, Texas and at the conclusion of five hours you are friends. It's really a complete experience. It's not just carrying the bags."

Indeed, while times have changed, the caddie role at Pebble Beach today remains the same. As it was in the beginning, Pebble Beach caddies still know the ins and outs of some of the world's trickiest greens, and they still literally know the distances at Pebble Beach to a tee. They're the hosts of a golf gala like no other.

The only real difference between a Pebble Beach caddie in the 2000s and a Pebble Beach caddie from the early 1900s is time. Time that, as any Pebble Beach caddie of any era will tell you, only adds more and more to the legend and lore of "The Kingdom of Golf" every day.

## The Legend

As the annual host of what is today the AT&T Pebble Beach National Pro-Am, Pebble Beach Golf Links has seen its share of autograph hounds.

Ray Romano of the hit CBS show *Everybody Loves Raymond*? Got it. Actor Kevin Costner? Got it last year. Phil Mickelson? On the mantel. Tiger Woods? Under the pillow.

It wasn't too long ago, however, that it was a Pebble Beach caddie who was the center of attention on the fabled course.

For veteran Pebble Beach caddie Casey Boyns, the trip to the lights fantastic began back in 1966, when a then 10-year-old red-headed kid began playing with and caddying for his dad, Leonard Boyns.

At the time, Boyns' caddie duties mostly involved driving the cart, but a mere two years later the kid was driving the ball past everyone else in his dad's group. As a result, Leonard Boyns bought his son a set of golf clubs, and the kid soon was teeing off with the rest of them.

"I loved it," said Boyns of the game. "I remember I couldn't go to sleep at night. I'd be thinking too much about playing the next day."

As for his caddie career, things were also heating up. While still only 12 years old, Boyns looped in his first Crosby Pro-Am by carrying the bag of Dr. Richard Gelb—the amateur partner of professional Gibby Gilbert—in the 1968 Pro-Am.

"I remember I was just a kid. I had no yardages and didn't know a thing about the greens at Pebble," Boyns recalled. "In today's terms I would have been a 'bag-toter.' All I knew was how to carry the bag. Other than that, I didn't know a thing."

After playing at nearby Pacific Grove High in his teen years, Boyns headed to the University of Utah, where he graduated with a degree in commercial recreation management. His next stop was a golf course, where, after landing a job, he hoped to start climbing the ladder in regards to the golf business.

Not soon after, though, Boyns would have second thoughts.

"I had become an assistant pro, but in the end I didn't like it," Boyns said. "I didn't like being inside. The money wasn't that great—long hours and low pay. I just didn't like it."

During that fateful year, Boyns also got pushed along by a friend from his college days who had previously entered the golf business.

"I remember the guy kept telling me reasons to not get into the business aspect of golf," said Boyns, a native of Carmel-by-the-Sea. "It was this and it was that, and in the end it would all be no good."

Stuck between being inside and outside, Boyns returned to his roots—taking on a job as a caddie at Pebble Beach.

"It turned out that I kind of got stuck, but it was a good stuck," Boyns said. "Through the years, being a caddie had helped my game, and my game had helped in being a caddie."

Regarded as the player among his peers, Boyns first showcased his own skills on the course in 1987, when the then 31-year-old would capture the Northern California Golf Association Amateur Championship at nearby Spyglass Hill.

Two years later, in 1989, Boyns won the prestigious California Golf Association State Amateur Championship at Pebble Beach. Previous champions of the State Am included

Ken Venturi (1951 and 1956), Johnny Miller (1968), and Mark O'Meara (1979).

"The experience I had on the course from working as caddie no doubt helped, but looking back it was a kind of fluky win," Boyns said. "That year, I pretty much won the event with my play on the greens. I don't think I three-putted all week and I made all the little ones."

While the State Am win in 1989 would open eyes, it was in 1993 that Boyns cemented his nickname as "Legend" among his peers. Having already been crowned the best of the Golden State once before, Boyns opened the 1993 California State Amateur Championship as medalist after firing rounds of 70-73. A few days and few matches later, Boyns was remarkably again the king of the state, joining an all-time list of only 10 players who were medalist and champion in the same year.

Following his second triumph at the State Amateur, Boyns was greeted by Pebble Beach Company officials holding bottles of champagne. As a bonus, Pebble Beach officials also set up complimentary accommodations for the two-time champ and his wife, Sara.

"The difference the second time around was that I just hit the ball good all week," Boyns recalled. "Other than that, I just two-putted them to death. I'd figured, let them make the mistakes."

With his second win, any notions of a fluke were long gone. So much, in fact, that the veteran looper of numerous Pebble Beach National Pro-Ams was suddenly the celebrity of Pebble Beach.

"After the second win, I remember more and more people wanted me to caddie for them. They'd want me to take photos with them and sign autographs," said Boyns, who regularly loops for former San Francisco Giants owner Bob Lurie during the AT&T Pebble Beach National Pro-Am. "I would get all kinds of people asking for me to caddie for them. There were people who couldn't hit a golf ball a lick that wanted me on the bag."

More than a decade after his big wins, the Legend is still

*Casey Boyns hasn't just caddied at Pebble Beach. The two-time California State Amateur champion (1989 and 1993) has also won there. (Courtesy of Pebble Beach Company.)*

looping Pebble Beach. And while he may not be signing so many autographs these days, Boyns continues to do what he's always done—guide players through the beauty and beast that can be Pebble Beach Golf Links.

"Everyone's always nervous on the first hole at Pebble," Boyns said. "I just tell them to relax. I say, 'Hey, it's only Pebble Beach; it's just another golf course.'"

If anyone knows Pebble Beach Golf Links, it's Boyns. Now a resident of Pacific Grove, Boyns has played the fabled layout nearly 1,000 times, and he has walked the course somewhere around 10,000 times.

"Looking back, Pebble Beach has been very good to me," Boyns said. "Not only have I caddied Pebble, but I've also won at Pebble Beach as a player. It doesn't get much better than that."

## The Foot

Looking back, Ray Mednis likes to describe his decision to become a caddie at Pebble Beach as self-defense. Somewhat fitting, being that Mednis would forever leave his mark at Pebble Beach with what would become a legendary kick.

The year was 1973, and fresh off a stint in the U.S. Army at nearby Fort Ord, Mednis found himself trying to make ends meet. The then 35-year-old Michigan native then landed a job at Pebble Beach as a cart man.

"I needed to pick up some extra bucks, and I always loved the game," Mednis said. "I was making something around three bucks an hour, which barely covered the rent, but it was an income. I knew I had to be doing something."

While still a cart man, Mednis soon began getting to know the caddies more and more, and he liked what he heard.

"There were about eight to ten caddies at the time, old-school guys, and on days off or after 3 P.M. in the summer they would all get to play free golf. Free golf at Pebble Beach," said Mednis with a ring of excitement in his voice. "Well, when some of the regulars would later be unavailable, I started packing. Not long after that, I told myself to hell with the cart stuff. I just wanted to loop."

A year later in 1974, Mednis would get his wish, devoting all of his time to bagging the Beach. A mere year later, he'd work his first Crosby Pro-Am, looping in the same group as 1950s sensation Bob Goalby.

Goalby, a PGA Tour fixture during the 1950s and 1960s, was at the time like Arnold Palmer and Chi Chi Rodriguez known as much for his unorthodox swing as his success on the course. "I just remember him being very demanding," Mednis said. "Things had to be done a certain way."

As for Mednis, who turned 66 in 2004, it wouldn't be long after the 1975 Crosby that he perfected his own swing using of all things his sneaker.

While caddying for a regular player during the Pebble Beach drought years of the mid-1970s, Mednis and his loop would eventually end up standing on the back end of the somewhat hourglass-shaped green at the uphill, par-4 eleventh hole. With the drought conditions, the greens were faster than the tongue of an auctioneer, and to make matters worse, the pin was tucked up toward the front of the green more than fifty feet away.

"He had a fifty-footer for birdie, but with the pin in front I knew it was lethal. As a rule of thumb, any pin near the front of a green at Pebble is for the most part deadly," Mednis said. "Well, he of course asked for a read. I told him, 'With the speed, this is my guess. Nice easy hit and ignore the break.'"

As the player stroked his putt, the ball rolled toward the cup, rolling on and on. Eventually, the player ended up near the front edge of the sloping green, still eight to ten feet away from the cup.

"Once it got going, there was no way to stop it," Mednis said. "It was on its way."

On a whim and a prayer, however, Mednis had a feeling that his read was correct. While the player went on to look at his sudden long putt for par, Mednis took a ball out of his pocket and dropped it on the green almost precisely from where the player had putted.

With a quick kick that would make soccer legend Pelé envious, Mednis sent the ball rolling directly into the cup. "He just looked at me and said, 'Okay, Foot.' I didn't say another word. I mean, what the hell could I have said," Mednis said.

With one stroke, another legend in the caddie barn at Pebble Beach had been born, yet Foot wasn't done playing his part at Pebble Beach.

A few years after his defining incident on No. 11 green at Pebble Beach, Foot was on the bag looping for Tom Kite's father during a 1970s Pro-Am. On the tee at No. 9 in the midst of the Cliffs of Doom, the younger Kite stepped up to show his dad the way.

"It was one of the clearest days I could remember. Not a cloud in the sky," Mednis recalled. "Well, Tom hits his tee shot and all of sudden you see feathers flying everywhere. Where the seagull had came from, I still don't know. Anyways, so Tom's ball ricochets and heads straight down the right side of the slope of the fairway, which used to be junk. Here his ball is screaming dead center and then it suddenly goes off on a right angle. It threw him off a bit, for sure. He had this look like, 'What the heck?' and at the time I was like, 'Holey, moley!' I mean there wasn't another bird around for miles."

Not too long after his experience with the Kites, Mednis would experience a bit more weirdness. During the 1977 Pro-Am, Mednis found himself looping for none other than actor James Garner, star of the hit shows *Maverick* and *The Rockford Files*.

"So here we were in the midst of a [Pro-Am] celebrity pairing. There was Jack Nicklaus and former President Gerald Ford and Arnold Palmer a group ahead. The crowds are going crazy," Mednis said. "Well, on No. 14 Garner hits his second shot into the gallery. As we get to the ball, it ends up it had landed next to a girl that's lying on the ground. It looked like she was asleep. As we walk towards the ball though, the girl reaches up and grabs Garner right in the crotch. As we get over the ball I asked him, 'What'd you think about that?'"

"Garner looked back at me and said, 'Well, you know when it comes down to it, that's how I make my living.' Jim was a great guy to caddie for. The only time he would ever show a temper was when he hit a bad shot."

Having seen or been a part of just about anything that could happen on the links, the one-time cart guy would eventually become a hot ticket as a caddie. So much, in fact, that at one point Mednis considered the option of looping as a regular on the PGA Tour. In the end, however, the humble Mednis would cling to his roots.

"There was a time where everyone kept trying to tell me that I should go on Tour. They'd say, 'But there's so much money you can make,'" said Mednis, who despite stepping away from Pebble Beach in the early 1990s is still a favorite among today's Pebble Beach caddie corps. "Going on Tour would've never worked for me. It wasn't my style. For me, being a caddie at Pebble Beach was all about the joy of the game. Some guys do nothing and they make it big, while some guys do everything and make nothing. I did what I wanted to, and I wouldn't trade it for anything."

## The Nut

It wasn't a midlife crisis. It was an epiphany.

In early 1992, Scott Houston, a former business owner and once the executive director of the Monterey Peninsula Chamber of Commerce, suddenly found himself working for a Monterey-based hotel management company.

While at work one day, Houston, at the time 40 years old, was fidgeting within the confines of his office.

"Here I am sitting there in this stupid red leather chair, and then it hit me. This is nonsense," Houston said. "So I began hitting a few chip shots in the office and began thinking, 'What would I like to do? What would make me the most happy?' I knew I loved being outside and I knew that I loved the game of golf."

A mere three days later, Houston walked into the Pebble Beach Company offices looking for work. Following a brief meeting with then Pebble Beach caddie master Neil Allen, Houston landed the job that had for so long tugged at his heart. It was actually his second attempt at being a caddie.

While growing up in Connecticut in the early 1960s, Houston had at the age of 12 tried to find work as a caddie at Wee Burn Country Club in Darien. At the time golf legend Jimmy Demaret was the head pro. In his first go, it would become trial by fire, literally.

"I'd told Demaret that I had caddied before, so at first I got hired. Well, when it came time for me to make my first loop, I went over to get the player's bag, and it was one of those huge, heavy bags. As I picked it up, I remember the club pro looking over and screaming, 'You've never touched a golf bag in your life! I can see it!' I got fired on the spot. It remains the only time I've ever been fired in my life."

Twenty years later, Houston again tried to enter the caddie ranks, at of all places world-famous Pebble Beach Golf Links.

Suffice it to say, the second go would prove that Houston's heart had been right all along. His life's calling had been answered.

"That first day at Pebble Beach, I remember coming home and jumping up and down. 'I'm a caddie at Pebble Beach! I'm a caddie at Pebble Beach!' It would take me three years for the butterflies in my stomach to finally go away," Houston said.

A few years later, however, the butterflies would be back. Not in the excitement of just being a caddie at Pebble Beach, but because of his loop.

While having already carried the bags of big names such

*Former Pebble Beach caddie Scott Houston and Arnold Palmer await their chance on the green at No. 2. Houston and Arnold Palmer would team up over a dozen times at Pebble Beach Golf Links.* (Courtesy of Scott Houston.)

as former Dallas Cowboys star Roger Staubach and former Boston Red Sox legend Carlton Fisk, to name a few, the re-born caddie was one day assigned to carry the bag of a certain player by the name of Arnold Palmer.

"I remember someone came into the caddie barn and told me I'd been assigned to Palmer," Houston said. "My first reaction was, 'You mean Arnold Palmer? The King?' I got so nervous my teeth began to sweat."

Palmer, one of the co-owners of Pebble Beach Company, and Houston would meet on the first tee that day. "I introduced myself, and Arnold says, 'Pleased to meet you.' As we go on, the more and more I heard on the course was, 'Scott, what's the plan here?' I'd give him the club and he'd hit. Well, of course after a while we get to No. 16 and we're in the fairway. At that point Palmer looks over and says, 'Scott Houston, what have we got? That is your name right, Scott Houston?' I was flabbergasted. I mean, he knew my whole name. I was a person to this man. Not just some schlup carrying his bag."

Immediately after the verbal exchange, Palmer would go on to knock a 7-iron onto the green in easy range for a birdie. Following that, The King just gave his caddie a wink.

"There's only a few icons obsessed with what they're doing rather than being obsessed in being an icon," Houston said. "After that whole exchange I knew the kind of icon I was looping for. I wasn't just a caddie or a number. I was a person. That's how he is."

With word spreading quickly that The King was playing, the new duo would arrive at their final destination—No. 18—amid a flurry of Palmer fans. Already having experienced the Palmer-way, Houston would see it defined even more.

"During that round, there had already been people flocking to see what was going on. They knew that The King was out playing Pebble Beach. I mean, there were cars pulling over on 17-Mile Drive just to get a look. The gallery kept growing," Houston said. "As we finished, he gave me his ball and glove. Then, he looks up and sees this crowd around the green, which by then was pretty big. As we're wrapping things up he asks me, 'Where'd all these people come from?' To him it was like, 'What's the big deal? I'm just another person out here playing some golf.' That's Arnold Palmer."

In the long run, Houston has looped for Palmer over a dozen times. And it was during one of those rounds that the golf nut in Houston would finally be released.

After teeing off, Houston and "The King" walked together toward the eighteenth green for Palmer's next shot. Following Palmer's approach shot to the eighteenth green, Houston took the divot.

At home, Houston sealed the piece of turf in a Ziploc bag in an effort to preserve it forever. The divot's name? Arnie.

"I kept that divot in my office at home in Pacific Grove for years. I remember I gave it lots of Miracle-Grow, plus some Coors Light," Houston said. "I'd cut him with my mustache

*Caddie Scott Houston and Arnold Palmer have teamed up over a dozen times at Pebble Beach.* (Courtesy of Scott Houston.)

scissors. I mean I nurtured it. On foggy days, I'd take it out to (Carmel Valley-based) Rancho Canada when I'd go to hit balls just to give it some sun."

As for the Arnie divot, the piece of turf survived a few years, enough time to help Houston earn 2002 *Golf Nut of the Year* honors. Awarded by the Golf Nut Society, the Nut of the Year competition ranks members for their fanatic dedication to the game on a point system. Former recipients of the title Golf Nut of the Year include 1986 winner Michael Jordan.

"I remember I showed the head Nut the divot and he just about lost his mind," Houston said. "That was about enough for him. Other than that, it was stepping away from my previous work to do what I'd always wanted to do."

Along with the Palmer divot and simply his decision to drop a lucrative job to pursue his dreams, Houston's Golf Nut resume includes being a member of the Professional Caddies Hall of Fame, being one of few members to play Pebble Beach Golf Links, Cypress Point Club and Spyglass Hill at night and hitting seven shots in seven different states, a feat Houston would accomplish along the East Coast.

Amid the accolades, however, the longtime Peninsula resident witnessed the demise of Arnie. Despite care as given to a child, the pampered divot finally succumbed to unknown causes. "I had the roots sent to an agronomy college in Pennsylvania," Houston said. "I also had an obituary written up. It was a sad moment. About four years later, I found myself returning to Arnie's spot. I sprinkled some dust."

In 2003, Houston moved to Florida. On occasion, however, The Golf Nut can still be found at Pebble Beach. Most recently in 2004, Houston looped the legendary course for none other than New England Patriots quarterback Tom Brady during the annual AT&T Pebble Beach National Pro-Am.

"Looking back, I was always supposed to be a caddie, and here it is that I'd land at Pebble Beach," Houston said. "Being a caddie at Pebble Beach has been the most poignant career that I've ever had. It's been beautiful. I mean, I've helped boxer Marvin Hagler get his gloves on. I've sat on the bench of the

Boston Celtics and in the dugout of the Boston Red Sox. And then I've had my experiences with Palmer. Did I end up making the right move in becoming a caddie at Pebble Beach? Put it this way, I always knew there was a reason for me becoming a caddie."

## The Player

While some caddies become players, some players become caddies. In the case of longtime Monterey Peninsula resident Steve Carter, it was the latter scenario that eventually landed him within the confines of the caddie barn at Pebble Beach Golf Links.

For Carter, the caddie life began in 1990, when, at the age of 20, he began looping after getting a lead from legendary Monterey Peninsula College men's golf coach Luke Phillips. "I was playing on the MPC team at the time, and Coach Phillips told me about a job," Carter said. "I've been doing it ever since."

Carter began his caddie career at nearby Cypress Point Club, looping that course for over ten years. He made the move to Pebble Beach in 2001. "Much of the public has a misconception as what we do and who we are. When most people think of caddies, they think of caddies as they are portrayed in movies. We're actually trying to be more professional than ever," Carter said. "As a caddie you have to know golf and you have to know the yardages, which can be tricky. You also have to be able to get the player to relax."

While Carter has come a long way as a looper, he has also come a long way as a player. So much, in fact, that he once played Pebble Beach for high stakes. After graduating from Monterey High, Carter enrolled at MPC, playing under Phillips during the 1989–1990 Season. At that point, Carter was still discovering his swing. On a team that featured ten players, he was the tenth man.

"I was terrible," Carter recalled. "I really didn't see too

much action." Still trying to figure out his own swing, in 1995 Carter began stopping by the prestigious Pebble Beach Golf Academy to visit with renowned golf instructor Laird Small. The director of the Academy, Small is annually a member of the Top Teachers list of both *Golf Digest* and *Golf Magazine*. In 2003, Small was named the national PGA Teacher of the Year.

"He [Small] basically helped me with my posture and set-up," Carter said. "After that, I began hitting balls every day for about four months straight."

The hard work and patience paid off. That same year, Carter qualified for the California State Amateur at Pebble Beach. He also earned a spot in the United States Mid-Amateur Championship. "My game had completely turned around," Carter said. A year later in 1996, he returned to MPC at the behest of Phillips and finished the season ranked No. 3 in the Coast Conference.

It was in 1999, however, that Carter got the opportunity he was waiting for. The 1999 U.S. Amateur was to be played in his own backyard, using both Pebble Beach and Spyglass Hill for the medalist rounds. "I'd played the courses and I'd worked the courses so I was really confident," said Carter, who earned a spot in the championship by shooting a 2-over-par 142 (74-68) during two intense qualifying rounds at Pasatiempo Golf Club in nearby Santa Cruz. "Pebble and Spy are two courses that I know inside-out."

On the first day of stroke play qualifying, Carter indeed felt right at home. While most of the field struggled with the brutal conditions at Pebble Beach, Carter opened stroke play with a comfortable 73. The next day, however, fate and Spyglass Hill dealt him a cruel blow. Battling tight fairways and thick rough, Carter finished round two of the stroke play portion of the 1999 U.S. Amateur with an 80, missing the cut for match play by one stroke. "Even though I failed to reach match play I still walked away with the feeling that I had accomplished a lot," Carter said. "The whole experience was a huge confidence builder."

Buoyed by his performance, Carter looked to make more noise a year later, trying to qualify for the 2000 British Amateur at Royal Liverpool Golf Club and Wallasey Golf Club. Again, he opened strong thanks to a 71 at Wallasey. On day two, however, he again faltered, carding an 86 at Royal Liverpool and missing the cut by seven strokes.

In shooting for a spot in the 2000 U.S. Amateur at Baltusrol Golf Club in New Jersey, he missed qualifying by four strokes. Still, in 2001 Carter made the decision to turn professional. Like many aspiring pros, he would however run into a major problem—lack of funds.

"I reached a level of golf that required me to travel to golf tournaments all around the country. Problem was, I couldn't afford it," Carter said. "I turned pro thinking that a sponsor would be easy to find. I was wrong."

Following an extremely brief pro career, Carter later in 2001 applied for reinstatement as an amateur. He had to wait eighteen months, but his wish was granted. These days, Carter can still be found on the course as a player, but for the most part he's sticking with his caddie duties at Pebble Beach.

"I plan on playing more amateur golf events in 2006," Carter said. "For now though, I'm going to be a caddie. For me, being a caddie at Pebble Beach means getting to work in one of the most beautiful places on earth on one of the most famous golf courses in the world, each day walking in the footsteps of the greatest golfers of all time. How many jobs offer that?"

Indeed, whether holding the sticks or carrying them, The Player has made, and will make, his presence felt.

## The Caddie Master

Neil Allen had no idea what he was getting himself into. Then again, he did.

For Allen, the forging of what became a lasting relationship with the caddies of Pebble Beach Golf Links began in

1989, when the then 27-year-old was hired as part of the re-nowned customer service division at Pebble Beach Golf Links.

While Allen spent his first year basically cleaning carts, if needed, he would take to the links as a caddie.

"I came to realize pretty quickly that being a caddie was a little more complicated than I thought it would be," Allen said.

Having started with a few sips, it was in 1991 that Allen would get a full taste of the Pebble Beach caddie experience when he was named as the new caddie master of the storied links. And while Allen knew he was in for a test, he also knew the benefits of a passing grade. After all, the guy he was re-placing as caddie master, Rich Cosand, moved up to the rank of head professional at nearby The Links at Spanish Bay.

"I remember at the time that it was one of those jobs that nobody wanted," Allen said. "It was basically about trying to manage a group of guys that weren't used to being managed. Guys become caddies for a number of reasons, and one of those reasons is freedom. Being where I was and knowing where I wanted to go, it was somewhat a clash of lifestyles. Looking back though, it was one of those clashes that resulted in a happy marriage. It was one of the circumstances where opposites did attract."

As caddie master, Allen, like past caddie masters at Pebble Beach, effectively served as the policeman of the cad-die barn.

In a nutshell, that meant among other things: hiring cad-dies, getting the caddies out on time, getting them to the right players, and making sure there were always enough caddies on hand for the day.

"As a caddie master, you try to get to know caddies and the players. Then you try to match personalities. For example, you don't want to send a player you know who has a temper out with a caddie who's also a hot-head," Allen said. "You want to give the player a caddie that will help the player have the greatest experience possible."

Like any leadership position, there were times however when things didn't always work out to plan; or the caddies, being independent contractors, simply didn't want to cooperate. In those instances, the caddie master's role sometimes involves firing caddies.

"One time I ended up firing a caddie. There were just too many offensives on his record," Allen said. "Well, he went on to threaten me. So here I am headed home one day and when I arrive his car is parked in front of my house. I fully expected this guy to be in my house waiting for me. I went in and checked through every closet, making sure he wasn't there. Turned out, he was over at the neighbor's just visiting."

While Allen escaped any physical wrath, he was soon dealing with mental anguish from the same caddie. Well, at least sort of. "As it turned out the caddie would eventually bypass me and go on to file complaints with Pebble Beach officials," Allen said. "Thing was, while he was in meetings with those officials he would try to secretly tape the conversation. Not with a mini tape recorder but with one of those old box-like recorders. Let's just say he didn't end up making the cut."

Like any leader the new caddie master would indeed have his run-ins, yet there were also the good times, even if it did involve a bit of policing.

"I remember one caddie we had at the time would show up each day at six o'clock in the morning, and you could tell he was happy. He'd probably had his last sip of something less than an hour ago," Allen said. "So when I'd arrive I'd ask him, 'Well, are you ready to work?' He'd look at me and say, 'Oh, no Neil. I'm not here to work.' After a while I knew his plan. He just wanted to hang around the guys in the barn, and he was professional enough to know that he wasn't able to go out on the course."

The same caddie, however, got his say one night.

"Every year we'd have an annual meeting of the caddies. We'd get all the guys together and go over all the rules and regulations, what the expectations were, the uniforms, the conduct, appearances, etc.," Allen said. "During that meeting, we'd also approach certain caddies and tell them, 'If you're drunk, don't show up for work.' Well, at one of those meetings that same early morning caddie showed up lit. You could tell he'd been hitting on something. Well, during that meeting the caddie went into a filibuster. He just kept going on and on. Finally, a higher up Pebble Beach official asked me to take him home. Suffice to say, the caddie went on to talk the whole way home. It was like he'd never left the meeting."

Not surprisingly, Allen, like those before him, quickly learned the ups and downs of being a caddie master at Pebble Beach Golf Links.

Yet like those before him, Allen also came to appreciate the intricate work performed by the caddies; an effort that was no doubt yet again noticed by Pebble Beach Company officials in 1999. That year, Allen would follow in the footsteps of Cosand, this time being named head professional at the eldest of all the Pebble Beach Company golf family courses— Del Monte Golf Course.

"Looking back, I'd describe my days as caddie master at Pebble Beach as two-a-day football practices. At the time it may not be so much fun, but years later you look back and appreciate what was accomplished. In my time as caddie master, I more than came to appreciate what the guys out there are doing. There's an art to reading the greens and knowing the course at Pebble Beach, and the caddies are always ready to bring out the brush," Allen said. "As if that isn't enough, the caddies at Pebble Beach are also masters in psychology. They know when to make the situation light or heavy. They'll know a player before they've even stepped on the first tee. Had I never been the caddie master, I may not have ever learned these things. The majority of courses throughout the U.S. don't have caddies, so the head pro probably hasn't had the experience. I know what having a caddie means. I've been there and I've worked with the caddies. I don't regret it for a moment."

# 14   The Caddie Cup

Some might call it the greatest four-course tournament in the world: Pebble Beach Golf Links, Cypress Point, Spyglass Hill, and The Links at Spanish Bay. In reality, it's all part of the annual Caddie Cup.

"Show me a better lineup anywhere," said Pebble Beach caddie Damon Lee. "This is as good as it gets."

Played annually since 1992, the Caddie Cup has become an annual rite for caddies working in the Del Monte Forest. The event was founded by former Pebble Beach Company tournament director Ducky O'Toole as a way to celebrate those who carry the bags. Has it ever.

"At the time there had always been competition on the course between the caddies, but those competitions were always at individual courses," O'Toole said. "Plus, back then there really wasn't anything for the Pebble Beach caddies. I wanted to do something to honor the guys."

Playing for the cup, each squad is comprised of four caddies representing Cypress Point, Spyglass Hill, The Links at Spanish Bay, and Pebble Beach Golf Links, with each foursome being determined by a qualifying round at Del Monte Golf Course.

The four groups then compete at each of the four venues in best-ball, foursome, stroke play. Both net and gross scores are compiled to determine who will have the ticket to bragging rights the rest of the year.

"Along with the courses we get to play, what makes the event so fun is that everyone is involved with the scoring," said Cypress Point caddie Jesse Perryman. "If one guy's going good and the other three aren't, it really doesn't matter. It's truly a team event." As for "going good," many of the caddies have proved time and again that perhaps someone should be carrying their bags.

In 1996, it was Pebble Beach looper Todd Gjesvold matching Ken Venturi's course record 62 at Del Monte en route to finishing the championship with a total score of even par. A few years later, it was looper Casey Boyns' turn, as the two-time California State Amateur champion (1989, 1993) turned in a four-day score of 1-over par.

"That was one more reason I wanted it to happen," O'Toole said. "I knew some of these guys were players." Now a part of tradition in the forest, the Caddie Cup keeps rolling along each winter. "Put simply, it's the greatest opportunity for us as caddies," Tim Springer said. "Everyone looks forward to it because it's a great way to end what has been a lot of good golf years for us."

# Across the Pond

On the heels of the success of the original Caddie Cup, Pebble Beach loopers decided to take it a step further in 1998 by offering up a challenge to their overseas compatriots—the caddies of St. Andrews. As Pebble Beach caddie Bob Keenan explained that year, it was time for caddies on both sides of the pond to do more than "just read greens, rake bunkers and carry clubs. As a caddie, you plug along and you work every day and you really get unnoticed in the golf industry," Keenan said at the time. "It's nice that a group of caddies from Pebble Beach who have been around the game a long time and really love the game are actually taking part in something of value and meaning, something significant."

It was then Pebble Beach caddie master Mike Lehotta who came up with the idea for an International Caddie Cup. Earlier that year, Lehotta sent letters to two of America's other most prestigious golf clubs—Augusta National in Georgia and Pine Valley in New Jersey. Both rejected the offer.

"They said 'We have a rule that you can't play without a member and blah, blah, blah,'" Lehotta recalled. "I said, 'It's a golf course. Just give us a tee time.'"

Frustrated, he wrote to St. Andrews, considered to be the birthplace of golf. Lehotta never expected a response, but within three weeks St. Andrews officials agreed to the plan and established plans for a two-day, Ryder Cup-style tournament on the Old and Jubilee Courses. Included in the plans were also dinners and luncheons for the Americans.

"I just thought it was a superb idea," said St. Andrews caddie manager Richard Mackenzie. "We see it as a working-man's Ryder Cup."

While St. Andrews selected its competitors from a group of over two hundred fifty, Pebble Beach choose from forty-five.

"We have some good players, but we definitely feel like underdogs being that we're going over there to play them," said longtime Pebble Beach caddie Chester Gillette at the time.

"I'm not going over there to kick butt," said looper Scott Houston at the time. "I'm going over there to shake hands and for the camaraderie. It's really to embrace the birthplace of the game."

When it came time to tee off for the Cup, the home-course edge showed quickly in a tournament that captured the attention of golf fans throughout the United Kingdom and Europe.

It was the first time any of the caddies at Pebble Beach had teed off at St. Andrews, and a few were surprised by the characteristics of the Old Course's greens. Six of the greens on St. Andrews Old Course are shared by two different holes.

"Sometimes you didn't know what green to shoot at," Pebble Beach caddie Tim Springer said. "Over there, you can have a putt that's one hundred yards out."

The squad from St. Andrews went on to soundly defeat the Yanks 13-7. With the win, the home-team Scots won the prize—a Scottish drinking bowl called a quaich.

A year later, on the eve of both courses hosting the 2000 U.S. Open and 2000 British Open, it was time for the Pebble Beach loopers to display a bit of their own home cooking.

With Scotland-like weather whipping over Pebble Beach, the Yanks turned the tables with a 25-11 convincing win of their own.

That time, just as confused were the caddies from St. Andrews.

"Even though both courses are considered links courses they're totally different," said St. Andrews caddie Cameron Imber. "The greens here [at Pebble Beach] are tiny."

"It's pretty much what I expected," said St. Andrews looper Paul Ellison, who fired a 6-over 78 in his Pebble Beach debut. "But on the greens there are some very tricky reads."

As for the blustery conditions at Pebble Beach, that was nothing for the laddie from Scotland. On day one of the Caddie Cup II, winds at Pebble Beach were blowing upwards of twenty-five miles per hour.

"The wind here is like nothing," Ellison said. "You're actually more sheltered."

Although each side was admittedly playing for pride each year, all of the contestants agreed that the main point of the event was to unite caddies from all points the world over. "They may be competing against one another on the course, but afterward they're all sitting side-by-side enjoying a pint of beer," said former Pebble Beach caddie master John Pietro, who, along with Lehotta, was instrumental in organizing the event.

"It unites us," Imber said. "It's nice for us to be out here playing instead of working."

# 15   Dawg and Phantom

In the year 2001, Pebble Beach Golf Links lost two of its greatest caddies—Donnie "The Phantom" Gahan and Bob "Dawg" Robare. Gahan, a native of Boston, had worked at Pebble Beach for more than twenty years. "Phantom was rather quiet but extremely personable," said former Pebble Beach looper Kris Shreiner. "He used to have this saying, 'It's OK to lose your money on the golf course, just don't lose your mind.'"

Fellow Pebble Beach caddie Casey Boyns also remembered Gahan as pretty quiet but admitted that The Phantom had his moments.

*In the year 2001, Pebble Beach Golf Links lost two of its greatest caddies—Donnie "The Phantom" Gahan* (left) *and Bob "Dawg" Robare* (right). (Photograph by Mike Lehotta.)

"One time Phantom was looping for two guys, and there were two other guys in the foursome in a cart," Boyns said. "Late in the round, one of the guys in the cart asked Phantom for some yardage. Phantom replied, 'Why don't you ask your cart?'"

"Phantom was the kind of guy that if you looked at him and didn't know him, you'd be scared. But if you looked at him and knew him, you'd want to give him a kiss," said another caddie. "They both had an intimate relationship between themselves and the golf course that only a few have ever had. I mean, they'd know before the round whether or not the sand in the bunkers was packed or loose."

Dawg, also a Massachusetts native, arrived at Pebble Beach in the early 1970s following a tour of duty in Vietnam. Along with being known for his gruff personality, Robare was also known for his involvement in founding an annual golf tournament held on the Monterey Peninsula that benefits families of veterans.

"Dawg loved to romance his players and would try to get them to do what he wanted them to do," Boyns said. "Both of them were great caddies and will always be missed."

As it was, shall it ever be...

# Caddie Hall of Fame

In 1999, the Professional Caddies Association established a World Caddie Hall of Fame section located at the World Golf Hall of Fame at the World Golf Village in St. Augustine, Florida.

Ralph Coffey, who caddied for Lanny Wadkins at the 1977 PGA Championship at Pebble Beach, was inducted in 1999. The Golf Nut, former Pebble Beach caddie Scott Houston, was inducted in 2002. Bruce Edwards, who caddied for Tom Watson at the 1982 U.S. Open at Pebble Beach, was inducted in 2003.

Founded in 1997, the Professional Caddies Association's mission is to provide caddies, their families, and others with additional income opportunities, high quality benefits, services, and certification through educational and communication programs worldwide.

> PCA Worldwide, Inc.
> 23 Malacompra Road
> Palm Coast, Florida 32137
> 386-446-8721

Founded in 1987, the Professional Tour Caddies of America represents more than 150 full-time caddies who work on the PGA Tour.

The PTCA, which is based in Tennessee, provides benefit programs such as health, disability and retirement insurance to caddies. The organization also strives to improve business conditions and family security for caddies.

"Caddy Central", a motor home that provides meals and information during regular PGA Tour stops, is also available to members.

> Professional Tour Caddies of America
> 6180 C Hixson Pike #312
> Hixson, TN 37343
> 1-423-400-6992

# Bibliography

*Augusta Chronicle*, April 1999.

Brown, Scott, with the *Monterey County Herald* Sports Staff. *The Major: 7 Days at Golf's Greatest Championship*. Chelsea, MI: Sleeping Bear Press, 2000.

*CBS News*, June 13, 2003.

*Des Moines Register*, July 1991.

*ESPN Golf*, www.espn.go.com

*Golf Digest*, August 2004.

*Golf Today*, August 1998.

Hotelling, Neal. *Pebble Beach Golf Links: The Official History.* Chelsea, MI: Sleeping Bear Press, 1999.

*Monterey County Herald*, November 18, 1966.

*Monterey County Herald*, August 7, 1977.

*Monterey County Herald*, August 31, 1986.

*Monterey County Herald*, January 31, 1995.

*Monterey County Herald*, March 8, 1996.

*Monterey County Herald*, June 11, 2000.

*Monterey County Herald*, June 17, 2000.

*Monterey Life*, February 1990.

Netland, Dwayne. *The Crosby: Greatest Show in Golf.* New York: Doubleday, 1975.

*PGA Tour*, www.pgatour.com

*USA Today,* June 13, 2003.

USGA, *2000 Championships Media Guide.*

*USGA News*, April 8, 2004.

www.kiwicaddy.com

# THE FORGOTTEN
# HALF OF
# change

# THE FORGOTTEN HALF OF
# change

ACHIEVING
GREATER CREATIVITY
THROUGH
CHANGES IN PERCEPTION

## LUC DE BRABANDERE

Dearborn™
Trade Publishing
A **Kaplan Professional** Company

President, Dearborn Publishing: Roy Lipner
Vice President and Publisher: Cynthia A. Zigmund
Acquisitions Editor: Jonathan Malysiak
Senior Project Editor: Trey Thoelcke
Interior Design: Lucy Jenkins
Cover Design: Jody Billert, Design Literate, Inc.
Typesetting: Elizabeth Pitts

Published by Dearborn Trade Publishing
A Kaplan Professional Company

**Library of Congress Cataloging-in-Publication Data**

Brabandere, Luc de, 1948–
   The forgotten half of change : achieving greater creativity through changes in perception / Luc de Brabandere.
     p. cm.
   Includes bibliographical references and index.
   ISBN 1-4195-0275-1
   1. Management—Philosophy. 2. Change. 3. Perception. 4. Creative ability in business.   I. Title.
HD31.B7198   2005
658.4'063—dc22

                2005000524

*This book is dedicated to*
*Arthur Janta-Polczynski (1949–2004)*
*who gave me so many ideas.*

The author can be reached at de.brabandere.luc@bcg.com

Cartoons from www.cartoonbase.com

My thanks to all my partners in the Boston Consulting Group,
and a special thanks to Erik Calonius and Richard Hill,
without all of whom this book would not have been possible.

# Contents

**A** few years ago Bill Gates came to Brussels.

The head of Microsoft Belgium decided to mark the occasion by organizing a conference meeting for one thousand customers and users. Two months before the conference he asked me if I would be willing to give a short speech, first to present a few provocative, stimulating, and surprising ideas on developments in IT, then to introduce Bill Gates to his Belgian audience.

Of course, I accepted. My passion for ideas knows no bounds, and a few weeks later I was ready to make a creative presentation on the relationship between man and machines.

On the eve of the great day, around 8 o'clock in the evening, the phone rang at home.

"You've forgotten to send the slides of your presentation, and Bill Gates would like to see them," said the head of Microsoft Belgium.

My reply was immediate: "Most people in Belgium and France know full well that I never use slides. I prefer to practice the art of oratory as was done in old times. I've got clear ideas and I'm ready for my presentation tomorrow."

Silence.

"So . . . you have no slides?"

"No," I said for the second time. "The spoken word and the written word are two different things. I use both but I never mix them. I give speeches, and I write books. The ideas are the same, but the way I express them is different. When I speak, it's in real time. When I write, it's in delayed time—it's as if I were someone else."

Silence.

I was aware of the acute levels of worry building up on the other end of the line. So it was actually possible to make presentations without using PowerPoint! What's more, in front of the spiritual father of Power-Point? At that very moment, I realized that something had shattered in the mind of the person I was speaking to. That something has a name: a *stereotype*.

A stereotype is an idea that has taken shape one day and matured over time—a stable idea, or a basic judgment. Stereotypes are the atoms of thought; they are the actual condition of thinking. All too often, we forget that our ideas are stereotypes. That's when the misunderstandings occur.

I decided to be as comforting as I could: I didn't want to hurt my Microsoft host. So over the phone we drew up a short series of some ten slides. It's easy to do. I have clear ideas, and a logical sequence for the way they're set out. The next day I made my presentation live, without text, standing in front of the audience of one thousand. After me, Bill Gates used PowerPoint. Maybe, when he was listening to me, he thought he should have done the same as me. But I'm sure you understand why he was obliged to use slides.

Parenthetically, another IT supremo, Lou Gerstner of IBM, clearly understood the stereotype-reinforcing potential of PowerPoint. When he arrived at the company's Brussels headquarters, shortly after taking over to get a first briefing from IBM's European business unit managers, he flatly refused to let them use the system. He needed to know what kind of people he was dealing with, and he wanted to hear, observe and challenge the real thing.

So why do I tell the story about Bill Gates? Precisely because this book is a lot about stereotypes, and what we have to do to look and get beyond them.

Little revelations like my Microsoft experience come to me every day. They always have done. Creativity has been my passion since I was born and, for my 50th birthday, my dream came true: I made creativity my career. I now earn a living from my passion for new ideas. I like to understand where these new ideas come from and why, sometimes, they don't come; who has more of them than other people; how certain companies benefit from them to change the world; and so on. An IT engineer and mathematician by training, I worked for 20 years in the worlds of finance and technology until I became Director-General of the Brussels Stock Exchange. For me, my mid-life crisis was also the shattering of a stereotype.

I slowly passed from one life, where I enjoyed my career while being creative, to another where being creative was my career. The investment

I made in myself was enormous. Psychoanalysis, authorship of four books, and a complete cycle of philosophy studies—these were all essential. When you want to make ideas your career, you can't ignore the history of ideas and the incredible adventure of concepts.

Creativity in companies is what I do for a living today, but I'm far from being the only one—fortunately, since creativity is the life force of enterprise. What is original and special in what I do comes from the interface between this passion that has always been in me and the currents of thought which have always been around me.

I was born in 1948—just like cybernetics! In that year Norbert Wiener published a seminal book with that title. He defined the discipline as the science of control and steering, and shed light on the importance of feedback mechanisms. My first contacts with control loops date back to my engineering studies, but I immediately had the feeling that this systems approach would never leave me. I didn't realize at the time the extent to which systems theories would fascinate me.

Again and again, I would study information and communications theory (Shannon, *et al*), game theory (Von Neumann, *et al*), ecology, linguistics, and so on. All these disciplines use systemic language to drive their respective scientific fields further forward.

But the most important thing for me was still to happen. That was meeting those people who put the concepts of feedback, paradox, and system to therapeutic use: the School of Palo Alto.

I read books by Watzlawick, Bateson, Hall, and others. Even if their objectives, confronted with suffering and illness, were far removed from mine, they were still facing the same problem as I was in the world of business: change.

One of their ideas appears to me to be of fundamental importance: to change, we have to change twice. Not only do we have to change things, but we have to change the way we see things.

One day I had a real revelation: I made the link between Palo Alto and my work. This is the key to the book you hold in your hands. I told myself that companies that want to change also have to change twice. Innovation is their people's capacity to change reality, and creativity is the capacity of these people to change their perception of reality. While parallel, the processes are totally different, and they have to be rediscovered and the difference appreciated.

Now that I had this puzzle clear in my mind, I could devote myself more wholly to the piece of the puzzle that is change in perception—the instant of the new idea, creative and disruptive.

Since then I've had moments of great satisfaction. One was after a speech I made in Stockholm during the final session of a CIES Congress, the annual event in the distribution sector. I had the honor of sharing the floor during two hours of plenary session with Desmond Tutu, the South African bishop and friend of Nelson Mandela.

After I had spent 60 minutes presenting the key concepts of creative thought to 500 big bosses of industry (without slides of course!), Desmond Tutu took the floor, and—I'm still getting over it today—asked the audience to give my ideas another round of applause.

The reason, he said, was that when apartheid was abolished in South Africa, the overwhelming majority of the country's inhabitants could only envisage two possible scenarios.

1. A general amnesty, forgetting all the crimes committed during this dark period in history, as if nothing had ever happened.
2. A systematic use of the judicial system with charges and/or imprisonment for all the crimes committed.

Desmond Tutu presented the first option as unacceptable, and the second option as impractical. Then, referring to the presentation I had just made, he explained how creative Nelson Mandela and his team had been. Rejecting the second option, which had seemed inevitable, they had the idea of setting up a body to be called the Truth and Reconciliation Commission.

No forgetting, no revenge. A third way—and a new idea. Desmond Tutu chaired this commission for years with one objective: forgiveness (the theme of his presentation on the day). Forgiving is not forgetting. Forgiveness means listening to every detail of everything a victim has suffered, as expressed by the perpetrators, and then renouncing the idea of revenge.

All the sessions of the commission have been recorded on film. Certain moments are almost unbearable.

Desmond Tutu explained to a hushed audience what creativity meant at the end of the South African tragedy. Everyone present understood just what it was about the archbishop that made him someone really extraordinary, and what it took to be a Nobel Peace Prize winner.

Even more for me, of course, this moment is laden with emotion. Happily, tragedy is not the backdrop of daily life in companies. Since I've been doing this work—become what you are, as Nietzsche said—I've realized to what extent humor is present when ideas are born.

Being a philosopher of creativity is a bit like climbing a mountain that has no peak. As I'm extremely conscious of the limits of what I can do or get done, in 1999 I contacted the Boston Consulting Group. I wanted to apply the message of Palo Alto, and the need to change twice, to myself.

That turned out to be a very good idea!

The result is the present book, the product of a long drawn out process of observation, reflection, and investigation—a process that is still going on. I approach my theme in eight steps, each of them in a separate chapter.

Chapter 1 describes the underlying precept: While we are all acutely aware these days that the world is changing around us—many of us, in fact, are party to making this happen—our perception of, and adjustment to, these changes has to keep pace. To face up to the future—let alone the present—you can learn from the past. The work of such disparate thinkers, ancient and modern, as Heraclites, Francis Bacon, and the Palo Alto school helps point the way.

The world is possible without you, but you are not possible without the world. In Chapter 2, then, I want to tell you something about the world today—how it is not only changing, but changing so rapidly that it offers great opportunities to those of you who are ready to take them.

In Chapter 3 I explain how the human mind is wired, as it has been for thousands of years, to make snap judgments and maintain outdated ideas. Once we recognize these traps—which often appear as harmless, even helpful, stereotypes or paradigms—we are better prepared to deal with them.

In Chapter 4 I examine the warning signs that appear when the reality we hold dear becomes increasingly at odds with real life. These warning signs are valuable, because they give us an important heads-up to the coming paradigm shift. If you recognize them first, and make the right moves, you can get ahead of the pack.

In Chapter 5 I explain how the brain is truly two-sided, and how the creative side differs from the logical, judgmental side. In this chapter I explain how you can take control of the creative process, making the moves that create perceptual changes, paradigm-shifting ideas and brand-new products. The surest way to get a good idea is to have many ideas. There's a lot in that!

In Chapter 6 I explain how a process of astonishment and questioning can lead you to one of these unique Eureka! moments.

Chapter 7 is a "So what?" chapter. I will explain how you can turn your company into an "ideas factory," how in fact it has to become an ideas factory to survive in this competitive and fast-changing economic environment.

Finally, Chapter 8 tells you how you can do the same thing for yourself.

# 1

# CHANGING TWICE

*"The Egyptian pyramid's form shows clearly that–already in
antiquity–workers tended to work less and less."*

**Anonymous**

**W**hat's the time, please?

I don't know, it changes all the time!

Change is a very old subject. For thousands of years, thousands of people have talked about it—philosophers, writers, and now thousands of consultants. So why another book on change? How dare I write yet another book on the subject?

My reply is that even change is changing. There are new things to say about change, as I will explain in the following pages.

The philosopher Montaigne said that no writer should say "my" book, but rather "our" book, since the work of any writer is built on what has been written before. That's the case here. As Isaac Newton said, "If I have been able to see further, it was only because I stood on the shoulders of giants."

In my case I am standing on the broad shoulders of many great philosophers, from Aristotle and Plato to Kuhn and Koestler. Of these, three serve as the bedrock of my observations. One of them is Greek, one is English, and the last is not an individual, but a group of individuals, and they are American. The Greek lived in antiquity; the Englishman in the 16th century; and the Americans in modern times.

# HERACLITES

The Greek is Heraclites, who was born in 530 BC in the seaport town of Ephesus, now in Turkey, to a wealthy and distinguished family. On reaching maturity, Heraclites renounced his status and position in life, retired into the mountains, and started to record the components of a radical new philosophy (which he would leave anonymously on the steps of the town temple in the middle of the night). At the time, the reigning philosopher in Greece was Parmenides, who believed that change was impossible. "*Hen ta panta,*" he wrote—all things are one and never change. There is no becoming, only being. His philosophy became known as the Parmenidean Rest, or Parmenides' Motionless One.

You can imagine how reassuring that philosophy was to many Greeks. It meant that life was stable, essentially immutable, and certainly predictable. It was a philosophy, furthermore, that made sense—at least by the standards of ancient Greece.

Heraclites felt that Parmenides was wrong, however. His reply to Parmenides, in fact, was "*panta rei*"—all things flow. "You can never walk into the same river twice," he wrote, "for other waters are ever flowing on to you." He also said, "The sun is new every day. Everything changes." Throughout Greece the debate between Heraclites and Parmenides was hotly contested, and in a way, it is still today.

Today, of course, most of us recognize that Heraclites was right—things do change. Today we see continents drifting, genes mutating, chemicals combusting, and black holes collapsing. We may not dip our toes into the river as often as Heraclites did, but we surf the Internet frequently, and we know that if we step away for even a moment and then immerse ourselves again, the whole nature of time and space will have changed.

In fact the world is changing much faster now than in Heraclites' time. The first acceleration occurred when the agrarian world segued into the industrial world. The second and far more dramatic jump occurred when the industrial world transmuted into the digital world. While electricity and the telephone took some 50 years to reach 50 percent of American homes, e-mail and DVDs were adopted by most Americans within a mere ten years.

A mere ten years? The way things are going, we will soon be counting change in terms of months rather than years.

It's not just products, but entire companies as well. Economist Joseph Schumpeter coined the phrase "creative destruction" to describe the rapid life cycle and death of companies. We have seen this phenomenon increase exponentially in the last generation. Just 50 years ago most U.S. companies stayed on the S&P 500 list for an average of 65 years. Today they survive about ten years before being bumped off. Not long ago, computer companies released their new models every two years. Then annually, then biannually—and before long, almost continuously.

Indeed, products mutate with every change of popular taste. People switch lives and careers as never before. Ideas come in and out of vogue in perpetual fast-forward. Remember when factories were made of brick, and banks of granite and marble? Nowadays factories are prefabricated, corporate offices have no walls, and banks—well, many banks (and stock exchanges)—no longer even need a physical presence. They can survive just fine in cyberspace alone.

So it *is* a river that is flowing, but a much faster river than Heraclites could ever have imagined.

You're entirely free to disagree with Heraclites, but if you do so, we can't go any further together. If you agree, then we can share an interesting journey.

## FRANCIS BACON

The second philosopher that I defer to is Francis Bacon. He lived from 1561 to 1626, and was a contemporary of William Shakespeare. While the bard communicated his thoughts through the characters he had strutting and fretting upon the stage at the Globe Theatre (and through his many sonnets), Bacon was a prolific essayist. No subject was beyond examination by the perspicacious Bacon. He wrote about falling in love, controlling anger, envy and health, and life and death. He was also England's attorney general under the steely rule of Queen Elizabeth I.

Bacon is most famous for his writings on a new way to think about science and loosen information from the grip of nature. The method he advocated, the "scientific method," consisted of creating a hypothesis that experimentation would either prove or disprove. At the time that he advocated this line of inductive reasoning (which he called *novum organum*), the brightest scholars in England—even those who had tutored

Bacon at Oxford—believed that everything worth knowing had already been written about by Aristotle and, if you needed an answer, you just looked it up there. Bacon tells a story of a group of monks who wondered how many teeth the average horse possesses. When the monks discovered that Aristotle had not covered this topic in his writings, one of them suggested they go out to the stable and count the teeth of the horses there. According to Bacon, who may have been exaggerating, the monk was expelled for this outrageous suggestion.

How many of us know that it was Francis Bacon who coined the phrase "knowledge is power"?

The point is that, while Heraclites argued that change was not only necessary but inevitable, Bacon pushed the ball further forward by arguing that, not only was change inevitable, but we could actually investigate it in nature—and even, through experimentation, make it happen. Today Bacon is regarded as the founder of science. He believed that experimentation could be the work of many people, building on one another's discoveries gradually, and that this process would improve the condition of man.

At the same time, this extraordinary man said, "We must obey the forces we want to command." Bacon acknowledged that there are external influences—like nature and change—that we have to understand if we want to harness them. His humility was a recognition of the realities that surround us.

I worked a couple of times with Bertrand Piccard, the balloonist who was the first to circumvent the globe, and he explains that when you are somewhere in the middle of the Pacific and you want to make a right turn with your balloon, you don't have the energy to do it. The only way you can make the turn is by looking for winds at another altitude—the jet stream can push you there. That's what Bacon was saying. A company's relationship with the Internet or with globalization is analogous—the company cannot influence the Internet, it must submit to it in order to harness it.

Once Bacon developed the idea that things could be changed, his imagination stepped forward with a vast number of possibilities. To think that, half a millennium ago, Bacon was already seriously contemplating that, sooner or later, we would be able to do the following:

- Slow the aging process
- Increase life expectancy

- Cure diseases thought to be incurable
- Raise the pain threshold
- Tackle obesity
- Transform mood and inspire happiness
- Increase and enhance the potential of the brain
- Transplant one species to another
- Create new species
- Accelerate germination
- Accelerate the ripening process
- Influence atmospheric forces and the birth of storms
- Manufacture new textiles for clothes
- Create artificial minerals and cements
- Get people to work together happily and productively
- Etc., etc.

If Heraclites had definite ideas about what is and what will be, it is Bacon who for the first time came up with ideas about what to do about the future. He was an applied philosopher and a convinced empiricist. He caught a cold while feeding frozen snow to a chicken, just to see what the result would be.

# THE PALO ALTO SCHOOL

Many people have thought about change and resistance to change. In *The Prince,* the book that Machiavelli published 500 years ago, he said, "Nothing is more difficult than to change the order of things." Today people say that the only ones to embrace change are babies when their diapers are wet. The image is different but the observation is the same.

In the 1950s a group of American psychologists and therapists banded together to start the Mental Research Institute. Among them were Paul Watzlawick, John Weakland, Gregory Bateson and Richard Fisch. Because they lived and worked in the Palo Alto area of Northern California, they became known as the Palo Alto school. Significantly, they were working on ways of treating schizophrenia.

In 1975, Watzlawick, Weakland, and Fisch published what would become a landmark book in Europe, titled *Change: Principles of Problem Formation and Problem Resolution.* This book offered a profound theory, one that touches not only on psychology but on change as well.

The inspiration for Palo Alto was the theory of logical classes or types developed by the English philosopher Bertrand Russell. To begin to understand this logic, let's take an example: "This sentence has seven words." True or false? False, of course, because the sentence has five words. Which suggests that the contrary is true: "This sentence does not have seven words." True or false? Surprise, surprise: this sentence is false too, because it has seven words.

We are surprised by this, because normally, if we say something and then say the contrary, one of them is going to be true. Evidently there are cases where neither is true—and this is called a *paradox*. According to Russell, this happens when you have something called an *auto-reference:* when a proposition includes a comment about the proposition. The only way to get around this dilemma is to introduce two levels: the thing itself and the comment about the thing.

Another example of an auto-reference is "This sentence is not a French one." Translate it into French and it's no longer true.

In the thinking process, says Bertrand Russell, you need to operate at two levels to avoid problems. Let's imagine, for example, two little boys playing a game with just one rule: say the opposite of what you think. Imagine now that one of the children really wants to quit. So he says, "I want to stop." The result is confusion: Is he playing the game, in which case his message is "I want to go on," or is he expressing his feelings about the game itself?

The Palo Alto school used this concept of two levels to take a fresh look at systems. Their ideas made them famous. They included a *law of communication* (it's impossible not to communicate—even by not speaking, you convey a message, which is, "I don't want to talk to you") and the concept of the *double bind* (when one level goes in the opposite direction; e.g., an instruction to "be spontaneous").

A good example of the double bind is a situation where a husband receives a gift of two ties from his wife. He has no option but to wear one of them first. Whereupon the wife says: "I was sure you wouldn't like the other one!" That's a double bind.

A third Palo Alto idea was the *law of change*. According to them, there are two kinds of change. The first change has to do with *reality*. This kind of change, called Type 1, is produced within a system that stays the same. If it modifies a component, it still follows the rules. Retroactive feedback protects the system and helps it keep its balance. That's why Palo Alto became famous for the statement, "The more something changes, the more it becomes the same." (*"Plus ça change, plus c'est la même chose."* Somehow it sounds better in French.)

The second change, however, is the one that really counts, and is also the focus of this book, the change in *perception*. For it to happen, at least one of the rules of the system—a hypothesis, a judgment, or a stereotype—has to be broken. This Type 2 change is sudden, sometimes unforeseen, and leads to a new representation of reality.

These two types of change are totally dissimilar. Type 1 is continuous, Type 2 is discontinuous. We tend to go on seeing things in the same way until one day, quite suddenly and with a mental rupture, we see it differently. Take a personal relationship, for instance. It may deteriorate slowly over months or years without your being aware of any change. Then suddenly it hits you: it's over. Or an enjoyable hobby that you have when, as happened with me, you suddenly realize *this* should be your job. Or the awful discovery, after staring at yourself in the mirror one day, that you are no longer the young Turk you thought you were—in fact, you're middle-aged! And how often have you said that a child is growing up quickly when, of course, those extra ten inches were not just added the night before!

One change is possible without the other, but Palo Alto went a step further: If you want to change, you have to change twice. You not only need to change the reality of your situation, you also need to change your *perception* of this reality. That is the essence of this book.

Consider people who always arrive late. They could do a lot of things to change the "reality" of their situation. They could get an appointment book, or wake up earlier for meetings, or schedule more time between meetings. But change is not just a matter of better organization. If they limit their change to action only, they will arrive late again within weeks, back to their old bad habits. To really make the change, they need to change the way they look at punctuality. This is a Type 2 change, when being on time is perceived as efficient and no longer as a constraint. Only a Type 2 change of this kind makes a Type 1 change irreversible.

Let's take some other examples. If you want your son to study French, you can give him private lessons (Type 1), but the teaching will be much more efficient if he falls in love with a French girl (Type 2)!

When you hire someone, the first day it's a question of how do *you* . . . ? But later it becomes how do *we?*

A politician who loses a big election and wants to make a comeback also has to change twice. First he has to find a new way of making a living for a while—that's reality. He also has to change the way he looks at his previous failure. This is very similar to losing a parent: a kind of mourning. You have not only lost a parent, but you now see the world differently. Mourning is not a matter of changing reality: the parent is still dead. By mourning you begin to see the future differently, without the loved one.

That's the micro level. Let's look at some examples of macro changes. For example, if the president of a bank wants to merge with another bank, he has to organize a double change. The president can start by merging reality—computers, accounting systems, and so on, which must be compatible (Type 1). But that's not enough. As long as the employees still see themselves as ex-employees of the old banks, the new bank doesn't exist (Type 2).

Similarly, a company is not a world company unless everyone sees it as one company, not a company of diverse national offices drawn together under one banner. The efficiency of a computer system is a matter of the quality of the system multiplied by the desire of people to use it. The quality is reality, the desire is perception. If one of the two is missing—if you have an excellent system no one wants to use, or the other way around—you have failure.

There are many such examples, but what they have in common is that you always have the two levels. On one side things, and on the other the way people look at those things. Let's give credit to Heraclites and Bacon. Both of them were aware of this second aspect, the importance of perception. Heraclites said, "If everything was smoke, we would learn through the nose." Bacon said, "People tend to believe what they hope to be true." And they said that many centuries ago.

The Palo Alto law of change is valid for all kinds of systems. The group started looking at the family as a system and they noticed that sometimes, if one of the children was smacked, this helped the system retain its stability. It's a paradoxical and highly provocative thought that a smacked child could contribute to the stability of a family.

What the Palo Alto group was doing was adopting a holistic approach to their problem. Examining things holistically is not something we do that easily (people from Asian cultures often charge Westerners with losing the point by being too analytical). By being holistic to the problem confronting them—in this case using a systems approach—the Palo Alto researchers were able to uncover a few of the many paradoxes that lurk beneath the surface of everyday life.

While the efforts of the Palo Alto group were mainly devoted to mental and behavioral problems, I believe their contribution can be equally dramatic for the business world. Companies also exist in two worlds—the world of reality, where things take time, and the other world of perception, of mental shifts.

# A SYSTEM OF IDEAS

Something amazing is happening! This book is entirely dedicated to the change process in the business world and yet, so far, I have not used the words *creativity* or *innovation*! But I will, as I go deeper into the book. It's inevitable now that I'm about to talk about another application of Palo Alto vision: *a system of ideas.*

Like all other systems, a system of ideas looks at first for stability and survival. A new idea is, more than anything else, a source of turbulence. A system is probably better disposed to accept more of the same (Type 1) than something different (Type 2). It is open to innovation, but reluctant about creativity.

How do I distinguish the two? Well, look at this chart:

### CHANGING

| Reality | Perception |
|---|---|
| Is called *innovation* | Is called *creativity* |
| Requires *action* | Requires *thinking* |
| Is a challenge for a team | Is a challenge for an individual |
| The process is continuous | The process is discontinuous |
| Takes a long time | Takes an instant |
| Delivers something new to the system | Envisions a new system |
| Its impact is measurable and certain | Its impact cannot be measured |
| Project management is required | Brainstorming is required |
| The fuel is practical ideas and useful suggestions | The fuel is questions, surprises, strange and incomplete ideas |
| The role of a consultant is to cause action | The role of a consultant is to encourage reflection |

Directing a company or managing a project is a task that takes place in two separate dimensions. There is the daily management, made up of decisions that constantly improve the process. Here the manager acting for his or her company is making things happen. But there is another level of management that takes place in parallel with the first and that is just as important. Here the manager is inventing the future, developing scenarios, looking for new ideas. This is the manager thinking for his or her company, to change the way things are seen.

Reality and perception are the two vital ingredients of effective management. They are the dual dimensions shaping the ultimate responsibility—change—which will itself inevitably come at two levels. Innovation is the approach whereby a team manages to change reality. Creativity is the way an individual succeeds in changing his or her perception. To innovate is to make something new in the system; whereas to be creative means thinking up a new system.

Innovation is linked to action, creativity to thinking. Innovation can be continuous; creativity will inevitably be discontinuous. As Picasso said, to create you must break. Creativity is not innovation. But, as we said about the two types of change, you can indeed have one of them without the other.

- *Innovation without creativity.* If you copy someone else's idea, you are not creating—you are innovating. The bank I used to work for decided, one day, to open on Saturday mornings. That was innovation without creativity.
- *Creativity without innovation.* Thinking of using a mouse to replace a keyboard, as was the case at Xerox' Palo Alto research park (the climate must be stimulating there), but without turning it into a product.

So creativity is not innovation, but don't forget that you have to change twice. How is this possible if the processes are so different?

It took about 50 years to move from sailing ships to steamships. Resistance to change from sail manufacturers resulted in ships with more and more masts. During the transition period, hybrid ships took to the waves. In 1833, for example, the *Sphinx,* a ship equipped with three masts but also with a funnel for a steam boiler, brought the Luxor obelisk to France to be erected in the Place de la Concorde.

FIGURE 1.1 *The Transition from Sails to Steam*

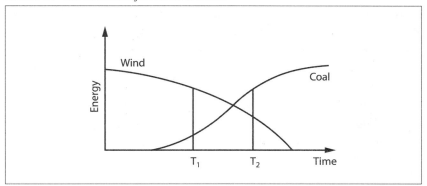

Imagine a curious onlooker who sees this hybrid ship sail by. How does he perceive its double source of energy? If it's the first time he's in the presence of a ship of this sort ($T_1$), he will see the engine as something that could be useful on a day with no wind. On the other hand, if this is the hundredth ship of the kind that he has seen ($T_2$), he will think of the sails as something that can always be used if the engine breaks down. Which means that the same boat can be perceived in two different ways, and that, one day, as he sees more and more of these steamships, he will reverse his opinion of what he sees as the emergency option (steam not sails) and there will be a break in his perception.

This phenomenon of course varies from one person to another. Early adopters who are fanatical about new things will adjust quickly. On the other hand Panurge's sheep will resist taking the plunge but in the end—even if they are forced to—they will change their minds too. Whether people are rash or fearful, their thinking evolves in a discontinuous manner, but the rate of evolution is different. When we add up millions of instances of discontinuous behavior that almost overlap with each other, then we can explain the apparent continuity of the way the world changes.

The move from fax to e-mail, from silver halide film to digital photography, or from the check to electronic payment—all these transitions are comparable with the process we describe when looking at sail power and steam power.

Today, a car is jam-packed with microprocessors. So when we want it serviced, whom do we go to? Do we need a mechanic who has a good knowledge of electronics, or we do we need an electronics specialist who is handy with engines?

In his book *The Age of the Bleep,* Bruno Jacomy asks this question: How do people view a car key with a built-in transmitter that bleeps? Why do they still need the key? The answer is always the same: just "because," the underlying judgment being that we cannot get rid of the past with just one click.

To demonstrate this, it's worth noting that Peugeot cars still have a three-figure number (205, 504, 708), where the middle number is always a zero. The reason? The zero is where you used to put the crank handle in to start their early automobiles. Incidentally the latest Peugeot model is designated 1003. Wags say this is so that you can now fit in a two-pin plug.

For similar reasons, we today have situations that are equally inexplicable, but in different ways. The taps for water and for gas open in different directions. The keyboards on a calculator and a telephone are different—the line with 123 is the bottom line on a calculator, but it's the top line on a telephone.

The early railway carriages had as many doors as compartments because they were based on the stagecoach. Automobiles didn't have a flashing turn signal, but were equipped with an arrow indicator inspired by the vision of a driver's arm stuck out of the window. The British still build their automobiles to drive on the left mainly because Napoleon had the idea of getting people to drive on the right, and they didn't like Napoleon (who had quite logically decided that it was better to have horse-drawn carriages drive on the right so that the coachmen's whips didn't get entangled with the whips of oncoming traffic).

You don't have to believe the hoary old "railway gauge/Roman horse cart" hoax to understand that the present is often, in fact, the past under a crust of new ideas. The potential of electricity was simply harnessed at first by adding a motor to a nonelectric tool; we can see that in the early calculators and sewing machines. The first electric clocks simply used the current to move the weights. So you can add new things to a system but, one day, you will have to think up a new system.

This mental, sometimes sentimental, attachment to the past—rather than thinking ahead—is evident in the way things have been named. Today it seems decidedly odd to speak of a railway locomotive as an "iron horse," but at the time it made sense. Today we talk about "the information highway," so, despite appearances, we're still stuck in the past. It would be better to talk about *infoducts,* as I did in my first book.

As long as we're wedded to an existing idea, we make the best of it. A good example is the U.S. phone system. The big cities have area codes like 212, 213, and 312 simply because they were easier to call up with the early rotary-dialing phones.

That's analytical thinking, but the real breaks and quantum leaps come when we think holistically. Teleworking is not only the sum of work and telecommunications; it's asking questions in the context of our professional activities in a world that has cables going in every direction. The future is not adding up ideas, but multiplying possibilities!

When I was a child, when we went on holiday, we would stop at a gas pump. Today we have a break at a service station. That's much more than a semantic change—it really is a break. We no longer think of it as a place where we fill up with fuel; we think of it as a place where we stop. That changing perception opens the door of our imagination, although it doesn't get rid of the petrol pump.

The reason the National Geographic Institute shop in Paris is so full of ideas is because, one day, the Institute stopped seeing itself as a manufacturer of maps, but as a mine of information and tools for travelers, sportsmen, and hikers. They now sell hiking shoes, compasses, and knives, as well as maps.

Limoges is the French capital of porcelain. We think of porcelain as the raw material for ornaments, chinaware, and statues. But, one day, somebody in Limoges realized that porcelain could be used for insulation, a key element in the electrical industry, and the international Legrand organization, a major manufacturer of electrical connectors and accessories, was the result.

Similarly, Xerox entered a new era when it started to see itself as a document company, as did the Century 21 real estate company when it went into rental collection. Only recently, the UPS courier company launched into laptop computer maintenance. Surprised? When you analyze it, speedy laptop repair, including sourcing of replacement parts, is much more a logistics problem than a technical one.

Ideas are born when a producer of champagne realizes he's selling good times, when a hotel owner discovers that a traveler can be a client even if that traveler doesn't stay the night, when a refrigerator manufacturer tells himself he's "selling cold," when a car manufacturer concludes that he's selling mobility, and when a traditional industry sells not only material but also the information that goes with it.

**FIGURE 1.2** *Changing Twice*

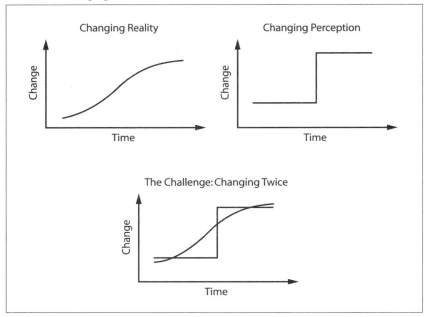

In diagrammatic form, all these examples look like Figure 1.2.

Even if you agree with all this, it doesn't mean you will avoid problems in the future.

Think for a moment how Bill Gates became involved in the world of the Internet. In the early 1990s, Microsoft seemed to have it made. The company had conquered the world of personal computing by selling the operating systems—first DOS, then Windows—that run PCs. It was worth $70 billion and had about 20,000 employees. Even Bill Gates was entitled to think the party would go on forever.

Yet even back then, the Internet was beginning to gather a fan base—first among computer nerds and hackers, then gradually to a broader network of academics and researchers. This was the reality that was slowly taking shape.

The word *Internet* gradually entered the common vocabulary, and we can assume it was being heard with greater frequency in Microsoft's corporate hallways.

Then, in 1994, a company called Netscape sprang out of nowhere. Its first product was the Netscape Navigator. With this so-called browser you could work your way round the World Wide Web.

We can imagine Bill Gates driving home at night, thinking, hmmm, *surfing* the Internet . . .

It took a year for the significance of the Internet browser to germinate in Bill Gates's mind, but in 1995 he finally got it: The Internet was not just an interesting device; it was The Next Big Thing.

Once Gates recognized the paradigm shift—i.e., had changed his perception—he made some swift moves to bring Microsoft into line. On December 7, 1995, Gates assembled his troops at the company's Seattle headquarters, along with top industry analysts and reporters. He was about to tell the world that Microsoft would stop everything—turning its back on millions of dollars already invested in R&D—and turn its full attention and creative resources to conquering the opportunities of the Internet. He said it was time to change reality.

As we can see from these examples, business is always affected by the outside world, and business leaders must adjust or lose. The first thing is to be aware of the outside world—Chapter 2—and keen to the signals that suggest your business may be out of synch.

How do you get ahead of the process—Chapters 3 to 8—changing the world rather than being changed by it? You have to be the driving force behind perceptual change. You have to be the hammer of change—not the nail!

## KEY POINTS IN THIS CHAPTER

- The great philosophers can help you.
- Change is not an option.
- The options are: what and when.
- You have to change twice: perception and reality.
- Innovation is not creativity!

If you want to feel what it feels like when you hit that point of changing twice—where your reality, which was just slogging along, suddenly takes a leap forward—consider the diagram below.

What do you see? A small cube in the bottom left-hand corner? Probably. Now turn this page slowly in a clockwise motion. Keep your eyes fixed on the diagram.

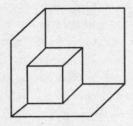

All of a sudden a new shape appears. Keep turning. When the shape is upside down, many people find it has become another shape.

This new concept challenges our assumptions—it's a break in continuity, a turbulence. A gentle movement of the cubes doesn't change the image we have of it. The world changes and we don't see it, and then all of a sudden we see the change in the full light of day.

You can say a number of things about this little geometrical-metaphorical manipulation:

- We see cubes when there aren't any! This drawing is two dimensional (by definition), but comes across as three dimensional.
- Even if the figure is the same, two different people will often see it differently.
- The transition from one way of seeing to another is brusque; there's a small shock.
- Even when he or she knows all about them, the viewer can't easily shift from one form to the other. We are not in total control of the way we see things.

So there it is. The world's oldest problem posed once again: the strange relationship between the universe and the people that live in it, between the environment and the person who is looking at it, between the subject and the object. This binomial situation is the foundation on which philosophical thought is built. The world on one side, the way of seeing the world on the other. In other words, reality and perception.

# 2

# A NON FINITO WORLD

*"Economics explain how people make their choices,*
*sociology explains that people cannot make choices."*

**Bertrand Russell**

I was traveling on the California Zephyr over the Rocky Mountains one summer (I find it hard to break the European habit of climbing onto a train rather than into an automobile). The train was winding its way through the snow-capped peaks when I saw something extraordinary: the grey, weathered ruins of an expansive industrial complex that had obviously been abandoned to the elements for a long time. When I asked the conductor about it, he said the building had been an ice factory, one that had cut ice from the nearby lakes and shipped it by rail to the growing population of America's west coast. The business model was very simple: During the winter you just wait, in the spring you cut the ice, in summer you sell the blocks, and in the fall you enjoy.

Then one day, or more accurately over a period of some years, the ice business had melted away. Refrigeration, the production of cold air with chemical refrigerants and electrical energy, had been discovered. From that day on, ice-making in the cold stretches of the Rocky Mountains was doomed.

The owners of the ice factory, I'm sure, didn't take the challenge to their business and their way of life lying down. They probably tried to make ice more efficiently. They may even have invested in making the plant larger, to benefit from economies of scale. Perhaps they struck up new relationships with retailers on the other side of the mountain to boost their sales. It must have been a dramatic day when they finally closed the doors of the ice factory that I was passing. But those doors did close, and the building died.

The ice factory, I realized, had become a ghost, a physical representation of how futile it is to keep going in one direction when the world is heading in another. You cannot put wings on a steam locomotive and make it an airplane, nor can you turn a business of shipping lake ice into one where ice is made with refrigerants passing through miles of copper coil (well you could, but there would be no economic advantage in doing this deep in the Rocky Mountains). The discovery of chemical refrigerants had changed the world, which is evolutionary, and the ice factory— like the discarded shell of some sea creature—just stayed where it was.

Of course, you couldn't expect the cutter of ice to invent the refrigerator. It wasn't the mail, after all, that invented the fax (or e-mail, or FedEx) and it wasn't even IBM that invented the PC (in fact, today's IBM has now sold off its entire PC business to the Chinese Lenovo organization).

I didn't have to go to the Rocky Mountains to see this kind of thing; it goes on all around us. I used to be the manager of the Brussels Stock Exchange, a neo-Grecian temple with an impressive marble stairway leading up to great doors of oak and brass. The building is now empty too, the stock exchange having moved. It is just used occasionally for cocktails, conferences, and seminars. There is no stock exchange in Brussels anymore; it has gone digital.

I told you in Chapter 1 that, despite the changes that have gone on in the world since the beginning of history, the changes of today are both different and greater than ever before. That is why we need to take heed of them. As Francis Bacon said, "We must obey the forces we want to command." If we want to stay in charge of our destinies, we have to learn to anticipate the changes going on all around us.

In Europe—a part of the world that I know well from my frequent travels—the frontiers are disappearing fast. The concrete of the Berlin Wall has been knocked down, the border controls between countries are vanishing, goods and services are moving freely. Students move from one country to another, from one language to another. Similarly, the walls protecting monopolies are crumbling away.

But it's not just in Europe that the barriers are breaking down. Twenty-five years ago, the three modes of information—code, sound, and image—each required a separate transmission network—telex, telephone, and cable—and different storage media—punch card, groove, and film. The tools were separate, distinct, and segmented, while the information they carried was global, whole, and multiple. This partitioning, in contradiction with the very nature of the information, was technically inevitable at the time.

The next technological stage, the widespread use of binary code, changed everything. This was the thesis contained in my first book, *Infoducs* (*Infoducts* in English), which Anne Mikolajczak and I published in 1984. This has been borne out since, and is being typified again by the disappearance of Europe's frontiers.

Then came digital information, which can change its state, share the same network, use the same medium. The immediate consequence of this is that a second type of barrier is surmounted, the one that sets the limits on technology. Where is it no longer applicable? Where does it stop being useful and start being useless? It's very simple, if I dare say it—cyberspace is everywhere. You can't *not* be there. All of which makes the advertisement welcoming us to cyberspace rather banal, to say the least.

It is intriguing to wonder whether the digital age has spilled over into society in unseen ways. For instance, can you still trace the borderline between professional and private life? Are you reading this book for work or for leisure? Where do cosmetics stop in the drugstore and start in the pharmacy? Where is the dividing line between the lending library, and the library café, and the bookstore? What is the difference between applied science and basic research? What is the difference between inside and outside? You can't throw your waste a long way out any more, because there is no far away and there is no outside. The ecosystem is one, there is one ozone layer, and the global village has no suburbs.

The fences are down. Solid separations now seem ephemeral. There are a thousand possible ways between two points. We have to wave farewell to privileged entry, because we are all privileged to go everywhere. What are the limits of an activity today? What is a market segment, a financial center, a zone of responsibility, a professional sector? Schemes become vague, images blur, and we don't know how to focus the lens. When I was a banker, the financial community consisted of bankers, insurers, and brokers, and each job was clearly defined. Today there are no barriers between them.

We always hear people talking about "stepping out of the box." That is supposedly the practical function of creativity, but the ability to step out of the box presupposes that there is indeed a box! Today, there is no box! Now we have to double or square our imagination. It is no longer a question of what to do about a problem and, because there are endless possibilities, what even constitutes a problem?

In the country I had a dog, which used to take a sly pleasure in jumping over the garden fence and escaping into the neighboring fields. One day I decided to remove the ugly wire netting which no longer served any useful purpose. Imagine my surprise the next day when I saw my dog jumping up at the exact point where the fence had been, with the same sly pleasure (possibly to remind me that the French words for *dog* and *cynicism* come from the same root)?

Before you laugh at him, think a moment! Maybe he's laughing at us, incapable of getting out of the boxes that we make for ourselves, stuck in buildings which no longer exist, squatting inside fences which disappeared long ago, and shut inside imaginary walls.

## NON FINITO

The disappearance of barriers is just one of many changes. Another is what Michelangelo ought to have called *non finito*.

A large number of Michelangelo's statues are unfinished. The *Four Naked Slaves* for example—which were meant to adorn the lower part of the tomb of Julius II and are today preserved in the Florentine Academy—give the impression that they are emerging from the marble. The heads and torsos have been drawn out, as if to allow the statues to breathe, while the rest of the body is trapped in the marble, waiting.

A number of hypotheses have been proposed to explain the large number of Michelangelo's unfinished statues. Some of the theories are simple: an unexpected fault in the marble, the artist's intention to imitate ancient sculpture where only one side was visible to the public, a change of mind, the death of a sponsor, lack of time, or even a sudden move by Michelangelo to another city.

For some people this unfinished state—this *non finito*—has a more fundamental reason. The sculptor despaired of being able to achieve the perfection he dreamed of. Michelangelo is said to have stated that, "the science of a great man is judged by his fear of not being able to execute something exactly as he believed he could." Or did he, rather, consider he had met his objective despite it not being finished? Or was he afraid of the negative results of going on with his work?

We will probably never know, all the more so since the degrees and forms of *non finito* are different in every case. By deliberately conserving a part of the original block, Michelangelo kept a memory of the raw and unformed material from which his statues were born, thereby accentuating the delicacy of their forms still further. Auguste Rodin even saw in the *non finito* the metamorphosis of material reality into reality of a purely spiritual nature.

If Michelangelo was afraid of spoiling the "little light of the marble" with one stroke too many of the chisel, *non finito* is not exclusive to sculpture. If you need convincing of this, you only need to listen to Schubert's Unfinished Symphony.

Gaudi didn't leave behind any plans for his cathedral in Barcelona, started in 1882 and never finished (he died suddenly and banally under the wheels of a streetcar). The French mathematician Pierre de Fermat had fun taunting posterity with his "Last Theorem" in a marginal note: "I have discovered a truly remarkable proof which this margin is too small to contain." And how many writers have abandoned a novel in draft? No wonder the French novelist Daniel Pennac lists in his "ten undeniable rights of the reader" the right not to finish reading a book.

Even philosophers—voluntarily or involuntarily—have had to give up finishing their work. "*Raynalde, non possum*"—"Reginald, I cannot"—are the words with which the master work of Saint Thomas of Aquinas stops, as we cannot really say it ends. These are in any case his words to the colleague who reproaches him for setting down his quill before he has finished his *Summa Theologica*. For Saint Thomas, philosophy is always on the move, always unfinished. It is nonknowledge that, once it becomes knowledge, can no longer be communicated.

What a stunning assertion! To say that an unfinished state is a sign of great talent, the expression of elaborate art, even the obvious proof of genius. Don't finish what you're doing! So that's it, the supreme step, the attitude that marks you out for perfection. It's a pity we didn't know about it sooner!

When we were children, we weren't allowed to go and play until we had finished our homework or meal. As adolescents, we would dream of traveling, but we were told to finish our studies first. Ah, so that explains it! That's why our taste for the spontaneous was beaten out of us, along with our natural tendency to sketch things out, and our wise propensity for putting off till later something we have started, simply to be able to start something else. *They* wanted us to finish, but *we* wanted not to finish—*non finito.*

It's a pity they deprived us of this pleasure of the approximation or rough version. For, in the world we're heading into now, the *non finito* is an even safer way of life than it ever was in the past. When the future is uncertain, when—paradoxically—the only reason to continue forecasting the future is to be able to change it, isn't it grossly pretentious to want to finish what you're doing?

Industrial processes have already built in the *non finito* and dubbed it "on demand." Production is latent and stays in a potential state until the client decides to start it up. The number of options is such that the car is only assembled, or the computer put together, after the order is signed (see the discussion of Dell in Chapter 7).

The *non finito* is strangely modern. It's an attitude that consists of just being ready, since we don't know how to forecast any more. It is in opposition to the sinister "we don't move so long as we don't know where we're going," where *non finito* would say "let's in any case do what has to be done," even if it can't be finished. *Non finito* is humility confronted with one sole certainty: we don't know what's going to happen. *Non finito* is the will to act while leaving the future open, the habit of writing in pencil rather than in ink, actively participating in a world that is becoming, without knowing what it's going to become. In the end, *non finito* is respect for others, and the liberty we grant them to finish in their own way.

Let there be no misunderstanding here. I am not seeking to defend those who sell software full of errors, nor the common practice in some countries of not constructing the top story of your house in order to avoid taxes. Nor am I making the case for those major reforms that are constantly put off until there's "a better time," or those enormous abandoned building sites like the Tower of Babel. No, *non finito* has nothing to do with procrastination, the lazy and systematic habit of putting things off until tomorrow. *Non finito* is the result of a decision, a deliberate choice in a world in which there are fewer fixed structures and more projects.

If this is provocative, don't worry—more's coming! I think I have convinced you that *finishing* is not a good idea. My next point is to show you that *beginning* is no longer possible.

I think, for example, of my contact with the director of a dairy concern. He wanted to organize a brainstorming session with his colleagues on the impact of the Internet on his area of activity. "When I think of the Internet," he told me, "I don't even know where to start."

We can understand what he means. Should he see the Internet as a new way of selling, of organizing, of finding information? Was it an opportunity, an irrelevance, or a threat? Who should be in charge of the file: the IT director or the head of communications? In fact, is there even a file? Should he try to sell e-cheese and yogurt.com? The poor man seemed completely lost.

## THE NEW NEW ECONOMY

It used to be so easy: There was a beginning, there was an end, life was linear. After the Old Testament there was the New Testament. After plane geometry there was spatial geometry. To learn mathematics, you started with figures. To learn to write, you started with the alphabet. The history of Rome started with Romulus and Remus. The history of the Crusades started with Godfrey of Bouillon. Learning Latin started with the first declension, and Mendeleyev classified atoms in increasing order of electrons.

The third principle of the French philosopher Descartes is very clear on this point: "Develop my thoughts through order, starting with the simplest objects and those that are the easiest to know, and then rising little by little—by degrees—to the knowledge of more complex things."

The problem today is that cyberspace and real time call for a different approach. Today networks are enmeshed, broadcasts are in loops, and crossroads are either spaghetti junctions or roundabouts. When we say there's no one on the end of the line, it's not because there isn't someone there, but because there's no end to the line. Think globally, act globally. Everything goes round and round. Some people no longer know if it's NGOs against GMOs or the other way round.

So today's world calls for thinking beyond Descartes. Holistic thinking, total thinking, which takes account of the elements and the relationship between the elements, action, and retroaction.

It is in the sense of *non finito* that we have to see that the world is changing and still continuing to change. There is a new New Economy. Even if a great deal of hope or money has been frittered away, this is by no means a return to the starting blocks. In no way can we expect a return to the Old Economy.

At Newton's funeral, Laplace declared that there would never be a second Newton, because there is only one world to discover! It is true that the works of the English genius had something startling about them. What nerve! He actually dared break a principle that was 2,000 years old! To dare to affirm that an apple that falls and a moon that doesn't fall both obey the same law within the same system of physics! This goes totally against Aristotle, who affirmed that there was a world cut into two: perfect and eternal in heaven, corruptible and mortal on earth.

With Newton, the metaphor of the world as a machine found its zenith. Eyeglasses and watches, which were still tools for Galileo and Huygens, took on the status of models. Science, which was the first to use machines to understand the world, now moved on to an understanding of the world seen as a machine.

It was a machine for sure, but one that wasn't so complicated, with cogs and levers only capable of going forward and backwards in a symmetrical way. Replace a plus by a minus in Newton's equations and you have an apple that falls upwards into the tree and a moon that turns back on itself.

The consequence of this mechanical and mechanistic view of things is that it becomes possible both to predict the future and go back into the past. All that has to be done is to be aware of the present and know the law that governs the universe.

This perception of physics gives rise to three philosophical questions, which we can all ask ourselves.

1. Who made the machine?
2. What is the machine for?
3. What happens to man's freedom inside the machine?

While Newton went in search of God as the answer to the first question, he was inclined to abandon the other two.

It was only in the 19th century that the metaphor of the world as a machine gave way to another: that of the world as a system. Carnot with his theory of heat and Darwin in his approach to the living world brought new words to science: evolution, dissipation, irreversibility.

Perpetual motion as defined by Newton is denounced as a practical impossibility. Time from now on only has one direction—there is no reverse gear without a corresponding effort in terms of energy. The world is now a system that consumes energy and wears out. If there is still room for a machine in this metaphor, it is no longer a well-oiled clock, but more of a noisy, smoky steam engine that one day or another will stop or blow up.

So it is that the philosophical discussion unblocks because, if there is fortuity, there is no longer determinism. As a result there is some room for a kind of liberty in mankind, and there is space for a debate on the objectives of the system and of the machine.

It's not Newton, with his fixed and reversive laws, that we should be looking at now. No, it's Darwin we should look to as our guide to reflection, for the Internet revolution is irreversible. Time and space are now definitively different, the number of access-points and users of the Internet continues to grow, and entire sectors of the economy—small ads, air transport, auction, the post—are no longer what they were. An entire generation has rediscovered what enterprise actually means, and millions of adolescents will never be consumers in the same way we were.

A new New Economy is bubbling under the surface—the Internet, Act III. After the expanding bubble and the exploding bubble, serious things are starting to happen. After the Internet machine, let's make way for the Internet system. It's a strange new world, and we need to adjust our mental settings a bit.

The generation after mine, for instance, only has a vague feeling of a theft when it copies something. Is ownership theft, or is theft ownership? There is no law that is really tenable when a major portion of the population sees very little moral reason for it. In the Internet ecosystem, billions of ideas exist because billions of ideas exist. You can only write a book once you've read hundreds of books. Could you compose a song if you'd never heard somebody sing?

Amazon.com now offers the reader the option of ordering the book, not by using a keyword but a key phrase. In other words a phrase taken from the work that the reader is looking for. This means that Amazon has digitally stored the entire contents of hundreds of thousands of books.

Contrary to the traditional economy, here abundance breeds abundance, and consumption increases stocks. Rarity does not increase value, on the contrary. Culture is no longer private property. A singer is all the more enhanced in everyone's eyes if pirates, of any type, distribute his or her music for free. Maybe we have to see creation as a service, almost a gift, and no longer as a product.

Perhaps the New Economy will simply encompass the old one without disrupting it. Perhaps without culture, generosity, people helping one another—incomprehensible for the market economy—this new market wouldn't work. Maybe artists are happy to be in direct contact with their audience via the Internet and, in this way, free themselves from their agents, intermediaries, and distributors.

Perhaps all the laws relating to intellectual property are counterproductive to creation, or would Andy Warhol still misappropriate the big international brands to make art from them? Maybe there is no market growth without something that slips through the system? Perhaps profit will go hand-in-hand with freedom from now on and we will have to replace the word *property* with the word *relationship*.

Today we speak of "open source." So what's going on? Would openness be the ideal attitude? Everything started when a Finnish programmer named Linus Torvald decided that IT was going down the wrong road. He was convinced that a community that turned in on itself had no future, and that owning the monopoly for an indispensable application was no more ethical—or feasible—than owning the rights to a spoken language, to the human genome, or to philosophy.

So Linus wrote an open operating system to challenge the monopolies of the time (the operating system within a computer is the basic program, one which allows all the others to be used; it is in many respects the source of the source.) In a historic e-mail dated 25th August, 1991, Linus Torvald made an offer to an ill-defined community to come and discover his work and take it off his hands. This of course was his right (his author's right). You can imagine the smiles this provoked at Microsoft when the rumor of his open ambition reached their ears!

In his message he used the word *free* to describe his system and distinguish it from the proprietary systems. From that day onwards, the words *open source* and *free software* have been almost inextricably interlinked. That day saw the beginning of an ambiguity because *free* does not only mean liberated, but also *free of charge*. It's probably the first meaning of the word that Linus Torvald had in mind.

At the heart of the philosophy—because that's what it is—there are three things to be shared:

1. *An objective.* A need is identified and a group takes part in the project.
2. *A job.* The task is segmented or built into an architecture for participation.
3. *The results.* The output of the collaboration is available to everyone, and it's up to everyone to try to improve it.

The unprecedented behavior of these programmers will probably change the world, because the spirit behind them will inspire other communities. The open source approach can be used to write a recipe book, a novel, or—why not—an entire encyclopedia.

Mathematicians can try to prove together that all even numbers can be the sum of two prime numbers (as far as I know, Goldbach's "binary" conjecture still holds). Investigators can solve a crime together. But why stop there? NASA uses lots of volunteers to analyze the surface of Mars. So why shouldn't there be open source to find a vaccine or to construct a plane?

Perhaps open source is not as brand-new as we might think. For centuries, most wise men, from Euclid to Newton, seemed to share this same ideal. The first version of the Oxford English Dictionary was the subject of countless exchanges of mail between etymologists of all origins.

We don't have to perceive the Open Source approach as an anticapitalist, antiprofit, or Other World movement (even if it is in part). Perhaps, on the contrary, it is the conclusion of a real market economy that reconciles freedom with speed.

We're used to seeing the statement "All Rights Reserved" at the beginning of every book. Will we soon begin to see the expression "Certain Rights Reserved" take its place?

The problem of intellectual property—and of excessive intellectual property—has been tabled as an issue. In Chapter 6, we refer to discovery, invention, and creation as finding something else that *was*, that *is going to be,* and that *might be,* respectively. Three dimensions, prompting numerous questions of a new kind:

- Can the discovery make money for the person who makes it?
- Does a systematic patent system for inventions encourage or discourage innovation?
- Is software invented or created? If it is a creation, then is it subject to a protection similar to copyright?

As the laws governing patents are not the same as those governing copyright, we can imagine that intellectuals will have a preference for one or the other in order to protect their property.

A patent is a title which accords its owner exclusive rights on its use for a given period, but it also obliges the inventor to make public the details of the invention one day. It's understandable, therefore, that software companies prefer to file for copyright, which is a form of legal protection that gives a work an intellectual or artistic character, and which accords its author the right to levy a fee.

FIGURE 2.1 *Patent versus Copyright*

|  | **PATENT** | **COPYRIGHT** |
|---|---|---|
| **Conditions**<br>Formalities<br>Substantive | Deposit<br>Invention<br>Novelty<br>Inventive step<br>Industrial character | None<br>Work<br>Expression<br>Original |
| **Ownership** | First to file | Flesh-and-blood creator, but exceptions |
| **Rights** | Bundle of rights extending to the idea | Economic rights (reproduction and communication to the public)<br>Moral rights |
| **Duration** | 20 years from filing | 70 years after the death of the author |
| **Publication** | Mandatory | Discretionary |
| **Cost** | High | Low |

Copyright Alain Strowel

There is an important new nuance that arises here between copyright in the French sense of the word and copyright in the American sense. The former is focused on its author, whereas the latter is focused on the work itself. In the first case the rights truly belong to the author and he or she cedes these for a fee allowing the work to be exploited. At death, the rights pass on to the heirs, and after 70 years they fall into the public domain.

Likening a computer program to an intellectual work at first sight doesn't seem to make much sense. But it is difficult to keep abreast of this subject. By the time you read these words, the laws may have changed once again. Beyond the copyright that protects a literary work, these companies want to patent the *idea*, the concept that underlies their software.

It's as if the publisher of *Harry Potter* wanted, from now on, to stop anyone from writing a novel in which the hero is an apprentice magician. Excessive action in the copyright area can only bring about a reaction in the form of *copyleft*. This pun was just too tempting for Richard Stallman—possibly the real founder of Open Source, an almost unknown soldier in a war against monopolies, and the mentor of Linus Torvald.

The partisans of *copyleft* contested an idea that is particularly widely accepted. Whether we talk about a book, a CD, or video, the stereotype is that a pirated copy is a copy that hasn't been sold. But that's not the case, these people tell us. A pirated copy at least results in the legal sale of an additional copy!

It's true that for ease, presentation, or speed, buying from a shop is much better than shabby photocopies or recordings with no cover notes. Will the ethics of ideas allow for the theft of ideas? In the publishing world, the greater the noise and circulation a work enjoys, the more it sells.

Where does Adam Smith fit into all this? His law of supply and demand seems to be particularly badly applied here. During the stock market bubble, the greater the increase in start-up shares, the more people bought them, which is contrary to the principle of this law. Moreover we've never had so much talk before of free things: free newspapers, free transport, free music, free telephone, free software. Of course gratuity in the absolute sense doesn't exist. It's just become a figure of speech, a way of presenting things.

Traditionally, economics and commerce have built in one criterion that is inherent to every sellable item or good: its rarity. The first step in looking at an ideas economy—music, images, text, counsel, information, brands—is therefore based on a supposition: the need to create rarity artificially when there is none.

The multinationals are engaged in a permanent struggle with counterfeiters, pirates, and photocopiers; it's a never-ending combat over copied software, generic medicines, and downloaded music. It only needs a technician or editor to want it, and a new film will be on the Internet before it's even shown in the cinema.

Encryption, secret codes, trademark law, court cases—everything has been tried. In vain? Has profit become an outmoded notion? Certainly new kinds of motivation are emerging. In any case, the absence of a legal framework for intellectual property didn't stop Euclid, Saint Augustine, Michelangelo, or J. S. Bach from working and producing.

If actors got back on stage, if singers spent more time performing in public (without lip-synching, preferably), if philosophers gave more lectures, would we really be the losers? What if the production of a new version of software automatically meant that the previous version became available free of charge? Consultants are like artists. They sell what people can't steal from them: their point of view, their energy, and the talent at the moment they give it.

Perhaps the foundation of the Old Economy was secrecy or nondisclosure, while the e-economy still remains to be discovered. That's not just a matter of adding electronics to the economy. Probably we'll find that, within it, the e-economy breaks down into micro-markets, without fixed pricing, and a return to ethics, taxation, and a new critical look at control mechanisms. Plus, of course, some surprising mathematical equations, and an enormous breath of fresh air for new ideas, new approaches, and new concepts.

## STARTING POINTS FOR CHANGE

If you want to see change, you need a fixed point—of which there are four—to start from. Let's use them to examine some very old questions, for which we used to have very easy answers.

1. Where are things?
2. When do things happen?

3. Why do things happen?
4. What is true, and what is false?

The answers to these four questions are becoming increasingly difficult.

## Space

*Space* used to be an easy-going concept. For a long time it was limited to three dimensions, compartmentalized, defined by boundaries on each side. Now, suddenly, it has all been shaken up. It's now globalized, unlimited. It's even become cyberspace.

Ecology shows us that there is no longer an "elsewhere." In the realm of economics we have replaced the concept of "each of us at home" by "everyone everywhere." Technology allows an item of information to be everywhere, which means nowhere, ungraspable. Aviation allows us to fly nonstop to the other side of the planet, only to phone back for news from the country we've only just left. We don't know where we are any more.

What happens to transport costs when you go to work by phone? Can a teleworker claim the cost of a modem on an expense form, instead of the kilometers traveled? What does it mean to tax a virtual company or have small ads paid in euro/$cm^2$?

Even the frontier between intranets and the Internet is indefinite, if not indefinable. Can we actually *go* into cyberspace if it's everywhere? What is a financial location these days? What does it mean to shift location in a market, if the choice of site is less and less important? Are we not all destined to become people of no fixed abode in the long term? Is it not companies like Visa that have got it right: we don't know where it is, but we see it everywhere?

## Time

*Time,* too, used to be a stable sort of concept: uniform and universal, measurable and measured, content to flow at its own rhythms. Today the pendulum is very confused. How can it swing in a society that functions in "real time"? Moreover, what was time like *before* it became real, at a time when you'd sometimes say you didn't have the "material" time to do something? An automatic cash dispenser allows you to check your bank balance and to have, in real time, information dated the day before (at best!). And many daily newspapers now make their archives available for consultation in real time!

Time is not the same for everyone any more; it's static for some, dynamic for others. "A long time," as identified by the French historian Fernand Braudel, is no longer just a reference. There isn't any "after" any more, just like there's no more "elsewhere."

Time is money! But is it really? Today, richness would appear to be more about speed. What do the clocking-in machines in companies actually check? As if long-expected creativity was a matter of minutes! Just in time—just in time for what? Are we heading for the kind of careers sportsmen have—retired at 35? It doesn't really matter to some people, including the 17 percent of Americans who, according to a 2004 *Newsweek* poll, think the world will come to an end in their own lifetime.

In the future will it still be possible to "lose" time or lose one's time? We are losing our time bearings, like when we watch a continuous TV news channel like CNN, for example.

CNN makes a mockery of time zones like a fly makes a mockery of an air pocket. CNN clocks only have one hand—the minute hand. The right time is news time, and that's all that matters. The newsreaders don't say "good morning," because there's no morning, and they don't say "good evening" because there's no evening. They'll say "it's night-time in America, midday in the Middle East, and morning in Europe" or something like that. They say "welcome" 24 hours a day and they don't say "good-bye," but "see you soon." On CNN, time doesn't exist any more than space does. Where *are* all these morning and evening speakers, anyway? In the United States, in "duplex," on mission, or on a time-delay? CNN is perpetual-motion media. The clock has only one hand.

Time and space are no longer reliable instruments of measurement. You only need to ask a taxi-driver and his passenger, stuck in a traffic jam, what they think of it. And if speed is one day defined as space divided by time, it will be amusing to see cyberspace divided by real time—and what's left of accountancy plans or career plans!

## Causality

Man has always liked to understand the why of things. Which *cause* produces which effect? Which hypothesis can lead to which conclusions?

Unfortunately, things are getting complicated here, too, though we don't really know why. There is a newcomer joining the traditional causes and explanations: the effect of retroaction or feedback. By this I mean the permanent confusion between action and reaction, and the impossibility of reaching a conclusion. Exactly in the same way as the publication of an opinion poll can modify the results of an election, information channels allow for events to be interfered with so that they themselves change.

How many more times are we going to hear that fog caused an accident, or that information technology is the cause of unemployment? How many more times is the airport going to announce that a plane will be leaving late because it arrived late? The dollar falls because the dollar falls, doesn't it? (See Aristotle's four causes at the end of this chapter.)

## Perception

The fourth lookout point—*perception* of the environment by its human occupants—is also now recast in a radically different way. We could even go so far as to close the old debate that consisted of opposing real and virtual, since specialists are now developing virtual reality!

Paradoxes are all around us. The digitalization of information, for example, enables us preserve it, to keep it in perfect condition. But in some ways this absolute truth can produce absolute deception.

A few years ago, during the Oscar ceremony in Hollywood, we witnessed the nomination of *Farinelli,* the castrato with the synthesized voice created by computer from a woman's and a man's voice. Didn't *Forrest Gump* receive accolades, the film in which the hero shakes President Kennedy's hand thanks to virtual and impressive editing of images shot 30 years before?

False sounds, false images—is that the information society? The computer can now resurrect John Lennon and many others, put John Kerry alongside Jane Fonda, and whiten the skin of black model Naomi Campbell so that she can work for a lipstick brand. Digital electronics also corrected Gérard Depardieu's French accent to make him speak perfect English in the film *Vatel* (ensuring more than equal honors since Depardieu had earlier linguistically dubbed the voice of English actor Kenneth Branagh as Henry V).

# A NEW RENAISSANCE

Space, time, causality, perception. This sort of reflection never ends—and certainly should not be allowed to end.

It would seem that the very foundations of our life and society have shifted. Information is now the key resource and we are obliged to rethink all these structures, since the concepts on which they are based are no longer what they were.

In a knowledge society, what in fact happens to property, competition, work, teaching, working together, authority, solidarity, ethics?

To want to change the world is, paradoxically, to confirm the most ancient of traditions—we've been doing that for centuries. So what do these new changes in change really mean to us?

In the last few years we have witnessed a renaissance of philosophy. Is this a pure coincidence or is it that we needed to rediscover this old passion?

The (re)discovery of thought developed by man over the centuries has the potential for making an enormous contribution at a time when we are embarking on a new renaissance. The pace of events is accelerating and there is increasing confusion between what is urgent, what is important, and what is essential.

- Information technology has an influence on the way we *write*, since text processing enables us to make rough versions that are not definitive. You can craft your message a hundred times on the keyboard and liberate your ideas, without any concern for the number of deletions or the cost of corrections. The ability to recycle old texts, to copy, cut and paste, to eliminate, unpaste and uncopy is also significant.
- IT also influences the way we *calculate*, or the fact that we no longer need to. Instead of strict arithmetical skills we now rely on our sense of orders of magnitude to know when something's wrong. The direct formula has given way to a process of trial and error.
- The way in which we *communicate* is evolving. E-mail accelerates written exchanges between those people who are connected to it. But what will happen to people who are not connected, or who have been disconnected? How does a child who has been given a mobile phone cut the "cord" that links him to his parents?

- The way we *speak* is also affected. Language is tending to lose its flavor and is gradually being saturated by a form of English that is itself increasingly colorless. Little by little, *security* is replacing *reassurance, high-performance* is replacing *excellent, governance* is replacing *conscience,* and *sustainable* is replacing *sustained.*
- Finally, information technology is having an effect on the way we *think.* Just one example: Knowledge no longer has to be memorized on paper with all the constraints of sequence and linearity. This can have both good and bad implications in the long run. The text of Pascal's *Pensées* reached us more or less intact, but what is by no means certain is the order in which the French philosopher thought them up. We can see that ordering his thoughts in one way, rather than another, could give a different impression of his, well, thought.

Today, knowledge can be stored in a much more abundant form. In a database or in hypertext, it can keep all the connections that link it—in all senses—to the components of that knowledge. Socrates never wrote anything, probably so as not to modify or degrade his level of thought. Even so, the computer would have been a useful tool for memorizing things; he could have committed them to disk without having to make arbitrary decisions on sequence or order of priority. Perhaps this all boils down to the fact that what can be thought out so well can't be expressed at all!

On the point of creativity, "founding fathers" like Alex Osborn, Arthur Koestler, and Edward de Bono made major contributions, but they now look rather "pre-IT." Computer-assisted creativity is a brand new discipline and the Internet, the seventh continent, is only limited by our imagination.

In more general terms, what we need is an entire philosophy of Information Technology and networks. In his book *Le Contrat naturel,*[1] Michel Serres champions the idea that, following on the social contract by which Man surrendered some of his individual freedom in favor of a community-based way of living, and following on the scientific contract by which Man accepted that part of Truth comes from experiment or demonstration, Man must also recognize nature as a full partner and sign a third type of contract.

Today, Man probably may need a fourth type of contract, a "digital contract." There is an urgent need to reflect on the relationship between man and machine. This reflection must be a match for what the machine has become: universal, real-time, woven with retroactive effects and paradoxes. This reflection can only happen in tandem and must, of course, start with a fundamental question: in the end, who is doing the programming—is it the user or is it the computer?

The sense of unease and disorientation we all feel today is rooted in a number of different things. One of these is our incapacity to entirely understand, and therefore effectively control, institutions that are changing in a changing world. The difficulty for us, these days, is to find the master switch to all those changes that are now passing us by.

We find it difficult to accept the shortcomings of a number of institutional systems—of an economic, legal, and political nature—when the media spotlight falls on their tendencies to excess, to change course and to alienate us all. Yet, when they were set up, most of us seemed satisfied with them.

Suddenly we find justice is less just, social security seems less secure and even less social, and democracy gives the impression of no longer being very democratic. There are explanations for this within the systems themselves, and these explanations are also often in the news. But there are also explanations outside, including the relatively sudden shifts in the four pillars on which these systems were built: space, time, causality, and perception.

So where are ideas in all this? They were at the origin of the Internet, that's for sure. Teilhard de Chardin—as long ago as 1955—saw human individuality as an element and as a step towards the total meeting of minds. Moreover his "noosphere," a sphere of reflection or conscious invention, was the inspiration for Marshall McLuhan, who ten years later was to make the metaphor of the global village world-famous. The French Jesuit and the Canadian philosopher shared a techno-scientific optimism and a complete trust in science, also shared by many people today. Turning their back on humanism, techno-philosophers see men as a neuron in a globalized cortex, as they imagine the subject becoming lost in the structure. In this thesis, the unification of minds would continue; it's the Gaia hypothesis of a global brain and of a planet which thinks, of the barrier disappearing between matter and life, and machines becoming prostheses.

The laws of evolution would also link up with laws of the market; the result of this convergence would be cyberspace. The digital era would have all its qualities, and it would simply be a matter of letting things happen. Be patient and the Internet will be the finalization, the omega of human culture, the ideology to end ideologies. Technological blindness is so comforting.

Clearly this is not my position. To disseminate ideas is one thing, to have ideas is another. A fishing rod, a gearbox, and a photocopier don't have ideas. The Internet doesn't have ideas, either.

Copyright © www.cartoonbase.com

## KEY IDEAS IN THIS CHAPTER

- Frontiers are disappearing.
- Maybe it's better to leave things unfinished.
- You can't explain anymore why things happen.
- Creativity of the "how" is replaced by creativity of the "what."
- There is a new New Economy.

Even Aristotle would have been surprised by today's world. Aristotle said that all things are made of four elements or causes—material, formal, efficient, and final. A statue would be made of marble, in the shape of the emperor, with blows from the sculptor's chisel, for final presentation in the town square.

Since Aristotle's time, this pattern has held true. Look at the automobile, which Aristotle could hardly have imagined 2,500 years ago. The materials used—despite being high-tech composite materials and a mix of computer chips—do not negate the spirit in which Aristotle defined the material cause.

The form cause has also survived. The arrival of unions and assembly line production has not contradicted the Aristotelian idea of the efficient cause (which is not, may I remind you, a synonym for efficiency). The Greek philosopher would probably not even object to the efforts of a robot fulfilling the role of the third cause.

The final cause simply defies time. Just as the statue completes the acclaim of the great man or woman, the car does so for the customer in the same way. In fact, isn't it said that owners sometimes resemble their cars?

Yet for the first time, the world may have changed to the extent that Aristotle's observation about the four elements is no longer true. Computer hardware and in particular, software, for instance. In terms of the material, what is the importance of silicon or the laser today? Prices are dropping, and they may end up dropping to the point that we get our PCs free. The future is in software. Should we put the idea to Aristotle of an immaterial (intangible) cause?

What has become of form? Where is the added value in the on-screen graphics and the design of a laptop, or in the architecture of circuits and the structure of software? This all comes as cold comfort to Apple, which was never compensated for having the design of its Macintosh software stolen by competitors.

Third, where is the efficiency coming from? The manufacturer or the user?

The final cause is also hard to establish. The goal of the designer of a machine is to allow an unknown user to achieve his or her goals. The new versions of software are just updates addressing bugs found or wishes expressed by the final user (who is not actually final).

The model of Aristotle's four causes applied to computers reveals a confusion on the causes that may be definitive. Everything happens as if the third and fourth causes function in a loop, which Aristotle probably thought about but set aside in a second go-round for technical reasons—the absence of an Internet at the time?

It is even possible to envision a large-scale analogy. Cyberspace, which is so much in the news today, is made possible by the widespread use of digital networks in real time—where any action, even an incomplete one, causes a reaction. This force of retroaction, of feedback, seems to be the cause of the great mutations we are now experiencing. Perhaps the fifth cause?

Today the economic world really has no more time left. The emergence of digital networks makes McLuhan's vision concrete: the global village has replaced a planet full of local diversity. In the past, when a small business said it had a window of opportunity, it was imagined to be in space. Now, the windows of opportunity for small businesses are in time. But the consequences of this planetary wiring could be impressive. Several years ago Barings Bank, the venerable British institution, disappeared. A trader in Singapore who got increasingly entangled in major transactions broke the bank, something that was thought possible only in a casino.

As an explanation for this explosion/implosion, the analysts cited the Kobe earthquakes and the upheaval—in every sense of the term—it caused in the Japanese economy. But this is not enough—it is the *combination* of the catastrophe and the real time of finance networks that led this bank into the unstoppable loops of feedback, beyond human control. The situation was complicated by the vulnerability of software systems to deliberate cheating.

This incident illustrates the need for fresh reflections—25 centuries after Aristotle—on cause and effect.

By-products have always existed—Thales of Miletus sold options on his harvest—but the planet was not "relational" at the time. But are they useful in protecting yourself against the volatility of the market, or are they at the root of this very volatility? It will never be possible to answer this question. At least the ancient Greeks discovered that it was better to leave corn production (with its attendant risks of rats, weevils, ergot, and the like) to the Slavs and the Egyptians, and to concentrate instead on the production of olive oil and wine, both of which tend to be impervious to or improve with age.

The role played by the Kobe earthquake and the inversion of trends that followed can't explain everything either. It is a good idea to read how Voltaire speaks of the 1748 Lisbon earthquake and of the influence it had on Western thought. There are always earthquakes. Maybe what is missing today are philosophers.

A squirrel is hiding behind a tree. All you can see is its head, and it is looking at you. You want to see the animal a bit better so you move a quarter-turn round, in the arc of a circle. Inevitably the squirrel also moves 90 degrees and you find yourself back in the same situation. But you don't give up, and you pursue your circular route through three more quadrants—and there you are back at your starting point. Despite going all the way round, all you will have seen is the squirrel's head. Maybe you're disappointed, but as a reward for your efforts you have presented yourself with a superb philosophical question: have you gone around the squirrel? You've gone around the tree obviously. But have you circled the squirrel?

All the great writers and all the great texts must be put to the test of the present. The *Critique of Pure Reason* (1781), for example, a major work in which Immanuel Kant tried to answer the question of the potential of knowledge, seems as current as ever.

$$7 + 5 = 12$$

This equation, however elementary, is at the heart of one of his great questions. Does the fact that we obtain 12 actually add knowledge to the mind of the person who calculates it, or is this simply a reformulation of the 7 + 5 that already exists? To Kant the answer appears simple: the result of the addition, the 12, is a new piece of information that teaches us something, in the same way as physics or a chemistry experiment would, even if the information arrives *a posteriori* in this case.

Of course, Kant's argument has been contested since. Where would philosophy be if it didn't thrive on the constant disagreement of its greatest thinkers? Giants such as Bertrand Russell have stated that 7 + 5 = 12 is a proposition that provides no more knowledge than the claim that the diagonals of a square are the same length, because this definition stems immediately from the definition of a square.

Still, while we're at it, why don't we try and reconcile these antagonistic positions by proposing a third possibility! Looking from an IT point of view at this equation, which might appear simplistic at first sight, suggests that the result of the addition actually contains *less* information than the part on the left of the equals sign.

Indeed, the expression 7 + 5 contains, besides the result, 12, the path that leads to it. The 12 on the other hand, having emerged as the sole survivor of this arithmetical operation, no longer knows whether it is the product of 24 divided by 2, of 15 minus 3, or of any other equation. This little paradox at least has one merit, that of providing a critique of automatic reason.

# 3

# SEEING IS BELIEVING?

*"We don't know who first discovered water,*
*but we can be sure it was not a fish."*

**Marshall McLuhan**

In Chapter 2 we saw how today's world is changing faster than ever before, certainly faster than anything that Heraclites, Bacon, and even the Palo Alto founders saw in their times.

The paradox is that, while the world is changing faster than ever before, the human brain is pretty much the same old instrument it has been for hundreds and maybe thousands of years. That's too bad, because the brain is the only tool that lets us change our perceptions, and changing perceptions, as I have said, is how we get new ideas.

In this chapter I want to describe how the human brain is "hardwired" to think in a certain way. Then I will explain how this function extends to the "software" of the brain, which explains why we form stereotypes and paradigms, and cling so loyally to them—even in the face of evidence that proves them false.

We can easily prove from some simple examples that all of us tend to react to given visual stimuli in the same way. Well, almost all of us, since researchers have come across some strange communities that, due to their environment, grow up differently.

The left-hand arrow in the famous Muller-Lyer illusion (shown later in this chapter) is interpreted by most of us as if it were the corner of a room seen from inside. Yet African Zulus, used to living in round huts, are not subject to this illusion to the same extent. (The illusion is that the shaft of the arrow on the left looks longer than the one on the right, yet they're the same.)

Pygmies living in the heart of dense jungle, when transported to an open landscape, see distant objects as small and try to reach out to touch the horizon. The phenomenon inevitably also extends to conceptual things. Benjamin Lee Whorf, the American linguistics researcher, discovered that the Hopi Indian "has no general notion or intuition of time as a smooth flowing continuum in which everything in the universe proceeds at an equal rate, out of a future, through a present, into a past."

Indeed perception is linked with, and influenced by, culture. The American Indian vocabularies of Navaho and Taos, for example, have only one word for blue and green. The anthropologist Clyde Kluckhorn claimed that, "anyone who wants to understand the Navahos at all must know something about their language and the way it molds thought, interests, and attitudes." Another American anthropologist-linguist, Edward Sapir, declared, "The fact of the matter is that the 'real world' is to a large extent built up on the language habit of the group."

Back to our examples of visual stimuli. When not unduly influenced by culture or experience, all of us tend to respond in the same way. The first point is that it is impossible for us not to make patterns. The brain does it for us. Consider the images in Figure 3.1.

In (a), do you notice that your mind immediately sees a rectangle, although one doesn't exist? In (b), does your brain try to make the four dots into a neat box, although there isn't one there? In (c), does you see a white bar across the word *IDEA*—although there is no white bar?

FIGURE 3.1 *Visual Stimuli*

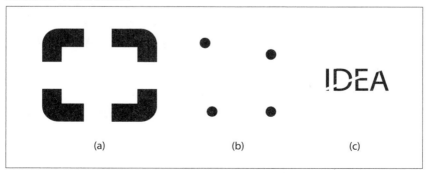

(a)          (b)          (c)

In each of these instances, the human brain is taking what amounts to a leap of faith. There's something deep in evolution behind all this. Perhaps it is that a human being, to survive, cannot always wait for all the lines to be connected.

The brain actively looks for patterns under various conditions. There are hundreds of laws governing perception, too complex to list in this book. But here are seven of the most important.

## I. The Law of Proximity

A first law is that of grouping by proximity. Elements considered to be close enough together are linked together in the same unit.

In Figure 3.2, the fact that the dots are close together in (a) encourages us to place them spontaneously in groups of two, rather than imagining two symmetrical structures containing three elements, or even three groups of four elements. The configuration in (b) can be seen in at least three different ways. We could see three horizontal rows that are staggered in relation to each other, a group of different series of points set in diagonal lines, or three parallelograms. It is proximity that makes us recognize the second possibility, the diagonal units.

## 2. The Law of Similarity

We can also associate elements displaying similar characteristics, and make groups based on similarity. This organizational principle often wins out when set against the first law. These two laws, far from being in opposition, are often complementary.

In Figure 3.3, (a) is seen as a line of columns, as the distinctive appearance of the dots is more persuasive than the distance that separates them. In (b), the same effect makes it easier for us to see horizontal rows.

FIGURE 3.2 *Association by Proximity*

FIGURE 3.3 *Association by Similarity*

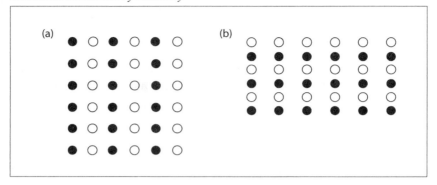

## 3. The Law of Common Fate

A third element that can have an impact on the way our perceptive units respond is movement. In the animal world, this law is everywhere. A camouflaged animal knows almost instinctively that it will only remain indistinguishable from its environment as long as it stays still—as soon as it moves, it will be detected.

In form recognition we also tend to associate elements, objects, or characteristics that are sometimes very different from each other but that are nevertheless to be found within the same "movement," even in the paradoxical situation of this movement being immobile! It is perhaps in this area that we get an insight into the way the constellations were born.

## 4. The Law of Continuity

Perceptive organization tends to prefer regular continuity to abrupt change by grouping together elements that in themselves are dissimilar, but which seem to "belong together" and form a type of continuity. The Law of Continuity reinforces the Law of Common Fate in this way. The principle of continuity makes us tend to link together the curved line in Figure 3.4, and, only then, to relate the result to the straight one.

## 5. The Law of Simplicity

One of the ways of explaining this phenomenon is to look at the need for simplicity, which is apparently within each of us. When differ-

FIGURE 3.4 *Continuity and Common Fate*

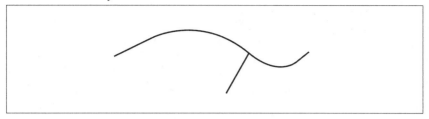

ent interpretations are possible, the first one to take shape in our mind is the simplest. In this way the image on the left in Figure 3.5 is perceived as a parallelopiped, a simple object in space, while the one on the right is seen as a design, a simple object in a plan.

It takes us a fair amount of observation time before we begin to see the left-hand form totally in the right-hand one, as one of the edges of the form (which we can't see anyway) appears to be missing.

If you ask a group of people which capital letter is represented by a figure that has been folded as in Figure 3.6, most of them will probably say L, whereas it could just as easily be the letter F upside down.

## 6. The Law of Orientation

This law can be subdivided into two basic principles: first, the smaller of two surfaces is generally perceived as being a figure on a larger background, and secondly, a figure which is positioned along vertical and/or horizontal axes is more easily perceived as the larger figure on a smaller background. It should be noted that the second type prevails over the first.

FIGURE 3.5 *Association by Simplicity*

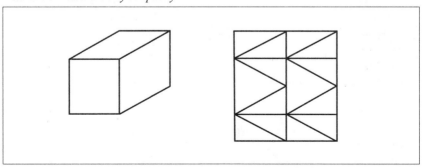

FIGURE 3.6 *Letter L or Letter F?*

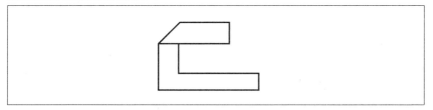

So in the left-hand image in Figure 3.7, the black surface, which is smaller than the white surface, is easier to see as a black rotor on a white background. If you turn it 45°, a larger white rotor appears on a black background.

## 7. The Law of Symmetry

According to the Law of Symmetry, the symmetry of the figure is the key element for the most spontaneous recognition of the form.

In Figure 3.8, the dots in (a) that are closer together appear to form a line, while the dot on the left does not appear to belong to this grouping, as it is so far away. The moment we add another dot in a symmetrical arrangement, (b), a new geometric shape appears, and there can be no argument about the fact that all the dots clearly form a part of it.

# THE GRAMMAR OF SEEING

In his book *Eye and Brain,* British neuropsychologist Richard Gregory asserts that perception is "a dynamic searching for the best interpretation of the available data. . . . The brain is in large part a probability computer, and our actions are based on the best bet in a given situation." As you can see from the above examples, your brain is constantly trying to make sense of the world, pulling disparate information in and searching for a pattern to it.

FIGURE 3.7 *Orientation and Background*

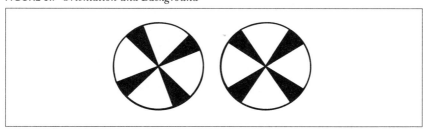

FIGURE 3.8 *Association by Symmetry*

(a)                              (b)

The brain obviously likes—and builds—coherent structures, forms, and unities. Psychologist Gaetano Kanizsa has christened the ability of humans to draw a pattern from disparate points *The Grammar of Seeing.* Some 100 laws governing how humans pull disparate shapes into patterns have now been established. The literature on the subject is vast.

Gestalt theory (*gestalt* means "form" in German), in fact, states that finding a new idea is about finding a new form. Finding an answer, meanwhile, is just like moving from one structure to another. It's a matter of reorganizing our field of perception.

Take a look at the lines in Figure 3.9.

While they are not connected you can see a lot of different things. The beginning of a map, a chair, a maze, or the letter H. And now that you see the H, you will probably not be able to make the figure revert to simply three unconnected lines. The same is true of an idea—there is something irreversible about it. There is always a before and an after.

Suppose I now add another line, as in Figure 3.10. Fans of the H theory will see this as a kind of vandalism.

But if you think it's a maze, you'll now be happy to see some progress in construction.

Reinterpreting these few laws of perception allows us to reduce them to a holistic principle of information theory. It represents the unique principle of being economical with the information, which drives us to recognize in any image the most regular, the simplest, the most symmetrical, or the most probable geometric structure.

FIGURE 3.9 *Gestalt*

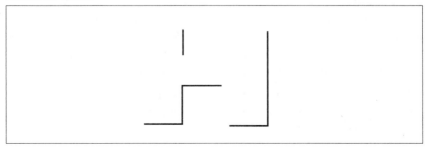

FIGURE 3.10 *Gestalt*

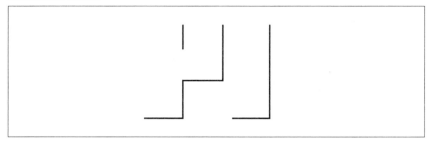

The study of the mechanics of perception is certainly not confined to the theory of form. Researchers have also been able to identify other phenomena.

Look at the black squares in Figure 3.11. Can you see the grey dots at the intersections? That's normal. Now look at one of the grey dots. Does it disappear as soon as you try to focus on it? That's normal, too.

We call these *optical illusions* and they are pretty common. It's not so obvious that the dots in the center of the drawings in Figure 3.12 are the same size.

Two thousand years ago the Greeks built curves into the columns of their temples to make them look straighter. Today, to make it clearer to drivers that a traffic circle is coming up, there's a sign with a broken ring. The step from optical illusion to paradox was made long ago.

Mapmakers are well aware of this. Imagine that you have to depict ten individual houses along a road. At a certain scale, the ten small black squares will be perceived as a continuous line. So the cartographer shows six distinct little black squares. These give the observer an impression closer to reality: by taking out four houses the mapmaker is doing a better job of hinting that there are ten individual houses in reality.

That's what these few pages are all about. Our way of seeing the world is governed by strange laws, which we have to know about. Behind all the figures we have shown lurks the reality of everyday life.

The black dots could be your clients, the broken lines could be products, the dotted curve could be your competitors. You could be influenced by a case of symmetry here or a case of simplicity there. It's no coincidence that creativity was once defined as being a revolution in seeing, or indeed as second sight. Today, competitive advantage can consist of being able to see something before anyone else, to observe faster, to be the first to be surprised.

FIGURE 3.11 *An Optical Illusion*

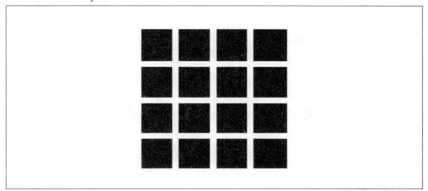

Look closely at Figure 3.13. At first sight, it's just a collection of black smudges. But stop for a while and give yourself the opportunity to take a second look. Try to construct a coherent whole.

Do you now see a cowboy on horseback, facing to the left? That's it.

Now that you can clearly see the rider, try not to see him again, and just see the collection of black smudges. In short, try to return to the state you were in just a few moments ago.[1]

What's the point of these exercises? It's simply this. There's a six-fold analogy between the construction of images of this sort and the construction of ideas.

1. You will never see the cowboy if you don't believe these kind of things exist.
2. They are difficult to find.
3. It's easier in a group.

FIGURE 3.12 *An Optical Illusion*

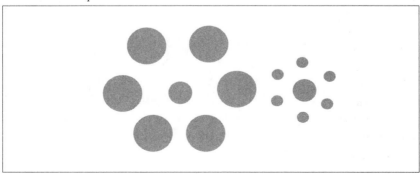

FIGURE 3.13 *Smudges*

4. They have an irreversible trait to them.
5. They appear all of a sudden.
6. And, finally, both the new image and the new idea are made up of elements that are not in themselves new.

Look how a plan for a holiday emerges. One day you see it clearly, when you couldn't see it the day before. In fact, you knew *a priori* all the components of the project. The new "idea" is simply the combination of the timing, the destination, the means of transport, and whom you're going to take with you.

Let's go into the metaphor in a bit more detail. Imagine now that those smudges represent your market, your customer base. The market has looked the same to you for years, so you have your own habits and ways of dealing with it.

Imagine now that your fiercest competitor suddenly sees the potential for a new image in your market. You know the rest of the story? Within months, you see your competitor come up with an idea that you are forced to acknowledge is brilliant. "But how did he think that up?" you ask yourself. It's quite simply because he saw something else.

Creating a new concept or looking at something differently are identical steps. The art of thinking is one of creating new forms. The effort required to see things differently is rather like grasping the 3D image in a stereogram, where you have to decouple your vision, staring at the image rather than focusing on a specific point (it helps to start close to it and move gradually back). The process is complicated by the fact that, as with a perception shift in everyday life, you don't know what you're looking for.

Isn't Plato's theory of ideas still called the Theory of Forms today?

If you show the smudge image to a smoker who is a Marlboro fan, he will probably see the cowboy instantly. This shows that part of our perception is programmed like a computer. Let's start with this first.

From the examples above, it is obvious that the brain jumps to conclusions. For the most part, the brain's compulsion to find the pattern and the coherency in random and scattered data is a good thing. In fact, it is the element that makes the Eureka! moment possible.

But at other times, the brain's persistence can inhibit our ability to find new ideas.

Thinking is about processing forms—small ones (*stereotypes*), medium-sized ones (*patterns*), or big ones (*paradigms*).

## STEREOTYPES

The word *stereotype* arose originally from the image of the printing press: *Type* refers to the letter character. *Stereos* in ancient Greek means solid. So a stereotype was a good thing—a useful device that withstood wear and tear.

In everyday life, stereotypes are important. In fact, we could not live or think without stereotypes. In the tumble of thoughts that flow through our minds, we need categories—labels—to simplify concepts that would otherwise stop us dead in our tracks. Like the steel rods that reinforce concrete, stereotypes structure the way we think. Without stereotypes, we would simply be incapable of thinking!

No wonder the brain skillfully condenses the word *Kansas* to a few simple symbols and the word *love* to a few pulsating thoughts. No wonder that all that is left of that memorable summer vacation a few years ago, or the novel we read several months ago, is an image or two. There's no way round it. The memory has faded away and, in so doing, has solidified. We can no longer change the way we now think about the place we visited or the book we read. It would require what physicists call a quantum leap to change that stereotype now.

Yet the same characteristics that animate stereotypes enfeeble them. That is why even the word *stereotype* has a negative connotation. It is cliché, hackneyed, stale, threadbare.

What are the characteristics of a stereotype?

- A stereotype is a judgment. It takes the form "A is B." It may be a factual judgment, such as "Ireland is a rainy country," or a value judgment, for example "Singapore Airlines is well run."
- A stereotype is reductive. It is no more than a few words strung together. There's no room for nuance, for details, or for exceptions.
- A stereotype is produced in a collective space. If it is not shared, it doesn't exist. A false idea is certainly a real fact, but it is also a fact of society.
- A stereotype endures. That is why it has negative connotations. It is very difficult to change or eliminate. Say *movie star, Texan,* or— heaven forbid—*management consultant* and a prefabricated image rises up. Most likely it is erroneous, because no single mental image covers all movie stars, Texans, or even management consultants.

So this is the problem with stereotypes. Our mind manufactures them continuously. We couldn't think without them. Yet they are mirrors that distort thought and cause intellectual illusion. We have to break them to think freely. Edison challenged the stereotype that, to produce light, you had to have fire. The key to his invention of the incandescent light bulb was to find a way of *preventing* the filament from burning.

In their most literal form, stereotypes are "packaged" encapsulations of perceptions that—rather like packet switching in telecommunications—simplify the processes of storing and transmitting ideas, and serve as common currency between people. Even if we claim to be politically correct, many of us still harbor ideas about people from other cultures that, at best, represent a very vague approximation of the reality and, moreover, brutally exclude all the exceptions contained within that culture.

In his famous book *We Europeans,* English interculturalist Richard Hill explains some of the attitudes and behaviors that underlie the creation of European stereotypes: "Such cultural mindsets, reflecting seminal attitudes and prejudices, have roots that go deep into a country's collective subconscious." He quotes a Sicilian proverb recorded by Francis Bacon (him again!) and others in the 17th century (by which time the Sicilians had had the opportunity to observe both the French and the Spanish as occupiers of their island): "The French are wiser than they seem, and the Spaniards seem wiser than they are." Five hundred years on, this clever and well-constructed stereotype still strikes home.

Stereotypes are, by definition, a step removed from reality. It is important that the person who uses them—and we all do—remembers that that is what they are and nothing more.

## PATTERNS

Patterns can be sinister: they're everywhere and sometimes, when they're not, our brains still make an effort to detect them! Suppose, for example, I ask you to rate the countries of the world in terms of their GNP. There's a fair chance you'll include Russia in the first ten, probably because you will start off by visualizing the sheer size of the country. Well, it's not! From the latest figures available, Russia comes 19th, after India, Australia, the Netherlands, and Brazil.

Suppose you are talking about the life expectancies of different animals (one of the examples cited in Roger Van Oech's book—see the Bibliography). As you probably know, the elephant lives to a relatively ripe old age (50+), whereas the mouse is lucky if it survives more than two years. There's a pattern there? The larger an animal, the longer it lives? Well, maybe. But even many of the smaller species of tortoises have an average life expectancy of over 50 years (some of the Galapagos species live to be nearly 200). So the pattern is unreliable. Yet it's extraordinary how important the principle of a pattern is in our own lives.

## PARADIGMS

Paradigms—which tend not to have the same negative connotations as stereotypes—are in fact, unfortunately, an even greater trap. Where a stereotype may catch us with a small and specific falsehood, a paradigm traps us in a larger and more significant one. *Paradigm*, in Greek, is παραδειγμα, meaning concept, model, or example. The word took on new strength in 1962, however, when the Austrian pundit Thomas S. Kuhn published *The Structure of Scientific Revolutions,* a book whose significance has continued to grow ever since.

According to Kuhn, the history of knowledge is not linear; learning does not take place in a continuous manner. Although researchers and scientists work within a given framework most of the time, occasionally they are no longer able to explain certain phenomena. They are faced with paradoxes, and cannot make any meaningful progress. That is when the time is ripe for defining a new context for thought. In two words—introduced by Kuhn—it is the moment of the *paradigm shift*.

Quite often, a new paradigm is catalyzed through the work of an exceptional individual. Geniuses from Newton, Lavoisier, and Darwin to Freud and Einstein have each, in a unique way, helped humanity pull itself out of a rut in which its thinking is getting stuck.

Other equally important paradigm shifts are not crystallized by one particularly striking figure or another. The spread of universal suffrage or the awareness of the limits of our ecosystem, for example, are also paradigms.

So applying the concept of paradigms to the economic system is not simply a temptation. It is absolutely self-evident to anyone who steps back a little, observes the vast changes occurring at the turn of this millennium, and recognizes the breaks and discontinuities in the world's evolution.

From the spread of telecommunications networks to the globalization of the market economy, to new ecological constraints, emerging political and monetary structures, the only recently recognized importance of the nonprofit sector, and the increasing role of the media—everything points to a profound transformation of the context of work, challenging every individual to define his or her personal strategy for change.

Paradigms, then, tend to limit us or blind us to the changes in the outside world.

# SEEING THE WORLD

We are building forms all the time we look at the world. We should beware, because this is also changing our perception of the world!

## Seeing versus Perceiving

The eye is not a perfect camera. Furthermore, it's the entire personality of the "cameraman" that gets in the way. Everything that he or she is—and has learned, seen, or experienced—adds distorting mirrors to his or her perception. As all of us have found, all we need to do is hear about a brand and, suddenly, we come across it in a shop where it's been sitting on the shelves for a long time.

It's enough to decide to buy a Renault and suddenly start seeing more and more of them on the roads. The day I learned I was about to become the father of twins, I suddenly realized the streets were full of two-seater pushchairs! If your back is hurting you, you'll be amazed to realize how many people share back problems. Those people who find you looking tired often do so because they think that they themselves look tired.

Because we don't see well—even when we've got perfect eyesight—our perception deforms things, foreshortens and fogs our view, leads us into errors. A full moon close to the horizon looks much bigger and follows us in the car, mirages appear in the desert, the train next to us moves off and we think our train is going backwards. It's not what we love that is beautiful, it's the fact that what we love is beautiful!

## Seeing versus Believing

Beyond the facts, one's convictions get caught up in the story too. The relation between the verbs *believe* and *see* is not a one-way affair. We believe what we see—that's for sure—but sometimes we see what we believe. If you believe that somebody is good, you see the goodness in him or her.

This is such a powerful mechanism that it can go as far as distorting the object. It's like a little girl who is pushing the jigsaw piece as hard as she can to get it into the puzzle. It's not the right one, but she's adamant in her belief that it is.

Edgard Morin gives a nice example in one of his most recent books. He was suddenly taken with an urgent need to answer a call of nature right in the center of Paris and was delighted to see a sign marked *urinoirs* (urinals) on the other side of the boulevard. He was brutally reminded of the laws on perception when he got to the other side of the street and saw that, in reality, the sign read *luminaires* (light fittings). I thought of him one day when I was cycling along a road with a lot of trucks thundering by. I was delighted, eventually, to see the sign for a cycle path. But when I got up to it, I realized it wasn't a pictogram of a bicycle, but the figure 100, denoting the distance I had traveled.

## Seeing versus Knowing

The relationship between the verbs *to see* and *to know* is also interesting.

An engineer will never tackle a problem in the same way as a lawyer, an accountant won't deal with a question the way a pianist will, whatever the problem or question may be. What we have experienced in the past forms the "axes" of our system for the future, and that's still the case! Despite the fact that we have known for 500 years that the earth revolves around the sun, we nevertheless continue to see the sun setting. This all goes to confirm the thesis of the neurobiologist Fodor, who insists that the various cerebral faculties do not communicate with each other.

To prove it, he often refers to optical illusions such as the Muller-Lyer one in Figure 3.14. Even if you *know* that the lines have the same lengths, you still *see* different lengths. Research has shown that the illusion works even with birds and fish!

## Seeing versus Hoping

Let's carry on because the verbs *to see* and *to hope* are also connected in a very strange way. We see and we believe what we want to be true much more easily.

As long ago as the 16th century Francis Bacon—yes, him again!—stated that people prefer to believe what they prefer to be true.

A weather forecast that announces good weather is on the way will be given more credence than one that announces the opposite. The sales of economic newspapers go up when the stock exchange does well. A reader spends much more time on the newspaper articles that he or she agrees with.

A long time ago in Delphi, the oracle worked exactly the same way. A traveler exhausted after a long journey would consult the oracle for the answer to a personal question, and the ambiguity of the answer would always allow the pilgrim to interpret it in his or her own way—and allow for the oracle to be right!

Enthusiasm for the Internet can easily be understood in this way. Whatever our point of view—entrepreneur, teacher, terrorist, anticolonialist, pensioner—the Internet gives many reasons for hoping.

FIGURE 3.14 *The Muller-Lyer Illusion*

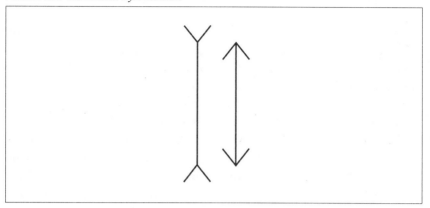

What conclusions should we draw from all this? *You don't see the world as it is, you see it as you are.* This sentence—which can be found in a number of works, including the Talmud—is a good way of expressing the issue: the way that man (the subject) looks at the world around him (the object).

## PERSEVERARE HUMANUM EST

Now perhaps you can see that the human brain, while trying to make coherence efficiently out of the chaos around us, oftentimes misleads us. We not only get false impressions, we often get boxed in by inaccurate stereotypes and paradigms. This is the paradox of our human "radar"—the ability to discern keenly, yet to be fooled at the same time. Let me explain.

It probably happens, from time to time, that you make a mistake. With hindsight you realize you have made the wrong decision, jumped to a conclusion too fast, overestimated one factor or underestimated another. You feel you've been trapped or wrongly informed, and you swear—but a little too late—that you'll never fall for that one again.

So from time to time you commit an error of appreciation, show a lack of judgment. But, so what? If it is human to err, then you can be sorry that you are human, just like the rest of us. Take Thomas Edison, for example, one of the most brilliant minds of the 19th century, an ideas factory, a veritable chain production unit for patents, the inventor of the lightbulb, as we have seen, and of the gramophone. Though he could bring perfection from the laboratory to the commercial production stage, he refused to believe in the advantages of alternating over direct current.

Even the great Albert Einstein made mistakes, though it was he who declared that knowledge was less important than imagination. Intelligence, if well informed, is worth double, which in his case was a considerable amount. Yet he nevertheless refused to move away from the form of physics that he had constructed. He always denied the probability dimension by stating loudly and clearly that God didn't play dice.

A third example is the physicist Heinrich Hertz, the discoverer of electromagnetic waves. One day someone suggested to him that he should use his invention to transmit messages from one point on the globe to another. He politely replied that it was not a bad idea, but that waves are propagated in a straight line, while the Earth is round. The "sweet dreamer" Alexandr Popov tried anyway and concluded that it *was* possible. It didn't occur to Hertz that electromagnetic waves would bounce back off the ozone layer.

If you sometimes happen to make a mistake, you are not the only one. In fact, you're in very good company.

While humanity is prone to forecasting catastrophes, it often appears in retrospect that it is the forecast itself that was, well, catastrophic.

*Errare humanum est.* But so is *perseverare.* On the other hand, *diabolicum est*—it's devilish—not to ask questions. How does it come about then that we make mistakes? Why do geniuses, large and small, skid off the road of reasoning, leave their logic-bound trajectory, and end up stuck in the mire of fatal obstinacy?

The answer seems to be the same for all of us. We can say, without any risk of making a mistake (!), that it is not a question of intelligence, but rather one of our perception of the world around us. The least reflection, the simplest act of reasoning, feeds on information reaching us through the senses, and it is apparently these that are sometimes unreliable.

We see and hear things in a variable way, and certainly differently from one another, because only the hardware is common to all of us. We can even become blind or deaf when confronted with some situations that will be glaringly or blaringly evident to others.

It is therefore hardly surprising that, from time to time, we do get stuck. We can't see clearly and seem to bump into things that should be obvious; we can't hear properly and we miss opportunities. So when, after making a mistake, we swear that we'll never let that happen again, we simply commit another error of judgment. For this is how human nature is made. *Perseverare humanum est.*

## THE PARADOX OF STRATEGIC VISION

Let's look at all this a bit more closely and listen to it a bit more attentively. Everyday life is a huge theatre full of optical and acoustic illusions.

We have to admit that sight and hearing don't work neutrally, constantly, and through 360°, like the radar on a yacht's mast. It seems much more that our senses are attracted or magnetized in line with our personal context. The speed with which we find our name on a list, spot a familiar face, or recognize a voice in a crowd: these are all demonstrations of our senses' total lack of objectivity. Our eyes see what they want to see; our ears hear what it's nice to hear; and the worst type of deaf person is the one who only wants to hear one thing.

Everything seems to converge towards one obvious conclusion: We perceive the world in a particular, individual way. Every preconceived idea, every stereotype, every prejudice is like a pair of spectacles with deforming lenses or like directional loudspeakers. They make us short-sighted or hard of hearing.

Someone we don't like needs only to open his mouth and we find his idea uninteresting. On the other hand, a bank with an efficient head office has a head start over the others when it comes to attracting our savings. In the same way, figures which are well presented seem better. They're all optical and acoustic illusions.

Even more worrying is the fact that every long-term strategy, every successful achievement, every breakthrough that wins recognition changes the way we see things, too.

The consequences of all this are immediate, instant, and irreversible now, today, for your company. There is a name for this type of danger; it's called the paradox of strategic vision.

We should look at this right away, as it concerns us all. A vision of things is indispensable for every project and for every strategy, whether it's individual or collective. But this vision is also the thing that hinders us in seeing what could prove essential for the future.

A word of explanation. These same mechanics can be found at every level of endeavor, for even a strategist is a human being with a laudable ambition to succeed and a perfectly understandable hope of well-being. He therefore seeks to comfort his vision of things, to complete the 'form' that he has built for himself *a priori* (remember the letter H?), especially if this has proved to be a good one, rather than call into question the assembly of ideas and rules which have standardized his thinking. Sometimes this vision will act like a filter, at other times like a prism.

You'll recognize this yourself. When a daily newspaper looks into a controversial subject like motorway speed limits and, in the interests of objectivity, invites two guest contributors to defend opposite sides of the argument, are you not subconsciously attracted to the texts that you are going to agree with *a priori*? Be honest here: do you read the other contribution right to the end?

A comparable phenomenon can be seen in the boss of a company or organization. In 1977 Ken Olsen, at that time CEO of Digital Equipment, stated that, "there is no reason that people should one day have a computer at home." This declaration, made at a congress of the World Future Organization, is a good illustration of the dangers that can lie in wait for a leader. Ken Olsen had heard the news that some students were trying to put together the first personal computer, but he didn't find this significant, quite simply because it didn't fit his personal conceptions of IT. These conceptions had already led him from success to success for over twenty years. Men like Ken Olsen use the "cut-out" method of working. Such people, for example, when leafing through a magazine, would apply one of two options: either tear out pages for later reference or throw them away. This summary treatment was based on their own vision of what was important and not on the intrinsic value of the information.

We all know the law of conservation of energy. Perhaps we ought to pay a little more attention to the law of conservation of laws (inertia is indeed a force!).

Abraham Maslow once said, "When the only thing you have to hand is a hammer, it is very tempting to treat things as though they are nails." When we consider the power of some of the tools that certain leaders have at their disposal, we can understand the difficulty they have in liberating themselves from the clutches of the paradox of strategic vision. Escaping from it without contributing a solution. Because you can never resolve a paradox—you can only reframe it.

Indeed, everything happens as if ideas have their own gravity, as if reasoning has weight, and as if information has polarity, taking on a positive or a negative charge according to how it suits us personally, according to what we want or don't want.

If an opinion poll produces negative results for a politician, he or she will question the reliability of the institute that carried out the poll. If, on the other hand, the results are good, the politician won't think of challenging the seriousness of the study, but will quote his or her rising ratings at every opportunity.

The same goes for companies. Negative figures published by an accounts department will cast doubt on the competence of the people who set up the system, while results that are better than expected will remove any lingering doubts about the usefulness or the quality of the system.

We cannot live without a vision of the world, a conception of things, a representation of our environment. In fact, we can't do without it, if we are to achieve any major objectives. But be careful. There are two sides to every coin, even when it is a well-thought-through strategy.

Advertising makes great use of the phenomenon of interpretation. Advertisers often play on the various ways people will interpret images or slogans to appeal to a wider range of audiences. This filter has always operated, at all levels. The more successful an approach proves itself to be, the greater the role played by the filter.

A company CEO made an appointment with her CFO so that they could go together to visit a difficult client. The time to leave for the meeting came and went, and still no CFO (who was usually as punctual in his timekeeping as he was accurate in his bookkeeping). Partly as a way of killing time, and partly to soothe her nerves, the CEO switched on the radio.

"Gridlock in town. . . ." came over the airwaves. These circumstances forced her into taking a more philosophical view of events, so she took out some work and started to read. In fact, though, the CEO had actually made the appointment for another place, where—punctual as ever—her colleague was waiting for her. What had happened?

Once again, that devilish "filter" raises its head. The information the CEO heard on the radio had taken on too much importance, because it didn't challenge her conception of things at that moment. On any other day, that particular piece of information would probably have gone in one ear and out the other.

**FIGURE 3.15** *The Paradox of Strategic Vision*

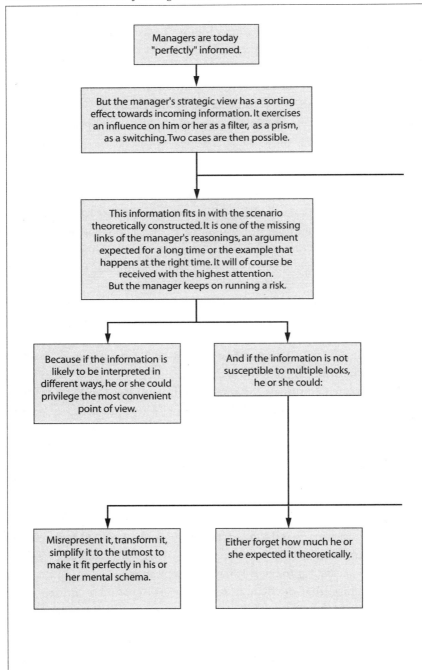

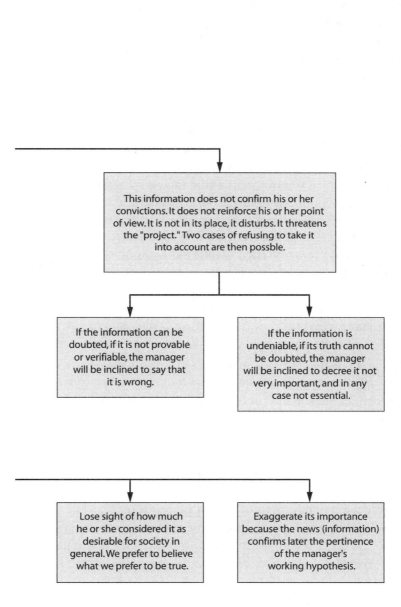

This information does not confirm his or her convictions. It does not reinforce his or her point of view. It is not in its place, it disturbs. It threatens the "project." Two cases of refusing to take it into account are then possble.

If the information can be doubted, if it is not provable or verifiable, the manager will be inclined to say that it is wrong.

If the information is undeniable, if its truth cannot be doubted, the manager will be inclined to decree it not very important, and in any case not essential.

Lose sight of how much he or she considered it as desirable for society in general. We prefer to believe what we prefer to be true.

Exaggerate its importance because the news (information) confirms later the pertinence of the manager's working hypothesis.

A lot of bad decisions are not due to a lack of information, but rather to the way our mind works!

A final example. When an author is on the verge of completing a book, as is my case now, and has spent an enormous amount of time assembling the index, do you think he is capable of hearing a new piece of information that may force him to reorganize his book? No!

All these examples have their place on a chart, laid out like a (good or bad) decision-tree.

We deal with our convictions as though they are material goods. We inherit them, we adopt them, protect them and keep them in good working order. Our schemes of thought—and in particular the cause-effect relationship—are like steel reinforcement rods. They strengthen and above all increase the resistance of all the personal concrete made of stereotypes, *a priori,* inhibitions, rites, and customs. Our value systems are at risk from dogma, routine, mania, and taboos we scarcely understand.

Ah, perception! One day an executive from a multinational tendered his resignation for a very simple reason: Fed up with living to the rhythm of quarters and the figures that are inextricably linked to them, he decided to live to the rhythm of the seasons. It's the same difference between a boss who says "I decide" and a boss who says "I choose." It's the same, but it's not the same.

Calling an office table a "hardware support" sometimes allows us to switch budgets and move from the furniture budget line to the IT line, therefore enabling us to get a new table.

Finally, think how we can all see ourselves in our horoscope (in fact it doesn't matter much which sign we look at!) and consider the extent to which an author can, in totally good faith, feel he or she has been cheated and plagiarized by another author.

## KEY IDEAS IN THIS CHAPTER

- There are hundreds of laws of perception.
- Some are "hardware," but most of them are "software."
- You don't see the world like it is; you see the world like you are.
- We think only with forms: stereotypes, patterns, and paradigms.
- A lot of bad decisions are not due to a lack of information, but rather to the way our minds work.

Because stereotypes are often slightly (or extremely) askew from reality, they often work their way into jokes. One goes like this: A European asks a colleague to describe his idea of heaven. The man thinks for a moment and says, "Heaven is a place where the British are the policemen, the French the cooks, the Germans the mechanics, the Italians the lovers, and it's all organized by the Swiss!"

Content with this answer, the European then asks his colleague for his idea of a European hell. The latter considers this momentarily and replies, "Hell is where the British are the cooks, the French the mechanics, the Germans the policemen, the Swiss the lovers, and it's all organized by the Italians!"

This is particularly unfair on the Italians because, when they really care about something, they are better organizers than anyone else.

## *T*he *W*orld *of* *F*orms

### Stereotypes, patterns, and paradigms

| | | |
|---|---|---|
| rumor | belief | rite |
| prejudice | model | principle |
| theory | methodology | constraint |
| standard | reference axes | popular know-how |
| protocol | convention | habit |
| doctrine | hypothesis | tradition |
| dogma | a priori | custom |
| ideology | mania | taboo |
| norm | routine | experience |
| expertise | common sense | myth |
| value system | | |

These forms may be positive, negative, or neutral, large or small.

Courtesy of Larry Gonick

# 4

# SURVIVING THE SUCCESS

*"I love work. I can watch somebody working for hours."*

**Tristan Bernard**

**P**art of my job is to think about the future with the people I'm working with, and I'm constantly surprised to see how many journalists and even writers focus on the past—and then reach the conclusion that almost everything is finished. In recent years we have seen a continuous stream of stories predicting that the end is near. At the very moment of sending this book off to the publisher, I have the 2004 Christmas issue of *The Economist* in front of me with a cover story on "The End of the World"! In this case, for once, the publication has its editorial tongue in its cheek.

It all started in 1992 with Francis Fukuyama's book *The End of History*. According to him, democracy and market economy are the final steps of a long journey. There we are, nothing can be better and that's it. But the title set the tone. One of the articles in the 1996 100th anniversary edition of *The Economist,* "The End of the Telephone," put into perspective the incredible value added of joining up networks, and the waste of telephones used only for telephoning. The "end of distance" in a sense.

In May 1999, the same publication had "The End of Private Life" on the front page, and in April 2004, "The End of Cheap Money." And now "The End of the World." There's no end to "The End"!

About the same time, the very French *Challenges,* an economics magazine published by the Nouvel Observateur group, devoted an editorial to "The End of Minitel." Squeezed between television on the one hand and the PC screen on the other, there was no longer room for the little black and white screen that, in its millions, had earlier launched French telematics into orbit.

Switching continents doesn't seem to change points of view. The magazine *Wired,* the plugged-in monthly for the wired-up reader, announced "The End of Products." In a long interview, Alvin Toffler, the futurologist who has been predicting for some time that the past is definitively past, judged that "mass production" has given way to "mass service."

That's not all. Still in the same period, the French *Futuribles* devoted a long article to "The End of Territories" and "The End of the Nation State." In today's game, open to global competition, the ethnic demands of smaller groups in search of their own identity confront nations facing the possibility of fragmentation, challenge social groups with the threat of being uprooted, and in some places are encouraging the emergence of region-states and even city-states.

Since then, there has of course been *The End of Work,* announced by Jeremy Rifkin, and *The End of Money,* forecast by Joël Kurtzman. According to the latter, currency circulates so fast that it doesn't exist, and real profits are today located around the traditional accountancy system, in a series of budget commitments that are partially measurements and based on mathematical formulas that their users don't entirely understand! There's a lot about that is rather disorienting—but don't worry, because the widespread use of GPS (Global Positioning System) means the "end of the compass"!

In May 2004, the American *Newsweek* emblazoned its front page with "The End of Europe" (what?) and, three weeks later, with "The Death of the Bistro," maybe feeling that you could have too much of a good thing. In August 2004, *Forbes,* not to be outdone, ran a cover story titled "The End of Power." Maybe . . .

The list of *The End of . . .* could go on for some time. Who's going to write "The End of Writing," a thesis that will study the impact of word processing on style and on literature in general? Or "The End of Holdups," a study that will show that computer-based crime offers opportunities that are in a totally different league from mere armed raids? Or

"The End of Film," a description of the project that links all the cinema screens across the world to broadcast a menu of the latest Hollywood productions. Or "The End of Counters," an analysis of the changes going on in all public administrations under the influence of more and more networks? Then the end of the blackboard, the end of medical diagnosis, the end of author's rights, the end of brands, . . . ?

There is also a need for a little pamphlet, "The End of Politeness," when you see your e-mail invaded by advertising, or a guest to a dinner party getting out a mobile phone in the middle of the meal.

It's obvious today that IT is changing everything, including Information Technology! We could also write "The End of Programming," given the number of tools that are available today. In fact, somebody just published *The End of Software*.

Does all this make you laugh? Yet, even the most serious journalists are today using the rearview mirror as a forecasting tool.

*Scientific American* gave the title "The End of Proof" to an article dealing with the demonstration of Fermat's theorem. For three centuries, mathematicians have been wanting to demonstrate that the equation $X^n + Y^n = Z^n$ had no solution for n higher than two. (In other words, no cube is the sum of two cubes, and so on.) A researcher presented a computer-assisted demonstration that was so long that today certain doubts remain as to its rigor—that's a great paradox for you!

In any case, *The End of Science* is coming soon, according to John Horgan[1]. And at the last count there were more than 6,000 references including *The End of* on Amazon.com. Who's going to write a book called *The End of Amazon,* I wonder?

In 2000, to celebrate the Millennium, a team from an international management consultancy (not my own) came out with a book called *The End of Change*! That could make life a lot easier, but, believe me, it's not going to happen.

We should be amazed at these expressions from the past we use to tell ourselves that the past is finished. Anything in fact is grist to creativity's mill. Grist? Mill? It must be several centuries now that the expression has been used to mean the capacity to jump at any opportunity. It's precisely because the expression hasn't changed that we can see the extent to which everything else changes.

Hundreds of examples, you will agree, could help fuel this thesis on the dynamics of language.

The systems approach can benefit hugely from this archaeo-literary view. It can demonstrate, for example, that health has a price, or that the traditional accountancy of companies sometimes reflects extremely large financial flows very badly. It shows that somebody who wants to go farther will sometimes have to dismount, that large projects require large sacrifices. And the different systems of Social Security sometimes give the impression that someone who risks nothing wins everything! Is it any wonder that we are seeing a decline in innovation and enterprise?

Today, all that ends well isn't necessarily *that* well, because the rest of the world doesn't stop inventing, and time doesn't necessarily heal all wounds. Sometimes you have to change a winning team. No news can means bad news, and the next time you refer to something as being "child's play," take a closer look at what your kids are playing with!

However, certain proverbs bear up well to today's complexity. If troubles never come singly, it's because of feedback. As we all say, he who sows the wind will reap the whirlwind. This is all because of the recently discovered Chaos Theory. If no man is a prophet in his own country, it's because his home country is a closed system.

There's a silent conspiracy going on to encourage us to go on doing things the way we've always done them. It can be summed up in its most elementary form as the "if your only tool is a hammer, everything looks like a nail" syndrome. Thomas Edison, quoting the English painter Joshua Reynolds, said, "There is no expedient to which a man will not resort to avoid the real labor of thinking."

Oftentimes, you just need to stick your head out of your shell and look around. It's funny how few people do this. I was recently in downtown Boston when I noticed that one store, which used to be open 24 hours, had cut back its hours so that it was closed at night. That didn't seem significant until down the street I found another store that had cut back on its hours. Suddenly a lightbulb went on in my head. Something negative was happening to the retail market in downtown Boston. I don't know what it is (or was) but I sensed something in the air.

These are the kinds of warning signals we need to be sensitive to. Think of the most recent space shuttle tragedy. How many warnings were there that the heat-resistant tiles might pose a problem? There were a lot of these warnings, yet they never made their way into procedures that could have prevented the crash.

FIGURE 4.1 *Weak Signals*

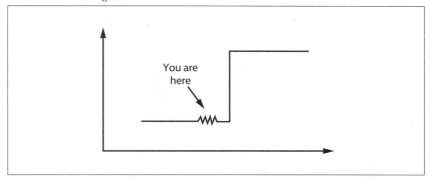

Rather than an "End of" mentality, we need a "Beginning of" attitude. We have to be ready to respond to the early signals, the beginning of the beginning.

## EARLY WARNINGS

In the spring of 1883, some sailors who were navigating between the Indonesian Islands of Java and Sumatra noticed a peculiarly smooth, rolling wave action that was unfamiliar to them. Casting their eyes toward the uninhabited volcanic island in the distance, they remarked that white clouds of smoke were rising from the lush green vegetation. No one was unusually alarmed, however.

Then the warning signals became more acute: pumice and ash started to spew, and there were hints of slight, earthquake-like tremors. Some of the ships left the area, others didn't. On August 27, the volcanic island—Krakatoa—exploded with the force of a hundred nuclear bombs, launching a tsunami wave 135 feet high against the coast of Japan and sending dust into the atmosphere that turned the sunset blood-red for a year.

In most cases, nature sends out warning signals when a big change is coming. The problem is that most people tend to ignore them, or at least respond so slowly that they are caught off balance.

Bacon, again, said 500 years ago that there were four reasons why people continually withdraw from an active exploration of change. He described them as false gods, or idols, that affect us with the same strength as truth:

1. The tribal idols (*idola tribus*) issue from human nature. They distort knowledge in different ways: they overrate the familiar, look for the *why* rather than the *how*, place ideas lower down the scale than passions, limit the senses, and have a tendency to be abstract too hastily.
2. The idols of the cave (*idola specus*) can be traced back to individual nature (what we would today call psychology). They are born of upbringing, habits, and events during our lifetime. They are what make us generalize a particular method of explanation to the bitter end, adopt stereotypes, press us into analysis or synthesis, and lead us to make the most of the past, or alternatively of things that are new. In short, these are our preferences when it comes to thought.
3. The idols of public places (*idola fori*) come from society. They pollute language by causing words and things to become confused and giving ambivalent meanings to words. In this respect, Bacon notes that mathematicians manage to escape from these idols, but that we cannot avoid resorting to them when attempting to define natural realities. Meanwhile the renovator of science, who makes the case for improving the use of mathematics, already brings the qualitative and syllogistic physics of Aristotle into discredit.
4. The idols of the theatre (*idola theatri*) can be traced back to the defective rules and theories of demonstration accepted merely by virtue of the authority of the author. Today we would say that these are the idols of fashionable theories and politically correct thinking with which everyone agrees.

What is true of individuals everywhere remains true when the same people interrelate in the corporate world. There are times when a company begins to realize that the stereotypes, concepts, and paradigms on which it is based are beginning to age—and not gracefully. In some cases, the paradigms are completely obsolete.

The bigger the company, the greater the tendency to sweep these rumblings under the rug. Any catalog of bygone companies—former greats like Pan Am, ITT, or the present stumbling giants like AT&T, Kmart, and many of the major airlines—reveals a common predicament: They failed to climb out of their outmoded concepts, paradigms, and stereotypes before the floorboards gave in.

How certain were the major airlines of the 1960s and 1970s—Pan Am, Eastern, Braniff, among others—that the regulated airline industry would always be there to provide a safe economic harbor for them? How certain were the major airlines in the 1980s—Delta, United, American, and others—that the upstart low-budget airlines would not invade too much of their space? How certain were the airlines at the end of the 1990s, in fact, that passenger volume would continue upward without any significant interruptions? They were certainly subscribing to Parmenides' theory of permanence, not Heraclites' theory of change.

Part of the reason that people and companies don't anticipate or even respond to change is that, while the world is changing continuously, the perception of such change can only happen from time to time. We don't see the warning signs, or at least we are not aware what these signs imply.

So what are these "weak signals" that indicate a mismatch between our assumptions and the real world? What are those little pieces of information that can save you and your business, if you take them into account? There are at least five situations you should watch out for:

1. *Minor defects.* If customers start complaining about a product, the manufacturer is in much the same situation as the 17th century German astronomer Johannes Kepler when people challenged his theory of the laws of planetary motion. Everyone thought the earth orbited the sun in a perfect circle, but Kepler's calculations showed that this was not precisely the case. If they were right, his observations and theory were wrong. Our manufacturer has the same problem with customers who complain about a defect, however minor. Rather than suggesting that they are a bunch of difficult so-and-so's, he would do well to listen to them. They may be trying to help. After all, the customer is always right. As it happens, in this case, Kepler was right. The earth circles the sun in an ellipse.

2. *Dissonance.* EuroDisney was dissonant in the ears of many Europeans. European efforts, meanwhile, to install pro soccer in the

United States also struck a sour note. When dissonance can be heard, it's generally a warning of failure ahead. It can happen when a franchiser imposes too strict rules on his franchisees: Mc-Donalds learned the hard way that its famous arches were too much for some particularly civic-minded administrations.

3. *Serendipity.* Some of the greatest discoveries in mankind would have gone unheeded but for the alertness of certain individuals. With the help of a photographic plate accidentally placed near a source of radiation, the ever-curious Marie Curie discovered radium. Dr. Plunkett of DuPont stumbled across Teflon when gas he stored in a cylinder solidified over night; he had to cut the cylinder open next day with a hacksaw to reveal its secret! The bubble jet technology used in inkjet printers was discovered by a Canon researcher when he unintentionally touched an ink-filled syringe with a hot soldering iron, causing an air bubble to form and eject the ink.

4. *Paradox.* The 16th century French chemist Antoine Lavoisier set out to challenge the "phlogiston" principle, according to which the combustion of an object results in a loss of weight. Lavoisier sensed the inherent paradox in the theory and, using an empirical approach, proved that some products weighed more than the original, thus disproving the theory. Another example of paradox is provided by America's steel industry, which by the early 1960s had reached its apex, accounting for more than half of the world's total steel production. A mere ten years later, Big Steel was in big trouble. The problem was that the American steel industry, fat and happy, had misjudged the changes underway in steel production worldwide. Big Steel could have adopted any or all of these new changes, but it didn't. When Asian and European steel makers invested in Basic Oxygen Furnaces, which could heat steel in one-sixth the time of U.S. Steel's open-hearth furnace, Big Steel stayed with open hearth. When word came that the Japanese and Germans were pioneering a radical technology called continuous casting, which vastly reduced the costs of making steel ingots, Big Steel didn't budge. Then when Nucor, a start-up company in Birmingham, Alabama, developed an audacious "minimill" that made steel products at a fraction of the cost of Big Steel and started nibbling away its markets, Big Steel—blinded

by its conviction of economies of scale—laughed off the challenger as a preposterous pipsqueak, not realizing that the paradox of small size and greater efficiency could be a reality. In the end the Japanese, the Germans, and Nucor's minimills defeated Big Steel. The mighty American industry, which had lit up the valleys of Pennsylvania for a century with its red glow, virtually collapsed. "What the steel industry did over the period of the late '60s and the '70s was rely too much on history," recalled one steel executive. "There were quarters where you would lose money or make damn little for what you had invested. But it was always, 'It will turn around. Just don't tinker with the toy'."

5. *Boredom.* When a concept or idea that was once bright and shiny begins to lose some of its glow, when the concept slowly becomes worn out, boredom sets in. World Fairs, for instance, were once the grandest events on earth. The Chicago World's Fair and the St. Louis Fair, the Paris Fair, even the New York World's Fair of the 1960s were hits. So what happened to the Hanover, Germany, and Lisbon, Portugal, fairs of the 1990s? They flopped. The fairs were just as good, but the world had tired of World Fairs. This happens all the time. The Lego block—once called the toy of the 20th century—is the same little cube of plastic that it was years ago when Lego sold hundreds of millions of them to little kids. The Lego block may be the same, but the kids are different now. They want Game Boys and action heroes—and Lego had no real answer! It's paradoxical but, if everything seems to be going too well, you need to be extra careful. Because, if nothing special is happening and there are not even any weak signals around, that itself should be a warning sign!

These five types of weak signals/warning signs have one thing in common. People tend to disregard them, to treat them as irrelevant (see the paradox of strategic vision in Chapter 3). They will have doubts about the instrument used rather than about the theory behind it. They will ask Kepler to double-check his night observations of the sky, not question Copernicus's principles that are challenged by these observations. That's how we miss opportunities and make mistakes.

Recently it was discovered that many stomach ulcers are not caused by stress or spicy foods (as the medical community had insisted for years) but by bacteria, a condition that can be cured with antibiotics. This theory was only proven when a brave young doctor from New Zealand by the name of Barry J. Marshall injected himself with the stomach bacteria and then took antibiotics to cure his condition. Even then, in 1984, the medical profession took several years to acknowledge that it had been wrong.

In the business world, theories that we thought to be true are very often found to be false. One of the big theories of the New Economy, for instance, was that first movers would always capture the market. That turned out to be untrue. Another was that market share was all that counted—don't worry about profits. That turned out to be false as well, and turned many dot-coms into "dot-bombs."

Be open, watch all those weak signals happening around you. Pay attention to all those little defects, strange dissonances, tiny paradoxes, curious accidents, and unexpected hints of boredom. I'm sure that now you can see them around you. Don't think they're unimportant. So many articles titled "The End of . . ." must be a warning sign!

## THE BREAKS

The future of a company is often thought of in incremental terms— a bit more of the same thing. A bit more efficient, a bit faster, a bit better looking, a bit more sophisticated. This is all very good, and suggestions are always welcome!

But I believe you are convinced there is one part of the future of this company that is not covered by continuity. One element of what is to come will be the result of something else—a *break* with its own existence.

There are breaks that we choose, and there are breaks that we are subjected to. Breaks we want and breaks that we put off. But, one day or another, there will have to be a break in the path to growth.

These future breaks are silently taking shape, and a quick glance at the past enables us to measure how great the variety of these breaks may be. We could also place these breaks in different categories, resulting from situations that are different too.

IT professionals of my generation will remember that, if you wanted to produce a table of figures on the IBM 360, you had to write a program—lines and lines of specifications in which all the parameters of the table were set out in advance. When the first spreadsheet appeared—it was called VisiCalc if my memory serves me right—it had the same effect on us as an earthquake.

What a shock! You could produce a table by building a table! People who had their noses stuck in their keyboards had forgotten this. This first type of break consists of going back to one's roots, the homeland of the original idea. We will therefore call this (we are, after all, talking about computers) going back to BASIC.

There was the same feeling about the development of Apple Computers. First there was the Apple II, which set the scene for the home computer.[2] More notably, ten years later, came the appearance of the Macintosh and its amazing graphic interface. Amazing? Yes and no. What it does most of all is remind us that the number 1 work aid is the desk, with files and a trashcan.

Sometimes things are simpler, and going back to basics happens of itself. The Rubik's Cube—significantly the work of a Hungarian, a remarkably creative race—was invented in 1974. Over 250 million Rubik's Cubes were sold in the early 1980s, and it came back in vogue with the following generation. Not many commercial products enjoy this privilege of relaunching without any modifications. Even the scooter only came back after a pretty major overhaul—and a gap of some 30 years.

Another way of making a break with what exists consists of changing the rules of the game. Low-fare airlines are a good example. Why have different types of airplane? Why sell tickets through networks of agencies? Why use only the main—and therefore expensive—airports?

This example is a good way of showing that certain decisions can be taken independently of the world around us. It's not an external event that suddenly means we only keep one type of plane. On the other hand, other rules can only be broken if something new appears outside the company. It was the Internet that made it possible to short-circuit the travel agent.

In all such cases, changing the paradigm means we have to reject all the old hypotheses set in the "quick-drying concrete" of the way we work. This is what Polaroid did: why wait hours—or even days—for that photo we just took? It's now a dated example, but history has since repeated itself with the arrival of digital photography.

This second type of break reminds us of what physicists call a quantum leap. I call it the Fosbury flop.

Areas of activity often have fences around the outside. Rupture for rupture's sake. But why not cut through the barbed wire of the way we work? Why not feel our way around the side of the way we work? It's like the big IT companies that start in consultancy, or Caterpillar and Michelin in the shoe business, or Amazon.com, which decides to market its own search engine.

Sometimes the grass really is greener on the other side of the fence. That's what the millions of cows supplying Danone will tell you, at least. In the beginning was BSN, a glass manufacturer that moved away from its original business of containers to focus on content. It moved from the yogurt jar to the yogurt in the jar, and abandoned other forms of packaging in favor of what was being packaged.

This third type of break is the one practiced by *managers sans frontières,* the nomads of the investment world, and we'll refer to it as the "prairie next door."

This prairie might be a mountain pasture. The Compagnie des Alpes, the world leader in the winter sports sector (Tignes, les Arcs), is moving into other seasons. It wants to be involved all year through in family entertainment and has acquired the Astérix amusement park, the Grévin wax museum, and "France Miniature."

While we're at it, why do we not simply just go somewhere else, very far away, to see if we can't find the future there.

There's no amicable way of parting with one's habits. We have to break off the relationship. Maybe it's because the way we dress is closely linked to our habits that Luciano Benetton decided to look elsewhere and make huge investments in the highway business.

In any case it seems that this is the age of musical chairs when it comes to breaks! Bouygues, the king of the French motorways, has started to invest heavily in telecommunications (television and mobile telephony). And isn't Coca-Cola moving into online music sales? Starbucks, meanwhile, has gone into the music business as an extension of the Starbucks "experience."

This fourth type of break has meant that the German steel giant Preussag is now a leader in the tourism sector. That sounds like a leap into the Great Unknown!

A break can sometimes be the result of a new link between two distant worlds. As we shall see in Chapter 6, this is where we find Arthur

Koestler's "bissociation." Inventing, he would say, most often means combining in a new way the things that are said the most frequently.

When Philips teams up with other companies to develop new products, the public—which likes genuinely new ideas—is struck by the bissociation. Examples are the joint venture with Nivea (Beiersdorf) to launch a new type of shaver with built-in shaving cream; with Douwe Egberts (Sarah Lee) to launch Senseo, a new type of coffee machine; and with Inbev—the merged Interbrew (Belgium) and Ambev (Brazil) companies—to market the Columbus home beer dispensing unit.

Philips even has a corporate alliance department to make this approach more systematic. It has the right to be proud: Senseo has become an incredible success. Philips had previously been watching its sales of coffee machines freefall, and Douwe Egberts was not enthused by the way its coffee sales were developing. But that's no reason for them to rest on their laurels! A court hearing in 2004 gave Sarah Lee's competitors the right to sell coffee refill pads for the Senseo.

This fifth type of break often causes tension between two cultures that are sometimes very far apart. This requires a great deal of energy—let's call it the electric arc!

These examples are all the result of companies that have been able to make a break with what exists. That leaves one more case to deal with: the case where there was nothing! When an idea sprouts outside any existing structure or tradition, a bit like a rumor. We don't really know how, or why. Let's call this SARS: Special Awareness for Real Surprises.

The textbook example is Linux, the free software discussed in Chapter 2.

Clearly, this sixth type of break is of a different kind. It even poses the fundamental question: Is a company capable of the break that is needed, or even vital? Could Microsoft have considered launching Linux? There are grounds for thinking not. It's not the public radio that invented independent radio stations, or the post office that invented faxes and UPS, and it's not local movie theaters that invented the video recorder.

But there too, there is a way of differentiating the manager from the strategist: the former manages continuity, the latter deals with discontinuity.

# KEY IDEAS IN THIS CHAPTER

- Try to escape the "end of" syndrome.
- The world is changing, not the way we think.
- Beware the different types of weak signals.
- A part of the future is not covered by continuity.
- There are many ways you can shift to the next good idea.

# 5

# THINK TWICE, IT'S ALL RIGHT!

*"Nothing is more dangerous than an idea, when all you have is one idea."*

**Alain**

The creativity evoked in speeches by management, labor, students, ministers, or professors is often just wishful thinking. What a shame! Creativity is something we can all agree on.

One of the reasons for this is a misunderstanding of the tools available. There is a methodology for putting creativity into practice, managing ideas in the same way as we manage any other resource. It is based on a very simple concept: the brain is a two-stroke engine. The second stroke is the one that is familiar to us. It's the moment when the brain selects, compares, sorts, plans, and fights against waste; it's the moment of decision. But the first stroke of the engine is the one that deserves attention. It's where the brain imagines, dreams, suggests, opens horizons, and anticipates. It's the time of exploration that presages real change.

The two strokes alternate endlessly. One is just as important as the other, but they can't mix, or the mechanics of the idea will self-destruct. Both stages of thought are essential, particularly in meetings where people become creative because it's a matter of showing that an idea *isn't* good. How many times have we heard "You can't really mean it!" said to someone who means exactly that?

Let's continue with an observation: Not a single idea is "born good." What do I mean by this? Simply that there are two stages to the idea process. The first is the generation of ideas—lots of them. The second is the refinement of these ideas into what I call "good ideas."

James Watt, for instance, wasn't the first to explore steam power, but he was the first to make a dependable steam engine. Similarly, Wilhelm Daimler didn't invent the internal combustion engine (actually it was a Belgian, Etienne Lenoir, who first thought of burning fuel inside a cylinder and thereby driving a piston), but Daimler won lasting fame, for he developed an engine that propelled a carriage.

When 25-year-old David Sarnoff came up with the idea of radio as an entertainment medium in 1916, he was already standing on the shoulders of many innovators. "I have in mind a plan of development which would make the radio a household utility much like the piano or phonograph," he said, "the receiver being designed in the form of a simple radio music box which can be placed in the parlor."

When Steve Jobs and Steve Wozniak created the Apple II computer in 1977 it was an idea shaped from many others (including the Altair, considered the first personal computer, along with their own Apple I). Because the Apple II was the first personal computer that really worked—and was capable of breaking the paradigm dominated by the IBM 360 mainframe—Jobs and Wozniak grabbed the laurels for a really good idea.

So there is a difference between *new* ideas and *good* ideas. Etienne Lenoir's internal combustion engine was the *new* idea; Daimler's was the *good* idea. The Apple I was the *new* idea; the Apple II was the *good* idea. You can use this framework for anything: The concept of ecology, as presented in Rachael Carson's *Silent Spring* for instance, was the *new* idea, but the development of the environmental movement in politics and society was the *good* idea.

It's not possible to summarize instructions on how to use creativity, but you can start with the idea of cerebral "Ping Pong." Just as becoming bilingual is an effort that may require years of work, becoming "bicerebral" is a long adventure, during the course of which you discover the art of creating innovative teams, developing methods to spark imaginations, and even creating an ideas bank. A long adventure, to be sure, but what a pleasure to invent the future together!

The brain is a two-stroke engine. The first brings you from *good old* to *new,* the second one from *new* to *good new.* The first stroke is imagining new ideas, lots of them, without subjecting them to judgment. The second stroke is judging, analyzing, and refining these ideas into good ideas.

You need imagination and judgment—but not both at the same time! You cannot judge a new idea instantly (it's got nothing to do with morality or ethics), because it makes no sense to judge something that is only *pretending* to be new.

The resistance to new ideas is based on a misunderstanding. Yet it's human to fear the consequences of a change in perception! Let's go back for a minute to the Palo Alto school I introduced in Chapter 1.

The Mental Research Institute studied resistance to change. Taking inspiration from group theory and from the theory of logical types, the Palo Alto team reached the conclusion that change is a phenomenon that is possible and should therefore be analyzed at two levels.

1. A Type 1 change is produced within a system that stays the same. If it modifies a component, it still follows the rules. Retroactive mechanisms protect the system and help it keep its balance.
2. A Type 2 change, however, alters the rules of the system thanks to a new representation of this system. If this rupture sometimes appears illogical, that is because it is viewed in the light of Type 1 changes.

Literature is abundant on the applications of this model to family therapy and group communication, but it is also pertinent to the subject at hand here.

The organization of ideas or thought is also a system dedicated to self-preservation and determined to keep its balance. Confronted with a new idea, it will trigger a counteridea to neutralize it. Only a Type 2 change can accept the aggression—the surprise of an unanticipated idea, an unexpected revelation—but this requires a change in perception.

Think about the Apple iPod. The conventional wisdom—at least in the record industry—was that the way to solve the Napster problem was to put the downloader criminals in jail. In terms of Palo Alto thinking, that is a Type 1 solution. The Type 2 solution, the perceptual change in the whole argument, was arrived at by Steve Jobs with the iPod—make a clever device that encourages people to pay for downloads rather than stealing them.

**FIGURE 5.1** *Two Strokes*

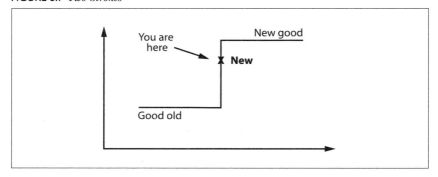

Creativity is like a foreign language. If a company wants its people to be bilingual, it can organize courses, select favored students, demand use of the new language in meetings—in short, work on the day-to-day reality (Type 1 change). But the effort may be in vain. The essential thing is to understand the perception of the people involved. Are they convinced that a second language is indispensable to the company, even useful? That is the mandatory stage, the most important aspect of all (Type 2 change). You may not even need someone who speaks the language to convince them! That shows how distinct these two levels of change are.

## CONVERGENT AND DIVERGENT THINKING

There is a big difference between the processes involved in creating new ideas and those of good ideas.

Some people call this the difference between the right and left brain. I would propose that, as suggested by J-P Guilford, it is the difference between divergent thinking and convergent thinking.

Convergent thinking is the one we are most comfortable with. It is the process that we read most about in management and business books. It is the topic of seminars and the reason for corporate reshuffling. Convergent thinking, as one part of the change process, is there to take ideas and put them to work.

Divergent thinking, on the other hand, is harder to pin down. If convergence is logical—which it is—divergence is magical. You can't organize with it, but you can stimulate it.

FIGURE 5.2 *Divergent and Convergent Thinking*

| Divergent Thinking | Convergent Thinking |
| --- | --- |
| Explore | Judge |
| Observe | Assess |
| Imagine | Analyze |
| Invent | Classify |
| Dream | Compare |
| Exaggerate | Select |
| Provoke | Avoid waste |
| Associate | Calculate |
| Model | Plan |
| Combine | Decide |
| Disturb | Choose |
| Visualize | Determine |
| Doubt | Organize |

To create change, the two cycles have to alternate endlessly. The best way to have a good idea is to have a lot of ideas.

But don't mix the two ways of thinking. Harmonized thought is harmful in and of itself. When opinions merge, when viewpoints resemble each other, when differences vanish, when standards become uniform and uniforms are standardized, the little that remains from the occasional clash of ideas sheds very little light. As with electricity, the creative potential is the function of a difference that must be maintained between the two kinds of thought, the one allowing for invention, the other for judgment.

So it's a matter of harnessing the potential of plural thought that manages the *for* and, much later, the *against,* providing rhythm to divergence and convergence, alternating quantity and quality. Inventing and criticizing are two entirely different functions that cannot be done simultaneously, even when time is running out.

Management of the full thought cycle—magical *and* logical—is more than ever the challenge for all political, business, or union leaders. Too much convergence can lead to catastrophe, but the same is also true for too much divergence. Companies have disappeared in the IT sector because they wanted to go on doing the same thing without listening to the market. Others never even really made an appearance; they were incapable of finishing a product, no matter how promising it was!

If the word *creativity* comes up again and again in their discussions, why don't they use the methods to enable them put it into practice?

There is a time for reflection and a time for action. In other words, a time for doubt and a time for decision. Both are necessary and justified, but they are not really compatible.

Change becomes difficult when it is the same people doing both exercises. Can someone freely think up a new structure, create a new system, imagine new functions while knowing he or she has to be part of that structure, be involved in the system, or even perform one of the functions? Isn't that person automatically condemned to suffer like Stephan Zweig's chess player who tries to play by himself—to be first on one side, then the other?

Maybe our problems come from the fact that our decision-makers fail to recognize the importance of doubt, and those capable of doubt want to make decisions on their own. Then, in the world of management, many other things get in the way, such as wishful thinking, emotional overinvestment, selective hearing, and filtered information.

Democracy also depends on separation of the various powers of decision. Everyone has to find his or her rightful place and fulfill his or her rightful role. Plato knew failure when, in Syracuse, he tried to apply his concepts of the life to society. Newton, who spent dozens of years in the Houses of Parliament, took the floor only once, and that was to ask someone to close the window! Einstein understood this lesson and declined the invitation he received to be president of the newly formed state of Israel.

It's not a surprise that we meet so many couples in the business world. They have the same values, but different thinking skills. Bill Hewlett and Dave Packard (HP), Charles Rolls and Frederick Royce (Rolls-Royce), Gordon Moore and Andy Grove (Intel), Paul Dubrule and Gérard Pelisson (Accor), Bill Bowerman and Phil Knight (Nike), Jeff Bezos and Jeff Wilke (Amazon), Larry Page and Sergey Brin (Google). *Success is built on divergence and convergence.*

Creativity is a question of harmony among talents, of alternation between competences, of passageways among disciplines. In short, it is the acknowledgement of the indispensable contribution of "The Other." It will only survive if companies allow and accept the discussion of ideas.

If too many thinkers are mute and too many senior managers deaf, it can only be because that rigorous and symmetrical space is missing where the *respect for the ideas of some* rubs shoulders with *respect for the responsibility of others.*

Copyright © www.cartoonbase.com

They are many books about the *divergence-convergence machine.* I have selected an exercise that demonstrates the concept and simultaneously illustrates the potential for rediscovering creativity in the Information Age.

The problem is very easy (at least to understand!). Pick numbers from the twelve listed below so that their sum equals 100.

| 51 | 36 | 3 | 15 |
| 9 | 17 | 63 | 6 |
| 53 | 42 | 33 | 72 |

You probably don't feel comfortable with this kind of problem. Rest assured, most of us have the same reaction. But those of you who can't come up with the answer should still be asking yourselves questions.

First, what's the point of math? The knowledge you need to answer this problem is "elementary course" stuff. So, what's the point?

So what use is computer science? Imagine you have a computer. Offhand, what else could the computer do but try out all the possibilities?

FIGURE 5.3 *Killer Phrases*

Great idea, but not for us.

We have tried that before.

The boss will never go for it.

Competition will eat you alive!

Do you realize the paperwork it will create?

It'll be more trouble than it's worth.

Yes, but . . .

We have always done it this way.

I have a better idea.

It'll never work!

Who do you think you are?

It isn't your responsibility.

Don't be foolish.

It's not in the budget.

We haven't got the manpower.

What will people say?

Put it in writing.

I'll get back to you.

The last person who said that isn't here anymore.

That's not my area.

Get a committee to look into it.

It doesn't meet our quality standards.

Why don't you go home early today?

Obviously, you misread my request.

It's totally irrelevant to this situation.

Play is frivolous.

That's relevant, but it's unproven.

It's proven; still it's dangerous.

It's true that it's safe, but it's not sellable.

That's not in your job description.

Don't waste time thinking.

I'm the one who gets paid to think.

Be practical.

Let's stick with what works.

Follow the rules.

I think you've got a brick loose.

To err is wrong.

It's not the high priority.

You must be kidding.

That's not logical.

Don't be ridiculous.

You don't really understand our problem.

I'm not creative.

It's all right in theory, but . . .

Avoid ambiguity.

You're too young.

Oh, yes, I had that idea a long time ago.

Too academic.

Women!

Is it supported by research?

It's my way or the highway.

How many of these subsets are there? More than you think. To put it more accurately, there are two to the twelfth power ways—precisely 4,096—to pick the numbers from among those listed. That's fairly easy to prove.

To do this, imagine a very simple case in which we have just three numbers. In this scenario, there are eight ways of selecting numbers. Aside from none and all, there are three ways to select one number and three ways to select two, for a total of eight possible choices.

This leads us back in time, because the figures (1, 3, 3, 1) come straight from Blaise Pascal's famous triangle:

$$
\begin{array}{ccccccc}
 & & & 1 & & & \\
 & & 1 & & 1 & & \\
 & 1 & & 2 & & 1 & \\
1 & & 3 & & 3 & & 1
\end{array}
$$

This can be extended indefinitely, simply by adding two contiguous numbers to determine the value of the one below it. This triangle has a number of important properties, but the one of greatest interest to us is the sum of the elements in a line. The following addition (1, 4, 6, 4, 1) yields 16 (2 to the fourth power) and the recurrence shows that the sum of each line is, in fact, equal to 2 to the $n$th power.

If you are a math fanatic, you can rush on to another famous and beautiful demonstration in the solutions to the exercises at the end of this chapter.

So, there are indeed two to the twelfth power (4,096) ways of selecting numbers from the dozen listed above.

Testing them out is, of course, one option. You can easily imagine that if we had a hundred numbers, for example, finding the answer would be simply out of the question. In fact, there are many problems of this kind. Allocating frequencies to independent local radio stations, determining whether a number is a prime number, checking account entries, minimizing the length of a railroad network, are all part of the same discipline, where the trial-and-error method is both inevitable and, at the same time, impractical.

The same problem can be child's play and a real puzzle by turns. It all depends on the size of the initial data. One interesting relationship worth studying is the link between the calculation time needed and the amount of information processed. Almost all scenarios are possible.

FIGURE 5.4 *Increasing Volume of Data and Complexity*

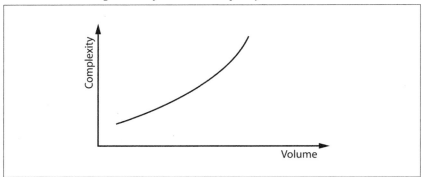

Sometimes, the complexity of a problem is independent of the volume of data. This is the user's dream—and a nightmare for the computer salesman who can no longer argue the need for such an investment! Assigning a new license plate number, for example, requires an effort that in no way depends on the number of plates in circulation.

More often, the calculation time increases in proportion to the volume of data processed. This is a linear function, as in the case of a sum where doubling the numbers to be added up simply doubles the work to be done.

In most cases, however, complexity increases faster than the information at hand, as shown in Figure 5.4. Sorting a million cards represents a great deal more work than a thousand separate sorting procedures for a thousand cards, and a company that grows threefold will have to implement an accounting system that may be ten times more complex than the one it replaces.

In most problems, the calculation time increases much faster than the volume of the data involved.

The little exercise above clearly illustrates this snowballing effect. The number of possible combinations explodes—mathematicians call this a combinatorial explosion—and, beyond a certain threshold, this kind of problem outstrips the capabilities of even the most powerful computer.

The expression would probably qualify as a "nuclear explosion" in the case of chess, where anticipating even just ten moves in advance is simply beyond the present state of computer science.

Contrary to what we might be tempted to think, the limits of a calculation today are very rarely associated with the difficulty of the calculation. Most often, the limits are reached because of the volume of data to be processed, the astronomical number of times that the same simplistic calculation has to be repeated.

So this is the point where we need to look at the question again and draw on our creativity, which, provided we feel confident about it, will always give us the edge over any machine.

To return to the initial problem—*just change your perception!* Try not to see 12 random numbers, but look for something strange, a pattern. A lateral approach to the 12 numbers reveals indeed that all of them are multiples of three, except 53 and 17, which are multiples of three plus two. Eureka!

This is because 100—the total we are asked to come up with—is a multiple of 3, plus 1. The solution, therefore, will necessarily include 53 and 17. It's the only way to create a multiple of 3 + 1, or 70 in this case. The complement (30) soon appears as the sum of 6 + 9 + 15.

This twelve-number problem is one of the games a British Airways flight attendant used to give children to keep them quiet for a while.

This little exercise also shows the absolute need for creativity in the information age. The use of the *lateroscope* helps us override the limits of the machine, when the creative moment periodically interrupts the algorithm. In fact, there was no logic involved in thinking suddenly of multiples of three. If that had been the case, the computer could have been programmed accordingly. The key, rather, was the conviction that a second look at the problem would find the alternative to the "brute force" that seemed necessary at first glance.

The computer scientist's utopia in fact is to find, for a given problem, a method with a calculation time that doesn't depend on the size or volume of data to be processed and that will solve a system of three equations with three unknowns just as fast as a system of two equations with two unknowns.

A good example is a tennis tournament organized by direct elimination, where we want to know the number of games played, including the final. Assuming there are 80 players, some of them are going to have to play qualifying games in order to get into the first round. The cumbersome method consists of doing the addition: one final, plus two semifinals, plus four quarter-finals, and so on, including the qualifying matches if the number of players is not a power of two. The creative method, by contrast, is immediate. (See the solution at the end of this chapter.)

FIGURE 5.5 *Complexity and Creativity*

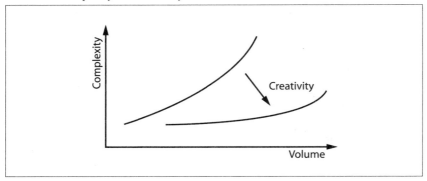

Creativity in cyberspace is the reflex that consists of attempting to change methods rather than change machines.

In computer science, creativity is the process of changing the algorithm to handle a larger volume of data in the same calculation time. It is the reflex that consists of rethinking the software rather than investing in hardware.

The Voyager II space probe, launched in the early 1970s, took twelve years to reach the Neptune suburbs and illustrates the acceleration of the pendulum. Even if, during those twelve years, the earth's population increased by about a billion people, at the other end of the solar system that period certainly seems minute, tiny.

The space probe was fitted with an onboard computer with 32 KB of memory! Its entire computing power consisted of what is now available in a wristwatch. At NASA, there was a team of computer scientists whose special mission was to have as little training as possible, to remain unaware of progress, and to reject any form of evolution. They must be the only programmers in the world who were happy to be working without any new systems at all. Thanks to this, they were able to modify the satellite's programs by remote transmission for a long time.

Familiarization is certainly one of the risks inherent in technology. It is likely that all the research departments in the world, if you happened to pose the question, would now insist that it is utterly impossible to send a spacecraft to Neptune with only 32 KB of memory.

Let's summarize. When an answer is required for a specific problem, give the "magical thought" a chance. Don't go headlong into a logical approach. Basically there are only two types of judgment: "yes but . . ." and "yes and. . . ." There are thousands of ways to say "yes but . . ."—just take a look at the list of the killer phrases in Figure 5.3 and add your own! I recommend, of course, the "yes and . . ." reflex. It doesn't mean "yes," it simply means "thank you." Thank you for bringing me out of the box, for having opened a new door.

When I run this twelve-numbers exercise, after a couple of minutes a participant often says, "Hey, they are all multiples of 3." It takes only a millisecond for another to say, "Yes, but 17 is not," and so loses the opportunity to find the solution. However, a "yes and 100 is also not" reaction could have led to success.

# OXYMORONS

There are hundreds of killer phrases. A classic one is "avoid ambiguity!" I love it, ambiguity, because it brings us back to Heraclites.

Our education has given us a bad image of ambiguity. The message received at school was clear: we have to eliminate ambiguity. There are friends and there are enemies. It's one or the other. A door has to be either open or closed. We must choose. The entire logic of Aristotle adheres to this condition alone. Descartes only wanted to deal with clear and distinct ideas. Woe betide vagueness, or even worse, contradiction!

However, their illustrious predecessor Socrates was a little less categorical on this question, and even left the door half-open or half-closed for oxymorons. Instead of condemning either rash cowardliness or intellectual ignorance, he replies—when asked what a virtue is—that it can be found between two extremes, one of which is insufficient and the other excessive. Courage is located somewhere between cowardice and rashness, and wisdom, where it exists, is somewhere between ignorance and intellectualism.

An oxymoron is a stylistic figure. It is the crystallization of a paradox in a composite expression that merges two words that in theory are incompatible, like for example *dead-alive* or *hot-cold*. As Victor Hugo said, "Melancholy is happiness at being sad."

The oxymoron is used more than we might think. We're not even aware of it when we speak about *jumbo shrimps, constant variables, open secrets, abstract images,* or *plastic glass.* Less charitable souls would add to the list *administrative efficiency, postal service, automobile sport,* and *military intelligence,* or even Microsoft Works.

Indeed the temptation to invent an oxymoron is sometimes far removed from poetry. A *clean war* or a *surgical strike* are formulae invented with the sole aim of getting people to forget that a conflict is necessarily brutal, horrible, and sordid.

Literature is of course flooded with oxymorons. Verlaine spoke of the "damp spark," Mallarmé of "sterile rain," Shakespeare of "sweet sorrow," "tragical mirth," even "hot ice," Corneille of "obscure clarity," Balzac of the "ignorant sage" and the "unbelieving priest."

Gérard de Nerval defined melancholy as "a black sun." Writers pushed the game of language even further; a figure of style allied with a contradiction had its uses! Oxymorons defy logic, but nevertheless make a contribution to clarifying thought. The oxymoron therefore isn't a dead end but, on the contrary, an invitation to think further ahead.

Boris Cyrulnik, a French ethologist, reminded the public of this a few years ago in his book *Wonderful Unhappiness.* The subject is serious: what happens 20 or 30 years on to children who have been subject to deep trauma? An extensive survey seemed to show that, for around one-third of them, the wound they suffered in childhood gradually became a source of energy, because they found in the unhappiness they knew as children a powerful force, and were helped in realizing this by the person who held out a hand to them. Boris Cyrulnik was a Jewish child during the Second World War, so he knows what he's talking about.

The oxymoron is ambiguous. It's not necessarily balanced; one of the two elements is likely to engulf the other. It's not an ambivalence like love and hate, which can exist side-by-side symmetrically between lovers. Nor is it the "double bind" the Palo Alto school was talking about. The famous verdict "be spontaneous" is built up of opposites of equal intensity—the order not to obey orders. No, wonderful unhappiness is lopsided; it limps. The child who has had a terrible emotional blow breaks in two. In the best of cases part of the child suffers forever and dies—and the other, hit less hard, reacts with redoubled energy.

The oxymoron needs both of its component terms in order to exist. Strangely, it can then generate great strength. Michelangelo was a perfectionist who left many of his works unfinished. Nearer to us, certain sportsmen attribute their success to *relaxed concentration.* Bill Clinton amassed great political power though his *unfaithful loyalty.* We all have our faults and qualities. Perhaps we have to go a little bit further and see some of our qualities in our very faults.

In its semantic dissonance, the oxymoron is striking, and the energy set free can be enormous. This is true in both individual and collective terms. An efficient organization is characterized by a "rigid flexibility" and a "hierarchical network." It only recruits "experienced youngsters" and, during the summer, it organizes "working holidays" with an "internal university" dedicated to "virtual reality."

On a more global scale, the challenges within our society all seem to fall within the remit of the oxymoron.

What should we make of the incredible possibilities of biotechnology? We hear people say that they're neither good *nor* bad. No, we should see them as good *and* bad. The law of business is the law of the strongest, and is in essence unjust. However we have had to invent "fair trade" and "ethical investment." The resources of our planet are limited. So we need "sustainable development" in order to avoid "humanitarian disasters," even if these are just many contradictory juxtapositions.

Sartre said that we were condemned to be free. Today we realize it's even worse than that, because we're condemned to live with the oxymoron.

I'm sure you're convinced now that creativity is "organized disorder."

## KEY IDEAS IN THIS CHAPTER

- You need your two brains, even if they don't like each other.
- No single idea is born good.
- Imagination is about quantity, judgment about quality.
- The best way to have a good idea is to have a lot of new ideas.
- Try a "yes and . . ." reaction before any kind of "yes but . . ."
- Discover the power of the oxymoron.

## Ten Paradoxes of Creativity

The art of being a great boss can be summed up, essentially, as the ability to identify, manage, and move beyond the paradoxes that are typical of the exercise of creativity. The paradoxes are:

1. Encouraging divergence while ensuring convergence.
2. When it comes to being inventive, vast multidisciplinary knowledge is a plus. So is the total absence of knowledge.
3. There is more in two heads than in one, and more in three heads than in two. But, at some point, the effect is reversed. A crowd doesn't invent anything.
4. To create, comfort is essential. So is the lack of comfort.
5. A computer will be programmed better to the extent that its user manages to deprogram himself or herself.
6. Creativity is freed in people who manage to switch off their critical faculty. Yet, creative people have a highly developed critical faculty.
7. Human creativity can help us build a better future, but people are never so creative as when it comes to destroying things.
8. An absence of creativity may lead a company to catastrophe. An excess of creativity may bring it to disaster.
9. We want creativity. We fear it too.
10. Creativity is as old as the world itself, yet is the essential tool for bringing a new world into existence.

Here is a little exercise commonly used in seminars: how to measure the diagonal of a small parallelepiped box using a ruler.

The reactions are generally quite varied. A participant who has a vague recollection of Euclidean geometry proposes using the Pythagorean theorem and calculating the square root of the sum of the squares of two sides of the triangle ad hoc. Another participant who is irritated even more by Pythagoras than by the exercise itself suggests just breaking the box. This would let you have the answer, of course, but it would cause irreparable damage. A less violent variant could consist of piercing it with a needle or a straw.

To avoid creating an unwanted hole, a participant suggests putting the box in front of the overhead projector. The shadow measured on the screen could lead to the result, provided the diagonal of the box is kept perfectly vertical and you remember Thales's theorem and the properties of similar triangles.

A member of senior management, annoyed by the turn of events, will undoubtedly propose calling someone. The habit of delegation helps (in the case where a seminar is attended by members of an executive committee, this idea is generally the first one on the table).

A slight variation in the question influences the sequence of answers. If the parallelepiped object presented is a brick, block glass, a dictionary, or a piece of wood, the suggestions will not arise in the same order although the problem is identical. In any case, there is another instantaneous solution! (See the solutions to the exercises at the end of this chapter.)

If the "lateral" method does not come to mind initially, this is probably because of its doubly paradoxical nature. Any mathematical knowledge or hierarchical comfort is an obstacle in the path to the easy method. The solution is outside the problem. It is so tempting at first to use your knowledge and then, when a question is asked, why go anywhere else if the answer is there? After all, an accounting mistake is corrected in accounting, and a problem with a machine is fixed on the machine, right? Well, not always.

The link between creativity and paradox is devastating. Perhaps creativity is paradox. As soon as a truth seems to be established, a creativity technique is perfected, or a method is found to yield good results, it becomes urgent to prove that sometimes the opposite also works. This is at the risk of leaving the world of creativity and entering the world of algorithms, where machines are only expected to show that they know how to run a program.

To illustrate this new assertion, we go back to our exercise. It consisted of doubling the system, of creating a virtual twin system where everything became simple. To show that there is no method there but there is creativity, here is another little exercise. An overly simple approach exists in it as well. It consists of doing exactly the opposite! Out of the two systems, it is necessary to create only one.

The story takes place in the Alps. An experienced mountain climber decides to climb the one mountain that she has never managed to conquer. Only one path is possible, but it is a tortuous one. Some parts are easy and can be traversed quickly, while others are steep and progress is slower. The ascent, including various pauses and breaks, lasts 12 hours. Leaving at 7:00 AM, the mountain climber reaches shelter at 7:00 PM. After a night of rest, she decides to go back down to the village.

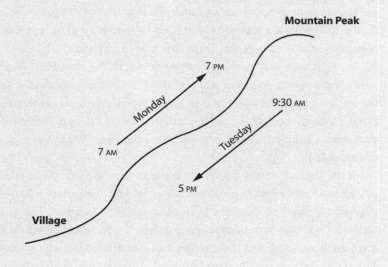

This is much less tiring and, just for fun, she decides to make the descent without stopping. Leaving at 9:30 AM, she reaches the bottom of the mountain at 5:00 PM. Here is the question: Is there a place on the path where the mountain climber passes at the same time on both days?

It's not easy! The speeds are variable, the pauses come at different points, and the descent is shorter. (See the solution at the end of this chapter.)

The juxtaposition of the two exercises is no coincidence. There is no formula for creativity. One approach might be suitable for one situation, while the opposite might work in another.

The next scene takes place in court. Two litigants are invited by the judge to present their version of their conflict. The first describes the facts partially, showing the other party to be in the wrong.

"I understand you perfectly," says the judge. "You are absolutely right."

"What?" asks the second litigant. "I haven't been able to speak yet and you have already told my opponent he is right?"

The second litigant then refutes point by point the accusations of the first litigant, showing that he himself was right in all respects.

"I agree," said the judge. "If this is the way it was, then I am with you completely. You are absolutely right."

The clerk of court then taps the judge on the shoulder and tells him that it is impossible for both parties to be absolutely right.

"You are absolutely right," answers the judge.

## **S**olutions to the **E**xercises

1. Another nice demonstration has been handed down to us by the inimitable Isaac Newton. The development of his binome $(x + a)^n$—which is to algebra what the Beethoven's Ninth Symphony is to music—gives us an immediate answer when we go $x = a = 1$.

2. 79! It involves seeing that the answer is in the question! If you look at a tennis match through a lateral thinking lens, then you see that the only objective of each match is to knock out one of the players. So, as all the players bar one have to be knocked out, the number of matches played will be the number of entrants minus one! This is a case where the time to calculate the answer doesn't depend on the size of the problem.

3. It's enough to put the box on the corner of a table, and slide it over a distance equal to its width. In this way you create a space that is identical to that of the box. You can then place a ruler in this space to measure the distance. Too simple an answer to be obvious? Yes and no. One day a child suggested plunging the box into mud.

4. If there is a difficulty with this one, it often stems from a refusal to listen to the question itself. The brain starts looking *where*, and not *if*, such a place exists. Let's make one system out of the two. Let's imagine the two days as superimposed, like two photos on a camera that we'd forgotten to wind on. What happens? Something extremely simple: All the evidence points to the fact that the two climbers (Monday's and Tuesday's) will pass each other, and at that time, they'll be at the same place at the same time, of course. The answer to the question asked is therefore: Yes, of course!

# 6

# THE MAGIC OF IMAGINATION

*"When we don't understand what's happening,*
*let's just pretend we're the organizer."*

**Jean Cocteau**

**H**ow do you create a wonderful fountain of ideas? What's the magic behind imagination?

In the 19th century, many people wondered whether a horse, at full gallop, had all four hooves suspended at any one point, or whether one hoof was always in contact with the ground. The question was not answered until 1872, when railroad baron Leland Stanford, to settle a bet, hired photographer Edward Muybridge to freeze the motion of a horse at full gallop. When the sequence of photographs was developed, the world had its answer: The hooves did indeed leave the ground.

It's a bit the same when it comes to thought. We may talk about those little ideas trotting around inside our head but, more often than not, our imagination is galloping along, throwing up ideas and giving an impression of instantaneity. It's as if all our mental hooves are off the ground. But this, in fact, is not at all the case. The various breakthroughs made in the so-called cognitive sciences enable us to analyze to a small degree the birth of a new idea, the process we call *thought*. Between *no idea* and *an idea* there is no bridge, no simply constructed arch. There are, rather, a number of stages that we can distinguish and identify precisely.

FIGURE 6.1 *Astonishment*

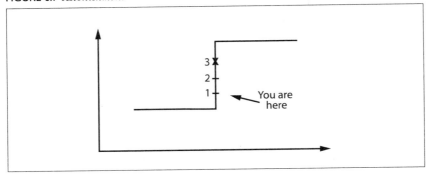

Let's take three of them. They form an equation:

Astonishment + Questioning = New Ideas

*Warning:* Imagination can be fostered by adding a fourth stage to the process; it's called *creativity techniques* or *methods*. But that's a discussion for another time.

Astonishment is not only the origin of almost every idea, it's an ability we all have within us. By this we mean the potential for experiencing surprise, blurting out "Jeez!" or "Hey!"

Perhaps you know people who don't seem to get surprised often. If you ask, "Anything special?" they will most often answer, "No, not really." "What's new?" will usually provoke the answer, "Oh, nothing much." If you ask, "How are you?" the answer will be "It's Monday . . ." or, if you work in a multinational, "Business as usual." This type of reaction is not exactly stimulating for the neurons, but it is through these instances of numbed thought and dormant reflections that we see where the real start line for imagination is situated, and we can find our way to the starting blocks of creativity.

Schopenhauer once said, "To be a philosopher involves being capable of being surprised at routine events, at day-to-day things, and setting for oneself as a subject for study everything that is most general and ordinary." At the start of thought there needs to be a state of openness to things, chronic and voluntary doubt, and a gentle, nagging worry. Peace of mind needs to give way to confident worry, to pleasure in ideas and to attention without tension. It is impossible for two Mondays to be identical, or for there to be absolutely nothing new. There is always something to report.

FIGURE 6.2 *Identifying Four Types of Astonishment*

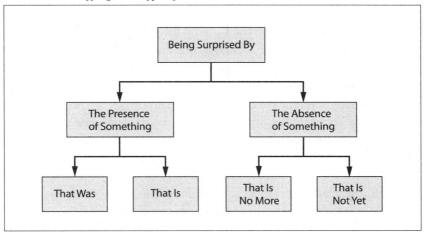

Astonishment is a gift we can give ourselves or other people. The characteristic "Hey!" of a mental leap bears witness to this. It really is a present we are asked to hold. Present in both senses of the word: a gift, and something now!

Ideas only grow in soil with high astonishment content, fertilized by curiosity. But soil can be varied and of many types, so the creative person has to be constantly on the watch for anything that moves and surprised by anything that doesn't. There are four types of astonishment, and they are all positive and can all be told apart by their use of the verb *to be* (see Figure 6.2).

1. You can easily be astonished by the presence of something that *is:* it's perhaps the easiest of the four types of "all of a sudden." A bad cup of coffee, a client who looks different, a strange noise. Something happens that is picked up by the senses, a difference is flagged up, and you feel surprise. It is, for example, the surprise of a Belgian tourist who, every time he goes to stay in France, is astonished to find that they still use checks.

2. More problematic is astonishment over something that *was* for a long time, but which you had not remarked until now. For years, you've been taking the same route to work. Every day, morning and evening, you find yourself going along the same roads, passing the same shops. One day, someone says to you, "Listen, as you're going that way, could you stop off at the jeweler's and pick

up the watch I ordered?" Astonishment. A jeweler's? I never noticed. But sure enough, on the route that you think you know by heart, at the number you've been given, there really is a jeweler. So you're astonished, although nothing has changed from yesterday to today! Nothing? Not really, because your perception has changed. Another example is the logo used by the Carrefour supermarket chain (see Figure 6.3). You always see it, rather vaguely, as an ace of spades on its side, until the day someone tells you it's a capital *C.* Astonishment once again, though in this case too nothing has changed. Nothing? Something has changed: the view that you yourself now have, the way of seeing something that hasn't changed. There is a small variant on this phenomenon: While surprise can sometimes come from another view of something that hasn't moved or changed, it can also sometimes come from observing a change that is real but minute, and which bears no proportional relation to the amount of astonishment it causes. Suddenly one day you notice that a child seems to have grown, a man you know seems to have gone bald—although neither the growth nor the hair loss are instant phenomena. The change in reality is slow; it is the change in perception that is sudden.

3.  Do you remember when the Apple logo had rainbow stripes? Did you notice one day that the colored stripes had disappeared? (See Figure 6.3)

4.  Perhaps the real challenge is astonishment of the fourth type— the kind which one can experience when confronted with something that *is not,* vis-à-vis some unexploited potential. Procter & Gamble launched a Pampers box, which, once empty, could be used as a doll's house. That was because someone, one day, was surprised to see that the inside of the carton wasn't being used. This last type of astonishment should be a privileged sort, for the new rules of the economy are opening up enormous opportunities for ideas. Twenty years ago, being creative was all about finding an original "how." Now, more and more, being creative involves finding a new "what." There's a divide. The challenge used to be the answer, but now it's becoming the question. Creativity, which for a long time was defined as the art of "getting out of the box," has to be reinvented, simply because there are fewer and fewer boxes. Astonishing, isn't it?

FIGURE 6.3 *Logos*

This division into four groups provides us with an interesting perspective on the creativity of great scientists. Four examples:

1. When he arrived on one of the Galapagos Islands, Darwin was surprised to see tortoises that were very different from those on other islands only a few kilometers away.
2. Copernicus, by comparison, was surprised one day to see the sun "set"—when people had been seeing the same thing for thousands of years.
3. Freud drew the attention of his patients to things they had forgotten or subconsciously rejected.
4. Carnot, watching a steam engine, suddenly said there must be a thermodynamic theory that helped explain the disappointing output.

All four were inspired by astonishment—Darwin in a new situation, Copernicus in a traditional situation, Freud and Carnot in a situation where something was missing. Aristotle must be pleased. In his *Metaphysics,* he said, long before any of the others, "The starting point of all sciences is the astonishment at the fact that things are what they are."

Creativity was one day defined as a revolution in the way we look at things. But this conspiracy should not be limited to future Nobel Prize winners; the insurrection has to appeal to everyone, because every individual's senses can contribute to the imagination of us all. You have to be the scientist of your own life and be astonished four times: at what is, at what always has been, at what has disappeared, and at what could be!

A supermarket can be a good laboratory. Consider your attitude toward the products you have no intention of buying. This illustrates the four instances quite clearly. It is easier to be astonished when a new product appears in the shop than when an old product is revamped. It is even more difficult to note that a product has disappeared from the shelves, or that it has never been put on sale. "Nothing surprises me any more," we hear people say when they are getting desperate. Quite the contrary: they should let themselves be surprised by everything, and then hope would return. "Nothing to be surprised at," people sometimes say, believing that things are logical. On the contrary, there's always something to astonish us—and, in the process, these things become magical.

Take away surprise and we have no ideas. There's nothing, three-fold nothing: nothing to report, nothing to think, nothing to do. You may think everything's chugging along nicely but, in reality, you're going round in circles. "Nothing new?" is not the right question. You should be asking "What's new?"—and the ideas will follow.

So be astonished, and astonish the others. From time to time, read a newspaper that you normally never read, go to a meeting of a political party that isn't yours, take a different route to a destination that is not where you normally go, read the job offers even if you're not looking for a job, watch football in another language. The things in life are so important, but it doesn't say anywhere that they always have to be the same. Be astonished and you will be surprised how much good it does you! Even if it doesn't get you anywhere.

Five last remarks about astonishment:

1. One astonishment may hide another—as the signs on French railway crossings used to say: *"un train peut en cacher un autre"* ("one train can hide another"). Believe me, that could be one great big surprise. That's exactly what happened to Galileo. Watching a church chandelier swaying in an air current, he rightly concluded that the time taken for one swing was dependent on the length of the supporting cable and not on the width of the swing. Had he not been so taken up with his discovery, he might also have noticed something even more significant: that the direction of swing changed as the day progressed, with the earth rotating under the chandelier!

2. Even Galileo couldn't make the entire thinking trip on his own—and we are not even Galileos. So don't hesitate to express your astonishment—that's also a gift, because your astonishment can sometimes help someone else have the idea.

3. Be careful—astonishment is much more like a shooting star than a comet. It is unpredictable and doesn't necessarily come back periodically. Keep your senses trimmed.

4. A group will never be astonished; surprise is an individual faculty. Confronted with someone else's astonishment, people say "Well, *I* never," or sometimes "Well, *you* never," but never "Well, *we* never."

5. While astonishment is essential, it is not of course enough, for it doesn't automatically induce questioning. A feeling of a missed opportunity or a wasted chance comes up after the event: "I'd said that, but . . ." or "It's true they'd told me that, but . . . ." This is the "but" of the idea that didn't come along, despite the invitation being there.

When an astonishment occurs there are two possibilities: either you don't have any doubt in your own mind and you lose the opportunity to have the idea, or you do have some doubt in your mind and profit from the astonishment. There will be a next step, most probably a question.

For example, if a customer comes into your office and you see he's angry. You may react by thinking that he has a problem at home. In this case the astonishment won't lead to anything.

Remember: convictions = addictions!

## A QUESTION IS MORE THAN A QUESTION

When I'm running a seminar, I often notice that people rush to a conclusion by taking a question for what it is. That's not a good idea, since the question that comes to mind may not be the best way to start the brainstorm.

The purpose of thought—and often the purpose of a work contract—is to provide an answer to the questions asked. That's even more reason to pause for a few moments to consider whether a question might be a loaded one, predetermining your thoughts on the item under consideration. The only mental exercise some people take is jumping to conclusions!

We should remember that a question is much more than a question.

When people realized there was room for cheaper airlines, their brainstorming could have started with the question "how do we estab-

FIGURE 6.4 *Questioning*

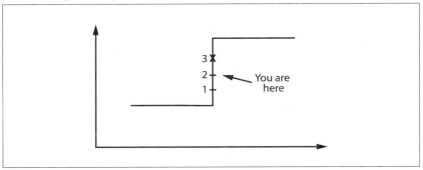

lish a low-cost airline?" Instead, they asked "how are we going to get people to fly that usually take Greyhound?" You immediately sense that the second question is the better one. It's more specific, it's accessible to the senses. You see and feel the Greyhound!

Sometimes the most effective way of dealing with a question is to reformulate it. One efficient reformulation consists of making the question visible, staging it, creating a situation in which the senses can grasp it. A service society took it upon itself to deal with the difficult problem of sales to the public sector by organizing a creativity session. Very few ideas came out of this until the moderator painted a verbal picture of a breakdown in an elevator containing the elevator company's sales delegate and the client's director-general, and the ensuing (and unexpected) dialogue. Ideas poured out because, suddenly, it was possible to see the problem.

This type of approach is anything but new. King Hiero II of Syracuse one day asked Archimedes, a mathematician by training, if his crown really was made of pure gold. Archimedes reformulated the question from a problem of quality to one of quantity: to weigh the crown and compare its weight to an equivalent volume of gold. But with the instruments he had, it was impossible for him to measure volume.

The famous "eureka" involved him using his bathwater as a unit of measurement. He got the solution because he put the question differently. Legend has made Archimedes the first man to realize that it's often the problem that is the problem.

Another example of reformulation was given by Karl Dunker one day in 1945 (this has to be put into the technological context of the time): "How can we destroy a stomach tumor using rays without damaging the healthy tissue?"

A problem posed this way often stays unanswered. But the same question reformulated in the following way: "How can we reduce the intensity of the rays in those parts of the body not affected by the tumor" set the researchers on a different path—the path of a lens located outside the body, focusing the rays on the center of the tumor.

Another idea that was also taken on board was to use three orthogonal rays (like the three edges forming the corner of a box). Each ray would have a third of the intensity required to destroy the tumor, which would therefore have to be positioned at the exact point where the rays came together, the only point where the intensity would reach 100 percent.

Reformulating the question can usefully be spiced up with a few constraints. It can, for example, be asked in another language, with children's talk, or by choosing to do without one letter of the alphabet.

So, ultimately, the father of reformulation is not Archimedes, but Socrates. In one of his many dialogues, the philosopher asks someone to take a given square and build another square out of it with double the surface area. As we would probably do over two thousand years later, the slave reasons "a little more of the same thing" and tells himself the problem is to extend two sides by a distance that needs to be determined.

Since the time of Pythagoras, the Greeks have known that this method is irrational (the side of a double square is $\sqrt{2}$ larger than the first one) and Socrates suggests thinking differently. He gives the slave some hints—more precisely, he poses the questions in a way that prompts the slave to take a step back and think creatively, to change his point of view in order to see the problem better. Instead of doubling the original surface area, divide it into two equal parts and quadruple the result. This gives the right answer!

So the easy method consists of looking at things differently, of changing perspective—in short, of being creative. (The next time you have to build a square of exactly 24.5 cm$^2$, you will remember me and solve it in a second.)

A couple of years ago, NASA gave us another example to illustrate the principle. How should we decelerate a spacecraft to land on planet Mars? How do we make it strong enough not to disintegrate? The question apparently focuses on how we keep the spacecraft from crashing, but the real question is how do we land it? If we focus on that question, dis-

**FIGURE 6.5** *Creatively Doubling the Surface Area*

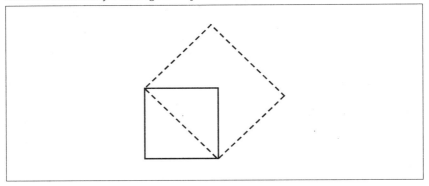

integration is not the prime concern. In fact the answer was remarkably creative and counterintuitive. Girded with airbags, it simply bounced—as happened with Pathfinder.

So, instead of asking his students for the right answer, Socrates suggested they ask the right question. He distinguished five types of questions and encouraged his students to choose the right one.

1. *A question to help you understand the point of view presented.* What do you understand by that? Can you give an example of . . . ? How do you explain that?
2. *A question aimed at testing the solidity of the argument.* Why do you think that . . . ? Is there proof that . . . ? How can we justify that?
3. *A question to lead to other clarifications on what was said.* What would someone who disagreed say? Can you reformulate . . . ? And if someone suggested . . . ?
4. *A question to draw attention to the implications and consequences.* Is there a general principle that . . . ? What would be the consequence of . . . ? Is it consistent with what was previously said?
5. *A question about the discussion itself.* How does it help us? How could we sum things up at this stage? Are there other questions?

Do companies that want to make themselves "intelligent" always give themselves the resources necessary? It's a worthwhile question. A fair number of discussions seem to be guided in only one direction, and the natural flow of ideas seems to be from top to bottom.

It should be recognized that answers may often be arranged but the questions generally are not, and management is more partial to a researcher who finds than a researcher who seeks. It's forgetting that the collective thought in a company should be nourished by an unceasing and balanced dialog between those asking and those asked, just as the usefulness of a question-and-answer session at the end of a conference or seminar depends only partly on the skills of the speakers or experts. Whatever the subject of a meeting, the "question" should always be on the agenda. It should be dissected, analyzed, X-rayed.

Sometimes a question is called devious. But could it be anything else? The person asking it, the relationship with that person, the tone used, all contribute to giving a question an orientation, momentum. A question asked already has its own idea of the answer, but is it yours?

Do this test. Ask someone to make a quick sketch of a little dog. Most of the time it will be a profile with the head on the left, although this was not stipulated. This appears to be linked to our Western up-bringing which teaches us that time's arrow goes from left to right (as we have been doing since the beginning of this book) and which at-taches more importance to the head than to other parts of the body.

The difficulty is sometimes to be found in the form and not the con-tent. The way the question is asked sometimes has more impact on our thoughts than the question itself does.

There are closed questions, which lead to yes or no (Do you want to go to Belgium?) and open questions, which lead to open ideas (What do you want to do when you are in Brussels?). In brainstorming sessions, you should never start with closed questions, because all you will get is yes or no. So you have to ask questions about the question itself, to see whether you're not leading in an unwanted direction. If you don't want to reformulate it, lighten it, open it up, invert it, to avoid having the ques-tion answer for us! The nature of the question is grounds for suspicion.

I was so happy—one of my clients said that because of me, everyone at his Monday morning meetings who wants to put a point on the agenda has to do it with a question. Imagine the issue is budget, but it must be put as a question. So the person has to consider: what is the problem with the budget? The person has to think about it a bit, even before the meeting begins.

To help you realize how devious a question can be, below are nine different characteristics a question can have, and some little exercises ac-company them. Take them as metaphors; identify the traps in your daily life with its problems that you do not want to fall into. Remember, questions are not neutral—they are loaded.

If, by the way, you start to think this chapter is about mathematics, it's not; it's also about ideas and how your brain functions!

## I. Wrong-Way-Round Questions

A question is by definition directed, meaning it has direction.

It can be presented in forward or reverse. So the same question can provoke different reactions. Because abundance in ideas is the objective here, why don't we try both?

Take two similar people. Ask the first to give a rough estimate of the product without providing the time to work it out:

$$2 \times 3 \times 4 \times 5 \times 6 \times 7 \times 8$$

Ask the second person, in a separate room, but with the same very short time limit, to estimate the value of the product of:

$$8 \times 7 \times 6 \times 5 \times 4 \times 3 \times 2$$

The results given by the first person are generally lower—by a large margin—than those of the second. I'm sure you have the same intuition. Don't, therefore, try to say that these questions have no direction! As you can see, they do!

Convention suggests that we tackle the problem from the left, but sometimes climbing the left face of a problem proves particularly laborious. This is then the occasion to try the creative (i.e., opposite) face—all the more so since the risk is safe!

It is sometimes useful to turn a question round, to tackle the problem from the other side. It's easier to multiply by two than to divide by half. Also, a project called "new computers" will boost its chances of success *de facto* if it is renamed "getting rid of the old computers."

When we have envisioned what would be the results of a policy to *reduce* working time, it can be useful to look at the consequences of another policy, namely to *increase* leisure time. It is, in effect, exactly the same question.

As early as 1654, Pascal was recommending this type of approach to Fermat. "Rather than calculating the probability of an event taking place," he wrote, "it is sometimes easier to calculate the probability of its *not* taking place." Then subtract it from one.

So the next time your car is stuck behind a flock of sheep, don't ask yourself "How can I get round them?" but instead "How can I put those sheep behind my car?"

## 2. Overloaded Questions

This kind of question is one that is burdened with useless figures. It not only makes reflection difficult, but it sometimes steers us to the wrong answer or completely down the garden path. Sometimes we are given too much information. We should not make the mistake of using all the information we have (even if our education told us to).

Let's take three examples.

1. A farmer has 17 horses. All but 9 are dead. How many are left? This kind of puzzle, which we loved in childhood, is still a lesson for adults. Do we not feel a sort of temptation within us, a force even, pushing us towards subtracting 9 from 17—even though a smile breaks through a second later?

2. A drawer contains red and blue socks in a 60 to 40 percent proportion. If you close your eyes, how many socks do you have to take out the drawer to be sure of having two of the same color? Three, of course. The "60 to 40 percent" means something, but it's irrelevant! In this case it's easier if you remove the information.

3. A driver buys a second-hand car for $3,000. Shortly afterwards, she sells it for $3,500. For a reason that is not important for the story, she is forced to buy back the car, for which she pays $4,000 this time round. But a few months later she manages to part with it for the sum of $4,500. What is the profit the driver makes on the entire operation? (If you want to use euros, no problem for me, the impact is the same.) See the solution at the end of this chapter.

How many times have you fallen into the trap of believing that overabundant information is useful, and, in fact, must be used? Sometimes the situation is exactly the opposite, as we shall see in the next exercise.

## 3. Underloaded Questions

Consider the diagram below, the most popular exercise in creativity (if you don't know the answer, buy the book of one of my competitors). How can you connect these nine dots with four lines, without taking your pencil off the paper?

The answer is that you have to move your pencil *outside* the virtual square.

Who said you *couldn't* move your pencil outside the square? Nobody. Indeed, we often fail to find the answer to problems simply because we put arbitrary borders around them that we think we cannot cross. When buying a birthday present, for instance, how often do we have trouble finding the right gift when we are searching within the "boundaries" of the top ten CDs, or books that are literary prize-winners? There are, after all, infinite numbers of other presents to buy.

Let me illustrate this by another exercise. In a desert area somewhere on Earth, an explorer covers a distance of 1,000 miles southwards. He then moves 1,000 miles east. Finally, after a third journey of 1,000 miles, this time to the north, he realizes he is back at his starting-point. What is his starting-point? (If you want to use kilometers, no problem for me, the impact is the same.)

This little problem evokes vague memories in the form of spherical triangles, and quickly suggests the answer should be the North Pole or possibly the South Pole. But the danger is to remain there. See the solutions at the end of this chapter.

## 4. Impossible Questions

Certain problems are qualified as unsolvable, and certain questions quickly give the impression there is no answer. Yet hundreds of books full of exercises like this are there to remind you that accounting puzzles, IT brain-teasers, even commercial riddles may also have their solutions.

FIGURE 6.6 *A Damaged Rug*

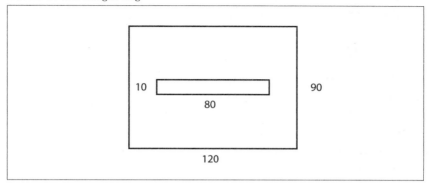

A superb little rectangular Oriental carpet has been badly damaged by a chemical product. The part left intact looks like the diagram in Figure 6.6.

There is a slit down the middle. The owner, something of an optimist, realizes right away that what's left, if properly handled, can be restored. He takes a pair of scissors, cuts the damaged carpet into two parts, and puts them together to form a perfect square with one-meter sides. Theoretically, it's possible since $90 \times 120 - 800 = 10,000 = 100 \times 100$. How does he do it? See the solutions to the exercises at the end of this chapter.

The point is that a question that seems impossible to answer is sometimes *not* impossible. People too often throw their hands up at the first pass. You must persevere!

## 5. Zoomed-In Questions

Life in most companies doesn't leave much time to step back and reflect. This, unfortunately, is because it's true that a specific case or a precise example is easier to deal with than a more general problem or even a generic one. However, sometimes the opposite situation arises. In such cases theory can be more efficient than practice, the *macroscope* more suitable than the microscope, and long sight less of a problem than short sight.

Let us suppose, for example, that you are asked to prove that 313,313 is divisible by 13. If you get too close to the figures, so to speak, you will very quickly recognize the similarity between the numbers and realize that they only feature the figures 1 and 3. You will probably also take a much more difficult route to solving the problem, even if you do come up with the right answer. (See the solution at the end of this chapter.)

## 6. Similar Questions

With the first five kinds of questions, we have limited ourselves to detecting the "instant load" of a question and have learned to be wary of its momentum. But some questions also have a past, a memory. They may look like another question, or may prompt the use of a conventional method.

Ask someone, for example, what the following figure means:

# T

He or she will probably refer to the letter *T,* rather surprised that the question has even been asked. Then ask what this represents:

# TT

Two *T*s, probably again. But if you had done things differently, showing the so-called double *T* first, what would have been the response? Telegraph poles, antennae, the letter $\pi$, a Greek temple, a table with a space down the middle? Difficult to say *a priori.* You will agree that the probability of getting the answer "double *T*" is much greater if you have already shown the *T* on its own. Because memory, being what it is, steers thought in familiar directions.

In a company, if the boss holds a meeting and tells his team, "Let's put together next year's budget," the chances are high that they will work from last year's budget. If he phrases his request differently, "Let's create a budget that makes us more competitive," he is asking an open question that will elicit a far more creative reply.

## 7. Identical Questions

Questions that come after each other—and look like each other—rub off on each other.

Sometimes you even need to find a different way of answering the same question. The answer can be totally different, simply because the environment has changed.

FIGURE 6.7 *Same Question . . .*

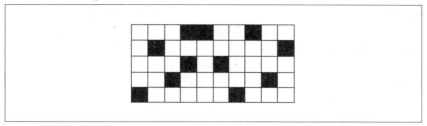

You are asked, for example, to count the number of black squares in Figure 6.7. You find this easy enough, and the question comes up so frequently that you have developed an extremely efficient method that makes you the regional black-square-counting champion! Then all of a sudden, the one in Figure 6.8 appears. Equally all of a sudden, the method you have long found best doesn't work any more! Though the problem is exactly the same, the world (reality) has changed.

Another example comes from accountancy. The idea of "writing off" means taking into account the depreciation of an asset. As a building gets older, it's logical to reduce its value on the balance sheet. For software, however, aging can only be measured in relation to external events; for example, the arrival of a competitor's product that is better or cheaper. But look how software is depreciated on a balance sheet!

Some companies sometimes fall into this trap from time to time because of their gigantic size. They become supertankers that are so big that the crew can't even see the sea—and, by definition, the other ships.

## 8. "Stupid" Questions

A place also needs to be set aside for all those questions that once perplexed you so much that you felt like jettisoning them from the back of your brain. Even if they fit well here, they come from a very different region of the noosphere.

FIGURE 6.8 *. . . At Different Times*

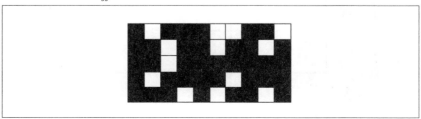

These kinds of questions are often answered with a smile, just to help us cope with the dizziness they provoke. They are destabilizing and worrying, and are divergent to such an extent that convergence can't even start. But, quite simply, they are beautiful. Perhaps, as in other disciplines, there is room for a level of *applied* creativity—the art of the unexpected answer—and a level of *pure* creativity: the art of the new question!

Children are here to prove that this art is innate to all of us. Here are some examples of their "whats" and "whys."

- What does the wind do when it's not blowing?
- Why is the sky blue?
- Why are there so many species of dogs?
- Why do I have identical shoes?
- If five-sixths of the planet is covered in water, why do we call it *Earth* and not *Sea?*
- 3/10 + 4/10 = 7/10. So, if we get 3/10 and 4/10 in different school tests, why doesn't that make 7/10?
- If there's no one there to hear it, does a falling tree make any noise?
- Why does glass break?
- Why do we have eyebrows?
- Why is the word *short* short, whereas the word *incomprehensible* isn't incomprehensible?
- Athens and Rome have such a similar history, so why was there no Greek Empire?
- Why were European towns more harmonious before there were town planning laws?

FIGURE 6.9 *New Idea*

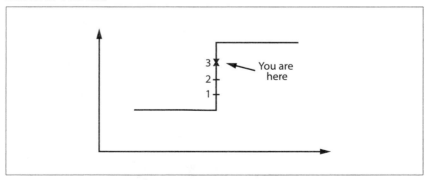

## 9. "What If?" Questions

Some questions do not have to have obvious answers—or answers at all—to mobilize our creativity. In fact they are ideal as warm-up questions in group discussions. For example, I once asked the executives of a petroleum company, "What if oil had been discovered before coal," The world today could be totally different—there would have been no steam locomotives, for example, as availability of oil would have made smaller engines immediately feasible. But the real point is that it made these managers think.

- What if the Romans had invented the steam engine (they were almost there!)?
- What if we never died?
- What if there was suddenly no gravity?
- What if the solar system became unstable?
- What if we never forgot anything anymore?
- What if Pontius Pilate had had more guts?
- What if a pack of cards had four colors—blue diamonds and green spades?
- What if light traveled at the same speed as sound?
- What if NASA started making cars?
- What if all the R&D people in IBM transferred to marketing?
- What if copyright didn't exist?
- What if we had six fingers?
- What if they were only one currency unit on earth?
- What if Immanuel Kant had died at the age of 40?
- What if we only could say 50 words a day?
- What if nobody agreed to be a teacher any longer?
- What if Columbus had arrived on the west coast of America?

Sometimes I adapt this approach a bit and run a "scenario" exercise: Your company disappeared in 2010. Why?

# BIRTH OF A NEW IDEA

The French have a nice word for it: *trouvaille*. It means "something found with happiness." We would talk about a "finding" or a "stroke of inspiration." It's a word that is inextricably linked with the exhilaration that goes with the moment that we see the light, that the penny drops. It is the mental click that accompanies sudden intuition, the first few seconds when we realize that something new is possible. The *trouvaille* is the idea of an idea, a new concept's birth certificate, discontinuity, a break. It's no coincidence that the icon for an idea is a lightbulb, as a lightbulb can only have two states, lit or unlit.

Sometimes we have been waiting years for that moment—a moment that can also mark the start of a process of reflection that can also go on for years—but once it's there, it changes everything. There is a "before" and an "after." The Eureka moment—the flash—corresponds to a change in perception. The world around us stays the same, but not the way we see it. It's the same mechanism at any point on the scale, from the great idea that can change the world to a small one that improves something in our daily routine.

Lawrence of Arabia shouted "Aqaba" and told himself that the town (today it's in Jordan, then it was held by the Turks) could be taken by coming from inland through the desert. Cantor, the mathematician, was forced by his convictions into understanding that certain infinities are bigger than others. Handel was "taken over" by his *Messiah* project. There are many other examples.

All of them went through the experience of finding something with a sense of relief and joy. It's just like the delight you experience when you manage to put the last piece in a Chinese puzzle, or when you finally understand the intricacies of a complicated form from the Internal Revenue Service.

It's not just the size, scale, or impact that characterizes a new idea. There are also a number of other differences.

- Certain findings are more necessary than others. You get the feeling that the steam engine was always going to be invented, whereas Scrooge McDuck was only one possibility in Disney's imagination.
- Einstein was capable of explaining his theory of relativity, while Paul McCartney was never able to describe how he came to compose *"Yesterday."*
- The R&D departments of the big pharmaceutical companies are in competition, while writers and painters are more like rivals.

With these three statements we can already identify one type of finding: creation. We can define it as the "possible new idea." Extraordinary as it may seem, such finds are fortuitous—no offence to admirers of Beethoven, but the world would still be possible without his Fifth Symphony.

If we turn to findings that are imperative, then we can make a distinction between finding something that is going to be, and finding something that already is. This defines and makes the difference between *invention* and *discovery*. Galileo used an invention, the telescope, to make a discovery, the phases of Venus. In the same way, Christopher Columbus had a compass with him when he discovered the Americas.

Discovery is more the domain of scientists, while invention is for company bosses who need to find what is going to be, and find it before their competitors do.

There are some other interesting questions. Who's the owner of the new idea? A discovery should not belong to anyone—here is the crux of the debate about the human genome. Invention is protected by patent, and creation by copyright (see Chapter 2). As financial conditions can vary greatly, we can understand the motive of big IT developers in having their product placed in the more lucrative of the two categories, if not in both!

Other distinctions are possible. Sometimes the finding is a unique concept—it can be a discovery (infinite calculus), an invention (the wheel) or a creation (Harry Potter). Sometimes, the finding is a bissociation, and this can also be a discovery (electromagnetism), an invention (the surf board) or a creation (theater improvisation combining theater with ice hockey).

As with any model, there are a number of criticisms that can be made of the breakout in Figure 6.10.

- Is a mathematical theorem discovered, invented, or created?
- There are discoveries in sociology (this is the aim of large-scale surveys where correlations emerge).
- There are some creations in corporations (e.g., Acela, Nutella).
- There are creations that artists *have* to create. Picasso said he could not have *not* painted *Guernica*.
- The borderline between invention and creation is a vague one (e.g., the Post-It note).

FIGURE 6.10 *Discovery, Invention, or Creation?*

|  | Discovery | Invention | Creation |
|---|---|---|---|
| **Existed** | yes | no | no |
| **The 'other one''** | competitor | competitor | rival |
| **Necessary** | yes | yes | no |
| **Explainable** | yes | yes | no |
| **Intellectual protection** | — | patent | copyright/ author's rights |
| **Field** | science | technology management | art |
| **Examples where there was no problem** | radioactivity | Post-It notes | "Hey Jude" |
| **Examples of answers to a problem** | hieroglyphics | iPod | the Louvre pyramid |

This book is all about innovation, *new* ideas. If that's obvious in the case of invention or creation, it's not the same for the other category: we can indeed also discover objects that are already there, like Tut-ankhamen's mummy, the dark side of the moon, oil, more oil, the wreck of the Titanic, hidden cave paintings, or buried treasure.

We can classify these things, because the coincidence of the discovery, the novelty of the object discovered, or even the identity of the discoverer can vary from case to case. The questions have been asked. Who owns something that is updated? Is it a discovery or a rediscovery?

But the focus of this book is invention—and now, at least, we understand better what is the first step in the process.

At the beginning of invention there is a new relationship, an original link between different things that have often been said before. Plato remarked on this, a long time ago. "A new idea," he said, "is a new form." The affirmation remains valid, but it needs to be nuanced. The inventor of the steam engine neither discovered steam nor the system of cranks and connecting rods. He invented a new combination and put together, for the first time, things that had been kept separate until then. Such new *matter-to-matter* links remain, of course, the domain of research. Remember Philips (Chapter 4)?

But a massive new field of possibilities is opening up: the *matter-to-information* links. The automobile sector has started to mine this rich vein: GPS, the keyless car, and so on. Information about the car is becoming the differentiating factor, more than the car itself. For example the OnStar GPS/cellphone in-car system, in addition to navigational and other services, signals emergencies at the trigger of an airbag. Everywhere, information can enrich matter. For so many years, being creative consisted of playing with molecules to invent new products. Today, it involves assembling molecules and bytes to invent new services.

As Koestler said about bissociations, "The more common the part, the more striking the whole!"

## KEY IDEAS IN THIS CHAPTER

- The eureka moment comprises several steps.
- Rediscover the power of astonishment.
- Raise questions about the question.
- Look at your problems with the eyes of an artist.
- Dare to bissociate.

### Solutions to the Exercises

1. When this question is asked in a group, it generally produces two answers. However, the majority tends to estimate the total profit at 500 dollars, which is the profit made on the second sale, because the three first operations would appear to cancel each other out. It's then time to start the story again in a slightly different way, and tell the adventure of the garage owner who buys a Renault for 3,000 dollars, sells it for 3,500, and then buys a Peugeot for 4,000 to sell it for 4,500 dollars. The group will be unanimous in calculating his profit at 1,000 dollars. Now is the moment to ask yourself what the difference is between the two exercises. Clearly, there isn't any, apart from the fact that the first question was loaded with irrelevant information—the fact that it is the same car is of no importance.

2. Surprise, there is an infinite number of possibilities! Let's take a parallel exactly 1,000 miles long. It exists somewhere in the south hemisphere. Then let's take another parallel exactly 1,000 miles to the north. All points of this second parallel meet the criteria and are a possible solution to the exercise.

### Solutions to the Exercises *(continued)*

3. All you need to do is to cut the damaged carpet in the form of a staircase, cutting steps 20 cm long by 10 cm high, to form two parts A and B, as in Figure 6.11. These two cut pieces can then be assembled as shown to make a perfect square with one meter sides.

4. Calmer consideration, or even a more detached one, will perhaps note that the number 313,313 is curious, as it has the form *abc,abc* and therefore is worth a thousand times *abc* plus another *abc* (i.e., a total of 1,001 times *abc*). This means that it is divisible by 13, whatever *a, b,* or *c* are (since 1,001 is divisible by 13).

FIGURE 6.11 *Cutting the Rug*

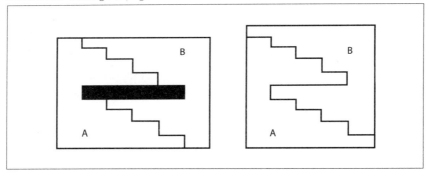

# 7

# AN IDEAS FACTORY

*"If a fight breaks out between you and the world,*
*you should place your bets on the world."*

**Franz Kafka**

**R**ecently, the world became aware
of the "transit of Venus," as the astronomers called it, the rare moment
when Venus slipped between the earth and the sun and the three heav-
enly bodies aligned. On TV that night one astronomer, still visibly reel-
ing from the emotion of the event, shared his joy with the viewers, some
of whom had also seen the pea-like object creeping across the disc of the
sun. The expert reeled off a few statistics and proudly announced that
the next two transits of Venus would take place on June 6, 2012 and
December 11, 2117.

This news was followed by the weather report, when a graceful
young woman brought us back down to earth: "On Wednesday we're
likely to see some showers." How odd, I thought. We're perfectly sure
that a transit of Venus will take place in seven years, but we don't know
with any certainty what the weather will be like in two days' time.

## UNCERTAINTY IS THE ONLY CERTAINTY

For as long as man has been looking ahead, the future has been presented to him in two segments. The first part is predictable: the seasons,
short-term population growth, the repayment of a debt contracted at a

fixed rate of interest. The second part is not: the way consumers will re-act, the choices of the electorate, the timing of earthquakes or volcanic eruptions.

One thing that is certain, however, is that uncertainty is increasing. This is particularly true in the case of consumers. There are at least four reasons for this.

1. Consumer values have changed. Loyalty to one supplier, for ex-ample, is no longer a foregone conclusion or even an attitude that is desirable. It is just one possibility among many.

2. The information at the consumer's disposal is now limitless. Making comparisons has never been so easy—the use of informa-tion networks can even eliminate fixed prices! Just as on the stock exchange, the price offered for travel today changes mo-ment by moment. The price varies according to the number of seats available, the weather, the loyalty of a client, or the chang-ing priorities of a supplier. Let's take this idea to its extreme: the phenomenon of floating prices will not be limited to travel alone. The western, privileged part of the economic planet may gradually come to resemble a giant trading room, with hundreds of millions of participants, and no price will ever again be known in advance (unless the purchase is made on the futures market!).

3. With the increase in standards of living, consumers tend to climb all five levels of Maslow's famous pyramid simultaneously. After fulfilling their aspirations for survival and security (levels 1 and 2), they slowly seek to fill the gaps of belonging, recogni-tion, and personal blossoming (levels 3 to 5). But the higher a consumer climbs the pyramid, the more uncertain his or her re-sponse becomes. We can predict that someone who is thirsty will buy water (levels 1 and 2), but what about fashion (level 3)? What is the consumer ready to do to set himself or herself apart (4)? What wild project is finally going to carry the consumer away (5)? It is possible to predict what someone needs, but it is much more difficult to predict what, for that person, is comfort—and even harder to imagine what that person considers luxury.

4. The consumer is increasingly resistant to attempts at classifica-tion. Sociology is not really comfortable with its categories. Thirty years ago, you could make out a coherent whole by look-

ing at the school someone went to, the healthcare fund that person chose, and the newspaper he or she read. Knowing the three individual elements allowed us to deduce a fourth. Today, any rationale underlying such choices is less the result of ideological convictions, but a matter of considerations of a very different nature: price, accessibility, fashion, quality of service, and so on. There is enough coherence in the eyes of the people themselves, but it defies categorization by onlookers!

Banker in the morning and volleyball trainer or actor in a theater group in the evening, the same person can love cooking and still buy frozen meals, He can have both a luxury bike and a bottom-of-the-range car, and be fanatical about the Internet, yet have numerous magazine subscriptions. She can be affiliated with a state insurance scheme, call herself a Christian, vote for the Greens, send her children to an international school, and consider herself entirely consistent!

Stereotypes are crashing down one after another, and attempts to slice the world up into separate segments are increasingly unrealistic. In all of this we run up against the problem of identity. What *is*, today, a computer specialist, a retired person, a philanthropist, a consultant, a Belgian, a sportsman, an ecologist?

Everything contributes to making the client a moving, unpredictable, and mutating target. The attitudes of *homo sapiens* resist equations, their zigzags cannot be modeled. They become *homo zappens*!

Are companies really ready for this? To check let's use a metaphor.

When a crack suddenly appears in a building, two explanations are possible. Either the building was badly constructed with poor materials—someday a wall collapses or a wooden frame begins to warp—or the cause is external; a solidly constructed building has simply cracked because of an earthquake.

The analogy is tempting: Many companies today are damage-prone. The hunt for guilty parties inside the organization is not necessarily the right way to proceed. Not a few of these companies were built at a time when an earthquake was inconceivable. But, under the rules of the New Economy and technology, that is exactly what is happening. A networked world is a world in tension. While actual earthquakes are latent, tremors are both certain and unpredictable. Companies now need to be built to earthquake-proof standards.

In the past, the business world was a calm one. Supply and demand curves would gently meet each other, not too far from the office or the factory. Suppliers and clients got together at the business club. Their relationships were stable, and so were the interest rates. Competitors were called "colleagues," poor credit risks were rare, and a person's word was better than a bank guarantee.

Seniority was synonymous with quality. A downtown location reflected abundant equity. You dealt with a banker the way you dealt with your confessor: asking questions was impertinent, comparing prices smacked of bad manners, and haggling was unspeakably crude. Big companies looked after their clients, when manufacturing their products left them a bit of spare time. Every delivery ended with the ritual "see you next time," so certain was the next order. Those days are long gone!

Today, the business club has been franchised by a multinational and one-third of the clients are not even English speakers. The stock exchange reverberates with the bids, "know-how" has given way to "know-who," and the question of "what's our competitor up to?" is replaced by "who is our competitor?" Nothing is a sure thing any longer; everything has to be tried and tested again and again. These days, a lot of young people start their first job reluctantly, intending to tackle a career seriously later on. Youngsters don't even like to hear the word *job*. They go to New York the way Parisians used to go into the forest at Fontainebleau. (You may remember the cartoon showing a young consultant who, feet up on the desk and with a PC in his lap, hails a colleague and tells him, "If my boss calls, ask him what his name is.")

In the past, the business environment was a relatively serene one, and you could think of the enterprise as settled in place, once and for all. Today, nothing is stable and you have to continuously rethink the enterprise, equip it with adaptive mechanisms, make sure it is capable of learning. Today you have to build earthquake-proof companies because they are the only ones capable of providing a client with sustainable products and services.

Let's take another metaphor (it's my job, isn't it?).

In the past, a company was like a rocket launched from the moon to Mars—i.e., a target whose behavior was perfectly predictable and which could be reached through space without running into the slightest disturbance. If the launch was OK, you just had to wait.

It reminds me of when I started my career at the *Générale de Banque* in the early 1970s. My boss told me that the 3-6-3 law governed the banking sector (borrow at 3 percent, lend at 6 percent, and play golf at 3 o'clock). Little by little this law has seen changes. From 4-5-6 (which was annoying in the winter), it has now moved to 4.99-5.01. In other words the margins have been seriously squeezed—and there's not even much room left for golf!

Today, the enterprise is more like a subspace rocket launched against a zigzagging missile—i.e., a target whose behavior is unpredictable, and which can only be reached in an environment racked by violent winds. To adopt another metaphor and echo Canadian ice hockey star Wayne Gretzky's famous phrase: "Is it really possible to know, not where the puck is, but where it's going to be?"

The two meanings of the word *revolution* clearly apply—both revolving and blowing up. Whereas once it was possible to predict a client's docile orbit, today we have to adapt to the client's demands, because client behavior is now unexpected, erratic, chaotic, even unknown. Moreover, violent winds are blowing through the economy. This double phenomenon can only be addressed by changing the type of rocket. We need to use a target-seeking model, adapted to the "imperfect" economy.

From now on, reality will contain air pockets—and survival, the sign of the "success" of a system, will be impossible without feedback mechanisms that continuously detect the gap between what is and what was supposed to be. By so doing, it will correct the resources consumed (the word *resource* should be understood in its broader sense and include the matter-energy-information trinomial) and how the system consumes them.

FIGURE 7.1 *Preparing for Uncertain Futures*

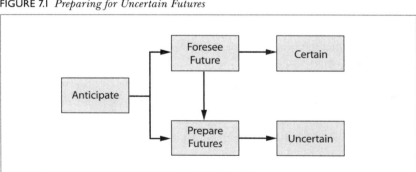

Uncertainty has no limit apparently, yet the top responsibility of the manager, more than ever, is to anticipate. How does he or she get out of this impasse? By a big mental shift from a *forecast* mind to a *prepare* mind!

# FEEDBACK AND CONTROL

To understand this better let's use—guess what?—another metaphor! (*Meta* means "elsewhere" in Greek and *fero* means "transport." The Greeks thought this was the best way to think, and they were right!). This time let's think in terms of how you set a temperature in a room. Imagine you want 68°F tomorrow. You have two options. Either you look at the weather forecast and try to adjust the heating system, or you install a thermostat—and you're no longer reliant on what's going to happen. This leads to an intuition: we can get out of the impasse by using a feedback system.

If you have feedback, you don't have to worry as much about uncertainty. As always in this book, whenever I introduce a new concept, I try to go back to the main thinker, in this case the pioneer was Norbert Wiener. He wrote a book in 1948 called *Cybernetics* and, if we talk today about cyberspace, it's because of him. (Wiener coined the word *cybernetics* by deriving it from the ancient Greek word *gubernau*, which means "piloting," and is present in the word *government*!). The book's subtitle was *The Science of Control and Feedback Systems*. It's not by chance that Wiener belongs to the same "systems thinkers" galaxy as the Palo Alto school I introduced in Chapter 1.

One of Wiener's posited problems, for example, was to imagine someone pouring wine into a friend's glass while keeping the distance between the bottle and the glass constant. A certain amount of effort is needed to hold the bottle at the proper distance from the glass. But a few seconds into the pouring, the bottle weighs less. To reduce the effort and maintain the distance, the pourer needs to relay information from his hand and arm to the brain, which then adjusts the degree of exertion. This is continuous feedback, a "looping" of information.

What's also interesting in the subtitle of the book is that it contains the word *control.* This makes the point that an effective regulated system has two elements: one is assessing, the other reaction. They have to be separated. When you drive home in your car and you see that the fuel

FIGURE 7.2 *The Old Economy*

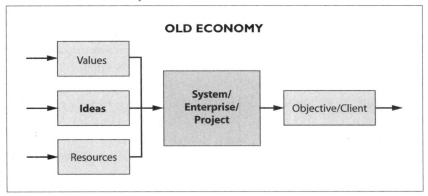

gauge is low, you may decide to refuel tomorrow. In any case, one thing is measuring and assessing, the other is taking action.

With this concept we can begin to understand today's economy better. In the Old Economy, feedback wasn't particularly necessary. You thought up an idea, built a factory, and delivered the product to the customer. Ergo, the Model T, the factory, and the consumer. That was the Old Economy. It worked very well, precisely because the needs of the customer were relatively easy to predict. (See Figure 7.2.)

That's why we can see that, at the beginning of an economic success, there was often a major idea: soda ash, electricity, or vaccines gave birth to countless industrial empires still around today. The creative genius of Solvay, Edison, the Pasteurs, and others made its mark on history in this way. But the regrouping of the economy around *information* is likely to make this sort of adventure less and less probable, for two reasons at least. Growing and definitive uncertainty demands prudence. Every new idea is necessarily constructed on hypotheses and therefore has to integrate the fragility of these hypotheses.

The second reason is that the *informational* nature of many of these new ideas makes them very susceptible to counterfeiting. It is easy to steal information—and, in a certain way, we do not deprive the owner of his or her property. Ideas therefore have a much shorter lifecycle. They create competitive advantage that is sometimes only measured in months. New ideas remain the source of wealth, for sure. But, even more, it is the capacity for generating them that is the determining factor. If, in the past, a company made sales because it had cheaper products to offer, in the future we will see sales that provide services that its competitors don't offer—yet. Competitive advantage has to be constantly reinvented, and this motion is becoming perpetual.

A big part of the effort is to build in a cybernetic system—one that feeds back information. Wal-Mart, for instance, has several of the biggest supercomputers ever made, just for consumer feedback. Harrah's, the world's biggest gambling enterprise, prides itself on its customer card system. Gary Loveman, Harrah's CEO, is not your typical gaming boss; he has a Ph.D. from MIT and an MBA from Harvard. What has made him dominant in his industry, though, is the implementation of a program whereby people who gamble are given a card that feeds back to the computers everything they eat, drink, play, and so on. It gives Harrah's the ability to anticipate what the customer will do next.

A great chef will tell you that his worth is not so much in the dishes he is capable of serving, but above all in his capacity for inventing new ones. Have you ever heard of Spanish chef Ferrán Adriá? His restaurant is called Bulli. Many people consider him the best chef in the world. What's his strength? Cooking extraordinary meals? Inventing new meals? Well, he closes his restaurant six months a year because he always says his value is not cooking but inventing. He is not a shrimp and salad factory; he is an ideas factory

The New Economy is really different. The customer is unpredictable, so you have to measure all the time. You have to check the difference between what is and what could be. That's the control part. Then you can bring in new ideas—and you feed them back into the system.

There are four ways to get feedback from a client:

1. *The client may take the trouble to tell you.* Perhaps the most important source is the dissatisfied client. The complaints department is where the most brilliant people in your company should be. But complaints are becoming rare. The old proverb, "no news is good news" is out of date. "No news signals a catastrophe—the client has gone elsewhere!" is probably more accurate. Numerous alternatives are open to the dissatisfied client. Schopenhauer—with whom it is not always necessary to agree—says we are bound to suffer. Either we don't have what we want and we suffer, or we no longer want what we have and are bored. The client who suffers may be helped by having a need satisfied but, if the client continues to be bored by the perfection of the supplier, what is to be done?

2. *You may have to intrigue or reward the client to get the feedback.* That's why we reward those clients who respond to a survey.

3. *The feedback may even be automated.* Large Client-Relationship-Management-type databases store everything known about the client, so that marketing becomes "one-to-one." That's where you record the reactions of the client who decides to go into business with you. But automation is still far off, however. Even if you have been the "client" of the same automatic teller for years, the machine doesn't greet you by name, and it asks you every time if you want a receipt (even though you always give it the same answer). The "click" economy is theoretically more earthquake-proof than the "brick" economy, but it still needs someone to do something.

4. *The feedback may be disguised.* The client thinks he or she is receiving, but in fact is giving. This is not a brand-new idea. When your wine merchant offers to put the bottles in your cellar for you, isn't that also an opportunity for the merchant to see just what you have there? When Bill Gates invites you to send e-mail reports to his company, it's not to do you a favor. It's you who are doing him one, by sending him your comments on his software. And when a large chain of stores agrees to pay you the difference if you find the same article cheaper elsewhere, the few pennies paid out are doubtless very little in comparison to the information it receives. The next time you leave your business card at a trade show, hoping it will be drawn from a box for a prize, remember that someone else wins at every draw: the manager of the show's mailing list.

You also need to get feedback from other sources too:

1. The focus can be on the company itself, what we call management control or quality control. The word *contrôle* in French is actually a poor choice, because it has more the sense of taking charge than simply monitoring what is going on. The expression "lack of control" is imprecise. Is it a failure by the person looking at the control panel or a mistake in the design of the control panel itself? After an accident, we often ask, "Who was at the controls?" The question really should be, "Who defined the control procedures?"

2. The focus can be on other sources outside the company. This is what is called *intelligence,* a concept that should be construed in its broadest sense:

- *Technology intelligence.* Can the same thing be done another way?
- *Competitive intelligence.* How do the others do it?
- *Market intelligence.* How is the consumer changing?
- *Financial intelligence.* Can our interest rate assumptions be verified?
- *Organizational intelligence.* What is the impact of a new software package?
- *Legal intelligence.* What are the legislative trends?
- *Government intelligence* Are subsidies in the offing?
- *Commercial intelligence.* What type of project is being launched abroad?
- *Social intelligence.* Why are they making this claim?
- *External intelligence.* What risks do we face?

The difference between 1 and 2 is clear. Management control is designed to correct errors in past assumptions. Intelligence, on the other hand, is designed to correct the error of not having made an assumption.

The immediate consequence is that an error isn't what it used to be. Making a mistake used to be a case of wrongly estimating a parameter. From now on, making a mistake is about failing to build in correction and improvement mechanisms.

Is it so easy? Should we simply put in loops everywhere to solve problems? Yes and no. Unfortunately, there is some bad news about feedback. Using feedback everywhere increases uncertainty. In France you can't have a poll the last three days preceding an election because the feedback could influence the election. The nuclear power plant in Chernobyl exploded because the Russians couldn't control the complexity of the feedback. Feedback also increases energy consumption; the system burns a lot of energy just getting feedback.

With feedback everywhere we are in a chicken-and-egg situation. If you asked economists why people buy options on the market, they would probably answer that it's because of volatility. With an option you take less risk. But if you asked them why there is so much volatility, they

FIGURE 7.3 *The New Economy*

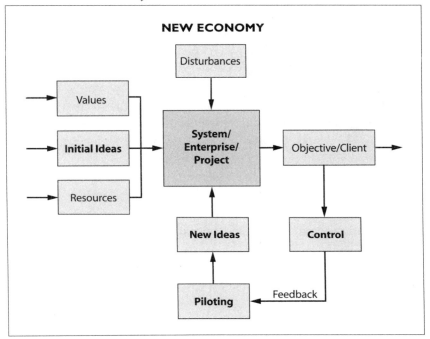

might answer, "because there are so many options." So we shouldn't pose the old question, "which came first, the chicken or the egg?" We should eat them both because, with the use of feedback, you increase your independence from complexity, but you also increase the complexity itself. There is no alternative.

As you can see in Figure 7.3, one thing is critical: the capacity to assess the output. We should look closely because, in some situations, this is not so easy.

Take the PC business, for example. Changing the rules of the game is what Dell did when it broke into the PC business. It cut out distributors, went straight to the users, and encouraged them to specify and buy exactly what they wanted. So users no longer buy off the shelf; they buy off an assembly line!

Dell didn't stop there. Anticipating the slender margins in PC sales, the company simply kicked the warehousing habit, eliminating the stereotype that "inventory is a form of security." Even suppliers' stocks held in Dell plants don't go onto the company's books until a forklift truck pulls them off the rack for the assembly line! In fact, total inventory time amounts at most to two or three days: 6 to 8 hours traveling across the assembly line, 18 hours being shipped to a 'merge' center where the product is packaged with a monitor and shipped on to the customer.

Dell's openness to change and its preparedness for uncertainty was best illustrated by the company's anticipation of the 10-day labor lock-out at the United States's West Coast ports in 2002. Sensing trouble, it alerted a real-time network of suppliers and shipping partners, fielded a "tiger team" of ten roving logistics specialists, and chartered a fleet of 18 Boeing 747 jumbo jets at a cost that later proved to be less than half the rate that applied once the lockout had started.

Through a brilliantly anticipated and equally brilliantly organized strategy, worked out in close collaboration with its suppliers and shippers, Dell survived this ten-day lockout with about 72 hours' worth of inventory—and fulfilled all its orders on time.

# MEASUREMENTS

Before you take measures, you have to have measures. You have to be informed to be able to decide. You have to have instruments to fly a plane. The ambiguity of the word *measure* covers a dual necessity: You need knowledge of what really is happening (measuring your environment) and the desire to make changes (taking the relevant measures).

Even if there is a sequence involved, one does not imply the other. Two quite different activities are involved, with different challenges and different responsibilities. The evaluation will be all the better if the evaluator doesn't have to make the choices, and the decider who doesn't have to investigate first will make a better decision.

We are all pilots and have our own instruments. The instrument panel, the numbers and statistics, are only vague representations of reality. Most often, they are inexact and imprecise. They make you think of Arthur Koestler's monitor screens or Plato's metaphor of the slave imprisoned in a cave who thinks the shadows on the walls are reality until he escapes and sees the sun! The terms *inexact* and *imprecise* are not interchangeable, by the way. Exactness deals with conformity to reality, while precision reflects how many numbers follow the decimal point.

While weakness in precision can be corrected by the use of more precise tools, problems with exactness force us to make a real effort of the imagination. In such cases, it is the choice of the measurement units themselves that is being challenged. This is not a new problem, far from it. It is the eternal problem of accommodating both a world that changes and a man-on-the-street who resists.

Pierre Bourdieu, a French philosopher, once gave a very good illustration of this conflict. The painters of the *Quattrocento* of the Italian Renaissance had to fight with their patrons not to be paid according to the size of their paintings and the cost of their paints (we know this from reading contracts that are still available today).

Six hundred years later, the question of the relevance of different ways or units of measurement is still current.

In the 35-hour work week debate in France, one hypothesis seems to have been accepted by all parties: time measures work. But, every day, this assumption becomes a little less true. For a growing portion of the workforce, the time of work, measured in hours and minutes, is only one parameter among many.

As purely physical fatigue in the workplace has diminished greatly, we face the paradox that a person at work is resting when standing still! But other types of effort are involved. Work is more abstract, interactive, and unpredictable; the boundary between work and nonwork is becoming blurred; and knowledge and imagination are decisive. Simply asking the question "how much time does it take to have an idea?" makes the point that work time is a measure inherited from a world we are now leaving behind us.

Insidiously, without our noticing, work risks being measured in terms of speed. In other words, work of perfect quality done slowly has zero economic value!

Another area where the indicators seem to be entirely out of date is, of course, the environment. Man is driving the planet at top speed without a fuel gauge. In reaction to such adolescent behavior, the World Wildlife Fund (WWF) suggests using a "living planet" index to provide a quantified response to the question of how fast the earth is losing its natural resources. The answer is a stunning one. From 1970 to 1995, the sustainability index fell by 30 percent. Moreover the natural equilibrium in two areas has already been disrupted almost irreversibly: fish consumption and carbon gas emissions have outrun sustainability.

The WWF index clearly shows the absurdity of an index like GNP (Gross National Product) which, in the case of an oil spill for example, goes up twice, first by the amount of fuel lost and then by the funds spent cleaning it up (http://www.panda.org)! The WWF proposes to replace the GNP by the "footprint" as a measure (see also http://www.footprintnetwork.org).

This also brings up the difference between efficiency and effectiveness. The first is seen from the perspective of supply, the second from demand. Which of the two is more important? The number of houses built or the number of people who have a house, the amount of food produced or the number of people who are no longer starving, the number of tons of waste collected by a garbage truck or how clean the street is? As you see, it is easier to quantify efficiency than effectiveness.

Let's return to companies. How many words and adjectives achieve unanimity simply because they are not "measurable"? Increase personnel motivation, client satisfaction, language proficiency, effectiveness of research—everyone agrees on such goals, but how to get there? The answer comes in one word: criteria.

If a jogger, for example, asks a doctor to suggest how fast to run, three types of answers are conceivable.

1. Not too fast.
2. A maximum of 130 heartbeats per minute.

The first answer is not measurable, the second impractical, so there must be something else.

3. When you jog, you should always be able to talk to another runner.

This third answer is of a different type. It is neither meaningless hogwash nor is it overloaded with numbers. It is a criterion, and a criterion allows evaluation in a particularly important area characteristic of human relations. It is verifiable, but not measurable.

Imagine you think it would be useful to have your assistant learn French. Between the meaningless "You need to make a serious effort" and the measurable "Spend two and a half hours a week on French," there is room for a criterion: "In six months, you should be able to handle calls from French-speaking callers."

A criterion has many advantages. It can take many forms, and it makes it possible to exercise authority on the basis of a relevant evaluation. Hogwash gets you nowhere, while a measurable criterion can lead to disagreement (why two and a half hours and not two hours?) or fraud ("window dressing").

Take the most recent list you have of your company's objectives and divide them among these three categories. To know where to put them, you have to know how the success or failure of each objective will be evaluated. The criterion zone is probably the smallest. Therein may be a key to your future success.

Thinking in this way, the quality of the water in a river might be evaluated by whether it has fish or not (and not by now many particles per cubic foot of a particular pollutant). You can say that a garden is big enough if you can safely build fires in it. You can decide that a consultant is good if the client calls back. You can establish that there is support for a group project if each of its members can explain its objectives in public. You can say a newsletter is interesting if its recipients make copies of it, that a report is good if the client looks at it and keeps it, that a filing system is good if others can find what they're looking for. You could also say that a small or medium-sized business is sound if it has very little contact with its banker.

Long ago, an industrialist dreamed up a wonderful criterion for determining the quality of the prototype of a new sound recording system: his dog had to be able to recognize "His Master's Voice"!

FIGURE 7.4 *Measuring Goals*

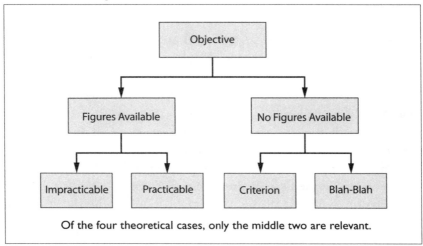

Of the four theoretical cases, only the middle two are relevant.

Criteria don't necessarily have to be binary. Like the Richter scale, the Beaufort scale, or even Maslow's pyramid, gradations are possible. Knowledge of a language increases if it is respectively read, understood, spoken in private, spoken in public, and written. Likewise, a writer can measure his "weight" in a bookstore by whether his books are absent, in stock, on display or—the ultimate satisfaction—if his name appears on a sign in a section containing all his works.

## ALIKE BUT DIFFERENT

Now we know that good feedback systems are the key to organizing a company, and we also know that a competitive edge can only be maintained if a company is an ideas factory. This leaves a last point: Can we really afford to be different at any time? We're back to the oxymoron approach, because we need to be both the same and different!

Let's start by trying a freshly squeezed orange juice. An immediate reaction is that it's delicious. In any case, it's nothing like whatever you can drink out of a bottle, a carton, a can, with or without bubbles—all those drinks that use the name "orange juice" because the juice itself is powerless to sue in court.

Second experience: Let's listen to a melody played in front of you by a cello virtuoso. An immediate pleasure—it's magnificent. In any case, it's like nothing you can hear from a CD, a Walkman, a hi-fi unit, with or without Dolby, playing all those recordings of a melody that probably ought not to have been recorded.

Two experiments, one conclusion: technology can't do everything. Two experiments and one personal opinion: so much the better!

The orange juice and the cello are fighting back—each in its own category, at the two extremities of the matter/information binome. They laugh at multinationals and unnerve the people who have to deal with innovation. Despite the enormous budgets they have at their disposal, researchers still haven't succeeded in packaging either of them. The flavor of orange juice and the vibration of a bow on a string still escape digitalization. Like the lemurs, those primates from Madagascar who die as soon as they are caged, they will not give in.

The orange juice and the cello might therefore be the standard bearers, a kind of Asterix and Obelix confronting an emperor Mondialus Globalus seeking to impose his *pax technologica,* and their fight is a just one. Besides the lower quality of products that have fallen victim to excessive productivity or mechanization, it is their uniformity and banality that intrigues and annoys us. For the drive to standardization today goes far beyond the boundaries of technology. Uniformization may seem subjacent, derived, perhaps secondary, but it is part of the great transformation going on in the world. A "heavy trend," as the sociologists might say. Too heavy?

On the one hand, more uniformization could have its good side. This is what we say when we can't plug our electric razor into a European power socket, when we can't compare two different mobile phone or credit card contracts, when we can't buy a pair of trousers of a certain size without trying them on (sometimes they're cut long in the leg, sometimes in the Italian style), or when we're studying logic and chemistry and the symbols or nomenclature change from one author to the next. We would even go as far as to sing the praises of uniformization when we're forced to drive on the left in England or to convert miles and nautical miles (not the same thing!) into kilometers, or when we have to give up trying to open a document on a Mac because it was made on a PC.

On the other hand, uniformization isn't as good as all that. This is what we say when we bite into an apple that has no taste, when we limit our vocabulary to two hundred words so that we can say it in English, when we curse the disappearance of bookshops and the meager, identical selection of books we see in department stores. We would even go as far as to curse uniformization when we have to pay five times the price for a new car door or trim simply because they're not "standard."

Uniformization does have a paradoxical side to it. The trainers and Walkman, jeans and T-shirt, that both parents and children are wearing—just as much Western youths as those from the countries that otherwise reject the Western model. What is fashion if it isn't an invitation to look the same by making yourself different in the same way?

Uniformization therefore seems:

- *A good thing.* It allows us to communicate more easily, to pay everywhere in the same currency, to save energy and raw materials; uniformization is indeed ecology.

- *A bad thing*. The one and only apple is just a pip's throw away from the one and only way of thinking; diversity is the very condition of life; uniformization is a negation of ecology.

Are we at an impasse? No, of course not. One of the common threads running through the history of philosophy is precisely the conviction that, in nature, all processes are the result of tensions between opposites. The texture of the thread has certainly varied, and the color and thickness too. Sometimes the thread has actually snapped, but the tussle is as a weaving of thought between light and darkness, between good and evil, or more generally between thesis and antithesis. Anaximander, who died around 540 BC, was impressed by opposites, the continual combat between hot and cold, dry and wet. But Heraclites once more pushed things further with the affirmation that, "conflict is the father of all beings, the king of all beings." He therefore made fire the primordial substance, 25 centuries before global warming started.

We are not in an impasse. We just need to watch out: uniformity one day was born out of boredom. Let's ally rigor with creativity, let's be militant supporters of the power of difference. A Christmas present doesn't need to be a CD from the charts or a book that's won a literary prize. A hotel isn't better because it's got 250 identical beds. Sending a greeting card doesn't have to be a procedure, even if the envelope is a post-office-approved standard.

## KEY IDEAS IN THIS CHAPTER

- Uncertainty increases, but you still have to anticipate.
- You used to make forecasts; now you have to be prepared.
- Organizing feedback is the way to do it, even if there is a price to pay.
- Nonstop creativity is required.
- You need measures even when there are no figures available.
- Be the same, be different!

# 8

# THE "IDEAL" MANAGER

*"Would we think a great deal, and would we think well,*
*if we were not thinking—so to speak—with other people?"*

**Immanuel Kant**

**'D**on't come to my company; we have too many ideas already!" This is a comment that has often been made to me and illustrates a common paradoxical problem. Creativity is acknowledged today as essential for the survival of a company, but management sometimes fears having to manage the abundance of ideas generated.

Some people even consider more creativity is useless, arguing that there are already lots of ideas in the organization that haven't been addressed. All these reactions bear witness to the same confusion.

To bring matters to a logical conclusion, these managers should only hire colleagues with no ideas—or the traffic jam of existing ideas will just get worse. Even better, they should hire people good at destroying other people's ideas so that, with a little patience, things will get back to normal.

Can you have too many ideas? Have you ever heard a manager complaining about having too many buildings, too many computers, too much money, or too many trucks? No, on the contrary, the manager would see these things as opportunities. Yet the opportunity embodied in a good idea is limitless.

FIGURE 8.1 *Typology of Ideas*

| | |
|---|---|
| Generated in the company | Generated elsewhere (clients, suppliers, etc.) |
| Proposed by one person | Proposed by a team |
| Can be used locally | Can be used elsewhere |
| Applicable immediately | Applicable later |
| Provide a new answer (suggestion) | Provide a new question (surprise) |
| Are truly new | Exist elsewhere (benchmarking) |
| Improve what already exists (something better) | Suggest something new (something else) |

Having accepted the importance of professionally managing their material assets, information, and human resources, companies now face a major new challenge: how to manage ideas. Even if this resource is particularly hard to handle, as we have seen in Chapter 7, it is only good ideas that will allow companies to create and maintain a distance from their competitors.

Ideas are the fuel of added value, the indispensable ingredient of little things with a big impact. But they are fragile, ephemeral, and chaotic.

Where do we start? Maybe with a basic statement: everything can be found here, in the world of ideas. Some are small ideas—either from the back of your head or pulled out of your sleeve—but they may get bigger one day. Others are waiting, in raw form, to be dug up from among so many other ideas inherited from anonymous donors. Then there are "harnessed" ideas, and ideas that seem utterly crazy, the result of wild brainstorming.

The important thing is to find the meaning behind the idea. Because it is not unusual for an idea that seems to be going nowhere to be "surprised" out of its immobility and join another one, an idea that is heading somewhere. Sometimes a somber idea gives way to a luminous one, or an idea that "glitters" turns out, indeed, to be pure gold.

Rather than leave things to chance, why don't we manage these nuggets of information like professionals? In the information society, the gold standard has gone forever.

# CREATIVE RIGOR

I know you may feel that managing new ideas is difficult—perhaps the most difficult thing imaginable—but obstacles to new ideas should not be seen as such. New ideas spring naturally from the toughest situations. Michelangelo himself said, "Art is born of constraint—and dies from freedom." In other words, hardship is the fertile soil of creativity.

Ravel composed his entire *Bolero* using only one tune, and afterwards wrote his *Concerto for the Left Hand* (dedicated to the brother of Ludwig Wittgenstein who lost his arm in an accident). Manuel de Falla produced his superb *Miller's Dance* from *The Three-Cornered Hat* in the course of an evening, after Diaghilev rejected his original composition.

Rigor and creativity are two words we're not really used to seeing together. We think of creators as souls who lay on their backs and dream. Yet, imagination can get on very well with discipline, and creativity can feed happily on the type of rigor that doesn't smother it but sets it in a clear framework.

In poetry, there's the example of the alexandrine. It's hard to imagine a vise that squeezes writing so tightly as these two lines of six beats. Yet this almost painful rigor has led to some of the most beautiful verses in literature.

Victor Hugo, for whom "form is content, risen to the surface," explained in two magnificent lines the paradoxical effect of constraint which, rather than blocking imagination, serves on the contrary to provoke it:

> "And I didn't fail to realize that the angry hand
> That delivers the word, also delivers the thought."

> [Et je n'ignorais pas que la main courroucée
> qui délivre le mot, délivre la pensée.]

In our time, thanks to OuLiPo (*Ouvroir de la Littérature Potentielle*, the workshop for potential literature), we have seen the reinvention of the duo "rigor and creativity" in a way that is perhaps more original but by no means any easier. Georges Perec's novel *La Disparition*, for example, manages to go from beginning to end without once using the letter *e*. Perhaps even more remarkable is that the English translation, *A Void*, succeeds in doing the same thing: no *the, he,* or *she,* no words ending in *-ed,* totally *e*-less.

Modernity drove another of the workshop's members to write an entire story using only the letters on the left-hand side of his *azerty* keyboard (incidentally, it would be entertaining to ask someone to type the text quickly and see what happens). The OuLiPian approach consists of injecting constraint in order to stimulate unexpected creation, to force the system out of its routine way of working. Just try writing at random, even if it's only one sentence (the book can wait):

- Alternating vowels and consonants systematically.[1]
- Subjecting yourself to the constraints of a prisoner who only has a very limited stock of paper in his cell and refuses to use any letters that extend above or below the center line (i.e., only letters like *a, c, e,* or *m,* and not *b, g, l,* or *q*).

OuLiPo is also a great lover of palindromes, those short phrases that read the same forwards or backwards:

- A man, a plan, a canal: Panama. (a tribute to Ferdinand de Lesseps)
- Are we not drawn onward, we few? Drawn onward to new era?

For OuLiPo, only constraint turns writing into an art, and all the rest is literature!

All the arts have their rules: Greek tragedies and Cicero's speeches, Renaissance frescoes and Bach's concertos, temples, tapestries, and sculptures. All works classed as beautiful or grandiose have hidden within them a constraining structure and an implacable discipline.

The directors of low-budget movies can tell you how lack of money can be an excellent stimulant for the imagination. When you have to evoke the Andean Cordilleras or a naval battle without being able to show or reconstruct them, the producer has no option but to surpass expectations.

In a similar way, doesn't the obligation to present one's ideas on slides in companies add something to the quality of these ideas? Each slide has to be coherent, both in itself (for example, a few points and a conclusion preceded by a little arrow) and in the presentation as a whole. It has to be limited, structured, and make the logic of the argument come to the fore. (I know this statement may seem a paradox since

I explained in the preface why I never use Powerpoint, but at this stage of the book, that will no longer surprise you!)

It's the strictest football referees who allow the players to liberate their talents to the greatest degree. In the same way, company managers who decide on, and respect, the limits to their reflection actually contribute to the quality of their thoughts.

Creativity, then, isn't just something that lets you think. It's much more about thinking *better*. To answer a question that's asked all the time, I constantly emphasize the fact that a new idea doesn't necessarily need new resources. It's quite often possible, even within the strictest of limitations, to detect degrees of newly found liberty. History abounds with examples of situations where it was precisely because of a shortage, poor conditions, or a lack of resources that an idea was born.

When a quartz watch wants to alert its owner to the fact that the battery is running out, it could stop, it could go backwards, or it could change the date to 32. But this would be detrimental to the "watch system," which would not be very watch-like any more. So it was decided to opt for a solution that makes four-second jumps every four seconds. In this way the message gets across while the watch continues to show the correct time and date.

Similarly, a school could choose to combine two classes with two teachers instructing simultaneously. This is an idea that would not require any extra resources but, if you feel within you a natural tendency to find this idea unacceptable, relax: you're only human!

Sometimes the participants at an in-house seminar are asked in turn to describe the strengths and weaknesses of their respective departments. This takes the same time as doing two complete rounds of the table—first the strengths, then the weaknesses—but, in that case, the coffee break halfway through will be conducted in a completely different atmosphere: everyone will be saying that the people involved have nothing but good qualities and it's the system that's to blame.

An IT company decided one day to replace the individual photos on their experts' CVs with a group photo of the entire team. Perhaps the success of Twix can simply be put down to the fact that the snack bar has now been replaced by two half-bars.

This capacity for creativity within constraint is all the more important because one of the main trends in today's world is to standardize and uniformize.

How can a subsidiary maintain its personality when the parent company hands its communications strategy to an advertising agency on another continent? How can a franchise operator who has to follow entire manuals of rules and procedures still be creative—that is, astonish clients? How can we leave enough space for new ideas despite ISO 9000? Do what you say and say what you do. Quality and creativity can and must both be total.

In the literature on the subject—and notably in the classic book by Alex Osborn—the four rules for brainstorming are presented as follows:

1. Express yourself; don't keep any ideas cooped up inside you.
2. Don't judge or evaluate an idea that's only just been voiced.
3. Be constructive and positive about another person's ideas.
4. Look for quantity in ideas, not quality.

The complicity that has to exist between creativity and rigor suggests that a few more rules may have to be added:

- Start on time; finish at the scheduled time.
- Use the services of a trained, neutral facilitator.
- Ask the "owner" of the problem to present it and to set the boundaries for reflection.
- Keep refocusing on the theme of the meeting.
- Note everything down and circulate a memo on the session.
- Ban mobile phones!

Good brainstorming sessions take place at 9 AM on Monday mornings with the real people responsible, and not late Friday afternoon with anybody who's still around. The future is at this intersection between rigorous creativity and creative rigor. As Leibniz said, "music is the pleasure the soul experiences when it is counting without noticing."

## THE RIGHT WORD

There are certainly additional ways in which a greater degree of rigor would be beneficial. For if management tools, information networks, and modeling can contribute to improving company performance, language is another resource that could benefit from a bit more thought.

The words, phrases, and verbs all of us use are not always well chosen or even adequate. Imprecise, clumsy, or virtually meaningless words are often used in internal communications when the correct choice of vocabulary is of great importance. In common speech—often delivered too fast—a number of words are used interchangeably. Nuances merge into each other and the little differences that prompt creativity are no longer there.

The overhasty choice of a noun or adjective, falsely synonymous with another one, gives rise to imprecision. The use of the wrong word is inefficient and to make a habit of it can have nasty consequences. How many times do we tell ourselves, "I don't have the time," when we really mean, "I don't want to"? How many times do we tell ourselves it's *important* when it's simply *urgent*? Urgency and importance are not measured on the same scale. Similarly a *dangerous* situation must not be confused with a *risky* one, *immaterial* and *virtual* are two very different things, a consultant's *approach* has nothing to do with his *approximation*. And is there a difference between *regularization* and *regulation*?

While the use of real synonyms can sometimes enrich communication, the wrong use of one word in place of another can provoke errors. This is the case, for example, of *stability* and *equilibrium*. Two words that certainly conjure up calm, even harmony, and are often interchanged. But isn't that overlooking the possibility of an unstable equilibrium?

At the same time these synonyms are not entirely false, and approaching a problem from the point of view of vocabulary can be a good way of encouraging creativity. If we're thinking about unemployment, let's look for the nuances between the words *job, trade, profession,* and *work.* If we are looking at skills acquisition, let's examine how the words *education, apprenticeship, training, upbringing, instruction,* and even *pedagogy* are differentiated.

The exercise can be very rich, provided it is done in a rigorous and not rigid way!

## CREATIVITY AND INNOVATION REVISITED

As I pointed out at the beginning of this book—and now aided by the momentum provided by the paragraphs above—it's important to remember that creativity is different from innovation. It is difficult to conceive of one without the other. Unless all levels of an organization open their minds as completely as possible to the two types of thought—divergence and convergence—the flow of creativity will be reduced to drips. On the other hand, if the "innovation circuits" are not yet installed, if the ideas can't circulate, people's frustrations will be stains on the walls of indifference.

From the young intern to the experienced foreman, from the researcher to the marketeer, the imagination of one person often rests on the surprise of another. But, to continue the hydraulic metaphor, "suggestion pipelines" are not always enough on their own. Sometimes the delivery rate drops, and the flow of ideas dries up. This is when creativity techniques should come into play. They act as the pump, guaranteeing the pressure of the collective imagination.

Creativity and innovation have some important things in common. Both are idea processes, and neither should be limited by technology. Nor should either of them be limited to products. Creativity and innovation should concern all a company's personnel across all its activities. Both are systems developments and so may benefit from the guidance of an outside consultant. The essential thing is to distinguish between the two (see Chapter 1).

If the right climate is indispensable to creativity, it's a real charter—almost a contract with itself—that will guarantee permanent innovation in a company. This charter can specify, for example, the percentage of time people can spend on their own projects, the percentage of product sales to be made within five years, the annual amount of internal venture capital, and so on.

A well-constructed charter can lead to an amazing shift in corporate culture. Not only can innovation get a company to the point where it brings out new products and services on an ongoing basis, it can also become the center of gravity for the entire organization.

But once a charter has been established, everyone involved has to translate the spirit of innovation into his or her area of the business.

- The controller or CFO should establish performance indicators: savings generated, or even original ways to determine and manage budgets tied to pay and to prices.
- The HR director should rethink offers of employment, reorient selection tests (how do you detect creativity?) and, for existing personnel, align evaluation procedures or the methods for defining new objectives. He or she should also learn the creativity profile of

each person in order to create better teams and, of course, initiate training programs on brainstorming methods and techniques.

- The facilities manager should ask whether the premises encourage new ideas.
- The IT manager should open up the network and create an accessible ideas bank.
- The R&D manager should understand that new ideas may also come from outside the R&D department.
- The design manager may suddenly realize that an old and popular product needs new packaging, or may decide to modernize the logo.
- Everyone should find an original way to share the message with colleagues.

Reading this, you will realize we are back with the "change twice" message of the Palo Alto school. Creativity is a Type 2 change, which is possible only if accompanied by a new representation of the world. Innovation, on the other hand, is a Type 1 change—it is survival in the perceived world. In its most consistent form, innovation is sometimes called *Kaizen.*

Creativity and innovation are indispensable and the link joining them is doubly paradoxical.

- *Creativity is an individual step.* An idea is born in the head of a person. Yet creativity works best in groups, preferably in live seminars. It leads collectively to a change in perception. But, as the saying goes, "you can lead a horse to water, but you can't make him drink."
- *Innovation is a collective process.* Yet it depends on everyone involved contributing individually to change the corporate reality.

A person may be called creative and a company may be called innovative. It's inappropriate the other way round.

It's no use trying to find out which is more important or deserves higher priority. One can't be perceived or conceived without the other. Creativity and innovation are not complementary skills; they are efforts to be multiplied. If either is insufficient, the outcome will be disappointing.

To innovate is to make something brand new in an existing system. To be creative is to think about a new system. It's not by chance that, even if there was such a word as "creativation," the verb "creativate" would still not be an active one.

# OPEN TO SUGGESTION

At the heart of any innovative company there has, of course, to be a suggestions system. This is the catalyst for staff creativity; the resulting "precipitate" is the company's success. Many of the studies and achievements in this area deserve greater attention than they already receive.

Suggestions systems do not come "off the peg." They have to be put together from a set of functions and modules that find their place within the company, and that can be fitted into the existing space and molded into shape. They should themselves be part of the system, without upsetting it, and must be taken on board by management. A suggestions system is a genuine part of the reality of a company and should be the object of a specific communications campaign.

The route taken by a suggestion is a long one. Step by step, a suggestion can be:

- Encouraged (among those who are required to participate)
- Submitted (recorded, numbered, acknowledged)
- Accepted (according to the criteria set by the company—for example: it should be related to the company's operations, it should not be anonymous or slanderous)
- Selected (considered valid and possibly kept for the future)
- Applied (implemented, made eligible for the annual suggestions award)
- Generalized (be applicable also to other parts of the company)
- Rewarded (the subject of public recognition)
- Patented (you never know!)

This process takes time, so it is important that every participant in a suggestions system knows where his or her suggestion is at any point. Waiting for an Amtrak train is less of a pain if there's a little light showing which station the train is in, and how long you're going to have to wait.

It is essential to place a number of modules along this route.

## The Encouragement Module

The Maslow system (see Chapter 7) can be used to boost creativity in a company. An ideas suggestion program is very easy to examine under the *macroscope*, and staff motivation can be fed in turn by five different types of incentive message.

1. Add to your pay packet with bonus payments.
2. Your ideas provide a guarantee for our future.
3. Be part of a winning team.
4. Become the hero of the staff party.
5. Discover the pleasure of seeing your ideas put into practice.

Encouragement can also work on a more personal level, with the support of a mentor, who may or may not belong to the company.

## The Reward Module

Three sorts of reward can be envisioned along this route.

- A small symbolic gift for any idea that is accepted
- An idea put into practice, which would receive a larger reward
- Once a year, an idea is selected and feted at a party (this could be called 'I-Day')—in this case, there should be a substantial reward

The importance of symbolic rewards (of the first type) is linked to the two stages of thought we discovered in Chapter 5. Both "new" and "good" should be rewarded.

Indeed, "magic thought" is a type of thought that should also be rewarded. Most prizes—including the most prestigious of them all, the Nobel Prize—crown an achievement, an idea that has been brought to maturity, the culmination of an entire cycle of thought. But this way of encouraging innovation puts the emphasis very much on convergence and quality. There also needs to be positive recognition of divergence and quantity.

Walt Disney understood this very well. He would send a dollar to anyone who sent him an idea, whatever it was. A child who suddenly discovered that a camel's back looked like a cogwheel was encouraged to let Disney know. The creator of Mickey Mouse would first send a greenback and a thank-you note to the idea's author, then file the idea under "camel" and "'cogwheel." When one of the ideas happened to turn up, the cartoonist would be only too happy to feature two camels rotating on one another's backs.

To stimulate plenty of ideas in your organization, you can raffle a bottle of champagne among the people who put ideas in the suggestions box. Perhaps you can commit to making a donation to a charity named on the suggestions slip by the participants.

The reward can also take on another form, however—recognition. For example, if an office is reorganized as the result of a suggestion, a simple "before" photo on the wall, showing how things were prior to the change, can act as a stimulus to action to anyone passing by.

## The Training Module

If everyone has to "play creativity" at some point, then there is a need to train the trainers. Rather like a first-aid team for ailing meetings, the trainers have to be clearly identified and available, be entitled to a number of privileges and, of course, must have been through the experience themselves.

## The Management Module

Like any system, all aspects of a suggestions system need to be constantly evaluated, guided, and enhanced in response to recommendations from the participants. The system can only work if it is a long-term project supported by a consistent process of data collection, including:

- The number of ideas per employee
- The staff participation rate
- The average time for implementation
- The implementation rate
- Savings achieved per idea
- Savings achieved per employee
- Comparison with the sector average
- Geography and history of new ideas

# THE OTHER HALF OF CHANGE

A suggestion system on its own, even a perfectly managed one, doesn't make the boss an ideal manager. To deserve this title, he or she has to remember throughout that change has its often forgotten side. I can now summarize the whole book with a full description of the model I outlined in Chapter 1. (If you only want to keep a few pages of this book, I recommend these.)

Running a company or managing a project is a task that straddles two distinct dimensions. There is, of course, daily management, consisting of decisions made to improve the process on a continual basis. This is where the director *acts* for the benefit of the company.

But there is another level of management, parallel to this, and just as essential. This is the level where the manager invents the future, imagines change, seeks out new ideas. This is where the manager *thinks* for the benefit of the company. As we have seen a couple of times, while action is most often presented as continuous, thought, on the other hand, evolves in leaps and bounds, as a genuinely new idea sends a shock wave and shakes things up. In the end, successful companies evolve up a steady slope and up a stepped staircase, both at the same time.

So real change within a company is, by necessity, achieved at two levels. But changing reality is, in its essence, a continuous process, whereas changing perception is essentially sporadic. The following model explains how these two mechanisms—at first sight apparently incompatible—work together (see Figure 8.2).

In the beginning there is the idea, the concept (1), which must be stabilized to allow the action aimed at changing things to take place (2). Reality evolves continually, even if from time to time there is a tremor, a failure, or a change in location (3). Perception by comparison is made up of an assembly of stereotypes, inflexible in their essence, that are challenged from time to time by doubt, anxiety, or, of course, external events (4).

One day strategic vision is exhausted and contributes less and less to keeping things moving (5). This is the moment to take a close look at the weak signals (6), because a perceptual break is indispensable.

The energy for change can come from inside the organization, but sometimes the opportunity or the constraint comes from outside, from a world where things are constantly moving on (7).

FIGURE 8.2 *The Process of Change*

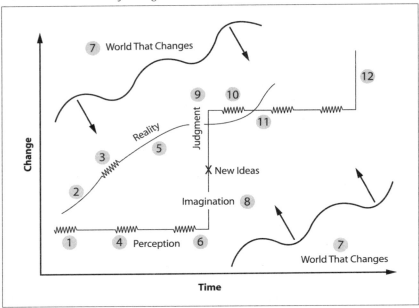

The inevitable change of paradigm occurs when the creative leap takes place. The time of imagination produces a great number of new ideas (8) and the time for judgment will decide on *the next idea* (9).

Thought then enters into a new period of calm, even if a few corrections are still necessary (10). A new strategic vision takes over from the old one and allows the company to enmesh with growth (11).

That only lasts for a moment, for Heraclites is right that history never repeats itself, but it never stops! (12).

You cannot "bathe twice" in the same river of strategic vision. Moreover, the model is true even when everything is going downhill (but that doesn't add anything—and isn't good for the morale).

## DEFINING YOUR STRATEGIC VISION

I began the book with the help of three philosophers. I then referred, in the course of these pages, to many others. That's not by chance!

Philosophy makes numerous contributions to management. One of these could be the need to use the right word in the day-to-day language of the company, as the philosopher is concerned with well-defined concepts.[2] Strategic vision, for example, is often the subject of discussion, negotiation, and presentation. But are we sure we're all talking about the same thing, and what is it, when all's said and done? I would like to propose a definition, using these twelve characteristics.

1. Drawing up a strategic vision is above all an intellectual process. It is located in the *world of thought,* and not in the world of action. Its objective is to change the way we see things (perception) and not things themselves (reality). To allow the second phase to take place (rolling out the project), the vision has to be "snapped" and frozen in time, because we can only build something if we accept there will be no further changes in the plans.

2. All reflection is based on a system of *values;* that is, a set of ideas that we construct from what is desirable. It is essential to express these convictions clearly. Sticking to these recognized values is a *sine qua non* for strategic vision.

3. Thought has its own laws. If we want to construct a strategic vision, then we have to defer to it. As ideas develop more like a stepped staircase than a steady slope, a new vision implies that there is a *break* with the old one. What is broken is a stereotype—at least one—that supported the previous strategy.

4. A strategic vision has to be easy to understand and *coherent.* At its start, it must not contain any internal contradictions or hidden ambiguities; otherwise it is doomed to fail in confusion.

5. The first challenge it will have to face is that of *credibility.* Whoever discovers it will immediately have to be able to see it as feasible, in particular through a clear demonstration of what the available resources are.

6. A strategic vision only exists if it is *shareable* among those it concerns. It only exists if they take ownership of it. It has to motivate, it has to be easy to understand, and easy to get across. It gives everyone involved room to be creative and a space for personal development.

7. Good *communication* is essential; a strategic vision has to appeal to the emotions. So why don't you put it in pictures and communicate with both sides of the brain?

8. It has to be visible from the outside—to clients, suppliers, public opinion—and so on—and has to provide information on the spe-

cific characteristics of the company, on the project itself, and on the *difference* it will make. It can be crystallized in a strong phrase (while avoiding the temptation to create a slogan!).

9. With all due respect to those who dream of the absolute, a strategic vision is *limited* in space and in time. It is defined by limits that are set down in advance and knows it is not eternal, and that—just like its predecessor—it is based on a certain number of hypotheses that will one day no longer be verifiable. In short, it knows that it, too, will end with a break.

10. A new strategic vision contains qualitative elements that go beyond traditional measuring instruments. There are no figures to allow us to evaluate how things are progressing. Nonquantifiable objectives should therefore be accompanied by *criteria*, if they are not to become wishful thinking. These criteria will allow permanent comparison of what is, with what was supposed to be.

11. Growing uncertainty is a fact, and so a strategic vision is necessarily incomplete. Because the unknown cannot be taken into account, it will be fitted out with *correction mechanisms*. While we can "pre-view" what is certain, we can "pre-pare" for the uncertain.

12. The characteristics set out above say nothing of the quality of the vision being constructed. There comes a time for *validation*. Is the vision ethically acceptable, practically feasible, or economically tenable? Moreover, quite simply, is this the right moment? A positive response leads to a decision, and the decision leads to action.

To make a long story short, a strategic vision is a representation, an ambitious image of a future state that is radically preferable to the current state. It becomes a reference, and in so doing, provides a set of concepts that allows every employee to approach his work thoughtfully and effectively.

If you keep this definition in mind, the forgotten half of change will be forgotten no more!

# KEY IDEAS IN THIS CHAPTER

- You have to manage the unmanageable.
- Rigor and creativity are good friends.
- Beware false synonyms.
- Don't forget the second half of change.
- You need to build your own suggestion system.
- Now you can finally define your strategic vision!

Copyright © www.cartoonbase.com

## Chapter 2

1. Serres, Michel. *Le Contrat naturel.* Flammarion, Paris, 1992.

## Chapter 3

1. As a respecter of copyright, I have searched for years for the identity of the graphic artist who created this image. But in vain. So if he or she, or an agent, comes forward, I will be happy to send a bottle of champagne in compensation.

## Chapter 4

1. Horgan, John. *The End of Science,* Broadway Books, New York, 1997.

2. In fact there was an Apple I (see Chapter 5).

## Chapter 8

1. Perhaps better suited to French (e.g., *il avala du lapin avec une salade de kiwis et un ananas*) than to English [translator].

2. Aristotle even proposed defining what a definition is, and deduced from it the notions of category, genus, and species.

Ackoff, Russel L., *The Art of Problem Solving*, John Wiley & Sons, 1978.

Barker, Joel Arthur, *Paradigms: The Business of Discovering the Future,* Harper Business, New York, 1993.

Bloomer, Carolyn M., *Principles of Visual Perception,* Design Press, New York, 1990.

de Brabandere, Luc, *Le Plaisir des Idées,* Dunod, Paris, 2004 (nouvelle édition).

——*Le Management des Idées,* Dunod, Paris, 2004 (nouvelle édition).

——*Le Sens des Idées,* Dunod, Paris, 2004.

Gilhooly, K.J., *Thinking Directed, Undirected, and Creative,* Academic Press Limited, London, 1988.

Hill, Richard, *We Europeans,* Europublic, Brussels, 2005.

Hinton, Perry R, *Stereotypes, Cognition, and Culture,* Taylor & Francis, Philadelphia, 2000.

Jacomy, Bruno, *L'Âge du Plip: Chroniques de l'Innovation Technique,* Editions du Seuil, Paris, 2002.

Koestler, Arthur, *The Act of Creation,* Arkana, London, 1989.

Kuhn, Thomas, *The Structure of Scientific Revolutions,* The University of Chicago Press, Chicago and London, 1996.

Jeanneney, Jean-Noël, *Une Idée Fausse est un Fait Vrai,* Odile Jacob, Paris, 2000.

Jones, Morgan D., *The Thinker's Toolkit,* Times Business, New York, 1995.

Lafontaine, Céline, *L'Empire Cybernétique,* Editions du Seuil, Paris, 2004.

Norman, Donald A., *Things That Make Us Smart,* Addison Wesley, New York, 1994.

O'Connor, Joseph and Ian McDermott, *The Art of Systems Thinking,* Thorsons, San Francisco, 1997.

Pousseur, Jean-Marie, *Bacon: Inventer La Science,* Belin, Paris, 1988.

Sander, Bernie, *A Wake-Up Call for Idea Champions,* Innovation Transfer, Ottawa, 1994.

Thompson, Charles "Chic," *"Yes, but . . ."* Harper Business, New York, 1993.

Thorne, Paul, *Organizing Genius,* Blackwell Business, Oxford, 1992.

Von Oech, Roger, *Expect the Unexpected or You Won't Find It,* Berrett-Koehler, San Francisco, 2002.

Watzlawick, Paul, John Weakland, and Richard Fisch, *Changements, Paradoxes, et Psychothérapie,* Editions du Seuil, Evreux, 1975.

Weinberg, Gerald M., *An Introduction to General Systems Thinking,* Dorset House, New York, 2001.

Wiener, Norbert, *Cybernetics or Control and Communication in the Animal and the Machine,* MIT Press, Cambridge MA, 1982.

Wujec, Tom, *Five Star Mind,* Doubleday Canada Limited, Toronto, 1995.

# WAFFLE STREET

## THE CONFESSION &
## REHABILITATION
## OF A FINANCIER

# JAMES ADAMS

ISBN–13: 978-1-937458-71-3

Printed in the United States of America.

This publication is designed to provide entertainment value and is sold with the understanding that the publisher is not engaged in rendering legal, accounting, or other professional advice of any kind. If legal advice or other expert assistance is required, the services of a competent professional person should be sought.

—From a Declaration of Principles jointly adopted by a Committee of the American Bar Association and a Committee of Publishers and Associations

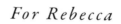

*For Rebecca*

# DEBT

*Etymology:* Old French dette, ultimately from Latin debita, plural of debitum, from neuter of edebitus, past participle of debere; to owe.

*—noun*

- Something that is owed or that one is bound to pay to or perform for another: a debt of $50.

- A liability or obligation to pay or render something: My debt to her for advice is not to be discharged easily.

- The condition of being under such an obligation: His gambling losses put him deeply in debt.

- Theology: An offense requiring reparation; a sin; a trespass.

# ACKNOWLEDGMENTS

*The author wishes to thank the following individuals:*

His wife, Becky, for her unflagging support throughout this quixotic endeavor.

His parents, Jim and Jane Adams, for providing feedback on several economic essays.

Benjamin Gibbs, for suggesting the book's title.

Gregory Osmond, for introducing him to Amy Cook at Sourced Media Books.

Jean-Baptiste Say, whose reputation this volume hopes to reclaim.

# CONTENTS

# PREFACE

Some seven years ago in a smoke-drenched back room of a twenty-four-hour diner, I scrawled my first batch of notes from my table-waiting shift on the back of a meal order ticket. I did so with a faint hope that I might ultimately accumulate enough worthwhile anecdotes to publish a book-length memoir.

Several months into my foodservice stint, the stories continued to pile up, but I had no clear idea if—or how—I would be able to thread them together to create a meaningful narrative arc. But then two things happened.

First, I was able to discover more of Edward's (the gruff master grill officer) backstory as his skepticism toward me gradually began to dissipate and we formed a bona fide relationship of mutual respect that happily continues to this day. More than any other figure that I encountered in my six months at the store, Edward embodied the capacity of honest labor to redeem a soul. I hope that, bawdy anecdotes aside, *Waffle Street* does justice to his qualities.

Second, when I wasn't recording restaurant vignettes, I was reading as much economic theory and financial history as I could get my hands on in an effort to discern how the global economy arrived at the precipice of total implosion in late 2008. As I stumbled upon one long-lost economic truism after another, I found them unexpectedly illustrated by interactions with customers and dialogues with my coworkers.

When I began preparing *Waffle Street*, I set out with the primary intention of offering the general reader a few good laughs at my expense.

As pen went to paper, however, I succumbed to an irresistible urge to infuse my table waiting account with economics, because the reality of the former was constantly reinforcing the theory of the latter. Omitting discussions of Say's Law, I felt, would deprive readers of my greatest on-the-job epiphanies.

My own bias notwithstanding, not all readers are terribly interested in a comparative survey of the ideas of Adam Smith, John Maynard Keynes, and Milton Friedman. If you aren't in the mood for financial pedagogy, just skip ahead to the next tale of waffles and hash browns when you encounter it. No harm done.

Economics, I'm told, would also have provided a less-than-compelling story arc for the recent feature film adaptation of the book. Instead, the screenwriter and directors created the plot device of my attempting to purchase the restaurant from the existing franchisee. Of course, that creative liberty raises the viewer question: how much of what the movie depicts actually transpired?

Rather than address each discrepancy, let me say this: what follows in these pages, save for the pseudonyms for persons (and in this edition, the restaurant chain and its trademark dishes), is entirely true. I'll leave it to the reader/moviegoer to reconcile the differences herself.

It's my hope that you find both the book and film versions of *Waffle Street* entertaining and edifying. If you're reading this after viewing James Lafferty in the role of yours truly, I'll take no offense if you envision him in the pages ahead. I have to imagine it makes for a more enjoyable read.

James Adams / April 2016

*Chapter 1*

# PINK SLIP

*"The sense of helplessness which unemployment brings
to a man is an affliction of the spirit even heavier than
the material loss which accompanies it."*
**HENRY CLAY**

If initial appearances were any indicator, Friday, January 16, 2009 was well on its way to being an aberrantly upbeat day in the capital markets. Bank of America confirmed it would receive $138 billion of government aid to mitigate losses related to its purchase of Merrill Lynch. Citigroup reported an $8.3 billion quarterly loss as its management announced plans to split the sprawling financial conglomerate in two. Bank of America and Citigroup shares rose 12% and 17%, respectively, as investors were heartened by the government support and restructuring plan.

Over the course of the trading session, news of more trouble in the real economy broke. Electronics retailer Circuit City announced its imminent liquidation, which meant that the economy could potentially lose another 34,000 jobs. Bank of America also offered a decidedly melancholy outlook on its earnings call. CEO Ken Lewis explained that higher unemployment levels meant higher losses on BofA's credit card loans. If history was any guide, the projected 8% unemployment rate meant that the bank would likely write off in excess of 8% of its credit card portfolio. Lewis's only semi-sanguine remark was an expression of hope for "early signs of stabilization" in the second half of 2009.

As the market digested the likelihood of continued (and accelerating) loan losses, Bank of America and Citigroup shares both plummeted. BofA closed down 14% from its opening level; Citi dropped 9%. Another day in paradise. It was a story I had seen many times over the previous eighteen months: rays of light quickly consumed by the vicious circle of souring debts and rising unemployment.

The only thing that really made this day any different from the others since June 2007 was a phone call I received at 10:30 a.m. The head of our marketing department asked if I had a few minutes to talk to him. I had been working fairly closely with him on some investment strategies that we could pitch to potential clients. I could only assume that he wanted me to brief him on my progress with some of the marketing materials.

While climbing the staircase which bridged our trading floor to the offices upstairs, I was intercepted by my direct supervisor, who gently placed his hand on my back and joined me in my ascent. I suppose it's a testament to my naïveté, but I didn't realize something was awry until I finally stepped into the marketing director's office and found the company compliance officer seated on the sofa. "Great," I thought. I expected to get reprimanded for neglecting to fill out some authorization form before distributing a pitch book to a prospective client. Or worse, I might be upbraided for checking for status updates on Facebook. I knew my habit was unprofessional, but that program was so uncontrollably addictive.

"This isn't good news, is it?" I asked sheepishly. "I'm afraid not," he replied. "How long have you been with the firm?" he asked. "Since March of 2006 . . . that makes it almost three years." "Wow. Time has really flown. You know, in that time, you've done consistently great work for us." He paused. "And it really kills us to do this."

I don't exactly remember how he began his next sentence. It was along the lines of, "As you know, our assets under management have declined, and revenues have consequently fallen."

I knew then that my days at the firm had come to an abrupt end. I was reassured that my termination was in no way related to my performance. After all, I had survived two previous rounds of layoffs. But given the eleven-hour days that I had been working on the aforementioned new products, I considered myself a fairly integral part of a resurgent marketing effort and wasn't anticipating being cut. (Admittedly, I could have abbreviated my workday had I not spent so much time reading economic theory; but, I was helplessly drawn to it in a sincere effort to understand why the global financial architecture was rapidly crumbling.)

My only prior experience with a layoff had been three years before. At the time, I was employed by a large, publicly traded life insurance company that was merging with a competitor. I had been involved with a high-profile deal that had recently closed, and I was told that my severance was not a reflection of any ineptitude. Despite the reassurance, I took the layoff very personally, cycling through the customary stages of grief: incredulity, despair, anger, and acceptance. My return to emotional normalcy took about four months. I was a man who took his career very seriously. Perhaps I even defined myself by the rate of my ascent on the corporate ladder. Clearly, I had a lot to learn about life.

As the director continued to express his regrets about my departure, I found my sense of shock gradually supplanted by another sentiment: relief. I couldn't understand it. To date, this had unquestionably been the best experience of my career. The company was replete with smart, good-hearted people with whom I relished working. Senior management had afforded me tremendous opportunities for professional growth. I was planning on being with the firm for another twenty years. So why did I feel this way?

I retreated to a vacant office and called my wife in the middle of her shift at the hospital. She took the news much harder than I did.

"Are you serious?" she asked repeatedly between sobs.

Only twelve hours before, we had both agreed that it was time for us to start a family. Money wasn't going to be an immediate concern; we had accumulated enough savings to service our expenses for a while. Nonetheless, her dream of becoming a stay-at-home mom seemed to have been summarily dashed. We realized that for the time being, she would need to continue in her position as a nurse while I would assume more responsibilities around the house. I knew she didn't hold me personally accountable for the setback, but I still felt that I had disappointed her. After expressing my apologies and providing what meager reassurance I could, I grabbed my pea coat and headed out for a walk.

I crossed the granite-tiled lobby, pondering an irony. Alpha Managers (a pseudonym) had been growing so quickly a year ago that we required more space to accommodate the additional personnel. Within months of completing the move to the beautiful new downtown office building, the firm announced the first layoffs in its quarter-century history. I emerged into the bright winter day and spent the next hour sauntering around the business district, reflecting on my tenure with the company.

When I joined the firm three years ago, I had grudgingly consented to a small salary reduction with the understanding that my diligence would be subsequently rewarded. The pay cut was a minor blow to my ego, but it was a small price to pay for admission into a prestigious firm that offered considerable prospects for advancement. "We want to have dozens of millionaires at Alpha Managers," our CEO had said in one meeting.

It wasn't empty rhetoric. By the end of my first year with the company, I received a promotion to vice president. Shortly thereafter, the CEO had described me as "a rising star" when he introduced me to a client. Then, in early 2008, I caught what was supposed to be my big break: I was placed in charge of a high-profile project to develop a subsidiary enterprise which would have culminated in a public stock offering. Only a few weeks before my termination, the endeavor had appeared very close to reaching fruition.

I finished my stroll, passing a parking garage containing my new 5-series BMW. I had bought the car at my father's behest over New Year's weekend. Although I offered the mild protest that my nine-year-old Volvo was running just fine, he insisted that a rising executive needed a vehicle commensurate with his position to create a positive image for visiting clients. I eventually conceded, noting that it would have been nice to have had a luxury sedan when I had recently entertained some investment bankers. Three weeks after the purchase, it was clear that I had gotten ahead of myself.

It's a funny thing when your coworkers hear that you've received a layoff notice. They react in one of two ways: 1) they are quick to wish you well in your next endeavor, or 2) they cease to acknowledge your existence. Women with whom I had previously enjoyed casual, flirtatious banter were suddenly reticent to even make eye contact. The phobia must have been born of a conviction that pink slips are as contagious as shingles.

I was given a week to pack up my belongings, transition my responsibilities to colleagues, and say my goodbyes. Maybe I should have, but I didn't feel awkward as I sorted through the miscellany of documents in my cubicle. Still, it was a little disappointing to think that, in some female eyes, I had gone from being the office eye candy to its resident leper. But even leper colonies have their advantages. In my case, the newfound solitude afforded me a lot of time to contemplate my sense of peace.

Over the past seven years, my career path had caused my wife and me to relocate to three different cities. Including intra-city moves between apartments and houses, we had packed and unloaded all of our possessions more than six times. The logistics of the transfers became increasingly depressing with each move.

During our first two relocations, the thoughts of life in our new home sustained us and seemed to make the sofas lighter as we loaded them into the U-Haul. By the fourth move, however, we found ourselves handicapping the time until my next assignment in corporate America.

While sincerely longing to establish a genuine homestead, we had seemingly been consigned to the fate of bivouacking for the rest of our married life. I wasn't in the Army, after all. But perhaps this was the lot of financial mercenaries, as well.

$ $ $ $ $ $

The investment profession is comprised of two classes of practitioners: 1) product manufacturers and 2) product distributors. Hedge funds, insurance companies, and mutual funds are product manufacturers. In the industry, they are referred to by the umbrella term, "asset managers." Their personnel usually have titles like "chief investment officer," "portfolio manager," or "securities analyst." Financial product distributors come in the form of stockbrokers, financial planners, and life insurance agents. They receive brokerage commissions for selling mutual funds and insurance policies; advisory fees are earned for placing money on behalf of clients.

Although stockbrokers and insurance salesmen have modest licensing requirements, no such examinations are necessary to work as an asset manager or financial advisor. And except in the case of insurance companies, asset management companies have no liability for the performance of the securities that they manage. Likewise, distributors are not on the hook for the performance of the asset managers' products that they sell or recommend. In short, being an asset manager or financial advisor is akin to practicing unlicensed medicine, dentistry, or law with no chance of ever being sued for malpractice. Except that you can make more money.

If you tell me what aspect of financial services that an individual works in, I can give you a pretty accurate general idea of what kind of person he or she is and what his or her school days were like. Asset managers tend to be intellectual, math-oriented, introverted types who dress rather casually. During high school, future asset managers populate chess clubs, student newspapers, quiz bowl teams, and the Model

United Nations. They are often teachers' pets. In their leisure reading, they embrace the fantasy and science fiction genres, primarily because twenty-third-century women are more interested in a man's brains than in his ability to throw a football. The blossoming asset manager has a high intelligence quotient but a generally limited capacity for scoring chicks. In short, these people are on the receiving end of a lot of wedgies.

Stockbrokers and financial planners, on the other hand, are extroverted, well-dressed types. They are smooth talkers. In high school, they held student government offices that entailed no real responsibility but nonetheless made them look respectable to college admissions officers. They served as captains of football and lacrosse teams and dated girls on the homecoming court. They gave a lot of wedgies to the sci-fi crowd, who would eventually pay psychologists a lot of money to mollify the consequent emotional damage.

My own high school experience was a contradiction in terms. I was an unapologetic participant on the quiz bowl team (PA state champs, 1994!), but I also played four years of lacrosse. Though I became team captain my junior year and was named MVP my senior year, I was made to endure the requisite freshman hazing outside a McDonald's on the return from a road trip to Baltimore. In an act of Providence, the upperclassmen spared me the ignominy of having my underwear retailored with a lacrosse stick. Instead, they were content to duct tape me to the front of a Ronald McDonald statue in a semi-prostrated position. Eighteen years later, I can still vividly recall several kids in the jungle gym adjacent to the restaurant pointing and laughing at the spectacle of me being molested by America's preeminent corporate icon. While my boxer shorts emerged from the incident with all threads intact, my dignity didn't fare so well. But all things considered, I was a pretty lucky fellow.

I entered Wake Forest University in the fall of 1995 intent on pursuing a degree in history, which had been my favorite subject in high school. During my second semester, I took a macroeconomics course and was absolutely intrigued. I remembered how much discussion in my high school history classes revolved around economic events. Everything in politics, it seemed, boiled down to money.

**Macroeconomics** is the study of the behavior of national economies. It is concerned with the wealth of countries. **Finance**, in contrast, is the study of getting rich yourself. An ability to speak in macroeconomic jargon enables you to sound sophisticated while bantering with your buddies at fraternity parties. Pursuing a degree in finance enables you to convince the girls at the party that you are on the fast track to becoming a rich man without the nuisance of attending medical school. When it came time to declare a major, the choice was clear.

After completing my finance degree, I spent the first five years out of college in the investment departments of two life insurance companies. As a credit analyst, I poured over the financial statements of corporations to determine whether or not we should purchase their bonds. (A **bond** is a debt instrument issued by a borrower to a group of lenders.)

Admittedly, it wasn't particularly glamorous work, but I loved it, anyway. How could I not? I got paid to read all day and pause occasionally to place a forty-million-dollar bet with somebody else's money. It was the perfect gig for an intellectually curious man who could temper his bravado with a healthy dose of skepticism.

Along with my colleagues in the corporate bond group, the investment departments were staffed with commercial loan officers and mortgage securities traders. The commercial loan officers lent money to real estate developers while the mortgage securities traders purchased and sold pools of residential loans that had been "securitized" into mortgage bonds.

While nearly everyone in the investment department could fairly be described as a nerd, mortgage traders unfailingly proved the geekiest of the lot. They take pride in being versed in the high-level math necessary for modeling mortgage prepayment patterns. Mortgage traders consider guys like me dumb brutes because corporate bond math only requires basic algebra. They're right, of course, but that sort of lame bragging really makes you want to give them a wedgie.

The only people below the mortgage guys on the insurance company social totem pole are the actuaries. Those guys would kill for a mortgage guy's social finesse. Contemplating the typical high school experience of an actuary presents a legitimate theological conundrum. That is, when you consider what his social life must have been like in grades 9–12, you don't leave much room in the universe for a merciful God. This model for projecting future financial career paths based on high school experiences may strike you as terribly simplistic and unreliable. In a future edition of this book, I will include a full-blown statistical analysis to substantiate my thesis. In the meantime, you'll just have to have my claims anecdotally corroborated by your nearest actuary. Just don't press for details when memories of his senior prom result in inconsolable sobbing.

After a long day of trading bonds and teasing actuaries, most of the nights during my insurance years were devoted to educational pursuits. I spent the first five months of 2002, 2003, and 2004 studying for the Chartered Financial Analyst (CFA) examinations. After successfully passing each of three six-hour tests and completing thirty-six months of qualified work experience, I received my CFA charter in late 2004. According to the CFA institute, I had demonstrated a knowledge of economics, statistical inference, financial accounting, investment analysis, and portfolio management. Most importantly, I had earned the right to affix "CFA" to my name on business cards. The institute promised that the designation would afford me instant credibility in financial matters for the rest of my life. Of course, should I ever neglect to pay $300 in annual dues, the institute also promised to censure me for unauthorized usage of those three letters.

A year after completing the CFA program, I enrolled in the executive MBA program at the University of North Carolina-Chapel Hill. The dean assured us that our degree would greatly increase our marketability in the corporate world, notwithstanding that prospective employers would (correctly) interpret "executive program" as a thinly veiled euphemism for "night school."

I genuinely liked my professors and classmates, but I can't say that I approached the curriculum with as much zeal as the other students. That's not to say that I didn't enjoy studying business—I always have. But shelling out fifty grand to analyze companies in the halls of academia seemed ridiculous given that I had already spent the past five years doing it professionally.

But as much as I could complain, my access to the UNC network paid immediate dividends after my layoff from the insurance company in 2005. Thanks to their career services department, I landed my dream job. Alpha Managers had started in the early 1980s as an investment advisor to commercial banks. The firm's competitive advantage laid in its expertise in valuing mortgage-backed securities before the vast majority of market participants had figured out how to do it.

Its early successes soon enabled the firm to branch out into discretionary asset management—i.e., the firm was making trades on behalf of its customers without having each one individually approved by the client. By the time I joined the firm in early 2006, Alpha Managers' assets under management had crested $30 billion. We managed separate accounts for large institutional investors, both domestic and international: state and corporate pension plans, banks, insurance companies, even sovereign wealth funds. We also ran several pools of commingled assets, including two mutual funds, several hedge funds, and a few limited partnerships comprised of Japanese banks.

My assignment in the firm's product management group was to service $20 billion of those assets by representing our trading desk to clients, investment consultants, and Wall Street brokers. I provided verbal and written commentary on the performance of forty bond portfolios whose strategies covered nearly everything under the sun. Occasionally, I participated in marketing efforts by designing pitch books and visiting prospective clients.

The work itself was extremely interesting, but the best part of the job was being surrounded by so many intelligent, ethical people. I cannot overemphasize what a pleasant anomaly this was. As far as most financiers are concerned, the phrase, "What shall a man give in exchange for his soul?" is not a rhetorical question. I'm willing to bet that sixty percent of the personnel on any New York trading desk can provide a ready answer in terms of square footage in the Hamptons.

When housing prices began to drop in early 2007, mortgage bonds soon began to follow suit. Initially, I explained to our clients that the declining bond prices were primarily the effect of selling by investors that had borrowed heavily to finance their positions and were now forced to repay their debts. The market would rally, I declared, as soon as the waves of forced selling had subsided. As the months passed and mortgage bond prices continued to tumble, fulfillment of my prophecy appeared increasingly implausible. I'm not sure my reassurances sounded any less pathetic than Linus's promise to Charlie Brown that the Great Pumpkin would arrive with gifts on Halloween night—if only the believers proved patient enough.

As the economic situation continued to deteriorate, many of the bonds we had purchased began to incur severe principal losses as overextended homeowners neglected to make their mortgage payments. Many of our investors terminated their accounts, taking their now severely depreciated portfolios with them.

Two years of watching our clients flee and chronicling what appeared to be the last days of capitalism had exacted an acute emotional toll. For the first time in my life, I had lost my capacity to speak about anything with genuine conviction. When apprised of my severance from the firm, I didn't feel terminated; I felt emancipated. The millstone of mortgage debt had finally been cut loose from my neck.

My first day at home had a seemingly auspicious beginning. Just after my wife had left for work, a man knocked on my door and introduced himself as a neighbor from down the street. He had locked himself out of his car and needed a ride to a friend's house. This was the silver lining to the layoff, I thought. I had been so busy with my job and my evening MBA program that I had largely neglected my social life. If nothing else, a little time off work would provide an opportunity to make some new friends in the community.

When she returned home from the hospital, I delivered a report to my wife on my new station as a domestic. Rather than providing me with a grocery list, she had given me carte blanche to purchase whatever items I deemed prudent. I had neglected to procure our usual sundries, returning instead with six cases of ramen noodles which now sat on our dining room table. Although neither of us had eaten ramen since college, I explained to my wife that our new cash flow constraints should emphasize frugality over nutritional content. She politely demurred. Additionally, I also had to account for crashing our computer's hard drive and getting swindled out of twenty-eight dollars by a man posing as our neighbor.

I retired to our upstairs loft and nestled in my recliner. I picked up the latest issue of *The Economist* and began reading about the financial crisis. For the first time in nearly a decade, the financial press had become leisure reading rather than a work requirement. It didn't matter. Now, more than ever, I was captivated by the riddle of the markets.

$ $ $ $ $

When I was previously laid off in 2005, I was given several months to look for new work. Thus, I was able to start a new job at Alpha Managers on a Monday morning after spending the previous Friday at the insurance company. This situation, in contrast, constituted bona fide unemployment. I had a few leads on some well-paying gigs in the bond market but absolutely no desire to pursue any of them. A headhunter contacted me regarding a job in corporate finance, but I had scarcely submitted my resume before the position was filled by another candidate.

After a few days of catching up on leisure reading and running errands, I found myself thoroughly bored and decided to search out the county unemployment office. I couldn't find any government bureau under "Unemployment" in the White or Yellow pages. I turned to the blue government pages and eventually found a listing for the "Employment Security Commission." That struck me as the appropriate euphemism for "where to get your handout," so I gave them a ring.

After ten frustrating minutes of navigating automated telephone menus, I decided to see the Employment Security Commission for myself. A ten-minute drive brought me to the front door of the office where two signs prohibited the possession of knives, firearms, and nunchucks. I entered the foyer half expecting a sepia-toned room full of men wearing trench coats and fedoras queued up for a bowl of soup.

Instead, I saw ten people lined up to speak with a husky woman situated behind a large reception desk. I took my place at the end of the line and glanced around the office. To my left, thirty people sat at tables in an austere lobby. To my right, unemployment claimants met with counselors under hanging placards which read "Placement Services," "Workforce Investment Act," "Veterans Services," and "Career Resource Center." Despite the close proximity, I couldn't hear any of the conversations.

The receptionist handed me a form, which I quickly filled out and submitted. Then I took a seat at a nearby table. The place was eerily quiet, particularly given the large number of claimants in the waiting room. To my surprise, many of them were accompanied by their spouses and small children. Maybe the family had only one car, or perhaps the dependents had simply come to offer moral support for their breadwinner during a stressful time. I wouldn't say that a pall hung over the place, but there was clearly a general feeling of sobriety. No one read or made idle chat; they just sat there.

I desperately wanted to know everyone's story, but I was constrained by the solemnity of the place. The melancholy demeanor of my fellow claimants left me with the distinct impression that any playful banter would not have been appreciated. These people needed this money to feed their families. I, on the other hand, needed it for . . . why did I need it, after all? I had just received two months of severance pay, my wife earned good money as a nurse, we had no debt at all, and I could live off my cash savings for many years.

Just as I had begun to contemplate my need for state handouts, my name was called. I informed the woman behind the desk that I desired to file an initial unemployment claim and that I was utterly clueless about the process. She was thoroughly patient and helpful. I was advised that my severance package would disqualify me for unemployment benefits for the next eight weeks. Before my discouragement could fester, she threw me an unexpected lifeline. "Now there is a way around this regulation," she said. "If you are pursuing continuing education, this requirement is waived and you qualify for immediate benefits."

Continuing education? I was intrigued. My expression must have conveyed my interest, because before I could solicit further information about this convenient loophole, she was already explaining how to exploit it. If I presented proof of enrollment in a class at the local technical college, I could return tomorrow with full eligibility to have my claim paid. Given my previous salary, I would qualify to receive $450 per week. And as fate would have it, Community Tech was located only several hundred yards from the State Employment Commission. I don't know whether it had been situated there by design or sheer coincidence.

I left the office and headed down the road in pursuit of higher learning. I had no idea what sort of curriculum would be required or what the classes would cost. In any case, it didn't seem that I had much to lose by investigating the opportunity.

As I traversed the campus in search of the Continuing Education facility, I remembered a conversation I had with my late grandmother in my middle teenage years. In the most respectful tone I could muster, I posited the immorality of taking state handouts—in her case, Social Security. "I paid into it for decades," she had coolly replied.

Fifteen years later, I stood condemned by my own conscience. To make matters worse, the state hadn't even deducted unemployment insurance premiums directly from my paycheck; my employer had paid them on my behalf.

According to the registrar's office, I was mistaken in my assumption that my beeline from the unemployment office to Community Tech was anomalous. As a matter of fact, most of their new enrollees had also been laid off recently; few of them were fortunate enough to receive severance packages. The registrar handed me a class registration form and a course catalogue. On its cover, a man constructed a wooden frame for what appeared to be a large bookcase.

Inside, I discovered a veritable cornucopia of scholastic opportunities. The course offerings ranged from the vocationally oriented (carpentry, medical coding, real estate appraisal) to the liberal arts (history of Western art, applied acoustic guitar), to the recreational (scrapbooking, wine appreciation, salsa dancing). While a number of the classes looked genuinely interesting, I suspected that only a handful would satisfy the Employment Commission requirements. To my complete shock, I was told that enrolling in any single class offered in the course listings would make me eligible for unemployment benefits.

"What about this one?" I pointed to a course description: "Make treasure from trash? In this fun and creative class, you will learn to make keepsake treasures using recycled materials. Discover your creative side, have fun, and save a little space in the landfill by reusing cast-off items to make art with a personal touch."

"Now there's no way a 'garbage art' class could possibly be construed as continuing career education," I asserted.

She assured me that as far as the state was concerned, it was totally legitimate. Ten minutes later, I had enrolled in a six-week sewing course. (Yoga had been my first choice, but those classes had quickly filled.)

"You're absolutely sure that this will enable me to receive my unemployment checks?" I asked, still incredulous.

"It counts," the registrar affirmed. "Are you surprised?"

"You bet I am. In my eight years in finance, I've never seen a real arbitrage before."

$ $ $ $ $ $

**Arbitrage** represents an opportunity to make risk-free profits without any investment. It is the Holy Grail of finance. Arbitrage profits are made by exploiting the pricing differential of identical goods in different markets, without using any of your own capital. It works like this: borrow cash to purchase the good in the market where it is underpriced. Simultaneously, enter into a contract to sell the good in the other market, at which it can be sold at a higher price. In essence: buy low, sell high, with no risk of loss.

In the nineteenth century, the Rothschild family frequently arbitraged the gold market. One family member borrowed gold in London, which was immediately sold for cash. At the same time, another Rothschild agent purchased the same amount of gold at a lower cash price in Paris. The Parisian gold would then be delivered to the family's creditors in London. The family reaped a handsome profit without ever risking any of its own capital. If you perform a Google image search on Rothschild European estates, you can quickly gain an appreciation for the immense profit potential of arbitrage.

Typically, true arbitrage opportunities arise only from knowing something that no one else does. By placing five brothers in different financial centers, the Rothschilds created a unique information network unparalleled in Europe, which readily lent itself to the practice.

Currency exchange rates, oil futures contracts, and stocks of merging companies can all be arbitraged. Unfortunately, in the digitized age, genuine arbitrage opportunities are typically very small and quickly exploited by the Wall Street dealer with the brawniest computer. The only way to consistently make large arbitrage profits is by trading stocks on inside information. Insider trading ensures risk-free arbitrage profits but concurrently creates a risky legal situation for the parties involved.

Arbitrage opportunities are the magical leprechauns of finance—you will receive a big pot of gold if you can just find one.

Everybody wants to believe in them, and a few people actually do. Unfortunately, arbitrage opportunities, like leprechauns and free lunches, are never seen by anybody sober. Nevertheless, finance professors and hedge fund managers use the word indiscriminately, because using French terms is an easy way to make yourself appear sophisticated to your audience. Technically speaking, arbitrage denotes "no money down, risk-free profits." In contemporary Wall Street parlance, it has come to imply any trade which involves the purchase of one asset with the simultaneous sale of another.

Despite the abuse, I can't blame the Street for casually throwing the word around at client conferences. "IBM's cash bonds are cheap to their five-year credit default swaps; there's clearly an arbitrage opportunity" sounds a lot more dignified than, "Hey, a leprechaun just ran down that hole. If you're fast enough, you can still catch him." In my case, the leprechaun and pot of gold had taken the form of a kindly middle-aged bureaucrat and the North Carolina State Treasury, respectively. The trade worked like this: Buy class time for $59. Sell class time back to the state for $1,800, thereby netting a tidy $1,741 in profit. Execute the trade again next month.

After completing my course registration, I promptly returned to the State Employment Commission offices. As I strode through the door, I was intercepted by a hefty bureaucrat in sweat-stained trousers.

"Can I help you?" he asked gruffly.

"I'd like to officially apply for unemployment benefits," I said.

"It's too late for that today," he snapped. "This office closes at 5 p.m. sharp." He cast a derisive glance at my course registration form as if to indicate that he knew that I had just spent the past hour gaming the state welfare system.

"It's 4:15," I said casually. As far as I was concerned, if the state felt genuinely obligated to compensate me for reinventing myself as a seamstress, I was in no position to refuse the offer.

"We quit taking applications an hour before closing time. If you really want a check, be here at 8:30 a.m. tomorrow," he said disdainfully.

$ $ $ $ $ $

I returned for my orientation session the following morning. After a half-hour wait, I was ushered into a back room and seated around a conference table along with ten other claimants. We were shortly joined by an administrator who briefed us on the nuances of the claims-filing process. As she started to speak, I noticed a framed poster of FDR signing the Unemployment Insurance (UI) Act. "1935–1995: UI is 60!" it declared.

The administrator explained that Employment Security Law required all claimants to actively seek work before they could draw unemployment benefits. For each week of benefits claimed, we had to file a weekly certification verifying face-to-face contacts with two different prospective employers. If these criteria were met, the state would deposit money on a bank card the following Monday morning. As far as I could tell, my account would still be credited even if I didn't actually intend to accept the job offer.

If we did gain part-time employment, we were permitted to work up to 23 hours a week so long as our wages did not exceed our earnings allowance. Most importantly, we had to maintain meticulous records of our work search claims for the next five years or the IRS would have a field day should our tax returns ever be audited. After enumerating all of the procedures and caveats, she proceeded with an illustration: "Now, let's say you apply at McDonald's . . ."

As she went on to explain the nuances of unemployment insurance, my thoughts drifted away from the lecture. Her hypothetical scenario had completely sidetracked me. I tried to imagine myself filling out a

McDonald's application. It seemed so cliché. Then again, I didn't have any better ideas. So that's what I did. I applied to work at McDonald's.

Nothing on the McDonald's menu is gourmet cuisine, but I've always loved it, anyway. Economists, on the other hand, might describe the fare as an **inferior good,** meaning that the public generally consumes more of it during periods of macroeconomic distress. And so it was in the last quarter of 2008. American Express Co. reported a 79% drop in quarterly net income, citing higher loan loss provisions and a 10% decline in customer spending. In contrast, Mickey D's reported an 11% increase in its fourth quarter operating income, driven by a five percent increase in same-store sales (a key performance metric for retail establishments). It's too bad for AmEx that Ronald only accepts Mastercard and Visa.

Despite the occasional litigation over excessively hot coffee, I can never recall McDonald's integrity being seriously called into question. The main knock on the company is that its menu will inexorably, albeit slowly, kill you. The health risks were brought to the attention of the general public by Morgan Spurlock in a 2004 documentary entitled *Super Size Me.* Spurlock, as director-cum-protagonist, physically demonstrates the perils of eating all of his meals at McDonald's for thirty consecutive days. To no one's surprise, he gains twenty-four pounds and utterly compromises his circulatory system in the process. The backlash generated by the film precipitated a prompt discontinuation of the Super Size option, wherein a customer could dramatically increase the size of his soda and fries in his combo meal for a mere 39 cents. A great victory against excessive American consumerism had been won.

It's too bad Spurlock didn't make a documentary about the perils of the consumption of McMansions by overextended homeowners. I will forever maintain that paying 99 cents for a double cheeseburger (that's only two-tenths of a cent per calorie) represents a much better deal than paying $500,000 for a 4,000-square-foot house (that's $125 per square foot). Consuming too much of the former may result in cardiac arrest, but excessive consumption of McMansions resulted in a nationwide financial crisis.

As I was out running errands, I happened upon the McDonald's outlet where I had dined at least bi-weekly for two-and-a-half years before my company relocated its office. It wasn't the healthiest diet, but then again, a three-dollar lunch tab was hard to beat—as was the two-minute stroll across the meadow which separated my office building from the restaurant. A lake was accented by a fountain, an omnipresent gaggle of geese, and an occasional turtle or jumping fish. Inasmuch as twenty-first-century corporate America can be, it was positively bucolic.

Notwithstanding the occasional misstep into a goose dropping, I found the brief amble to be quite relaxing. I hadn't dined at this particular franchise since our office had moved seven months ago, and I was excited to reacquaint myself with an old haunt. I still recognized most of the faces behind the counter. I presented myself at the register with the same element of swagger that a sailor displays to a dockside paramour after returning from a long deployment at sea. After receiving my food and exchanging pleasantries with a Latino attendant who had recognized me, I asked for an application. "Qué?"

"Could I get an application please? For employment."

She paused. "What?" I had spoken clearly, but she was obviously puzzled.

I didn't know much Spanish, but figured it was worth a shot. "Uh, uno aplicación, por favor?"

"For . . . you?"

"Yes."

Startled, she turned to look behind her before quickly resuming eye contact. "Just a minute, please." She retreated to the back of the restaurant and quickly convened a powwow with three other employees. After two minutes of talking and casting furtive glances in my direction, the woman returned with a two-page job application and the contact information for the local franchisee.

I called the store owner the next day. An amicable woman, Jane and her husband, Max, had been McDonald's franchisees for twenty-two years and currently owned seven restaurants in the area. Prior to being bitten by the entrepreneurial bug, they had both been public school teachers. Over the course of our conversation, I realized that Jane and Max were undoubtedly in a more favorable financial position than most of the principals at the firm from which I had just been dismissed. I had nearly forgotten you could get rich without ever once trading a mortgage bond.

She inquired about my background. I gave her a brief synopsis, concluding that I was tired of the capital markets and was now contemplating doing something else with my life—maybe even becoming a McDonald's franchisee. I needed to find out if I had the chops for real work before forever consigning my career fate to the movements of numbers on a computer screen.

Jane laid it on the line for me. You could certainly do well owning a McDonald's store, but it was clearly a lot of work, as in, sixteen-hour days, seven days a week—and a lot of personnel-related headaches. Yes, the current recession would mean good times for Mickey D's for the foreseeable future, but Ronald had no panacea from the vicissitudes of commerce. In addition to negative publicity from the *Super Size Me* muckraking, Jane had seen a fair amount of hard times during her tenure. She asked me what, if anything, I knew about the restaurant business.

I had to confess that I had never worked in foodservice per se, but I tried to preemptively squelch Jane's concerns about my inadequacies by feeding her some line about my having briefly worked in the "food logistics industry." Translation: I spent the summer after my junior year of high school in my father's warehouse salvaging forklift-damaged pallets of yellow mustard, onion rings, and other foodstuffs.

"Oh, I see," she said, her voice intonation conveying unveiled skepticism. Ultimately, Jane referred me to the store supervisor, to whom she had delegated all hiring decisions.

I spoke with him the next day. "We're always looking for people," he said. Encouraged by the demand for my services, I filled out my application with great alacrity and dropped it (and an updated resume) off at the restaurant the following night. I didn't hear anything over the weekend, so I left the manager a voicemail on Monday evening. I kept myself pretty occupied the rest of the week running long-overdue errands. By Friday, it finally dawned on me that I hadn't heard back yet from the store manager. I took the neglect rather personally.

Later that night, I found myself watching a YouTube video of a presidential town hall meeting in Florida. President Obama fielded the last question from a second-semester college student, who dreams of a post-collegiate career in broadcasting. Julio has been laboring at his local McDonald's for the past four-and-a-half years and lamented his inability to find another gig. What would the president do for him?

*That lucky jerk,* I thought. I had five more years of formal education than Julio but couldn't even land a face-to-face interview with his current employer. You would think that cleaning broken cases of Hellman's mayonnaise from a warehouse floor would leave me qualified to do something in this economy. Private high school, college, and the Chartered Financial Analyst curriculum evidently hadn't. And neither had MBA school. I turned from the computer to glance at my MBA diploma.

On one hand, I was grateful to have completed the program before the school implemented a $15,000 tuition hike. On the other hand, when the advanced degree on your resume doesn't even get McDonald's to return your phone calls, you have to wonder if a full refund isn't in order. If, however, I did land a fast food gig, I desperately wanted to arrange a little field trip for the introductory finance class.

I had a delectable vision of thirty graduate students crowding into a McDonald's, where I would be diligently scrubbing the grill. The professor would say something like this: "Here is an alumnus of the same MBA program that you are currently enrolled in. He currently earns $6.50 an hour and works a fifty-hour week, fifty weeks out of the year. Assume he pays no taxes. Now assume that upon graduation, you get the same job that he has. Given the $70,000 you pay for your degree, what is the payback period on your investment?"

I finally heard back from the store manager a full week after I had submitted my resume, which had apparently been misplaced by one of the night shift crew members. He asked me to complete an online version at the McDonald's website and assured me that he would be in touch within forty-eight hours. After our conversation, I returned to the Employment Security Commission to submit my final leg of paperwork before my benefits commenced. I never turned it in.

After a one-on-one meeting with a benefits counselor, I bumped into an office manager who introduced himself as the employment supervisor for Veterans' benefits. He graciously agreed to answer a few of my questions about state employment conditions, ushering me into an office where a wall plaque attested to his prior service in the Marine Corps.

He informed me that the North Carolina Employment Security Commission's coffers had been depleted by the unanticipated surge in unemployment claims. It was so bad, he said, that the state would soon be forced to turn to Washington for additional funds. I solicited his economic prognosis for the state. The economy had to get better soon, he reasoned. When I pressed him to justify his sanguine outlook, he could only offer that the alternative was too unpleasant to seriously consider.

As the supervisor continued to outline his agency's budgetary woes, I could feel the enthusiasm for my arbitrage opportunity begin to wane. I thought back to the faces of the people in the lobby. They needed the money to pay rent and feed their kids. Granted, the past two years of my job had proved extremely taxing, and I did feel somewhat entitled to a break from the mayhem. But unemployment insurance had been established during the depths of the Depression in order to help needy families get by. The original intent had never been to furnish a paid vacation for people of means.

Worse, I couldn't help but feel a growing sense of culpability for my role in the economic downturn. There was no way to spend the state's money without feeling guilty for having accepted it in the first place. Before the supervisor concluded our meeting, I had already decided that I'd accept the McDonald's job. Assuming, of course, that they'd offer it. And that my marriage would survive the endeavor.

$ $ $ $ $

"So you want nothing do to with the financial services industry, anymore?" my wife asked.

"Not for the foreseeable future," I replied.

"But why?" she responded, adding that this information would have been nice to know prior to supporting me through three CFA examinations, many job relocations, and two years in business school. I could only agree. How could I adequately respond that I had lost my confidence and had no intention of playing a game that neither I nor anyone else it seemed could understand, anymore?

It wasn't that I was a naïve ingénue unaccustomed to market turbulence. After all, I had cut my financial teeth in a terrifically ugly market in late 2001. On Sunday, September 9th, my boss and I traveled to New York City to attend a bond market conference held the following Monday and Tuesday at the Metropolitan Club. Thankfully, the only fallout we experienced from the terrorist attacks was a prolonged stay at a luxury hotel in midtown Manhattan. The most harrowing aspect of the whole episode was making the thousand-mile road trip back to Birmingham with a man who insisted on providing accompaniment to every song on the radio. As a rule, portfolio managers are not gifted vocalists.

In the weeks and months after we returned to our office, our Bloomberg terminals were constantly flooded by news of accounting scandals and corporate bankruptcies. The Enron, Tyco, and WorldCom debacles unfolded and the domestic airline industry imploded. A year into my job, I represented the insurance company in the debt restructuring of U.S. Airways after it filed chapter eleven. By 2009, I considered myself a financial market veteran (inasmuch as you can be a veteran of anything at age 31).

But the turmoil seven years ago had, for the most part, been contained to a few miscreants in the energy trading and telecom sectors. Bernie Ebbers, Dennis Kozlowski, and Jeff Skilling were undoubtedly bad guys, but they weren't reflective of corporate America in general. Relative to the financial events of late 2008/early 2009, the corporate malfeasance episodes were a pleasant dream. Something was different this time. Very different. Pillars of the financial system had toppled like helpless dominoes. Those that remained were severely cracked, and the thought of spending another year watching the government spackle them in a vain effort to restore their structural integrity held little appeal.

The distinguishing characteristic of the current environment was that the economic foundation was shifting so drastically from week to week that you could no longer place an intelligent wager. Alpha Managers' chief investment officer had succinctly described it as an "Ike Turner market." I couldn't help but concur. It really was like being in a relationship with a temperamental lover: moderately uplifting one day, then terribly abusive the next.

Some part of me still wanted to believe that if I could just be patient, maybe my mercurial boyfriend, Mr. Market, would eventually become a nice guy. But in my heart of hearts, I knew that fidelity would never be his strong suit. And while I was willing to get back together with him at some point in the future, I refused to do so until I better understood his nuances. For the time being, a hiatus was clearly in order. I needed to distance myself as far from the financial profession as possible, so why not food service? If writing bond market commentary had a polar opposite, then it was probably serving Chicken McNuggets.

I must reiterate that my quarrel with the market wasn't simple shell shock at having spent the past two years at the epicenter of the meltdown. Rather, the frustration stemmed from a genuine concern that no political, academic, or business luminary could state with sincere conviction that the financial system was viable.

For its part, the media had ably covered the particulars of the crisis. But with each opinion piece that I read, I became increasingly convinced that the pundits were all omitting something terribly fundamental from their analyses.

I devoted much of my newfound discretionary time to scouring local bookstores and Amazon.com for titles that might help me to complete the puzzle. Over the next few weeks, several of the volumes provided valuable insights, but the integral revelations wouldn't arrive until I was chest deep in my next vocation several months later. Nearly two years have since passed, but I still marvel at the source of the illumination. Only by taking a job wholly unrelated to finance was I finally able to truly appreciate the first principle of economics: the Law of Markets.

$ $ $ $ $

The **Law of Markets** is perhaps best understood by way of illustration. Imagine an island inhabited only by two men, each of whom owns a small plot of land. One of the men uses his land to grow coconut trees, while his neighbor elects to cultivate pineapples. For several months, each man lives entirely in isolation, consuming only his own production. Understandably, he tires of eating the same kind of fruit day in and day out. Then one day, the men get together and decide to trade several coconuts in exchange for a few pineapples. An economy has just been born.

An **economy** is a system of production arrangements and production exchanges. On the island, each man labors on his farm to produce one type of fruit. By exchanging some of his production with the other farmer, he may consume both kinds of fruit. The production of pineapples by one farmer creates an opportunity for the other man to sell his coconuts.

Obviously, the farmers could not eat the fruit without first planting and harvesting it. Ergo, production is the cause of consumption.

Demand, in the economic sense, is not equivalent to a capricious materialistic desire. If all that were required to procure an item were mere longing for ownership, every sixteen-year-old kid would be driving a new Ferrari. Rather, true demand is driven by the willingness to work in order to supply more goods.

On our island, the supply of pineapples constitutes the demand for coconuts—i.e., if the pineapple farmer wants to eat more coconuts, he must first grow more pineapples to give the other farmer in exchange. The only alternative means of acquiring the coconuts is to borrow or steal them. If the coconut farmer lends the coconuts, he will only do so with the agreement that the pineapple farmer repay him in the future. That is, he will trade his own production today for a claim on the other man's production in the future. But whether it occurs in the present or the future, the creation of value is always the basis for demand. Here, then, is the Law of Markets: *production is the cause of prosperity and wealth; consumption is the effect.*

The first modern economist to state the proposition that the production (or supply) of a good creates the foundation for demand was a French businessman named Jean-Baptiste Say. First published in 1803, Say's *Treatise on Political Economy* asserted that "a product is no sooner created, than it, from that instant, affords a market for other products to the full extent of its own value" (p. 134). In personal correspondence, Say later wrote, "As the amount for which we can buy is equal to that which we can produce, the more we can produce the more we can purchase" (1820, Letter 1).

Because he popularized the concept that the power to consume depends entirely on the power (and willingness) to produce, The Law of Markets is also referred to as "Say's Law." Most of us have often heard it expressed colloquially in phrases such as "you can't get something for nothing." It is, undoubtedly, the most intuitive principle of economics. Incidentally, it is also the one most neglected and abused. Despite its clear immutability, it is a rule which nearly everyone—including myself—attempts to violate it at some point in his life.

In our two-man, two-product island economy, the farmers can directly exchange their production with each other in a barter system. Under a currency system, the farmers add an intermediate step: they exchange their production for money. **Money** is anything for which someone is willing to trade his production. In a more developed economy (e.g., one with hundreds of producers and products), the presence of money greatly facilitates the exchange of production.

Money serves as a medium of exchange by which people indirectly exchange their separate productions. One person produces, then sells his goods or services in exchange for money, and subsequently uses that money to consume someone else's production. In Jean-Baptiste Say's words, "Money performs no more than the role of a conduit in this double exchange [of production]" (p. 138).

Produce > Sell Production (for $) > Consume Production (with $)

In addition to serving as a medium of exchange, money also represents a store of value. That is, money should retain its purchasing power over time, or at least not lose it very rapidly. Lastly, money is a **unit of account,** meaning that it can be used to measure the amount of a good or service. For example, a dollar could measure a loaf of bread, a half gallon of gasoline, or a liter of soda. A unit of account provides a means of expressing prices, costs, and profits in a common language. We can even express time in units of money. Assuming a laborer receives $15 per hour for his wages, then four minutes of his labor is also worth one dollar.

Any commodity which can function as a **medium of exchange, store of value,** and unit of account can serve as money. Gold and silver have served as money in many societies. Money has also taken the shape of alcohol, tobacco, and even livestock. But regardless of its form, it is only a mechanism of trading one production for another. As Say explained, "money is but the agent of the transfer of values."

After exchanging their production for money, many people do not immediately spend their money on consuming the production of others. The excess of their production over their consumption is known as savings. That is,

Production – Consumption = Savings.

Savings represent a decision to defer one's consumption until a later point in time. In the interim, savers can do two things with their money: hold it or invest it. Everyone should maintain a reasonable amount of cash on hand for emergency needs. But generally speaking, a large cash hoard does the saver no good. He is not enjoying consumption, and he is not putting his savings to work in his behalf.

To the extent that people choose to save rather than consume, the supply of capital increases. **Capital** is savings that has been (or is waiting to be) recycled into investment. Just as with any other good, the price of capital is determined by the amount of its supply relative to demand. The price of capital when it is loaned to a borrower is known as the **interest rate** on a loan. A higher savings rate increases the supply of capital, putting downward pressure on interest rates. That is, the more money that some people save, the cheaper it becomes for other people to borrow.

When savers lend their money, they transfer the power to consume to a borrower, who then spends the money. Broadly speaking, borrowers try to invest the funds in assets that will assist in the production of other goods and services. A bakery may purchase a more efficient oven, or a factory may purchase software which increases its manufacturing efficiency. Spending on vocational training (e.g., medical school tuition) can also be an investment. But whatever the form it takes, investment spending should follow one general rule: increase productivity.

By producing, saving, and channeling savings into productivity-enhancing forms of investment, we increase our capacity to consume in the future. Jean-Baptiste Say described spending on current wants as "unproductive consumption," while investment spending was "reproductive." Inasmuch as savings are reinvested in these reproductive uses, output per worker increases, and the economy grows. An economy's total output is measured by multiplying the average productivity per worker by the number of workers. The total output is usually referred to as the **gross domestic product,** or GDP.

Total Economic Output (GDP) = Output per Worker x Number of Workers

Aside from increasing productivity, the only other means of raising an economy's output is to increase the workforce population. As with other items, labor can be imported or manufactured domestically. The former process is known as "immigration," and the latter is known as "childbearing." Forgive the pun, but it is wholly true that childbearing represents the ultimate form of reproductive investment.

While Jean-Baptiste Say is traditionally given credit for first articulating the principle that production must always precede consumption, any good rabbi can tell you that the concept dates from antiquity. Moses recorded it 3,500 years ago in the third chapter of Genesis. After Adam and Eve partake of the forbidden fruit and become aware of their nakedness, God dispenses a series of punishments. First, the tempting serpent is sentenced to crawl upon his belly and eat dust all the days of his life. Second, Eve is cursed with acute labor pains. Lastly, Adam is informed that the ground has just been cursed for his sake.

In that last curse, the salad days of capricious dining from every tree in the Garden of Eden come to an abrupt halt. Henceforth, God declares, "In the sweat of thy face shalt thou eat bread, till thou return unto the ground." Exiled from the Garden, Adam is now consigned "to till the ground from whence he was taken." Until the end of the earth, man and woman must labor for their sustenance. East of Eden, there is no such thing as a free lunch.

So the last thing man learns prior to his expulsion from Paradise is the grand, immutable principle of economics: Say's Law. Although God didn't actually state that "production is the basis of consumption," it is clearly the doctrine being imparted. Regrettable though it may be,

Adam's condition has been shared by all mankind ever since the Fall: someone has to bake bread before anybody is going to eat a sandwich.

$ $ $ $ $ $

Or Big Mac, as the case may be. I tried to put McDonald's out of my head by spending the next two days running errands and catching up on leisure reading. As much as I tried, I was unable to convince myself that eagerly anticipating my next interaction with the manager was fundamentally different than a homely girl waiting next to the phone on the off chance that her crush might call.

Besides quick service restaurants, I had only considered one other alternative career move. I had excelled at making door-to-door sales during college; perhaps I still had a knack for them. Whenever my fraternity was faced with a budget deficit, we turned to selling doughnuts. While most of my frat brothers considered the endeavor a terrible chore, I relished hawking glazed Krispy Kremes in female dormitories.

Watching a calorie-obsessed fitness freak gradually acquiesce to my repeated entreaties was particularly gratifying. "Just look—no, smell— these warm doughnuts," I'd say, provocatively waving the open box in front of the poor coed. As her resolution began to dissolve, I laid my trump card:

*"Why, you've practically earned them with all that time you just spent on the treadmill. Please don't deny yourself the pleasure. We both know you want them."*

While I did more than my share of helping to replenish the fraternity coffers, money was the least gratifying element of the job. The best part was envisioning a customer's inevitable remorse after singlehandedly devouring the full dozen, despite having promised herself that she would save half of the box for her girlfriends. No wonder the devil approaches his job with such alacrity.

Friends told me that I had aged pretty well in the eight years since I had finished college. Nonetheless, I had serious qualms about resuming campus doughnut sales. An eighteen-year-old freshman who opens her door to discover a thirty-something man holding a large plastic bag (which she doubts is full of doughnuts) would probably shoot him with pepper spray before he could even make his sales pitch.

If I couldn't hack it in door-to-door sales, perhaps there was another viable alternative. Earlier in the day, I had driven past an adult novelty retailer that had opened just a few weeks ago. A window sign indicated that they were still in a hiring phase. I'm ashamed to admit how seriously I actually considered applying. Ultimately, I was dissuaded by a window display featuring a leather-clad mannequin clutching a riding crop. It was too reminiscent of the bond market.

Before my ruminations could lead me any further into a morass of self-pity, I had an epiphany. When thrown back into the dating pool, the natural response is to immediately turn to the most familiar names in one's black book. This is a mistake. The best bet for a solid romantic adventure is to look up an ex-girlfriend that you haven't thought about in years. No passion reignites so quickly and passionately as the one that got away.

Surely the same principle applies to dining establishments, I reasoned. McDonald's had sufficed as lunchtime fare during my corporate years, but only because I had forgotten how sublime dining out could really be. As I reflected on my fond memories with an old college flame, I knew exactly what had to be done. I would reintroduce myself to my long lost true love: Papa's Chicken & Waffles. Although its storied history really deserves to be told by a Herodotus, Livy, or Flavius Josephus, I'll try to do it justice in their absence.

In 1960 (five years after McDonald's opened its first franchise store), Jason Hank Kramerson opened the first Papa's Chicken & Waffles in a Charlotte, NC suburb.

"Papa" Kramerson wanted to create a "good food, fast" dine-in experience. Unlike McDonald's, all Papa's food would be cooked fresh, made-to-order, and delivered to the table by a friendly waiter.

Despite the increased demands of order customization, Kramerson was determined to rival the meal preparation time of drive-in restaurants. He was also insistent that all Papa's stores operate around the clock and remain open every day of the year. Furthermore, customers could order anything from the fifteen-item menu at any time of day. For anyone who wanted them, cheeseburgers were served at 5 a.m. and waffles would come out of the iron at midnight.

Kramerson's formula worked beautifully. By 1965, there were four Papa's outlets in metro Charlotte. Shortly thereafter, the company began to franchise its stores and established twenty restaurants by the end of the decade. Today, Papa's Chicken & Waffles boasts 1,700 locations across twenty states. While its stores are still primarily concentrated in the Southeast, Papa's has locations as far north as Pennsylvania and as far west as Phoenix. Metro Charlotte now has over fifty. The chain is so popular in North Carolina that major intersections frequently have two stores situated on opposite sides of the same street.

The brick exterior of the Papa's is accentuated at the top by a white façade, which bears the restaurant's name in bright red lettering. Many locations have double-length parking spots to accommodate truck trailers and recreational vehicles. No store has a drive-through window, although servers will gladly prepare take-out meals for a ten percent surcharge.

Inside, one wall is lined with four booths, each of which can accommodate four patrons. The four-and-a-half-foot "high bar" offers barstool seating for six customers directly in front of the grill. Eight chairs line the adjacent "low bar," whose top is three feet from the floor. Another row of three booths connects the high bar with the wall opposite the first row of booths, making a grand total of 42 seats. The interior walls are decorated with pictures and artistic renderings of menu items. A watercolor of a hen perched on her nest attests that Papa's is the South's leading restaurant seller of chicken breasts (over 10,000 a day), no mean feat for a chain primarily renowned for its breakfast fare. Another proclaims that the company has served over 300 million waffles since inception.

Besides its eponymous feature menu item, Papa's is renowned for its nationally acclaimed hashbrowns. The hashbrown potatoes may be cooked "in the round," i.e., inside a circular steel cookie cutter roughly five inches in diameter. Alternatively, they are "scrambled" on the grill without the constraint of the metal ring.

The scrambled hashbrowns experience is typically augmented with a variety of toppings. The plate can be flavored with onions, cheese, tomatoes, diced ham, bacon, tomatoes, mushrooms, or Caleb's chili. (Caleb was a Papa's employee who won a chili cook-off in 1978. The company appropriated his recipe shortly thereafter.) The company claims that variously combining these additives creates over a million ways to prepare hashbrowns. As I haven't done any permutation math since high school, I'll have to trust it on this one.

The most common add-ons are onions and cheese—that's "scrambled, seasoned, and blanketed" in Papa's vernacular. More intrepid diners (including myself) order "home run hashbrowns," meaning that all seven additives are concurrently piled on the plate. In addition to being incredibly delicious, nutritionists should note that this meal represents all four food groups—a fact I used to justify my indulgence in a double plate at the beginning of every shift for two months.

Outside of placing its trademark red-and-white icon on interstate exit signs, Papa's Chicken & Waffles doesn't employ official advertising campaigns. It doesn't need to. Its cult-like following has spread by word of mouth. Many devoted customers have even held their wedding ceremonies at their regular store. In lieu of tossing rice, the custom is to throw grits at the newlyweds. Etiquette dictates that the grits are not cooked beforehand.

Papa's reciprocates the customer love. The company's website and calendars feature regular customers who have dined at Papa's restaurants every day for decades. "Regular" patrons who dine there every day of the week receive a 10% discount; some stores even extend the discount to "weekday regulars" that neglect to visit on Saturday or Sunday. (I hold that to be a particularly magnanimous gesture.)

The company also maintains a twenty-four-hour Customer Call Line at 1–888–PAPAWFL. If you ever have a dire need to unravel the enigma of a "waffle sandwich" at 3 a.m. on a Tuesday, you can speak to a live operator who will happily field your question. (I did this, myself, recently. It turns out that it's an otherwise-standard ham and cheese sandwich, which is grilled inside a waffle iron.) If you are dying for more Papa's lore, you can tour the company museum at the original restaurant location in Charlotte. It is primarily used for internal corporate events, but public tours are available by appointment.

Guided campus tours given to high school seniors offer no real clue as to how or where the enduring memories of the college experience will be produced. Eight years after my graduation, I can't think of any particularly memorable incidents at the gymnasium, student union building, assembly hall, or classrooms. Categorically, the only anecdotes worth relating all happened late at night.

As all bona fide Southerners know, there is no better way to conclude a night of carousing than to pile six friends into a car at 2 a.m. and head to the local Papa's for a plate of hashbrowns. In such a setting, the banter inevitably proves three times as entertaining as a typical dinner conversation at the university cafeteria. In the first place, at least two people in your party are still likely to be inebriated and, therefore, amenable to tomfoolery.

More importantly, your server is accustomed to waiting on imbeciles like you and your friends, meaning that the ramifications of any obnoxious behavior are relatively limited. One notable exception: while he typically enjoyed a lively repartee with Papa's Chicken & Waffles waitresses, my fraternity brother was nearly expelled from a Winston-Salem store for turning a pecan waffle into a fashion accessory. (Oddly, pouring syrup on his bare chest while belly dancing for the hapless server hadn't been sufficient cause.)

Infatuated by such reminiscences of my glory days, I hopped in my car and made a ten-minute drive down the road. As are most Papa's Chicken & Waffles outlets, the restaurant was situated just a few yards from the interstate exit. I had driven past the diner on many occasions since moving to town three years ago but had never ventured inside. In fact, I hadn't eaten at any Papa's location in several years.

I parked my car and entered the restaurant. A waitress and a cook attended to a handful of patrons, who were scattered across the counter seats and booths. I asked the waitress, Mary, for a word with the manager. She informed me that the best time to catch him was the following day at 2.30 p.m. I asked if she knew about any available jobs.

"Papa's is always hiring," she said.

"What do you mean, 'always'?"

"I mean the managers are constantly looking for more folks. Cooks, servers, whatever."

Call Barack Obama. I had just solved the nation's rising unemployment problem.

"Really? In that case, I'd like an application."

"Sure, let me get one for you." She reached under the counter and produced a pale green piece of paper not much bigger than a 3 x 5 index card. I accepted it and quickly scanned it over.

"There's no writing on the back side of this," I observed.

"Yeah. Is that a problem?"

"No. I just thought it would be a little longer."

She assured me I was holding all of the requisite paperwork. I surveyed the restaurant again, trying to get a better feel for the establishment.

"Are you hiring at this store, or are your available positions only at other locations?"

"We're looking for people at all of our area stores."

"Really? How many are there around here?"

"There's three alone inside the city limits."

I turned to see a grizzled man holding a cigarette with two inches of ash reclined in the corner booth.

"Oh," I said. "I thought there was just the one."

He shook his head in gentle reproof. He leaned forward and drew on his cigarette.

"You see, you got Papa's all around the capitol area." He then proceeded to list the city and street of each outlet within a 60-mile radius—twelve in all. I had to admit, I was pretty impressed. I didn't even bother to memorize my wife's social security number. He was certainly a devoted customer. Or else...

"You don't work for *The Michelin Guide,* do you?" I inquired.

"No, I work for Roadway Trucking. Why?"

"Just wondering."

I thanked the waitress for her time, nodded respectfully to the Connoisseur, and exited the restaurant. I returned home, laid the application on my kitchen counter, and took another look. It was decidedly succinct. Under "education," all I had to do was circle a number indicating years of schooling. Oddly, the last number was "14." There were no pesky boxes in which the applicant would have to report completion of an MBA program. I circled "12" and moved on. Five seconds more, and I was finished.

I returned at the appointed time the following day. The manager was not in, although the assistant manager, a forty-something woman named Debbie, agreed to meet with me. After a brief review of my application, she invited me to join her in the corner booth where the Connoisseur had been seated the previous day.

"So you're looking for work, huh?"

"I am."

"You ever work in a restaurant before?"

"No." I confessed, trying to keep a confident demeanor.

I braced myself for a thorough scrutinizing.

"What were you doing at your last job?" She paused, eyeing me.

"You have had a job before, right?"

"You know that international banking crisis that's been in the news lately?"

"Yeah."

"Well, it's kind of my fault. I mean, not the whole thing, but I was one of the people involved."

"Oh?" Her eyes widened. "What were you doing?"

"You know those bad mortgages?"

She nodded.

"My firm bought a bunch of them for banks. And for pension funds. And for mutual funds. And for some other people. And now I'd like to do something completely unrelated to mortgage bonds. Or any kind of bond." I lowered my head, hoping that my gesture of contrition might curry some favor.

Debbie looked at me with wonderfully sympathetic eyes. "You're one of those millions of people that just lost their job recently, aren't you?"

I nodded solemnly.

"Well, you can start at 8 a.m. Monday. Wear a white shirt, black pants, and black shoes. The shift runs until 2p.m."

I was ecstatic. My confession had surely softened her heart and swept away any doubts she may have been harboring. On the other hand, maybe Papa's Chicken & Waffles would hire anybody. Debbie explained that I would be in a training program for the next few weeks and cautioned me against being complacent in the face of a steep learning curve. (That's not exactly how she put it, but you get the idea.) I reassured her that the restaurant would receive my full intellectual commitment. I figured if I paid any attention to what I was doing, I couldn't do any more damage to restaurant patrons than I had done to institutional investors. As long as I wasn't going to cook and there wasn't a bond in sight, what could possibly go wrong?

After administering a few more instructions, Debbie let me go. I waved goodbye to my new colleagues and returned to my car with a spring in my step. On the way out, I stopped to examine the music catalog of a juke box situated near the store entrance. I had forgotten that every Papa's has one. *How cool is that?* I thought. *For all its supposed sophistication, the bond market didn't even have good music, much less a juke box.*

I spent the drive home daydreaming about squandering my tips on Randy Travis songs. I didn't even particularly care for country music, but the idea was liberating nonetheless.

While trying to remember how many tunes I could purchase for a dollar, I realized that I had neglected to ask Debbie a very important question. Though the application had said something about "above average wages," I had no idea what I was going to be paid, or how much I could expect to earn in tips. Then it dawned on me—I didn't care about the money. What really mattered was that I had officially put the bond market behind me and had begun a new chapter in my life.

*Chapter 2*

# LEARNING CURVE

*"When the going gets weird, the weird turn pro."*
**HUNTER S. THOMPSON**

My family members were universally supportive of my sabbatical from the capital markets. "Finally, you're doing something I actually understand and can wholeheartedly endorse," my father crowed. I had expected as much from him. This was a man who agreed to accompany my mother on her frequent 400-mile treks to visit me at college on the sole condition that he could patronize the Papa's. (At the time, the company had no stores in my home state of Pennsylvania.)

"I think it's terrific," my mother said. "You're going to find out what the real world is really like." My brother found the situation deliciously ironic. "You'll be waiting tables on a lot of college-aged jerks. You remember how obnoxious we were back then."

"I remember how obnoxious *you* were," I said.

My sister, a usually serious type, broke into uncontrollable laughter. "You have no idea what the heck you're getting into, do you?" she sneered.

"Probably not," I conceded.

"That place is going to kick your butt," she prognosticated. I had to acknowledge that she was probably right.

Despite her jibes, my sister did have one major concern: Papa's still had a smoking section in nearly all restaurants whose state laws permitted it.

"Cigarette smoke is really bad for you. You can get heart disease that way," she warned.

"The bond market will kill a man faster than second-hand smoke," I retorted.

One other voice haunted me. Three years ago, the director of the career development office at my graduate school had issued an ominous warning to a roomful of MBA students. "Don't ever take a step backwards in your career," he cautioned. "It can permanently impair it."

At the time, I had received his comments as words of wisdom. Now, they seemed like a fetter restraining me from enlightenment. Every time I moved two steps ahead in my path to the corner office, the rug had been pulled from beneath my feet. I was sick of playing by the rules. Besides, I wasn't taking a step back down the corporate ladder; I was throwing myself down four flights of stairs. It was time to see if fate would respond better to some reverse psychology.

$ $ $ $ $

I showed up for my first day wearing the only white polo shirt in my closet and a pair of black cotton pants that I hadn't worn in at least six years. I took a seat at the low bar and completed a packet of paperwork. After I returned it to Debbie, a man in his late twenties introduced himself as Matthew, the store manager. He invited me to accompany him to the employee break room where I was joined by another new employee. A hefty man in his mid-twenties, Tim had previously worked as a cook at a local country club where he had earned $20 an hour. As a new "grill officer," Tim would be making less than half of his previous wage.

Like Tim and me, Matthew had also fallen on hard times. Prior to Papa's, he had been a construction supervisor in Florida. The money had been great, although his employer was "crooked as hell" and eventually went under. Matthew was perfectly amicable, though I could tell by his repeated stares at the Jupiter Yacht Club crest on my polo shirt that he was anxious to discover my history.

"And what did you do at your last job?" he inquired.

"Well, you know how most of the homes you built were sold to people that really couldn't afford them?"

"Yeah."

"Well, my last shop gave them the money to do that."

"Oh." He thought for a few seconds, then shot me a broad smile. "Well, I bet it was fun while it lasted, right?"

"Sure was," I said.

Matthew grew increasingly warm toward me after this brief exchange. Evidently, our shared culpability for the economic meltdown had endeared me to him. But instead of reminiscing about "the good old days" and lamenting his current situation, he gave one of the best workplace pep talks I've ever heard in my life. As French author Antoine St. Exupery once admonished, "the best way of building a ship is not to order people to collect wood and assign them tasks, but rather to teach them to long for the endless immensity of the sea." And that's what Matthew did. He painted an alluring portrait of life at Papa's, a veritable siren song.

"You can make a lot of money here," he began. "And I'm not playing with you boys. I'll be honest, it was hard for me when my last company went under. I didn't know what to expect when I came aboard. But let me tell you something. If you work hard, and you produce, you do have opportunity. I started out just like you guys not that long ago, and now I'm the store manager." He proceeded to relate numerous anecdotes about how the company consistently rewarded its top performers with managerial positions. In many cases, managers even went on to run their own franchises. Matthew praised the business acumen and dedication of the company's founders. As someone who has heard a lot of canned speeches delivered by corporate managers, the sincerity of his tone was completely unfamiliar to me. He had genuine respect for the men running his company—in particular, CEO J. Hank Kramerson.

A voracious consumer of his company's products, Hank dines a Papa's nearly every day of the year. He is renowned for dropping into his stores unannounced, where he spontaneously pours customers' coffee, grills waffles, and washes dishes. Hank requires that all senior Papa's executives work holidays, including Christmas and New Year's. In his view, the demands placed on rank-and-file employees should not exceed those placed on upper management.

I was wholly unprepared for this sort of praise of executive management. In the corporate world, nobody talks about senior company officers in such a flattering manner—unless, of course, they're present. As Matthew continued extolling the virtues of the top man, I got the distinct impression that Hank would have to immediately resign should Papa's ever list on the New York Stock Exchange. In my experience, a man with that much humility could never thrive in a corporate boardroom.

The only coffee-pouring anecdote about a CEO that I ever heard had been markedly less flattering. Rising from his chair in the middle of a conference meeting, the president of an insurance company beckoned his secretary from her desk down the hall. When she arrived at the conference room, he directed her to prepare his coffee, notwithstanding that the service cart had been situated directly behind him all along. In the time required by this superfluous act of her fealty, the CEO could have simply poured his own cup and consumed half of it.

After wrapping up the grand corporate vision of Papa's Chicken & Waffles, Inc., Matthew concluded his speech where he started it: with an appeal to greed. If we were motivated, he claimed, we would soon be living high off the hog like Debbie. Yesterday, she had raked in a hundred dollars worth of tips during an eight-hour shift. After including her $2.13 hourly wage, her average earnings were better than fifteen bucks an hour. Furthermore, because most of her tips were in cash, the IRS would be none the wiser if she elected not to report some of them.

As someone who normally expresses tremendous skepticism at any promotional pitch, I was surprised by how much Matthew's speech won me over. I normally carried less than fifty dollars of cash in my wallet, so the idea of physically holding in excess of a hundred bucks at one time was quite alluring. More importantly, I really liked the idea of being able to give the taxman the slip. It was only after I bothered to do the math on the drive home that it dawned on me. Even if I worked really hard, my income would never amount to more than a fifth of what it had been just a few weeks before.

$ $ $ $ $

During our first week on the job, Tim and I divided our time between watching training videos in the back room and shadowing our trainers on the breakfast shift. Despite a generally mirthless demeanor, Debbie proved a patient mentor. I followed her to each table, placing the silverware as customers arrived and fetching drinks after they had placed their orders. Most of the table waiting process was fairly prosaic. The real difficulty, I learned, was in memorizing prices and properly calling in orders to the cooks.

Unlike most contemporary restaurants, Papa's does not utilize computers to facilitate communication between servers and cooks. Instead, servers stand on a specified floor tile (a rooster giving a big thumbs up) and verbally relay the orders for their table. This is a three-step process. First, all of the meats are aggregated. The server calls "DRAW," followed by the requisite number of cheesesteaks, hamburger and sausage patties, bacon strips, and so forth. The grill officer then retrieves the meats from the refrigerator and places them on the grill. Secondly, hashbrowns are ordered with a "PLACE" and the appropriate number of servings. Lastly, the server yells, "SET" and indicates the particulars of each dish to the grill officer.

The cook marks the plates using a proprietary system wherein condiment packets represent meat and eggs. Mayonnaise indicates bacon or sausage, depending on its position; ketchup signifies a cheesesteak; a butter cup indicates a T-bone, and so forth. The arrangement of the packets indicates the temperature of the meat and how the eggs are cooked. Any egg or meat plate not marked for hashbrowns is assumed to be receiving grits. Waffles are always called last.

Similar orders must be consolidated as much as possible. For example: three customers order scrambled eggs. One of them would like cheese in his eggs and a bowl of grits, while his two companions prefer hashbrowns in lieu of grits; one of them wants wheat toast. The proper call is: "Set an order scrambled on three. Make one cheese; make two a plate; make one plate wheat." The grill officer then calls back the order to the server to verify that he has set the condiment markers correctly. At no time during the process does the grill officer view the order ticket.

It's really an ingenious system in many respects. It eliminates the need for a computer, while leaving the server in control of the order ticket so that he can tally the meal cost and make any subsequent additions. Unfortunately, the process has a drawback—namely, a large number of idiosyncrasies on the menu. For example, you must always remember a regular order of bacon is comprised of three strips. However, when bacon is being added to a sandwich (e.g., to a cheeseburger) only two strips are required. In that case, the server requests a "half order" of bacon. The BLT sandwich is the exception to the rule, as it receives a full order. Of course, the "bacon lover's" BLT receives five strips—an order and a half. Got all that?

At the end of every shift, each server submits a test, which requires him to write the abbreviation and price of nearly every menu offering. Initially, it's a laborious process because you are constantly referring to a master pricing sheet. But committing this information to memory has tremendous value to a server, who does not want to be forced to consult the pricing sheet during the middle of a busy shift. Even once you master the ordering system (which took me well over a month), it's still difficult to place an accurate order call on nights when you're operating on five hours of sleep.

After the breakfast crowd subsided, Debbie told me to take a seat at the low bar as she retreated to the back room. She returned a minute later with a large black binder under her arm.

"Read this," she said, placing *The Rise & Shine Manual* on the counter. "For the next four weeks of your training program, this is your Bible."

"Is it okay if I pretend it's the Qur'an?" I asked. "The paperwork I filled out yesterday said that Papa's doesn't discriminate on the basis of religion."

She looked confused. I explained that the Qur'an was the primary text of Islam, a religion whose adherents numbered in the billions. I neglected to mention that a devout Muslim would not assume a vocation that involves serving prodigious amounts of bacon and pork sausage.

"You can call it whatever you want, so long as you read it," she said.

$ $ $ $ $

I spent the next two hours immersing myself in the 200-page training handbook. The first few pages outlined general principles for creating a quality dining experience. *The Rise & Shine* alleged that regardless of how well the food was prepared, servers who neglected to bathe on a regular basis might endanger their gratuities. I also learned that delivering a customer's check along with his food provided a subtle hint to pay his bill as soon as he was finished eating. By encouraging faster table turnover with this tactic, Papa's would garner more revenue, and I would earn more tips.

Beyond explaining rudimentary serving skills, *The Rise & Shine Manual* imparted optimal temperatures for brewing iced tea, grilling hashbrowns, and maintaining the chili pot. The manual committed me to memorizing each of them and concluded each chapter with exercises to test my knowledge. There was even an "honesty pledge" for me to sign. I wondered if anyone, anywhere, in a capital markets job ever had to make such a vow. My brain, for one, cannot conjure a mental image of a Wall Street bond trader making a public commitment to professional integrity without a conspicuous smirk on his face.

Matthew abruptly broke my study session by informing me that the franchise owner would be in later that afternoon to inspect the premises. Accordingly, the grill officer and servers would have to clean the store from top to bottom before his arrival. I was assigned to wash windows.

"I hate to do this to you," Matthew said to me, "but we all need to be looking as hygienic as possible when this guy shows up. So that means you have to wear appropriate headgear during the review. Unfortunately, the visor we ordered for you hasn't arrived yet, so I'm afraid you're going to have to wear this for the time being. Sorry, but it's the only alternative."

He was right to have made the preemptive apology. A wedge-shaped paper cap is the kind of item that you only wear if you lose a bet or you're too senile to be cognizant of your appearance. As a normally very fashion-conscious fellow, I was taken aback by how few reservations I had about donning it. After all, if you're going to swim in a freezing pool, you might as well jump headfirst into the deep end.

No sooner had I emerged from the employee break room sporting my new accoutrement than a regular customer named Bert decided to critique it.

"What're you wearing that funny hat for?" he snickered. I had to concede that I looked pretty lame. The wedge cap made me look more like a 1950s-era soda jerk than a contemporary Papa's employee. On the other hand, it wasn't really fair that a man wearing camouflage pajama pants and tan combat boots should call my fashion sense into question.

"Well, Bert," I said, "management told me to 'keep it sexy' when they agreed to hire me, so I'm trying to fulfill that mandate as best I can."

I strode to the front door and began washing its panels. After thirty seconds of cleaning, I turned around to find Bert staring blankly at me from the high bar. My remark had obviously disarmed him, and it was clear that he was thinking really hard about what I had just said. Apparently, Bert did not realize that it's impossible to denigrate a man who no longer considers dignity to be any sort of a virtue. I smiled at him and sprayed a few more squirts of cleaning solution onto the glass.

I'm sure that it loses luster for people that have been doing it for thirty years, but for me, washing windows and sweeping floors proved an unexpectedly satisfying experience. I had spent the previous twenty-four months cleaning up bond market messes via conference calls, lengthy emails, and five-page memoranda. Cleaning up physical messes, rather than financial ones, was a welcome change of pace. On the surface, it may seem less glamorous, but at the end of the day, what difference does it make whether you're cleaning up after a mortgage trader or a trucker? At least the latter would tip you in cash and not bust your chops every time you interacted with him.

Undoubtedly, the best part of my new job was a culinary perquisite. During our shifts, we could eat nearly any menu item that we wanted at no charge. Pork chops, steaks, or chicken would cost us a few dollars, but for everything else, the price was free and quantities were unlimited. All you can eat hashbrowns? That passes for nirvana in most parts of Arkansas.

The only problem with this otherwise unbelievable fringe benefit was the ambiance in which said hashbrowns were consumed. Employees were required to eat in the back room of the restaurant, whose decorations consisted of soda syrup bladders, a rusty $CO_2$ tank, two industrial sinks, and a wall calendar extolling the loyalty of a twenty-year regular customer. Over the course of twenty years, he had consumed an estimated 6,000 waffles and 15,000 cups of coffee.

Accentuating the Spartan décor was the omnipresent odor of cigarettes. When the room wasn't saturated with the smell of live

Newport menthols, it was caked with the smell of stale smoke. After several days of nearly choking to death, I decided to cast the situation in different terms. Instead of considering the carbon monoxide exposure as an express lane to heart disease, I decided to think of it as an amenity. Purchasing two packs of cigarettes would have set me back ten bucks, so I figured that consuming a pack's worth of secondhand smoke probably had a five-dollar retail value. In a week's time, my eyes and lungs had adjusted to the adverse conditions. Given that all of the other employees smoked, asking them not to do so in my presence would have been a major imposition. I only expressed my disdain on one occasion as a pregnant coworker ignited a cigarette in front of me.

"When are you due?" I asked. "In another four months," she responded. I cast a scornful glance at her Newport cigarette and watched her follow my eyes as I let them deliberately wander to her protruding belly.

"I'm just trying to get rid of my last carton," she said, blushing. "Honest."

"Of course," I said. "It would be a shame to let good tobacco go to waste."

$ $ $ $ $

Despite my occasional misgiving about their smoking habits, I was genuinely enjoying time with my new colleagues. They were very patient with me as they imparted skills like judging whether a pot of coffee was fresh or stale based on its smell. Most of them were quite incredulous at my claim that because I never drank coffee, I didn't even know how to brew a pot. In short order, I earned a reputation as a serious eccentric. Rumors began circulating that I had been through some serious hell in the financial markets, which had left me in a state of mental disrepair.

My general ineptitude notwithstanding, my only work-related injury during the training period was a minor cut on my index finger. I had been eavesdropping on an economic conversation, causing me temporarily to lose my concentration as I diced salad tomatoes. Oddly, listening to middle-aged smokers discuss a precipitous drop in the Baltic Dry Container Index and the declines in their retirement accounts proved much more painful than the laceration.

As expected, the juke box turned out to be a small treat, containing a robust selection of country, pop, and hip hop. If no one placed any coins in it for more than twenty minutes, it began to play spontaneously Papa's-themed ditties. Some of them were shameless marketing propaganda like, "Where Else Would You Go for Cheese Grits?" Other tunes took a more comedic approach: "I Just Saw Elvis at Papa's Chicken and Waffles." (Within weeks, I would come to realize that a cameo appearance by the King would rank fairly low on a list of absurd late-night happenings at the store.)

I was impressed by the broad swath of appeal cut by the juke box's country music tunes. Old and young, male and female, black and white all deposited coins to hear, "She Thinks My Tractor's Sexy" or the Dixie Chicks's "Goodbye, Earl." I would never have expected to witness a young black man dressed in gangbanger attire enthusiastically singing along to "Forever and Ever, Amen."

"I didn't take you for a Randy Travis fan," I said playfully. "Do you have him on your iPod?"

"Oh, no, I'm not," he said, blushing. "I never even heard this song before."

I had caught him redhanded. "That's funny, I swore I heard you reciting the lyrics like you were already familiar with them."

"Well," he stammered, "I picked up the tune after a minute or two. I gotta admit it's kinda catchy."

I turned from him and began bussing a table where a woman in her mid-twenties was finishing her meal.

"Thank you, Brother," she said as I removed a plate.

"I'm sorry, I don't recognize you from any family reunions," I responded.

"Oh, I don't think we're biologically related. I call everyone 'Brother' because I'm a communist."

"Really? I thought that 'comrade' was the preferred term."

"That's true, but I prefer 'Brother' because it expresses the same sentiment with a more familiar term."

"I see. Do you happen to know if the Soviets addressed their political dissidents as 'comrade' after they tossed them in the gulag?"

She smiled. "That wasn't *real* communism. People always mess up when they try to implement good ideas . . . even capitalists," she said with a wink. "People are fundamentally bad. That's why Thomas Hobbes advocated a powerful state—to keep people in line."

"It's certainly true that free markets only work when there is some base level of trust among the participants," I said. "But the power of the state can never coerce people into moral behavior. That's a deeply repugnant notion, even if it was advocated by American presidential advisors like John Kenneth Galbraith."

"Well, how would you make people decent?" she asked.

"I would defer to George Washington. In his farewell presidential address, he asserted that religion and morality are indispensable supports to political prosperity. A republic works best when its citizens are taught correct principles in their families and are then left to govern themselves. When the majority of the people are fundamentally decent, then the only necessary role for government is the protection of property rights."

"Amen, Brother."

I continued. "People forget that Adam Smith, the father of capitalist thought, was a moral philosopher first and an economist second. He believed that the free market was the best mechanism for improving the aggregate well-being of society."

She stared at me for a while before venturing an opinion. "Jimmy, you're too much of a philosopher to be working at a Papa's Chicken & Waffles."

"And here I thought I was working at Papa's *because* I was a philosopher."

The Communist smiled and advised me that she would return for another meal within a few days. I had high hopes for her. While the statist doctrines of Hobbes and Marx had caused some minor cognitive impairments, it appeared to be nothing that Adam Smith and a few plates of hashbrowns couldn't remedy.

$ $ $ $ $

Adam Smith is generally recognized as the founding father of **Classical economics.** Classical economists believe that individuals should be left free to pursue their own economic self-interests with minimal interference from the state. Prior to Smith's time, economies were typically managed under mercantilist philosophies which held that governments should play a protectionist role by encouraging most exports and discouraging certain imports.

In contrast, Smith held that markets are best left to regulate themselves. This belief is sometimes referred to as laissez-faire, a French expression meaning "let it be." Smith's novel ideas on free enterprise and free international trade were expressed in the seminal *An Inquiry into the Wealth of Nations,* published in 1776. The classic tome on capitalism, *Wealth* revolutionized economic thought and inspired much of Jean-Baptiste Say's *Treatise on Political Economy.*

But while he was the intellectual parent of laissez-faire capitalism, Smith was first and foremost an ethicist. Seventeen years prior to writing *Wealth,* he had penned *The Theory of Moral Sentiments,* a treatise on the nature and motives of morality.

Smith argued that despite man's natural inclination to selfishness, all human beings possess an innate concern for the welfare of others. Morality, he explained, consists of the development of this natural endowment of sympathy. Sympathy encourages people to cultivate good relations with their fellow human beings and provides the basis for social order. (If this philosophy sounds vaguely familiar, it's probably because you heard some version of it expressed in Sunday school. "To love our neighbor as we love ourselves is the great law of Christianity," *Sentiments* asserts.)

*The Wealth of Nations* served as an economic corollary to the broader philosophical views espoused in *Moral Sentiments.* Its great philosophical contribution is that voluntary economic transactions benefit both buyer and seller. That is, no one will purchase a good or service unless he assigns a value to that good above the price he is paying. Similarly, sellers will not continue to offer their goods unless the sales price exceeds their cost of production. Furthermore, laborers in the employ of the sellers also benefit from wages earned in the production process. Led by an "invisible hand," each of these economic actors pursues his own **self-interest,** concurrently benefiting himself and society as a whole.

Consider a contemporary illustration. Papa's Chicken & Waffles offers the "Winnie K Special," which is arguably the greatest breakfast value in the continental United States. For just $7.00, diners can enjoy two eggs, toast, and their choice of grits or hashbrowns AND waffle or biscuit and gravy AND two sausage patties or three bacon strips. It's almost too good to be true. The customer parts with his dollars because he values the food more than his cash. For its part, Papa's offers the meal because its cost of production is below $7.00, so the company turns a profit on the sale. Waiters serve the Winnie because we value the (anticipated) tips resulting from our labor more than we prize our leisure time. Everyone wins: customer, business owner, and laborer. Despite acting in their own self-interests, a universally beneficial outcome is attained by all. It's pretty amazing when you think about it.

By offering its customers a delicious breakfast at a reasonable price, Papa's revenues have increased precisely because the stores attract a loyal customer base that relies on the restaurant chain to produce an affordable, quality product. The same condition holds for the servers: on average, increased attentiveness to customer desires yields higher tips.

Customers, in turn, will receive better service as they patronize the store more frequently and reward servers with large gratuities.

In the aforementioned example, each participant (restaurant, waiter, customer) is acting in his own self-interest *by serving other people.* In Smith's view, these sympathetic actions are fully consistent with pursuit of individual self-interest and form the basis of economic interaction. Commerce requires cooperation, which is fundamentally grounded upon sympathy and trust.

In the absence of sympathy and trust, however, the wheels of industry grind to a halt. You will not patronize a restaurant if you are unwilling to entrust the cooks with your food preparation. The restaurant, in turn, is reluctant to serve customers that it believes may walk out without paying. Papa's will not hire a cook without having faith in his ability to properly prepare a meal. Similarly, the company would be hard up to find willing cooks if prospective employees believed that their payroll checks wouldn't clear.

To Adam Smith, a free market implies "free of excessive government interference." To a **selfish** person, the free market means "free of scruples." While self-interested behavior benefits all parties in a free economy, selfish behavior does not. Selfish behavior is personal aggrandizement *at the expense of other persons.* Unlike self-interested behavior (which benefits all parties—capitalist, laborer, and customer), selfishness is a zero sum game.

In the short term, selfish behavior seems to pay off. A restaurant can temporarily fatten its profit margins by deliberately overcharging its customers, a worker can steal from his employer, and a customer can save a few dollars by neglecting to tip.

But while selfish people may reap short-term economic benefits from their behavior, selfishness has an immediate drawback: it renders one fundamentally incapable of experiencing true joy. Instead, selfish people experience a debased version of happiness derived from the accumulation of whatever good they presently covet. In the long term, of course, selfishness catches up with the offending party. The unscrupulous restaurant will see its business erode, the dishonest employee will eventually be fired, and the stingy customer will receive increasingly mediocre service.

Unfortunately, contemporary society often conflates selfishness with self-interest, forgetting that capitalism—as envisioned by Adam Smith—is a fundamentally *moral* economic arrangement. As long as individuals behave in a self-interested (rather than selfish) manner, more economic freedom enables greater levels of happiness and higher standards of living.

In contrast, state-managed economies produce widespread misery and low standards of living for one simple reason: no one has any economic incentive to serve anyone else. As far as I can tell, Russia only produced two worthwhile goods during eighty years of Communist rule: crude oil and Tetris. (Sorry, matryoshka dolls don't count.)

In addition to making reproductive investments in machinery that was productivity enhancing, Smith explained that much of the gain in living standards in a capitalist system arises from the intelligent **division of labor.** As the types of work performed become increasingly specialized across a broad pool of workers, the volume and quality of output both increase.

Smith observed these productivity gains when he visited a pin factory. He estimated that by dividing the manufacturing process across ten specialized laborers, the men were able to produce between 240 and 4,800 times as many pins than if they had made them independently of each other. It makes you wonder what those guys could have accomplished with a really large grill and a few truckloads of uncooked hashbrowns.

$ $ $ $ $

A typical Papa's shift operates with half the number of employees as Adam Smith's pin factory. Labor tasks are divided amongst five employees: two grill officers and three waiters. The former group is responsible for food preparation; the latter, for its distribution. Like most other restaurants, Papa's has "side work" assignments for its servers. In addition to our table waiting duties, servers are expected to refill napkin holders, replace empty condiment bottles, sweep floors, bus tables, and so forth. They are also charged with serving as dishwashers and cashiers.

Having no previous retail experience, I had never operated a cash register before. But as far as I could tell, our machine operated differently from the registers which I had encountered as a customer at other restaurants and retail outlets. Normally, the process goes as follows: 1) The clerk rings up each individual item on your tab. 2) He punches a button to calculate the total, which appears on the register screen. 3) You hand the clerk an amount of currency and/or coin equal to or exceeding your total, which he then keys into the register. 4) The amount of change due appears on the register display.

Our register wasn't quite that fancy. For some reason, it only had a step #2, so the onus of calculating the check total and the correct amount of change fell entirely to the register operator. For this reason, most servers used a calculator, which they kept in their apron pockets or on the counter next to the register. Unfortunately, as I discovered during one of my first customer checkouts, they weren't terribly dependable.

No sooner had I started to sum the tab than I realized the keypad had been totally compromised by waffle syrup. The "3" and "7" keys would not return to an upright position after I pushed them; the number "5" key refused to depress altogether, despite my repeated efforts to force it down with a knife butt. I decided to resort to manual addition before my customer's visible impatience increased any further.

I showed up for work the next day proudly brandishing my Hewlett Packard model 12c financial calculator. Since acquiring her eight years ago during my first week on the job as a junior credit analyst, the HP 12c had remained with me throughout my entire bond market career. She had seen me through all three levels of the Chartered Financial Analyst exam, two years of business school, and countless hours of capital market mayhem. In her past life, the HP 12c had been used to calculate capital gains on sales of forty-million-dollar blocks of corporate bonds. Now she was consigned to spending her latter days computing taxes on nine-dollar restaurant tabs.

As a new recruit, I wore a pocketless cook's apron in lieu of the pocketed version worn by tenured servers. Regrettably, the absence of an apron pocket meant that I had to keep my beloved calculator on the cashier's counter. It was the last place I ever saw her.

A few hours after my shift ended, I realized that I had neglected to bring the HP 12c back home with me. No matter, I thought.

No one would want it to take it, anyway. The machine operated via "reverse Polish notation," meaning that the keys had to be punched in an unconventional sequence to perform even basic arithmetic. It had taken me several weeks to master this skill, so I presumed that a casual thief would be deterred by the sheer frustration of trying to operate it. I thought wrong.

Although I realized that any investigation into the calculator's whereabouts would likely prove utterly futile, I decided to ask around, anyway. I began my inquiry with Betty, a wonderfully pleasant server in her late forties. Upbeat and gregarious, she always sent departing customers off with the phrase, "Have a blessed day." It was evident that she really meant it. Even when she was tired, I never heard Betty utter a cross word about anyone. Which isn't to say that the job didn't wear her down from time to time. During her four-year stint, she had quit her job on five different occasions. But despite her repeated public resignations, she always showed up for her next shift, anyway. You have to admire that kind of tenacity.

In recognition of Betty's faithful service as a "five-star waitress," the district manager had presented her with a single star pin, which Betty promptly affixed to her hat. And while the bright red star undoubtedly differentiated her from the other servers, it seemed to proclaim Communist partisanship rather than five-star waitressing. "Betty, did you happen to see a Hewlett Packard calculator in the store this morning? I can't find it anywhere."

"Oh, you mean that real fancy looking one that you had yesterday? I had never seen a calculator like that before," Betty said.

"Yeah, she was a real beauty," I said morosely. "So you haven't seen anyone using it to run amortization schedules?"

"I can't say that I have, hon. Then again, if I knew what you were talking about, I could give you a definite answer." She paused for a minute, studying my features. "You don't look like the typical server here," she said finally.

"Oh? Why is that?"

"You just don't have the *Papa's look.*"

I had never been so insulted. French aristocrats have dueled with less provocation.

"What's that supposed to mean?" I could feel a grin slowly creeping across my face.

"I didn't mean anything bad by it. You just look more like a scientist to me. Or maybe the vice president of a corporation."

"Betty, we just met. Don't you think it's a little soon to malign my character?"

"I didn't mean nothin' by it. I think scientists are great. But what are you doing here?"

"I'm on work release."

"From jail? A guy like you? I don't believe it."

"From the bond market. It's a lot like jail, but the uniform's less comfortable and we don't get any yard time."

She shook her head. "Whatever you say, honey." "Honey." I really liked that. She called everyone "honey," but it still made me feel special.

$ $ $ $ $

I couldn't be entirely certain why I failed to project the "Papa's Chicken & Waffles look," but an objective review of my attire offered a few clues. I had substituted a white button-down shirt for the polo shirt I had worn during my first three days on the job, which probably made me look more corporate than I had intended. Following a company policy mandating black shoes, I had worn the same Brooks Brothers cordovan leather pair that had served me for seven years in the bond market. I thought they added a classy touch to the uniform. Another server had pointed out that my feet would fare much better with a cheap pair of dark cross-trainers supplemented by Dr. Scholl's inserts. He was right of course, but at the time I was in an extremely frugal mindset. After a few weeks, I came to see the wisdom of his advice. I broke down and bought the cheapest pair of black sneakers I could find.

The impetus for my purchase was not sore feet. Rather, the smooth sole of my dress shoes had crossed paths with a wayward onion ring the night before. Hearing the patrons laugh at me as I picked myself off the floor was all the motivation I needed to shell out a few bucks for an oversized pair of skateboarding shoes. They looked absolutely ridiculous. I consoled myself with the thought that I probably looked better standing erect in a fifteen-dollar pair of skater shoes than lying down on the floor of the Papa's wearing my five-hundred-dollar Oxfords.

Donning my button-down shirt didn't prove to be a great idea, either. In short order, it was totally compromised by coffee and chili stains. Coupled with the loss of my financial calculator, I had consecrated about $140 worth of personal items during my first week of work. In that same period of time, I had put in twenty hours at an hourly wage rate of $6.55. (As a trainee, I was ineligible for tips and was therefore paid the minimum wage.) After seven days, the privilege of employment at Papa's had cost me about ten bucks.

$ $ $ $ $

Whether or not she readily admits it, everyone spends a significant portion of her life thinking about money. Most of the meditation is devoted to personal cash balances. Few of us pause to consider money's peculiar role in a global economy; those who bother to do so are often left to cynically conclude that money is the closest mankind will ever come to a universal religion. Although he may spend most of his time masquerading as deity, money's true place in society is better understood by way of anatomical metaphor. In the human body, millions of cells constitute tissues.

Organs, in turn, are comprised of various tissues. Each organ contributes a unique product to the rest of the body. The liver and kidneys produce hormones, the pancreas generates insulin, and so forth. The output of each organ is introduced into the blood stream, which then transmits the output to the other organs. By distributing each organ's production to the other organs, blood plays a crucial role in the body's production processes. Blood, while producing nothing itself, provides the means by which the various components of the body can interface. In the absence of blood, the lungs and pancreas would have to directly touch in order to exchange oxygen for insulin.

Whereas organs are comprised of tissues made from cells, industries are made up of companies, each of them consisting of numerous workers. Each industry produces a unique set of goods required by other parts of the economy. The "Real Economic Output" is the sum of the production of each of the cells, or workers. Each industry's output is distributed through the "bloodstream" of money flow. That is, money is simply the mechanism of introducing each worker's production into the body of commerce. An economy's **money supply** is analogous to the amount of blood in the body.

In economic terms, money is exactly like the circulatory system. It creates nothing by itself but is the indispensible conduit by which each worker's output is ultimately transmitted to other workers. In the absence of a monetary system, each worker would have to barter with another worker in order to exchange his output. It would be horribly inefficient.

Blood pressure is an important means of assessing the health of the blood flow. Many factors can affect blood pressure, but for purposes of illustration, consider just two: blood volume and heart rate. All else equal, a larger amount of blood in the body places greater stress on the arteries, causing blood pressure to increase. (Conversely, loss of blood will trigger a decline in blood pressure.)

When the body exerts itself through cardiovascular exercise, the lungs and other organs increase their production. The heart rate rises as the body circulates a fixed amount of blood at a faster pace in order to distribute the higher level of output. The blood courses through the arteries at a faster rate, causing arterial stress. The result: higher blood pressure. After the athlete finishes her workout, organ production slows, and the blood pressure declines.

Just as blood pressure rises when blood is added to the body or the heart rate increases, the "Price Level" of the economy's goods and services will rise as money is added to dollar circulates at an increased rate. A rise in the Price Level is known as **price inflation.** A decline in the Price Level is known as **price deflation.** The rate at which a dollar circulates through the economic bloodstream is referred to as monetary "Velocity."

The relationship between an economy's output, money supply, price level, and velocity is captured by the **Equation of Exchange:** Money Supply x Velocity = Price Level x Real Economic Output. The Equation of exchange is generally abbreviated as: $MV = PY$. Let's consider a few illustrations of the interplay between these four factors.

As a child matures, his organs grow as the body produces more tissue. Accordingly, the body will generate a larger quantity of blood to service the greater flow of output from each organ. If the body failed to increase the amount of blood in circulation, the adolescent would display low blood pressure. Likewise, if an economy's output grows without a comparable increase in the money supply, the Price Level will fall—i.e., deflation will result. ($MV = P{\downarrow}Y{\uparrow}$)

Deflation means that a dollar now purchases more goods and services than it used to. This is a great condition if somebody owes you money. The dollars that you will receive from your debtor will now buy more things than they did when you originally made the loan. Of course, deflation is not so much fun if you owe money. You can think of deflation as a tax on borrowers.

In the late nineteenth century, the United States experienced deflation for this very reason: the U.S. economy grew at a faster rate than its money supply. Deflation was the major political question in the 1896 presidential election, because falling prices raised the real debt burden on Midwestern farmers who were making mortgage payments on their property.

The farmers turned to the Democratic nominee, William Jennings Bryan, who promised to create some inflation to help them repay their debts. Bryan lost the 1896 race. He lost again four years later, and again in 1908. However, it's not fair to label Bryan as a born loser, as he achieved a measure of success in 1900 with the publication of L. Frank Baum's *The Wizard of Oz*. (He served as the inspiration for the Cowardly Lion.)

Now imagine the maturing child's blood supply rises at a faster rate than his organs are growing. He will have more blood servicing a smaller number of organs; the excess fluid will generate a higher blood pressure. Similarly, an economy whose money supply rises at a faster rate than its real output will experience a higher price level. The result: inflation. Inflation means that the dollar's purchasing power has declined because it takes more dollars to purchase the same amount of goods. ($M\uparrow V = P\uparrow Y$)

Inflation is a borrower's best friend, because it's easier to repay a loan if there's more money floating around. On the other hand, inflation really stinks if you are a lender, because your debt will be repaid in devalued dollars. You can think of inflation as a tax on savers.

While nineteenth-century America experienced frequent deflationary episodes, inflation has been the predominant condition during the twentieth century. The most memorable episode occurred during the mid- to late-1970s. The United States government had accumulated a large amount of debt in order to fund a bevy of government welfare programs and a war in Vietnam. Rather than overtly raising tax rates on its citizens, the Federal Reserve simply printed more money, which it then used to purchase the government debt.

Because the increase in the money supply outpaced the rate of economic output, each dollar purchased fewer goods.

Between 1973 and 1980, the dollar lost 55% of its purchasing power. Anyone who had been saving cash for a rainy day—or even a haircut— was decimated. The tragic result was an entire nation groomed like Lhasa Apsos.

If inflation increases too quickly, businesses and laborers will no longer accept "money" in exchange for their production, as its value becomes increasingly dubious. Alternatively, if deflation occurs too rapidly, people will hoard their cash instead of spending or investing it. Many economists used to suggest that the inflation/deflation problem should be approached by setting an inflation target and then printing the amount of money required to generate that rate given the anticipated level of economic growth. If only it were that simple.

In the first place, economic growth is difficult to project because you don't know beforehand exactly how much workforce population and productivity growth will occur over a given time period. Even if economists could predict economic growth with absolute certainty, there's another issue: all of the components of the exchange equation interact with one other, so the problem is fundamentally unsolvable. The big wild card in the system is the velocity of money—how many times (on average) that a dollar moves through the marketplace over the course of a year.

The primary driver of monetary velocity is **cash preference.** Cash preference, also known as "liquidity preference," indicates the desire of consumers and businesses to hold cash, rather than spend or invest it. As people cling to more of their money, its velocity falls as the cash moves through the economy at a slower pace. On the other hand, if the cash preference declines, then money will circulate at a faster velocity.

When people anticipate that inflation will rise because the money supply is increasing faster than the economy is growing, they are more inclined to spend their dollars rather than hoard them. If a computer is going to cost more in six months, you are more likely to purchase it now—because you expect that your money's purchasing power will deteriorate in the interim. The fear of rising prices encourages you to spend your dollars today because they will be worth less in the future. In other words, your cash preference is low.

As consumers or companies reduce the amount of time that they hold money before they spend it, the velocity of money increases. Money is now changing hands at a faster rate; the higher velocity enables inflation to become a [partially] self-fulfilling prophecy. That is, the very expectation of inflation can result in higher prices. ($MV\uparrow = P\uparrow Y$)

While inflation expectations tend to lower cash preferences, expectations for a slower economy produce the opposite effect. If your job security becomes increasingly uncertain, you will think twice before parting with any cash. Consequently, the velocity of money slows during recessions, creating modest downward pressure on consumer prices. ($MV\downarrow = P\downarrow Y$)

Every few decades, economists forget how the interplay between production, money, and inflation actually works. I'm not sure why, but they seem to have an insatiable need to develop these alternative explanations rather than to embrace the one that readily accounts for centuries of economic phenomena. Fortunately, medical doctors are not so anxious to reinvent the wheel when it comes to physiology. I can't imagine suffering from chronic pain and seeking advice from prominent physicians, only to discover that none of them knows for sure which one of my organs introduces oxygen into my bloodstream.

$ $ $ $ $

After two weeks under Debbie's wing, my training period was over. Matthew presented me with a cherry red, short-sleeved polo shirt bearing the Papa's rooster mascot emblazoned on the left breast. "Wear this with pride," he said, handing me a white visor and a red nametag, which read: "Papa's Little Helper, JIMMY, Team Member Since 2008." It was slightly larger than my old business card, which had read: "James Adams, CFA, Vice President, Product Management Team." How far I had come.

"You're ready for action now," he declared. "I certainly hope so," I said. I wondered why my tag stated that I had begun my employment the previous year. As I scrutinized it, I realized that my name hadn't actually been engraved. Matthew had simply printed off a label and taped it over my predecessor's. It seemed like kind of a bad omen. In any event, I was grateful for the inaccuracy. If customers perceived I had some tenure, maybe I would garner more credibility. I sorely needed every ounce of it that I could muster.

Most restaurants experience most of their volume during two spans of rush hours: an 11 a.m.–1 p.m. lunch rush and a 5 p.m.–9 p.m. dinner rush. By 11 p.m., most of the patrons have headed home and the employees have begun to clean the establishment. The restaurant is typically vacated by midnight and will not reopen its doors for another ten hours. In contrast, Papa's does most of its sales during a 9 a.m.–12 p.m. breakfast rush and a late-night rush from 11 p.m.–3 a.m. At no time does the store ever close.

Given these unconventional rush hours, the most prudent way to acclimate a tenderfoot server to Papa's is to start him waiting tables during a "second shift" which runs from 2 p.m.–9 p.m. (First shift runs from 7 a.m.–2 p.m.; third goes from 9 p.m.–7 a.m.) For the next two weeks, Tim and I were assigned to work second shifts along with Mary, the waitress who had given me the application form during my initial visit to the store. I hadn't seen her since then and was anxious to ingratiate myself with the girl who had facilitated my career transition.

I supposed that we didn't have much in common. She was finishing her senior year of high school, which made her too young to consider any of my bond market anecdotes the least bit entertaining. But in my naïve optimism, I supposed that I could surmount our age disparity and her mercurial disposition by applying some timeless Dale Carnegie principles. In *How to Win Friends and Influence People,* the author posits that the fastest way to make others warm to you is to encourage them to talk about themselves as you make a sincere effort to learn about their interests.

"Read any good books lately?" I thought it a safe opener.

"I *hate* to read."

"Really? 'Hate' is a strong word."

"I prefer movies. The only book I've read recently was *The Caramel Seduction.*"

I hadn't encountered that title in the *New York Times* book review, so I had to ask. "Oh? What's it about?"

"It's erotica."

"You don't say. I thought it might have been a biography of Milton Hershey or some other confectionary mogul."

"There's no one named 'Milton' in this book," she said reprovingly.

"Of course," I said. "'Milton' is a name best suited to economists, not Casanovas."

She stared blankly at me for a few seconds through the thick lenses of her tortoise shell glasses. When she finally solicited my literary interests, I had the distinct impression that she wasn't asking out of politeness, but out of a desire to ascertain the cause of my idiotic suppositions.

"I don't read much fiction," I said. "I mostly read the financial press, books about history or economics, and the occasional theological treatise."

"Sounds boring. You mean you don't read any novels?"

"Hardly ever. The last novel I read was *Atlas Shrugged.*"

"Is that erotica? 'Cause that's a good title for a romance novel." In truth, Ayn Rand's magnum opus does contain three or four love scenes. But something told me I would regret encouraging her in this line of dialogue.

"I'm afraid not. It's more of a libertarian screed against the perils of socialism and government bureaucracy."

"And you liked reading that?"

"It wasn't too bad. But I thought that the author's earlier work, *The Fountainhead,* was a much better read."

"*The Fountainhead?* Never heard of it. What's it about?"

"It's about an architect."

"An architect? Those guys that draw buildings?"

"That's right. This architect refuses to compromise his professional integrity despite being incessantly buffeted by his adversaries. It's an inspiring tale of surmounting obstacles and staying true to a vision, no matter what."

She placed a finger on her lip for a few seconds, a pensive look on her face. Maybe we could have a stimulating conversation after all.

"So does the architect seduce anyone?"

I removed my visor and gently pressed my forehead against a nearby refrigerator. Two thoughts came to mind: 1) it was going to be a long night; and 2) Dale Carnegie had obviously never worked at a Papa's Chicken & Waffles.

$ $ $ $ $

While I made vain attempts at literary banter with Mary, Tim was learning the finer points of grill operation from a mustachioed Papa's veteran. Despite being a pack-a-day smoker, Edward Jarvis barely showed thirty-five of his nearly fifty years of age. An otherwise average build was accentuated by broad shoulders and sinewy forearms.

Edward was one of the store's only two "senior grill officers." The designation indicated a complete knowledge of the plate marking system, all menu items, abbreviations and prices, and the experience of having cooked $3,200 worth of food over the course of a ten-hour shift. He was also a "relief manager," meaning that he was authorized to change out the cash register drawers at the end of each shift.

Edward was leagues brighter than anyone else in the store. In addition to managing the grill, he provided trenchant (albeit usually ribald) commentary on all customer and employee activity. After watching him deliver endless innuendos and colorful euphemisms over the next five months, I eventually concluded that his talents would have been better applied to writing bawdy fortune cookies than cooking omelets.

As the resident alpha male, Edward was quick to reprove words or actions that were inconsistent with good service, although he was generally willing to overlook infractions that had no direct bearing on the customer's experience. Alternatively, if he concurred with another's sentiment, he sanctioned it with a deep, low "yeeeeaaauuuh." Three full seconds and a subtle head bob were required to expel the guttural affirmation.

Edward's extremely gruff voice made it exceptionally difficult for me to understand him. To say the least, his gravelly intonations and my penchant for daydreaming made for an interesting workplace dynamic. Half the time, I was unaware that he was addressing me. When he did have my undivided attention, I couldn't readily interpret his dialect.

"Jimmy, hand me that bama ring."

"The what?"

"The bama ring. The one you just pulled out of the dish washuh."

I passed him the only item I saw. Apparently, "bama ring" was Papa's speak for *bain marie,* which is a fancy French term for a translucent plastic bucket used to hold waffle batter or condiment packets.

In the majority of cases when communication did miraculously occur, I was usually being issued a reprimand.

"Jim-may, you're makin' too many visits to the stock room. One minute you're getting paper towels. The next minute, you're headin' back for ketchup. Then for straws. Make a list and save yourself two trips. Aren't you a college boy? Use your head, Man."

When he wasn't chastening me for superfluous energy expenditure, he was expressing disbelief at my inability to locate any given item in the store, even when it was situated directly in front of my face. I explained to him that I had the exact same problem when I combed through the refrigerator at my house. My wife considers my idiosyncrasy to be a sort of charming defect. Edward didn't find it quite so endearing.

Edward had been a frequent armchair psychoanalyst in his youth but eventually yielded to paternal counsel that such endeavors were useless.

"My father taught me that the surest and fastest way to go crazy in this world is to spend your time trying to figure out why a mofo is doing this, or why he's doing that," Edward said. "There are more strange cats out there than there are hours in the day, so you can't afford to speculate on the brain waves of every wild animal that comes down the pike."

Edward had earnestly tried to follow this admonition, but apparently his interaction with me caused him to fall off the wagon. He just couldn't believe that someone with my educational credentials could be so utterly clueless when it came to the practical aspects of life.

I explained that in my previous career, I had dealt exclusively in abstractions. When researching a company, I preferred to study its Securities Exchange Commission filings rather than its annual reports because I felt that the pictures contained in the latter would compromise my objectivity. I didn't care how a company's widget looked, smelled, or tasted. I only cared how much cash the firm generated by selling them. The only reality I was concerned with had been a completely intangible one.

"If you're so good at abstract thinkin'," Edward said, "Did you see the big crash coming?"

"I expected a slowdown, but not necessarily a crash."

"Is that a yes or a no?"

"No, I guess not, Edward."

He directed me to follow him to a booth that had recently been vacated. "Can you see all these syrup stains?" he asked, pointing to the table.

"Yes."

"Outstanding. Even though you can't find anything else in the store, you're still more valuable in here than you were at your last job. Now grab a wet towel and get to it."

I wiped down the table, trying to recall an occasion in high school or college when I had seen the Socratic Method employed so brilliantly. The Connoisseur sipped coffee in the same corner booth where I had first encountered him. He scratched several lottery tickets, stared into space, tapped the ashes off his cigarillo, poured some creamer into his coffee mug, then began scratching more tickets. He repeated the cycle three times over the course of an hour before finally punctuating it with an amble to a nearby gas station. He promptly returned with another fistful of lotto tickets and resumed scratching.

Several of my coworkers had recently apprised me that the Connoisseur's affinity with Papa's was not entirely driven by his appreciation for our cuisine. The district manager (who oversaw our store and two others) had purportedly offered him free coffee in exchange for keeping an eye on the employees during second shift. I was advised that any mischief would summarily be reported to the higher-ups.

I couldn't help but think that this arrangement was completely unnecessary. In the first place, customers only have to pay $1.50 for a bottomless cup of coffee, so it would take a truly desperate person to sell out for less than that sum. Second, if any associates were actually stealing cash from the register, a manager would know within hours because the cash register was balanced at every shift change. Drawer shortages were immediately recorded, and the shortfalls were deducted from the paychecks of all salespersons working on that shift.

I was cleaning orange juice that had spilled behind the coffee machine when the Connoisseur finally broke his silence.

"Didn't you used to be a stock broker?"

I paused for a second, carefully weighing my response. I didn't know if he was making honest conversation out of boredom or practicing his subtle form of espionage.

"No, sir. I have never been licensed to sell securities." I resumed wiping the counter.

"Well, I heard you used to do stocks."

"I worked in the bond market. I never touched stocks during my career." I dropped my dishtowel and turned toward him.

"Stocks are for children," I said. "You can do a lot more damage with bonds."

I explained to the Connoisseur that bad investments aren't really dangerous unless large institutions are borrowing vast amounts of money to buy them—that's when things get particularly nasty. My only saving grace was that I hadn't actually bought the bonds myself; I had just been a press secretary for those that did.

"Well, it's not your fault then," the Connoisseur asserted. "You were just doing the job you were assigned."

"Isn't that the 'Nuremberg defense?'" I asked.

"What?"

"The Nuremberg trials. After World War II, the Nazi leaders were charged with war crimes in an international court. They pleaded innocence on the basis that they were only following orders."

"Oh. Well, you don't look like a war criminal to me."

"That's tremendously reassuring. Do I look like a white collar criminal?"

"Not anymore you don't. Papa's shirts have red collars." He nodded at my new uniform.

Maybe the Connoisseur was right. Perhaps serving good food to the taxpayers that were footing the financial bailout caused by guys like me was a legitimate form of restitution. Perhaps my new uniform symbolized redemption from my past transgressions.

I had barely finished thanking him for his kind words when Edward reminded me that my sidework assignment for the evening included cleaning the restrooms.

"Since things are pretty slow at the moment, you might as well get started now," he said, handing me a bottle of disinfectant. Redemption, indeed.

$ $ $ $ $

In addition to purloining financial calculators, employees were occasionally known to take toilet brushes—even used ones—from the store without permission. In their stead, management had furnished me with old dish towels which were to be immediately discarded after usage. I put on a rubber apron and latex gloves, grabbed two of the towels, and headed into the ladies room.

I emerged from the lavatory ten minutes later. "Well, that was a thrill," I said to Edward. The experience had given me legitimate reason to wonder how women ever earned their reputation as "the fairer sex."

"You must not get out of your house a lot," Edward replied. "Haven't you ever had a real thrill before?"

"I guess you could say so. I jumped out of an airplane on five occasions."

I briefly related my experience in the Wake Forest "Demon Deacon Battalion" during my freshman year of college. I had participated as a "walk-on" cadet, meaning that in exchange for not receiving any pay, I was able to participate in the ROTC program without signing a formal contract with Uncle Sam. It also meant that my name was not sewn on to any of my uniforms, and that none of the Army officer cadre took a particular interest in ensuring that I received the same training as all of the other cadets.

My deficiencies as a soldier were quickly made manifest during my first field training exercise at Fort Bragg. I was the only cadet in the battalion with no clue about how to clean an assault rifle. One upperclassman was kind enough to do it on my behalf, notwithstanding his irritation by my use of the word "gun." In the Army, I was told, a soldier can only refer to his M–16 as a "weapon" or a "rifle." I went along with the terminology. But for all intents and purposes, it still seemed a lot like a gun.

Later that weekend, I had the opportunity to use my "weapon" on the firing range to qualify for marksmanship certification. About halfway through the qualification, I felt my stomach beginning to rumble. I ignored the sensation and shot a few more times at my designated paper target. As I was calculating the number of remaining rounds in the magazine, my innards began to spin in earnest. There was no more disregarding nature's vociferous call; Army food had gotten the best of me. Fortunately, my supervising officer was kind enough to let me adjourn to the latrine.

I had been in the latrine no more than five minutes when I heard my fellow cadets assembling to board a bus to return to the barracks. The senior officers had started a head count. It was only a matter of time.

"Hey, where's Adams?"

"Uh, I think he's in the latrine, sir."

"Well, tell him to hurry up. We're all waiting."

There are undoubtedly worse things in life than contending with an acute case of diarrhea when a surly Army sergeant bangs on your bathroom stall and demands that you finish immediately, forcing you to waddle thirty yards into a busload of fifty people who are aware of your plight and are thoroughly enjoying themselves at your expense. But I can't think of any right now.

I had anticipated this scenario when my stomach made its first outcry on the firing range. But my prescient awareness of the ridicule utterly failed to prepare me for the humiliation when it finally came. On the other hand, the illness did provide a perfect alibi for my failure to qualify as an expert marksman.

At the end of my freshman year, I was summoned to the captain's office. The results of the "cadet competence" poll were in. The Captain bluntly informed me that I had been voted the worst cadet in the entire battalion. The news didn't come as a big shock. What *was* surprising was that the captain went on to ask me if I would like to take three weeks out of my summer to attend Airborne School at Fort Benning, Georgia. I wouldn't receive any pay for attending, but there were a few perquisites, namely, "three hots and a cot."

"You can't beat that!" the captain said enthusiastically.

He was a lousy salesman. My mother's cooking was undoubtedly better than whatever the Army chefs would prepare, and lodging in the barracks would be less commodious than my bedroom at home. But I was flattered that the ROTC officers thought I still had the potential to be a good soldier. Granted, my Army career had gotten off to a shaky start, but I had been given an opportunity to redeem myself. I thought back to a biography of General Custer that I had read in the fifth grade.

Like me, Custer had also been at the bottom of his class (albeit at West Point). Despite the rough start, he went on to become a distinguished cavalry officer during the Civil War and the nation's preeminent Indian fighter. I was heartened by his example. The book had also mentioned that Custer's illustrious military career ended abruptly at some place called Little Bighorn on what you wouldn't call a high note, but I tried not to dwell too much on that point.

A week after my talk with the captain, another cadet apprised me that unless we sent a cadet to Fort Benning for the last three weeks of June, our battalion would lose a slot at jump school for the next few years. Apparently, the ROTC cadre had already made the offer to every other cadet in the battalion before finally extending the opportunity to me. So much for delusions of military grandeur.

Thirteen years after the fact, I still remember my time at jump school quite vividly. Most days were spent running, practicing parachute landing falls in sawdust pits, and standing around waiting for orders. By the end of three weeks, I had gotten pretty good at all three activities. The two constants were the heat and the humidity. We were told to drink copious amounts of water to prevent heat exhaustion.

One soldier who neglected to follow this counsel collapsed outside the mess hall one morning after physical training (PT). That was all I needed to see. Unlike so many youngsters, I was going to learn from other people's mistakes, rather than become dehydration's next victim. I decided to drink two canteens of water the next morning before we began our PT session. I was a wise man.

As we jogged the mile from the barracks to the PT area, my sense of wisdom gradually yielded to feelings of intense bladder pressure. There is nothing like running that exacerbates the need to go. Each step sends a shock up the leg, and you get the sensation that barbarians are taking a battering ram to your crotch. Tomorrow, I decided, one canteen of water would suffice. In the interim, I needed to get to a bathroom. Badly.

My platoon sergeant would have none of it. Despite my repeated implorations, he refused to let me visit the latrine until after we had finished PT and our morning run. I would have to wait it out for another fifty minutes. I was doomed.

I had heard stories from other soldiers about what to do in these types of situations, which occur fairly often during long hikes in basic training. The consensus was that the best option was to keep moving along with the group, relieve yourself in your trousers as surreptitiously as possible, and hope that nobody noticed. So that's exactly what I did.

Everything was going along according to plan until I reached the chin-up bar. After knocking out three repetitions, a sergeant from another platoon confronted me about the conspicuous spot on the front of my fatigues. He commanded me to drop from the bar and began his interrogation.

With a completely straight face, I did my best to assign the blame for my incontinence to my squad sergeant, who was too incredulous to be angry with me. He instructed me to run back to the barracks, change, returning in time for our group run. Aside from some brief ribbing, the incident didn't create too much of a stir. It was a small price to pay for a substantial quantity of relief.

Within a week's time, I was standing in the doorway of a C–130, eagerly anticipating the rush of my fourth jump. After my chute deployed, I checked the direction of my drift and adjusted the angle of my body to prepare for the imminent landing. The Sergeants Airborne had instructed us to never look at the ground before landing; staring at it causes you to extend your legs, greatly increasing the chance of a broken bone. Instead, we were to focus on the horizon and brace for impact. Confident in my landing preparations, I permitted myself to relax and enjoy the panoramic view of the Georgia skyline for a full minute. As I was relishing the view, I felt my body mildly lurch forward. Had the wind just shifted?

My question was summarily answered with a prompt face plant into the Drop Zone. The tilled soil of the field had partially broken my fall, but my head was throbbing nonetheless. Through the fog of my headache, I vaguely remembered that the first thing that the jumpmasters had trained us to do after hitting the ground was to detach our parachutes from our harnesses.

As if on cue, a gust of wind suddenly swept across the earth. My chute promptly inflated, dragging my body across the field at what felt like twenty miles per hour. After struggling for a few seconds, I was finally able to roll onto my back and engage the chute releases. I turned onto my side and began spitting out a mouthful of dirt.

As I rubbed my forehead in a futile attempt to assuage my headache, everything suddenly became very dark. I looked up to discover the frame of a horribly large, muscular sergeant, whose physique was broad enough to completely obstruct the noonday sun. He demanded that I pack my chute into its stuff sack and clear the area, giving me ten seconds to do so. I staggered around, desperately trying to comply with his orders while he impugned my masculinity with the aid of a bullhorn.

I'm sure the whole spectacle must have been terribly amusing to a casual observer. At the time, I could only ruefully contemplate paying a very steep price for three hots and a cot. But after one more jump, I was finally awarded my coveted silver wings and returned home. I had no reservation about promptly returning my uniforms to the ROTC office when I resumed college in the fall. I had come to interpret my ineptitude with firearms, adversity with bodily functions, and undignified parachute landings as God's less-than-subtle way of telling me that he simply hadn't fashioned me for a life in the military. Between my inability to see things directly in front of my face and my mind's penchant for incessantly wandering, I was a sniper's dream come true. Instead of serving waffles in North Carolina, I would have undoubtedly been a grease spot in Fallujah by now.

Had I been a more competent soldier, I could have served a valuable role in the economy as a member of the Armed Forces. As *The Wealth of Nations* explains, governments should protect physical property (including, of course, life) by providing for the national defense and providing a justice system. Adam Smith asserted that governments should also enforce private contracts and protect intellectual property by granting patents and copyrights to inventors and authors.

The defense of private property is absolutely essential to a functioning free market. When each economic actor knows that the wealth generated by his production will be protected by the law, he will become more productive. In the absence of this guarantee, businesses and individuals will be far less willing to risk their capital in the reproductive investments which promote economic growth. Instead of a military career in which I would have protected American capital, I eventually opted for finance, a vocation in which I allocated capital on behalf of savers.

And while finance has historically been a more lucrative endeavor, it is certainly no more prestigious than soldiering. Yes, you get to wear expensive suits and use fancy terms like "LIBOR," "swap spreads," and "convexity hedging." But you don't get to shoot at any bad guys without concurrently guaranteeing yourself a prison term. And, unlike the Army, should you happen to wet your pants during your financial market workday, your colleagues on the trading desk won't let you live it down after twenty-four hours. (I never actually saw anyone lose control of his or her bodily functions during my eight years in the bond market, but I'm sure a few probably came close on several occasions.)

Edward seemed to appreciate my Army anecdotes, but he still felt that my parachuting experiences needed some spice. "So, of the five times that you jumped outta that plane, were you naked on any of those occasions?"

"No, Edward, the Army made us wear camouflage uniforms."

"Well, when you jump out of a plane in the buff, *then* you can call it a thrill. Don't hardly count if you was wearing clothes at the time."

I couldn't quite follow his line of reasoning. But, as I would soon learn, Edward was consistent in his belief that nudity was a prerequisite for any worthwhile endeavor.

## Chapter 3

# ONE FLEW OVER THE PAPA'S CHICKEN AND WAFFLES

*"Banking was conceived in iniquity and born in sin."*
**JOSIAH STAMP, DIRECTOR OF THE BANK OF ENGLAND**

After two more weeks working second shift, Debbie approached me with a proposition that would radically alter the course of my life. According to the grill officers and other servers, I had made substantial progress with my table waiting skills. If the reports were indeed accurate, she believed I was ready for reassignment to the 9 p.m.–7 a.m. third shift on Thursday, Friday, and Saturday nights.

The initial leg of the shift wouldn't be markedly different from the second shifts I'd grown accustomed to, but I would have to be prepared for a considerable spike in volume after the local bars closed at 2 a.m. Because of the brisk pace, this offer was extended to only the most competent servers. In fact, Debbie said, I should think of this opportunity to earn large tips from profligate drunkards as "something of an honor."

I appreciated her flattery. Despite my initial fumbles, my rapid ascension up a steep learning curve had been recognized. I would soon learn, however, that being asked to work third shift was not an honor in the same sense as being asked to speak at a Rotary luncheon. Rather, manning the Papa's on early Saturday mornings with two cooks and two other servers is honorable work in the sense of 250 Texans defending an old Spanish mission against a Mexican army force ten times their strength. Third shift isn't about servers earning tips any more than a firefight is about soldiers receiving combat pay. Like a gun battle, third shift is about one, and only one, thing—survival.

To my knowledge, no motion picture has ever attempted to recreate the social dynamic of a Papa's Chicken & Waffles at 3 a.m. on a Saturday morning. Fortunately, the penultimate scene of Oliver Stone's Vietnam War epic, *Platoon,* provides a suitable proxy. Cinemaphiles will recall that a hopelessly outnumbered U.S. Army battalion watches helplessly as its position is overrun by hundreds of frenzied North Vietnamese troops. In desperation, the beleaguered commanding officer finally instructs the Air Force to expend all of its remaining ordnance inside the perimeter of his firebase. The scene concludes with the terrain being wholly consumed in the fiery blaze of a napalm airstrike.

I can't tell you how many early Saturday and Sunday mornings I spent entertaining fantasies of a squadron of F–4 Phantom jets strafing the restaurant in similar fashion. If you can imagine Papa's employees and patrons in the roles of the American soldiers and Vietnamese belligerents, respectively, then you have a pretty accurate depiction of my weekends.

At 2:30 a.m., the restaurant doors explode. Within fifteen minutes, sixty barflies and club hoppers occupy a diner with seating capacity for only forty-two persons. I and two other harried servers struggle to placate them as they drunkenly clamor for service. Plunging into the maelstrom, I ask myself which part of my job description contains the phrases "crowd control" and "hangover mitigation."

A young man boasts of the beauty of a lady that had recently given him her cell phone number. His colleague is unimpressed.

"Yeah, she had a tight little body, true dat. But the girl is missin' way too many teeth," he responds.

The Casanova goes on to extol her other virtues (the list is decidedly brief) and argues to his confederate that bicuspids are overrated to begin with.

I glance down to discover an obese girl I waited on 45 minutes ago is cradling her face in her crossed arms next to a half-eaten plate of cheese eggs. I lean over the counter, trying to ascertain whether or not she is still breathing. Before I can get close enough to gauge vital signs, she erupts, flailing her arms wildly.

"Security!" she blurts out. "Look, Man, if you're going to harass me like this, I ain't payin' for my raisin toast."

No sooner have I begun to offer my apologies than her face collapses back into her forearms. I retrieve two orders of scrambled eggs from the grill, passing by another narcoleptic customer who is snoring audibly. I deliver the eggs to a girl with ubiquitous tattoos and eight visible body piercings. She offers me a large tip in exchange for desecrating her companion's double cheeseburger while she adjourns to the restroom. I politely decline the offer.

A white man contends with two black women that his struggle to obtain company health insurance benefits for his gay partner is every bit as important as Rosa Parks's quest to desegregate public buses. The girls demur, and a civilized political discussion quickly degenerates into threats of fisticuffs.

"Security!" the corpulent patron yells again.

For many a drunkard, deciding what to eat is no small feat, and placing a correct order is practically a Herculean task. As I wait on a man in a camouflage t-shirt which regrettably fails to cover his navel, the value of menu pictures immediately becomes manifest.

"I'll have a cheesesteak," he says emphatically, while tapping his index finger on a photo of a different menu item.

"You mean you'd like a Texas bacon egg and cheese sandwich?" I ask.

"Yeah, I want a cheesesteak," he says.

I invite him to examine the menu more closely.

"Yes, that's what I pointed to," he said. "A cheesesteak sandwich."

"Would you like the sandwich that comes with bacon and fried eggs and American cheese served on Texas toast?"

"Yeah. Y'all don't call that a cheesesteak sandwich?"

"We call it a Texas bacon egg and cheese sandwich."

"Really? 'Cause 'cheesesteak' is a lot easier to say. Bacon egg and cheese is too many syllables, Man."

I concede the point and turn to his friend, who is comparably inebriated. As he struggles to customize his hashbrown order, our dialogue quickly degenerates into an Abbott & Costello sketch.

"Make 'em scrambled, sleazy, and blanketed."

"I'm sorry, did you just ask for 'sleazy' hashbrowns?"

"Yeah, Man—just like it says on the menu. Sleazy it with that . . . stuff."

"Onions?"

"No, no onions. Just sleazy 'em for me."

"Sir, seasoned hashbrowns contain onions. That's what 'seasoned' means."

"That's what I said, Man. Carpet and sleazy them, just hold the onions."

I turn to the last man in the booth, who appears to have some semblance of sobriety.

"Do you know what he's talking about?" I ask.

"He's just tied on one too many beers. Today is his birthday."

"That's cool. Did NASA give him the day off work?" I decide to call in an order of scattered and covered, hoping that he's too intoxicated to notice the difference by the time his plate arrives.

Distracted by a group of college girls performing a horrid cover of a *Destiny's Child* song, I inadvertently scald a customer's hand with a plate containing a cheesesteak sandwich.

I apologize profusely and provide him with burn ointment from our first aid kit. His check is discounted by ten percent, the maximum amount permitted by company policy.

"You know," his friend says reprovingly, "this man is a keyboardist. His fingers are his livelihood. He should probably sue you."

I hand him a five-dollar bill out of my pocket, considering the payment a cheap insurance policy against getting my tires slashed.

Other customers show greater magnanimity when I fumble a delivery. While placing several drinks on a table where two couples are seated, I knock a glass of Coke onto the booth seats. The young man barely vacates his seat before the soda splashes.

"I'm awfully sorry," I apologize. "It's a good thing you've got such fast reflexes."

"No sweat Jim," he responds. "Wouldn't a been no harm even if the pants had gotten soaked. The odds are real good that my trousers and drawers are coming off in about ten minutes anyhow."

His male companion howls in laughter as his date playfully slaps him. I thank him for his patience, and for creating such a delightful mental image. For some reason, my brother's collegiate hijinks of hellraising at Papa's no longer strikes me as particularly humorous.

I stave off a gaggle of hungry, impatient customers by excusing myself to attend to the cash register. Ringing up the second tab, I discover that the credit card machine has just run out of tape. For the rest of the night, all customers must pay cash. The news is not well received.

The only effective means of fighting the mob is an extremely potent air conditioning unit. When the barflies get really out of line, we set the thermostat to the low 60s. Generally, the frigid temperature shifts their focus from harassing servers to maintaining their own body heat. Still, there are some nights when nothing short of the concentrated blast of a fire hose would squelch the din. Edward barks a series of contradictory orders at me. If I am ringing out a customer at the register, I should be taking an order. If I am taking an order, I should be picking up food from the grill. If I'm picking up an order, I should be ringing out a customer.

Things aren't any easier for him at the grill, where he is swamped in a flood of orders.

"Wait staff, drop your own waffles!" he cries, indicating that the responsibility for pouring batter into the waffle irons now lies with the servers. This command is the military equivalent of "fire at will!" or, more accurately, "every man for himself!"

In the four feet of space separating the high bar from the grill, servers call in orders and pick up food as grill officers set plates and place hashbrowns onto the grill. The frenzy is reminiscent of a commodities exchange; I can only marvel that the plates emerge unscathed. Seemingly, the laws of probability would dictate that several of them should be dashed to the floor in pieces.

As the melee escalates, we keep all of the waffle irons constantly filled with batter (whether or not waffles have been ordered) just so we will have them on hand to readily placate impatient customers. I call in an order, pour batter into two irons, then return to the floor to attend to a customer. I retrieve the waffles when a timer sounds three minutes later, noting that the elapsed time is the same length as the round of a prize fight. It certainly feels like I've been in one.

By 4:30 a.m., all customers have vacated the premises, and the store is eerily quiet. The recent decadence is attested to by a floor strewn with used napkins, hashbrowns, bent silverware, syrup splotches, and the occasional afro pick. Within another hour, the early Sunday morning crowd trickles in. Many of these patrons carry Bibles and say prayers over plates of food that others had cursed only a few hours before. I refill their coffee as subtly as possible so as not to interrupt their scripture study.

As they read psalms, I am floored by the irony of our store's hasty transformation from Bacchanalian festival to house of worship. I remember St. Paul's admonition that believers should not keep company or eat with drunkards, which raises two questions. Does it violate the spirit of Paul's teaching if the believers and drunkards dine in the same establishment within forty minutes of each other? More importantly, was there a Papa's in ancient Corinth that inspired this piece of doctrine?

$ $ $ $ $

Relative to the Friday and Saturday night ruckuses, Thursday shifts were downright sedate by comparison. Absent the frenetic rush of a bar crowd, customer flow was much more manageable, enabling me to consistently deliver food within five minutes after taking an order. The confluence of greater customer satisfaction and sobriety won me much larger gratuities. On Friday and Saturday nights, I typically wrote between fifty and fifty-five tickets and left the restaurant with $80 in tips. On Thursdays, I only averaged about thirty tickets but usually earned closer to $90 or $100.

Occasionally, an extended lull in activity provided me with sufficient time to eat a quick meal during the middle of a shift. Tim had graciously prepared all of my food during our training period, but his goodwill expired shortly thereafter. Left to cook my own hashbrowns, I always came up short in my attempts to emulate his performance. Reticent to burn yet another batch early one Friday morning, I solicited his help.

"Not now, Jimmy. I'm watching something go down." Ten minutes ago, an old Lincoln sedan had pulled into the parking lot, prompting me to grab napkins and silverware to set a place for the driver when he entered the store. He never did. The reason became evident as a jeep pulled up next to him and a fistful of cash was passed through his window. In return, the Lincoln driver handed the other man a brown paper bag.

"Looks like our Papa's just got a drive-through window," Tim chuckled.

As the cars drove away, he turned to the grill and began my tutorial.

"It's not that hard to cook hashbrowns. Now grab a spatula and listen. Drop one ladle of oil on the grill for every scoop of hashbrowns. After a few minutes, put the cubed ham on the grill. Just before the ham is done cooking, flip the hashbrowns and add in all the toppings you want. When they're finished, mix in the ham cubes, then put the cheese slices on top."

It sounded easy enough, but my finished product proved woefully inadequate on several fronts. The ham was undercooked; and while the hashbrowns had gotten hot enough to burn, they hadn't been sufficiently warm to melt the cheese I had placed on top of them.

"I don't know, Tim. These hashbrowns don't look as good as the ones you make."

In an apparent response to my comment, Tim began to flail his tattooed arms and recite rap lyrics. I understood them to mean something to the effect that his culinary prowess warranted my adulation. Or that Rome wasn't built in a day. Or that I was just stupid.

"Yeah, I clearly messed up. So what should I do with the plate?"

"What do you mean? I'm the grill officer on this shift, and that's part of my reported food cost. If we throw 'em out, that money's gonna come out of my pocket. So you're eating them or nothin', boy."

This seemed terribly unfair. In the bond market, no money managers are required to eat their own cooking—no matter how sick their customers get.

It took me a few more weeks of trial and error until I could properly implement Tim's instructions. In the interim, I expanded my repertoire by asking Edward to teach me how to make a bacon, egg and cheese sandwich. Under normal circumstances, I suppose it's a fairly easy skill to learn. However, the endeavor becomes markedly more difficult when your tutor intersperses his instructions with commentary on *Friday the 13th* films.

"Where do these clowns think they're gonna run to? Jason grew up in the woods 'round Crystal Lake. The boy knows every tree. Now, they're innocent victims, no question 'bout that. All I'm saying is that if they're stupid enough to really think they can escape by running into the forest, then Jason is doing the world a small favor by taking them fools out of the gene pool."

The grill's spatula was too large to be of any use in the frying pans, so making eggs over easy required a cook to flip them in the air with an adroit flick of the wrist. This isn't a skill you pick up overnight. As fascinated as I was by Edward's application of Social Darwinist concepts to horror movies, his remarks proved an unfortunate distraction. After two unsuccessful attempts at turning the eggs, I finally got them airborne and landed them both inside the pan.

"Edward, I did it!"

"Third time's da charm," he said, smiling. "If the circus can teach a bear to ride a bicycle, I can teach you to fry eggs."

"No doubt, Edward."

"No doubt, suh."

I noticed a small aperture between the flames and the grill. Glancing down, I could see several discarded egg shells and overcooked bacon strips.

"Edward, would you mind if I throw my eggs down this little chute here?"

"No problem, suh, that's what it's there fo'. Just make sure you throw the yolk in the pan, and the shells in the trash."

He grabbed my shoulder lightly, spun me toward him, and looked me straight in the eye.

"If you throw the yolk in the garbage, and the shells in the pan, you're gonna be eating a crunchy-ass sandwich."

"Yes, Edward, I suppose it would be crunchy."

"Yeaauuuh. Of course, if you want it like that, I ain't gonna stop you."

$ $ $ $ $

Besides larger gratuities and free classes at Edward Jarvis University, Thursday nights offered the perk of quality customer interaction. Friday night banter, while colorful, was unfailingly formulaic. "We were at this club/concert. We drank so much beer/liquor. There were these three/four girls. It was so crazy/awesome. In the history of the world, no one has ever done anything as cool as we did tonight, ever." The narrative never deviated much.

Conversely, weeknight patrons always had a unique story. A man in his late twenties debates whether or not to follow his girlfriend to Tampa, where she had recently relocated. A group of Yankees are making a pilgrimage to an old family homestead in a less-traveled part of the state. Or, my personal favorite . . .

A man wearing a trench coat staggers through the door. He promptly seats himself at the high bar and begins casting furtive glances over his shoulders. His eyes are quite bloodshot, but I don't smell any alcohol or smoke on his breath. This is going to be interesting.

"Are you alright, sir?"

"I'll be alright as soon as I get a biscuit in me. I just seen my daddy's ghost."

"When?"

"About five minutes ago."

"Where?" I look out the front windows. "Here?"

That's all the store needs, I thought. A specter lurking in the parking lot. The poor soul had probably died of food poisoning and has now come back to haunt the responsible parties. It's bad enough dealing with churlish drunkards on the weekends. But if the weekday shifts include confronting the supernatural, then I'm going to have to resign my commission.

"No, Man, in my bedroom. I just woke up to find my daddy at the foot of my bed just starin' at me. And he been dead fo' five years."

Thank goodness. Papa's was not, in fact, haunted. The man informs me that he has been thinking of his father in recent days. While shocked by the apparition, he is still deeply grateful to have seen his father, albeit in an ethereal state. I now realize he has been crying. In my tenure at the store, he is the only customer whose eyes are bloodshot from tears rather than substance abuse.

The man's sorrows are promptly consoled with a sausage, egg, and cheese biscuit, a dish renowned throughout the South for its palliative effects. Ten minutes later, he is on his way back to bed, another poor soul whose burdens have been lightened in our sanctuary.

I do not use the term "sanctuary" with as much sarcasm as you might suspect. Papa's Chicken & Waffles really is a haven for folks at the end of their ropes. People came to us with all sorts of problems, at all times of the day or night. At any given time, we could function as a sort of third-tier emergency room, church, motel, or concert hall. But the particulars are incidental. Our congregants know that no matter what their problem, be it insobriety or encountering a dead relative, they will always leave our stores in a better disposition than when they arrived. Hashbrowns, you see, are the universal salve—a veritable balm of Gilead.

Countless immigrants have found hope in these assuring words inscribed on a plaque inside the Statue of Liberty: "Give me your tired, your poor, Your huddled masses yearning to breathe free, The wretched refuse of your teeming shore. Send these, the homeless, tempest-tossed to me, I lift my lamp beside the golden door!"

Of course, poetess Emma Lazarus had no idea that the promise made in her 1883 sonnet would ultimately be fulfilled inside the four walls of a Papa's restaurant. Where else can you find tired, poor, and tempest-tossed individuals congregating inside a golden door? Verily, the prophecy has come to fruition.

Regrettably, I must acknowledge that "wretched refuse" is a term applicable to at least two percent of our clientele. (On weekends, that number approaches five or seven percent.) But there is respite for all, whether or not the patron deserves it. In short, Papa's serves as a kind of YMCA for people who don't like swimming or aerobics. Seriously.

At 9:30 p.m. one Friday night, a woman in her late forties enters the store pulling a suitcase behind her. She removes her raincoat, sits down in a corner booth, and orders a cup of coffee. I deliver it and inquire if she will be eating dinner tonight. A bottomless cup of coffee will suffice for the evening, she says, opening a paperback novel.

Within two hours, the novel rests, pages down, on the table, and the woman's head is tilted backwards against the wall. She emits a faint snore through her gaping mouth. I look forward to watching her slumber being abruptly curtailed by a horde of barflies. But when the stampede arrives three hours later, the commotion doesn't cost her an ounce of sleep. I'm not sure whether to be impressed or dumbfounded by the feat. At 6 a.m., she finally resurrects and demands another cup of coffee.

"Aww, this is stale. I'm going to need you to brew a fresh pot for me," she demands.

"Certainly, ma'am. As soon as I get this order of eggs out to another table, I'll take care of that for you."

"No. I need that coffee right now," she says in a surly tone. I brew it for her and ask if she's planning on having breakfast with us this morning. She's not, which just leaves one remaining question. "Are you partial to *The New York Times* or *The Wall Street Journal?*"

"What difference would that make?"

"We offer a national newspaper as a courtesy to all of our overnight guests. I just need to know your preference."

"I'll have to think about that," she says. "But I'll let you know." Nothing in this world is more irritating than trying to criticize someone's manners, in a decidedly non-subtle way, only to have your insults go completely over their heads. Edward, as always, has been monitoring the entire dialogue.

"Jimmy, you shouldn't talk to the customers like that," he admonishes.

"Should I have offered her *The Washington Post,* instead?"

"You got a good point, but she is still a paying customer."

"Are you serious, Edward? She orders one cup of coffee all evening, sleeps in the booth like some kind of vagrant, and then has the nerve to complain this morning because the coffee's not fresh. I came this close to asking her if she wanted me to change the linens in her booth."

Edward smiles. "Well, I won't say you wouldn't be justified in doing that, but it behooves you to keep a cool head about you, no matter what the customahs say or do."

As much as I could complain about a small number of them, I genuinely *liked* the vast majority of my customers, particularly the regulars. There was Fat Albert, a nineteen-year-old retail stock boy who always arrived at the beginning of my shift along with his brother and their mutual friend. The three of them sat at the low bar, where they manufactured sweetened iced coffees, creating a terrific mess in the process.

They were in dire need of finishing school, but nonetheless every receipt of a cheeseburger and every coffee refill was unfailingly acknowledged with a "thanks, Man," or "'preciate it." After their departure, a very pleasant middle-aged woman came in for eggs and coffee after her shift ended at the local FedEx terminal.

Later in the evening, we received occasional visits from the Spy, a short, rotund fellow that took particular pride in repeatedly advising everyone within earshot that he worked for the government. On two occasions, I overheard him attempting to impress his dinner companions by threatening rowdy customers on the other side of the store.

"I know people that could take care of that guy for us," he'd whisper under his breath.

The only thing that the Spy enjoyed more than steak and hashbrowns was implicating the CIA in every mundane piece of global news. I couldn't help but solicit his information sources.

"Who exactly did you say that you work for?" I asked.

"The government," he said. "Federal government," he added with a wink.

The pace of his response was familiar. "Bond . . . James Bond," he seemed to be saying.

When I pressed for details about his occupation, the Spy informed me that any further disclosure would inevitably culminate with a phone call to my next of kin. I thanked him for his magnanimity in providing such a subtle warning and refilled his Diet Coke.

I came to understand that the Spy lived in the sort of imaginary world that most people abandon during their elementary school years. He wasn't walking into a Papa's restaurant with a prostitute at three in the morning; he was strutting into a Monte Carlo casino with a beautiful woman who may or may not be a Russian double agent. I couldn't decide whether it was pathetic or admirable that a middle-aged man could still have such an active imagination.

The Spy's fashion sense and physique were at conspicuous odds with his swagger. He usually wore sweaters with geometric designs—the horribly gaudy sort that Bill Cosby popularized during the second Reagan administration. He didn't have Daniel Craig's mysterious eyes, chiseled jaw, or bulging pectorals. Instead, big eyes sat above rosy cheeks, and a potbelly protruded below a cluster of isosceles triangles on his sweater. He didn't belong in a James Bond movie; he belonged in an animated Disney film (perhaps as a woodchuck in Bambi's entourage).

Whatever my opinion of him, the Spy was absolutely convinced of his own importance. I never discovered his exact vocation, but I'd bet cash money that he works as a meter maid somewhere in the District of Columbia.

At the bottom of my list of favorite regular customers was a colorful duo of Repo Men.

In my old career, "repo men" were guys that worked on the "repo" desks of Wall Street broker/dealers. A repurchase agreement, or "repo," is a way to borrow money using a bond as collateral. It works like this: I own a U.S. Treasury bond with a market value of $1 million and want to borrow money. Merrill Lynch offers to buy my bond today at a price of $1,000,000, on the condition that I will repurchase the bond from them in three months at a price of $1,010,000. The higher repurchase price represents my interest cost. Effectively, Merrill is lending me money at a three-month rate of 1% ($10,000/$1,000,000).

Of course, "repo" can also stand for "repossession," rather than "repurchase." In the Papa's Chicken & Waffles context, Repo Men do not lend money for lower Manhattan brokerages using Treasury bonds as collateral. Rather, they seize collateral on behalf of third-party creditors. On Wall Street, Repo Men rise very early in the morning and take commuter trains to work. At the Papa's, Repo Men drive pick-up trucks in the middle of the night to their reclamation assignments. In lieu of pressed shirts and Zegna suits, they wear Nascar t-shirts and jean jackets. In fact, the Wall Street and Papa's Repo Men have only one thing in common: if you don't pay your debts, you can be sure they will seize their collateral. Immediately.

As completely nocturnal creatures, it only made sense that the Repo Men would patronize the only 24-hour establishment in town. I suppose I should have been grateful for their business. I wasn't. The Repo Men were two of the lewdest human beings I have ever met. They almost never ordered food and contented themselves by waxing philosophical in incredibly profane terms.

By "waxing philosophical," I don't mean that they were debating epistemology or metaphysical issues. Rather, their dialogue was generally confined to matters of professional ethics—e.g., "if I'm seizing a vehicle, and I run over the neighbor's dog as I'm backing out of the driveway, whose fault is it? When you stop to think about it, that animal's life would never have been placed in jeopardy if the guy had been paying his bills on time."

Beyond animal rights, the Repo Men also opined on matters of gender equality.

"Only a coward initiates an attack on a woman," one of them posited. They were, unquestionably, the noblest words I ever heard come out of his mouth.

"Now, on the other hand," he continued, "If she's man enough to hit you, then she's man enough to get hit right back."

So much for chivalry.

When not considering life's weightier questions, the Repo Men directed their energy towards the grill officer and wait staff. Innuendo and verbal sexual harassment were hurled at everyone with no provocation. I recall a much higher level of decorum in my high school locker room after lacrosse practices.

For whatever reason, I was the lone exemption from the Repo Men's taunts. Some perceivable element of indignation in my countenance may have convinced them I wasn't worth the effort, or maybe they just felt bad for me because they knew about my previous career track. Of course, I should appreciate the uncharacteristic benevolence that they extended, but all I can do is lament that they never gave me a chance to use any of my premeditated comebacks.

One of my would-be retorts involved pointing out that when one has been in the repo game for more than a decade, the corporate advertisement on his truck should reflect a capacity to correctly spell "repossession." But somehow, calling their attention to the fact that their vehicle needed another "s" painted on it didn't seem sufficiently denigrating.

Though I never exchanged any antagonistic remarks with them, every conversation with the Repo Men was painfully awkward. No matter how hard I tried, I simply couldn't relate to them.

"Hey, Repo Man. How's your night been treating you?" "Oh, it's been a great one so far. This girl came out of her house while we were taking her Corvette and . . ." he stopped, bursting into laughter.

"And what?"

"It was great, Man. We made her cry *and* throw up."

"That's terrific," I said flatly. "That must have been really neat to see firsthand."

Apparently the Repo Man construed my tone as some sort of chastisement. "You misunderstood me. It wasn't like she was doing both at the same time. She cried first, *then* after she collected herself for a minute, she puked all over the car."

"Oh," I said, forcing a smile. "That makes all the difference."

"Of course it does. Don't get me wrong, I'm in this for the money, but it's the little perks like that that really make the job so worthwhile."

He left the store a half hour later to chase down a wayward Chevrolet, offering Edward a cautionary word on the perils of Chlamydia on his way out. As I cleaned up the sugar granules and empty creamer cups the Repo Man left behind, I wondered if he had refrained from mocking me precisely because his livelihood depended on people like me. After all, Repo Men spend their time cleaning up the messes left by financiers who make loans to people that have no business receiving them. By cleaning up after a Repo Man, I had just completed the circle of economic justice.

### $ $ $ $ $

When they weren't belittling my fellow employees, the Repo Men spent much of their time deriding a forty-eight-year-old regular customer named Kathy, whose orange hair, large blue eyes, broad face, and constant requests for free drinks brought to mind a feral tabby cat soliciting a saucer of milk. At 10 p.m. every night (and I do mean every night), Kathy entered the store and seated herself at the end of the low bar. You could set your watch to it.

Kathy didn't consume anything other than Diet Coke on most nights. On the rare occasion when she did eat dinner at the store, she usually ordered a double plate of plain hashbrowns, always paying in cash. Apparently observing the cooks and servers was entertainment enough for her, because she never read, listened to music, or initiated conversations with the other patrons. She was perfectly content to stare at us as she smoked cigarettes and bounced her leg.

Kathy was consistently polite and patient throughout the early morning rush hours, prefacing all of her requests with, "Whenever you get a chance, Jimmy, would you please . . ." The calmness and civility were a welcome relief amidst the din of the nighttime revelers, creating a soft spot in my heart for her.

After seven hours of watching "Papa's Chicken & Waffles Follies," Kathy spent her last hour at the store providing comedic fodder for a cohort of morning coffee drinkers. After an hour of enduring their barbs, she promptly retired at 6 a.m., always donning a pair of earmuffs before departing. (To my mild surprise, the earmuffs were still being worn on June mornings.)

My interaction with Kathy took an unexpected turn on an early Sunday morning when she came up two dollars short on her dinner tab and asked me if I would be willing to lend her the cash she needed to make up the difference. I gave her two bills without thinking much of it. Kathy patronized the store every night, so I doubted that she would skip out of town. And even if she did neglect to repay, my wallet could withstand the loss of principal.

If nothing else, it was a small token of appreciation for a customer who never harassed me about anything.

I didn't give any thought to the loan until the following week, when Kathy approached me again to solicit a five-dollar borrowing. I reminded her that she still owed me two dollars and that additional lending wouldn't be prudent for either one of us until the first debt was settled. Still, I didn't want to appear callous to my favorite customer, and I had always enjoyed loan underwriting during my insurance company years. Before I knew it, Kathy and I had signed an agreement establishing a revolving credit facility.

Admittedly, most loan agreements are not signed on the back of a Papa's order ticket, but my rudimentary document covered the loan conditions nearly as well as some of the 200-page corporate bond indentures that I've read. Under the terms of our contract, Kathy could borrow—at any time, for any reason—up to five dollars from the Bank of Jimmy. Not one additional cent of credit would be extended beyond that mark. After signing the contract, Kathy immediately drew down an additional three dollars, with a promise to repay me during the following week.

$ $ $ $ $

In 1912, J.P. Morgan expressed his views on loan underwriting in testimony before the House Committee on Banking and Currency:

Committee Counsel: Is not commercial credit based primarily upon money or property?

J.P. Morgan: No, sir; the first thing is *character* (emphasis added).

Committee Counsel: Before money or property?

J.P. Morgan: Before money or anything else. Money cannot buy it.

Committee Counsel: So that a man with character, without anything at all behind it, can get all the credit he wants, and a man with the property cannot get it?

J.P. Morgan: That is very often the case.

Committee Counsel: But that is the rule of business? J.P. Morgan: That is the rule of business, sir. As the country's preeminent banker, Morgan knew whereof he spoke. In a financial context, **character** refers to a borrower's trustworthiness. The term "credit" derives from the Latin *credere,* which means "to believe" or "to trust." A creditor's belief in a borrower's ability and intention to repay his debts provides the foundation for finance. In the absence of trust, borrowers and lenders will not get together.

In addition to character, three other factors are considered in the process of underwriting a loan: capacity, collateral, and covenants.

**Capacity** refers to a borrower's ability to service and repay his debt obligations. Bankers use several metrics to gauge this ability.

**Collateral** represents the assets pledged by the borrower to the lender. Should the borrower default on the loan, the lender can seize the collateral and sell it to a third party.

**Covenants** are the terms under which the loan is extended. For example, a borrower may promise not to incur any additional debt without first obtaining permission from his current lenders.

Together, these factors constitute "the Four Cs of credit." A potential borrower that can satisfy these criteria is considered "creditworthy."

When I first studied the Four C's as part of the CFA curriculum, I read that "character" and "capacity" were the most important aspects of credit analysis. Intuitively, that seemed right. You need to know a man's intentions and his ability to execute on them. Covenants are merely a check to keep him honest, and collateral serves as an airbag to cushion the blow should the borrower prove unable or unwilling to make his payments.

While assessing character is admittedly a somewhat nuanced and subjective process, assessing a borrower's capacity to repay debt is a fairly prosaic endeavor. If you can bear with me for a few minutes, I'll show you how.

$ $ $ $ $

Business lenders are primarily focused on three questions: (1) How does the company's operating income compare to its debt service costs? (2) How long would it take the company to completely pay off its debts? (3) What is the value of the company's assets relative to its debts?

Of course, there are infinite variations on these metrics, but these represent the major components. The loan officer (or credit analyst) begins by examining the company's balance sheet, which is a snapshot of its assets and liabilities (debts) *at one point in time.*

### ACME CO. BALANCE SHEET

| Assets | Liabilities (Debts) | Equity (Capital) |
|---|---|---|
| Property, Plant, & Equipment $2,000,000 | Bank Loan at 5% Interest $1,000,000 | Common Stock $1,000,000 |

The lender will also examine the company's income statement, which depicts its financial performance *over a period of time* (in this case, one year).

### ACME CO. INCOME STATEMENT

| | |
|---|---|
| **Sales** | **$1,000,000** |
| **Cost of Sales** | **($500,000)** |
| **Selling, General, and Administrative Costs** | **($200,000)** |
| **Operating Income** | **$300,000** |
| | |
| **Interest Expense** | **($50,000)** |
| **Income Before Taxes** | **$250,000** |
| | |
| | |
| **Income Tax Expense** | **($100,000)** |
| **Net Income** | **$150,000** |

Given this information, we can get a good feel for the company's credit risk:

**Debt service coverage.** Operating income reflects the amount of money earned from running the business before any interest or tax payments are made. In 2009, Acme generated $300,000 in operating income but paid only $50,000 in interest, meaning that it covered its interest expense six times over ($300,000 divided by $50,000). That's a pretty good margin of safety for a lender.

**Time needed to repay debts.** The company's net income roughly captures the amount of cash that it generates in a year—in this case, $150,000. Assuming the company can continue to earn this much income, Acme would need 6.7 years to repay its entire bank loan (liabilities of $1 million divided by $150,000 of income). Not bad.

**Value of debts vs. assets.** Assuming the reported asset values are a fair gauge of their market values (this is not always the case but suffices for this illustration), then liabilities of $1 million divided by assets of $2 million = 50%. Again, a fair number.

All in all, Acme looks like a decent credit risk. We don't know what widgets they sell, and frankly, we don't need to care unless their sales are declining dramatically. If they've sold a lot of widgets in the past, they'll probably keep selling a fair amount of them in the future. The main things we should worry about are rising expenses and increasing debt.

While the particulars vary somewhat, mortgage candidates can be evaluated using a similar array of credit metrics. Assume a prospective homebuyer has a gross salary of $100,000 and brings home $70,000 after taxes. She has saved $60,000 for a down payment on a $300,000 home and would like to borrow the remaining $240,000. The total annual payments on a 30-year mortgage at a 6% interest rate are $17,270.

Again, we start with some financial statements (although these are pro forma because the loan has not yet been approved):

## HOME BUYER BALANCE SHEET

| Assets | Liabilities (Debts) | Equity (Capital) |
|---|---|---|
| House $300,000 | Mortgage at 6% Interest $240,000 | Down Payment $60,000 |

## HOME BUYER INCOME STATEMENT

| | |
|---|---|
| **After-tax income** | **$70,000** |
| **Living expenses, ex-housing costs** | **($36,000)** |
| **Discretionary income before housing costs** | **$34,000** |
| | |
| **Mortgage payments (annual)** | **($17,270)** |
| **Discretionary income** | **$16,730** |

Now, let's ask the same series of questions that we asked the corporation: can the borrower service the debt? How long will it take the buyer to repay the debt? How large is the borrower's debt relative to her assets?

**Debt service coverage.** The homebuyer will be paying her mortgage using the income that she retains after paying taxes and other living expenses. Therefore, we compare her "discretionary income before housing costs" relative to the size of her estimated mortgage payment. The homebuyer is expected to have $34,000 in income before housing costs, nearly two times the size of the mortgage payment ($34,000/$17,270 = 1.97). Should she experience a decline in discretionary income due to a pay cut or an unforeseen expense, the debt service coverage ratio would fall but probably still remain high enough for the borrower to continue to pay her mortgage.

**Time needed to repay debts.** Should the borrower apply all of her discretionary income to prepaying her mortgage, she could fully repay the loan in roughly fourteen years. Loan balance of $240,000/$16,730 per year in discretionary income equals 14.3 years. (This calculation assumes that the borrower's income does not decline and/or her expenses do not rise.)

**Value of debts vs. assets.** If the borrower defaults on the mortgage, the bank will foreclose on the house and sell it for cash. The larger the borrower's down payment, the greater the bank's recovery in the event that the home is placed in foreclosure. Assuming that the house was appraised at its selling price ($300,000), the mortgage loan-to-value is 80% ($240,000 loan divided by a $300,000 asset). If the borrower immediately goes into default, the bank will not lose money on the loan as long as the value of the house does not decline by more than $60,000.

In recent years, most mortgage bankers became less disciplined in applying these time-tested underwriting criteria, relying instead on sophisticated computer models that could (ostensibly) project loan default rates better than the three aforementioned ratios. Rather than focusing on debt service coverage ratios and borrowers' repayment ability, the new models were heavily reliant on accurate estimates of home price appreciation rates.

Until 2007, these models appeared to work very well because American home prices had experienced a steady upward climb. Even though many homeowners lacked the ability to service their debts, mortgage default rates remained low because the rising housing prices enabled the borrowers to readily refinance their mortgages. When housing prices began their precipitous decline, the lenders that had taken a corner-cutting approach to underwriting were hung out to dry.

I had no intention of making the same underwriting mistakes with my loan to Kathy. Even though the only collateral she could offer was a half-eaten plate of hashbrowns, I could take great comfort in the knowledge that she had the capacity to repay me. After all, I had personally verified her income stream.

Every morning between 5:30 and 5:45 a.m., I swept the store, gathering a considerable amount of dust, napkins, and change (usually north of 70 cents) during the process. When I had completed sweeping all of the debris into the center of the floor, I would retrieve the dustpan from the corner. In the five seconds that I needed to grab it, Kathy would bolt from the end of the low bar, snatch all of the coins from the trash pile, and scurry back to the bar. I was considerably impressed by the speed of her movement, although her attempts at subtlety during the process left much room for improvement.

By consistently garnering the 70 additional cents of daily income, I knew that Kathy could repay her five-dollar loan after a week of scavenging the fruits of my dust pile. Clearly, the *ability* to repay was not in question. Kathy's *willingness* to honor her debts was a more complicated matter, however.

As I was drafting the loan agreement, Kathy had informed me that she had been struggling with some mental health issues for the past few years. I can't say I was terribly surprised by the revelation. Anyone whose primary source of weekend entertainment consists of people watching at Papa's Chicken & Waffles is probably due for a clinical evaluation. I wondered if too many nights spent in the store were the cause (or result) of her breakdown.

I didn't hold Kathy's illness against her, as I had felt my own sanity slipping away in recent weeks. Hearing the juke box play "Syrup for Strawberries" and "Where Else Would You Go for Cheese Grits?" for the thousandth time is enough to make anyone long for the comfort of a padded room at the psych ward.

It wasn't until a discussion with the Repo Man two weeks later that I became aware of the severity of Kathy's condition. Her appearance was two hours overdue, so I asked the Repo Man if he knew anything about her whereabouts.

"What day of the week is it?" he asked.

"Wednesday. Why?"

"Oh, that explains it. Every other Wednesday afternoon, Kathy surfs the electric wave. She's probably still recuperating."

Failing to grasp the metaphor, I pressed him for details. Kathy, he informed me, regularly received electroshock therapy.

While her eccentricity was undeniable, I assumed that the Repo Man was pulling my leg. But just to be on the safe side, I asked Edward if he knew anything about her treatments.

"You heard right, Jimmy. They've had that broad in an electric helmet for the past eighteen years," he said.

After corroborating the Repo Man's claim, Edward went on to tell me that Kathy had recently been employed by a Target store. Her employment had been abruptly terminated for stealing from the cash register. When I informed him that I had extended her five dollars of credit, he simply shook his head. Before approaching me, she had already hit up nearly every employee in the restaurant. In all, Edward estimated, she probably owed the cooks and wait staff in excess of a hundred dollars.

So I had just loaned money to a woman with acute mental illness, who also happened to be a thief. Beyond that, I already had a line of other creditors in front of me.

"If everything you said is correct, Edward, I don't suppose this contract is worth the paper it's written on," I said, producing the revolving credit agreement from my pocket.

After a few seconds of perusing the document, he broke into hysterical laughter.

"And you . . . you . . . used to . . . invest money . . . for a living?!" He was laughing so hard that he had to force out the words in staccato. He announced my financial arrangement to Tim and another server, who found it similarly hilarious.

"Hey, I got a similar document in my back pocket!" Edward continued. "A man sold it to me for ten dollars. It says I get a cut anytime somebody pays the toll to cross the Brooklyn Bridge. But I'm still waitin' on that first royalty check . . . must a got lost in da mail."

He smacked me on the shoulder and leaned into my face. "Jimmy, if that's how you been investin' money all of these years, maybe you better off at Papa's Chicken & Waffles after all."

$ $ $ $ $

I finally saw Kathy again the following Saturday night. She tapped her fingers nervously on the bar top as I delivered her obligatory Diet Coke.

"Good evening, Kathy. How have you been?"

"Not so good. My head's really been out of sorts lately," she said.

"Didn't you tell me that 'out of sorts' was the status quo?"

"No, it's been worse the past couple of days. I've been doing a lot of sleepwalking."

I didn't consider sleepwalking particularly abnormal behavior, but I had to admit that Kathy's condition seemed a bit acute. She had awakened that morning to discover that her bathroom doorknob had been forcibly detached and that a pair of jeans had been deposited inside the bowl of her commode.

Kathy spent several minutes trying to unravel the enigma of how she had managed to remove the doorknob given that she kept no tools whatsoever in her apartment. I nodded politely as she continued her speculations, but all I could think about was the imminent write-off of a certain five-dollar loan. Although I already had testimony from two credible witnesses, I couldn't help but ask her to verify the accounts of electroshock therapy. I normally didn't ask my customers such blunt personal questions, but given that my economic interests were at stake, an exception was clearly warranted.

I only had to provide the subtle hint of missing her presence on Wednesday night to cajole Kathy into providing an enthusiastic description of her shock therapy regimen. It was clearly the highlight of her week. The electric currents, she explained, produced a calming effect that assuaged her severe anxiety. She spoke with the same passion that most women use in championing the restorative effects of a body wrap treatment at a day spa. She was such a convincing advocate for the procedure that I was half inclined to ask her who I needed to speak with to receive a few volts myself.

"Oh, before I forget, Jimmy, here's your five dollars." She reached into her pocket and presented me with a handful of coins. I could scarcely believe my eyes. I thanked Kathy for her prompt repayment, desperately trying not to think about where the coins might have recently been.

Reaching into her other pocket, Kathy produced her copy of our loan contract and held it up proudly. She explained that, beyond their palliative effects, the shock treatments also sharpened her short-term memory.

"You didn't think you were going to get your money back, did you?" she teased playfully.

"The thought never crossed my mind, Kathy," I said. I tried to imagine what J.P. Morgan would make of this whole situation.

"Jimmy, I've got one more question for you."

I braced myself for another drawdown on the revolving credit facility, but she took the conversation in an unexpected direction.

"I was on a walk last night and I heard a bird chirping. I'm trying to figure out what kind it was. Do you know what bird makes the sound 'whoo, whoo, woooo'?"

I studied her face for a minute, trying to ascertain if this was some kind of trick question. "I believe that an owl makes that sound, Kathy."

A look of absolute shock overcame her. "Are you sure? I could have sworn that it was a cardinal or a blue jay."

$ $ $ $ $

As our sales volume declined after the school year ended, we were increasingly able to handle all of our patrons with just three servers. Occasionally, a superfluous fourth server would be reassigned to work his/her shift at our airport location a few exits down the interstate. It was a newer, cleaner store whose management team had been in place for several years. To say that they did things more professionally would be a gross understatement.

While my regular store kept an inventory of six or eight prepared salads in the refrigerator, the airport store maintained a stock of fourteen. I can barely express how inexcusable I find this practice. In my opinion, Papa's Chicken & Waffles shouldn't even serve salads. They are horribly incongruous with everything else on the menu, an effete touch which detracts from the experience of capriciously gorging on breakfast food in the middle of the night. Driving to a Papa's to order a salad is every bit as lame as flying to Paris only to consume a Big Mac and Coke once you reach the Champs-Elysees.

Instead of taking a free-for-all approach to the cash register, airport management limited its operation to two persons in an effort to keep drawer shortages down. They mandated that we verify the numbers of all customers phoning in an order prior to cooking any food. Servers did pretentious things like garnishing bowls of chili with complimentary saltines packets. The wait staff didn't bicker with the grill officers, patrons, or even with each other. The sanitation score was a nosebleed-inducing 97.5. In short, the store was a model of customer service, efficiency and attention to detail. I found it all somewhat nauseating. The place just felt too sterile to be considered a bona fide Papa's.

It wouldn't be fair to dismiss the location as hopelessly bland, however. It was in close proximity not only to the airport, but also to three different night clubs which provided the majority of its early morning customers. Recently, two young men had gotten into a row over a female's affections which culminated in one of them brandishing a firearm in the parking lot. Perhaps the store had some redeeming value after all.

In addition to the occasional gunplay, the airport Papa's had one other entertaining feature—the Linebacker, a six-foot, broad-shouldered, fourteen-year company veteran (by far the longest tenure of anyone I had met personally). The Linebacker took no crap from anyone. Surly customers were shown to a booth, then deliberately ignored for the next twenty minutes. A playful remark from another server was immediately met with a crass comeback. Even the grill officers, who normally call the shots on the restaurant floor, gave the Linebacker a considerable berth. Incidentally, the Linebacker was also female.

The Linebacker and another waitress were assigned to the cash register while I was given charge of maintaining the dish pit when not tending to customers or taking call-in orders. It was amazing how much the client demography differed from eight miles down the road. On the two occasions that I did work at the airport, I was struck by the number of New Yorkers patronizing our establishment.

There are just a handful of Papa's restaurants north of the Mason-Dixon Line, and none in New York or New Jersey. As far as the meatheads from Long Island were concerned, we were a major tourist attraction. Many of them had never consumed grits. I was glad to have their patronage for two reasons. Firstly, they tended to be very good tippers—it's much cheaper to eat in North Carolina than in New York City. Secondly, they served as a powerful reminder that I hadn't missed much by not pursuing my financial career in that part of the country.

On my first night at the airport, I was bantering with one Empire State resident about the cost of a Bloomberg terminal when I had to excuse myself to answer the store telephone.

"I need an order o' hashbrowns." the voice said. "I also need to speak with a good server. I doubt you have anyone good in the store right now, but I suppose I'll ask anyway."

It took me about two seconds to identify the caller. It was Edward. He was terribly curious to know how I was faring without his supervision. I assured him that for the time being, all was well. He congratulated me, expressed his skepticism about my prospects, and hung up.

The rest of the evening passed without much incident. The airport store didn't have a regular cohort of early morning coffee drinkers, enabling us to clean up with little interruption before first shift arrived. After cashing out one of the last customers, the Linebacker surveyed the store, then turned her gaze toward me. "You know, I'm tired of watching you wash dishes," she sighed.

"Well, what would you rather watch me do?" I asked innocently.

"Do you *really* want an honest answer to that?" she asked, poking me in the ribs.

I put down a dish and turned toward her. With a large grin on her face, she bounced her eyebrows several times. I was pretty certain I knew what she was intimating.

I had to tread lightly here. On one hand, I thought the excuse of being happily married could quickly get me off the hook. On the other hand, recent experience had taught me how volatile some women were and how quickly situations could escalate. I couldn't afford to reject her too forcefully. If push came to shove, I would be giving up at least forty pounds of muscle mass to this dame, so an altercation was out of the question.

I decided to steer the conversation toward economic matters. In college, I had found this to be an effective method for quickly dispatching aggressive coeds. I could only hope that I hadn't lost my touch.

Fortunately, my ploy worked beautifully. To my great surprise (and relief), the Linebacker proved unexpectedly eager to wax philosophical on banking. Her mother had opened a savings account for her as a child, which she promptly closed at age eighteen. Since that time, she had kept every cent she owned on her body at all times. She had several reasons for this practice, chief among them a belief that banks had been designed for the sole benefit of Semitic peoples. I assured the Linebacker that the greatest banker in American history, J.P. Morgan, had been a consummate WASP. She had never heard of him.

The Linebacker's biggest reservation, though, lay in her resentment of financial intermediaries. Granted, she didn't use the term "financial intermediation," but that is exactly what she described.

"What is the point of me putting my money in the bank so that they can pay me one percent on my money and turn around and lend it to someone else at five percent? They're gonna use my money to make all that money for themselves just for sitting on their butts? I don't think so. If I'm gonna lend anyone money, I'll do it myself."

I explained to the Linebacker that banks added value to their depositors in two ways: 1) Banks can create a diversified loan pool across a broad array of borrowers. This diversification of risks helps to protect the lenders' principal. 2) The bank absorbs the first 10% (or so) of credit losses on the loan pool, providing yet another means of defense. She already knew this but remained unsold on the idea.

"If nothing else," I said, "your money is safer in a vault than it is at your house or on your person."

"I doubt that," she asserted.

"Look," I said, "if the bank gets robbed, your deposits are insured by the FDIC, which is effectively backstopped by the federal government. What happens if you keep all of your cash in your shirt pocket and then you end up getting mugged?"

"Would *you* mug me?" she asked soberly. I had to concede that she had a real point. Had Jack the Ripper made a move on her, this woman would have easily stomped his face in.

We conversed for a few minutes before our conversation was interrupted by a ringing cell phone. The Linebacker, it turned out, had a better half. While we had spent the night waiting tables, the LBBF (Linebacker's Boyfriend) had been out clubbing. He had spurned the advances of an admiring female, much to her chagrin. No sooner had the LBBF turned his back than the scorned woman commenced bludgeoning him with a beer bottle. The police were summoned after he retaliated with fisticuffs.

After a few hours in jail, the LBBF bailed himself out—presumably by using a chunk of the life savings which he always kept on his person. He was very constructive on his prospects for acquittal on grounds of self-defense. I never found out whether he was exonerated, but I'm confident that the whole incident could have been avoided by diverting his admirer into a dialogue on the banking system.

$ $ $ $ $

"Neither a borrower nor a lender be," Polonius tells his son Laertes in Act I, Scene III of Shakespeare's *Hamlet*. Anyone that has ever loaned money directly to another person will immediately recognize the wisdom in this timeless piece of advice.

A lender does not stand to materially benefit from making a single loan. In exchange for a fixed (and usually modest) rate of return, he risks losing his entire investment. For a lender, the best possible outcome is simply getting all of his money back from the borrower. An investment that contains a large amount of downside relative to a small amount of upside is said to have an **asymmetric payoff**; the risks and/or aggravation substantially outweigh any possible benefits.

Romancing your boss's daughter is the classic example of an asymmetric payoff. You don't have to ponder the matter too long before you realize that the prospective benefits fall far short of the potential headaches involved. Potential upside: minimal; potential downside: considerable.

The best way to mitigate the asymmetric payoff inherent to lending money is by pooling lending activities. When an investor lends money to a large number of borrowers (rather than a mere handful of them) the riskiness of his investment declines dramatically. Assuming the money is generally loaned in a prudent manner, the number and diversity of the loans will alleviate the effects of a few defaults.

The pooling of credit risk benefits borrowers as well as lenders. Because the loan diversification will cushion the impact of individual defaults, lenders are willing to charge a lower average interest rate to each borrower.

Investors can lend out their money to a pool of borrowers by purchasing shares in a mutual fund that purchases loans or bonds issued by corporations, municipalities, or governments. The mutual fund manager acts as the investor's agent as he selects the securities for purchase on his behalf. However, the fund manager is not liable for the performance of those investments; the saver bears all of the risk. Effectively, the saver is lending directly to the pool of borrowers.

Rather than lending directly to borrowers via mutual funds, savers can place their money with a **financial intermediary,** who in turn lends it out across a pool of borrowers. A **commercial bank** is the most common type of financial intermediary. When you deposit your money in a bank, you are lending money directly to the bank, who in turn lends to the ultimate borrower. That is, the bank simultaneously borrows AND lends, thus forging a **chain of debts.** (Incidentally, this practice flouts both sides of Polonius' dictum.)

*Owe money to*        *who owe money to*
Bank borrowers > Commercial Banks > Depositors

Before they got into the money lending business, early banks were in the business of providing physical security for precious metals. Depositors placed gold (or silver) in the bank vault, where the bullion could be better protected than at their own homes. In exchange for the gold, bankers gave their depositors a receipt which was redeemable for the exact number of ounces placed in the bank's care. The gold receipts issued by banks were known as "banknotes." A liability of the bank, they represented a claim on its assets—gold. Far less cumbersome and less prone to theft, banknotes began to supplant gold and silver coin in commercial transactions. *Banknotes had become money.* Banknotes which are backed entirely by precious metals stored in a vault are sometimes referred to as **warehouse money.**

Because the public was content to use banknotes as money, only a small number of depositors exchanged their notes for gold on any given day. Observing this phenomenon, the bankers soon conceived a better use for the gold which had been sitting idly in their vaults. They would lend it out and earn interest on their depositors' funds.

Of course, the banks had to maintain at least some gold on hand to return to depositors that wished to redeem their banknotes. The amount of gold in the bank vaults earmarked for redeeming depositors is called the bank's **reserve.** As long as the depositors never redeemed their banknotes en masse, the scheme could work. **Fractional reserve banking** was born.

As its name implies, a fractional reserve bank does not maintain a 100% gold reserve against the value of the banknotes that it has issued. Instead of completely backing its liabilities with gold, a portion is instead backed with loans. Depositors, aware that some of their money was being loaned out, demanded that their banks should keep the "fractional reserve" of gold above a specified level, measured by a **reserve ratio.**

---

**NEWTOWN BANK**
**Balance Sheet - September 30, 2010**

| Assets | Liabilities |
|---|---|
| Gold   $10,000,000 | Banknotes          $10,000,000 |
|  | (100% Warehouse Money) |

---

The reserve ratio is the proportion of reserves relative to the bank's liabilities. This ratio dictates how much of the depositors' savings can be invested into loans. The remainder, or **required reserves,** must be kept in the vault.

The balance sheet indicates that Newtown Bank maintains only 1 million in gold to support the 10 million dollars of banknotes that it has issued. The gold reserves are just a "fraction" of the bank's liabilities: 1 million/10 million, or 10%. While reserve ratios have changed over time, they have historically varied between ten and twenty percent of deposits.

A bank with very high reserve levels is said to be liquid.

If the bank did not maintain adequate reserves, it faced the problem of **liquidity risk** if a large number of depositors simultaneously demanded their gold back.

Besides ensuring that the banks had enough gold to satisfy banknote redemptions, depositors had another concern: **credit risk.** Credit risk (also known as default risk) is the potential that a bank's borrowers will fail to repay their loans. If enough loans started to go bad, a bank's assets would soon be worth less than its liabilities. The face value of the banknotes would exceed the value of the loans and gold backing them. The banknotes would begin to trade below their face value, thereby destroying the depositors' wealth.

---

### NEWTOWN BANK
### Balance Sheet - October 30, 2010

| Assets | | Liabilities | |
|---|---|---|---|
| Gold | $1,000,000 | Banknotes | $10,000,000 |
| Loans | $9,000,000 | (10% Warehouse Money) | |
| | $10,000,000 | (90% Fractional Money) | |

---

In order to insulate themselves against loan defaults, the depositors required that the bank owners contribute their own gold to the bank vault. The bank owners' capital would serve as a buffer to absorb any losses from souring loans.

**Leverage** measures the ratio of a bank's liabilities to its stockholder capital. Newtown Bank's **leverage ratio** is 10.0 (10 million in banknotes divided by 1 million in capital).

If loan defaults rose to a level exceeding the stockholders' capital, the stockholders would lose their entire investment and the remaining losses would be absorbed by the depositors. The bank would go bankrupt, a condition known as insolvency.

## NEWTOWN BANK
## Balance Sheet - November 30, 2010

| Assets | Liabilities | Stockholder Capital |
|---|---|---|
| Gold   $2,000,000<br>Loans   $9,000,000<br>$11,000,000 | Banknotes  $10,000,000 | Stock   $1,000,000 |

Liquidity and credit risks were the two primary problems facing banks. They could fail for either reason: 1) inadequate reserves, or 2) insufficient capital to absorb loan defaults. But as long as a large share of the banknotes weren't being redeemed and the vast majority of its loans were being paid on time, the banks remained solvent and liquid. *Banknotes could continue to function as money.*

Of Newtown's *original* $10 million in depositor gold, only $1 million remained in the vault. (The other $1 million in gold was contributed by the bank stockholders.) The other $9 million in gold was loaned out. As Newtown's borrowers redeposited their gold at other banks, those banks in turn issued their own banknotes. Newtown Bank's depositors' gold was not only supporting its *own* banknotes, it began supporting *other banks'* banknotes, as well. As the scheme continued, a large quantity of banknotes was soon pyramided on a relatively small base of gold.

## Banks Really Do <u>Make</u> Money

Banknotes

$10 million

GOLD

$1 million

By fractional reserving, banks can transform $1 million in gold into
$10 million in banknotes (the gold reserve requirement is 10%).

Through the magic of fractional reserve banking, *banks were creating money on their own.* Savings were being recycled into investment [the bank loans]; new money [the banknotes] was the byproduct. Money was now inextricably intertwined with credit, and the fate of both rested entirely in the hands of commercial banks. Economic life was about to get a lot more interesting.

## Chapter 4

# YOU CAN'T BANK ON ANYTHING

*"All money is a matter of belief."*
ADAM SMITH

The great thing about cooking is that it is more or less a **natural science,** like chemistry, biology, or physics. That isn't to say there isn't an art to it—of course there is. But cooking is a talent that can be imparted. If a culinary numbskull like me can learn to prepare an edible plate of hashbrowns, the skill can be obtained by anyone with sufficient determination. (On the other hand, I suspect that Edward's conversational flair can only be obtained through a genetic endowment.)

Unlike cooking, economics and investing are **social sciences,** along with psychology, anthropology, and political science. While natural sciences are focused on the physical world, social sciences are devoted to understanding human behavior. For many reasons, the conclusions drawn by natural scientists are far more dependable than those made by social scientists.

In the first place, natural science experiments generally transpire in laboratory environments in which all pertinent variables can be perfectly controlled. If you mix a given set of ingredients in their correct proportions and heat them for an appropriate length of time at the specified temperature, you will generate a consistent outcome. Consequently, a patron can enjoy the same fare in a Pittsburgh Papa's in 2010 that he did in Greensboro fifty years ago.

Given the myriad of physical and psychological nuances of every human being, social scientists have a much more difficult time designing genuinely controlled experiments. In the human laboratory, no two situations are ever perfectly identical. Further, the variables (i.e., people) are constantly changing, and so is each person's relative significance in the system.

Secondly, the results of a natural science experiment can be evaluated fairly quickly. Eating a T-bone dinner is a discrete, one-time event. The steak's taste will immediately apprise the customer whether or not the grill officer has botched the order. In contrast, investing is an ongoing endeavor, so assessing the merits of a particular investment strategy will greatly depend on the time period being evaluated. The genius hedge fund manager who doubles his investors' money in one year is very likely to be the complete moron who loses 60% of it during the next one.

Most importantly, natural scientists' expectations cannot influence the outcome of any experiment. Regardless of what a grill officer *thinks* will happen if he sets the grill at an excessive temperature and does not adjust his cooking time accordingly, he will end up burning the food. Conversely, human experiences are constantly affected by the beliefs of social scientists; outcomes are largely dependent on reactions to past events. Human expectations for the future, based on past experiences, affect the future itself. This phenomenon of feedback loops between cause and effect is often called "reflexivity."

A perfect illustration of reflexivity in action is the film, *Back to the Future.* Marty McFly (brilliantly played by Michael J. Fox) is a harried adolescent who inadvertently travels back in time from 1985 to 1955. He spends several weeks with his then high-school-aged parents, trying to prevent their actions—as well as his own—from compromising their future marriage.

Marty carries with him a 1984 family photo, which enables him to determine how his maneuvers are paying off. As a result of his miscalculated actions, Marty's brother and sister soon disappear from the picture and his own body begins to fade. After another maneuver, Marty's parents finally kiss at the "Enchantment Under the Sea" dance, and he and his siblings are restored in the photograph.

A theme emerges during the film: however benign his intentions, Marty can never be sure how his slightest move in 1955 will end up affecting the lives of many people thirty years later. Such is the nature of life. Each change of our tack forces a subsequent reevaluation of the course upon which we're headed.

Societies, as well as individuals, experience the reflexivity phenomenon in their collective psychology. Since the dawn of mankind, material success and prosperity has fostered pride. As the arrogance increases, conventional wisdoms are disregarded in favor of tenuous theories propounded by social scientists. The longer the prosperity continues, the more outlandish the philosophies become. "We are wiser than our forebears, hence we are no longer plagued by their problems" is a common refrain during these periods.

Of course, the day of reckoning eventually arrives in the form of war, famine, plague, or economic calamity. Chastened, the populace begins to substitute humility for hubris and reevaluates its thinking. In due time, prosperity returns and sentiments of pride begin to creep back in.

## PRIDE CYCLE DIAGRAM

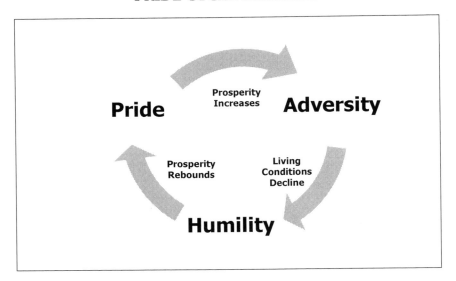

This **pride cycle** of affluence, followed by foolish excess, then decline and humility, is endemic to all civilizations. 3,500 years ago, in consequence of their pride and iniquities, Israelite settlers in Canaan were conquered by Philistine armies, losing the Ark of the Covenant in the process. Centuries of military and economic hegemony in Europe cultivated a similar spirit of hubris in the late Roman Empire. The egocentrism led Rome to betray her Visigoth allies, who eventually responded by sacking the city in A.D. 410.

Because of its propensity to undermine national and individual prosperity, a sentiment of pride should always be checked. Inasmuch as we curb our prideful feelings, we become wiser creatures. Inasmuch as we don't, we condemn ourselves to repeating the cycle indefinitely.

$ $ $ $ $

The most recent nadir in my personal pride cycle arrived on an April Friday morning. The grill officer and I had been hit with an aberrantly

high volume of customers immediately after the other server had left at
1 a.m. Consequently, I couldn't begin cleaning the store until ninety
minutes after my usual start time. When Debbie arrived at 7 o'clock,
I was still laboring in the dish pit. My salutation had been met with a
grumbled "morning" in response. She had been in a consistently foul
mood for the entire week.

"Why are you still washing dishes?" she snarled.

"I wrote 53 tickets last night. Mary didn't do any side work or dishes
before she left, so I got stuck with all of them."

"I see," she said flatly. She headed to the back room, where I overheard
Matthew ask her about several cash register shortages that had occurred
over the past few weeks. After a few minutes of conversation, I heard
my name.

"Jimmy's the common denominator," she said.

I was attempting to get some hardened chili to part from a steel pot
when she returned to the floor and hurled the accusation at me directly.

"Do you know how to count?"

"What?"

"Do you know how to count? And subtract? And make change?"

"I think so. That is, I remember doing exercises on making change in
Mrs. Diehl's first grade glass. But that was back in '83, so in all candor, I
may be a little rusty by now. Why?"

"We've had six drawer shortages over twenty dollars in the past two
weeks, and you were working on four of those shifts."

"Am I being indicted for theft?"

"Theft, no. But I think you may have some difficulty counting change."

That was the last straw. My MBA and CFA charter did not give me
omniscience in the capital markets, that I would allow. But the inability
to make change? Was she kidding?

Edward could label me "stupid" when it came to calling orders; that
didn't bother me because it was true enough. Impugning my capacity to
subtract was where I had to draw a line.

I briefly debated how best to defend my intellect. I could have pointed out that besides the 80% of my coworkers who were convicted felons, one was mildly cross-eyed, and the other (by her own admission) could not subtract without the aid of a calculator. I could have asked a rhetorical question: why would two major life insurance companies permit me to trade 50-million-dollar blocks of corporate bonds if I couldn't perform bond math, which is patently more complicated than making change for a ten-dollar bill?

I elected for a third route. I had paid fifty-one thousand dollars out of my own pocket to acquire an MBA. During orientation, the dean had assured my classmates and I that the skills attained during the pursuit of our degree would be applicable in our vocations. Now was my big chance. I would use principles of quantitative analysis inside the Papa's store. In retrospect, I think Don Quixote had much better odds when he charged the windmills.

"How many drawer shortages did you say there have been?"

"Six in the last two weeks. You were working on four of those shifts."

"Uh-huh. Debbie, are you aware that you need to have thirty observations to make any statistically significant statement about whether my presence is correlated with the shortages?"

"Maybe it's not to *you,* but to Papa's twenty dollars is statistically significant."

"That's not what I meant. You need to have at least thirty *incidents* of twenty-dollar-plus drawer shortages before you can legitimately correlate them with my failure to properly subtract."

"Whatever. All I know is the drawer has been short, lately, and you've been working several of those shifts." She returned to the back room and lit a cigarette.

I had heard the term "kangaroo court" before, but I never really appreciated it until just then. I guess I was mistaken that someone using fancy terms like "common denominator" would be well-versed in correlation coefficients. I just couldn't win.

"Y'all looking for help?" I turned to find a young man standing at the cash register.

"Given that we've recently fired three people, I'd presume the answer is an unequivocal 'yes.'"

"Are you the manager?"

"Goodness, no. I'm not even the assistant manager. *She* knows how to count; I'm still learning. But if you complete this form, I'll see that she gets it."

As I watched him fill out the application, a hand patted my back.

"You look tired," Matthew said. "It's obvious you had a rough night, so I went ahead and took care of your meat count tickets for you. Just take care of that last table over there and you can go home and get some sleep." He gestured to a booth where three graduate students had seated themselves.

"And don't worry about Debbie—she's just in a mood this morning. For what it's worth, I think you do know how to subtract." I thanked him for the vote of confidence and reviewed the young man's application. He had, of course, been convicted of a felony. His explanation: "Guilt by association. At the wrong place, at the wrong time."

Boy, could I relate to that sentiment. I was finally beginning to understand the necessity of the "no firearms on these premises" sign in the break room. I didn't even own a gun, but the idea of firing a few rounds into the lights above the high bar had become an appealing proposition.

The graduate students were excitedly discussing the results of an intramural basketball game when I sauntered over to their table. Their t-shirt logos and cocky demeanor evidenced their status as students in an eminent MBA program. "We are three sharks, ready to conquer an ocean of commerce," their body language said. All I saw were three naïve fish in a barrel, ripe for the shooting.

The dean of their business school had cofounded Alpha Managers twenty-five years ago and was known to frequently refer to the firm during his lectures. Students considered it a great honor to land a summer internship, let alone a permanent position, at the firm. I approached the booth with a modest hope, namely, that finding an Alpha Managers alumnus waiting tables at the local Papa's Chicken & Waffles would summarily destroy their model of the universe. This was going to be a lot of fun.

"Hey, how are you fellahs doing this morning? Any of you taking the investment class that the Dean teaches?" I asked in a ridiculously enthusiastic tone.

"Yeah, I'm taking it now," one said.

"Are you learning a lot?"

"I think so."

"That's good, I'm very happy to hear that."

"Hey, how did you know that the Dean teaches that class?"

"Oh, I used to work for his firm. Until two months ago."

His eyes visibly widened. "You were working at Alpha Managers?"

"Yes, in the Product Management group. Now could I interest you guys in some chocolate waffles? Or perhaps some hashbrowns?"

"Wait a minute. How did you end up working here?"

"That's not so important," I said. "What is important is that you boys start your day with a healthy, balanced meal."

"You *really* worked for Alpha Managers?" he asked incredulously.

This was going even better than planned.

"I'll tell you what, guys. You let me take your orders, and then I'll share a few anecdotes. Is that fair enough?"

They readily consented. I called their orders, brought out their drinks, then ducked into the back room. I sat down on the stool in the office, where I could observe their bantering behind the one-way mirror. Their demeanor was starting to shift from ebullience to confusion. I emerged back onto the floor, trying to maintain as straight a face as I could.

"So what happened?" one asked.

"We're going to have to drop you another waffle because we burned the first one. I'm terribly sorry about that, sir."

"No, I mean with your career."

"Well, I'm only a salesperson now, but with sufficient tenacity, I *could* be promoted to assistant manager in another eighteen months. If you wouldn't mind putting in a good word on my behalf with the manager, I'd sure appreciate it."

"Why aren't you at Alpha Managers, anymore?" The student to my right was getting visibly frustrated, and stifling my laughter was becoming increasingly difficult.

"Simple. As mortgage bond prices collapsed last year, our clients began closing their accounts. Our fees declined, so the firm couldn't support as many personnel. I got hit in the third wave of layoffs."

"But . . . you were at *Alpha Managers*," he protested.

"Yes. And now I'm at Papa's. What's your point?"

"But that . . ." he shook his head violently. "That doesn't make any sense. You guys were supposed to be super smart. I mean, some of the top academics in the country."

"Have you ever heard of the Black-Scholes option pricing model?"

"Sure, everyone has. The guys that invented it received a Nobel prize in economics."

"That's right," I said. "They won it in 1997. The following year, the hedge fund they founded had the most spectacular collapse in the history of Wall Street."

Founded with a billion in capital in 1994, Long-Term Capital Management (LTCM) posted several years of annual returns in excess of 40%. By early 1998, the intellectual brain trust had grown to nearly $5 billion in capital and $130 billion in assets, creating a leverage ratio of 25-to-1. That summer, LTCM's highly leveraged bets began to go awry. As its capital declined by more than 80% during the first three weeks of September, the fund's imminent failure threatened to compromise every trading desk on Wall Street. On September 23rd, the Federal Reserve Bank of New York orchestrated a $3.6 billion bailout by LTCM's creditors in order to prevent a total collapse in the financial markets.

"Academic credentials are no guarantee of good investment performance," I concluded. "Similarly, a stellar resume or an MBA degree from a leading institution does not ensure finding a job in a tumultuous economy."

I inquired how long the students had been in their program. The man to my left was in his first year; the two to my right were in their second (and final) year. One of them had secured post-graduate employment. I congratulated him on his good luck and leaned toward his less fortunate companion, framing my nametag between my thumb and index finger. It was within six inches of his eyeglasses when I resumed speaking.

"You see this?"

"Yuh . . . yeah," he stammered.

"Take a long, hard look at it," I admonished him. "In a few more months, it could have your name on it." I leaned back slowly.

The first-year student covered his mouth as he chortled. The soon-to-be-employed man sat agape. The third—in whose face I had thrust "Papa's Little Helper, JIMMY, Team Member Since 2008"—was visibly shaking.

I wished the men well on the rest of their journey through higher education and excused myself to the break room. A plate of hashbrowns, which I had hastily cooked four hours ago, sat waiting for me. As the store had no microwave, I had no way of reheating them.

In the course of my career, I have eaten at four- and five-star restaurants in New York, Atlanta, Las Vegas, and Tokyo. No meal served at any of those establishments has been nearly as satisfying as the one I consumed on that Friday morning. You see, a cold plate doesn't matter when your food has been seasoned with irony, the tastiest condiment of all.

"It is pride," C.S. Lewis wrote, "which has been the chief cause of misery in every nation and every family since the world began." As I have come to understand that the abuse of leverage is simply a manifestation of pride, I realize that truer words have never been spoken.

Instead of increasing their leverage solely by issuing banknotes, banks began to write other kinds of liabilities. These instruments—checking accounts, savings accounts, and certificates of deposit—enabled depositors to participate in the interest earnings of the bank's loan pool. Broadly speaking, these non-banknote liabilities also functioned as part of the money supply.

The weighted average interest rate that the bank earns on its loan pool is called the **interest yield.** The weighted average interest rate that the bank pays on its deposits is known as its **cost of funds.** The **net interest margin** is the difference between the interest yield and the cost of funds. If the interest yield of the loans is 5% and the cost of funds is 3%, then the net interest margin is 2% (5% minus 3%). Normally, banks earn net interest margins between two and four percent.

The net interest margin is the bank's profit earned for 1) the legwork involved in underwriting the loans; 2) using its stockholders' capital to absorb the loan losses; and 3) returning cash to depositors on short (or immediate) notice.

The return on the stockholders' capital is: Interest Yield + (Net Interest Margin x Leverage). By borrowing money at 3%, lending it at 5%, and leveraging their capital ten times, the bank stockholders earn a 25% return on their money (ignoring overhead expenses). Despite providing nearly 90% of the loanable funds, the depositors earn a paltry 3% return.

**NEWTOWN BANK**
**Balance Sheet - Dec 30, 2010**

| Assets | | Liabilities | | Equity | |
|---|---|---|---|---|---|
| Reserves | $2,000,000 | Savings Accts | $10,000,000 | Stock | $1,000,000 |
| Loans | $9,000,000 | | | | |
| | $11,000,000 | | | | |
| Interest yield: | 5% | Cost of funds: | 3% | Return on Equity: | **25.0%** |
| → | $550,000 | → | $300,000 | → | $250,000 |

If the bankers want to earn even higher rates of return on equity, they have three options:

- Pay depositors a lower rate of interest
- Lend money at a higher rate
- Use more leverage

We'll consider each of these options in turn.

**Pay depositors a lower rate of interest.** Generally speaking, this is the least practical option. Competition for deposits generally keeps banks from dramatically lowering the interest rates on savings accounts. Any large decline in deposit rates will be met with a wave of withdrawals as depositors seek a higher rate of return at another bank.

**Lend money at a higher rate.** In addition to contending for deposits, banks also compete with each other to lend money to creditworthy borrowers. Banks will lend at lower rates to persons that they believe have a high probability of repayment. (Remember the "four Cs": character, capacity, collateral, and covenants.) If the bank wants to earn higher interest rates, it must resort to lending money to persons or businesses of increasingly dubious character, limited means of repayment, and little collateral. A good example of indiscriminate lending is granting loans to persons of dubious mental health whose only form of collateral is a plate of half-eaten hashbrowns.

As a concession to the bank for assuming higher default risk, the less creditworthy borrowers will agree to pay higher interest rates. By making these dicey loans, Newtown could raise its interest yield by 1%, thereby boosting its shareholder return to 36%:

---

**NEWTOWN BANK**
**Balance Sheet - March 30, 2011**

| Assets | | Liabilities | | Equity | |
|--------|--------|--------|--------|--------|--------|
| Reserves | $2,000,000 | Savings Accts $10,000,000 | | Stock | $1,000,000 |
| Loans | $9,000,000 | | | | |
| | $11,000,000 | | | | |

| | | | | | |
|--------|--------|--------|--------|--------|--------|
| Interest yield: | 6.0% | Cost of funds: | 3.0% | Return on Equity: | **36.0%** |
| → | $660,000 | → | $300,000 | → | $360,000 |

---

**Use more leverage.** For every one unit increase in leverage, the stockholders' return increases by the net interest margin. In the example below, Newtown has increased its leverage from 10 to 15, causing its return on equity to climb from 25% to 35%.

---

**NEWTOWN BANK**
**Balance Sheet - March 30, 2011**

| Assets | | Liabilities | | Equity | |
|--------|--------|--------|--------|--------|--------|
| Reserves | $2,000,000 | Savings Accts $10,312,500 | | Stock | $687,500 |
| Loans | $9,000,000 | | | | |
| | $11,000,000 | | | | |

| | | | | | |
|--------|--------|--------|--------|--------|--------|
| Interest yield: | 5.0% | Cost of funds: | 3.0% | Return on Equity: | **35.0%** |
| → | $550,000 | → | $309,375 | → | $240,625 |

---

All else equal, easier lending standards will increase the demand for land, houses, and other long-term real assets (also known as **capital assets**) on which most individual consumers spend their loan proceeds. The same holds for business assets: factories, warehouses, machinery, timber, equipment, etc. The demand for these capital assets is largely dictated by bankers' ability and willingness to furnish the capital. The other source of demand for capital assets is borrower optimism. If individuals and businesses feel confident that a prospective investment will increase in value, they will be confident to make the purchase. Efficient use of capital assets is the engine of higher productivity and, therefore, greater wealth.

**Financial assets** such as stocks, bonds, and bank loans are claims on capital assets. Ergo, business optimism and readily available credit drive up the prices of financial assets and capital assets in tandem. A rapid rise in the prices of financial assets is known as **asset inflation.**

Asset inflation should not be confused with the consumer price inflation that we have previously discussed. Inflation of consumer products, i.e., those goods which are *immediately* consumed, results from the money supply growing at a faster pace than the volume of consumer goods. (Remember the Equation of Exchange? The "P" in the equation primarily consists of consumer prices.)

$$MupV = PupY$$

To summarize, the loan growth that occurs in the asset column of a bank's balance sheet is a major driver of asset inflation. The growth in the money supply that occurs on the liability column of its balance sheet (through the fractional process) is the major driver of **consumer price inflation.** Money is backed by bank loans, whose values are tied to the prices of capital assets.

| *support* | | *which support* | |
|---|---|---|---|
| **Capital assets** | **>** | **bank loanss** | **>** | **money** |

Bankers, while not renowned for being the life of most parties, are social animals nonetheless. Responding to the behavior of borrowers and other bankers, they are prone to alternating bouts of group optimism and pessimism. In their euphoric periods, bankers lend money on easier terms to increasingly less worthy borrowers, creating credit expansion. In more sober times, bankers are more discriminating in their lending decisions, causing credit contraction. The fluctuation between periods of credit expansion and contraction is known as the **credit cycle.**

Because asset prices are driven by both credit availability and speculator optimism, they are subject to self-reinforcing reflexive actions between speculators and their lenders. A rise in asset prices increases speculative fervor and demand for debt. Bankers, encouraged by the higher prices, lend speculators more money to purchase real estate, stocks, or other assets. The asset prices rise again, and the upward spiral continues.

Often, the asset prices reach a level that far exceeds any fundamental business justification. At this point, a prudent banker would be gravely concerned about borrowers' ability to repay their loans and quit extending credit. Instead, most lenders are content to rely on further asset appreciation. The party mentality has taken over.

It's safe and easy for most bankers to stick together and engage in the same reckless behavior. Of course, there are always a few who choose to remain sober rather than participate in the frenzy of easy credit and asset inflation. As the party continues, these people are often derided for failing to understand the "new paradigm." The sober bankers, while correct in their assessments, often become unpopular with their borrowers and shareholders alike.

In the short term, an illusion can become a temporary reality as long as it has a critical mass of popular acceptance—it doesn't matter if the emperor is really naked as long as everyone is willing to act as though he's actually wearing clothes. But as anyone who has been to high school is well aware, popular opinion and stupidity are frequent bedfellows. There is no long-term safety in numbers when the entire group is acting foolishly.

Sooner or later, reality strikes. The borrowers have insufficient cash flow to service their debts and begin to default on their loans. The rising loan losses deplete the banks' capital, constraining their ability to make new loans. Healthy banks begin to raise borrowing rates and tighten their lending standards. Highly leveraged banks, who had previously enjoyed high returns for their stockholders, suffer the most. They quit making new loans and, in many cases, call in existing loans in an attempt to raise their capital back to healthy levels.

### CREDIT CYCLE DIAGRAM

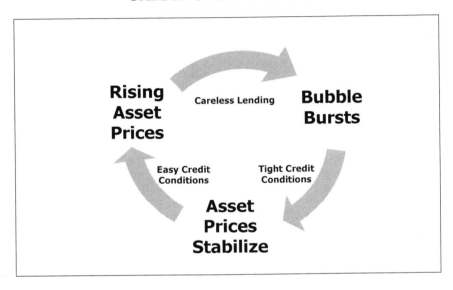

As banks begin to withdraw financing, asset prices begin to decline. Potential borrowers grow pessimistic, resulting in further deterioration of asset prices, causing banks to become even more reticent to lend. The virtuous circle of asset appreciation has turned into a vicious downward spiral. The greater the overpricing in capital assets and the greater the banks' leverage, the more painful the adjustment process becomes.

The lesson is clear. As long as humans inhabit the earth, the pride cycle isn't going anywhere. And as long as humans are running banks, the credit cycle will surely be there as well.

$ $ $ $ $

I realize some of my culturally deprived readers (namely, those living north of the Mason-Dixon line or west of the Mississippi River) may have never encountered a bowl of grits. Please allow me to educate you on a dietary staple of the God-fearing Red States. Traditional grits is prepared by boiling ground corn kernels into a sticky, viscous porridge and then adding butter and salt. Second only to NASCAR, this culinary masterpiece represents the South's greatest cultural achievement.

Papa's Chicken & Waffles customers consume over three million pounds of grits every year. I have seen them flavor their bowls with cheese, pepper, sugar, jelly, and chopped sausage patties. I have no personal recommendation on how grits is best consumed, because I don't eat the stuff.

My colleagues informed me that grits are also served daily at nearly all North Carolina penitentiaries. Ostensibly, grits are offered because it's a very inexpensive way for the state to keep the prisoners flush with carbohydrates. I'm inclined to think that their motives are far more odious. There's something about a whitish-grey bowl of porridge that smacks of a depressing nineteenth-century British workhouse (think *Oliver Twist)*. Serving plain grits every day must undoubtedly demoralize the prisoners, effectively pre-empting any temptation to riot. I imagine a cruel warden laughing mercilessly as he personally ladles every scoop.

Beyond their dull appearance, grits exhibit an annoying ubiquity. They end up *everywhere* inside a Papa's—on countertops, in between fork tines, even stuck on the back of order tickets. Even after a cup has been manually sprayed and run through the dishwasher, a grain or two inevitably remains clinging to its inside. Fortunately, the wayward granules can be readily camouflaged from customers by adding sufficient ice to the cups. But ice or no, burnt grits in a glass of water unfailingly draw customer ire, given their strong resemblance to dead gnats.

Because they are extremely adhesive and are always served at very hot temperatures, grits are the culinary equivalent of napalm. A grill officer told me (with a considerable degree of conviction) that the U.S. could completely extirpate Al Qaeda if we could simply manage the logistics of pumping large quantities into every hole in Afghanistan. I had to concede that the idea had merit. The image of terrorists drowning in a flood of the stuff is terribly appealing. But as I learned early one Saturday morning, they aren't the only ones that need to fear a hot bowl.

Although the high bar assignment made me accountable for only six seats, I also had the responsibility of covering all to-go orders. Normally, I preferred this job because the automatic ten percent gratuity added to take-out checks meant that at least half of my total customers couldn't stiff me even if they wanted to.

The main drawback to the high-bar gig was trying to assuage the jealousies that inevitably arose from dividing my attention to both dine-in and dine-out patrons. Given the already harried state of the restaurant, it was simply impossible to keep everyone happy. I was trying to communicate with a mute customer, who I believed was ordering a BLT sandwich, when we were interrupted by a girl to his right. "Where's my food?" her shrill voice demanded. She had ordered three strips of bacon and a bowl of grits ten minutes ago, but the grill had been so backed up that I hadn't yet been able to call in the bacon order. I advised her of the situation, scooped a bowl of grits, and placed it in front of her.

"I'll bring out the bacon as soon as it's ready. In the meantime, please enjoy your grits."

She looked at my nametag. "Whuh-oah," she said in a confrontational tone, eyeing my nametag.

"Uh, 'Jimmy,' is it?"

I nodded.

"Well, Jimmy, this is unacceptable. You need to bring out my bacon at the same time as my grits. I'm not going to put my bacon into a bowl of cold grits."

I assured her that I would bring a fresh bowl when the bacon was ready. At the end of our exchange, the mute man tapped my arm and pointed to his sweet tea. Signaling its bitterness, he puckered his lips and shook his head violently. Before I could offer to bring him more sugar, he gestured for my pen and scrawled out "Coke" on a napkin.

I called in the bacon orders for him and Grits Girl and brought out their beverages. The mute man nodded his head in gratitude; the girl wasn't so thankful.

"I hope you know I ain't payin' for this Sprite, Jimmy."

"Why is that?"

"You took too long getting it to me. You got to be faster if you want to get paid."

I put my hands on the counter and looked her right in the eyes. Eight consecutive weekends of this sort of churlish behavior had worn me thin. It had already been a long night, and I was in no mood to be addressed this way by a girl ten years my junior.

"Ma'am, I desperately want you to enjoy your dinner. But I'm new at this and I need a little information so I can optimize your Papa's dining experience. Would you kindly tell me if you would prefer me to bring your food promptly or slowly?"

"What kind of a dumb question is that?"

"Well, I'm a little slow on the uptake when it comes to understanding contradictory orders. First, you tell me I was too fast with your grits. Then, I take too long on the Sprite and you start bitching at me."

Her mouth fell open as her two friends gasped simultaneously.

"What did you call me?" she fumed.

"I didn't call you anything. But I did accuse you of bitching at me."

"I'll tell you what's going to happen now," she said coolly as she placed her hand around the bowl. "You're gonna wear these grits, Jim-may!" She began cocking her arm.

I had done a fair amount of amateur boxing off and on over the past eight years. I wasn't the most aggressive fighter, but I had become extremely adept at slipping punches. Dodging a bowl of grits wouldn't be any more difficult, particularly having been given advance notice of its arrival.

"You know, I brought those grits out so long ago that they're probably cold by now," I said flatly. "If you really want to scald me, let me get you a hot bowl first."

Before she could offer a rejoinder to my salvo of trash talk, a coworker threw his body in front of me, spreading his arms across my chest in the manner of a bodyguard shielding a VIP from an assassin's bullet. After making a few conciliatory remarks to her, he put his hand on my shoulder and walked me into the break room.

"You can't talk to the customers like that!" Tommy exclaimed.

I spent the next ten minutes receiving an impromptu lecture on appropriate customer interaction from a twice-convicted felon. My words had inarguably been inappropriate, but the infraction seemed minor given that my coworkers frequently used the f-bomb, n-bomb, and all the other bombs in front of customers with total impunity. It was a tough pill to swallow.

I returned to the floor and found my dissatisfied customer still sitting at the high bar. She was visibly surprised by my approach.

"I'm sorry for what I said earlier," I began. "Things get a little hectic in here on weekends and I can get impatient. My outburst was inexcusable, and I hope you'll forgive me. I'm still fairly new at this."

She gave me a deliberate nod.

"As a waiter, I'm not authorized to give you a free meal. But I would like to pay for yours," I said, placing a five-dollar bill on the counter. "I hope you'll visit us again soon."

"Well, Jimmy, I'll have to think about it."

A young man seated at the end of the bar overheard the conversation and decided to test the limits of my goodwill. "Hey man, I think you mighta been looking at me cross-eyed when you brought out my T-bone. How about covering my tab while you're at it?"

$ $ $ $ $

When the crowd subsided at 4:30, I rolled the mop bucket outside the store and began to replenish it with hot water from an exterior spigot. It was halfway full when Tommy caught up with me. I expected him to continue his sermon where he had left off, and I wasn't looking forward to it. Instead, I received an outpouring of empathy.

"I've had some customers say some awful stuff to me. But no one had ever threatened to algreen me like that girl did to you. She left me no choice but to throw myself in there."

"She threatened to do what to me?" "

The grits. She was fixin' to go algreen on you."

Tommy then explained to me the origin of the term "algreen." In the mid-1970s, soul legend Al Green was assaulted by his girlfriend as he was climbing into the shower in his Memphis home. The deranged paramour heaved a pot of scalding hot grits on poor Al, causing third-degree burns on his back, stomach and arms. As Green was writhing in pain on the floor, she fled the bathroom and shot herself with his pistol.

Al was rushed to the hospital and emerged from his convalescence several months later with a decidedly religious mindset. He forsook R&B, began recording gospel music, and became an ordained minister. So, to "algreen" someone meant that you were going to douse them with hot grits in hopes of burning them so badly that they would emerge from the experience with a newfound fear of the Almighty.

"Your problem is that you're trying to do too much," Tommy explained. "You need to focus on keeping a small number of customers happy instead o' trying to please everybody. It's better to let an impatient customer leave before they can place an order. Instead, if you start waitin' on 'em and they get frustrated, they'll probably walk out without paying."

"Or throw their food at you," I interjected.

"True 'nuff," Tommy said. "But whatever else happens, you gotta keep your cool. It's never worth lettin' folks get you so worked up you end up tellin' 'em off, no matter how much they deserve it."

He had a point. It's useless to tell someone to go to hell when they're already headed in that general direction.

I pulled my mop bucket back into the store and began mopping the floor. I had only been at it for a minute when Edward decided to interrogate me about the night's events.

"I saw you had a little trouble with the customahs last night, Jimmy."

"Edward, I can't take much more of this. These college girls are going to kill me."

"I don't blame 'em. I feel like killing you myself half the time when you mess up your calls."

"Yes, Edward, but at least you're reasonably polite about it. I mean, I used to work my butt off for Japanese clients, but they never got so nasty with me. And I lost them a few billion dollars. These girls freak out if their grits are lukewarm."

"Has any customers been speaking to you in Japanese?"

"No, Edward."

"And do you see anyone come in here wearing a kimono or carrying a samurai sword on their belt?"

"No, I haven't, Edward."

"And do you see any signs that say 'Tokyo' anywhere 'round here?"

"I can't say that I have, Edward."

"Then why would you expect to get treated like you was serving waffles in Japan? What was it Dorothy done said in that *Wizard of Oz* movie: 'Toto, we ain't in Kansas no mo.'"

"I believe that's what she said, yes."

"Well, you ain't in Kansas. And you ain't in Japan neither, so you'd better get used to it. Look, if you are accustomed to riding in a Cadillac," he said, turning an imaginary steering wheel, "and then you go mountain biking," he continued, moving his fists in small circular motions, "you should anticipate a bumpier ride. Ya see, a mountain bike don't have as good a suspension as a Coup de Ville."

In this case, Edward's logic was undeniably cogent. My new vocation had taken me pretty far through the looking glass. I had to be more conscious of the cultural nuances of my customers.

"You're right, Edward. I just don't understand why some people have to be so rude."

"Well, when the first Papa's opens in Tokyo, you can apply for a transfer. I'll even put in a good word for you with the corporate office. Then you'll be able to wait on all them polite Japanese folks."

"You'd do that for me?"

"Yeaauuuh," he said with a confirming nod. "It can be a little rough with those girls sometimes. But you'll be alright. Just be glad you don't have to fight off a pack of monkeys like the ones that ripped that scarecrow to pieces." He turned back to the grill and diced a cheesesteak patty with his spatula. "Flyin' monkeys. I hate those thangs."

$ $ $ $ $

For as much time as he spent upbraiding me, Edward appeared to genuinely enjoy guiding my transformation (however gradual) from hapless financier to server extraordinaire. The week after my run-in with Grits Girl, I overheard him enumerating my new talents in the sort of boastful tone that a master uses when cataloguing the tricks he has imparted to his new puppy.

"You ought to see him now," he said proudly to two young men at the high bar. "The man can wash dishes, set up the tables, wipe down the tables, serve the food, and even cook some of the food. Hashbrowns, waffles, burgers, eggs, he do that okay. Obviously, there's some things that still elude him. For example, omelets are still way over his head." The boys gave an understanding nod. "But he knows the price of almost everything on the menu. And the man does real good arithmetic—he can add with the best of them. He was a financial man in his past life, so he's got a knack with numbers, which serves to offset his weakness elsewhere. And there *are* still a few chinks floating around in his armor. Ain't that right, Jimmy Jam?"

As I started to respond, Edward advised me that his question had been purely rhetorical. He was merely using me as an illustration for an economics lecture.

"Take this man here," he said, pointing at me. "There's always work to be done, somewhere. The only question is what kind of job it is, where the job is, and if you're willing to accept the wage. As long as you're willing to adapt yourself to different kinds of work, then there really ain't no such thing as a recession," he posited.

$ $ $ $ $

The **business cycle** refers to economy-wide changes in production over a number of months (or years). During the upswing of the cycle, total output increases at a relatively fast pace, worker productivity rises, and unemployment generally declines. During a downswing, production declines as factory capacity and labor go unused. Companies shutter plants and lay off workers. A **recession** occurs when a deterioration in the economy's output lasts for two consecutive three-month periods.

During the late nineteenth and early twentieth centuries, there was widespread agreement among economists as to the causes of the business cycle. Recessions and unemployment were the result of unplanned mismatches in the structure of production (i.e., the type, location, and labor composition of output) relative to the structure of demand. This is known as the **Classical theory of the business cycle**. It is the most lucid explanation for why recessions occur, which makes you wonder why it hasn't been taught in university classrooms for the past seven decades. I myself hadn't encountered it in any form until I eavesdropped on Edward's lecture.

Prior to Adam Smith's writings, economic slowdowns were generally attributed to a scarcity of money and/or a general overproduction of goods. Smith had exploded the first myth in *The Wealth of Nations*. (Remember, producing more money only results in higher prices, not more production.) Jean-Baptiste Say developed his "Law" as a means of repudiating the "overproduction" fallacy. There could never be excessive production of all goods, Say claimed, only of particular goods.

Although Say didn't write extensively about the business cycle, Say's Law provided the foundation by which later economists understood it. As economies developed, production became increasingly specialized. Greater division of labor (and capital) enabled quantum leaps in productivity. Consequently, standards of living dramatically improved. People were able to consume more goods simply because they were producing more of them.

However, the division of labor and capital that Adam Smith heralded as the great driver of economic productivity had an unfortunate downside. In a developed economy, people do not consume most of their own production but rely extensively on trade. The welfare of individual businesses and workers depends heavily on their ability to find willing buyers for the goods which they produce. Therefore, each economic actor must forecast what sort of goods that others will desire for months (or even years) before he actually produces it.

For example, a woman who attends medical school and studies oncology is making a prediction that chemotherapy will be needed after she finishes her residency. Effectively, she is wagering that cancer will not be cured until many years after she begins to practice medicine. Of course, if a bona fide cure for cancer is discovered, she will find that the demand for her services will quickly evaporate.

Now imagine how the doctor's spending habits will change when the market no longer has a need for her specialty. Because she is no longer producing a valuable good, she will lose her ability to purchase the goods and services of others. The medical service that she had been supplying may have constituted a demand for a luxury automobile. If the doctor can no longer sell her services, the car dealer will soon find his own sales declining. As the car dealer sells fewer automobiles, the demand for steel and rubber will decline in turn.

The principle here is simple, yet profound: if one person fails to produce a desired good, she loses the capacity to purchase someone else's production. That is, *one person's supply constitutes another person's demand.* If one set of producers cannot buy, then another set cannot sell. So a disruption of supply in one market affects the supply in another market, and so on. Economically speaking, John Donne was absolutely right in stating that "no man is an island."

As the doctor's situation illustrates, production miscalculations are quickly transmitted from one individual or business to another. Because one person's production is another's consumption, a reduction of output in one industry reverberates throughout other sectors of the economy in a chain reaction. Declining supply in one sector reduces the demand for products in other sectors.

Production miscalculations can occur as the result of a sudden "disruptive" technological breakthrough, as in the case of the hypothetical cancer cure. But in most cases, the errors usually occur as a result of the pride/credit cycle. Rising asset prices cause too much capital and labor to be allocated to a "hot" industry (such as the housing market in recent years). *The greater the misallocation of capital and the more leverage employed, the greater the adverse repercussions in the broad economy.*

While *relative* overproduction of undesirable (or unprofitable) goods may temporarily occur, a *general* overproduction of goods is not possible. Economic downturns do not occur because an economy has produced too much of everything. Resources become idle only because they have been producing *certain* goods that are no longer in demand.

A general "demand failure" is never the cause of recession, because supply is always the basis for demand. The problem of recession is that supply exceeds demand in particular segments of the economy. Companies that fail to supply the correct type of goods, at market-clearing prices, will be left with unsold inventories or unused labor. Consequently, the "unused" laborers soon receive layoff notices.

It's easy to deride the market as a callous, faceless institution that cares only about profit and nothing for an individual's job security. But that attitude betrays a misunderstanding about what the market really is. "The market" is really just another name for "the people," and it is the most purely democratic institution on earth. You can think of each dollar as a vote. The number of votes you receive is a function of how much worthwhile stuff you produce for other voters. If you are making a product that is in high demand, but is in short supply, you will garner a lot of votes in the form of dollars.

By equating "the market" with "the people," recessions can be understood as a referendum on the economy. The question being decided is how society will allocate its resources. The electorate casts its votes for businesses that generate value in the form of high-quality products and/or competitive prices. Those companies that produce undesirable products or whose sales cannot cover their production costs are voted out of office.

Some nineteenth-century economists believed that recessions and unemployment resulted from overproduction of all goods. Recessions, they claimed, resulted from being too productive! Of course, this notion is a total canard. Think about it: if recessions were caused by making too much of everything, then society would be in a constant state of depression and our standards of living would not have improved exponentially over the past two centuries. Say's *Treatise* provides the key to surmounting recession and unemployment: "when a nation has too large a quantity of one particular type of product, the means of disposing of them is to create goods of another variety" (p. 155). *The appropriate response to recession isn't to quit producing; it is simply to begin producing different items.* Economic recovery arrives as businesses rationalize their costs, re-price existing products, and offer new products that are in demand.

Recessions, while uncomfortable for those adversely affected, are a necessary adjustment process. Capital and labor are redeployed from industries where there is too little demand into areas where there will be demand (at cost-covering prices) for the goods produced. In the oncologist's case, she might find gainful employment by working in another branch of medicine (or, in a worst-case scenario, by waiting tables at a twenty-four-hour dining establishment).

Economies consist of millions of products and countless types of labor. Some of these products will be demanded at certain prices, others will not. It is just that simple. The key to maintaining output and employment at high levels is to produce goods and services in correct proportions to each other. If these ratios of various types of production are correct, then all products will be sold at prices that cover their costs of production.

Recessions force companies to use their resources—namely, labor and capital—more efficiently. As these resources are reallocated to the changes in market demand, output increases and employment conditions alleviate. However, if potential workers are not offering the types of skills desired by employers, or if their wage and salary requirements are excessive, they will remain unemployed. Naturally, no one wants to admit that the labor skills they are offering are 1) undesirable or 2) priced too high. But if we truly believe Say and the Classical economists, then the onus lies with the unemployed man to restructure his production, just as Edward asserted.

Forty years ago, financial services comprised only 3% of total U.S. output. By 2007, the sector mushroomed to 7.5% of the nation's economy. Instead of building bridges or designing more fuel-efficient vehicles, mathematicians and engineers had been recruited to Wall Street, where they designed financial schemes to put people in homes that they simply couldn't afford. The reckoning of an untenable situation was at hand. The economy was enduring a massive restructuring of its production, and the adjustment process had robbed millions of other Americans of their livelihood. The type and cost of production that they had been supplying was considerably mismatched with the demand for that same output.

As far as my own job loss was concerned, the market clearly no longer demanded another PR man to furnish an optimistic assessment of the mortgage market. Accordingly, if I wanted to retain some capacity to consume, I was forced to produce a commodity for which a healthy market still remained: namely, cheap, quality breakfast food. Undoubtedly, the shift had been for the greater good of society.

A dramatic change in the field of your production can be a traumatic thing. When you have been engaged in one line of work for the best part of a decade, it's difficult to imagine yourself doing anything else. I tried to think of my new job as a career "restructuring," but after a few weeks, the word began to sound awfully euphemistic. After all, a root canal "restructures" your tooth. But for both recessions and root canals, the long-run benefits are well worth the temporary discomfort involved. Regrettably, economists have forgotten this truth for the past seven decades.

The primary responsibility of economists is to forecast and interpret recessions. They are particularly bad at it. To accurately prognosticate a nation's output involves a solid understanding of each of its industries and the dynamic interaction between each of them. Considering these innumerable idiosyncrasies across thousands of industries and millions of firms, you begin to understand why projecting the precise path of the economy is truly a fool's errand.

To create a patina of sophistication to hide their theoretical shortcomings, modern economists employ intricate mathematical models and fancy graphs to represent the aggregate economy. Lost in the math and the charts, however, is an appreciation for the diversity of goods and services produced, as well as their individual prices. Economists pay minor lip service to this "aggregation problem," and then proceed with their modeling just as though it never existed.

Below is a graphic representation of the broad economy taught in all macroeconomic textbooks. "Total output" represents the myriad goods and services in an economy which sell at a weighted-average "price level." Early in the term, college economic students are taught how to draw this "X," then spend the rest of their semester being inundated with bogus theories about business cycle fluctuations resulting from the movements of these two lines. The graph is a very convenient way to look at the world. Unfortunately, it wholly ignores all of the subtle but important nuances of economic reality—namely, the structure of production.

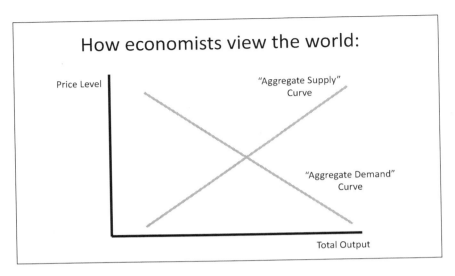

In this model, there is no diversity of industries, products, or labor. As far as the graph is concerned, a waffle and a BMW are the same product, sold at the same price. What a tremendously accurate depiction of the way things really work.

In the world of the graph, the movements of the aggregate supply and the aggregate demand curves are considered independently of each other. Regrettably, most contemporary economists have long since forgotten that economic demand is, has always been, and will always be determined by supply. Were they to reconsider the graph's value in the context of Say's Law, they would realize that only a fool would take it seriously.

Because most economists value elegant mathematics more than common sense, Say's Law and the Classical theory of the business cycle have been completely omitted from contemporary textbooks. My first exposure to these principles came from Edward, who had no formal training in economics. It's amazing how perceptive a man can really be when his mind hasn't been compromised by college professors. Then again, nobody understands the "no free lunch" principle of Say's Law better than the man who has just cooked three chicken sandwiches.

*Chapter 5*

# CRIME AND PUNISHMENT

*"No man for debt shall go to jail from
Garryowen in glory."*
**IRISH DRINKING SONG**

In celebration of its fiftieth anniversary in 2010, Papa's Chicken & Waffles commissioned its own version of Monopoly. "PAPA-OPOLY" was produced exclusively for company employees and has become a collector's item amongst die-hard fans of the restaurant. Game pieces include eggs in a skillet, cheeseburger, T-bone, pie slice, coffee mug, and iced tea. Waffle slices and company stores substitute for houses and hotels. A Papa's waiter adorns the one-dollar bill. Higher denominations feature company executives.

Store locations serve as property spaces. In lieu of Pennsylvania, Reading, B&O, and Short Line railroads are four company luminaries appearing in caricature, each accompanied by an eponymous menu item. The "Go" and "Free Parking" corner spaces have been renamed "Grand Opening" and "Free Refills," respectively. The other two corner spaces of PAPA-OPOLY are marked "Company Headquarters" and "Go to Company HQ."

While I appreciate the mandate to Waffle-ize the board, the game designers might have left the original "JAIL" and "Go to Jail" designations in place. At my store, every male employee except the manager and yours truly had spent time in a state or federal correctional facility.

My colleagues spoke of their prison time in the same manner that middle-aged suburbanites might reminisce about their high school football injuries. Tommy lifted his shirt to display two bullet wounds which he had obtained in separate gunfights, one of which had led to a conviction. As a rejoinder, Edward brandished a knife wound on his forearm and related an account of the prison yard brawl wherein he obtained it. After exhibiting their battle scars, they each went on to describe those that they had inflicted on their adversaries.

I briefly considered relating the time that I had incurred a severe bruise while making a game-winning save as the lacrosse goalie of my prep school team, but soon thought better of it. However dramatic my adversity may have seemed during high school, it paled in comparison to being kissed by a .38 slug.

Where ex-jocks might boast of passionate escapades with cheerleaders, Edward related several accounts of romancing female prison guards. After months of speculation as to why a female would seek employment at a male correctional facility, he had received an epiphany. No woman, he realized, would ever pursue that vocation unless she was absolutely desperate for attention. The romantic liaisons weren't exactly the stuff of Walt Disney films. Snow White doesn't share her first kiss with Prince Charming when she confronts him about the contraband she's just discovered in his foot locker.

Edward had briefly labored as a custodian and in the prison laundry before finally obtaining a kitchen job. He became head chef in short order, overseeing six other cooks as they served breakfast and lunch to eleven-hundred inmates. (And, yes, they did serve vast quantities of grits.) The job only paid a dollar for a day's labor, but Edward soon discovered a way to augment his income by fermenting orange and tomato juice mixes in the kitchen heating ducts. Within twenty-four hours, he could manufacture a four-ounce drink that would set even the largest convict with three sheets firmly to the wind.

While I was quite certain that Edward's distillery was in violation of prison rules, I couldn't help but admire his entrepreneurial spirit. Most of his beverage sales were dollar-denominated, but transactions were also frequently paid for in cigarettes, which were broadly accepted as currency. Although Edward wasn't in the habit of extending any form of credit, many inmates frequently loaned cigarettes to each other. In the penitentiary, however, tardy debt repayments were not met with the same level of clemency that they might have been on the outside.

Lenders taught borrowers a visceral lesson in the importance of honoring their debts by sabotaging a cigarette with a small ball of aluminum foil stuffed with shaved match heads. Halfway through such a custom-manufactured Newport, the deadbeat debtor's cigarette would explode in flames to tremendous comedic effect. The gag didn't always precipitate swift debt repayment, but at least the creditor could get a measure of justice.

Of course, Edward explained, this trick could be played on relatives as well as derelict borrowers. He had recently offered a modified cigarette to his sister-in-law, whose hair almost caught on fire as a result. Edward had nearly fallen off his chair convulsing in laughter; she found the prank considerably less amusing than he did.

"Some people just can't appreciate a practical joke," I offered.

"Well, that's women for you," Edward said.

In prison, Edward had taken a variety of vocational training courses that had enabled him to perform a wide array of tasks subsequent to his parole. Over the past four years, he had worked in construction, painted houses, and done a number of odd jobs which allowed him to showcase his new skills in plumbing and small-engine repair. When money became really tight, he took his pool cue to the local billiard hall and earned a few dollars playing eight ball. I don't know whether his wide array of talents would technically classify him as a "Renaissance Man," but he certainly had an unimpeachable work ethic.

Incidentally, Edward loathed the idea of anyone going on the dole, although not for reasons common to middle- and upper-class Americans. While most people have an aversion to public welfare schemes on the grounds that government redistribution of wealth is tantamount to theft by the state, Edward's justification was much more primal. In his mind, any man who accepted a handout despite being able to find work (albeit not in the field of his choice) was compromising his masculinity. Any self-respecting man, he asserted, should at least have the initiative to take on some part-time work as a gigolo. I can't (or rather, shouldn't) weigh in on whether he had done so himself.

$ $ $ $ $

If Edward epitomized the criminal justice system's ability to transform a shiftless man into a hard-working one, the store also had a case study in recidivism. On the weeknights when I wasn't working with Edward, I was paired with a thirty-five-year-old parolee named Maurice. While deviousness, infidelity, and penchant for larceny are not uncommon traits, very few people exhibit all of them. Maurice did. In spades.

Taken individually, each of these attributes was obnoxious. But aggregated behind an unapologetic Cheshire cat grin, Maurice's personality defects proved unexpectedly entertaining. He was the man you loved to hate—a ghetto version of J.R. Ewing.

In lieu of the double-breasted suits worn by Larry Hagman, Maurice sported flannel shirts and low-riding blue jeans that exposed six inches of his plaid boxer shorts. J.R. emerged from his Mercedes wearing a ten-gallon hat; Maurice rolled up to Papa's in a Cadillac Escalade and adorned himself with a black do-rag.

Maurice's favorite scam was giving free T-bone and sirloin steaks to his friends, who then paid a token amount of hush money to keep the servers quiet about the inventory theft. I regret to admit my inadvertent complicity in one of these transactions. I should have known that a game was afoot when Maurice magnanimously volunteered to wait on their table for me, but I had accepted his offer. Since I had seen him purloin my gratuities on two occasions, I figured that at least this time he would have to work for the money that he would have otherwise stolen from me.

When he wasn't engaging in unethical business practices or planning a tryst on his cell phone, Maurice spent his discretionary time sleeping in booths whenever the store was vacant. I didn't go out of my way to banter with him, but sometimes the dialogue found its way to me.

"People around here have been talking about you," he said. "They say you was a banker or something."

"Well, the people have their facts wrong," I said. "I used to write condolence letters to institutional investors."

"I thought that you only need to write condolence letters when somebody dies," he said.

"Well, they have to be written when money dies, too."

Maurice scratched his head. "So did you make good money writing the letters?"

"I did okay. But if I'd really wanted to get rich in finance, I would have blown up a bank," I said coolly.

"No kiddin'. I had a cousin that used to rob banks, but he just used a pistol. So if you wanted to blow one up, would you use dynamite or a grenade launcher?"

Evidently, Maurice was unfamiliar with this particular figure of speech.

"Blowing up a bank is entirely different from robbing one."

"So what's the point of dynamiting the vault then?"

"Look," I said in the most casual tone I could muster, "If you want to blow up a bank, you need to put on an expensive suit and convince the bank officers to let you invest their money. Then you take that money and use it to buy a lot of bonds. After those bond prices tank, the bank is left with no capital, causing it to collapse. Afterwards, the U.S. Treasury

Department, and in some cases a foreign government, has to rebuild it. That's what it means to blow up a bank."

"But you never blew one up yourself?"

While it was true that a number of Japanese bank clients had taken write-downs on mortgage-backed bonds that we had purchased on their behalf, none of them had actually folded as a consequence. Nonetheless, I couldn't help but wince as I read their quarterly earnings announcements; the results were still bad enough that I had to seriously wonder if they had caused at least one incident of boardroom seppuku.

"No," I confessed. "But I'm only thirty-two. I've got a lot of time to get back in the game," I said with a smirk.

Maurice eyed me as he stroked his goatee. After a few seconds of contemplation, he finally broke his silence.

"You're one bad mofo," he said, offering me a fist bump.

"True dat," I replied, punching his knuckles.

He headed back to the grill, shaking his head and repeating the phrase "blowing up banks." The large grin on his face and zealous tone in his voice led me to believe that he wished he had conceived the scheme himself. After all, bank demolition was undoubtedly more lucrative than accepting cash kickbacks in exchange for furnishing your buddies with free sirloin dinners.

I smiled. With some measured bravado, I had firmly established my street cred.

$ $ $ $

There are, broadly speaking, two ways to get rich in business: 1) start your own small business and expand it; or 2) work for a corporation and ascend the ladder over the course of your career. The first course necessitates a lot of creativity, managerial skills, long hours, and tenacity. The corporate route primarily requires the ability to politick, endure endless conference meetings with a straight face, write needless memoranda, and, most importantly, survive repeated rounds of musical chairs when the layoffs arrive.

But there's yet another route to a pot of gold without the nuisance of attending medical school. It requires little intelligence, formal education or political acumen. And here's the best part: its potential for generating wealth is virtually unlimited.

The model is simple: a speculator borrows a lot of money, uses the cash to purchase real estate, maintains or makes improvements to his lot, and waits for the value of the property to appreciate. If the bet pays off, the speculator keeps the profits. If the bet sours, any losses exceeding his investment cost are transferred to a third party.

Real estate is the most common type of capital asset financed by the banking system. In most cases, the borrower puts down a fraction of the purchase price of the land and buildings—typically, between 10% and 25% of the property's value. The remainder is furnished by the bank.

In the example below, an investor purchases a small shopping center for $10 million. He invests $2 million of his own capital and borrows the remaining $8 million. A $10 million capital asset—the shopping center—supports $10 million in financial assets, which represent claims on that property. (Remember, stocks, bonds, and bank loans are just stakes in capital assets.)

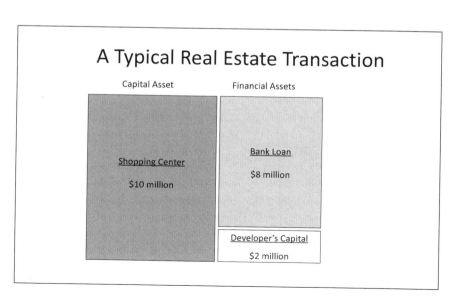

## A Typical Real Estate Transaction

Capital Asset      Financial Assets

Shopping Center

$10 million

Bank Loan

$8 million

Developer's Capital

$2 million

Here's where the story gets interesting. Not only has the developer borrowed money to finance the building purchase, but the bank has also borrowed money to finance its lending.

While the real estate speculator has a legal obligation to repay his debt to the bank, the bank has a concurrent legal obligation to repay its depositors. The bank is lending its money on a principal basis, i.e., on its own behalf. It is *not* an agent investing the money on behalf of its depositors. This point cannot be overemphasized.

On average, banks borrow roughly ninety cents of every dollar that they lend. In this case, the bank borrows $7.2 million from its depositors (90% x $8 million). These borrowings could be in the form of banknotes, checking accounts, or savings accounts. Each of these accounts is also a type of financial asset, and all of them constitute the money supply.

The developer financed a $10 million capital asset (the shopping center) with $8 million in bank debt. But the bank has financed the $8 million loan with $7.2 million of financial assets. Because a chain of debts has been created, a $10 million capital asset is now supporting $15.2 million dollars in total debt.

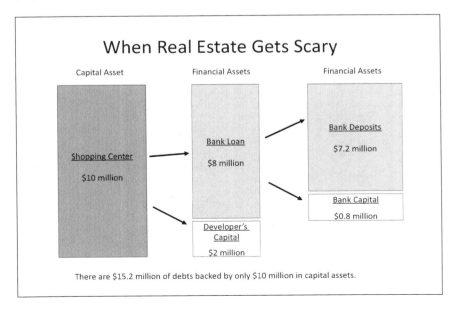

## When Real Estate Gets Scary

Capital Asset     Financial Assets     Financial Assets

Shopping Center
$10 million

Bank Loan
$8 million

Developer's Capital
$2 million

Bank Deposits
$7.2 million

Bank Capital
$0.8 million

There are $15.2 million of debts backed by only $10 million in capital assets.

If the developer can earn sufficient rental income from the shopping center to service his debts, he stands to earn a nice rate of return on his $2 million investment, particularly if the property climbs in price. If he sells the property for $13 million, he would earn a 150% rate of return ($3 million gain divided by his $2 million in capital). But regardless of how much the property's value rises, the bank will not see an extra nickel of interest income, and neither will the bank depositors. Despite financing only 20% of the investment's total cost, the developer retains all of the upside benefit.

During the expansion phase of the credit cycle, real estate buyers are incentivized to employ as much leverage as possible. In the example above, a buyer that puts down only $1 million and subsequently sells the property for $13 million will earn a 300% return on his capital.

*During asset booms, holders of both capital assets (e.g., real estate buyers) and financial assets (e.g., banks) will be strongly tempted to increase their returns by maximizing their leverage. As long as the boom continues, both levered real asset buyers and levered financial asset buyers will reap large economic rewards.*

As the downturn in the business cycle unfolds, our shopping center begins to lose tenants. (Some of them may have gone out of business; others may have found cheaper rent elsewhere due to recent overbuilding.) The diminished rent fails to provide adequate cash flow to service the bank loan. The bank forecloses on the property and sells it at auction. As long as the bank can dispose of the shopping center at a price above $8 million, its capital will not be threatened. If the bank sells at any level below $8 million, however, the losses begin to drain its capital.

In the down phase of a normal credit cycle, banks slow their lending and/or call in loans in an effort to replenish their capital. Because of bankers' rising cash preference (i.e., liquidity preference), depositor savings are no longer quickly recycled into investment, and economic uncertainty rises. In turn, businesses and consumers also become more judicious in their spending decisions, increasing their cash preference. As more cash sits idle in bank vaults and consumer pockets, money travels through the economy at a slower pace of circulation, or velocity.

The primary effect of the declining velocity is to place downward pressure on capital asset prices. Additionally, some consumer prices may experience moderate price declines as people scale back on discretionary purchases ($MV\downarrow = P\downarrow Y$). But in general, the prices of consumer sundries will not fall off a cliff. Even in a recession, most people aren't willing to hoard their cash to the point where it means foregoing purchases of toilet paper (although there may be noteworthy exceptions in some parts of West Virginia).

Here's where the story can get really ugly. As depositors learn that a large number of their bank's loans have started to go bad, they begin to get nervous. They know that as the bank's capital cushion is eroded by the loan losses, their deposits become increasingly unsafe. Accordingly, they begin to withdraw their money en masse in a **bank run.** Because most of the bank's assets consist of loans (rather than cash), it is unable to satisfy all of the redemption requests. The bank is now simultaneously experiencing acute severe credit problems (from the defaulting loans) and liquidity problems (as depositors redeem their checking and savings accounts for cash). In many cases, the contagion of fear spreads as a run on one bank sparks a run on several others.

There is something very unique and strange about money. It is created gradually in commercial banks through the fractional reserving process but can be rapidly destroyed through an erosion of confidence. During bank runs, bank liabilities cease to function as money. Businesses quit honoring checks written against the accounts of less reputable banks. Depositors redeem their accounts for cash, and the fractional reserving process is thrown into reverse, causing the money supply to shrink.

Just as blood transmits the output from one organ to another, so money enables the exchange of economic production. When the body hemorrhages large amounts of blood, the blood pressure drops, and organs begin to shut down. The economy exhibits similar effects when the public severs the "monetary arteries" in bank runs. When money is being destroyed, it becomes nearly impossible to exchange real production because money itself becomes the primary commodity in demand. Economic actors have little incentive to produce because they know that their potential customers will be hoarding their cash rather than exchanging it for production.

As a consequence of the "blood loss," the real economy shrinks rapidly in a pernicious downward spiral known as **debt deflation.** ($M\downarrow V\downarrow = P\downarrow Y\downarrow$)

As both the money supply and the real economy shrink, wages and consumer prices begin to drop precipitously. The decline in consumer prices puts another round of pressure on asset prices. For example, if bread prices keep falling due to money destruction, then the value of the bakery (the capital asset which produces the bread) must soon follow. So a drop in the money supply lowers the prices of capital assets.

*supports*
Money  >  Capital asset prices

Capital assets only have value to the extent that they represent a claim on money (in the form of rent or profits from production). But remember, in a fractional reserve banking system, the money supply is almost entirely supported by bank loans. And bank loans, in turn, are supported by capital asset prices.

*support*     *which support*     *which supports*
Capital asset prices > Bank loans > Money supply > Capital asset prices

Money is the link which forges the chain of debts into a triangle of interdependent liabilities.Once a triangle is constructed, the angles between the sides are permanently fixed, making it the strongest geometric shape. Unlike a rectangle, whose sides will bend or totally collapse under stress, the triangle responds to pressure by either

## The triangle is the strongest shape....

The
Economy

Money Supply

Capital Asset Prices

Bank Loans

### But each of the sides must be firm!

contracting or expanding. Its resiliency makes the triangle indispensable in architectural applications when strong supports are needed—e.g., bridge trusses. Of course, these benefits are entirely contingent on the resiliency of each of the triangle's sides. If one of them is fragile, the weakness spreads, splintering the shape into pieces. So it is with the economy: the money supply, asset prices, and bank lending must all be sound, or the entire system can collapse.

The commercial banking system creates two layers of debt behind one capital asset. During periods of asset inflation, this arrangement enables bankers and speculators to become fantastically wealthy through the magic of leverage.

During the reckoning of debt deflation, however, the correction in asset prices compromises the entire economy as the medium of exchange is destroyed.

*Here, then, is capitalism's dirty little secret: Creating multiple layers of debt enables immense private profits, while creating the potential for large losses that are socialized throughout the entire economic system. In an immoral arrangement, the sins of a minority are involuntarily borne by the masses.*

Adam Smith is not pleased.

$ $ $ $ $

Just as much as nationalism or religious zeal, money has been a primary driver of history. And yet, monetary events get tragically short shrift in history curriculums. I suspect that historians deemphasize the role of banking and money in their analyses primarily because they don't understand how it actually works (putting them in the same league as most economists).

The United States suffered through numerous bouts of debt deflation during the nineteenth century. These episodes are generally referred to as financial "panics" or "depressions." The labels are apt: if you wake up one day to find your entire life savings destroyed when your bank collapses, the natural reaction is indeed panic and depression.

Each of the "panics"—1819, 1837, 1857, 1873, and 1893—had the hallmarks of any credit cycle: prosperity and aggressive lending practices followed by souring loans and bank runs. I find the first two incidents particularly intriguing, because they are both linked to America's seventh President.

In late 1818, the U.S. Government was obligated to deliver $4 million in either gold or silver to European investors in payment of debts incurred for the Louisiana Purchase fifteen years before. The Second Bank of the United States, a precursor to our modern Federal Reserve, was required to make this payment on the government's behalf. Effectively, the United States Treasury needed to withdraw its money (i.e., gold) from the bank in order to repay its debts to the European creditors.

In order to meet this obligation, the bank was forced to demand repayment (in the form of gold) of loans that it previously made to commercial banks. In turn, the commercial banks had to demand repayment of loans which they had extended. As the Second

Bank of the United States called in its loans, a shockwave went throughout the entire economy. The flow of gold went as follows:

U.S. commercial bank customers > U.S. commercial banks > Bank of the United States > U.S. Gov't > European lenders

The ensuing "Panic of 1819" caused a severe contraction in bank credit. As the banks erased their liabilities (banknotes & deposits), money was destroyed, and prices fell. This was a tolerable situation if you held most of your wealth in the form of gold or you were a European who owned U.S. Treasury bonds. It was a bad situation if you had borrowed money from a commercial bank and had to pay it back in a hurry. Unfortunately, Andrew Jackson was one of those borrowers. Hard-pressed to repay his real estate debts during this period, Jackson developed a lifelong hostility to all fractional-reserve banks.

General Jackson, wildly popular for killing hundreds of British soldiers during the War of 1812 (and thousands of American Indians in subsequent years), was elected President of the United States in 1828. Jackson spent most of his first term coercing Indians into relocating west of the Mississippi River. He was also successful in coercing South Carolina to accept a punitive tariff by threatening to close its ports. Jackson's only political failure was one he couldn't settle at the point of a gun: despite his cajoling, the wives of his cabinet members refused to socialize with each other.

In 1832, Jackson was elected for a second Presidential term. Having subdued the British, the Indians, and the South Carolinians, but still unable to resolve the "Petticoat Affair," Jackson opted for another target. He decided to settle an old score with the Second Bank of the United States. His primary opponent was the president of the bank, Nicholas Biddle.

A Philadelphia native, Biddle was an intellectual prodigy. He graduated from Princeton University at age 15 as the class valedictorian.

A trained attorney, he spoke fluent French and prepared the majority of the report for the Lewis and Clark expedition. In the Pennsylvania legislature, he had campaigned heavily for public education. It's safe to describe Biddle as a "Renaissance Man." It's also safe to say that his bank never had any real chance of survival once Jackson trained his guns on it.

In early 1833, Jackson decided to withdraw all of the federal Treasury's deposits from the bank. Knowing that economic chaos would surely result, Treasury Secretary Louis McLane demurred. Jackson replaced McLane, but his successor also refused to make the move. Finally, a third appointee, Roger B. Taney, complied with the President's request. Having lost its largest depositor, the Bank of the United States was forced to call in its loans in order to accommodate the Treasury's demand for gold and silver specie. The resulting credit contraction threw the country into a recession.

The U.S. Senate censured Jackson on March 28, 1834, for his action in removing the deposits from the bank. The President defended his decision on the grounds that the national banking system was unconstitutional. He ascribed the economic malaise to the actions of Biddle, who he believed was "out to get him." Not everyone agreed with this explanation for the recession, which was more or less analogous to shooting a houseguest and then blaming him for bleeding all over your living room carpet.

The following January, an unemployed housepainter named Richard Lawrence attempted to shoot the President as he emerged from the Capitol Building. Both of the would-be assassin's pistols misfired, and Jackson promptly began bludgeoning the assailant with his cane. After being apprehended, Lawrence explained that after the President's death, "money would be more plenty"—meaning that credit conditions would ease absent Jackson's meddling with the Bank of the United States. Lawrence's trenchant economic analysis was spot on. Unfortunately, his credibility was summarily compromised when he claimed to be Richard the Third, an English king who had died three-and-a-half centuries before. The paint fumes, it seemed, had gotten the best of him.

Lawrence needed only to wait a few more months to see the re-expansion of lending. After the Treasury withdrew its gold and silver specie from the national bank, the money was deposited into a number of state-chartered banks managed by Jackson's political supporters. The "pet banks" wasted no time in issuing massive amounts of banknotes against their new gold and silver reserves. Much of the new bank credit was lent to speculators for the purchase of public lands, many of which Jackson had appropriated from the Indians.

The sale of public lands increased five times between 1834 and 1836, as a large portion of speculators purchased land from the government with paper money issued by the pet banks. Ironically, Jackson, who hated fractional-reserve banking, had provided the means of encouraging its widespread abuse.

*owed money to*    *who owed gold and silver to*

Speculators   >   Banks   >   Bank depositors

Unnerved by widespread reckless lending practices, Jackson decided to again clean house. On July 11, 1836, he ordered his Treasury Secretary (his fifth) to issue the "Specie Circular." The mandate declared that beginning in mid-August, the federal government would refuse to accept anything but gold and silver specie in payment for sale of public lands. Effectively, the federal government was declaring that it would no longer recognize private banknotes as money.

You can imagine what happened next. Following the government's lead, speculators began to redeem their banknotes for gold and silver. The banks called in their loans in a desperate scramble to meet a wave of depositor withdrawals. Capital asset values plummeted, bank runs ensued, and consumer prices collapsed as the money supply was destroyed. By the time the smoke cleared, over a third of the nation's banks had failed. A five-year depression—surpassed in severity only by the 1930s Great Depression—soon followed.

The depression had only begun to unfold when Jackson left office in March of 1837. In his farewell address, he railed against "indiscreet extensions of credit" which "engender a spirit of speculation injurious to the habits and character of the people." He lamented the "wild spirit of speculation in the public lands," noting that speculators tended to "withdraw their attention from the sober pursuits of honest industry."

Curiously, Old Hickory neglected to mention that much of the "indiscreet extensions of credit" were made by banks which Jackson had provided with gold reserves only a few years before. Another omission: Jackson had devoted much of the past eight years to confiscating lands from the Indians—the same lands, in many cases, favored by the speculators that he inveighed upon.

Asked what his most important accomplishment had been, Jackson replied, "I killed the bank." His two regrets? "I didn't shoot Henry Clay, and I didn't hang John C. Calhoun" (the Speaker of the House and Jackson's Vice President, respectively). To be fair, Jackson had dueled at least thirteen times in his life, so from his perspective, shooting someone was just another day at the office.

In recognition of his unmatched prowess at killing British, Indians, and the U.S. economy, the U.S. Treasury placed Andrew Jackson's portrait on the twenty-dollar bill in 1928. The Federal Reserve banknote was redeemable in gold or silver at the bearer's discretion. By 1971, the note was not redeemable for either. It was primarily backed by federal debt, which Jackson had fought so hard to eradicate. The man who despised fractional reserving and central banks now had his mug on a paper note issued by a central bank. What goes around really does come around.

[An interesting aside: Jackson's triggerman at the Treasury, Roger B. Taney, played an instrumental role in fomenting another financial crisis twenty years later. As chief justice of the U.S. Supreme Court, he delivered the majority opinion in the 1857 case of *Dred Scott v.*

*Sandford.* The ruling threatened to open up all western territories to slavery, causing the bonds of east-west running railroads to plummet in value. Many of those railroad bonds were held by large New York banks. Depositors became nervous and bank runs ensued, resulting in a financial collapse known as the Panic of 1857. Incidentally, the case also expedited the Civil War.]

$ $ $ $ $

*The Rise & Shine Manual* outlined a specified order for attending to customer needs. No matter how busy we were, all patrons needed to be acknowledged immediately upon entering the store. Customers waiting to pay at the register were given the second highest priority. Delivering orders was third, and taking new customer orders was last. And of course, all customers were to be served in the same order in which they arrived at the restaurant.

This system is perfectly viable for four servers attending to fifty civil customers late on a Sunday morning. But going strictly by the book at 3 a.m. on a Saturday morning is downright naïve. Waiting on fifty inebriants, you adhere to the dictum, "the customer is always right," at your own peril. As far as I was concerned, the tenets of *The Rise & Shine* went out the door as soon as the local bars made their last call.

The company manual stated that customers appreciate hearing "Welcome to Papa's!" as soon as they cross the store threshold. I had used the phrase consistently during my training on the first shift. Sure enough, customers usually waved or smiled when you greeted them. However, it's much harder to deliver the salutation with a straight face when your words are drowned out by four miniskirt-clad female diners hurling epithets at each other.

There was no standard operating procedure for dealing with this sort of behavior. Should you try to stifle the girls' animus by soliciting their orders? Their truculence might be quelled with a few waffles, although the issue of who will order first might fan the flames. You could simply wait for the fur to fly and then notify the police. But if you summon law enforcement every time someone gets really out of line, your customer base will be summarily halved.

On some occasions, I flouted company policy by attending to my customers based on their physical condition rather than their order of arrival. When a girl entered the store bearing a bruised cheek from an altercation at a club, I immediately brought her a cup of ice and took her order in front of several patrons who had already been waiting more than ten minutes. While they might have been offended, none of them expressed any indignation at my decision to triage.

"I woulda taken that other gal if it hadn't been for these," the girl said, pointing to a pair of zebra-print stilettos that she had placed on the low bar counter. "They threw off my balance."

"You'll get her next time," I said cheerfully.

There were other late-night contingencies that the manual utterly failed to address. What if the servers have been so occupied with taking and distributing orders for the past three hours that there has been no time to wash silverware? When you run out of forks, do you catch up with the dishwashing, running the risk that the food on the grill might go cold? Or should you deliver the ham and cheese omelet with a spoon, as I did at 3:45 a.m. on a Sunday morning? I had hoped that my delirious chuckle would garner a little sympathy as I explained the predicament to the customer. My apology didn't win me enough sympathy to garner a tip, but under the circumstances, I was grateful enough not to have been algreened.

Four a.m. quickly became my favorite time of day. Typically, its arrival signified that the last of the barflies had entered our doors. Once they had been served, I had a full hour to devote to my side work. However mind-numbing sweeping and mopping the floor might have been, I found it a delightful reprieve from customer interaction. No tip, however large, would have been adequate compensation for those coveted moments of tranquility.

At 5 a.m. every morning, the first of the Coffee Drinkers saluted the staff and took his seat at the low bar. Clad in a flannel shirt, B.D. was in his late sixties and had recently retired from a career consisting of a series of odd jobs. He was soon joined by two affluent, albeit casually dressed businessmen, Mark and Wallace. Lawrence, the only decaf drinker of the bunch, was generally quiet, although he occasionally favored the rest of the group with anecdotes from Vietnam. The youngest man in the group was forty-five-year-old Joey, who ran a heating and air conditioning service. Anticipating their arrival, I always brewed a fresh pot of coffee at 4:55, and poured each of their individual cups by the time they opened the restaurant door. Except for B.D., all of them smoked. None of them ever ordered breakfast.

The Coffee Drinkers harassed the employees, albeit in a far more benign manner than the Repo Men. Most of their conversation was focused on local politics and sports, particularly UNC basketball. For the most part I just listened quietly, though I was occasionally called upon as an expert witness when economic subjects were introduced. While not always Sunday school appropriate, the Coffee Drinkers' banter was a welcome change of pace from the barflies' dialogues. Decorum was always maintained, and most diatribes were thankfully brief.

The only genuinely surly member of the group was Joey, whose visage evidenced at least ten more years of life mileage than he claimed to have. He was horribly finicky about the freshness of his coffee and became incredibly indignant at the smallest triviality. When Mark cited a newspaper report on the county's low level of cumulative rainfall, Joey spent the next ten minutes profanely inveighing on the matter. I was willing to forgive the college-aged barflies for this sort of boorish demeanor, but I found it repugnant coming from a man twice their age. His crassness was particularly inexcusable given that he couldn't assign blame to a high blood alcohol level.

After downing three cups of coffee, Joey habitually retreated to the men's room for a full ten minutes before finally leaving the store at

6 a.m. His timing in this endeavor was particularly uncanny. Typically, the only available time that I had to clean the restroom was immediately after he had vacated it. I was left to bask in an aroma only slightly less offensive than his disposition.

While I finished cleaning the store, Edward lit a cigarette and seated himself next to the coffee drinkers at the low bar. He usually engaged in their playful banter, but every few days he would ask if they knew of any part-time employment opportunities. As he explained it, networking was crucial to finding gainful employment if you had spent any time in prison. In the absence of someone willing to vouch for the current state of your character, you would be summarily written off as a good-for-nothing ex-con.

"Papa's Chicken & Waffles is one of the few institutions that believe in giving a man a second chance in life," Edward said. "Most other places don't want anything to do with you once they know about your past mistakes."

I could empathize with him. I had spent several weeks trying to get McDonald's to take me seriously, but I couldn't even land a face-to-face interview with the manager. Papa's, on the other hand, didn't care that I had been a white-collar guy. My total lack of experience hadn't been an impediment, either. All they cared about was whether I was doing a good job for them today. It was wonderfully egalitarian.

In Edward's theology, the worst imaginable sin was wasting one's potential. While he was grateful to be out of prison and to be earning a real wage, he still had reason to be frustrated. It wasn't just the lower wage that he had to accept; circumstances prohibited him from applying his full array of culinary skills. He simply wanted to share the scope of his talents with his customers.

Perhaps his career frustration was the reason that Edward had been riding me so much. When I had tired of serving grits, he knew that I could readily switch gears and resume the easy gig of office life. Edward, on the other hand, had few viable alternatives.

The district manager had approached Edward about pursuing the management training program. After some investigation, Edward had declined the offer. He had done the math and realized that despite any tenacity that he might bring to the job, the probability of meeting the stipulated hurdles for performance-based compensation was simply too low. After factoring in the increased aggravation of supervising temperamental employees, it was a no-brainer. For the time being, he was perfectly content to remain a senior grill officer.

After bussing the Coffee Drinkers' cups, I generally left the store around 7:15 and arrived home ten minutes later. I spent the next three hours checking email, playing Tetris, and reading *The Wall Street Journal* online before finally retiring around 11 a.m. Nearly every one of my shifts concluded with tension in my lower back. Working three of them consecutively was unbelievably physically, mentally, and emotionally taxing. It took two full days for my mind and body to fully recover.

Russian psychologist Ivan Pavlov famously demonstrated the power of behavioral conditioning by using a bell to call his dog to his food. After a few repetitions, the dog started to salivate in response to the bell, even when the food was not present. Now imagine an interesting twist on Pavlov's experiment: ring the bell, show the dog a fresh can of Alpo, then beat him with the Sunday newspaper a few seconds after he makes it to the dish. Repeat ten times. On the eleventh occurrence, note whether the "ding" induces salivation or simply causes the poor mutt to mess in his pen.

I don't think anyone has done this research, but they need not bother. I can tell you exactly what the hapless canine will do when that bell rings: he will nervously look in all directions, frozen to inaction out of fear of offending his master. I know this because that was my reaction to a very similar set of circumstances.

During my first two months on third shift, I had developed an incessant nervous feeling which I could only shake for a few hours a day. The sensation was so intense that I could barely discern normal hunger pangs when they struck. Consequently, I had lost nearly ten pounds, a considerable amount of weight for my frame. Eventually, I came to understand that the bugaboo I was dreading was simply the early morning bar crowd rush.

In this life, there are things to act, and things to be acted upon. I had to decide which camp I was going to be in. Was I condemned to spend my days as a Pavlovian dog whose behavior was solely dictated by external stimuli? Or was I a free agent with the capacity to choose my own reaction to adverse circumstances?

Several employees took the edge off of third shift by using recreational drugs or alcohol before they showed up for work. Our store hadn't mandated a drug test in several years, so there was little risk of being caught. I had initially frowned on the unprofessional behavior, but at this point I could empathize with the inclination to self-medicate. There's only so much abuse a man can take before his sanity expires. I didn't entertain the idea myself, though—I've always been averse to chemical intervention in the brain. Drugs—legal and illegal—are a poor coping mechanism for life's problems. A real man, I decided, doesn't flee from reality: he confronts it head-on with snarky remarks. The best way to survive in hell is to poke fun at the devil whenever you can.

I have always been a terrible liar when my motive is covering my sins; I simply cannot do it with a straight face. When my intent is purely sarcastic, however, I can deadpan with the best of them. I perfected this trait during my college years by making the most outlandish claims possible to female guests at fraternity parties.

A standard act was to relate gruesome personal anecdotes from my Marine Corps service during the U.S. invasion of Grenada. I'm proud to report that most of the coeds bought my story, if only because they didn't realize that the invasion transpired when I was six years old. But whatever my listener's reaction, I always felt better for having spun the yarn. When you don't take yourself too seriously, you're much less likely to be offended by anything anyone else has to say.

The first opportunity to employ my new strategy presented itself the following Thursday. Three women sat at a booth, flanked by a three-year-old boy in a high chair. After the ladies ordered, I inquired if the child was going to require any food.

"Nah, Jimmy. He's just going to share with me. Didn't your mama ever feed you off her plate when you was his age?"

"No, ma'am, I'm afraid she didn't."

"Aaaw, that's too bad. Your mama loved you, didn't she?"

Her tone of voice was irritating in and of itself, but dragging my mother into the dialogue was totally uncalled for. The gloves promptly came off.

"She loved me enough to breastfeed me until I was ten years old. That's the hallmark of *real* maternal love, you know."

"No, she didn't do that, Jimmy. You just playin' with me."

"I wish that were the case, Ma'am," I said, lowering my head. "It's so difficult to afford these frequent visits to the psychiatrist on my salary."

Later that evening, a customer insisted that we remove all traces of pork from the grill before cooking his T-bone. As he scraped the grill for the third time in an effort to satisfy the request, I suggested to Edward that we secure a rabbinical blessing before finally pronouncing it kosher. The insulted customer refused to let me wait on him any further. I excused myself to the office, where I watched him eat his steak with his bare hands through the one-way mirror.

Edward advised me to use more discretion when making editorial remarks. I reminded him that I had suggested that the rabbi only bless the grill, not circumcise the customer.

"I was just having a little fun. It seems to me that the man overreacted."

He admitted that he had been amused by my remark but abstained from smiling, given the customer's temperament.

"If you're gonna make comments like that, you better grow eyes in the back of yo' head. You never know who's got a gun in their car."

Prison life had dramatically heightened Edward's consciousness of his surroundings. He knew exactly what was transpiring in every corner of the restaurant at all times. With the exception of the bar rush hours, he could always recite the make and color of every car in the parking lot at any given moment.

"Ya see, both of us can't afford to be playin' with the customers like that," he continued. "It would be bad enough if you got shot, but at least we could still keep the sto' open when the ambulance came. On the other hand, suppose I laugh and he comes back and blasts both of us. Now we got two men down and we'd have to close the store for at least three or fo' hours. That wouldn't be acceptable to management."

"What, having two chalk outlines on the floor?"

"Well, that too. But they really hate to close the sto' on account of anything."

As far as I know, a gunshot wound on the premises is the only legitimate justification for halting service at a Papa's. If you are inclined to test this theory, may I offer one piece of advice: to ensure store closure, the victim should receive at least two slugs. Management will likely interpret a single bullet as simply being the punch line of a practical joke.

Papa's never, and I mean never, closes. Every location in the country remains open twenty-four hours a day, 365 days a year. Christmas is one of the company's highest-grossing days of the year; servers and grill officer working the yuletide shift often receive $100 tips from regular customers. And while the bond market's pace unfailingly slows during most Jewish holidays, any given Papa's can be found celebrating Passover by grilling ten pounds of bacon.

I'm quite certain that Papa's Chicken & Waffles will be the last remaining testament to Western Civilization after the rest of it has collapsed under its own weight. Say what you will about its food, servers, or ambiance, but Papa's tenacity is unimpeachable. Our restaurant hadn't been closed for so much as an hour in more than five years. You probably think I'm speaking in exaggerated terms. I'm not. The year before I began my employment, a hurricane caused a twelve-hour power outage at our store. The generator kicked in, candles were lit, and hashbrowns were cooked. At another nearby location, an inebriated customer drove his vehicle right through the wall. Distracting though the spectacle was, service was never interrupted.

Although it may have eventually culminated in a bullet wound as Edward suggested, my facetious attitude proved quite therapeutic in the interim. Within two weekends of my decision to become the Teflon Server, I was wholly impervious to all complaints during the bar rush. I matched every ounce of customer impertinence with an increased measure of sarcastic indifference. It was incredibly empowering. A middle-aged man, observing my poise (and probably the dumb grin on my face) as I tended the register amidst the early morning din, wondered at me.

"It's amazing how you do that. What's your secret?" he asked.

"What's that?"

"How do you stay so calm when all these people are yelling at you all the time?"

"It's simple," I said. "After 2 a.m. I just think of them as animals."

Recent experience had taught me that it does not pay to conduct yourself as a tuxedo-clad English butler when you are outnumbered ten to one by a group of surly inebriants. On the contrary, you must act like a farmer dressed in bibbed overalls. Your job is to slop the pigs, and there can be no question about who rules the barnyard.

The following week, my equanimity won me another compliment with a monetary reward to boot. I had been waiting on a couple at the high bar when twelve boisterous high school seniors had materialized in three booths. Two of the boys were too restless to sit anywhere and spent an hour just running back and forth between their friends' tables. I coolly explained my rules of engagement to the kids and attended to them at an unhurried pace.

After the students left, I retrieved a credit card receipt from the couple at the high bar. They had given me a forty-dollar gratuity.

"What's this for?" I asked incredulously.

"I've been a cook at an upscale restaurant for the past two years," the man said. "None of our servers could handle three tables like that without completely freaking out. You, on the other hand, were as cool as Clint Eastwood in a gunfight. Those kids weren't going to leave you a hefty tip, but you certainly deserve one."

I performed less admirably the following week as I waited on a group of four middle-school-aged kids. After ordering a hamburger and hashbrowns, one of them made an innocent request for Parmesan cheese.

"Did you see anything on our menu that would necessitate us keeping Parmesan cheese on hand?" I asked.

"I just thought it might go well on my burger."

"Well, we do keep a small supply in the commissary, but we serve it exclusively with Oysters Rockefeller. Could I interest you in a plate?"

His friends laughed at my suggestion, and the kid shrank back into his seat. I felt bad. He was just trying to spread his wings by having a late-night dinner with his buddies, and here I was taunting him. Five minutes later, I delivered his food, along with an apology for my sarcasm. Standing up for myself was one thing; striking preemptively was another.

Even when I wasn't being particularly antagonistic, my fatigue and exasperation were getting the best of me. I was becoming impatient with Spanish-speaking customers who had difficulty ordering in English. A simple request for hashbrowns from a middle-aged construction worker threw me into a rage.

"Potatoes," he said, pointing to its menu picture.

"Hashbrowns!" I corrected him in a resentful voice. "These are called *hashbrowns!*"

My indignation wasn't justified in the least. My Latino customers were unfailingly courteous. They always thanked me for the smallest effort I made on their behalf and never neglected to tip. Penalizing them for any linguistic deficiency was simply callous. A cool demeanor may have been a prerequisite for waiting on the bar crowd, but referring to my customers as livestock was probably crossing the line.

A dose of charity was clearly in order. I decided to treat my customers the way I would want to be treated, giving them the benefit of the doubt until they broke my trust. Further, I vowed to take better care of my stomach in hopes of improving my disposition. Regardless of how crowded the restaurant became, I wasn't going to let my table-waiting responsibilities preclude me from eating for more than six hours.

From then on, whenever hunger struck, I simply called in an extra side plate of hashbrowns along with the customer order. After delivering the food, I retreated to the back room with the plate and a bottle of ketchup. Thirty seconds later, I was back on the floor with renewed gusto. Hashbrowns, like Popeye's spinach, have a tremendous capacity to reinvigorate the constitution in short order.

$ $ $ $ $

Despite my resolution to choose my words more judiciously, I couldn't help but indulge in occasional moments of unrestrained candor. After I finished calling in an order for two young women and their Japanese grandmother, Debbie informed me that it was my turn to clean the store lavatories. In particular, a toilet paper roll lodged in the base of a urinal required my attention.

After receiving my instructions, I filled three glasses of orange juice and placed them in front of the women at the low bar counter.

"Here are your drinks, ladies. Now if you would excuse me for several minutes, I need to fish something out of the urinal, and then I'll bring your food right out."

In retrospect, it wasn't the most decorous exit line I could have chosen. I entered the men's room and verified the problem. Unfortunately, the store was still short of toilet wands, and I had no intention of manually removing the obstruction. I asked a colleague, Lamarr, to cover the table while I devised a solution to my problem.

I exited the store through the back room and emerged into the cool morning dawn. I stood still for a minute, reveling in the fresh air and the hum of the highway traffic, which produced an unexpectedly soothing rhythm. The sun had broken through the clouds, illuminating the forested ravine which sat between our restaurant and the interstate. The idyllic scene was marred only by a large pile of hashbrown cartons, syrup jugs, and other miscellaneous refuse in the valley below.

I ripped a three-foot branch from a nearby bush and began stripping most of its leaves. Within a few minutes, I had manufactured a passable toilet brush. After I retrieved the toilet paper roll, I gave the commode bowl a thorough scrubbing. The handcrafted brush worked surprisingly well—despite applying a considerable amount of pressure to the porcelain, only a few leaves separated from the branch. Thoroughly pleased with myself, I proudly leaned the instrument in the corner of the restroom alcove. In my estimation, it added some much-needed ornamentation.

No sooner had I begun admiring my handiwork than Lamarr confronted me about his recently departed customers.

"What's the deal with that old Japanese lady?" he asked.

"What do you mean?"

"Her granddaughters tried to leave a tip, but she yanked their hands back just as they were about to set the money down. What gives? Did you offend her or something?"

"I can't imagine I said anything offensive," I said. "Hey, what do you think of this?" I said, pointing to my brush. "It only took me five minutes to make, but it cleans the toilets really well."

"That's great," he said. "Are you sure you didn't say the wrong thing before you gave me that table?"

"I might have. Are you sure their waffles weren't too crisp?"

"There was nothing wrong with the food. I just can't believe a classy woman like that would stiff us unless the service was bad."

His face made it clear that he held me accountable for their parsimony. Undoubtedly, he would not be pleased to learn that I had announced my intention to intersperse restroom cleaning with serving their food. Just as I was about to confess, I remembered an important element of Japanese culture that I had learned during a business trip to Tokyo the previous year.

"The Japanese never pay gratuities," I said. "Not to waiters, hotel bellboys, cab drivers, anyone. If a foreigner even attempts to tip, a waiter will refuse."

"I wouldn't refuse," Lamarr said. "They're not in Japan now, they're in America."

"Yeeeaaauuuh, " I said in agreement. It was the only comment that came to mind.

$ $ $ $ $

I had another small victory the following Friday morning when Matthew, the store manager, counted the drawer at the end of the shift. As the only server working that night, I had full discretion over the cash register. Instead of coming up short, the drawer's cash balance exceeded the sales by three cents.

"I've never had a drawer come out that close," Matthew said. "You know what that means?"

"It means that I probably don't need the remedial arithmetic class that Debbie suggested I take at Community Tech."

"That's right, pal," he said.

Vindicated, I skipped to the store exit with more spring in my step than a young man in love. Nine years of post-secondary education hadn't been such a waste after all. My mirth was suddenly preempted by a shout from the office.

"Hey, Jimmy, before you leave, I need you to do the bathrooms again this morning."

"Oh . . . right," I said plaintively. I trudged back inside and began donning a pair of latex gloves.

The despondency must have been written all over my face. Ever the consummate manager, Matthew decided to provide some much-needed comfort.

"Hey, Man, it'll only take a minute."

"Yeah, it's not a big deal."

"And besides," he continued, "you can use your stick again," he said, pointing to the alcove where my toilet wand was propped up against the wall. "That makes the job a little easier, right?" He gave me a smug grin.

I had to smile. For once, I had left a private possession on Papa's premises for forty-eight hours and no one had stolen it. Providence had finally begun to smile on me.

"Indeed it does, Matthew. Indeed it does."

That was the last conversation I ever had with Matthew. The following Tuesday night, his wife showed up at the restaurant to inform him that she was moving out. Their marriage had been under tremendous strain ever since he had lost his lucrative construction job, a fact he had freely shared with most of the cooks and wait staff. After she left, Matthew fled the store in a fit of despondency. No one has heard from him since.

Edward derided the departure as consummately amateur conduct. Matthew, he argued, should have completed his shift and submitted a two-week notice. Admittedly, the exit had been unprofessional, but I felt the situation warranted more charity. There simply can't be many things in life more depressing than being dumped by your wife of six years in the back room of a Papa's Chicken & Waffles at two in the morning. Receiving a Dear John letter written on your (former) best friend's monogrammed stationary seems downright humane by comparison.

Debbie's attitude changed dramatically after she began serving as interim store manager, following Matthew's departure. Her incessant criticism was replaced with a spirit of optimism and gratitude. She thanked me for my willingness to work extra shifts and clean the store in preparation for an inspection by representatives from corporate headquarters. In a separate conversation, she lavishly praised my honesty and apologized for having intimated that any previous drawer shortages had been my fault. It was a nice change of pace to hear her applaud my character and exonerate my math skills from all previous charges.

Within forty-eight hours of commending me for my integrity, Debbie was terminated from employment at Papa's for an ethical shortcoming of her own. As assistant manager, she had the responsibility of delivering weekly cash profits to the bank every Sunday afternoon. Shortly after the bank opened one Monday morning, the district manager was advised that the money had not been deposited. She inspected the store's safe to discover that in addition to several hundred dollars in profits, the $300 petty cash fund had also disappeared.

Scuttlebutt had it that Debbie had used the money for a drug purchase. Her indiscretion had not been a premeditated act of malice, but a momentary weakness due to a tragic addiction. I felt genuinely bad for her. She had frequently complained of the struggle to pay for her daughter's college tuition and could have used the higher income resulting from the official promotion to store manager.

After Debbie's abrupt dismissal, the district manager assumed the reins of the store. Previously, I had only had brief interactions with her during shift changes when she was filling in for absent employees. A fifteen-year Papa's veteran, Sharon had a reputation as being a skilled grill officer and a tough, but fair boss. She had been gracious enough to not press charges against Debbie on the condition that the store was remunerated for the stolen cash; Debbie's mother obliged on her behalf.

Sharon was willing to accommodate vacation requests given sufficient notice but had absolutely no patience for absenteeism. The first time I called out of work, I gave her six hours notice, citing a rib that had been badly bruised during a sparring session. Sharon was not pleased but accepted my excuse and wished me an expedient recovery.

My second call-out, also a boxing-related injury, evoked less sympathy. I knew the physical requirements of this job when I had taken it, Sharon said. If I chose to jeopardize my ability to work with my avocation, then I needed to seriously reevaluate whether I really wanted to stay on as a server.

The thinly veiled threat caught me completely off guard. Although I had lost my job on two prior occasions, I had taken cold comfort in hearing that my work had been par excellence. In all of my performance reviews, I had always been lauded as a thorough and dedicated employee. For the first time in my working life, I was being threatened with termination on the grounds of negligence.

Managing restaurant employees for a decade and a half, Sharon had undoubtedly heard every imaginable excuse for truancy. I couldn't fault her for being skeptical about my claim; sustaining two severe injuries over the course of three weeks probably sounded like a stretch of the truth. Eventually, she backed down after I offered to submit X-rays and hospital paperwork for her perusal.

Sharon's chastisement was a difficult thing to bear, if only because I couldn't argue with her sentiments on personal responsibility. The minute an employee started to complain about a problem, she immediately urged him to take a proactive approach to remedying the situation, himself, and intervened only after he had exhausted all other alternatives.

Whatever else could be said about her, Sharon knew how to handle people and run a business. She had no tolerance for b.s. and accomplished tasks with a considerable economy of effort. If she gave any of her employees legitimate cause for complaint, I never heard any voiced. I often pondered how much her managerial acumen would have been compromised by attending an MBA program.

In business school, Sharon would have been taught to manage employees using information gleaned from employee personality assessments. Once the data had been translated into color-coded pie charts and bar graphs, she would have learned to convene two-hour committee meetings with fellow executives to discuss how the charts could be used to resolve personnel issues. It was a much more sophisticated approach to managing people than her archaic method of holding employees personally accountable for their actions.

Since my argument with Debbie on statistical sampling, I had only conceived of one other application of material I had learned in business school—namely, the revenue potential of shared marketing arrangements. The classic example of this strategy is promoting Disney film franchises with plastic toys included in McDonald's Happy Meals. Because school-age kids are huge consumers of both fast food and animated media, the marriage works beautifully. Similarly, I envisioned Papa's teaming with the County Board of Health in offering a discounted cervical cancer vaccine with every Winnie K Special ordered between 2 and 4 a.m.

Whereas Sharon had greeted my second boxing injury with a stern reprimand, physical injury and illness had been met with sympathy from my former supervisors—with one notable exception. While I was working for Alpha Managers, I once showed up to work with a black eye garnered from an opponent's uppercut. I thought it gave me a certain element of cachet relative to most of my colleagues. The greatest weekend adversity that they could boast of on a Monday morning was posting a double-bogey on a par three at the local country club.

My boss gently reprimanded me for my recklessness. I was a professional, he declared, and needed to act accordingly. I assured him that despite the bruise, there had been no cognitive impairment, but that wasn't the source of his concern. In less than a week, our firm would be hosting a contingent of Japanese bankers. Our clients, he explained, would not be particularly pleased to discover that one of the men responsible for supervising their portfolios spent his discretionary time receiving repeated blows to the head.

There are exceptions, of course, but generally speaking, boxing is not a white-collar pastime. There were a few white-collar guys at each of the three gyms I've trained at, but they were decidedly in the minority. Wall Street types are much more inclined to boast about their golf game than their ability to deliver a powerful overhand right. Although I enjoy golf as much as the next fellow, I don't take the game seriously on the grounds that a man's handicap is a sorry proxy for his masculinity. You can discern a lot more about a man's character by how he responds to a barrage of punches than how he reacts to a ball landing in a sand trap.

Besides me, the store had two other servers that had been amateur pugilists. Tyrell had fought several bouts in Police Athletic League events, while Mike had been a very competitive Golden Gloves fighter in his youth. Both of them hailed from New York City and had been paroled after serving time in federal prison for drug offenses.

A thirty-six-year-old of medium build, Tyrell was the only child of a very devoted mother. In his own words, he grew up to become "the stereotypical young, drug-slinging, gun-toting black man feared by suburbanites." While he didn't make excuses for his past behavior, Tyrell did lament the absence of a positive male role model during his adolescence—he had known his father only by reputation.

After working eight months on first shift as one of the store's highest-grossing salespersons, Tyrell switched to third shift in order to pursue continuing education at Community Tech. He expected to begin work as a fiber optics technician as soon as his parole was finalized. Besides being articulate and highly motivated, he always maintained an admirable degree of composure. I first became aware of the latter attribute when a young black girl, claiming (erroneously) that she had been shortchanged an egg, hurled an n-bomb at him. In a manner worthy of Atticus Finch, he coolly reproved her for using the epithet and arranged for another egg to be added to her plate.

Of anyone I worked with, Tyrell's disposition seemed the least conducive to the life of a felon. After I shared this observation with him, he explained that he had always committed crimes methodically, rather than with the reckless abandon of his peers.

"That's why I went so long without getting caught," he added.

He had dealt drugs and committed other felonies for the best part of a decade without receiving a single charge. When he was finally convicted, it was by virtue of guilt by association with the actual perpetrator. The irony of serving time on account of someone else's offense—which had been less heinous than so many of his own—compelled him to become very religious. Upon his parole, he began playing the drums for worship services at a local church.

Mike was a six-foot-three, 240-pound, jovial man who was finishing his parole at a halfway house when I first met him. He had assembled an impressive 14–1 record as an amateur boxer and served as a frequent sparring partner of another amateur named Riddick Bowe. Only weeks before he would have turned pro, Mike was arrested for cocaine trafficking and sentenced to twenty years in federal prison. Riddick Bowe turned pro and went on to become the world heavyweight champion.

Although he was clearly remorseful for the sins of his past life, Mike didn't dwell on them. Indeed, he had the most consistently upbeat attitude of anyone in the store. When he wasn't serving home run hashbrowns, he spent his discretionary time developing his nascent record label. He had only been at it for a few months, but he already had two acts signed. I had to appreciate his attitude and tenacity.

While he was serving his sentence at a Federal Correctional Institution in Fairton, NJ, Mike made the acquaintance of an incarcerated former bank executive. His company, Silverado Savings & Loan, had been the poster child for a banking debacle popularly known as the "Savings and Loan (S&L) Crisis."

In the wake of substantial deregulation in the early 1980s, many S&Ls (a type of bank that specializes in residential mortgages) had made a series of imprudent loans, particularly in commercial real estate. Over the next ten years, 745 of the S&Ls went bankrupt as the souring investments burned through their stockholders' capital. Their depositors, however, were made whole by the American taxpayer.

Since 1934, the federal government had been insuring S&L deposits through an entity known as the Federal Savings and Loan Insurance

Corporation (FSLIC). Similar to the FDIC, the FSLIC charged a fee to member banks to insure against the risk of bankruptcy. As the crisis grew, the FSLIC quickly depleted its own reserves, leaving taxpayers to make up the difference. The final price of the tab ran in excess of $120 billion, one percent of which was accounted for by Silverado. The S&L bailout substantially contributed to large federal budget deficits in the early 1990s, marring the last years of George H.W. Bush's presidency (along with an economic slowdown exacerbated by the deteriorating credit conditions).

Incidentally, then-President Bush's son, Neil, had been a Silverado director. While serving on the board, Neil Bush had neglected to notify the board that a business partner was contemplating a $3 million investment in Bush's oil exploration company at the same time that Silverado was forgiving the man $8.5 million of his debts—on the grounds that he was approaching insolvency!

As a result of this and other incidents, an S&L regulator determined that Neil Bush had engaged in numerous "breaches of his fiduciary duties involving multiple conflicts of interest." He was not indicted on criminal charges, although Bush did settle a civil suit out of court with the FDIC for $50,000. The Resolution Trust Corporation Suit (a government entity that liquidated the failed S&Ls) brought a separate suit against Bush and other Silverado officers, which was ultimately settled for $26.5 million. Not all of Silverado's officers were so fortunate. For his role in the failed institution, Mike's cellmate received ten years in federal prison.

I don't know enough about the case to say whether other people were more deserving of a conviction. What I do know is that when someone's abuse of debt inflicts $1.2 billion of costs on hapless taxpayers, it stands to reason that someone should end up doing time. What I can't figure out, however, is why Mike should have served twice as many years for distributing drugs. The social costs of illicit drug abuse are high, but the social costs of debt abuse are downright astronomical.

Drugs, per se, are not intrinsically evil. Nearly every drug has a legitimate medical usage. Opium derivatives like morphine are essential to alleviating extreme pain; cocaine is used as a topical anesthetic in nasal surgeries. However, both of the aforementioned substances are ripe for misuse, and it's probably fair to assume that most of Mike's customers were not outpatient surgical centers.

Everyone recognizes that drug abuse generates social costs to innocent victims. In addition to adverse health effects on the user, drug abuse weighs on families, workplaces, and communities. Fathers neglect their children, employees become lethargic and dishonest, and theft and violent crime escalate as a consequence.

As a nurse, my wife has administered drugs to the relief of many suffering patients. Conversely, she has also attended to countless victims of substance abuse. As she has explained to me, drugs are only appropriately employed if three conditions are met:

- They are used for the right reasons
- In appropriate dosages
- Administered by a responsible professional

Just as doctors and nurses are charged with the prudent administration of drugs, financiers are charged to lend carefully. In its proper usage, debt finances what Jean-Baptiste Say called "reproductive investments," which raise productivity and enable a sustainable rise in living standards. This responsible application of debt benefits business owners, employees, creditors, and consumers alike.

Two centuries ago, Say noted that "Loans are sometimes contracted not for a productive investment, but for mere barren consumption. Transactions of this kind should always awaken the suspicion of the lender" (p. 346). Of late, the timeless caveat had been ignored, to disastrous consequences.

For the ten years ended in September 2009, banks increased commercial and industrial lending to business by 34%. Loans secured by real estate, on the other hand, grew by nearly 215%. As a share of total bank assets, commercial and industrial loans declined from 17% to 10%, while the share of real estate loans increased by a comparable amount—from 26% to 34%.

While some of the real estate lending may have financed business investment, a large share of it was used to finance speculation in the residential housing market. By allocating an increasing share of capital to fund real estate purchases, bankers created a large increase in housing prices. Thanks to the easy credit and speculative fever, Americans watched their home values appreciate. Through no real effort, they had become much wealthier. In the short run.

In the long run, wealth—the power to consume—derives from one, and only one, source: increased productivity. Unfortunately, houses are nonproductive assets. No one has ever increased his capacity to produce more goods and services by purchasing a 5,000 square foot monument to conspicuous consumption.

Labor followed the increasing amounts of capital channeled into the housing sector. A large segment of the economy was soon providing large-ticket consumer goods to persons whose demand was supported not by their own production, but by a misallocation of credit. In simplest terms, the housing bubble was simply a large-scale attempt to cheat Say's Law by abusing debt. The result: a reincarnation of the Savings and Loan Crisis on a much broader scale. And just like the last time, almost none of the perpetrators would go to prison.

As I talked with Mike about his experiences selling cocaine, I began to realize how much we had in common. As with most narcotics, debt is easily and frequently mishandled. Time and again, experience has demonstrated that its abuse can destroy individuals, communities, and entire countries. And that's exactly what professional financiers had done. They had destabilized society by distributing debt to the wrong patients, for the wrong reasons, and often in lethal dosages. They had become a cartel of consumer debt dealers. And I had been one of their PR men.

The Cartel was comprised of mortgage banks like Washington Mutual and Golden West Financial; Wall Street brokers like Bear Stearns and Lehman Brothers; and insurance companies like AIG. And the kingpins? None other than two agents of Uncle Sam, himself: Freddie Mac and Fannie Mae. The growth in the "retained portfolios" of these government-sponsored enterprises accounted for 40% of all new subprime mortgage securities in both 2003 and 2004—a veritable Mr. and Mrs. Escobar.

The Consumer Debt Cartel had enjoyed tremendous profits over the past three decades. As a percentage of total corporate profits, financial services climbed from a 10% share in the early 1980s to a 40% share by 2007. In the process, we facilitated an extraordinary increase in consumer debt levels. In 1980, the average U.S. household had 65 cents of debt for every dollar it earned. By 2007, the ratio had doubled: Americans had accumulated more than $1.30 in debt for every dollar of income. America had become a nation of financial drug addicts.

The recession, I realized, was simply the inevitable overdose after 30 years of building an increased tolerance to consumer debt. Sustainable recovery would only arrive after Americans had checked themselves into rehab and the structure of production adjusted accordingly. Too much labor and capital had been devoted to providing goods to people whose consumption was driven not by their own production, but by imprudent lending. Given the large misallocation of resources and the tremendous amount of leverage used to finance them, the adjustment process was going to be very unpleasant. The era of the capricious American consumer was about to end.

As Mike's case illustrates, convicted drug dealers often spend decades in prison, even for a first-time offense. Given cocaine's propensity to destroy lives, perhaps the sentences are warranted. But if sentences are truly commensurate with social costs, where does that leave irresponsible bankers? When high-profile financiers misallocate capital and blow up a large bank or brokerage, they don't end up in prison unless there has been a blatant case of fraud. More often than not, they usually land another seven-figure gig at a different Wall Street firm within a matter of months.

By threatening drug dealers with incarceration, the government dissuades a number of would-be distributors. However, those that are willing to flout the law can earn tremendous profits by selling into a market with an artificially limited supply. Like so many other young men in their demographic, Mike and Tyrell had started selling drugs because of this powerful economic incentive. I couldn't think much less of them for having done so. Had they been raised in an affluent Long Island suburb, they might have pursued an even more lucrative career in debt trafficking, done more damage to society, and never run the risk of imprisonment.

Over the course of my life, numerous people have told me that I would have made an excellent attorney. "You have a keen analytical mind," they said. "Why not practice law?"

My typical rejoinder was that I had a much greater interest in seeing justice served than the law enforced. Recent experience has been a vivid reminder of the distinction. For the life of me, I can't make sense of it all.

*Chapter 6*

# THE RESTAURANT OF LAST RESORT

*"Give me control over a nation's currency,
and I care not who makes its laws."*
ATTRIBUTED TO MAYER AMSCHEL ROTHSCHILD

I never saw anyone order three waffles until my fourth month at the store. The twenty-something bartender explained that he wasn't normally so ravenous, but extenuating circumstances had forced his hand. While he was pouring drinks the night before, his girlfriend had called to advise him that she was going into labor with their first child. To celebrate the good news, he spent the next six hours inundating his blood stream with alcohol.

After the first hour of heavy drinking, he had had second thoughts about the prudence of his actions. "I figured the doctors and nurses might get irritated if I showed up drunk to the delivery room. And besides, I probably should be sober when I meet my daughter for the first time."

Before common sense had gotten the best of him, the bartender reasoned that he could continue imbibing as long as he consumed a few waffles afterwards. Their spongy texture, he claimed, made them particularly effective at absorbing liquor from the stomach.

I commended the bartender for his sense of paternal responsibility and delivered him a fourth cup of coffee. He thanked me profusely for being "an angel of mercy" and began reciting an extemporaneous paean to our establishment. Papa's, he sang, was the only place at 3 a.m. where a man could not only detoxify his system, but enjoy doing so.

Although the vast majority of the 2:30 a.m. crowd had clearly tied a few on before visiting us, most of our customers didn't come with the express intent of sobering up. On occasion, however, the store could function as a surrogate emergency room. A week after my encounter with the bartender, two young men literally dragged an inebriated companion though the front door. They planted his backside on a chair at the low bar and carefully removed his arms from their necks. The drunk wobbled for a second, then promptly collapsed belly first onto the counter. We stared at him for a few seconds before one of his friends finally broke the silence.

"Hey, Jimmy. What should we do for him?"

Once again, I had been presented with a scenario for which *The Rise & Shine Manual* had failed to prepare me. I was barely competent as a server, let alone an emergency room nurse. All I could do was hazard my best guess.

"We'll let him sleep for five or ten minutes. After that, we'll check his vital signs to ensure he's still breathing. If so, we'll start him off with a glass of water," I said in a very professional tone of voice. "If he can handle that without incident, I'd like to administer a cup of coffee, with a little cream and lots of sugar. If he rallies within the hour, we'll give him a small plate of plain hashbrowns. Then we can discharge him."

The patient's friends nodded in agreement.

"And *you* wanted to take him to the hospital to get his stomach pumped," one of them said condescendingly to the other.

His friend conceded the error in judgment. It would have been foolhardy to pay for an ER visit when he could receive comparable quality care at our establishment.

"Uhhll," the drunk suddenly mumbled, straining to clutch a fistful of air.

"Listen. He's trying to tell us something," I said. I bent down and placed my ear next to his head.

"Efful," he groaned louder.

"What's he saying?" his friends asked.

There was a time when I too would have been puzzled by the cryptic sounds. During my first week on the job, I delivered a glass of water in a response to a young customer's request. As I placed it on the table, he glared at me.

"Ahsed ah nade uh . . . foke."

I leaned forward, hoping he'd take my cue to enunciate. "Uh foke!" he repeated.

Ten seconds later, I returned with his fork. I entertained the idea of responding in kind by soliciting his order in a thick Scottish brogue but thought better of it. After all, he was the customer. If I was going to work in sales, the onus lay with me to gain fluency in his language (whatever it may have been).

Following the "foke" encounter, I made a concerted effort to listen more closely to my customers and the break room banter. In a few weeks, I could readily interpret various guttural tones for the sundry menu items that they represented. For example, "fru pun" was a common request for fruit punch. By the time the drunk's cry of "efful" reached my trained ear, its meaning was as plain as day.

"Do you want a waffle?" I asked.

That was the magic word. He raised himself up on his elbows and gave a slow nod. I looked into his eyes, trying to gauge the severity of his condition by the glaze on his irises. Regrettably, he performed a face plant onto the counter before I could complete my assessment.

The act was reminiscent of an old Western film. The dying man, having crawled through the desert for days, uses his last breath to beseech a passerby for water before collapsing into the sand.

I delivered the waffle five minutes later, although the man slept at the bar for another hour before he finally consumed it. Within another hour, I had the profuse thanks of his companions for providing him with the energy he needed to leave the store on his own two feet.

Although most inebriated customers were sincerely appreciative of my early morning service, others had markedly less gratitude.

"The gova mint should shut y'all down!" an indignant patron exclaimed, when I advised him that we had just exhausted our inventory of chicken breasts. Customers were always incredulous when we ran out of chicken, pork chops, or take-out trays. Most of the time, they demanded free meals as compensation for the inconvenience. This was the first time anyone had suggested a store closure. Typically, I responded by offering my sympathies and tried to call their attention to another item on the menu. But this time, I didn't feel like backing down.

"If you really feel that way, why do you keep coming back so often?" I had seen him on the past three Saturday nights.

"Because y'all are the only place that's open at three in the mornin'."

He was right. I couldn't think of any other local restaurants that were open all night. And I couldn't imagine another establishment that would be so tolerant of obnoxious patrons, whatever the hour. Papa's was the only place where barflies could procure hot food at 3 a.m. They simply couldn't get it anywhere else.

Most regulars knew what to anticipate after the bars closed. If they wanted quick service, they would address their servers by name and offer a fat tip out of the gate. The uninitiated were much less sympathetic. In their minds' eye, being forced to wait longer than ten minutes for their food was an all-out assault on their civil liberties.

I knew where this sense of entitlement originated. It's three in the morning, and you're famished. Suddenly, it hits you like a bolt of lightning—Papa's is still open. Your brilliant epiphany deserves to be rewarded with expedient service. Unfortunately, half the town has had the same stroke of genius, so you have to wait your turn.

While the morning shift contributed the largest portion of the store's revenue, the graveyard shift wasn't too far beyond. The late-night crowd generated almost three-quarters as much sales as the breakfast crowd. Between 1 a.m. and 4 a.m., we had a monopoly on the restaurant business. Indeed, a large part of our profitability was predicated on our willingness to do what no one else would.

We were the Restaurant of Last Resort.

$ $ $ $ $

In 1873, Mark Twain published his only coauthored novel. *The Gilded Age: A Tale of Today* satirized the greed, political corruption, and real estate speculation which characterized late nineteenth-century America. Although it was met with less critical success than Twain's other oeuvres, the term "Gilded Age" became synonymous with contemporary economic and social conditions. Incidentally, its publication coincided with the onset of a long depression.

Earlier that year, President Ulysses S. Grant signed a Coinage Act which changed the nation's **monetary policy.** ("Monetary policy" refers to a government's management of the money supply and credit conditions.) Under the new law, the United States would back its currency only by gold reserves. Previously, paper money had been backed by both gold and silver specie. Overnight, silver lost its status as a reserve metal. Banks that had been using silver now found themselves under-reserved and were forced to call in their loans. A major financial firm named Jay Cooke & Company failed, and the money supply soon collapsed in a series of bank runs.

The country would endure another severe financial crisis in 1893 as a debt-financed bubble in railroad construction imploded. Fourteen years later, yet another large-scale panic broke after a group of stock market speculators defaulted on a sizeable loan to a large trust company (a type of lightly-regulated bank). The collapse of the Knickerbocker Trust sent shockwaves throughout Wall Street. Runs on several large banks and trust companies ensued, quickly engulfing the New York financial district in chaos.

The country's most prominent banker, J.P . Morgan, coordinated a desperate effort to provide reserves to faltering banks and trust companies. If the weaker financial institutions should collapse, he asserted, the stronger ones would soon follow suit. In his view, the only alternative to a bailout was a total meltdown of the banking system.

Morgan wasn't bluffing. A veteran of the Panic of 1893, he knew how quickly a single calamity could metastasize across many institutions. Not only had the banks, trust companies, and brokerage houses borrowed heavily from depositors, they also owed considerable sums *to each other.* The financial system, which was charged with recycling savings into reproductive investments, had become a tenuous chain of dominoes.

> *had borrowed from*            *who owed money to*
>
> Speculators   >   Trust companies & brokers   >   Banks
>
> *who in turn owed*
>
> >   Bank Depositors

At one point, Morgan convened over a hundred bankers and trust company officials to a 3 a.m. summit at his private library to design a $25 million relief program for the imperiled banks and trusts. They weren't going home until a resolution was reached—Morgan, they soon realized, had locked them inside. After ninety minutes of cajoling, the other financiers acquiesced and the reserves were provided. Through the sheer force of his will, J.P. Morgan had succeeded in preventing what would have been the largest implosion of money and credit since Andrew Jackson issued his Specie Circular seven decades before.

While the fallout from "The Panic of 1907" would have undoubtedly been much worse devoid of Morgan's efforts, it was bad enough for the government to take notice. The following year, Congress established the National Monetary Commission to investigate the causes of the crisis and propose an overhaul of the banking system.

After surveying the banking operations of several European countries, Commission head Senator Nelson Aldrich became convinced that the United States needed her own central bank. Working with several prominent bankers and economists, he submitted a proposal to Congress in 1911. The "Aldrich Plan" provided the basis for the Federal Reserve Act, signed into law by President Woodrow Wilson on December 23, 1913. The national bank, that "monster" which Andrew Jackson had so vigorously campaigned to destroy, had been resurrected.

Rather than concentrate power entirely in one entity (as the Second Bank of the United States had done), the new Federal Reserve System had its power diffused across twelve regional banks. The act required all nationally chartered commercial banks to purchase stock in their regional Federal Reserve bank, which would be managed by a board of directors. In turn, a seven-member Board of Governors would supervise the entire Federal Reserve System. Although the Board of Governors was comprised of Presidential appointees, the system was designed to be an independent entity that could act without prior approval from Congress or the White House.

Through the Federal Reserve Act, Congress delegated control of the money supply to the Federal Reserve System ("The Fed"). While many of the Fed's critics argue that its existence is unconstitutional, Article One, Section 8 of the Constitution grants the Congress "Power . . . to coin Money, regulate the Value thereof." The Constitution never explicitly defines money, although Article One, Section 10 forbids States from coining money or making "any Thing but gold and silver Coin a Tender in Payment of Debts."

The Federal Reserve banks would be entirely owned by private commercial banks, although their banknotes (Federal Reserve Notes) would serve as the official U.S. currency. Each Federal Reserve bank would maintain a gold reserve ratio of 40% of the value of its Notes and deposits. The Federal Reserve Notes could be redeemed for gold bullion at the U.S. Treasury Department in Washington, D.C. or at any regional Federal Reserve bank at the rate of $20.67 per troy ounce.

In the new banking regime, the Federal Reserve banks' notes and deposits constituted the nation's **monetary base.** Commercial bank deposits were backed by a fractional reserve of the monetary base, which was in turn backed by a fractional reserve of gold bullion. The monetary base accounted for roughly 20% of the U.S. money supply; commercial bank deposits comprised the remaining 80%. As long as the Federal Reserve was never faced with the threat of a run on its own gold reserves, the system was tenable.

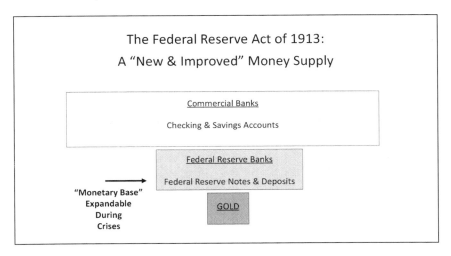

The Federal Reserve Act granted the Fed four important powers: First, it provided an **elastic currency,** meaning that the Federal Reserve banks could issue an increased volume of banknotes in time of crisis. Should nervous depositors begin to withdraw their money en masse, the Fed would step in as **Lender of Last Resort** and lend cash directly to the banks. By providing the commercial banks with reserves, the Fed would sharply reduce the risk of widespread bank runs and destruction of the money supply. When the panic subsided, depositors would resume lending money to the commercial banks, which would then use the deposit proceeds to repay their loans to the Fed. In theory, the downward spiral of debt deflation would never gain sufficient momentum to do serious damage.

Second, in addition to providing reserves to the banking system, the Fed also had power to set reserve requirements for the commercial banks. By managing these two factors, the Fed could manage the creation of money through the fractional reserve process. By limiting money supply growth to a modest pace, consumer price inflation would be contained.

Third, the Fed could set short-term interest rates by buying and selling U.S. government bonds and fixing the rate at which banks borrowed from its "discount window." (This power was later broadened in the 1930s to include managing the rates at which banks loaned their excess reserves on deposit at the Fed to each other.) As short-term rates fell, the cheaper borrowing costs tended to increase capital asset prices. Admittedly, the Fed couldn't exercise direct control over asset prices, although it could certainly affect them.

Fourth, the Act granted the Fed authority to supervise bank lending and establish capital requirements. The regional Fed banks were to ensure that each private commercial bank was following sound lending practices and maintaining adequate capital to absorb any potential losses. If capital buffers were not threatened by imprudent lending and/ or excessive leverage, banks would be seldom forced to call in their loans. The magnitude of the upswings and downturns in the credit cycle would be severely curtailed.

(**Money Supply**: Serving as Lender of Last Resort prevents money supply contraction. Setting reserve requirements limits money supply expansion. **Capital Asset Prices**: Lower short-term interest rates support capital asset prices. Higher short-term interest rates help prevent asset price bubbles. **Bank Loans**: Lending Supervision & Capital Requirements reduce probability of a crisis that would force banks to call in their loans.)

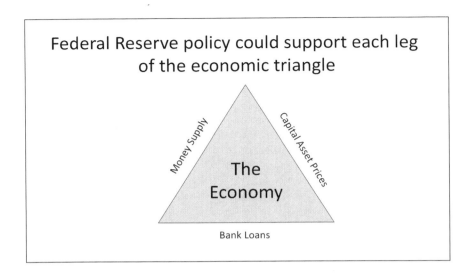

In this latter respect—smoothing extreme undulations in the credit cycle—the Federal Reserve would play the same role that the Old Testament prophets played in mitigating the pride cycle. Moses, Isaiah, and Elijah each preached humility and repentance in the midst of pride and debauchery. To the extent the people were humbled by their words and forsook their sins, they were spared from God's wrath.

So too would the Federal Reserve exhort the commercial banks to repent of reckless lending and overleveraged balance sheets. Their calls to repentance could take several forms: higher reserve and capital requirements, higher short-term interest rates, and tougher lending restrictions. During the downturns, the banks would receive clemency as these policies were reversed.

Of course, the efficacy of the Federal Reserve System was predicated on competent and courageous leadership at the Board of Governors. But since the time of Noah, calling bankers (or anyone else) to repentance has never been a fast track to popularity. However foreboding the weather forecast may be, very few people will readily board an ark while there's a good party going.

$ $ $ $ $

A few minutes after we passed the baton to the first shift on Sunday morning, the third-shift crew formed a break room queue to receive our weekly pay. In lieu of paychecks, the manager paid us cash money straight from the register. The going wage for servers was $2.13 an hour, and the tax withholding rate assumed that gratuities put our income at minimum wage level. The ten percent surcharge added to all take-out orders added a few more bucks, but I was still only netting about fifty dollars.

Not since I had picked strawberries and mowed lawns as a teenager had I felt such a visceral connection to every dollar in my wallet. Each one represented the fruit of recent production, and I became very finicky about parting with any of them. The great thing about paying with cash, rather than credit cards, is that removing the bills from your wallet encourages you to ponder whether you are exchanging your production for something of real value.

My unspent currency accumulated on my kitchen bar top for several weeks before I finally bothered to deposit it, along with several pounds of change, at the bank. I always enjoyed drawing a few stares as I pushed several hundred dollars in unsorted small bills across the teller counter. But the best part of the experience was my interaction with the hapless tellers.

"Welcome to Wachovia. How are you this morning, sir?" the young woman asked.

"Well, that depends. Is the bank still solvent?"

"As far as I know."

"Good." I wrote my cell phone number on a deposit slip and slid it across the counter. "Please call me if that situation changes before four o'clock today. I know how tenuous these things can be."

"You've got a lot of cash sitting in your account," she observed.

"That's very reassuring," I said. "I was afraid the bank might have managed to lose it."

"Perhaps you'd like to meet with one of our financial specialists who could help you put that money to work for you."

"You mean to tell me this bank offers investment advice?" I asked in feigned disbelief.

"Yes, we do," she said enthusiastically.

"And how long have you been doing that?"

"Oh, for at least the past ten years."

"I see you're now advertising yourselves as 'A Wells Fargo Company.'" I said, pointing to a poster behind the teller windows. "Correct me if I'm wrong, but didn't that merger occur just a few months ago?"

"Yes, we officially merged in April."

"I thought so. If memory serves, it was right after you tried to sell yourselves to Morgan Stanley and Citigroup. Your bank almost collapsed because you purchased a California-based mortgage lending company whose loan portfolio had been poorly underwritten. A large chunk of their option adjustable-rate mortgages went bad, depleting your capital base and triggering intense regulatory scrutiny. If I recall correctly, a few large depositors had even started a run on your bank."

"There were a lot of factors at work," she sighed. "You seem to know a good deal about these events."

"Yeah, that forty-thousand-dollar bath I took on my Wachovia shares kind of seared it into my memory."

"I'm sorry," she said apologetically.

"I'm not mad," I said. "But I am genuinely intrigued that a bank which decimates its own capital base through bad loan underwriting is in a legitimate position to counsel other people on how to invest their money. So I think I'll pass on the advice and just let the cash keep sitting there. What do you think?"

"I understand completely, sir," she said, handing my deposit receipt.

"In fact," I continued, "I'd like your complete assurance that you won't lend my money out at all."

"But then you wouldn't earn any interest."

"But then I wouldn't have to worry about you guys blowing it on bad loans, would I?"

"Will there be anything else, sir?" she asked in an exasperated voice.

"Yeah. Would you mind exchanging these two twenty-dollar bills for four tens? I always get nervous whenever Andrew Jackson is in my wallet. He's in the habit of destroying money too."

$ $ $ $ $

I would have been quicker to forgive Wachovia for their underwriting mistakes had it not been for a telephone conversation that I had with a woman in their credit card department the Friday before I started at Papa's. My card was approaching its expiration date, and the bank was performing its due diligence before issuing me a replacement.

"What is your current income?" the woman asked.

"I don't know. I'm starting a new job waiting tables on Monday, but I forgot to ask about my wage."

"Well, what was your income in 2008?"

"My total compensation was approximately $150,000. But I'm guessing that it will be markedly lower in 2009. To be honest, I have no idea what my new employer is going to pay me. But even in a best case scenario, I doubt that I'll bring home a quarter of what I had earned previously. "

"I'll just go ahead and put down what you made last year," she said. "That way, your credit limit won't be reduced."

I had thought that I knew a thing or two about sloppy underwriting, but this woman was setting the bar lower than I ever would have imagined possible. The banking industry had come a long way since my parents purchased their first home 35 years ago. At the time, my mother's pay stub wasn't even admissible on their mortgage application because the bank considered her income stream too tenuous—i.e., a 27-year-old married woman was likely to soon bear children and drop out of the labor force.

Bankers and borrowers both seemed to take money lending more seriously back then. Bank branches were constructed of granite and marble; all of the personnel wore suits. Today, bankers' lackadaisical approach to loan underwriting is reflected in their attire. The khaki pants and polo shirt worn by a Washington Mutual loan officer makes him virtually indistinguishable from a Starbucks barista. (For all of their other deficiencies, at least Wachovia employees still wear neckties.)

$ $ $ $ $

If I was indeed going to get my gratuity receipts to a level commensurate with Wachovia's six-figure estimate, I needed a game plan. In markets, you are always looking for patterns that can be exploited as trading opportunities. So it was with my customers—if I could gauge a customer's likelihood of leaving a large tip, I could devote extra effort to his table. Unfortunately, handicapping a customer's propensity to tip based on his appearance was an extremely difficult endeavor. A man dressed like a gangbanger may be just as likely to leave a large gratuity as a middle-aged man in business casual attire wearing a Rolex.

There were two demographics, however, that consistently tipped me well: gay men and obese Caucasian women. I was heartened by their generosity as it provided me with a career safety net. If my promised Tokyo transfer fell through, I could still expect to earn a pretty good living working at a store situated in Greenwich Village or any town in Wisconsin.

Getting stiffed didn't bother me so much personally. My wife still had an income and I had saved a lot of money from my prior career. But seeing my coworkers neglected by ungrateful customers always aroused my ire.

"I feel like a slave working on third shift," Tyrell said, bussing a table that had just stiffed him. "You kill yourselves for these people and get nothing for it. It's like a scene straight out of *Roots*."

I could appreciate his predicament. From what I had observed during my two-week training period, the breakfast crowd he was accustomed to waiting on had much looser purse strings than the barflies. At the end of a typical shift, Tyrell and I were averaging between seventy and eighty dollars. Lamarr had earned north of one hundred bucks, while Tommy was closer to two hundred. He attributed his windfall to having lived in town for thirty years and accumulating a robust base of devoted fans.

Lamarr's method for success was also straightforward. Because some customers would stiff the waiters regardless of the quality of service, the best bet was to assume way more volume than you can possibly handle. Instead of following *The Rise & Shine Manual's* prescribed method of calling in one table order at a time, Lamarr took orders from everyone within earshot and then jammed the grill with a ten-plate call. Unfailingly, the system resulted in a large number of botched orders and a very irritated grill officer.

Lamarr was a short man in his mid-twenties who had spent the previous eight years in the Navy. He claimed that his time in the service had saved him from getting himself "imprisoned or killed." Though his table-waiting skills had ample room for improvement, I couldn't impugn his work ethic. He always completed his side work assignments and offered unsolicited help to other servers with theirs. When I complimented his productivity, he responded by holding his two fists together in front of me. "H-A-R-D" was tattooed on the knuckles of his left hand; "W-O-R-K" was engraved on the right.

"That's what I'm all about," he declared.

"So you like to work hard?" a sultry voice asked. Lamarr and I turned to the high bar where a woman in her late forties was smoking a cigarette.

After Lamarr muttered an affirmation, the woman inquired about his current income level. After conceding that a competent waiter could earn a decent living, she advised him that he could tread a more lucrative path by taking part-time employment as a male escort. Like table waiting, the job required meticulous attention to detail. In addition to the obvious perk of carousing with beautiful women like her, clients paid in cash money, none of which would have to be reported to the IRS.

The invitation had barely escaped her mouth before Lamarr began listing his disqualifications. She continued to pressure him for a few more minutes as he fielded excuses at every turn. Exasperated, he eventually deflected her attention over to me. The woman swiveled around on her barstool and began eyeing me as I swept the floor. I couldn't help looking back at her over my shoulder. She scrutinized me as a cattle rancher at auction might consider placing a throwaway bid on a sickly Angus bull. After a minute, she spoke.

"Well, how 'bout it, Jimmy? Do you know how to meet the needs of a grown woman?" she asked in a skeptical tone.

A classy man would have rebuked her, citing his marriage vows and an unwavering commitment to his wife of eight years. But it was five in the morning, and I was too tired to explain that I had quit wearing my wedding band to the store a few weeks ago—manually unclogging the dish pit drain had been placing it in constant jeopardy. Besides, I doubted that she was the sort of lady to be dissuaded by my marital status. Instead, I simply offered to assemble a list of references from my college days with the caveat that most of the ladies' phone numbers were likely no longer in service.

While my number of local acquaintances couldn't begin to rival that of Tommy, I did receive a fair number of visitors. Church friends usually dropped by early in my shift, often bringing their spouses and children. For many, it was their first Papa's Chicken & Waffles experience. I thoroughly enjoyed tutoring them on our menu and championing my favorite items. The other servers were intrigued when I waited on a large group of my acquaintances. For some reason, they always assumed that any white customers with whom I had an obvious rapport were my cousins.

Business school classmates and erstwhile colleagues from Alpha Managers also dropped in. Most of them had heard about my new career path through the grapevine and wanted visual confirmation that my employment wasn't some elaborate hoax. For all they knew, the pictures of me in a Papa's uniform had been Photoshopped before being uploaded to Facebook. While they never failed to tip, my gratitude for their patronage was tempered by the knowledge that they had not been drawn to the store by a passion for hashbrowns. Having fallen a long way from my bond market perch, I had become the Elephant Man.

After devoting a few minutes to satiating their curiosity, everyone voiced support for my new vocation—with one notable exception. An ex-colleague informed me that a few of the younger guys at Alpha Managers bristled at my move. By taking this position, I had preemptively spoiled someone else's chance at finding gainful employment in a weak economy. In their view, a socially conscious person would not have taken the job from someone that needed it more.

It's difficult to fully convey my indignation at this remark. Rather than serving as an additional burden on state taxpayers by collecting unemployment insurance, I was under indictment for performing honest labor, instead. But the sorest spot wasn't that my sense of social justice was being maligned; it was that reasonably well-educated people could have reached such an erroneous conclusion.

If they had any appreciation for free markets or Say's Law, the young men never would have ventured such an ignorant opinion. To the first point, if I was a better employee than other potential candidates, then my absence would have been detrimental to both the store and the customers. To the second, the notion that the economy contains a finite number of jobs is wholly ludicrous. The only impediment to full employment is supplying the correct type of labor, at a clearing price, to markets where it is demanded. If anything, our store needed *more* bodies. Due to a recent spate of firings, employee workload had increased dramatically. For several weeks, we had been running both second and third weekday shifts with only one grill op and one salesperson.

Mary, the waitress with the penchant for Harlequin novels, had been sacked for neglecting her side work. Another waiter, Chris, had been terminated for leaving work midway through his shifts, showing up to work inebriated, and issuing an ultimatum to the manager. Two other servers had been fired for participating in kickback schemes like the one Maurice had going.

I was somewhat surprised to learn that the graft was so common. In the past four months, I had never seen any server steal anyone else's tips, nor had I seen anyone else accused of such a theft. Servers, it seemed, had a double standard when it came to property rights. It was expressly unethical to steal from another employee, but shortchanging your employers was considered fair game. As far as I knew, Maurice hadn't been caught, but his employment had been terminated due to a recent arrest. Apparently, possession of a firearm is a big no-no if you're a convicted felon.

Lois, a waitress who had joined third shift only a few weeks before, had been reported to federal agencies for augmenting her credit card gratuities. By scratching in a "1" in front of single digit numbers, she had transformed a two-dollar tip into a twelve-dollar one. This might have been a tenable scam, except for the fact that she had used the trick on nearly every receipt during her shift. Perhaps if she had previously worked in a restaurant, Lois would have known that eight consecutive customers leaving gratuities exceeding 70% of their tab is more likely to arouse suspicion than accolades for great service.

Then there was Carl, who had been canned for at least three reasons. For starters, he had driven the store's food costs through the roof by furnishing his pals with considerable quantities of free T-bones and personally consuming six to eight cheeseburgers on each shift. I can only suppose that his hunger was primarily driven by his incessant marijuana usage. Granted, a lot of people showed up to work with a buzz, but they were at least fairly inconspicuous about it. Carl, on the other hand, was barely functional. His eyes were constantly glazed, and his hat, apron, and every article of clothing always seemed to be falling off of his body.

The last straw came when Carl took horrible advantage of one of our regular customers. Biggie was a soft-spoken gentleman who dined with us two nights a week, always ordering three pork chops and double hashbrowns. He had earned his sobriquet, as his dimensions and manner of dress were reminiscent of rapper Biggie Smalls.

Several weeks after taking him into his confidence, Carl arranged for a group of his friends (presumably the same ones receiving the free steaks) to mug Biggie at gunpoint in front of his house as Carl watched from his car. After discovering who had orchestrated the attack, Biggie confronted him at Papa's several days later. Rather than bludgeon Carl in front of an elderly patron at the low bar, Biggie vented his frustration by slamming his fist into the front window of the store. The massive fracture gave the restaurant a terribly ghetto ambiance for the next 72 hours, but I have to admit that the blemish made for an interesting conversation piece.

The melodrama didn't draw much of a reaction from Edward. As far as he was concerned, the personnel turnover merely created an opportunity for him to earn more money. By substituting for the recently fired employees, he would log more than forty hours a week and increase his marginal wage by fifty percent. The staff shortage had also enabled me to earn some additional cash by picking up extra hours, but my major windfall came in the form of a new recruit who made me look like the world's greatest employee by comparison.

Jennifer had recently moved into an apartment with a roommate after being discharged from a rehabilitation facility. At one time or another over the past three decades, she had been addicted to every substance known to (and, in fact, including) man. To her credit, the effects of a life hard lived were largely obfuscated by her cheery disposition and a large quantity of makeup.

Jennifer's favorite publication was *The Slammer,* a weekly newspaper that "focuses on local crime in a straightforward, humorous and revealing manner." The publication primarily consists of mug shots of persons "charged with committing Felony and Misdemeanor crimes in the seven days prior to the issue date." You can purchase the North Carolina edition of *The Slammer* for only one dollar. It's a small price to pay to make you feel much better about your own life by comparison.

I had never encountered an issue of *The Slammer* before I met Jennifer. Thumbing through its pages, I found myself reconsidering why I was paying $130 for an annual subscription to *The Economist.* Matters of international political economy, while intriguing, simply cannot compete with your neighbors' dirty laundry when it comes to sheer entertainment value.

"Look at that boy there," Jennifer said, pointing to a booking shot of an unkempt miscreant who had earned the coveted "Mug of the Week" award. The picture was selected for two reasons: 1) although the accused had been charged with domestic battery, the ditors noted that he appeared to have been on the receiving end of fisticuffs; and 2) the assailant's middle name was "Demon." "What a hell of a deal," the paper quipped.

For someone so congenial, Jennifer displayed an astounding lack of social intelligence.

Besides calling Sharon at home at 3 a.m. to ask her to adjudicate a personal dispute with another employee, she frequently offered Edward her unsolicited opinion on all sorts of matters. Even when he and another male cook were rating women at the gas station on the other side of our parking lot, Jennifer couldn't resist interjecting. No matter how much disdain Edward showed for her comments, Jennifer never seemed to appreciate how angry she made him. He publicly criticized her every mistake, even her failure to stand directly on the designated floor mark when she called in her orders.

"Place one hashbrown!" she barked, squatting over the mark in a conspicuously wide stance.

"Yes, I believe you may have," he replied. "In your drawers."

"You're crazy, Edward," she said laughing. "Why would you think I did that?"

"Why else would you stand like you were straddling a dirty commode?"

Later that evening, two young men entered the store wearing only boxer shorts and shoes. I recognized them immediately as regular weekend customers. Two of their friends followed behind, laughing and documenting our reactions with their cell phone cameras.

"Are you guys going incognito tonight?" I asked.

"Yeah. If 'incognito' means 'without pants,'" one responded as he high-fived his companion.

Edward let them have their laughs for a minute before finally speaking up.

"Gentlemen, this is a public place. No on wants to see you in your underoos."

"I do," Jennifer contradicted him.

"Big surprise there," Edward muttered.

Although Jennifer had deflected much of Edward's chastisement away from me, he still found time to put me under the gun. Even arriving five minutes before my shift started would engender a reprimand for tardiness. Edward advised me that, technically speaking, I was supposed to arrive at work ten minutes early. As annoying as the reminder was, I had to admit that Edward certainly practiced what he preached. In our five months together, I never once saw him arrive for work less than fifteen minutes before his shift was due to start.

I took Edward's example to heart and began consistently arriving twenty minutes early, partially in an effort to placate him, but mostly to fill my stomach before the rush started. After weeks of practice, I had finally developed the ability to prepare a respectable double original cheeseburger and an oversized plate of hashbrowns all the way. In my humble opinion, my handiwork was comparable to that of a seasoned grill officer. I was very proud.

Edward had taken notice of my newfound skill set, as well. For several weeks, he had permitted me to cook my own orders whenever he was on a cigarette break. Acting as a surrogate for the great Edward Jarvis (and endorsed by the man, himself) provided a real sense of accomplishment. I didn't have the capacity to prepare anything as fancy as a T-bone or an omelet, but I could ably cook an order of eggs or bacon.

Beyond filling in for him during slow periods, I also tried to help out Edward during the rush hours by dropping my own waffles and marking my plates with the appropriate condiment packets whenever I could. I couldn't properly mark omelet and steak orders, but I was pretty adept when it came to eggs and sandwiches. He even commandeered my bread-buttering services when our traffic got really high. Try as I might, I could never do it fast enough for him.

"Jimmy, you need to butter that toast, not make love to it."

"Well, you know I bring a lot of *passion* to my work," I quipped.

He didn't appreciate the pun.

"You can do it in five seconds, Jimmy Jam. Instead, you puttin' that butter on so delicate I'd think you were smearin' it cross a gal's backside."

I was fairly certain that my new nicknames—"Jimmy Jam," "Jimmay," "Jimmy John," and on occasion, "Jim Jones"—weren't terms of endearment, but I didn't find them particularly derogatory, either. After all, Edward even scolded employees that procured scratch-off lottery tickets on his behalf for failing to purchase winning cards.

My favorite illustration of Edward's arbitrary chastening occurred over the phone at the start of a weeknight shift. Tyrell, like several other employees, did not own a vehicle and relied on his legs or public transportation to carry him to work. Although he was running late, he had to maintain a slow pace in order to accommodate a large female employee who was walking with him. He advised Edward of the situation, who would have none of it.

"If she's slowing you down that much, you ought to just pick up that big ole football and run it into the end zone . . . the end zone in this case being the store, Ty."

I pointed out to Edward that Emily was two hundred pounds if she was an ounce. "I used to carry cast-iron stoves on my back when I was just a teenager," Edward asserted. "She can't weigh any more than those did."

"What about the weight distribution?" I asked. "I would think that Emily is even more bulky than the stoves would have been."

"Naw, Jim-may. At the end of the day, it don't make no difference if it's a major appliance or just a big gal."

He sat down at the low bar and began eating the take-out sushi he had brought with him. I took the adjacent seat and offered my thoughts on the quality of the sushi I had eaten on business trips to California and Japan. Edward listened politely, asked a few questions about Tokyo, and began ruminating on the subject of kimonos. Specifically, why Japanese men were in the habit of wearing them around the house after work. (This is not PG material, so I'll leave my readers to speculate as to what his thoughts were.)

In a few more minutes, Edward was imparting a Biblical parable. "So this woman sold her soul to the devil and never aged. But she had a painting of herself that she kept in da attic," he said, gesticulating upward with his finger. "And every time that old broad did somethin' bad, instead of her gettin' a new wrinkle on her own face, the portrait aged instead."

I could only listen to so much of this before calling to Edward's attention that the story's actual protagonist had been a man and that the allegory in question was actually a nineteenth-century British novel entitled, *The Picture of Dorian Gray*. He continued to protest its Old Testament origin, so I let the claim slide. Whether written by Ezekiel or Oscar Wilde, the point was still valid: Faustian bargains simply aren't worth making.

Halfway through my dinner, Edward's discourse took an unanticipated turn from moral issues to medical ones. While I cleaned the hashbrowns from my plate, he elaborated on his extreme aversion to prostate examinations. He had a real flair for the dramatic, alternating between the roles of physician and patient as he acted out the scenario. His physical comedy was some of the best I'd ever seen, rivaling even John Belushi's finest work.

While few men look forward to said exams, Edward had more reservations than most. In his opinion, submitting oneself to even one doctor's scrutiny would put a man on a slippery slope of perversion. Over a course of months, the patient's deviance would snowball, culminating with his performance in a New Orleans burlesque show.

As I watched Edward's rendition of the can-can, I reflected on how lucky I had been to land a job that offered the amenities of free food and a front-row seat to a world-class comedy show. Generally speaking, I enjoyed Edward's social commentaries more than his personal anecdotes. Each of his tales was a little tall but still marginally credible when considered independently of each other.

When I compared the details of the separate accounts, however, matters began to get a little sketchy.

For example, Edward had made these separate claims regarding his father: (1) He had served as a Navy SEAL during the Vietnam War (the first SEAL teams were commissioned by President Kennedy in 1961); (2) he lived to be 88 years old; and (3) he died in 1981.

Any of these three statements, combined with any one of the other two, constitutes an entirely plausible scenario. That is, there are undoubtedly men who (1) died in 1981 at the age of 88; (2) served on SEAL teams during Vietnam, subsequently dying in 1981; and (3) fought in the Vietnam War, then died at age 88 (although this necessitates military service in their early forties during the early years of the war).

Considering all three facts concurrently, a most unlikely situation presented itself: a man born in 1893 begins his SEAL training no sooner than age 68 and finally dies in 1981 (most likely, he unknowingly succumbs to prostate cancer on account of refusing precautionary examinations). As we manned the store by ourselves one Tuesday night, I asked Edward about these discrepancies.

"You ask so many questions, you belong in Hollywood," he curtly replied.

I didn't make the connection between inquisitiveness and motion pictures. But I found it generally best to concede his claims rather than challenge them.

"Well, I don't know about cinema, but I do feel like I'm in a play, Edward."

"Yeah, I wouldn't be surprised to see you come in here one day wearing rouge and eye shadow all over yo' face."

"You've never heard the phrase 'All the world's a stage, and all the men and women merely players'? William Shakespeare wrote that."

"William Shakespeare is under stone."

"What?"

"William is under stone. He's dead."

"And?"

"The man is dead, so it don't really matter what he thought about nothing. Now if Moses had 'all the world's a stage' written on them tablets, then I might give it a second thought. But it ain't."

"Come on, Edward. Shakespeare's the most quoted man in the English language. I mean, don't you ever feel like we're in a play sometimes?"

He shot me a stern glance. I was going to have to build a more robust case.

"Take that guy that came in here last month. He saw his father's ghost, just like Hamlet did. Maybe he was a distraught Danish prince caught in the intrigues of court. I mean, there *are* similarities."

"I'll tell you what I know. That boy's been in here befo', and he ain't no Prince of Denmark. He stocks shelves at the supermarket." He turned to the grill and began scraping charred hashbrown residue from its surface.

"Just 'cause William Shakespeare said something don't make it right, Jimmy. If you spent as much time reading *The Rise & Shine Manual* as you do *Hamlet,* you'd be making two hundred dollars a shift."

When I first read *Hamlet* in high school, I felt a tremendous empathy for the titular character. But now, I had a closer bond with Yorick, the late court jester exhumed by Prince Hamlet in Act V. Closing my eyes, I could envision the shelf stocker sitting at the high bar several years hence.

He has just unearthed my skull from a shallow grave in the ravine behind the store, where I had been hastily buried by three female malefactors who had fatally algreened me three years before. He holds my pallid cranium aloft and begins his monologue: "Alas, poor Jimmy! I knew him, Edward; a fellow of infinite jest, of most excellent fancy; he hath served me a thousand biscuits. And now, how abhorred in my imagination it is! My gorge rises at it . . . I'll have a waffle now."

While I was contemplating the effect of grits on the decomposition process, a rotund patron moseyed up to the bar.

"Did I hear you all say you had a friend named Will that died and you need a headstone for him?"

"Why does it interest you?" I asked.

"I'm a stonemason," the man responded, pointing to his baseball cap. It read, "K & M Memorials: a shrine of memory for those who care."

"Yes, it looks like old Will is going to need one," I said. "Would you mind doing some work on the other side of the Pond?"

"I'll do work as far north as Washington D.C. Cutting stone on the other side of Jordan Lake is no problem."

I should have been more specific in my aquatic references.

"Will was a very important man," I asserted. "How do I know that your work is up to snuff?"

"It just so happens I have some of it with me," the Stonemason responded.

"Let's go outside and have a gander then," I suggested. I had assumed he was hauling a headstone in the bed of his pickup.

"No, it ain't in my truck; it's right here. Look, I carved these myself." He flashed a large grin and pointed to his upper incisors.

I stared at them for longer than a polite person should have. But since he would be immortalizing the greatest writer in the English language, it was imperative that a master craftsman be selected for the job. Also, I had never met a man who manufactured his own teeth before, and the opportunity seemed unlikely to present itself again for at least a few more weeks.

"They're very nice," I said, completing my examination. "I guess that only leaves two unresolved issues—your fee, and what kind of rock we want. Or rather, what Will would prefer, God rest his soul."

While getting the full court press from bond salesmen used to really annoy me, I actually enjoyed the Stonemason's high pressure sales pitch to spring for a granite headstone.

"You really shouldn't even be thinking about marble," he said.

"It might look nice at the outset, but it will start cracking after a few years pass."

"Well, this is the Bard we're talking about, so expense really is no obstacle," I said.

The fact that Shakespeare had been dead and buried for nearly 400 years seemed incidental at this point. We were getting down to the specifics of the epitaph when Edward finally interrupted us.

"Jimmy, why are you still bothering this man?"

"We're brainstorming on exit lines for our friend Will. Do you have any suggestions?"

"Yeah, I got an exit line. But it ain't for Will Shakespeare. Bus that table and leave this man alone."

I grabbed a wet towel and began applying some elbow grease to a coffee stain in a corner booth as Edward began to explain my mental shortcomings to the Stonemason.

"You see, that boy's in a parallel universe most of the time. He used to work in an office all day as a finance man, so he's been through that crash which we've all heard about. He's been here several months—which is time enough for most people to adjust—but his brain hasn't finished acclimatin' to Papa's."

The man nodded.

"He thinks he's in a Shakespearean production," Edward continued. "You see, that's how his brain copes with the big change in his life—he pretends he's an actor."

I thought the Stonemason might be upset that I had deliberately wasted fifteen minutes of his time, but Edward's intercession had its intended effect. He offered Edward his condolences, paid his check, and cast me a pitiful glance as he left the store.

$ $ $ $ $

Edward busted everyone's chops without much provocation, but his interest in knocking me down a notch had accelerated of late. The criticism reached a crescendo the following week when I responded to his "order up!" bellow at the grill.

"Is this plate mine?" I asked.

"Who else's would it be, Man?" he asked sardonically.

"I don't know. Jennifer's?"

"Have a look around, Jimmy."

Jennifer wasn't waiting on anyone at the moment, and she was the only other server working the shift. Edward was giving me the "what the hell is wrong with you" look. I had been reproved by him so many times that I could accurately predict the length of an impending diatribe by how long he stared at me before he began fulminating.

"You're right, Edward. It looks like Jennifer isn't busy, so by process of elimination, it must be my order."

"Why are you asking me these stupid questions? I know you're a college boy, so you can't be that dumb." The tone was unusually forthright, even for him.

"Maybe I am stupid, Edward. I'm just not as aware of my surroundings as you are, I guess."

"You got eyes, don't you? Do they both work?"

"Yes."

"Then why are you acting like you're retarded? You worked at a bank before."

"No, I worked at two insurance companies. And then at a hedge fund."

I don't know why Edward was so ambivalent about my inquisitiveness. Sometimes, he interpreted my curiosity as a desire to be thorough. At other times, an inquiry drew a stern glance and chastisement for wasting his time.

"So do insurance companies have a 'work for retards' outreach program? What was it they was teachin' you in college? That yo eyes is best used for reading Shakespeare and under no circumstances are they to be put to work spottin' waffles?"

"I admit that I can be a space cadet from time to time. But do you honestly think I've been sandbagging, just playing dumb in order to drive you nuts?"

"Yeaauuuh."

It was time to level with him.

"Edward, you've been at the store for five years. Maybe for you, or some of the other employees, this is a normal gig. But for me, it's brutal. I have to simultaneously be aware of my customers, the grill, the stock of silverware and straws, and a hundred other things. I need to have immediate recall of all the menu prices. I have to know the skill level of each grill officer so I know how fast I can call my orders. Despite a lot of pressure from the customers, and from you, I'm expected to execute all of these tasks perfectly every night.

"At my old job, I used to sit at my desk for three or four straight hours and focus on one task at a time. I could plan out my work flow for days in advance. In my eight years in the bond market, I was given a tight deadline out of the blue on maybe ten different occasions. This is nothing like any of that."

"You mean to tell me you done had the same job for the past eight years?"

"Not at the same company, but I was always working with large institutions in the same industry. I've never dealt with the public before under this kind of constant pressure. *This is the hardest job I've ever had.*"

It was true. My previous years had been spent poring over company 10-K filings, reading Street research, and writing performance commentaries for clients. I had dwelt exclusively in the ether. The transition from the abstract world to the concrete one had been jarring, to say the least.

Edward stared at me for a few seconds, gauging my sincerity. "Alright, I can appreciate your situation," he said finally. "You're just a fish that's jumped out of the water onto dry land and you're floppin' around helplessly. Now, from my perspective, I have to think that the fish is a fool for not stayin' in the pond in the first place."

"So if you happened upon a fish like that, would you filet him or throw him back in the water?" I asked.

"I'd teach him to breathe air," Edward said. "But I'd expect that with him being a fish, it would take a while to learn." He clapped his hand on my shoulder. "Don't worry, Jimmy, you'll get it right one of these days."

Edward's temperament became less mercurial in the weeks after our discussion. Not only did the intervals between his reprimands lengthen from fifteen minutes to a full thirty, but the tone of his criticisms softened considerably. However large my mistakes had been, I had finally received a measure of clemency. More deserving people have waited years before they get any.

$ $ $ $ $

During twenty-two years in major league baseball, Bill Buckner posted a respectable .289 career batting average and compiled 2,700 hits. The first baseman spent his eighteenth season with the Boston Red Sox, driving in over 100 runs and playing an integral role in his team's march to the 1986 World Series. At the bottom of the tenth inning in game six, the Red Sox led the New York Mets by two runs. Boston was one out away from winning a World Series Championship, their first since 1918.

On the tenth pitch of his at-bat, Mets center fielder Mookie Wilson hit a slow-moving ground ball toward first base. What should have been a routine play quickly turned into a rout. The ball rolled underneath Buckner's glove just as he squatted to intercept it. The Mets scored the winning run on the error, tying the series at 3–3. Two days later, the Mets won game seven, taking the World Series trophy to Queens. For the rest of his career, the untimely mistake would mar Buckner's name. Public forgiveness would not arrive until April 2008, when he threw out the first pitch at the Red Sox season opener. Their hearts having been softened by World Series championships in 2004 and 2007, the Boston fans gave him a four-minute standing ovation.

A similar tragedy to Buckner's befell an American economist named Irving Fisher in 1929. The first man to earn a Ph.D. in Economics from Yale University, Fisher was a pioneer in the field of monetary economics—i.e., studying how changes in the money supply affected production, unemployment, and price levels. (The MV = PY "equation of exchange" was his brainchild.) He also performed seminal academic work regarding the determinants of interest rates.

Beyond his academic life, Fisher was a successful inventor and a renowned advocate for diet, health, and hygiene. He coauthored a book entitled, *How to Live: Rules for Healthful Living Based on Modern Science,* which became a national bestseller. During the roaring bull market of the 1920s, he also enjoyed public notoriety as a stock market commentator.

In late 1929, Fisher famously stated that "Stock prices have reached what looks like a permanently high plateau." Just days after his prediction, the stock market plummeted more than 20%. For months after the crash, he continued to assuage investors with promises of an imminent recovery. In fact, stocks did not bottom until July 1932 and would not retrace their previous high until a quarter century after Fisher made his "plateau" forecast. His reputation never recovered from that singular gaffe.

Like Buckner's mishap during the World Series, one conspicuous public error eclipsed many of Fisher's great accomplishments. One of them, regrettably, was the debt deflation theory of depressions. Fisher had published his theory in a 1933 academic publication in an effort to explain a contemporary depression whose severity and duration hadn't been experienced by Americans in nearly a century. Unfortunately, the public largely ignored the discredited economist and his theory; instead, they heeded a voice across the Atlantic.

No single figure dominates the landscape of twentieth-century economics more than John Maynard Keynes. Not only did the six-foot, six-inch Engishman physically tower over his peers, he also cast a formidable intellectual shadow. In the mid- and late 1930s, he propounded a radical theory of the business cycle and depressions which would become economic orthodoxy within a decade. Perhaps no teacher in history, religious or otherwise, has enjoyed such a rapid acceptance of such revolutionary doctrine.

For 80 years, Classical economists understood that recessions were the result of imbalances in the structure of production (i.e., too much of this good, too little of that), exacerbated by the rapid contraction of bank credit. Heretics who claimed that recessions were the result of "insufficient demand" were dismissed as intellectual pygmies unable to wrap their heads around the first, immutable principle of economics:

that demand is always derived from production. And that is precisely where Keynes began his attack. He would later describe his magnum opus, *The General Theory of Employment, Interest and Money* (1936), as "a final break-away from the doctrines of J.-B. Say."

In the original version of his *Treatise*, Say had posited that "products are paid for with products" (p. 153). Recessions were born of "too many means of production applied to one kind of product and not enough to another" (pp. 178–79). Several variations of these concepts appeared in nineteenth-century economic literature as "The Law of Markets" or "Say's Law." However, the explicit definition remained an unsettled matter. Regrettably, this ambiguity made the concept easy prey for a straw man argument.

Keynes defined Say's Law as a "fallacy that demand is created by supply," and elsewhere as "supply creates its own demand." In his interpretation, Say's Law meant that everything produced would automatically be purchased. If this were true, he reasoned, recessions and involuntary unemployment would never occur. Because they are frequent occurrences, Say's Law must be erroneous. Keynes believed that the Classical economists had over-emphasized the role of production (i.e., supply) in understanding the economy. What was really important was consumption (or demand). When people produced more than they consumed, the Classical economist had assumed that the saved cash would find its way back into the economy in the form of investment. Savers lend money to borrowers, who in turn use the money to purchase investment goods (Savings = Investment).

In the Classical school of thought, a rise in the savings rate should have raised the supply of loanable funds, lowering interest rates and stimulating investment. However, Keynes noted that in a recession, the savings may not be recycled into spending on investment goods because a contagion of fear suddenly increases the demand for cash. That is, *Savings = Investment spending + Change in demand for cash.* In a deep depression, *money itself* becomes the primary investment of choice. As banks and businesses become increasingly unwilling to part with it, the wheels of commerce grind to an ever-slower pace. The cash hoarding causes the velocity of money to slow; consequently, prices and economic output both decline. $(MV\downarrow = P\downarrow Y\downarrow)$

Keynes attributed the increased demand for cash to "animal spirits," which was his term for describing the alternating phases of humility and arrogance in the pride cycle. He argued that if banks and entrepreneurs were too apprehensive to lend and invest capital, respectively, then a third party needed to remedy the situation. The government should use its **fiscal policy** to pull the economy out of the doldrums. (Fiscal policy pertains to how governments tax their citizens and spend money.)

Specifically, Keynes held that the state should run a **contra-cyclical** fiscal policy, meaning that governments should stimulate the economy against the tide of the business cycle. Taxes should be raised during times of economic strength, creating a budget surplus. When the economy slows, the government should draw down its rainy day fund and spend on public works projects. With proper application of the stimulant, governments could avoid massive economic boom-and-bust cycles that had plagued capitalism since its inception.

Even if the government had not run a budget surplus heading into a downturn, it should go into debt and serve as Consumer of Last Resort. Most traditional economists bristled at Keynes's notion that a government could somehow be doing its citizens a favor by spending money it didn't have. Even if there were some short-term benefit, wouldn't it merely create a debt that would have to be paid for in the long run? His rejoinder: "The long run is a misleading guide to current affairs. In the long run we are all dead."

Keynes maintained that the *type* of spending that government undertook wasn't important so long as the spending took place. In *The General Theory,* Keynes argued that if a government treasury "were to fill old bottles with bank notes, bury them at suitable depths in disused coal mines which are then filled up to the surface with town rubbish, and leave it to private enterprise on well-tried principles of laissez-faire to dig the notes up again . . . there need be no more unemployment and, with the help of repercussions, the real income of the community, and its capital wealth, would probably become a good deal greater than it actually is."

As the government made a purchase, it put cash in the hands of a private individual who would now be empowered to purchase goods himself. To the extent that the recipient of government funds in turn spent (rather than saved) his money, yet another round of spending would occur. The process continued in a virtuous circle which Keynes dubbed the "**multiplier effect.**" The government's deficit spending would result in a vast increase in economic output, such that the initial round of spending would pay for itself. Whereas Say believed that consumption was constrained by the volume of production, Keynes contended that the only upward limit on consumption was a willingness to part with one's cash.

While Keynes is generally credited with the idea of government contra-cyclical fiscal policy, the concept predates him by several millennia. An Egyptian pharaoh implemented it 4,000 years ago. Genesis 41 tells us that Pharaoh had been harrowed by a dream of seven lean cows devouring seven fat cows and a similar vision involving ears of corn. Frustrated by the inability of his magicians and wise men to interpret his dream, Pharaoh eventually turned to a young foreigner imprisoned in his dungeon. Joseph advised that the dream was a divine vision of Egypt's economic fate. After "seven years of great plenty throughout all the land," Egypt would be overwhelmed with seven years of grievous famine. He told Pharaoh to prepare for the dearth by storing a fifth of the annual grain production during each of the seven plentiful years.

Pharaoh, impressed with the young Hebrew's wisdom, immediately appointed Joseph ruler in Egypt. Joseph spent the next seven years gathering the surplus corn into city granaries. At the appointed time, the prophesied famine arrived—not only in Egypt, but across the face of the earth. The storehouses were opened and the corn was sold to eager crowds. Word spread and Joseph soon found himself distributing corn to hungry foreigners, as well. Egypt's thrift in times of plenty had enabled it to save the world from starvation.

Joseph's story is Keynesian economics at its finest. A prudent ruler stores his country's surplus from the boom years, and then uses the savings to feed his people during a subsequent bust. The policies work pretty well under a very limited set of conditions, namely: a country governed by an all-powerful monarch, who receives divinely inspired dreams on economic matters and has a prophet on hand to interpret them. In a country ruled by a Congress (whose dreams primarily revolve around reelection) and a president advised by less-than-clairvoyant economists, the system doesn't work quite so well.

In a 1934 article for *Redbook* magazine, Keynes wrote, "The very behavior that would make a man poor [deficit spending during a recession] could make a nation wealthy." The words were sweet music to political ears. In the name of "maintaining consumption" and fighting "demand failure," politicians finally had philosophical cover for their profligacy. Washington could justifiably gorge on debt at the slightest sign of economic slowdown. Elected officials and voters alike would soon become debt-addicted prodigals.

The attitude was wholly antithetical to Say's views on the role of government: "The encouragement of mere consumption is no benefit to commerce, for the difficulty lies in supplying the means, not in stimulating the desire of consumption; and we have seen that production alone furnishes those means. *Thus, it is the aim of good government to stimulate production, of bad government to encourage consumption.*"

Within a decade of the publication of *The General Theory,* Keynes had firmly wrested control of macroeconomic thought. The Classical doctrine—that recessions resulted from misalignments of the *structure* of production and the *structure* of demand, exacerbated by the liquidity and capitalization problems inherent to banking—was soon forgotten. Keynesian adherents spent the next forty years building their models of recession around fluctuations in the *level* of demand, rather than in mismatches between the *structure* of supply and demand. The concept of recession as demand deficiency, which Say's Law had been specifically developed to refute, would now become the lynchpin of modern macroeconomic doctrine.

As redefined by Keynes as "supply creates its own demand," Say's Law is clearly an untenable proposition. Everything that is produced does not find a ready buyer, and some goods cannot be sold at prices that cover their costs of production. If these conditions were true, then the noun "artist" wouldn't so often be preceded by the adjective "starving." Every would-be Warhol could find a satisfactory bid for his oil-on-canvas creations.

What Say had actually said was "a product is no sooner created, than it, from that instant, affords a market for other products *to the full extent of its own value*" (p. 134). That is, *desired* goods, which can be sold at prices which cover their costs of production, are the basis of all economic demand. By omitting an essential qualifier, Keynes completely misrepresented the first principle of economics and adopted a consumption-oriented (rather than production-oriented) worldview. In so doing, he opened a floodgate of spurious economic doctrine. And just as importantly, the moral implications of economic activity underwent a subtle, but crucial, shift.

In an economy with large-scale division of labor, a production-oriented person is focused on meeting the needs and wants of others. Those persons and organizations that provide others with goods *of value* earn the right to subsequently consume. A man who is preoccupied with service has little time to cultivate a sense of entitlement. Alternatively, a focus on consumption is an emphasis on immediate self-gratification. It's no wonder Keynes had emphasized the short run to the detriment of the long run. Accordingly, he also spoke derisively of saving and lending: "Interest today rewards no genuine sacrifice, any more than does the rent of land . . . But whilst there may be intrinsic reasons for the scarcity of land, there are no intrinsic reasons for the scarcity of capital." He maintained that market interest rates were "unjust" due to savers' large preference for cash.

Contrary to Keynes's assertion, interest *does* represent a genuine sacrifice: the willingness to temporarily forego consumption and risk one's capital. In order for money to be invested, it must first be saved. Interest is the reward for the delay of consumption and the risk of loss on an unpaid loan. The investment which flows from savings raises productivity, thereby enabling higher levels of future consumption. For this reason, Say had extolled the virtue of saving and subsequent "reproductive" investment spending.

Just like the private sector, government can engage in "reproductive investments" which create higher living standards through prudent allocation of capital. The interstate highway system is a noteworthy example. But in the majority of cases, government deficit spending merely funds current consumption for favored constituencies. In doing so, it saddles posterity with public debt with no prospect for a corresponding increase in living standards. The future generation will not enjoy the fruits of its own production because most of their income has been involuntarily earmarked to pay the tab for their grandparents' bender.

Toward the end of his life, Keynes saw firsthand the abuse of his well-intentioned ideas. After a 1944 meeting with President Roosevelt and White House staffers, he realized that politicians would be strongly tempted to abuse the principle of demand stimulus long after the exigencies of the Depression and World War II had passed. "I was the only non-Keynesian in the room," he lamented. Regrettably, he died in 1946 before he could emphasize the necessary caveats. But it was too late: the Pandora's Box of Keynesian Economics had been opened.

## Chapter 7

# ROMEO AND JULIET HEDGE THEIR BETS

*"If you have to prove you are worthy of credit,
your credit is already gone."*
**WALTER BAGEHOT, FIRST EDITOR-IN-CHIEF OF THE ECONOMIST**

I had committed most of the menu prices to memory within my first month at the store, although I still had to consult the cheat sheet when a customer ordered an esoteric item. Though customers seldom attempted to order off-menu, we were always willing to oblige inasmuch as the requisite ingredients were found in our kitchen. There was, however, one request which we categorically refused to accommodate: pancakes.

As with waffles, pancakes come in a variety of forms: German pancakes, crepes, Mexican hotcakes. All pancakes, like all waffles, are prepared by heating a batter comprised of flour, eggs, and milk. Essentially, they are both flat cakes prepared without the use of an oven. As far as I can tell, the only real difference between a pancake and a waffle is that the former is cooked on a flat surface, the latter in an iron. Given the similarities between the two, I was surprised by how severely the grill officers bristled at a pancake order.

In their defense, the only frying pans at Papa's were six inches in diameter: perfect for cooking two or three eggs, but far too small to quickly prepare a stack of pancakes. On the other hand, the 3-foot by 5-foot grill was unquestionably large enough to handle the order. After some cajoling, the cooks would generally acquiesce, but made their offer in a serious (and hushed) tone: "Okay, I'll make three of them this time, but just for that one table. And you have to swear not to tell anyone about this."

Initially, I couldn't understand why the cooks were more secretive about cooking pancakes than they were about discussing their parole violations and recreational drug habits. I subsequently realized that cooking pancakes is more likely to get you fired at Papa's. I'm not really sure why pancakes were such a taboo subject, although I suspect it had to do with our corporate nemesis, another twenty-four-hour establishment that specialized in breakfast food.

The International House of Pancakes (better known as IHOP) was founded in 1958, just two years before Papa's Chicken & Waffles. In addition to serving the eponymous pancakes, they also offer a few other dishes not served at Papa's: French toast, crepes, and cheesecake. The rest of their menu offering is quite similar to our own. IHOP has 1,400 locations, only 300 fewer than Papa's. While our geographic footprint currently encompasses roughly half of the states in the Union, IHOP has locations in the U.S., Canada, and Mexico. I suspect that in the eyes of management, the international presence makes them downright cosmopolitan.

Whereas Papa's Chicken & Waffles cooks artificial strawberry cubes into our half-inch thick waffles, IHOP serves thick Belgian-style waffles garnished with fresh strawberries. Papa's offers two varieties of syrup: plain and "warm." IHOP, in all its pomposity, keeps four flavors on each table: blueberry, boysenberry, butter pecan, and strawberry. It's downright obnoxious. And while I don't have any hard data, I'm willing to bet that hiring managers won't even take a second look at your application until you finish serving parole.

While they never conceded that it was a superior restaurant, Papa's servers would occasionally refer pancake-starved customers to an IHOP location 14 miles away. "But you didn't hear it from me," they added in a whisper. I never made the recommendation but came very close on one occasion when a recalcitrant middle-aged man believed that wearing a sport coat gave him the privilege of ordering off-menu during the three a.m. rush hour. I had repeatedly advised him that waffles were perfectly viable substitutes, but he refused to bend. Thankfully, his dimwitted girlfriend reproved him on my behalf.

"Honey, you are at *Papa's Waffles*. If you wanted pancakes, then you should have gone to the *Pancake* House. Or House of Pancakes. Whatever they call it."

She was immensely proud of herself for having made the observation. The glare that it drew, however, left no doubt that there would be strong words exchanged when they returned to their car.

$ $ $ $ $

At first blush, cooking a waffle is a prosaic endeavor. You apply a nonstick spray to a waffle iron, pour a ladle of batter in its center, close the lid, set a timer, and return three minutes later to remove that most sublime arrangement of simple carbohydrates—a golden brown waffle. It sounds so easy. (Then again, so does "buy low, sell high.") The fresh waffle contains a tremendous amount of moisture. Should you need to reheat one, never use a microwave for the job—always use a toaster oven, instead. The former will cause the waffle to emerge hot and soggy; the toaster will produce a much drier result, which is imperative for proper syrup absorption. Waffle irons can be horribly temperamental. If improperly calibrated, the waffles may cook too quickly, resulting in a burnt shell housing a doughy center. If the iron is not doused with sufficient amounts of nonstick spray before receiving the batter, it will not readily part with a cooked waffle. Additives such as chocolate chips, pecans, and artificial fruit chunks only complicate matters.

An eight-inch steel pick makes prying an obstinate waffle from the iron somewhat easier, but it's still a meticulous task. The tiniest slip frequently results in a second-degree burn, which often remains tender for more than a week. Edward had developed a more effective method for separating waffles from the irons. Delivering a quick palm strike to the tip of its coiled handle, the iron would pop open as the impact of the blow knocked the waffle free.

"Tricks of the trade, Jimmy," he said with a wink.

People were more finicky about their waffle orders than any other item. Our menu advertised "light waffles," which made many customers erroneously assume they had been prepared with buttermilk batter. What it actually meant was that we had left the batter in the iron for thirty seconds less than for regular waffles. A "dark" waffle was simply cooked for an additional minute. There was no "rare" or "medium well" type convention, which would have come in handy one Thursday evening. Instead, the customer resorted to an ad hoc approach.

"Make mine dark—but not too dark," he said.

"Could you be more specific, sir?" I asked. "I want to be sure that we get this right the first time."

"Yeah. I want it a little bit lighter than me." He pointed to his bare forearm. "Make it as dark as . . . Obama. Can you all handle that?"

"I'm not sure that we've ever tried," I said. "We'll do our best."

"I trust you, Jimmy. By the way, my girl also wants a regular waffle."

"She doesn't want it to resemble Bill Clinton in any way, does she?"

During his first two months in the Oval Office, Barack Obama had enjoyed widespread support amongst my customers and co-workers. However, his popularity was summarily undermined when he signed legislation raising federal taxes on cigarettes by 62 cents a pack. It was a pretty expedient way to alienate a demographic that thought of Newport menthols as the fifth food group.

I turned to call the order. "Edward, set waffle on two, make one. . . like . . . Obama."

"Jimmy, are you placing an order or talking politics?"

I walked over to Edward and whispered the peculiar request in his ear. He nodded, cast a glance at the customer, and poured the batter. In three minutes and forty-five seconds, he peeled the finished product from the iron and set it on a plate. I reached under the counter and produced a recent issue of *The Economist,* whose cover photo featured the President delivering a speech. I discreetly placed the magazine next to the waffle in an attempt to verify that it had been prepared to specification. I glanced quickly at the magazine cover, then at the waffle, and back at the magazine. I knew I didn't have much time before—

"Jimmy, what the hell are you doing reading a magazine when customers are waiting on their food? Take that order out right now!" Edward barked.

I placed the magazine in my apron pocket and set the plate in front of my customer.

"One presidential waffle," I declared proudly. "I hope it's up to par."

For only 45 additional cents, we prepared waffles with chocolate chips, pecans, and berries. All toppings were sprinkled into the iron after the batter was poured, thereby baking them directly into the core. Chocolate waffles enjoyed popularity across a wide array of demographics, while pecan waffles were favored by only a small minority of customers. Strawberry and blueberry waffles, while not an uncommon selection among sober patrons, were incredibly popular with the stoner crowd. I don't know what it is about THC, but apparently the more you have in your system, the more artificial berries your stomach requires.

No matter how liberal I was with a blueberry allocation, it was never sufficient for the always-finicky potheads. Notwithstanding this hang-up, they were much easier to wait on than the drunkards. For one thing, they always came in when the store was less crowded—usually between 1 and 3 a.m. on weeknights. And while they tended to be lousy tippers, the stoners had infinitely more patience than the barflies. Of all of our toking patrons, my personal favorite was the Cookie Monster.

Like his Sesame Street eponym, the Cookie Monster possessed an insatiable appetite and a set of irises that moved at random inside his eye sockets. It was truly a sight to behold. Careful though he was to order only as much food as he thought he could pay for, the Cookie Monster always came up short. Perhaps I should have been annoyed by his arithmetic ineptitude, but combined with his soft demeanor and general sense of helplessness, I actually found the trait quite endearing.

The Cookie Monster habitually ordered two or three items before asking me to furnish a subtotal. He then proceeded to count his money, and then asked me to repeat the total again. If he had sufficient funds, he would resume ordering until he thought he would break the bank. After he realized that the demands of his stomach exceeded the cash in his pocket, he would spend several minutes trying to decide what items to delete from his order. Naturally, by that point, I had already called it in to the grill officers.

I don't know if Cookie's deficient math skills were a function of poor primary education or the volume of cannabis in his body. During my first few encounters with him, I tried attending to other customers while he fecklessly attempted to reconcile his belly with his wallet. No sooner had the others begun to order than he would interrupt with questions about how canceling particular items would affect his total. Instead of forcing the other patrons to wait indefinitely and losing their business, I simply gave him carte blanche and covered the inevitable shortfall out of my own pocket. During my six months at Papa's, his was the only customer tab that I ever covered.

All Papa's checks have a note on both the front and back asking the customers to pay at the cash register. Most patrons complied with this request. Those that didn't either walked out of the store without paying or left cash on the table. When the Cookie Monster took the latter route, he could always be depended upon to leave an insufficient amount of cash and coin to cover his check. Unfailingly, the difference was less than fifty cents. I was only too happy to pay it for him.

Of the fifty tickets I wrote on most weekend shifts, an average of two of them went unpaid. Given our volume during the bar rush, it was all too easy for dishonest customers to slip out before we could notice. Of course, someone that leaves his check on the table also neglects to tip, but it wasn't the personal economic slight that bothered me. It was what the walk-out represented: theft. The unpaid check might as well have been a shattered window pane that bore testament to a break-in.

Edward taught me that it didn't pay to chase a stingy customer out to his car, because the kind of person that leaves without paying is often the same kind of person that has no compunction instigating violence when he is called out on it. The best way to address the problem was to try to remember the face of an offending party and refuse service if he or she ever returned. As a group of female bandits absconded from the premises, he simply offered the casual observation, "those four hoes just left without paying for their biscuits."

I turned to look at the offending parties to discover that he was actually using the term "hoes" in a descriptive, rather than a pejorative, sense. Their dress, tattoos, and body language fully conveyed the impression that they just finished strutting their wares up and down Hollywood Boulevard.

Although I eventually learned to heed Edward's advice and shrug off the incidents, there was one type of walk-out that always left me incensed. Occasionally, customers would place an order, decide they weren't willing to wait for it, and leave the store while their food was still being prepared. When the unclaimed food came off the grill, it went straight into the garbage.

Not only had the walk-out wasted my time, the cooks' time, and other customers' time, but the food itself had been wasted.

$ $ $ $ $

As Say explained in his *Treatise*, production represents the creation of utility, or value. By contrast, consumption represents the destruction of value. Any waste of material and labor, however minute, represents a real loss of wealth. A commonly held economic fallacy maintains that war is an economic boon because a wartime economy usually entails increased utilization of society's labor and capital. Although it is true that heightened military spending by governments may result in a temporary increase in reported economic output, no products of real value to consumers are being produced. Has anyone ever derived any value from "consuming" an artillery shell? Furthermore, the deaths of working-age humans always *subtract* productive capacity from an economy; they never add to it.

World War II has the distinction of generating the greatest manmade decline in living standards in human history. Unprecedented in scale and scope, the war affected every inhabited Continent on earth. Over its six-year course, 100 million troops were mobilized across a comparable number of countries. By its conclusion in August 1945, more than 70 million people had lost their lives. Freedom for the nations of Europe, North Africa, Asia, and the Pacific Islands had come at an inestimable price.

Inasmuch as the Allied victory had been achieved in European and Pacific battlefields, it had been won in American factories. In order to meet the demands of war, the structure of production had undergone an immense shift: a third of the goods and services produced in the United States during 1943 and 1944 were consecrated to the war effort. Government spending, which had accounted for roughly 15% of the economy in 1940, spiked to a nearly 50% share by 1943.

As measured by Gross Domestic Product, total output increased substantially. The economy grew at an average rate of nearly 12% between 1941 and 1945. The large government demand for material ensured that any man who was not serving in the Armed Forces could find ready employment in domestic manufacturing.

The torrid pace of economic growth and attendant decline in unemployment during the war years appeared to be a full-fledged vindication of Keynes's ideas. The Depression, the Keynesian narrative explained, had been caused by a precipitous decline in private spending. The country emerged only as a result of massive government expenditure which had plugged the gap between savings and investment.

Keynesian economic theory quickly gained broad acceptance in both academia and mainstream America in the postwar years. By the mid-1960s, it had become so predominant that the December 31, 1965 issue of *Time* magazine declared, "We are all Keynesians now," in a cover story. In the "New Economics," Say's doctrine was a misguided suggestion rather than a law, and Adam Smith's Invisible Hand suffered from frequent bouts of palsy. Accordingly, the public acquiesced to a larger role for government in managing the business cycle and regulating industry. The only alternative, they understood, was another Depression. But the Keynesian dogma would soon be challenged by a plucky heretic from the University of Chicago.

At barely five feet tall, Milton Friedman stood eighteen inches shorter than the colossal Lord Keynes. The diminutive stature was hardly a reflection of his intellectual power. The volume and scope of Friedman's contributions to economics, statistics, applied game theory, and political thought is truly prodigious and cannot be adequately chronicled in a few paragraphs. But perhaps his greatest achievement was popularizing laissez-faire ideologies of Adam Smith amongst a generation that had come to think of "the free market" as an expletive and of government as a panacea.

Keynes had once written that a master economist "must be a mathematician, historian, statesman, philosopher... He must study the present in the light of the past for the purposes of the future." If there was ever a man who met those criteria, Friedman was it. Unlike most economists—who had contended primarily on the basis of theoretical abstractions—Friedman employed a bevy of statistics and historical experience to substantiate his arguments.

In 1963, Friedman and coauthor Anna Schwartz published *A Monetary History of the United States, 1867–1960,* a 900-page tome that surveyed American history through the lens of money and banking. It was a laborious compilation of nearly a century of data on the domestic money supply, inflation rates, gold stock, and bank reserves and deposits. Armed with copious figures and a thoroughly researched historical narrative, Friedman explained the Depression in much the same terms that Irving Fisher had thirty years before.

According to Keynes, the Great Depression of 1929–33 arose from a global savings glut, particularly in the United States. Falling output, high unemployment, and collapsing asset prices were the symptoms of pessimistic "animal spirits." Skeptical consumers and investors preferred to sit on their cash rather than spend or invest their money, respectively. The increased demand for cash slowed its velocity, or circulation rate. In order to get the monetary bloodstream circulating goods and services again, the economy desperately needed the stimulant of government spending.

Keynes's argument for government intervention rested on the notion that the demand for cash was highly volatile due to the collective mood swings of a fickle public. The economic instability that resulted from these sporadic bouts of money hoarding was the main cause of depressions. Friedman would later describe the theory as "one of those very productive hypotheses—a very ingenious one, a very intelligent one," adding that "it just turned out to be incompatible with the facts when it was put to the test."

The "facts" Friedman was referring to were changes in the money supply. While Keynes had claimed that an increase in demand for money was the *cause* of depression, Friedman demonstrated that it was a *symptom*. As with all depressions, the real culprit in the 1930s was a deflating asset bubble (in this case, the stock market) magnified by the collapse of the banking system. The particulars differed from the 1837 and 1907 panics, but the storyline was clearly the same:

*had borrowed from*     *who owed money to*

Stock Market Speculators   >   Brokers   >   Banks

*who in turn owed*

   >   Bank Depositors

After the establishment of the Federal Reserve System in 1913, commercial bankers looked to the Fed (rather than private financiers like J.P. Morgan) to provide the banking system with reserves in times of emergency. Most of the cash was furnished by The Federal Reserve Bank of New York under the supervision of its president, Benjamin Strong. Strong had served as Morgan's chief lieutenant during the Panic of 1907 and had ably guided the bank from 1914 until his death in late 1928.

When the stock market crashed the following October, an internecine conflict erupted between the Reserve Bank of New York and the Board of Governors in Washington D.C. Instead of flooding the banking system with cash reserves as Strong surely would have done, the Board allowed the money supply to slowly decline by 3% over the next twelve months.

Friedman believed that the severe, but manageable, recession of 1930 would not have snowballed into a depression had the Federal Reserve provided emergency lending during a spate of bank runs late that year. Between 1930 and 1933, the Fed largely stood by as nearly 40% of America's banks collapsed, taking with them a third of the nation's money supply. At the exact moment that the Fed should have been lending cash to the commercial banks to ease their liquidity plight, it had barely budged. Why?

The Federal Reserve Act had stipulated that each Reserve bank would maintain a gold reserve ratio of 40% of the value of its liabilities (notes and deposits) at a statutory rate of $20.67 per troy ounce. In order for a Reserve bank to create additional money to lend to the commercial banks, it would need more gold reserves in its own vaults. However, the Act gave the Board of Governors authority to circumvent this rule. In times of crisis, the Board could suspend all gold reserve requirements for the Reserve banks for an indefinite period, enabling them to create an unlimited amount of cash. But before they could begin manufacturing Federal Reserve Notes and freely lending the new money to commercial banks, the Fed banks had to address one complicating factor: foreign investors, who were experiencing economic calamity in their own countries, had begun to redeem their Federal Reserve Notes for gold.

Rather than sit idly as its gold reserves were depleted by the repatriation, the Fed raised interest rates to entice the foreign investors to keep their money in dollar-denominated investments. In one sense, the maneuver worked beautifully: the higher interest rates attracted new gold inflows into the Reserve banks, causing the Fed's stockpile of bullion to rebound. Regrettably, the higher rates created tighter credit conditions in the U.S. economy and sent the debt deflation spiral on another leg downward.

After a modest 2% decline in 1930, the U.S. money supply collapsed in successive waves of bank runs over the next four years. In 1931, it fell by 7% and was followed by 17% and 12% declines in 1932 and 1933, respectively—a total drop of 33% from 1929 levels. As the banking system hemorrhaged the monetary blood, the productive organs of the economy shut down. Real output collapsed by 26.5% from 1929 to 1933; unemployment rose from 3% to a staggering 25%. The velocity (or "heart rate") of money also fell by nearly one third $(M{\downarrow}V{\downarrow} = P{\downarrow}Y{\downarrow})$.

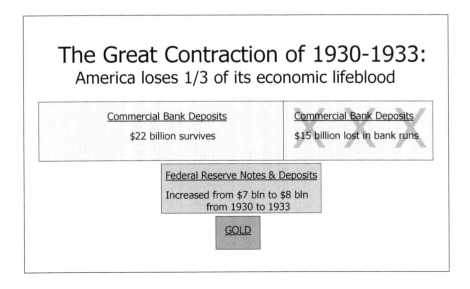

## The Great Contraction of 1930-1933:
### America loses 1/3 of its economic lifeblood

| Commercial Bank Deposits | Commercial Bank Deposits |
|---|---|
| $22 billion survives | $15 billion lost in bank runs |

Federal Reserve Notes & Deposits
Increased from $7 bln to $8 bln
from 1930 to 1933

GOLD

The deplorable state of the economy in 1932 enabled Franklin D. Roosevelt to defeat incumbent American President Herbert Hoover in a November landslide. FDR's first year in office was marked by a bevy of reforms which provided both liquidity and capital to the beleaguered commercial banks.

Additionally, the government also injected liquidity into the Federal Reserve banks via the Gold Reserve Act. The dollar, which had been pegged at $20.67 per ounce of gold, would henceforth be valued at $35 per ounce—a 40% debasement. By reducing the value of its liabilities (the dollar), the Fed was now awash in gold reserves and free to create new money.

With the advent of government bank deposit insurance and a now-accommodative Federal Reserve in early 1933, the bank runs halted, and the money supply stabilized. No longer forced by frightened depositors to call in their loans in a mad scramble for cash, banks were free to lend again, and the economy went on a tear. From 1933 to 1936, the U.S. economy grew at an average annual rate of 9.4%. Total output reached an all-time high, surpassing the previous record set in 1929. The unemployment rate fell from a high of 25.6% in 1933 to a low of 11% in 1937. After falling at an average rate of 6.7% per year from 1930–33, consumer prices rose by an average 2.7% per year from 1934–37 as the stock market increased fourfold.

As the economy mended, bankers added to their cash reserves in a precautionary move against a repeat of the bank run episodes earlier in the decade. By 1936, they were holding reserves at 20% of deposits, more than twice the regulatory-mandated level. In an attempt to boost public confidence in the banks, the Fed decided to raise the reserve requirement between August 1936 and May 1937.

Unfortunately, banks responded to the Fed's move by hoarding even more reserves. As the stockpiled cash sat fallow in bank vaults, lending dried up—and so did economic activity. In 1938, real output fell by 3.4% as unemployment climbed to 19%. A robust recovery was underway by 1939, but the market's natural healing process was soon overshadowed by war mobilization in the wake of the Pearl Harbor attack in December 1941.

As Friedman sifted through the historical data on the Depression, he noticed the same phenomenon that he had observed in other periods in American history: changes in the demand for money (as measured by velocity) were highly correlated with changes in the money supply. During episodes of consumer price inflation, velocity rose as the demand for money declined. In periods of money destruction, velocity declined as the demand for money rose.

*A Monetary History of the United States* made a convincing statistical case that changes in the money supply and the attendant contraction of credit were a major cause of depressions. Yes, money demand rose modestly during recessions, but it did not increase exponentially unless banking institutions were imperiled. Keynes had believed that bankers stopped lending and businesses quit borrowing to invest simply because they had lost their nerve due to melancholy "animal spirits." But Friedman's data brought to light a major omission of Keynes's analysis: during depressions, banks are severely encumbered by capital and liquidity constraints. They aren't simply *scared* to move; they literally *can't* move. *Sudden swings in the demand for cash were due to forced debt repayment by borrowers to their banks and by banks to their depositors,* not a nebulous "failure of aggregate demand" as Keynes had claimed. In the absence of war, demand for money was fairly steady as long as the banking system had a strong foundation.

If indeed commerce shut down on the whims of the market's animal spirits, then the Keynesian prescription of timely government spending could be justified. But if Friedman's diagnosis was correct, *government could play a more valuable economic role simply by ensuring that financial institutions were liquid and well-capitalized.* There would be little need for the drug of budget deficits as long as the economy didn't hemorrhage its monetary blood.

The postwar decades continued to bear out Friedman's hypothesis. In the absence of bank runs, the demand for money held remarkably stable from 1950 to 1980. Fiscal policy also turned out to be less important in determining economic growth than Keynes's followers had believed. When fiscal policy was at odds with monetary policy, the latter consistently proved to be the deciding factor. As far as economic conditions were concerned, decisions made at the Federal Reserve building mattered much more than what transpired on Capitol Hill.

The concurrent phenomena of high unemployment rates and high inflation rates in the 1970s dealt another blow to Keynesian theory, which had posited that recessions and elevated unemployment resulted from an increase in cash preferences. According to the Keynesians, greater economic uncertainty should cause more people to hoard their money, creating downward pressure on consumer prices. How could the demand for money be falling (as evidenced by the high inflation rate), if unemployment was high?

Simple, Friedman explained. Due to Federal Reserve policy, the money supply was growing faster than the real economy. The natural result of more money chasing a relatively flat volume of goods and services was an increase in the price level ($M\uparrow V = P\uparrow Y$).

Later in the decade, the Fed finally began to follow Friedman's prescription by slowing money supply growth. After an acute recession, inflation was bridled and robust economic growth resumed in the early 1980s, exactly as Friedman had predicted.

The analyses were conclusive: the Depression of the 1930s and the "stagflation" of the 1970s were not due to fractures in the Invisible Hand. In both cases, the true blame lay at the clubbed feet of the Federal Reserve as it mismanaged the money supply. Deficit spending was not an economic salve, but only a mechanism for diverting capital away from the private sector, creating superfluous bureaucracies and encumbering future generations with debt. "The government solution to a problem," Friedman wrote, "is usually as bad as the problem."

Due in large part to Friedman's efforts, free market ideology enjoyed a robust resurgence in the 1980s. Americans had justifiably learned to place limited faith in their government for having mismanaged the

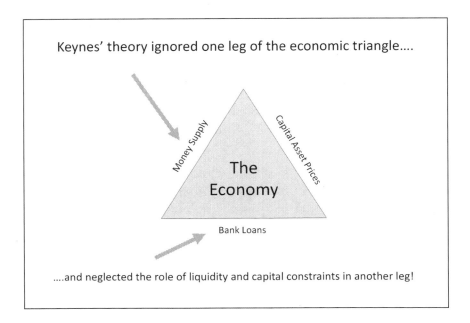

Keynes' theory ignored one leg of the economic triangle....

Money Supply

Capital Asset Prices

The Economy

Bank Loans

....and neglected the role of liquidity and capital constraints in another leg!

nation's money supply. But in the next two decades, they would learn that private bankers were just as human as the central bankers at the Fed, and the fallout of their mistakes could prove every bit as severe.

$ $ $ $ $

Of all of the unique individuals that I waited on during my six months at Papa's Chicken & Waffles, one customer's attire stands out in particular: lime green dress, wide-brimmed white knit hat, faux pearl necklace, and plastic wrist bangles. A gaudy ensemble, to be sure, but the drag queen could have probably still passed for a woman had a gray beard not blown his cover.

"You must like that lady at the high bar," Edward said in a hushed tone as I replenished the beans in the coffee grinder.

"Why is that, Edward?" I asked in a tired voice. I had grown accustomed to him maligning my sexual orientation when I bantered at length with any male acquaintance. By waiting on this guy, I was walking into a veritable minefield of harassment.

"Well, I see you keep licking your lips every time you talk with her."

I had cut the inside of my lower lip during a recent sparring session and had spent most of the shift subconsciously massaging the wound with my tongue. Edward was reticent to accept my explanation on the grounds that adopting such a suggestive mannerism while serving a transvestite could not have been a total coincidence. According to him, this was consistent with an observed pattern of behavior.

"There's a lot of things I've noticed about you, Jimmy. For instance, every time you mess up an order—which is something you do pretty often—it's always a gal's. I have yet to see you screw up when it's a man you're waiting on. Now why would that be?"

"Well, I'm not sure I know, Edward. Perhaps you've formulated a hypothesis of your own."

"Yeah, I got a hypothesis. My hypothesis is that you like dudes more than gals."

"So what might I do to convince you otherwise, Edward?"

"Well, that would make for a pretty long list, and I ain't got that kind of time. Maybe if you were to give first-class treatment to a man *dressed* as a woman, it would actually represent a small sign of improvement. By getting comfortable with a fake gal, you would be better prepared to handle orders from bona fide females."

With no other customers to attend to, I elected to wipe down my tables and cast the occasional furtive glance at the drag queen as he quietly consumed his omelet. I had never seen a real live one before. Admittedly, I didn't know a lot about cross-dressing, but it seemed like it was something people should do at home, or perhaps at a club that catered to that interest. More than anything else, I was intrigued by his age—he had to have been sixty-five years old if he was a day. I guess I had assumed that most practitioners would outgrow their habit by the time they received an AARP card in the mail.

It was only a matter of time until Edward nudged me again on the arm.

"I see you still got your eye on that rough-looking broad at the high bar."

"I was noticing the earrings she . . . he's . . . it's wearing—those gray studs."

"And you're thinking, 'hey, he looks cute in 'em, but I'd wager that they'd look even better on my ears.'"

"I was thinking that they look exactly like the Tahitian pearl earrings I bought my wife for Christmas last year. I'm going to ask her never to wear them again."

$$$$$

"An insurance company," an industry executive once told me, "is a hedge fund in drag." I didn't know what he meant at the time. After a few more years in finance, I began to get the picture. Insurers, banks, and other financial intermediaries all have the same mission: borrow at one rate and lend at a higher rate. It doesn't matter who you borrow your money from, or in what form. Those are details.

At some point in their lives, most people will purchase an insurance policy on their car, home, or life. But despite its ubiquity, few people understand how the insurance business works. The easiest way to think about insurance companies is to consider them as a special type of bank.

A bank, you will recall, earns its profits by borrowing from its depositors, lending out their money at a higher rate, and pocketing the difference.

An insurance company uses the same business model, except that instead of borrowing money from depositors, it borrows from its policyholders. When you purchase an insurance policy, you agree to make a regular payment called a **premium** to the insurance company. In exchange for the premium, the insurance company agrees to pay you a specified sum of money (the **claim**) in the event that the **insured risk**—a car accident, house fire, or untimely death—comes to pass.

By insuring (or underwriting) the risk, the insurance company is making a bet that the insured event will not transpire before the policy matures. Insurance companies use copious data and a team of actuaries to help them assess these risks, but they can never be 100% certain about what the future will bear. The uncertainty about the amount of money that will ultimately be paid out for insurance claims is known as **underwriting risk.**

The premium is the insurance company's compensation for assuming the policyholder's risk. The insurer tries to make a profit by charging a sufficient premium to compensate for the probability that the accident will occur. If the insurer charges an adequate premium, it earns an underwriting profit. If it charges too little relative to the risk it assumes, it will incur an underwriting loss.

Important as they are, underwriting profits are not how insurance companies earn most of their money. Rather, they earn it by lending out the policyholders' premiums—just as a bank lends out its depositors' money. But whereas banks lend out most of their money in the form of bank loans, insurance companies invest most of their money by lending to commercial real estate developers and purchasing bonds issued by large corporations. Once again, a chain of debts is forged.

|  | *Owe money to* |  | *who owe money to* |
|---|---|---|---|
| Corporations | > | Insurance Companies | > | Insurance Policyholders |

As a de facto bank, the insurance company faces the same set of challenges faced by banks, namely, credit and liquidity risks. If too many corporations default on their bonds, the insurance company's capital will be depleted, rendering it insolvent. And where a bank must maintain sufficient cash on hand to satisfy deposit redemptions, an insurance company needs to keep adequate cash levels to pay out its claims.

Whereas banks are contractually obligated to redeem the value of checking and savings accounts on demand, insurance companies charge steep penalties and require advance notice for customers that want to cash in their policies. This arrangement has made insurance companies much less prone to liquidity crises (i.e., bank runs) than commercial banks.

The major disadvantage of running an insurance company instead of a commercial bank is the greater uncertainty of liabilities. A bank knows exactly how much it owes each of its depositors. In contrast, an insurance company can never be precisely sure about the ultimate size of its liabilities due to underwriting risks. Accordingly, the most likely reason for an insurance company to collapse is if a large number of accidents occur simultaneously across the country. But should such broad destruction actually occur, it is probable that Armageddon has commenced and the claims department staff won't be showing up for work, anyway.

A nontraditional form of insurance known as credit default swaps (CDS) has proliferated in recent years. CDS are essentially bets on whether or not a particular "reference" bond (or loan) will make its scheduled payments of interest and principal. "Selling" default protection is akin to insuring the reference bond against default. "Purchasing" default protection is buying an insurance policy that pays a claim if the reference bond defaults. In most cases, neither the seller nor the buyer of credit protection actually owns the reference bond.

Selling default protection creates the same economic effect as purchasing the bond referenced by the CDS contract. If the bond defaults, you owe your counterparty money—the same amount you would have lost if you had actually purchased the bond itself. It's sort of like betting on the heavy favorite in a basketball game—you receive a small premium for doing so and, in most cases, your bet will pay off. But when the bet goes against you, the loss is fairly large. The main difference is that in the CDS market, you are wagering on corporations or home mortgages rather than the New York Knicks. (And Goldman Sachs is your bookie.)

When I started in the insurance business in August 2001, the CDS market was still in its infancy. Within three years, it had eclipsed the market for "cash" corporate bonds—i.e., the actual debt obligations issued by the companies themselves. By early 2009, the market had reached a notional value of $40 trillion, nearly three times the size of total U.S. annual output.

When I left the bond market in January 2009, five-year credit default swaps on McDonald's corporation traded at 50 basis points, meaning that you could earn $5,000 per year for insuring a million dollars worth of McDonald's debt until January 2014. On the same date, five-year CDS on U.S. Treasury bonds were trading at 65 basis points. Writing a comparable insurance policy on Uncle Sam's debt would garner an annual payment of $6,500.

This was perhaps the most horribly disconcerting set of price quotes that I ever saw during my bond market tenure. The Street was telling you that Ronald McDonald and friends had a better chance of surviving the economic holocaust than the United States Treasury Department. It seemed ludicrous at the time, but then again, who was to say that Timothy Geithner wouldn't be grilling Big Macs before the nightmare finally ended?

$ $ $ $ $

If Papa's Chicken & Waffles occasionally manifested elements of *Hamlet* on the weeknights, the early Saturday morning shenanigans of mischievous young lovers were more reminiscent of Shakespeare's *A Midsummer Night's Dream*. Girls really made themselves up for a night out on the town in the hopes of landing a man. A few of them skipped the clubs altogether and headed straight to the Papa's after party, where they could mingle without the nuisance of paying a cover charge. I could appreciate the rationale, but something about donning a slinky neon dress and a pair of stilettos for the avowed purpose of eating biscuits and gravy struck me as inherently absurd.

As a pretty girl in a short-hemmed pink dress took a booth seat, Edward leaned over my shoulder.

"There's a lot of beef on that cow," he stated.

Startled, I wheeled around to face him. "Edward, that girl has a perfect figure. What are you talking about?"

"What is a man supposed to do with beef?"

"What?"

"Beef, Jimmy. What do you do with beef?"

"I suppose that's not a rhetorical question."

"No, it ain't rhetorical. It's not even multiple choice. It's a question that every man your age should know the answer to by now."

The heat was on.

"Well, I suppose that one grills beef to the temperature he pleases, douses it with his favorite array of condiments, and then dines."

"That's right." He paused, waiting for me to draw the appropriate conclusion.

"So you're saying that a 'beefy cow' is an expression for a beautiful woman?"

"I'm glad to see your education hasn't entirely robbed you of your capacity to reason."

"You might be surprised, Edward. It's just that I've never traveled in circles where 'cow' was anything other than a pejorative term for a woman. I spent ten months in Romania, and it's considered quite an insult over there."

"It's also several thousand miles away. Is it time for another geography lesson?"

"That won't be necessary, Edward. I will gladly defer to your judgment." It stood to reason that challenging Edward on his use of idioms would be as utterly futile as questioning his position on Japanese cultural norms.

As we were bantering, another attractive female entered the store and joined her friend at the table.

"That girl makes the blood change directions," Edward said.

"I'm pretty sure I catch your drift on that one," I said.

"Yeaauuuh. You a smart man. You ain't 100% there yet, but you're coming along."

$ $ $ $ $

When coupled with effective flirtation, a lady's provocative dress frequently culminated with a male admirer offering to pick up the tab for her hashbrowns.

"Oh, sweetie, you shouldn't have," she'd reply, embracing him with all of the zeal of a silhouette in a DeBeers' commercial. In a few more minutes they would leave the store with their arms wrapped around each other's waists.

It was touching to see romance blossom. Hashbrowns, unlike diamonds, are not forever. But they're an indisputably cost-effective way to garner the love of a woman. At least at three in the morning. Cupid really is a knavish lad, thus to make poor females mad.

While our customers were busy offering, accepting, and rejecting romantic overtures, I spent every spare minute that I had washing plates, glasses and silverware in the dish pit underneath the high bar. Although convenient for maintaining productivity throughout the shift, the location had one major drawback. If the pressurized water struck a plate, pot, or cup at an awkward angle, several customers could be completely drenched by the consequent ricochet. (I made this mistake myself on several occasions.)

Although the volume could be daunting at times, I usually found washing dishes to be a very therapeutic exercise. There was only one element of dishwashing that I didn't appreciate: no matter how thoroughly I scraped the plates before spraying them, food particles always found their way to the bottom of the sink, clogging the basin. As the store had no dishwashing gloves, I was left to remove the grits, hashbrowns, and meat chunks with a bare hand from the ten-inch-deep drain.

After several handfuls of the detritus had been extracted, the remainder had to be gently cajoled down the drain with my index and middle fingers. And if that wasn't sufficiently grotesque, when I finally retrieved my hand from the abyss, stray grits clung to my forearm hair like fleas on a dog's back. After they had been cleaned manually, we ran the dishes through a high-temperature industrial dishwashing machine. But despite our thoroughness and high marks from state inspectors, many patrons still requested a glass of hot water to sterilize their own silverware before eating. Others eschewed metal silverware altogether, demanding instead the plastic utensils that we generally reserved for take-out orders.

While I could empathize somewhat with the germaphobes, I couldn't understand why so many of them were more concerned about the bacterial threats from our silverware than from the strangers that they took back to their apartments after dining with us.

Most of the romantic liaisons forged inside the walls of Papa's were made between patrons, but every so often a grill officer or server was the object of a customer advance. In our store, the preponderance of female attention was garnered by Tommy, the server who had shielded me from a bowl of hot grits. Not only did his good looks and congeniality win him two hundred dollars worth of tips on most Friday nights, he usually went home with several phone numbers, as well. If I was ever mildly envious of his monetary success, the drawbacks of Tommy's popularity became manifest at 4 a.m. on a balmy summer morning as he tended to a rotund lady at the cash register.

"Tommy, when do you think it's gonna clear up in here?" I called from the dish pit.

"Why, you need to be somewhere?"

"No, Man, but I'm starving. I'm feeling a double hashbrown all the way. When do you think the grill op will have time to make some for me?"

"Don't worry about it. I'll make 'em for you myself after it dies down."

"Thanks, I'd appreciate that."

I spent the next several minutes scrubbing iron skillets as Tommy exchanged playful banter with his admirer at the register. I couldn't hear most of the dialogue over the din of the dish hose, but it was quite evident from their facial expressions that she was throwing him a lay-up. While I'm not generally disposed to eavesdropping, I couldn't resist the opportunity to see if the portly lioness was going to catch her prey.

"That will be eight forty-nine. You payin' cash or credit?" he asked.

She reached a hand down into her low-cut blouse, fished around for a moment, and withdrew a credit card. The gesture was clearly intended to be seductive, but I have to say that it would only have had the intended effect on the most nearsighted of men.

Although television commercials proclaim that "Visa is everywhere you want to be," let me assure you that the card has also been at least one place to where no sober fellow would electively venture. Tommy asked her for a driver's license to verify the credit card ownership. None of the servers ever bothered with this gesture unless they had some ulterior motive.

"It says here you're twenty-nine years old. You don't look it."

"On the inside, I'm twenty-one and holding. But I am twenty-nine years old, legally."

Just as I was turning off the dish sink water, she delivered the coup de grace.

"Hey, baby, did I ever show you my tattoo?"

"Yeah, once before I think."

"Well, let me show you again." I had already observed part of the tattoo when the woman had dug her fingers into her blouse. The top of her left breast had the words "Mess with my heart," scrawled in cursive lettering above a graphic that I couldn't make out. I could discern a few circles, but the whole picture was an enigma. I would have been perfectly content to leave my curiosity unsatisfied.

Alas, she promptly yanked down her blouse and brassiere, causing an enormous boob to crash land on top of the cash register with an audible thud. The five circles I had noticed earlier constituted the chambers and barrel of a revolver pointed directly at the reader. Underneath the gun, I could read the rest of the phrase, "and I'll kill you."

A firm message. And if appearances were any indicator, decidedly firmer than the mammary on which it was engraved. For a woman ostensibly so worried about getting her heart broken, she sure was putting herself out there. Tommy politely refused her entreaty, chatted with her pleasantly for another minute, and sent her out of the store with a gentle wave.

After I had recovered from the stupor that the spectacle had given me, I spoke.

"Tommy?"

"What's up, Man?"

I had originally meant to ask him if our female patrons usually came on to him so strongly, but suddenly my mind switched gears. "Never mind about those hashbrowns. I'm not so hungry, anymore."

$ $ $ $ $

I had to hand it to Tommy. While his customer's sales pitch had rendered me catatonic, he had played it perfectly cool. Perhaps I shouldn't have been surprised by his poise. In our five months working together, I had yet to see it waver. No matter how severe the antagonism he received from customers or other employees, he simply could not be provoked to respond.

As I discovered in a conversation with him, Tommy had a very strong legal incentive to maintain his composure: he had been convicted of felonies on three separate occasions. Two of the convictions were for drug dealing; another was for breaking and entering. While he admitted his culpability on the former counts, the latter had been a special situation. The tenants had stolen some property from him a few weeks previously, so he spent several hours in the bushes outside their house waiting for them to leave so he could reclaim his possessions.

Given his criminal record, the smallest legal infraction (e.g., an assault charge) would guarantee Tommy thirty more years in a state penitentiary. He had no intention of spending the rest of his life behind bars and believed that amiability was his best defense against another term there. Should his disposition fail him, Tommy had also purchased an insurance policy that would prevent him from going back to prison.

During my five years in the insurance industry, I had never encountered the idea of insuring against a prison term. I knew that Lloyd's of London had some esoteric product offerings (Tina Turner has a Lloyd's policy on her legs), but this was beyond me. Before I could ask if he was sending premium checks to Travelers every month, Tommy explained that the "insurance" in question was more of a figure of speech.

"See my car over there?" he said, pointing to an old Cadillac in the restaurant parking lot. I nodded.

"Well, I got three guns in that trunk. Two of 'em are fully automatic. And I've got a couple hundred rounds of ammunition in there, too."

"I don't quite follow you," I said. "You're afraid of being cited for jaywalking, and yet you're comfortable with keeping automatic weapons in the trunk of your car?"

Tommy explained that he would never dream of brandishing the rifles unless he found himself in a situation wherein law enforcement officials were going to haul him back to the clink. In such a circumstance, he was fully prepared to go out in a blaze of glory a la Butch Cassidy.

"If it's going down, it's really going down, Man. I told the police, if they ever have to come for me again, they better bring a whole army with 'em. 'Cause I am going down swingin', Baby."

It was a fairly convincing argument. Tommy didn't have an MBA or a CFA charter, but when it came to managing risk, he was unquestionably canny. If the whole purpose of insurance is to protect yourself against risks, at some point it makes sense to take matters into your own hands rather than to depend on a potentially unreliable counterparty. Unlike many hedge funds that traded insurance derivatives with Bear Stearns and Lehman Brothers before their collapse, Tommy would be able to cash in his policy when it was most needed. I couldn't help but wonder how different his life would have been had he been raised in an affluent family and had attended the right prep school.

"Tommy, you could have been one heck of a mortgage bond salesman."

He smiled and blushed with pride. I didn't have the heart to tell him that he was doing a lot less damage to society by serving hashbrowns.

$ $ $ $ $

Although Tommy's disposition was generally quite pleasant, I couldn't help but be moderately concerned about his private arsenal in the parking lot. But if it was an unconventional approach to hedging, it was probably still an effective one. An acquaintance of mine had adopted a similar self-insurance program to hedge against skyrocketing gasoline prices by storing several drums of fuel in his suburban garage.

I had pointed out to him that gasoline fumes are highly flammable and that the potential savings from his hedging scheme were probably offset by the increased risk of his house burning down. I asked him to instead consider purchasing shares of Exxon, which would provide comparable protection against $200 oil without concurrently threatening the life of his infant daughter.

My friend's investment philosophy was also decidedly unorthodox. Rather than channeling his savings into stocks, bonds, or real estate, he had funneled his cash into another market. While I devoted my days to combing through broker research reports looking for attractive securities, he carefully sifted through flea market tables in search of vintage auto parts and highbrow pornography. He believed that scarce, quality items like '67 Ford Mustang mufflers and *Penthouse Forum* issues from the early 1990s were likely to appreciate over time. Like stocks and bonds, they could also be readily sold for cash on short notice. But they were better than securities in that you could also find practical uses for them in the interim.

When my friend first articulated this investment strategy, my reaction was incredulity followed by internal scoffing. Recent events have humbled me. I have to admit that if I did the math, his retirement fund has probably outperformed mine. I'm not ready to embrace the approach myself, but I would still really like to read a broker research report which contains a paragraph like this: "Broadly speaking, we do not perceive value in domestic equities. Rather, we advocate an overweight to emerging market debt, with a particular emphasis on Latin American sovereign issuers. However, we do find compelling pairs trading opportunities in domestic adult magazines. We recommend going long the June 1979 *Playboy,* offset by a short position in any Larry Flynt publication of the same era."

$ $ $ $ $

Beyond self-insuring against incarceration, Tommy was also conscious about managing the risks attendant with his personal life. To facilitate a high rate of girlfriend turnover, he maintained an inventory of five cell phones. This practice enabled him to broadly distribute his contact information while providing his exes with an alibi for why they were no longer able to reach him—he had changed his number.

Perhaps the tactic was somewhat reprehensible, but given the sort of women that were coming on to him, the strategy struck me as a complete necessity. When a woman tattoos herself in a preemptive threat to kill you over a broken heart, you really have to exercise the utmost caution when philandering. Hell hath no fury like a woman scorned, indeed.

"Yeah, baby, I'll be at the store 'til seven tomorrow morning," he said into phone #3. "Stop by anytime. Alright. Holla."

"Who's the lucky lady?" I inquired.

"You remember that gal that was in here a few weeks ago? The one with the tattoo?"

Given that most of our female patrons had at least one visible tattoo, I really wanted to give him the benefit of the doubt. Surely it couldn't be.

"You don't mean the one with the revolver inside her triple-D cup?

"That's the one. You remember her?"

I nodded slowly. How could I forget? Since her visit, I hadn't been able to eat a plate of hashbrowns without being interrupted by a harrowing vision of her .38 special. I couldn't understand why a man who was beloved by all of our female patrons would pursue this woman, whom I shall henceforth refer to as "Gunshot."

"I don't get it, Man. What's the appeal?"

Tommy offered a long-winded explanation whose rationale I could only partially follow. His sentiments echoed George Mallory, the English mountaineer whose burning desire to scale Mount Everest was justified with the succinct phrase, "because it is there." Given the size of his latest romantic quarry, the metaphor seemed to fit Tommy's situation only too well. (Mallory, by the way, died in close proximity to the summit; historians are still unsure whether or not he actually attained it. I could only hope that Tommy would have better luck in his climb, which I figured may prove comparably perilous.)

In addition to dating large women, Tommy's amorous nature had also once led him to romance a dwarf.

"Don't let the size fool ya," he testified. "Midgets is strong *everywhere.*"

I had to take his word for it.

Tommy was convinced that pursuing Gunshot was a worthwhile endeavor, so I wasn't going to waste my breath enumerating reasons to the contrary. For my part, I just couldn't envision any fruits from laboring in that field. Perhaps I simply lacked his intestinal fortitude. Then again, he had scars from two bullet wounds on his stomach and another on his leg, so he probably found her tattoo decidedly less intimidating than I had.

"That girl's alright," he continued. "The only thing else she wants from me is to see my papers."

While 'papers' evoked thoughts of passports or thoroughbred pedigrees in my mind, Tommy explained that Gunshot was looking for impeccable results from a blood test before she would agree to a second date.

This woman was really something else. Apparently, she had been giving him the full court press in the weeks since she had compromised my appetite. But despite her aggressiveness, the warning engraved on her chest and her demand for a clean bill of health evidenced a genuine commitment to hedging her bets. I wondered if she had previously worked as an options trader for Lehman Brothers.

I had the opportunity to ask Gunshot about her career path later that night as I waited on her at the high bar. Tattoo notwithstanding, she was very pleasant and highly complimentary of my capacities as a server. She had relocated to town a few years ago after earning an accounting degree from a college in Florida. So much for stereotypes about that profession.

"You seem a bit extroverted to pursue a career in accounting," I said.

"Yeah, I didn't enjoy that so much," she confessed. "Now I work in customer service."

After she retired from the store at 5 a.m., I asked Tommy about the state of their relationship. Despite his initial zeal, the night's dialogue had dampened his enthusiasm for their prospects together.

"She's twenty-nine and wants to have a baby before she's thirty. And she wants me to do the honors. But I already got enough mouths to feed. I don't need any more right now."

Tommy's love life was really none of my business, but I was still relieved for him. He had already fathered five children with three different women, so his reluctance to increase his brood was probably a wise decision.

While I concur with Thomas Paine's dictum that "That government is best which governs least," some of the events I witnessed on third shift occasionally caused me to reconsider the merits of public sterilization campaigns. Gunshot was amicable enough, but I just couldn't envision her brandishing that tattoo at parent/teacher conferences or bake sales at her child's school.

I sincerely hope that if and when she does birth a child, Gunshot elects to sustain her baby on formula rather than mother's milk. Granted, I'm not a trained psychologist, but I can't help but worry that a child who breastfeeds on the muzzle of a revolver may exhibit debilitating emotional effects down the road. That is, if playing a round of Russian roulette serves as a casual reminder to call your mom, you are probably in need of some serious psychotherapy.

## Chapter 8

# MEA CULPA

*"False principles are more fatal than even intentional
misconduct; because they are followed up with erroneous
notions of self-interest, and are long persevered in
without remorse or reserve."*
**JEAN-BAPTISTE SAY**

Shortly after I marked my fifth month at the store during the second week of July, Sharon delivered some bad news. Edward had been reassigned to the airport location, where he would remain for the foreseeable future. I was devastated. How could the third shift crew maintain its esprit de corps when our captain had been taken from our midst?

Edward's replacement only made the void left by his transfer even more conspicuous. The new grill op was very courteous, but his passive demeanor really left me at a loss. After months of listening to Edward's ribald observations and extemporaneous diatribes, the newfound decorum was positively unnerving. Yes, Edward had his defects—a critical temperament chief among them—but they were happily overlooked on account of his astronomical entertainment value.

Jennifer and I both agreed that the store just wasn't the same in the absence of our witty and charismatic ringleader. Despite constant bickering during their shifts together, Edward had still been gracious enough to provide Jennifer with a lift back to her apartment when she required one. Although she had initially been hesitant to defer to his counsel, Jennifer had to acknowledge that her quantum leap in professional competence was largely due to his mentorship. More than anything, she had been greatly impressed by his indifference to her feminine wiles as she tried to deflect his reprimands. (While Edward was no pushover, I'm not sure her methods were quite as persuasive as she imagined.)

Amongst its other effects, the exodus also left me with the responsibility of training new servers, one of whom had recently relocated to North Carolina from Wyoming. For the first few days, most of our conversations revolved around the distance between the two states. My rookie maintained that he had logged exactly 38,000 miles on his odometer over the course of four days of driving. I observed that his route must have been especially circuitous given that a 38,000-mile drive would have enabled him to circumnavigate the earth one and a half times.

Normally, I wouldn't let that sort of comment perturb me, but the precipitous decline in the quality of the banter was downright disgraceful. Granted, many of Edward's break-room anecdotes contained a fair amount of hyperbole, but he never said anything so patently ludicrous. But if most of the fallout from Edward's departure was tolerable, the abrupt sea change in the balance of power was not. No sooner had the transfer occurred than a grill officer named Larry began to posture himself as the Supreme Pontiff of Papa's Chicken & Waffles.

As Edward explained to me, most grade school bullies learn abusive behavior in their own homes before applying the same principles in the schoolyard. Larry was no exception. He had the meanest old lady in the Tarheel State. In Edward's words, describing the woman as "an extremely hard broad" didn't even begin to account for her brutality. In addition to the verbal abuse Larry took from her directly, she had two surly children from a previous relationship who followed their mother's lead in endlessly belittling him.

I witnessed the domestic abuse firsthand as Larry's girlfriend dropped him off at work. Sitting inside the store, I couldn't hear any of the dialogue exchanged in her minivan, but the body language was unmistakable—he was receiving a serious browbeating. After enduring two minutes of her lecture, he reached for the car door, muttering a retort. The defiance was promptly acknowledged with a backhand to his face.

Although he had been emasculated in his personal life, Larry had recaptured a modicum of his dignity with his recent promotion to the position of relief manager. Unfortunately, Larry interpreted this new assignment from "Miss Sharon" (of whom he now spoke in the most reverent tones) to mean that he should mercilessly criticize other employees whenever the slightest opportunity presented itself.

The gravity of Larry's rapid-fire chastisements was undermined by an acute lisp resulting from his total absence of canine and bicuspid teeth. The best way I can explain his speech is by challenging you to imagine how Daffy Duck would have spoken had he hailed from Queens and been under the constant influence of methamphetamines.

I first bore the brunt of Larry's unrighteous dominion as I dined on two chocolate chip waffles at the low bar. At the conclusion of an intense Friday night shift, the warm plate was nothing short of ambrosia. And then Larry walked in.

"Jimmy, what are you doing eating at the low bar? You're never supposed to eat on the restaurant floor while you're in uniform! It looks unprofessional to the customers."

Making my head motions as deliberate as possible, I glanced around the store. It was completely devoid of patronage.

"Larry, you're absolutely right. The minute I see a customer, I'll be sure to abide by that policy." I took another bite.

"Don't be disrespectin' me," he said. "I'm a relief manajuh and I won't hethitate to write you up to Mith Sharon."

$ $ $ $ $

Prior to his promotion, my only interactions with Larry had been brief exchanges during shift changes. Now he had gotten in the habit of relieving the third shift grill officer at 5 a.m., which meant that I had to spend the last two hours of my workday calling in my orders to him. A prosaic request for hashbrowns needlessly became a source of contention.

"Place two scattered please, Larry."

"Place two what?" he asked antagonistically.

"See if you can guess, Larry. What's the only menu item that we ever 'place' on the grill?"

Larry made it quite clear that he was in no mood for riddles and that all order calling protocols were to be respected when we were working together. Not only had I failed to specify my drop item, I was standing eighteen inches away from the colored floor tile from which all orders were supposed to be called. Thoroughly reproved, I took his demands to heart.

"I'm sorry, Larry, let me try this again from the top," I said as I walked over to the designated mark. I took a moment to clear my throat and started again. "My good sir, wouldst thou place two cupfuls of hashbrown potatoes?" I bellowed in an intonation that I generally reserve for addressing the British House of Lords.

"Now there's no need for smart mouthin'," he retorted. "You betta wath yo step or yo gonna find yoself in Mith Sharon's offith."

$ $ $ $ $

The full brunt of Larry's indignation came the following Thursday evening. No sooner had I arrived at the store than he handed me a document citing me and two other servers for neglecting our side work on a previous shift. To my chagrin, the other defendants had already signed the sheet, thereby conceding that the accusation was true.

Customer volume had been very slow on the Sunday morning in question. Energy that the servers would have devoted to waiting tables was instead applied toward thoroughly cleaning the restaurant. The three of us had actually taken a minute to compliment each other on how fabulous the place looked thanks to the recent application of our elbow grease.

I was apoplectic. I would have signed a document that cited me for insolence, but this was simply a dishonest indictment of great work performance. Using a tone I have never before used at the workplace, I called Larry a bold-faced liar in front of the other employees. He promised to immediately notify Sharon of my insubordination and lobby for my early termination.

As with any other job, working at Papa's meant enduring some hard times with customers, other employees, and managers. But in the aggregate, it had been a great adventure, and I had no intention of concluding my six-month tenure on a sour note. Before Larry could press the issue any further, I gave Sharon my two weeks' notice. She gave me several plaudits on my performance and assured me that I was welcome to work for her again in the future.

Although my contention with Larry may have provided the impetus for my resignation, I had been contemplating retiring my apron ever since my mentor's departure. As far as I was concerned, my technical education in the art of table waiting was more or less complete. The most important thing now was to meticulously record the financial lessons learned during my stint in foodservice.

$ $ $ $ $

A popular introductory economics text written nearly a century ago explained that "a cautious and conservative policy in the giving of credit is essential to the stability not only of the banks and their allies, *but of the whole industrial community.*" More than any other profession, bankers play a governing role in the body of commerce. Not only are they responsible for allocating capital to organs so that they may continue to produce, bankers also create money, which enables production to circulate from one producer to another. In short, bankers have a sacred trust which cannot be understated.

Unfortunately, bankers are inclined to break this trust during periods of prolonged economic comfort. As with most people, prosperity causes bankers to succumb to lapses in judgment and self-discipline. In their state of complacency, they begin to lend imprudently and assume higher debt levels on their own balance sheets. But despite the poor underwriting and greater debt, banks can get away with the heightened risk level until collateral values experience a large decline. In the interim, stockholders are content with the situation. After all, the upside to their share price is unlimited.

Bank depositors have a different view of the increased risk taking. For them, the best possible outcome is simply getting their money back. That is, their investment has negligible upside potential but a very large amount of downside risk. The reckless loan underwriting, coupled with insufficient stockholder capital, can quickly wipe out their life savings.

The fallout from irresponsible banking is not limited to shareholders and depositors. When a bank's solvency is imperiled by a souring loan portfolio, another group of people is soon hurt: business customers. Liquidity and capital constraints force banks to call in their loans, depriving even profitable businesses of financing. Were banks not so leveraged, the survival of good businesses would not be compromised.

Lastly, the general public suffers greatly from bankers' mistakes. When a large component of the money supply is lost in bank runs, the body of commerce goes into cardiac arrest. Output grinds to a halt as the economy hemorrhages its "monetary blood." The worst two depressions in America's history, the Panic of 1837 and the Great Depression of 1929–1932, were both exacerbated by 30% declines in the nation's money supply.

With the advent of deposit insurance in 1934 and a generally accommodating Federal Reserve policy subsequent to 1938, the

United States did not face a bank run for the seven decades ending in 2007. While the nation endured numerous recessions as resources were reallocated from one sector of the economy to another, each of the episodes paled in comparison to the acute deflations of the late nineteenth and early twentieth centuries.

In 1971, the Federal Reserve ceased to redeem its Notes for gold, enabling it to issue more dollars without concern that a run would occur on its gold reserves. Unencumbered by gold reserve requirements, the Fed consistently increased the volume of its liabilities over the next four decades. By doing so, the Fed provided commercial banks with the means to increase the money supply through the fractional reserve process. Presently, cash only constitutes about 20% of the U.S. money supply; the remaining 80% consists of commercial bank liabilities (checking and savings accounts) and money market funds.

As the money supply has steadily grown, inflation (rather than deflation) has become the rule for consumer prices. ($M\uparrow V = P\uparrow Y\uparrow$) While economists and politicians debate the optimal amount of inflation for a healthy economy, there is general agreement that a 2–4% annual increase in the price level is far preferable to the double-digit price declines experienced during nineteenth-century banking crises.

All things considered, the monetary system has worked pretty well since the Great Depression. Until recently.

$$\$ \ \$ \ \$ \ \$ \ \$$$

As explained in the last chapter, insurance companies are really a special type of bank that borrows money by selling insurance policies. Like commercial banks, insurance companies earn profits by lending at a higher rate than their cost of borrowing. In addition to insurers, there are a myriad of other bank-like entities that simultaneously borrow from one group of investors and lend to another. These financial institutions have been suitably named "shadow banks" by a prominent investment manager. Here's a sampling:

| Type of Shadow Bank | Example |
|---|---|
| Insurance companies | Allstate, Nationwide |
| Student loan companies | Sallie Mae |
| Commercial finance cos. | CIT, GE Capital |
| Wall Street broker/dealers | Goldman Sachs |
| Credit card companies | Capital One, MBNA |

(I have omitted pension funds, money market mutual funds, endowments, and sovereign wealth funds from this list. Unlike banks, they act as agents investing directly on behalf of their shareholders and beneficiaries. As a result, they cannot be forced to sell assets to raise liquidity or capital because they do not borrow money to finance their lending activities.)

The main difference between commercial banks and shadow banks is their mix of investments and methods of borrowing. You can find the types of loans and funding sources used by banks and shadow banks listed on their balance sheets, listed under "assets" and "liabilities," respectively. But make no mistake; it's all the same game: borrow at a low interest rate from one person and lend at a higher rate to somebody else.

| Assets/Loans | Liabilities/Funding Sources |
|---|---|
| Corporate bonds | Repurchase agreement (Repo) |
| Business loans | Asset Securitization |
| Residential mortgages | Bond |
| Mortgage-backed securities | Checking/Savings Accounts |
| Student loans | Certificate of Deposit |
| Commercial mortgages | Insurance Policy |
| Equipment leases | Annuity |

In addition to borrowing directly from creditors, shadow banks also use derivatives contracts to bet on the performance of an investment without actually purchasing it. A **derivative** is a financial instrument whose value is tied to the price of a commodity (e.g., oil) or a security (e.g., stock). Traditionally, if a commercial bank wanted to invest in the debt of IBM Corporation, it would use cash proceeds from customer deposits to purchase a bond issued by IBM corp. Today, a hedge fund can write a credit default swap (CDS) on IBM and obtain exactly the same economic effect—a leveraged bet on IBM's ability to repay its debt.

Instead of borrowing money from a depositor, the hedge fund is effectively borrowing the money from its CDS counterparty—typically a Wall Street broker/dealer. Through the derivatives market, the hedge fund has effectively become a bank. Nearly anyone can start one of these de facto banks as long as a Wall Street dealer is willing to face him as a derivative counterparty.

*make bets with*        *who owe money to*

Hedge Funds  >  Broker/Dealers  >  Money market funds

The number of shadow banks has increased exponentially in the past thirty years. In the early 1980s, commercial banks accounted for 70% to 80% of all the loans made in the United States; shadow banks accounted for the remainder. By 2008, the positions had reversed: 70% of the country's total loans were either originated or held by shadow banks, leaving commercial banks with only a 30% share. The trend was pervasive: even large commercial banks had established shadow banking subsidiaries known as "structured investment vehicles."

Shadow banks were susceptible to the same risks faced by conventional banks, namely: (1) insufficient capital to absorb loan losses; and (2) insufficient cash reserves (i.e., liquidity) to repay nervous depositors.

Moreover, shadow banks faced the same temptations that commercial banks encounter during the upswing of a credit cycle: making riskier loans and using more financial leverage.

"A sound banker," Keynes wrote in 1931, "alas, is not one who foresees danger and avoids it, but one who, when he is ruined, is ruined in a conventional way along with his fellows, so that no one can really blame him." Somewhere, he must be smiling.

Shortly after the close of the twentieth century, many bankers—both commercial and shadow—began to notice that, on a nationwide basis, housing prices had never declined year-over-year since the Great Depression of the 1930s. Admittedly, there had been a number of regional housing busts since then. But if an individual bank maintained a residential mortgage portfolio with sufficient geographic diversity, the total credit risk was manageable.

As with all other asset booms, the housing bubble was the result of a self-reinforcing feedback loop of naïve optimism. Speculator demand was fed by a large corps of bankers, who were increasingly confident that the bloated volume of credit devoted to the housing sector would prevent any dramatic price declines. Besides, the bankers reasoned, even if housing prices experienced a widespread precipitous drop, most of the American banking system would become insolvent. The country would be plunged into a severe recession, if not an outright depression. And while the public could pillory the financiers *collectively,* no single organization could be blamed for the entire debacle. In hindsight, they were exactly right.

Most commercial banks lent the money to borrowers directly:

|  | *borrowed from* |  | *who owed money to* |
|---|---|---|---|
| Home buyers | > | Commercial banks | > | Bank depositors |

Most shadow banks lent the money indirectly through mortgage-backed securities (bonds backed by pools of thousands of mortgages):

|  | *borrowed from* |  | *who in turn owed* |
|---|---|---|---|
| Home buyers | > | Mortgage securitization cos. | > | Insurance cos. |

Other shadow banks—particularly broker/dealers, hedge funds, and insurance companies—placed side bets with each other by selling credit default swaps (CDS) written on mortgage pools:

*Placed bets with regarding*      *who had borrowed from*

Hedge Funds   >   Broker/Dealers   >   Home buyers   >   Mortgage cos.

The actors and assets had changed, but it was the same story as in 1907:

*had borrowed from    who owed money to    who in turn owed*

Speculators   >   Trust cos. & Brokers   >   Banks   >   Bank depositors

1929 hadn't been too different, either:

*had borrowed from      who owed money to    who in turn owed*

Stock speculators   >   Brokers   >   Banks   >   Bank Depositors

Rather than recycling savings into productive investments, bankers had once again misallocated capital to finance speculation, this time in the housing market. As these loans were made and derivative bets were placed, chains of debt were forged across the entire financial system. In some cases, there were four financial intermediaries between the borrowers and the savers that ultimately provided the capital for the loan.

Here's a not-so-hypothetical illustration: A southern California resident borrowed money from a mortgage company to purchase a million-dollar home with no cash down. After lending him the money, the mortgage company sold the mortgage (along with many others) to an investment bank, which bundled the loans into a mortgage-backed security. The investment bank then sold the mortgage-backed security to a hedge fund. The hedge fund borrowed the money to buy the mortgage-backed security from a broker/dealer using a repurchase agreement. The broker/dealer borrowed the money to lend to the hedge fund by issuing commercial paper to an insurance company. Lastly, the insurance company borrowed the money from its policyholders to lend to the broker/dealer. (Got all that?)

Every month, the flow of borrower payments went something like this:

Homebuyer > Mortgage Co. > Hedge Fund > Broker/ Dealer > Life insurer > Policyholder

Despite the large number of middlemen, each of the shadow banks was able to earn a positive net interest margin (the lending rate less the borrowing rate) because the borrowing costs were progressively lower for each link in the debt chain:

- The homeowner borrowed the money from a mortgage company at a 6% rate.

- After a 0.5% servicing fee to the mortgage company, the hedge fund earned a 5.5% yield on its mortgage bond.

- The hedge fund paid a 5.2% rate on its repurchase agreement financing with the broker/dealer.

- The broker/dealer sold its short-term debt to the life insurance company at a 4.7% interest rate.

- The life insurance company credited its policyholders' accounts at a 4.0% rate.

| | Interest Yield | Cost of Funds | Net Interest Margin |
|---|---|---|---|
| Hedge Fund | 5.5% | 5.2% | 0.3% |
| Broker/Dealer | 5.2% | 4.7% | 0.5% |
| Insurance Co. | 4.7% | 4.0% | 0.7% |

While the interest margins were relatively small (ranging from 0.3% and 0.7%), each shadow bank could still earn a handsome return on its stockholders' capital. You can probably guess how they did it: by dialing up the leverage.

|  | Interest Yield | Net Interest Margin | Leverage | Return on Capital |
|---|---|---|---|---|
| Hedge Fund | 5.5% | 0.3% | 20 | 12% |
| Broker/Dealer | 5.2% | 0.5% | 25 | 18% |
| Insurance Co. | 4.7% | 0.7% | 15 | 15% |

Remember, return on capital is calculated as: Interest yield + (Net interest margin x Leverage).

In the short term, this arrangement benefited everyone. The homeowner got the money he needed to purchase the house, the mortgage company earned a nice fee for servicing the loan, and three financial intermediaries each earned attractive returns.

Of course, leverage has a major downside: it greatly reduces an investment's margin for error. As chains of debt were forged across the financial intermediaries, the potential for unfathomable disaster was set. A few bad mortgage loans could quickly metastasize into global financial ruin: one set of loans backs another set of loans, which supports yet another group of loans. When each participant's liability is someone else's asset, "upstream" problems can have sudden adverse effects on everyone living "downstream."

| Participant | Asset | | Liability | | Capital |
|---|---|---|---|---|---|
| Homeowner | House | 1,000,000 | Mortgage | 1,000,000 | 0 |
| Hedge Fund | Mortgage | 1,000,000 | Repo agreement | 952,381 | 47,619 |
| Broker | Repo agreement | 952,381 | Corp. Bond | 915,751 | 36,630 |
| Life Ins. Co. | Corp. Bond | 915,751 | Insurance Policy | 858,516 | 57,234 |
| **TOTAL** | | **2,868,132** | | **2,726,648** | **141,484** |

In this example, the bankers had created $2.7 million of liabilities against the same real asset, a $1 million house, which was overvalued in the first place! Little did the father of three realize that a wave of mortgage defaults in Phoenix, AZ and Stockton, CA could ultimately compromise the insurance policy he purchased to protect his family.

Before the 2008 crash, I once tried to justify this sophisticated layering of debt to my wife, who has spent the past five years laboring in hospital Intensive Care Units. It's really honest work, which has afforded her many incredible experiences. Regrettably, the vocation has left her completely intolerant of b.s., which renders her completely unsuited to appreciate the theoretical nuances of finance.

"This system sounds an awful lot like a Ponzi scheme," she observed.

I tried to explain that several really smart guys who had won Nobel Prizes in Economics (and who presumably understood risk and leverage much better than she did) were perfectly comfortable with these arrangements.

The credentials failed to impress her. She had just spent the afternoon explaining to a physician that despite a computer report indicating solid vital signs, a patient's condition is not "stable" if he also requires two pints of blood every hour to replace the amount he has been hemorrhaging. The (ostensibly) well-educated M.D. couldn't seem to appreciate that the computer data was neglecting to tell the whole story. In hindsight, I believe that the doctor should have pursued a career in economics, a field where a math fetish and a penchant for ignoring the obvious frequently earns you that coveted trip to Stockholm.

As usual, my wife's intuition was dead-on. The only thing that separates a bank from a Ponzi scheme is a thin layer of stockholder capital. The more leverage that each bank employs, the more quickly it becomes insolvent. And the more linkages between highly leveraged banks, the greater the potential for a system-wide catastrophe.

Most of the time, the system works because the vast majority of the "upstream" bank borrowers are able to pay their debts. But when borrower delinquencies reach a critical mass, the chain reaction goes off, and the entire scheme unravels. And that's exactly what happened during 2007–2009.

Cash-strapped homeowners found themselves unable to service their loan obligations. Powerless to refinance their mortgages amidst rapidly deteriorating housing prices, the borrowers began to default en masse. In the pattern of a nineteenth-century bank panic, commercial and shadow banks quickly found themselves simultaneously strained for both capital and liquidity.

Hamstrung by their own debts, the banks were forced to raise cash and capital by calling in loans and selling bonds. As the financing for capital assets (like real estate) was withdrawn, asset prices declined further, and the pernicious cycle of debt de-leveraging began to snowball. The situation was horribly reminiscent of the initial stages of the Great Depression.

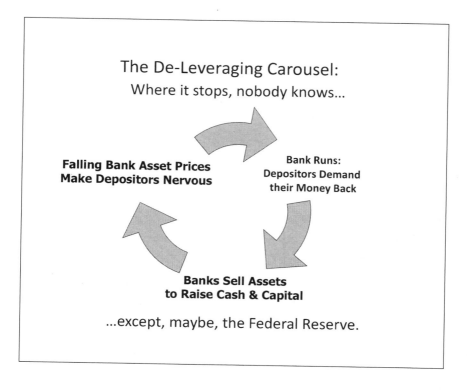

The De-Leveraging Carousel:
Where it stops, nobody knows...

Falling Bank Asset Prices
Make Depositors Nervous

Bank Runs:
Depositors Demand
their Money Back

Banks Sell Assets
to Raise Cash & Capital

...except, maybe, the Federal Reserve.

Fortunately, actions taken by the Federal Reserve and U.S. Treasury during 2008 were able to prevent a total implosion of the financial system. Fed chairman Ben Bernanke had spent much of his academic career studying the Depression, basing much of his own research on Milton Friedman's *Monetary History*. The "Bernanke Fed" implemented numerous emergency lending facilities to provide liquidity to the banking system and slashed short-term interest rates in an effort to raise asset prices and lower banks' funding costs.

While the Federal Reserve furnished the banks (both commercial and shadow) with liquidity, the U.S. Treasury concurrently provided much-needed capital. In some cases, the government facilitated the acquisition of insolvent banks by larger competitors by agreeing to absorb a share of failing loans. In other instances, the Treasury assumed majority ownership stakes in failing banks in exchange for replenishing their equity cushions, which had been depleted by large loan losses.

After proceeding in fits and starts, the measures ultimately worked. By providing liquidity and capital to imperiled financial institutions, government checked the debt deflation cycle before it spiraled completely out of control. But while the credit market turmoil was not magnified by the destruction of the money supply, the economic damage—steep production declines and a spike in unemployment— was acute nonetheless.

Constrained by credit losses and liquidity concerns, commercial and shadow banks severely rationed credit, resulting in a precipitous drop in investment spending. Beginning in the last quarter of 2007, private investment declined for seven consecutive quarters, the longest stretch in the postwar era. Responding to the heightened economic uncertainty and a dearth of credit, production fell dramatically. Between January 2008 and June 2009, total U.S. output (as measured by changes in real GDP) declined by nearly 14% as the national unemployment rate spiked from 5.0% to 9.5%.

By June 2009, U.S. residential real estate values had declined roughly $4 trillion from their zenith in 2006. Although the losses were considerable, they had been less than half those of the March 2000–October 2002 bear market in stocks, in which $10 trillion in wealth vanished in a comparable time frame. During that episode, however, the fall in output and rise in unemployment had been much milder. From April 2000 through December 2002, total U.S. output fell in only three of eleven quarters (the largest decline was a modest $-1.4\%$ in Q3 2001), while unemployment rose from 4.0% to 6.0%. The recession had been relatively brief and painless.

In the depths of the Great Depression, Irving Fisher observed that "overinvestment and overspeculation . . . would have far less serious results were they not conducted with borrowed money." His remark had proved eerily prescient.

Here, then, was the difference between the 2000–2002 stock market collapse and the 2007–2009 real estate collapse: debt. During the real estate bubble, banks and mortgage companies had often financed 90–100% of the purchase price of a home.

In contrast, the vast majority of stock market investment during the dotcom bubble had not been financed by intermediaries like banks and insurance companies. Because the decline in stock prices never posed a serious threat to capital and liquidity cushions, the banking system remained strong. Viable businesses were able to retain access to capital (albeit at occasionally higher interest rates), and the structure of production could readily adjust to a dynamic change in the marketplace.

The problem with debt is its manic tendencies. It plays servant one minute and master the next. When asset prices are rising, debt paves the road to fast riches for speculators and their bankers. But in a bear market, debt quickly becomes a debilitating fetter. Despite heavily discounted selling prices, potential buyers cannot bid because they themselves are encumbered by their own financial liabilities. Having bound themselves in chains of debt, market participants can no longer move. The "free market" is no longer free at all.

Imagine a lakeside community where each resident is responsible for disposing of his own garbage. Most of the homeowners pay a modest fee for a trash collection service. But one enterprising individual finds a way to reduce his expenditures. Under cover of darkness, he quietly disposes his trash in the lake. After a few months, several neighbors discover his scheme and confront him. He explains that he is just trying to keep his expenses down and that because he is just one person, the environment is unlikely to be materially affected by his waste.

The sympathetic neighbors acknowledge that any detrimental effects are insignificant in such a large body of water and agree to turn a blind eye. They return home and begin to contemplate his reasoning. Trash collection is an unnecessary expense, they tell themselves. They soon decide to follow his lead. The number of polluters gradually increases, and the dumping continues unchecked.

After several uneventful years, the residents suddenly begin to feel the effect of the lake's changing chemistry. Children become ill after swimming. Dead fish appear on the water's surface. The residents summon an ecologist to examine the water. Sure enough, he finds that it contains a high level of toxins. The once-beautiful lake has been compromised. Thanks to a few corner-cutting individuals, the entire community is now deprived of a precious resource.

In an unfortunate deviation from Adam Smith's vision of capitalism, the pursuit of selfish behavior has failed to produce a beneficial outcome for society. The lake dumping temporarily helped a few residents balance their household budgets; but in the end, the practice cost everyone else their quality of life.

Pollution imposes costs on others without their consent—in this case, the loss of use of the lake. Economists refer to these third-party costs as **externalities.** Essentially, externalities are a subtle form of theft that generally occur over long periods of time. Whereas you will be immediately aware of the costs associated with someone stealing your car, it may take several years to realize the costs arising from pollution.

One individual act of pollution often has a negligible effect on others. However, once enough polluters join the bandwagon, the ecological damage reaches a critical mass, forcing all of society to pay for the indiscretions of an irresponsible minority.

As the primary role of government is to protect private property rights, the state has a legitimate role to play in addressing externalities like water pollution. Regrettably, externalities prove a difficult problem to manage objectively. That is, deciding how much garbage each resident can safely dump in the lake before public safety is threatened quickly becomes an arbitrary matter. Some polluters will argue that their particular form of waste is biodegradable, and therefore more benign than their neighbor's.

Conceding the point, the government determines which types of refuse are the most ecologically hazardous and then establishes permissible dumping levels for each. It's a rational approach for a regulatory regime, but it allows little margin for error. By the time it is discovered that some varieties of trash are causing unacceptable damage to the ecosystem, it's too late. The lake can only be cleaned up at great expense to the public.

Permit me to disclose one of the most important, but least understood, principles of capitalism: *foolish investment, coupled with financial leverage, is a form of pollution.* Sooner or later, one man's bad debt becomes somebody else's big problem. If it is not preemptively contained, the cost of misused leverage is borne by all of society. As with other market externalities, government has an important role to play in regulating financial leverage.

Adam Smith, for one, recognized the dangers of debt and advocated banking regulation. Writing in his *Wealth of Nations,* he asserted that "those exertions of the natural liberty of a few individuals, which might endanger the security of the whole society, are, and ought to be, restrained by the laws of all governments. . . . The obligation of building party walls, in order to prevent the communication of fire, is a violation of natural liberty exactly of the same kind with the regulations of the banking trade which are here proposed."

State governments and federal agencies have constructed various sorts of "firewalls" by creating a myriad of financial regulators. Each of these entities attempts to manage financial leverage by establishing liquidity and capital requirements and restricting the types and terms of loans that each institution can offer.

Currently, the Federal Reserve Banks (in conjunction with the Board) supervise approximately 900 state member banks and 5,000 bank holding companies. However, oversight of the commercial banking system is shared with two other federal regulators: the Federal Deposit Insurance Corporation (FDIC) and the Office of the Comptroller of the Currency (OCC).

(Another regulator, the Office of Thrift Supervision, is being merged into the latter entity.) In addition to Federal oversight, most commercial banks are also subject to regulatory supervision by state agencies.

Insurance companies are regulated by a separate commission in each state in which they write policies. The regulations of the fifty state insurance commissions are somewhat standardized by the National Association of Insurance Commissioners (NAIC). Insurance holding companies, however, are not currently subject to any statutory limitations on leverage.

Student lenders and commercial finance companies are both typically subject to state and federal banking regulators. Typically, student lenders also fall under the regulatory purview of the Department of Education, while commercial finance companies may be additionally supervised by the Small Business Administration and/or the Financial Industry Regulatory Authority (FINRA).

Credit card companies are frequently overseen by the Federal Reserve Board, FDIC, and state bureaus. Government-sponsored Mortgage Companies were formerly supervised by the Office of Federal Housing Enterprise Oversight but as of 2008 are now regulated by a new entity called the Federal Housing Finance Agency.

Broker/dealers like Goldman Sachs have capital requirements mandated by their regulator, the Securities and Exchange Commission (SEC). Most hedge fund advisers are also registered with the SEC, although the organization currently imposes no liquidity or capital constraints on any hedge fund.

Inasmuch as the regulatory regime is highly fragmented, it is also markedly inconsistent in its approach to capital requirements. State commissions require insurance companies to hold a relatively small amount of capital against "AAA"-rated corporate bonds issued by companies like Exxon-Mobil or Johnson & Johnson. In contrast, bank regulators view mortgage securities much more favorably than corporate bonds. A bank must hold five times as much capital against a triple-A corporate bond relative to a comparably-rated bond backed by subprime mortgages.

Think about the reasoning implicit in this requirement: it is five times more likely that 3,000 subprime borrowers will make regular payments on their no-money-down mortgages than it is that the rest of the world will continue to fill their gas tanks or apply band-aids to skinned knees.

In addition to disparate risk assessments of investment assets, leverage limitations vary greatly across industry regulators. Most life insurance companies entered 2008 with total leverage of 10 to 20 times their capital base. Most large broker/dealers like Bear Stearns and Lehman Brothers had pre-crisis leverage in the range of 30 times capital (in 2003, the SEC had raised permissible levels from 10 times). The most unapologetic use of debt occurred at the government-sponsored enterprises (GSEs), better known as Fannie Mae and Freddie Mac. Adjusted for off-balance sheet obligations, these mortgage market behemoths were leveraged in excess of 50 times their capital base at the beginning of 2008.

As a young analyst, I had asked a mortgage securities portfolio manager how the GSEs could possibly justify such astronomical debt levels.

"The first bill everyone pays is their mortgage, and Fannie and Freddie both have high underwriting standards. It doesn't get much safer than that," she explained.

I conceded that the relative risk of the loans was safer than corporate junk bonds but pointed out that fifty times leverage didn't give the agencies much room for error.

"You worry too much," she said.

On September 7, 2008, their capital bases depleted by loan losses, Fannie and Freddie were placed into federal government conservatorship. The U.S. Treasury assumed a 79.9% ownership stake in the institutions in exchange for guaranteeing $5 trillion of their liabilities. The action ensured that investors holding Fannie and Freddie mortgage bonds would not lose one cent of principal. The portfolio manager had been right after all. As an investor, there really is no need to worry when Uncle Sam covers your losses. (The Congressional Budget Office estimates that supporting Fannie and Freddie will set American taxpayers back by $350-400 billion over the next ten years.)

Repugnant though it may be, bailing out large financial institutions is far preferable to enduring the financial pandemic unleashed by their failures. Had the government not shored up beleaguered banks during the crisis, the United States would have undoubtedly endured large-scale bank runs and destruction of the money supply, just as it had in the 1930s. Domestic production losses would have been much steeper, and the investment losses to large international institutions— including foreign central banks—would likely have fomented a serious geopolitical crisis.

Society also pays for bankers' mistakes in another, more subtle form: inflation. Between January 2008 and June 2011, the Federal Reserve purchased a substantial amount of government bonds and mortgage-backed securities, and loaned money to a number of embattled commercial and shadow banks. As it did so, the Fed's liabilities (i.e., the monetary base) grew from $890 billion to $2.8 trillion, a 215% increase.

Because the spike in "base money" replaced disappearing bank credit which had previously supported asset prices, the Fed's actions have created a windfall for stock market and commodity investors.

Understandably, many pundits fret about the inflationary effects of this "money printing." However, the total money supply hasn't increased dramatically because commercial bank lending has been contracting. Until that trend reverses, the increase in bank reserves is not likely to stoke an extraordinary rise in consumer prices. Nonetheless, the Fed's low interest rates have reduced the financing costs for speculators who have bid up the price of wheat, corn, and other basic foodstuffs. Low rates have also weakened the dollar's exchange value, making oil and other essential imports more expensive for American families.

The Fed has repeatedly stated its position that it would rather maintain an "easy money" policy for an extended period of time at the risk of raising inflation, rather than move to a "tighter" policy which would hamper employment growth. While the easy money policy may marginally help the unemployed by lowering borrowing costs for businesses, any consequent rise in consumer prices hurts people living on fixed incomes, particularly senior citizens. Effectively, the inflation serves as a tax on savers to the benefit of the borrowers (and, of course, their bankers).

Lastly, American citizens are covering the bill for bankers' transgressions in the form of Keynesian stimulus programs. As loan losses forced the private banking system to tighten the credit spigot, companies lost investment funding and laid off large numbers of employees. The declining business revenue and rising unemployment created political pressure for increased government spending designed to "bridge the gap" between a higher consumer savings rate and a falling level of private-sector investment. The intent of the stimulus was to buy time for the banks to strengthen their balance sheets. When their capital reservoirs are replenished, the government will presumably pass the torch of investment spending back to the private sector.

Some of the government spending has occurred automatically in the form of unemployment insurance, which enables individuals to continue a moderate level of spending when their income streams are otherwise compromised. Other forms of Keynesian stimulus, such as the American Recovery and Reinvestment Act of 2009, required new legislation. The Act provided a $500 billion expansion of federal spending coupled with $275 billion in tax credits and deductions.

When all of its forms are considered—bank recapitalizations, inflation, and stimulus programs—the ultimate cost of the economic rescue is likely to exceed one trillion dollars. Given their massive scale, the bailout packages drew considerable populist angst and demands for banking reform. After months of deliberation, Congress passed the Dodd-Frank Wall Street Reform and Consumer Protection Act, which President Obama signed into law on July 21, 2010.

Besides reshuffling chairs on the regulatory deck, the 2,300-page legislation seeks to impose more stringent capital guidelines on large financial institutions. By limiting their size and use of leverage—in both conventional and derivative forms—the Act is intended to reduce the probability of a "systemically important" institution's collapse. While the spirit behind Dodd-Frank (protecting average Americans from the fallout of financiers' risky behavior) is certainly commendable, the Act has been criticized as unnecessarily byzantine. Even more problematic, large banks have been aggressively lobbying against the implementation of its most valuable provisions: higher capital requirements and oversight of derivatives trading.

Despite Congress's best efforts, I have little doubt that the banking lobby will ensure that the leverage caps are not low enough to prevent another disaster. Whatever the exact form the new rules take, smart guys in lower Manhattan will scour them for loopholes and immediately begin creating new derivative instruments enabling traders to employ more leverage while still respecting the official letter of the law. When questioned about their behavior, the bankers will justify their actions by arguing that they are fighting Congressional tyranny in the name of increasing market efficiency.

I remember observing this sort of self-serving churlish behavior when I was nine years old. My mother had taken a friend and me to the local public swimming pool. At the entrance, management had placed a large sign about four feet from ground level. Written in large red letters were the words:

"Welcome to our OOL. Notice there is no "P" in it. Please keep it that way."

Although subtly couched in clever word play, the message was quite straightforward. All pee was supposed to be deposited in the bathroom. It seemed like a fair rule that everyone should adhere to. I, for one, didn't want to swim in someone else's urine.

After an hour of swimming, my friend waded over to me and whispered something in my ear. In a shameless act of civil disobedience, he had just violated the 'P' rule. He felt that any ordinance that restrained him from urinating in a body of water was clearly an all-out assault on his civil liberties. The water was too cold, he explained, and his discharge had provided a welcome respite from the frigid temperature. If the pool staff really intended to keep the water clean, he reasoned, they should have turned up the pool heater. Besides, he added, anyone ingesting his pee probably wouldn't notice the taste, anyway.

In his own mind, he was Gandhi, defying a tyrannical British empire on a salt march.

To any casual observer with a cerebrum, however, he was just a bratty kid too lazy to walk thirty feet to the bathroom. I don't know what ever happened to that boy, but I can't help but wonder if he eventually found employment in the capital markets group of a Wall Street bank.

I really shouldn't throw so many stones at bankers without disclosing the fact that I was once building a glass house of my own. During my last ten months with Alpha Managers, I was assigned the task of creating a particular type of shadow bank known as a "Mortgage Real Estate Investment Trust (REIT)."

There are several Mortgage REITs which trade on the New York Stock Exchange. They're pretty simple businesses and work as follows: Issue a bunch of stock to investors. Use the cash from the stock sales to purchase mortgages issued by Fannie Mae and Freddie Mac. Then borrow a lot of money from Wall Street dealers using repurchase agreements to buy 5–8 times as many mortgages as you initially purchased outright. Your profit is the difference between the interest earned on the mortgages and the interest cost of borrowing from Wall Street. It's a bank without a physical branch. All you really need is a telephone and a Bloomberg computer terminal.

The neat thing about Mortgage REITs is that they don't really have customers. They simply create another link in the chain between borrowers and savers:

Homeowner (Borrower)   >   Fannie Mae (Shadow Bank)   > Mortgage REIT (Shadow Bank)   >   Broker/Dealer (Shadow Bank)   >   Money market fund (Saver)

Another favorable aspect of this particular type of shadow bank is the total absence of credit risk. I didn't have to worry that the REIT's mortgage bonds would default—they were effectively guaranteed by the Federal government, which owns most of Fannie and Freddie. I wasn't concerned about our creditors demanding their money back, either. If the financial system got in a severe pickle again and broker/dealers quit lending money against Fannie and Freddie bonds, the Federal Reserve would assuredly create a new lending facility that provided the same service.

The only major risk the REIT faced was a sudden change in interest rates; all of the others would have been covered by the American taxpayer. But that's not even the best part. As long as management told the truth in our accounting statements, we faced no regulatory scrutiny whatsoever. It was a wholly unregulated bank, whose assets and liabilities were tacitly insured by Uncle Sam, but whose profits were entirely private. It was beautiful.

Or, rather, it would have been beautiful. In late 2008, I had all my ducks in a row, ready to launch the new venture. In another eighteen months, I would be an officer of a publicly traded company, making a few hundred thousand dollars per year. But as fate would have it, I was laid off before my firm could secure the seed investment.

I spent the first several weeks after my layoff contemplating just how close I had come to pulling it all off. But as more time passes, the less I lament the forgone wealth. If it represented anything at all, the deal's collapse was an act of grace. For whatever legacy I may leave to the world, at least it won't be forging another layer of debt in the global financial system.

$ $ $ $ $

As I entered the store to begin my last series of weekend shifts, I reflected on what had been the most extraordinary chapter in my professional life. Wherever I might next tread on my career path, it was highly doubtful that a future road would be replete with such interesting characters.

"What are you doing here?" a grill op asked. "You're not slated to work tonight."

I checked the schedule in the back room. Sure enough, my name was nowhere to be found.

"Well, I suppose that's it then," I said sullenly. "I guess I'll just go home." It was certainly an anticlimactic conclusion to a journey that had been punctuated by so much excitement. Then the store phone rang.

"Yes, he's here now," the grill officer said into the transmitter. "Alright, I'll tell him." He hung up and turned to me.

"Jimmy, you need to report to the airport. That's where you're going to spend your last three days. Say hi to Edward for us while you're out there."

So I was going to have one last hurrah with the World's Greatest Short Order Cook after all. I drove out to the airport, ecstatic about the propitious turn of events. When I arrived there, Edward explained that Sharon had transferred him to replace a lethargic and unreliable predecessor as relief manager. His commute had been lengthened by ten minutes, but he was amenable to the move as long as he was guaranteed a workweek of at least forty hours.

The only real drawback to Edward's new gig was that his new coworkers, while congenial, were decidedly less interesting than the crew at our old store. Accordingly, he had spoken to Sharon and personally arranged my reassignment. As her longest-standing and most dependable employee, she was happy to oblige his request. I was genuinely flattered.

While we had never worked together in that location, we hit our stride immediately. My calls were on point, Edward's callbacks were flawless, and volume was healthy, yet manageable, with nary a disgruntled customer in sight. It was the sort of picturesque scenario envisioned by *The Rise & Shine Manual.*

"Marking two chocolate waffles. Yee-hee!" Edward yelped in a high pitch. He had been adding Michael Jackson sound effects to his order callbacks in homage to the recently late King of Pop. In between orders, we passed the hours debating whether the Linebacker or the Giantess (another formidable dame who had recently joined the crew) would win in a fight, and how much pay-per-view revenue such a televised event could garner. We had come a long way since February.

During the lull before the Friday night rush, I was eating a cheeseburger in the break room when Edward suddenly volunteered information about which I had been curious for some time.

"I never told you why I went to prison," he began.

Nearly thirty years ago, Edward had committed a robbery which culminated in a tragic accident. Despite being only seventeen, he was tried as an adult and received a twenty-five-year sentence. He spoke of the event with a degree of sobriety and regret that I had never heard anyone express before. He didn't weep as he related the account, but the sincerity of his remorse was unquestionable. Edward made no efforts to exculpate himself or assign the blame to his parents or society. He freely acknowledged his guilt and had sought God's forgiveness for the crime on many occasions since.

It was a terrifying and yet strangely inspiring account. I don't know why he shared it with me. Maybe he just wanted me to appraise him as a fundamentally honorable man, despite his past mistakes. Whatever the reason he imparted his history, I was grateful that he did.

"The main thing I learned in prison," he concluded, "was that if you want anything in this world, you got to work for it in the first place. Greed will never take you anywhere good."

Later that night, Edward asked if he could borrow twenty-one dollars. I was surprised by his request. He had never tried to borrow money from me before, and I knew that he had a general aversion to debt. I wondered briefly about the use of proceeds but didn't bother to ask. I trusted him, so it didn't matter. I slipped him the two bills, all too eager to get rid of a banknote featuring a portrait of Andrew Jackson.

**$$$$$**

As I drove home, I pondered Edward's words. "If you want anything in this world, you've got to work for it in the first place." It was a poignant restatement of a now very familiar principle, one which we had both violated. Perhaps I hadn't transgressed as overtly as Edward had, but I had clearly been an accessory to the crime in my role as a financier. I had provided capital to enable people who tried to consume more than they had produced. In hindsight, the blowback was clearly unavoidable.

Speaking of the Ten Commandments, acclaimed film director Cecil B. DeMille said: "It is impossible for us to break the law. We can only break ourselves against the law." And that's exactly what Edward and I had done: we had broken ourselves against the Law of Markets.

While I can't speak on Edward's behalf, I can at least plead some degree of personal ignorance in the matter: it's difficult to respect a principle that you've never been taught. My freshman economics class at Wake Forest University employed a textbook entitled *Economics: Principles and Policy,* by William J. Baumol and Alan S. Blinder. The book devotes a paltry twenty-five of its 900 pages to the banking system. John Maynard

Keynes is featured prominently in a page-long biographical note; his theories comprise roughly ten percent of the text's total content. Page 559 contains a typical illustration of his doctrine: "Recessions and unemployment are often caused by insufficient aggregate demand."

No one who understands Say's Law would ever make such an assertion. If some fool uttered this ludicrous claim at a cocktail party, I'd laugh at the man and reprove him by dumping my drink right on his blazer. But when the fool in question is a former vice chairman of the Federal Reserve Board of Governors, the statement is more disconcerting than humorous.

Recently, I examined four contemporary undergraduate economics textbooks to find that Say's Law is mentioned in only one of them. Regrettably, the concept is amateurishly explained as "supply creates its own demand," and the author then proceeds to praise Keynes for liberating economics from the antiquated fallacy. How far we've fallen. In the mid-nineteenth century, Say's *Treatise on Political Economy* was the preeminent economics textbook at American institutions of higher learning, including Harvard University. Instead of learning sound doctrine, today's undergraduates are inundated with principles that will not bear the scrutiny of common sense and experience. Then again, common sense never proved a sufficient impediment to stop a determined economist.

In economics, as in other endeavors, we are often more inclined to embrace a principle based on its convenience rather than its veracity. Keynes's ideas of economic prosperity through government profligacy are very comforting ones. It's easy to blame recessions on "demand failure" and then prescribe a regimen of tax cuts, low interest rates, and higher government spending. It's a fun medicine to take, and one that politicians have become only too happy to administer. Unfortunately, it's a bad prescription based on a lousy diagnosis of the symptoms.

As individuals, Americans tried to violate Say's Law by elevating household debt levels to unsustainable levels. As a country, the United States is now attempting to break it collectively. In 2009, the federal budget deficit exceeded 10% of the nation's total output for the first time since World War II. It fell slightly below that level in 2010, but remains in the 10% range for 2011. Optimistic estimates project the number migrating to the 3-6% range for the remainder of the decade.

Our spendthrift approach is a lamentable deviation from the fiscal discipline of our ancestors. The United States government ran a budget surplus in sixty-seven calendar years of the nineteenth century. When the country was not at war, the country was in surplus 75% of the time, with the deficit never exceeding 1% of the nation's output. The trend continued for the first thirty years of the twentieth century. Budgets were balanced or in surplus 80% of the time, with large deficits being run only in 1918 and 1919 to fund military expenditures during World War I.

The track record worsened in subsequent decades as the government borrowed to finance FDR's Depression-era New Deal programs, World War II and wars in Korea and Vietnam. From 1931 to 1965, the U.S. Treasury ran deficits in more than three years out of every four. 1965, you may recall, was the same year that *Time* magazine declared the hegemony of Keynesian economic theory. The observation was prescient: the United States government has been a net borrower in nearly 90% of the years since then.

The unavoidable consequence of embracing the short-term gratification that Keynes championed has been a gradual erosion of the American economy's long-term stability. An ever-larger share of capital that could have been devoted to investing reproductively for tomorrow is now earmarked for expenditure today.

As of August 2011, U.S. national debt—the accumulation of years of deficits—stands at roughly 14 trillion dollars. When unfunded entitlement programs (e.g., Social Security, Medicare, and Medicaid) are included, the number rises to a staggering $62 trillion. If the status quo does not change, mandatory government spending on entitlements and interest on the national debt will exceed tax revenue sometime between 2030 and 2040, leaving no resources for national defense, law enforcement, education, and other "discretionary" items. At that point, the Treasury will need to issue new debt just so that it can keep paying interest on its outstanding obligations. The U.S. government will have become a Ponzi scheme.

In recognition of this threat, Moody's and Standard and Poor's credit rating agencies have recently warned that the United States is at risk of losing the Aaa/AAA status which has enabled it to borrow cheaply from foreign investors. Given that the agencies had also assigned the coveted Triple-A rating to countless pools of subprime mortgages, which now trade for twenty cents on the dollar, we should probably be in a state of outright panic.

In a 1938 essay titled "My Early Beliefs," Keynes offered a description of his undergraduate peer group at Cambridge: "We repudiated entirely customary morals, conventions and traditional wisdom. We were, that is to say, in the strict sense of the term, immoralists . . . we recognized no moral obligation on us, no inner sanction, to conform or to obey." Nowhere was this ethos more manifest than in his refusal to genuflect before the first law of economics.

But whatever else can be said of him, Keynes was surely right on one point—we are all dead in the long run. The question before us is whether we want to die of a self-inflicted overdose of his medicine. We can continue to follow the spurious doctrines of an economic pied piper, or we can acknowledge the simple truth that a burgeoning federal debt only postpones our inevitable arraignment before the Court of Economic Justice.

Neglecting to contemplate the negative consequences of short-sighted behavior will not make them any less likely to come to fruition. As it stands, the U.S. Government is on a collision course with Say's Law. I don't know when the crash will occur, but I have no doubt as to which of the two entities will survive the wreckage unscathed.

$$$$$

When I reported to sing my swan song at 9 p.m. Saturday night, Edward was nowhere to be found. Something was wrong; he was never late for a shift. He had mentioned that he had been investigating another job opportunity, so perhaps he had taken me in to his confidence only to borrow some cash before disappearing forever.

I tried to put the matter out of my head as I prepared an egg and cheese sandwich for myself, but I couldn't resist the temptation to repeatedly glance at my watch as my dinner cooked on the grill. 9:45 came and went. Still no Edward.

"I believe this belongs to you, suh," a familiar voice said behind me.

No sooner had I wheeled around than Edward placed two ten-dollar bills and a single in my hand.

"Edward, you're always at least fifteen minutes early for work. What gives?"

"They cut my hours back a little bit. My shift doesn't start 'til ten." He ran his eyes over my face. "Was you afraid you weren't gonna get your money back?"

"That never crossed my mind."

"I can tell you're lyin.'"

"Maybe a little bit," I conceded. "It's not about the money, Edward. Losing twenty-one dollars doesn't hurt. But misjudging a man whose character I respected . . . now that would have stung a lot."

After another pleasant ten-hour shift, I decided that cheese eggs and hashbrowns would be the perfect coda to my six months in the restaurant business. While I had served hundreds of orders of cheese eggs, I had never cooked or eaten a plate of them, myself. But they were such a popular menu item, and I wanted to see what all the fuss was about.

As I scrambled my eggs and flipped my hashbrowns, I permitted myself one final flirtation with Keynesian economics. My stomach had indicated a desire for food, which had led to the subsequent production. So maybe demand really did drive supply after all.

Before my meditation could go any further, a muscular arm reached across my chest and placed a hamburger patty on the grill.

"Excuse me, Jimmy. I'm just gonna fix a quarter cheese plate," Edward declared.

"Would you like me to make it for you?" I offered.

"No suh, that's alright. I'll make it myself. I've been eating my own cooking for thirty years, and I don't intend to break that habit this morning. But I thank you, anyway."

*I'm going to eat my own cooking. I'm going to eat my own cooking.* I repeated the mantra in my head. I had experienced a myriad of flashes of economic revelation in the past few months. But on this, my last day, the epiphany was particularly forceful.

I like to imagine that a six-month stint at Papa's Chicken & Waffles would have prompted Keynes to recognize that "demand," in the economic sense, implies more than a simple desire for a good. No one will sell you an item just because you want it. True demand means that you are willing to pay the price of production. It means that you must produce before you can consume. We can only eat inasmuch as we are willing to cook for ourselves or produce *something of value* in exchange for another's cooking. Sure, you can borrow a few bucks for a meal if you're short on change, but only if you're of sound character and have a willingness to produce to repay your creditor.

Jean-Baptiste Say had been right all along. Production drives consumption, not vice versa. I wonder why twentieth-century politicians had forgotten this simple dictum which had been so long revered by the Classical economists. In a global economy with large-scale division of labor, perhaps we are so dependent on the production of others that we forget the necessity of our own efforts. While contemplating a purchase, we often look first to a credit card rather than the sweat of our own brow. But Say's Law is best learned viscerally, by harvesting crops or cooking your own food. Most nineteenth-century American farmers must have understood the Law of Markets intuitively, just as Edward did.

We put the food on our plates and retired to the low bar. I suggested that a toast was in order, though I had absolutely no idea what to drink to. Edward thought for a few seconds before finally raising his cup.

"To the meltdown," he said.

After five months together, he still had the ability to catch me completely off guard.

"The meltdown? Why should we drink to that?"

"Think about it, Man. What are the chances that you woulda spent any time working at Papa's if the market hadn't collapsed?"

"Slim to none."

"And you've learned a lot since you been here, haven't you?"

"That's a gross understatement, Edward."

"So your journey was worthwhile."

"It certainly was."

"And on my end, it's been a real pleasure traveling together with you."

He offered me his hand, which I gladly accepted. "Well, I guess it's about time to roll out," he declared.

"Edward, could you wait here just a second? I've got something I want to give you before we part ways." I returned from my car a few minutes later and presented him with a DVD.

"Look at that there. Now that's alright," he said, holding his new copy of *The Shawshank Redemption*. "I love this movie and that boy Morgan Freeman, he's a fine actor. Now what are you giving this to me for?"

"Think of it as a memento of our time together. After all, it's a lot like our story, isn't it?"

"How do you figure?" he asked. "A young financier is thrown into a tough new environment. A veteran of the institution, doubting the tenderfoot's prospects for survival, takes him under his wing. Despite their differing backgrounds, the two form an unexpectedly strong bond as they confront the demons of their past. In the end, hope and tenacity finally pay off. Escaping the chains of past transgressions, they move on to better lives as their friendship carries them through to their redemption."

Edward smiled at me, then studied the DVD case for a few seconds. "You *do* kind of resemble this boy," he said, pointing to Tim Robbins's picture. "See you around, Jimmy Mac."

"Hey, you didn't call me Jimmy Jam or Jimmy Dean."

"No. You've been the Mac for several weeks now. Take care and beware."

After a final handshake, we retired to our vehicles. I waved to Edward as I drove out of the parking lot. As I pulled on to the interstate, I found myself suddenly overcome with a profound sense of gratitude. He was right to have toasted the meltdown. Had I not been laid off, I would never have met him, let alone the Repo Men, the Linebacker, and Crazy Kathy. Except for other finance nerds, my best career-related anecdotes would fall on deaf ears. No grandchild wants to hear lame anecdotes from the bond market about "the great yield curve inversion of aught five" or "the time LIBOR spiked to six percent in two days." My biography, while still bland in many respects, became markedly more exciting thanks to those six months.

For most people, "recession" carries a negative connotation. For me, however, the recent episode has come with a lustrous silver lining. I have learned a life lesson in true capitalism. As originally expounded by Adam Smith, capitalism works. It is a moral and just system of organizing human behavior. It promotes political freedom. It rewards creativity, initiative, and alacrity. It affords us a higher standard of living than any alternative economic system. At its heart, its ethos is one of serving others. When earned honestly, profits are merely a byproduct of diligent service.

True capitalism means that capitalists and financiers gracefully bear the consequences of their misallocated capital. The cure for recession isn't government profligacy; it is to reassign labor and capital to where they are most needed. And if you have an ounce of daring, the reallocation process can provide you with the experience of a lifetime.

I learned more about the true nature of productivity and economic organization by observing Edward's work ethic and pondering his casual restatements of Say's Law than I did from all my time in the bond market and from studying Keynes's half-baked theories during my undergraduate years. It is wonderfully ironic that the example and common sense of a paroled short-order cook could decimate the reasoning of the twentieth century's most influential economist. But perhaps I shouldn't have been surprised. After all, irony is the fundamental organizing principle of the universe.

One realization was painful, however. The next time I dined at Papa's, I would have to pay full price for my food. But, I reflected, that was an acceptable state of affairs. The triple hashbrowns were worth at least $2.25 to my palate. The restaurant would turn a profit on the sale, and my waiter would undoubtedly garner a healthy tip. Everyone would win in a confluence of culinary excellence and laissez-faire capitalism. Undoubtedly, Adam Smith and Jean-Baptiste Say would heartily approve. There was only one unresolved question in my mind: how would the Fathers of Capitalism take *their* hashbrowns?

# ARTICLES OF ECONOMIC FAITH

- Production is the source of all consumption. No good or service can be consumed without first being produced. Society's wealth can only grow by adding more workers and/or increasing their productivity.

- Money is only a mechanism through which society's producers exchange their productions. Any large, sudden increase or decrease in the volume of money inevitably creates adverse consequences for the volume of real production.

- Capitalism operates on principles of freedom and mutual edification for producers, consumers, capital, and labor alike. Ergo, it is a fundamentally moral system of production arrangements.

- The primary responsibility of governments is to ensure the protection of private property for all citizens.

- Productivity enhancements result from individuals' willingness to defer consumption and invest their savings into reproductive investments. The role of the financier is to facilitate and direct these transfers of capital. Capital should only be entrusted to persons of sound character.

- Because the vast majority of the money supply is supported by the assets of commercial banks, bankers have a sacred responsibility to ensure that their capital is loaned prudently.

- Bankers will be tempted to make riskier loans and employ more financial leverage when asset prices are rising. The worse the loan underwriting and the greater the leverage employed, the more profound the economic fallout when the credit cycle turns.

- Recessions and unemployment result from changes in the structure of production as it shifts to meet changes in the structure of demand. The key to maintaining output and employment at high levels is to produce diverse goods and services in correct proportions to each other.

- When financial intermediaries like banks misallocate capital using an excessive volume of leverage, the miscalculation imposes costs upon third parties without their consent. It is the proper province of government to prevent this imposition from occurring by regulating financial leverage.

# REFERENCES

Akerlof, George A., and Robert J. Shiller. *Animal Spirits: How Human Psychology Drives the Economy, and Why It Matters for Global Capitalism.* Princeton: Princeton, 2009.

Barbera, Robert J. *The Cost of Capitalism: Understanding Market Mayhem and Stabilizing Our Economic Future.* New York: McGraw-Hill, 2009.

"Banking Unsound Practices." *TIME.* April 29, 1991.

Baumol, William J. *Microtheory: Applications and Origins.* Cambridge, MA: MIT, 1986.

Baumol, William J., and Alan S. Blinder. *Economics: Principles and Policy.* Orlando, FL: Harcourt Brace, 1994.

Bernstein, Peter L. *Against the Gods: The Remarkable Story of Risk.* New York: John Wiley & Sons, 1996.

Bernstein, Peter L. *The Power of Gold: The History of an Obsession.* New York: Wiley, 2000.

Bremner, Robert P. *Chairman of the Fed: William McChesney Martin, Jr., and the Creation of the Modern American Financial System.* New Haven, CT: Yale, 2004.

Bruner, Robert F., and Sean D. Carr. *The Panic of 1907: Lessons Learned from the Market's Perfect Storm*. Hoboken, NJ: John Wiley & Sons, 2007.

Buchholz, Todd G. *New Ideas from Dead Economists: An Introduction to Modern Economic Thought*. New York: Plume, 2007.

Clay, Henry, and Eugene Ewald Agger. *Economics: An Introduction for the General Reader*. New York: Macmillan, 1921.

Cooper, George. *The Origin of Financial Crises: Central Banks, Credit Bubbles and the Efficient Market Fallacy*. New York: Vintage, 2008.

Ebenstein, Alan O. *Milton Friedman: A Biography*. New York, NY: Palgrave Macmillan, 2007.

Ferguson, Niall. *The Ascent of Money: A Financial History of the World*. New York: Penguin, 2008.

Foley, Duncan K. *Adam's Fallacy: A Guide to Economic Theology*. Cambridge, MA: Belknap of Harvard, 2006.

Fraser Management Associates. "Money Trust Investigation. Sub-committee of the Committee on Banking and Currency, House of Representatives, Washington, D.C., Thursday, December 19, 1912." Retrieved August 2010 from http://fraser.stlouisfed.org/publications/montru/issue/3642/download/53582/montru_pt15.pdf.

Friedman, Milton. *An Economist's Protest*. Glen Ridge, NJ: Thomas Horton, 1975.

Friedman, Milton. "Commanding Heights: Milton Friedman on

PBS." PBS interview. Retrieved 22 July 2010 from http://www.pbs.org/wgbh/commandingheights/shared/minitext/int_miltonfriedman.html.

Friedman, Milton, and Anna Jacobson Schwartz. *The Great Contraction 1929–1933.* Princeton, NJ: Princeton, 2008.

Friedman, Milton, and Rose D. Friedman. *Free to Choose: A Personal Statement.* San Diego: Harcourt Brace Jovanovich, 1990.

Greenspan, Alan. *The Age of Turbulence: Adventures in a New World.* New York: Penguin, 2007.

Griffin, G. Edward. *The Creature from Jekyll Island: A Second Look at the Federal Reserve.* Westlake Village, CA: American Media, 2002.

Hazlitt, Henry. *The Failure of the "New Economics": An Analysis of the Keynesian Fallacies.* Auburn, AL: Ludwig Von Mises Institute, 2007.

Kates, Steven. *Say's Law and the Keynesian Revolution: How Macroeconomic Theory Lost Its Way.* Northampton, MA: Edward Elgar, 1998.

Keynes, John Maynard. *The Collected Writings of John Maynard Keynes.* Edited by Donald Moggridge. Vol. 4: *A Tract on Monetary Reform.* London: Macmillan, 1971.

Keynes, John Maynard. *The Collected Writings of John Maynard Keynes.* Edited by Donald Moggridge. Vol. 7: *The General Theory of Employment, Interest, and Money.* London: Macmillan, 1978.

Lefevre, Edwin. *Reminiscences of a Stock Operator.* Hoboken, NJ: J. Wiley, 2006.

Lewis, C. S. *The Complete C.S. Lewis Signature Classics.* San Francisco: HarperSanFrancisco, 2002.

Lewis, Hunter. *Where Keynes Went Wrong: And Why World Governments Keep Creating Inflation, Bubbles, and Busts.* Mount Jackson, V A: Axios, 2009.

Lowenstein, Roger. *When Genius Failed: The Rise and Fall of Long-Term Capital Management.* New York: Random House, 2000.

Mankiw, N. Gregory. *Principles of Economics.* Mason, OH: South-Western Cengage Learning, 2009.

Meacham, Jon. *American Lion: Andrew Jackson in the White House.* New York: Random House, 2008.

O'Rourke, P. J., and Adam Smith. *On the Wealth of Nations.* New York: Grove, 2007.

Paul, Ron. *End the Fed.* New York: Grand Central, 2009.

Rosenbaum, S. P. *The Bloomsbury Group: A Collection of Memoirs and Commentary.* Toronto: University of Toronto, 1995.

Rothbard, Murray N. *Classical Economics: An Austrian Perspective on the History of Economic Thought.* Vol. II. Aldershot, UK: Edward Elgar, 1995.

Rothbard, Murray N. *The Panic of 1819: Reactions and Policies.* New York: Columbia University Press, 1962.

Say, Jean-Baptiste. *A Treatise on Political Economy.* New Brunswick, NJ: Transaction, 2001.

—. (1820). *Lettres à M. Malthus sur différents sujets d'économie politique, notamment sur les causes de la stagnation générale du commerce.*

Skidelsky, Robert Jacob Alexander. *Keynes: The Return of the Master.* New York: Public Affairs, 2009.

Smith, Adam, D. D. Raphael, and A. L. Macfie. *The Theory of Moral Sentiments.* Indianapolis: Liberty Classics, 1982.

Soros, George. *Open Society: Reforming Global Capitalism.* New York: Public Affairs, 2000.

Woods, Thomas E. *Meltdown: A Free-Market Look at Why the Stock Market Collapsed, the Economy Tanked, and Government Bailouts Will Make Things Worse.* Washington, D.C.: Regnery, 2009.

Made in the USA
Lexington, KY
18 August 2018